MW01202263

Encyclopedia of
PUBLIC
RELATIONS

Encyclopedia of
PUBLIC RELATIONS

Editor
Robert L. Heath
University of Houston

VOLUME 2

A SAGE Reference Publication

SAGE Publications
Thousand Oaks ▪ London ▪ New Delhi

For information:

 Sage Publications, Inc.
2455 Teller Road
Thousand Oaks, California 91320
E-mail: order@sagepub.com

Sage Publications Ltd.
1 Oliver's Yard
55 City Road
London EC1Y 1SP
United Kingdom

Sage Publications India Pvt. Ltd.
B-42, Panchsheel Enclave
Post Box 4109
New Delhi 110 017 India

Printed in the United States of America

Library of Congress Cataloging-in-Publication Data

Encyclopedia of public relations / edited by Robert L. Heath.
    p. cm.
"A Sage reference publication."
Includes bibliographical references and index.
ISBN 0-7619-2733-6 (cloth)
  1. Public relations—Encyclopedias. I. Heath, Robert L. (Robert Lawrence), 1941-
HD59.E48 2005
659.2'03—dc22

                                    2004009256

This book is printed on acid-free paper.

04 05 06 07 10 9 8 7 6 5 4 3 2 1

Acquisitions Editor:	Margaret H. Seawell
Editorial Assistant:	Jill Meyers
Developmental Editor:	Paul Reis
Production Editor:	Diane S. Foster
Copy Editor:	David Mason, Publication Services
Typesetter:	C&M Digitals (P) Ltd.
Proofreader:	Libby Larson
Indexer:	Jeanne R. Busemeyer
Cover Designer:	Ravi Balasuriya

Contents

Editorial Board

List of Entries

Reader's Guide

JARGON

REPORTS

RESEARCH AND ANALYSIS

THEORIES AND MODELS

Illustrations and Tables

Activism: Unidentified activists from the AIDS Coalition To Unleash Power (ACT UP) stage a demonstration on July 11, 2000, in Durban, South Africa, at the 13th International AIDS Conference. ACT UP called on the World Health Organization (WHO) to distribute antiretroviral treatments to poor countries.

Asia, practice of public relations in: Far Eastern Economic Review (FEER) journalists, British citizen Rodney Tasker (*left*) and United States citizen Shawn Crispin (*right*), attend a press conference at the Thai Immigration Bureau in Bangkok on February 27, 2002. Thai Prime Minister Thaksin Shinawatra insisted that Thailand had the sovereign right to expel the two foreign journalists over an article they wrote that touched on the government's relations with the country's revered monarchy.

Barnum, P. T.: A portrait of P. T. Barnum on a Barnum and Company circus poster that advertises an exhibit featuring "Great Jumbo's Skeleton."

Berlowe, Phyllis: Photo

Bernays, Edward: Photo

Bogart, Judith S.: Photo

Burson, Harold: Photo

Byoir, Carl: Photo

Collaborative decision making: Table 1. Common Techniques for Collaborative Decision Making

Committee on Public Information: Poster for "Under Four Flags," one of a series of films by the Committee on Public Information promoting the United States' efforts in World War I. Such films were used both as propaganda and as fundraisers for the war effort.

Communication management: Table 1. Six Domains of Communication Management

Communication technologies: Table 1. Technological Considerations in Designing Messages and Selecting Media

Community relations: Gray Panthers' founder Maggie Kuhn gestures and screams during her address to the Poletown Neighborhood Council in Hamtramck, Michigan, circa 1980.

Consumer/customer relations: Figure 1. Ten phrases to attract return customers.

Co-orientation theory: Figure 1. Co-orientation model.

Crisis and crisis management: Joe Allbaugh, Director of the Federal Emergency Management Agency (FEMA), briefs reporters on September 15, 2001, about the ongoing operations at the Pentagon in Washington, DC. Workers started to remove the collapsed portion of the Pentagon shortly after the briefing.

Crisis communications and the Tylenol poisonings: James Burke, Johnson & Johnson executive, displays a new tamper-resistant Tylenol bottle on November 11, 1982. Nearly eight months earlier, six Chicago-area people died of cyanide poisoning from tainted Tylenol tablets.

Cultural topoi: Table 1. Cultural Topoi Compared

Cutlip, Scott M.: Photo

Drobis, David: Photo

Dudley, Pendleton: Photo

Ellsworth, James Drummond: Photo

Environmental groups: Protesters at a 1990 Earth First! protest hold up a banner reading "Stop Redwood Slaughter."

Exxon and the Valdez *crisis:* Cleanup workers spray oiled rocks with high-pressure hoses after the *Exxon Valdez* ran aground on March 24, 1989, spilling more than 10 million gallons of crude oil into Prince William Sound.

Exxon and the Valdez *crisis:* An Exxon memo proclaims the rules of zero tolerance, posted after the 1989 *Exxon Valdez* oil spill in Alaska.

Federal Trade Commission: The former R.J. Reynolds cigarette advertising mascot, "Joe Camel," plays pool and smokes cigarettes in an advertisement for Camel cigarettes that covers a billboard in a field. The FTC and antismoking advocates pressured R.J. Reynolds to eliminate the "Joe Camel" campaign in 1997, accusing the company of using a cartoon character to attract young smokers.

Focus group: As a focus group in Needham, Massachusetts, watches an interview of Monica Lewinsky on televisions in 1999, members' reactions are displayed directly on screen in graph form.

Four-Minute Men: A 1917 poster for one of the Four-Minute Men speeches. President Woodrow Wilson recruited 75,000 speakers called Four-Minute Men to give short talks on United States war aims to the public at theater intermissions and other venues.

Frede, Ralph E.: Photo

Hammond, George: Photo

Health Belief Model: Figure 1. Health Belief Model.

Hill, John Wiley: Photo

Hoog, Thomas W.: Photo

Hunter, Barbara W.: Photo

Image restoration theory: Table 1. Image Restoration Strategies

Industrial barons (of the 1870s–1920s): Industrial baron J. P. Morgan (1837–1913), founder of U.S. Steel, shakes his cane at a passerby on a city street. Although Morgan is alleged to have said, "I don't owe the public anything," he called upon early public relations practitioner Theodore Newton Vail

to help save the American Telephone & Telegraph Company in 1902.

Integrated marketing communication: Table 1. Strengths of Alternative IMC Tactics

Involvement: Figure 1. Motivation-ability-opportunity model for enhancing message processing.

Labor Union Public Relations: Local 600 of the Congress of Industrial Organizations (CIO) electrical workers electrocuting an effigy of Hitler in a 1942 Labor Day parade. Public relations philosophy, strategies, and tactics have been used in struggles for organized labor and its goals.

Lucky Strike Green Campaign: Lucky Strike Cigarettes used a variety of campaigns to sell products in the 1930s, from promoting green—the color of their cigarette packaging—as fashionable for women to featuring Santa Claus as a customer, as in this 1936 advertisement. "Luckies are easy on my throat," Santa is quoted as saying. "There are no finer tobaccos than those used in Luckies, and Luckies' exclusive process is your throat protection against irritation . . . against cough."

Muckrakers (and the age of progressivism): American journalist and political philosopher Lincoln Steffens (1866–1936), who published many articles exposing urban political corruption. He was prominent among the writers Theodore Roosevelt called "muckrakers."

National Investor Relations Institute: Chairman of the Board of the General Electric Company, Ralph J. Cordiner (*center*), pounds the gavel here to open a meeting of share owners of the firm. Some 2,500 owners attended the 68th annual meeting of the firm. Flanking Cordiner are Robert Patton (*left*), President, and Ray H. Luebbe, Secretary. Cordiner established the first efforts at formalizing a company's communication program with shareholders in 1953.

Nongovernmental organizations (NGOs): Members of nongovernmental organizations (NGOs) wave fliers during a protest outside the conference room of the opening session of the World Trade Organization (WTO) conference in Doha on November 9, 2001.

Page, Arthur W.: Photo

Page, Arthur W.: Arthur W. Page's book, *The Bell Telephone System* (1941), explained the company's the financial policy and how it affected the company's mission to serve, including the public relations function. Nearly 200,000 copies of the book were sold in hardcover and in paperback.

Perjury: Senator Karl Mundt (R) of South Dakota, who was acting chairman of the House Un-American Activities Committee (HUAC) when the first testimony on the Alger Hiss–Whitaker Chambers investigation was heard, is shown in his office scanning the headlines that tell him of the jury's January 21, 1950, verdict in Hiss's second perjury trial. Chambers, a senior editor from *Time* magazine and an admitted ex-communist, identified Hiss and several other federal officials to HUAC as having been members of a communist cell whose purpose had been to infiltrate the U.S. government. The conviction made Hiss liable to a maximum sentence of 10 years in prison and fines totaling $4,000.

Plank, Betsy: Photo

Political action committees (PACs): United States President Bill Clinton addresses the 54th annual meeting of the Association of Trial Lawyers of America (ATLA) while in Chicago, July 30, 2000. The ATLA is regularly one of the top-spending political action committees (PACs).

Postcolonialism theory and public relations: An Indian protester uses a megaphone during a demonstration against the 1984 Bhopal gas tragedy in New Delhi on August 27, 2003. Scholars have pointed to the Bhopal tragedy as an example of postcolonialism because most mainstream public relations literature continues to depict how the company dealt with the crisis and maintained its line of communication with its shareholders and investors, while the voice of the victims of the tragedy is rarely heard.

Psychographics: Figure 1. Generational influences.

Public Affairs Council: Table 1. The Public Affairs Council, in Profile

Public Affairs Council: Table 2. Membership Composition

Public Affairs Council: Table 3. Most Active Members

Public Affairs Council: Table 4. The Components of Public Affairs: The Public Affairs Council's Fields of Expertise

Public health campaign: The U.S. Department of Health and Human Services' *Healthy People 2010: National Health Promotion and Disease Prevention Outcomes* is one of the major engines driving the prioritization of specific efforts in current health services and research.

Public Relations Field Dynamics (PRFD): Figure 1. Field diagrams of the perceived relational landscape.

Relationship management theory: Table 1. Dimensions, Types, and Models of Organization-Public Relationships

Roberts, Rosalee A.: Photo

Rules theory: Figure 1. Rules compliance continuum.

Spin: Prince Charles on a walkabout in Sheffield in 1998, with his Deputy Private Secretary Mark Bolland behind him (holding files). Described by the British newspapers as the prince's "spin doctor," Bolland left Charles's employ soon thereafter to set up his own public relations agency.

Sweden, practice of public relations in: Table 1. Some Facts About the Swedish Public Relations Association

Traverse-Healy, Tim: Photo

Vail, Theodore Newton: Photo

Warfare and public relations: President Woodrow Wilson (*left*) and George Creel, Committee on Public Information (more commonly known as the Creel Committee) leave the Royal Train at a station in the Alps on January 2, 1919, for exercise. Wilson formed the committee during World War I, made up of leading newspaper editors, advertising writers, and members of the public relations field as a means of spreading propaganda.

Wire service: A United Press International (UPI) Unifax machine was an early type of fax machine that used early photocopier technology, enabling the sending of picture data over phone lines and turning UPI into a "wire service."

Contributors

Rebecca G. Aguilar
University of Houston

Steve Aiello
Senior Counsel, Public Affairs
Hill & Knowlton,
New York

Linda Aldoory
University of Maryland

Robert V. Andrews
Retired Executive Director of
    Corporate Communications
Johnson & Johnson,
New Brunswick, NJ

Cristina Proano Beazley
Lafayette, LA

William L. Benoit
University of Missouri

Günter Bentele
University of Leipzig

Pamela G. Bourland-Davis
Georgia Southern University

Shannon A. Bowen
University of Houston

Glen M. Broom
San Diego State University

Amy Broussard
Communications Director
Louisiana Gulf Coast Oil Exposition
    (LAGCOE)

Brigitta Brunner
Auburn University

Lisa C. Burns
Lafayette, LA

Ann R. Carden
SUNY Fredonia

Craig Carroll
University of Southern California

Nicole B. Cásarez
University of St. Thomas

Cindy T. Christen
Colorado State University

W. Timothy Coombs
Eastern Illinois University

Teresa Yancey Crane
President
Issue Management Council
Leesburg, VA

Terry M. Cunconan
Central Missouri State University

Tiffany Derville
University of Maryland

Barbara J. DeSanto
University of North Carolina Charlotte

Eric P. Eller
Buena Vista University

Lisa T. Fall
University of Tennessee

Kathleen Fearn-Banks
University of Washington

Jack Felton
Institute of Public Relations
Gainesville, FL

Yan Feng
Lafayette, LA

Kathryn L. Ferguson
Duson, LA

Sherry Devereaux Ferguson
University of Ottawa

John P. Férré
University of Louisville

Emilee V. Fontenot
Houston, TX

Nancy Engelhardt Furlow
Elon University

Sabra H. Gill
Sabra H. Gill & Associates,
Houston, TX

Karla K. Gower
University of Alabama

Mark A. Gring
Texas Tech University

James E. Grunig
University of Maryland

Kirk Hallahan
Colorado State University

Tricia L. Hansen-Horn
Central Missouri State University

Henry Hardt
Buena Vista University

Rachel Martin Harlow
Lubbock, TX

William Forrest Harlow
Texas Tech University

Joy L. Hart
University of Louisville

Robert L. Heath
University of Houston

Keith Michael Hearit
Western Michigan University

Ray Eldon Hiebert
Colton's Point, MD

Catherine L. Hinrichsen
C&C Communications
Seattle, WA

Sherry J. Holladay
Eastern Illinois University

Tom Hoog
Chairman, Hill & Knowlton/USA,
Washington, DC

Adam E. Horn
University of Missouri, Warrensburg

H. R. (Holly) Hutchins
University of Houston, adjunct faculty
Retired Manager of External Relations
Shell Oil Company
Houston, TX

Cassandra Imfeld
SunTrust Bank
Atlanta, GA

Jim C. Jennings
CEO
Elizabeth Glaser Pediatric AIDS
    Foundation
Washington, DC

Peter Johansen
Carleton University

Garth S. Jowett
University of Houston

Dean Kazoleas
Illinois State University

Kathleen S. Kelly
University of Florida

Michael L. Kent
Montclair State University

Marilyn Kern-Foxworth
The Ad*tive
Silver Spring, MD

Katherine N. Kinnick
Kennesaw State University

Diana L. Knott
Ohio University

Bonnie J. Knutson
Michigan State University

Dean Kruckeberg
University of Northern Iowa

Margot Opdyche Lamme
University of Florida

Barbara Langham
Renaissance House International
    Public Relations
Houston, TX

Jaesub Lee
University of Houston

Kathie A. Leeper
Concordia College (MN)

Roy V. Leeper
Concordia College (MN)

Phyllis Vance Larsen
University of Nebraska—Lincoln

John A. Ledingham
Capital University

Greg Leichty
University of Louisville

Shirley Leitch
University of Waikato

Maria E. Len-Rios
University of Kansas

Charles A. Lubbers
Kansas State University

Lisa Lyon
Kennesaw State University

Woodrow Madden
Spring, TX
Past President of the Public
    Affairs Council
Retired, Public Affairs, Exxon Oil
    Corporation

John Madsen
Buena Vista University, retired

Dick Martin
Summit, NJ
Retired Executive Vice President of
    Public Relations
AT&T Corporation

Katherine McComas
Cornell University

Becky McDonald
Ball State University

David McKie
University of Waikato

David B. McKinney
Manager of Community
    Relations
Shell Chemical Company
Deer Park, TX

D. Gayle McNutt
Executive Director (retired)
Executive Service Corps of Houston
Houston, TX

Lisa K. Merkl
University of Houston

Maribeth S. Metzler
Miami University (OH)

Jerry Mills
Overton Brooks Medical Center,
Shreveport, LA

Mary Anne Moffitt
Illinois State University

Daniel A. Moss
Manchester Metropolitan
    University Business School

Judy Motion
University of Waikato

Debashish Munshi
University of Waikato

Michael Nagy
University of Houston

Bonita Dostal Neff
Valparaiso University

Amy O'Connor
North Dakota State University

Bolanle A. Olaniran
Texas Tech University

Nicki Orsborn
Westerly, RI

Michael J. Palenchar
University of Tennessee

Kelly M. Papinchak
Director of Communications
Schipul – The Web Marketing
    Company
Houston, TX

Kristine A. Parkes
Krisp Communications
Eagleville, PA

Wes Pedersen
Director, Communications
    and Public Relations
Public Affairs Council,
Washington, DC

Emma Louise Daugherty
    Phillingame
California State University,
    Long Beach

Betsy Plank
Betsy Plank Public Relations
Chicago, IL
Retired from Edelman
    Public Relations and from
    Illinois Bell Telephone
    Company
Founder of Public Relations Student
    Society of America

Kenneth D. Plowman
Brigham Young University

Donnalyn Pompper
Florida State University

Ann Preston
St. Ambrose University

Robert S. Pritchard
Captain, U.S. Navy (retired)
Ball State University

Jim L. Query, Jr.
University of Houston

Ashli A. Quesinberry
University of Georgia

Brad L. Rawlins
Brigham Young University

Bryan H. Reber
University of Georgia

Bonnie Parnell Riechert
University of Tennessee

Karen Miller Russell
University of Georgia

Michael Ryan
University of Houston

Lynne M. Sallot
University of Georgia

Charles T. Salmon
Michigan State University

DeNel Rehberg Sedo
Mount Saint Vincent University

Matthew W. Seeger
Wayne State University

Timothy L. Sellnow
North Dakota State University

Shirley Serini
Morehead State University

Melvin L. Sharpe
Ball State University

Jae-Hwa Shin
University of Southern Mississippi

Danny Shipka
Gainesville, FL

Margaretha A. Sjoberg
Executive Director
Swedish Public Relations Association

Jim Sloan
Senior Vice President, Corporate
    Communications
Hill & Knowlton Chicago

Michael F. Smith
La Salle University

Brian C. Sowa
Eastern Illinois University

Jeffrey K. Springston
University of Georgia

Krishnamurthy Sriramesh
Nanyang Technological University

Don W. Stacks
University of Miami (FL)

Benita Steyn
University of Pretoria
Kevin Stoker
Brigham Young University

Maureen Taylor
Rutgers University

William Thompson
University of Louisville

Tatyana S. Thweatt
North Dakota State University

Elizabeth L. Toth
University of Maryland,
    College Park

Tim Traverse-Healy
Director, Centre for Public Affairs
    Study

Richard H. Truitt
Truitt & Kirkpatrick
New York

Robert R. Ulmer
University of Arkansas at Little Rock

Betteke van Ruler
University of Amsterdam

Dejan Verčič
Pristop Communications,
Ljubljana, Slovenia

Marina Vujnovic
University of Northern Iowa

Hsiang-Hui Claire Wang
Syracuse University

Ruthann Weaver Lariscy
University of Georgia

Aileen Webb
Michigan State University

Candace White
University of Tennessee

Jos Willems
High School for Management and
    Public Relations,
Ghent, Belgium

David E. Williams
Texas Tech University

Brenda J. Wrigley
Syracuse University

Davis Young
Senior Counselor
Edward Howard & Co.
Solon, OH

MANAGEMENT THEORY

Management theory refers to the range of theories that help to explain the concept, purpose, and process of management in organizations. There are, of course, many definitions of management, with management as a concept and process arguably being traceable back to antiquity. However, the systematic development of management thinking is generally accepted to date from the late 19th century, when the emergence of the large industrial corporations created the need for more effective management structures and processes. Of course, the growing demand for management skills at that time and since has not been confined only to large private-sector businesses but has also been manifest within government, public, and voluntary-sector organizations, including schools, hospitals, and the like. As with management in general, the history of public relations as we conceive of it today was spawned in unison with management theory. As public relations has matured as a profession, it has become more firmly rooted in assumptions and processes relevant to management theory.

Perhaps the best-known definition of management is that advanced by the early management scholar Henri Fayol, who maintained that management involves "to forecast and plan, to organize, to command, to co-ordinate and to control" (1949,

p. 40). This so-called classical view of management implies that managers generally operate as essentially rational, analytical planners and decision makers directing the work of subordinates in such a way as to achieve pre-stated organizational goals. More simplistically, management can be seen as focusing on identifying and guiding those activities that transform business inputs into outputs. At one extreme, these activities are manageable on a day-to-day basis, with managers responding to problems and minor changes in operating conditions; this is called *operations management.* At the other extreme are *strategic management* decisions that will launch the firm on a trajectory that is expected to continue for a number of years; the long-term character of these decisions is what makes them strategic.

This classical view of management has come under sustained criticism during the latter half of the 20th century as empirical studies have revealed a quite different picture of what management involves and what managers do. Scholars such as Henry Mintzberg (1973), John P. Kotter (1982), Andrew Pettigrew (1973), and Rosemary Stewart (1976, 1982) have pointed out that, in reality, management is often a very frenetic, unstructured, and largely reactive activity in which managers are forced to engage in a constant process of negotiation, bargaining, and compromise to get things done. Indeed, Tony J. Watson (1994) suggested, "Managing is essentially a process of strategic exchange because it shapes the overall activities of the organization and how it functions in its environment through the continual and continuous exchanging of information, favours, material and symbolic resources" (p. 37).

Management scholars have tended to focus on identifying the generic elements or activities associated with the performance of management roles in organizations. However, as Colin P. Hales (1986) emphasized, management work is contingent upon, inter alia, function, level, organizational type, structure, size, and environment. Moreover, managerial work may comprise both *formal* and *informal* elements, although the distinction between formal and informal may not always be easy to sustain since managerial work is itself highly fluid. It is also important to recognize that the scope of management theory extends beyond the distinction between operational and strategic management and embraces elements of a number of other subdisciplinary areas, ranging from human resource management and marketing management to more narrowly defined fields such as leadership and knowledge management.

The distinction between operational and strategic management has important implications for how the role of public relations in organizations is understood. Much of the debate to date has focused on arguments advocating that public relations should have a seat at the top management table (the dominant coalition) and should be party to strategic decision making within organizations. Yet as Jon White and David M. Dozier (1992) acknowledged, public relations is often excluded from membership in the dominant coalition and, more important, from participation in strategic decision making. One of the principal reasons cited for such exclusion from the work of the top management team is the perceived lack of management skills and competencies among many practitioners. Indeed, a recent large-scale study of the UK public relations industry conducted on behalf of the Institute of Public Relations and the Department of Trade and Industry (DTI) found that only around 20 percent of practitioners claimed to have public relations representation at board level. Equally, the study found that in less than a third

(31 percent) of cases was public relations strategy a regular item discussed at board level, and in 56 percent of cases public relations strategy would be discussed at board level only if a major issue was involved. Perhaps more significantly, nearly half of respondents (47 percent) rated their public relations strategy-making ability as relatively weak—a finding which the study's authors suggested points to significant gaps in the management training and development provision for practitioners. Although these findings relate only to the UK public relations industry, it would not be unreasonable to infer that they may well reflect the situation found in public relations worldwide.

Thus the challenge for public relations practitioners hoping to achieve board-level recognition in what has become an increasingly professional and demanding corporate world is to move public relations away from a communication emphasis and develop a managerial focus both in the training and operating mindset of practitioners. Indeed, the manager's role in public relations has tended to be defined primarily in communication terms instead of the more generic skills associated with general management responsibilities. Thus the manager's role has been defined as a composite of the three practitioners' roles identified earlier by G.M. Broom and G.D. Smith (1979): expert prescription, communication facilitation, and problem process facilitation. Here the main attributes defining manager role enactment exclude what are recognized as the higher-order management competencies required of more senior managers in organizations: leadership, people management, and strategic vision. It is not necessarily the case that senior public relations practitioners/managers do not require these broader management skills, but rather that academic research has failed to look for them or to encourage their development. If public relations is to achieve senior management/board-level status within organizations, it seems obvious that practitioners will need to develop and demonstrate these broader, mainstream senior management skills.

—Daniel A. Moss

Bibliography

Broom, G. M., & Smith, G. D. (1979). Testing the practitioner's impact on clients. *Public Relations Review, 5,* 47–59.

Dozier, D. M. (1984). Program evaluation and roles of practitioners. *Public Relations Review, 10*(2), 13–21.

Dozier, D. M., and Broom, G. M. (1995). Evolution of the manager role in public relations practice. *Journal of Public Relations Research, 7*(1), 3–26.

Fayol, H. (1949). *General and industrial management* (C. Storrs, Trans.). London: Pitman.

Hales, C. (1986). What do managers do? A critical review of the evidence. *Journal of Management Studies, 23*(1), 88–115.

Kotter, J. (1982). *The general manager.* New York: Free Press.

Mintzberg, H. (1973) *The nature of managerial work.* New York: Harper & Row.

Pettigrew, A. M. (1973). The politics of organisational decision-making. London: Tavistock.

Stewart, R. (1976). *Contrasts in management.* Maidenhead, UK: McGraw-Hill.

Stewart, R. (1982). *Choices for the manager.* Englewood Cliffs, NJ: Prentice Hall.

Watson, T. J. (1994). *In search of management: Culture, chaos and control in managerial work.* London: Routledge.

White, J., & Dozier, D. M. (1992) Public relations and management decision-making. In J. E. Grunig (Ed.), *Excellence in public relations and communication management* (pp. 91–108). Hillsdale NJ: Lawrence Erlbaum.

MANAGING THE CORPORATE PUBLIC RELATIONS DEPARTMENT

To manage a corporate public relations department, a senior practitioner must be able to build what amounts to a business-to-business relationship between the department and senior management of the company. The manager of this department must serve not only the professionals who work in the department, but also his or her peers within the company's dominant coalition as well as the key business heads. The manager must use knowledge of public relations and management skills to deliver value to the business. At the same time, the person must guide, coach, and foster the professionals in the department. Managing the department puts this individual into a counseling role—even a marketing role—with others in senior management. Not only does this person have to at times educate and

reeducate others in management regarding what public relations is, but he or she must also assert how public relations can add value to the bottom line and build brand and reputation with key audiences. The person in this role is expected to foresee potential "image" problems and manage issues, as well as offer ethical advice for positioning the company to build, repair, or maintain relationships.

As long ago as the 1880s, major companies in the United States began forming budget and staff public relations departments. Originally these were often called publicity departments, a name that implies that their original objective was merely to publicize and promote the company and its business activities. Public relations activities were limited to press agentry, the use of one-way communication to tell the company's story.

Today, major and even small companies routinely have some variation on the theme of what we think of as a public relations department. As with managing agencies and building agency-client relationships, the principles underpinning the successful corporate department are knowable, but the size and style of a public relations department may vary. One size or template does not fit all. Several issues surround the ways in which the public relations department is positioned, structured, and managed within an organization.

At various times in the history of corporate America, public relations or public affairs departments became quite large, with big ones employing 100 members. Huge ones grew to have as many as 200 professionals who brought to service a wide array of talents and performed very specialized services such as editing or speechwriting. Large size assumes that the organization is willing to commit to and budget for a full-service in-house operation. Business downturns and changes of philosophy about what public relations is and can do for the organization often lead to reductions in the size of public relations departments. Senior practitioners often moan that the size of the department is cut at just the time volume is most needed.

At the very least, management entails budgeting to achieve definable outcomes. It requires the application of best practices to develop public relations functions and to implement them through strategies and tactics. In the broadest of terms, public relations as a professional practice is justified as part of the management cadre to the extent that it contributes to the net income of the business. It can help increase income and cut costs. Stressing this theme, Holly Hutchins (2001) prophesied that "today's public relations organization will not survive as an expense or overhead cost in the new corporate business model. The new business model demands that public relations be accountable" (p. 445). The management of public relations requires that the department be positioned, budgeted, and staffed to achieve definable outcomes that are in the interest of the business.

The name of the department often indicates its position in the company as well as its influence on other members of management, and on the other businesses. Ideally, it should be a separate department with its leader reporting to and being a member of senior management. Thus, the title of the senior person over this function should be at the officer level, such as Vice President of Public Relations or Vice President of Public Affairs. In many large companies, the major department is often called public affairs rather than public relations, which suggests that its scope goes well beyond traditional public relations and into the disciplines of government relations, corporate philanthropy, constituent relations, and others.

Additional options exist. Public relations may be part of the marketing department, and it may be subservient to advertising. This configuration is typical of any company with a heavy emphasis on consumer marketing. In other companies—for instance, heavy manufacturing—the lead department might be public affairs, with public relations, marketing, and advertising as subparts. An emerging trend is the joining of public affairs and human resources under one very senior corporate officer, typically from the public affairs side of the house. Up until just the past several years, these were very distinct and often competitive corporate services. Today, given the increasing interaction and synergies between the two functions in areas such as employee benefit communications and diversity

awareness, more and more public affairs and human resources departments are consolidating.

If there is a corporate-level public relations department, companies may also have public relations specialists, typically called community relations managers, working at key locations wherever the company operates. A large diversified manufacturing company or a holding company may have a corporate public relations department. In addition, each manufacturing site might have a small team of public relations professionals who specialize in building partnerships both with employees and within the community. Such has become the case as companies have become increasingly global.

Also, in this diffused model, senior personnel in locations distant from corporate headquarters may have at least minimal public relations training, particularly in dealing with the media. This management strategy assumes that senior members in scattered business locations "do" public relations even though they don't have that role specified in their title. They may have that role specified in their job description. These business managers may be responsible for understanding the public relations culture of the organization and the community, and they need to know what professionals they can call on to serve the needs of their local operations. Even limited knowledge of public relations can help them contract for the services of a local agency.

Thus, public relations can be positioned in various configurations within the company. It can be highly concentrated, featured prominently, or placed in subordinate roles and diffused throughout the organization. One size does not fit all. How public relations is designed and managed will reflect the business's public relations. How senior management defines and respects the contribution of public relations will determine how the practice is positioned and deployed to bring professional public relations services to bear on definable management objects and the corporate mission.

Corporate public relations departments are structured in ways that serve the needs and meet the value propositions of the company. At least that is the logic. One aspect of the structure of the department is the definition and allocation of specialties in the department. People are often organized by function and tactic. A large corporate public relations department might have many functions staffed by one or more persons. These functions might be community relations, crisis response, corporate communications, investor relations, media relations, government relations, and strategic philanthropy.

The corporate public relations department also may be structured by tactic. Some of the professional talent in the department may be pool writers who work on many varied projects as needed. Large departments are likely to matrix individuals so they work on their specialties as well as serve collectively on many kinds of projects. Matrixing can help to integrate talent by bringing different perspectives and specialties to bear on problems that require varied experience, skills, and knowledge. People may be assigned to various projects on a temporary or permanent basis. For instance, one or more professionals might manage the corporate Web site. One or more might write and publish the corporate employee magazine. In similar fashion, an individual or team might craft community relations pieces, supply information for the company intranet, and update the company history.

The senior person in charge of the public relations department needs a blend of management and public relations principles to guide her or his management style. Unfortunately, it is not unusual today in corporate America, particularly in the energy sector, to see non–public relations or communications professionals in the senior public relations leadership positions. Many companies approach the senior public relations job as a "pass-through" or "get your ticket punched" position for corporate fast-trackers coming from finance, manufacturing, or technical areas.

Many senior practitioners adhere to the principle that communication may not be the most important aspect of public relations. Exploring this theme, John Budd, Jr., observed that "communication is the last act in the process of public relations—a process that should appropriately begin with policy and decision-making" (1995, p. 178). In the effort to build lasting, mutually beneficial relationships, appropriate policies and actions must precede communication. Using counseling to advise the development of sound management policy is vital to making the organization good, prior to expecting it to speak well. To this end, public relations professionals should advise as well as help implement the business's strategic plan.

Dozens of studies and professional papers have addressed how the public relations department can best satisfy the expectations of CEOs. Practitioners know that CEOs may misunderstand and even overestimate what public relations is and what it can do for the company. In 1995, while examining the ways to please CEOs through sound public relations practice, Robert L. Woodrum stressed six qualifications for success. The manager needs to have *personality.* This person must be personable, confident, intelligent, energetic, and cooperative. He or she needs to be *driven*; the department head is more likely to succeed if he or she goes to work each day committed to specific outcomes and if he or she is someone on whom others can depend. The successful manager must be *results oriented.* Can this person set goals and achieve them through the application of subordinates' skills and knowledge? The manager must be a *team player.* In addition, Woodrum noted that this person must possess *solid communication skills.* Even though the person may do less and less writing as he or she matures into management, the person has to be articulate and able to get his or her point across—both to others in management as well as to subordinates. To be a successful manager, the person needs to be able to listen to and appreciate the points others are making. The person in this position will fail if he or she is not *analytical,* capable of identifying and dissecting issues. Moreover, this person must understand the *business* of being in business, that is, delivering value to his or her business customers, to the company's shareholders, and to other key stakeholders.

Three last challenges of managing the corporate public relations department are worth noting. One challenge arises because of the disciplinary experience and training of the person who holds this position. Studies and experience have indicated that the dominant culture of the business may unduly—and unfortunately—influence who is selected to head the public relations department. If the organization has an engineering culture, only people with engineering degrees and experience may find their way into senior management. Such persons may not adequately understand what public relations is, what it can do, and what its limits are. The same can be said if the department head has a law degree but limited experience and study of public relations. Add to this list the person who is expert in finance or management, but not public relations. Practitioners like to believe that the person who is most qualified to head the public relations department is someone educated and experienced in the profession.

A second challenge is positioning the department to receive adequate budget to accomplish its objectives. Two fundamental models prevail over how the department is budgeted. One assumes that the department is given a budget based on what it needs to do and can do to serve the interests of the business. A second model is to treat the department as a profit center—an agency-in-residence—instead of a cost center. As an agency-in-residence, the department has to compete for business by promoting and selling its professional services to others in the company. The challenge is to earn a budget as an external agency might by adding value to internal "clients" or "customers."

The third challenge is to know when to hire professionals as members of the company or to outsource services to agencies. Having a full-time employee employed by the company increases the likelihood that the person will understand and work for the culture of the organization. This person knows the company and its business. The person is often quite loyal, beyond merely generating billable hours for an agency. However, the wise manager knows that some talents or specialties are not needed every day, 2080 hours per year. Thus, the services of some individuals might be outsourced since it is unwise to employ those talents on a full-time basis. These talents can be employed as needed.

Management is a two-edged sword. It requires knowing what can be done through public relations.

It demands understanding the difference between a "public relations problem" and a management problem. Public relations, for instance, cannot use communication to solve a problem that is not a communication problem. Counseling management requires credibility, honesty, and experience to help executives understand that having effective public relations may require that changes be made in how the business operates, not just how it communicates.

—Robert L. Heath and H. R. Hutchins

See also Advertising; Community relations; Counseling; Government relations; Investor relations; Marketing; Public affairs; Public relations agency

Bibliography

Budd, J., Jr. (1995). Commentary: Communications doesn't define PR, it diminishes it. *Public Relations Review, 21,* 177–179.

Ehling, W. P. (1992). Estimating the value of public relations and communication to an organization. In J. E. Grunig (Ed.), *Excellence in public relations and communication management* (pp. 617–638). Hillsdale, NJ: Lawrence Erlbaum.

Hutchins, H. R. (2001). A new order for public relations: Goodbye cost center, hello profit center. In R. L. Heath (Ed.), *Handbook of public relations* (pp. 445–450). Thousand Oaks, CA: Sage.

Woodrum, R. L. (1995). How to please the CEO and keep your job. *Public Relations Strategist, 1*(3), 7–12.

MARKET SHARE

Market share is the proportion of any market that is achieved by a specific product or service of a company in the mix of competitors. Of all automobiles sold in the United States, for instance, how many were manufactured under the General Motors name? Even more specifically, market share can be determined for each individual model in an array of products. Thus, the market share can be calculated for Chevrolet and GMC (General Motors Company) pickups among all pickups sold in the United States. Even more specific market share calculations could be made by state or by demographic. Thus, market share in the most specific sense is a sheer accounting record of the portions of a market as it is divided among competitors.

Public relations is one of several business functions that provides strategies and tools that can be used to affect the market share enjoyed by any competitor in a specific market for goods or services. Differentiating between marketing and public relations was simpler when Edward L. Bernays was practicing, teaching, and writing about public relations. To quote Bernays, "Marketing is properly concerned with the distribution of products, public relations concerns itself with the distribution of ideas which may or may not include products" (1955, pp. 63–64).

The goal of marketing is "to attract and satisfy customers (or clients) on a long-term basis in order to achieve an organization's economic objectives" (Wilcox, Cameron, Ault, & Agee, 2003, p. 15). In other words, the goal of marketing is to maintain or increase the market share of a product or service, the proportion of consumers of a product category who consume the product of the client. Thus, integrated marketing communication—primarily a strategic blend of advertising and pubic relations—is used by each competitor in a market to try to increase its market share. Since market share is always a proportional calculation, the increase of market share by one competitor is achieved by the loss of market share of one or more competitors.

How public relations serves this marketing function is a matter of consideration and debate. At one extreme, any communication effort—even the use of events created purely for marketing purposes—can be employed. Customer relations, often a purview of public relations, can help keep or expand market share. Practiced in what many believe to be the most ethical way, the goal of public relations is to achieve mutual understanding and cooperation between the client and the array of publics—customers in this sense—who affect and are affected by the client. Convergence—the merging of public relations, product advertising, and strategic communication functions—is thought to be one of the ways to maximize the contributions of several related professions.

One of the strategic objectives of organizations working to increase their brand share is to first increase the mindshare customers have regarding their product in contrast to those of their competitors. Cornelius Dubois coined the term *mindshare* to represent one brand's standing compared with other brands in the opinion of potential customers. Mindshare, according to Dubois, predicts market share. Because product ideas are not the only types of ideas competing for share of mind, Bernays (1955) expanded the notion of mindshare to mean the share of peoples' minds relative to competing attitudes or ideas (p. 65).

Many authors and managers cast public relations in the supporting role of developing mindshare to be turned into market share. According to Thomas Harris, for example, public relations functions to raise awareness, to inform and educate, to gain understanding, to build trust, to give people reasons to buy, and, finally, to create a climate of consumer acceptance. Jordan Goldman located public relations within the marketing tools directly related to increasing market share. Philip Kotler described public relations as the fifth P in the four P's of marketing (product, price, package, promotion).

Wilcox et al. (2003) listed eight ways that public relations contributes to marketing and the development of market share:

1. Developing new prospects

2. Third-party endorsements

3. Generating sales leads through articles in the trade press about new products and services

4. Paving the way for sales calls

5. Stretching ad and promo dollars through use of publicity about the company and its products

6. Providing inexpensive sales literature because articles about the company and its products can be reprinted as informative pieces for prospective customers

7. Establishing the corporation as an authoritative source of information on a given product

8. Helping to sell minor products that don't have large advertising budgets.

Evins Communications, Ltd., and IT Management Global Corp. provided examples of an approach that blurs the boundaries of public relations and marketing. Both companies use public relations to generate brand or product awareness and then parlay that awareness into mindshare, which translates into market share. Retailers like Wal-Mart also engage in efforts to capture mindshare as a precursor to market share. To enhance its fashion image, Wal-Mart is tracking and releasing fashion forecasts.

However, when integrated marketing communication casts public relations in a supporting role to marketing in the development of mindshare to translate into market share, it is a step backward from the two-way symmetrical model of public relations to an asymmetric practice of public relations.

The marketing function is traditionally a one-way function with clearly delimited channels of communication. As James E. Grunig and Todd Hunt (1984) pointed out, "The marketing function should communicate with the markets for an organization's goods and services. . . . The major purpose of marketing is to make money for the organization by increasing the slope of the demand curve."

In consulting on public relations for two nursing homes, this purpose was shown to be superfluous. Nursing homes and extended-care facilities often have waiting lists. However, employee turnover, family perceptions, and government relations were significant influences on the nursing homes' abilities to survive and prosper.

J. E. Grunig and Hunt (1984) accurately captured the contribution of public relations in such instances: "Public relations saves money for the organization by building relationships with publics that constrain or enhance the ability of the organization to meet its missions. Public relations, therefore, should be concerned with all the publics of the organization."

The Public Relations Society of America defines public relations by saying that it "helps an organization and its publics adapt mutually to each other." Although this definition does not preclude the practice of public relations in support of efforts to build market share, it gives more than a nod to the two-way symmetrical model of public relations

and encompasses the public affairs and public information functions where there is no market share to be built and where expansion of market share is not an issue.

—Ann Preston

See also Advertising; Bernays, Edward; Brand equity and branding; Event; Integrated marketing communication; Public Relations Society of America; Symmetry; Two-way and one-way communication

Bibliography

Bernays, E. L. (1955). *The engineering consent.* Norman: University of Oklahoma Press.

Cuneo, A. Z. (2003). Wal-Mart gains on Payless turf. *Advertising Age.* Retrieved from the EBSCO host database.

Goldman, J. (1987). *Public relations in the marketing mix.* New York: McGraw-Hill Contemporary Books.

Grunig, J. E. (Ed.). (1992). *Excellence in public relations and communication management.* Retrieved 1991 from http://www.iabc.com/fdtnweb/pdf/Excellence.pdf

Grunig, J. E., & Hunt, T. (1984). *Managing public relations.* New York: Holt, Rinehart, and Winston.

Issacs, N. B. (2003, April 3). Brand marketing public relations firms form strategic alliance. PR *Newswire,* Retrieved from http://www.prnewswire.com

Seitel, F. P. (2001). *The practice of public relations.* Englewood Cliffs, NJ: Prentice Hall.

Wilcox, D. L., Cameron, G. T., Ault, P. H., & Agee, W. K. (2003). *Public relations: Strategies and tactics.* Boston: Allyn & Bacon.

MARKETING

More than 40 years ago, Theodore Levitt (1960) said that the purpose of business is to make and keep customers. It might seem that his admonition is just plain common sense, not some cutting-edge revelation. On the other hand, the growing competitiveness in all industries has led many firms to believe that the purpose of business is making money. The focus on profits, ROI (return on investment), growth in sales and number of units, mergers, buyouts, stock prices, and sophisticated business school jargon has drawn attention away from the real purpose of business: to make and keep customers. No one is suggesting that profit is not important. It is critical. Without profit—and cash flow—a business "ain't no more." Think of the following analogy: If you claim that the purpose of business is making money, you might just as well say that the purpose of life is eating. Eating is a requisite for, not a purpose of life. The same is true of profits. In other words, profits *follow* people.

Giving Levitt's perspective a marketing definition, *marketing is a process by which we make and keep guests at a profit.* This view confirms the marketing philosophy begun by the General Electric Company that became known as "the Marketing Concept." The Marketing Concept views the consumer as the focal point of all marketing activities. In his classic article "Marketing Myopia", Levitt (1960) reinforced this belief. Before this re-orientation was introduced, marketing focused on what the company could produce, promote, and sell, and it was called "the Selling Concept." Folklore of the day maintained that Henry Ford reflected this philosophy with his claim that you could have any color of Ford, as long as it was black. This basic switch in how marketing was viewed reshaped the field of marketing to focus on the "customer is king" philosophy. From this reorientation came such concepts as the practice of segmentation, target or niche marketing, competitive advantage, product differentiation, positioning or brand building, and consumer research.

Although many people may be influenced to try a brand for the first time through the media, loyal customers are made one at a time. This appears to be a mind-boggling task. Think about a hotel that checks in 800 guests a day, a brokerage firm that serves 2000 people daily, or the hundreds of thousands who walk through the gates at Disney World every day. The managers of these operations, and thousands more like them, must have knowledge, understanding, and managerial skills to establish a standard operating performance—notice this didn't say procedure—for customer satisfaction. The consumer who first walks through the door can be turned into a loyal customer only through well-selected, well-trained, and highly motivated

employees. Thus, in reality, it is impossible to separate marketing from operations/line management. They are two sides of the same coin. Every employee is both a salesperson and a goodwill ambassador for your business. In fact, to your customer, he or she *is* your business. Therefore, you have to view marketing as a process with three major functions:

1. *Identifying* opportunities to increase revenues and/or customer counts

2. *Influencing* customer choices through brand building and promotion

3. *Servicing* customers to develop loyalty, gain repeat business, and generate word-of-mouth advertising

Sometimes these functions are known as identifying, influencing, and servicing demand, where demand is defined as consumers who are ready, willing, and able to buy. Whatever the label, each of these three marketing responsibilities involves a variety of marketing tasks: research, positioning, packaging, differentiating, pricing, promotion, calendars, budgeting, and analysis—all of which serve the purpose of increasing customer count, that is, making and keeping customers.

IDENTIFY DEMAND

Business leaders know that a marketing information system (MIS) is the basis for effective management decisions. It stands to reason that if you develop new products, services, or concepts, the market had better want them and be willing to pay what you need to charge to cover costs and produce the desired ROI. You are in the business of solving customers' problems better than your competition does, so you had better carefully observe and listen to consumers and customers.

INFLUENCE DEMAND

Any basic marketing course teaches the "four P's of marketing"—Product, Price, Place, and Promotion. This model served us well in the past, but now there is a more complex and competitive business environment, so it makes sense to expand the paradigm of the four P's and think of marketing in terms of eight P's. The eight P's are tools to be understood, used, manipulated, developed, and perfected in order to reach the ultimate marketing goal of making and keeping customers at a profit. Just as you would use a hammer, saw, and nails to fashion wood into a piece of fine furniture, you use these elements to fashion raw marketing information into a successful marketing plan. You use them to influence consumers to come into your business and, once there, to influence what they buy.

People

The first "P" requires you to ask the question, Who are your customers and prospective customers? You need a clear understanding of their demographics, psychographics, and buying behaviors. Underlying the needs, wants, and expectations of these markets are changing lifestyle trends, which alter how consumers think about your products and brand. Just think of the healthy eating and fitness trend. Before we all started counting calories and fat grams, fried foods were *good*! Now, we may still eat them, but we think of them differently. In addition to trends, an important part of the People "P" is who customers "rub elbows with." Being like other people—the *right* other people—is part of why consumers buy a certain brand of jeans, join a certain club, or eat at a certain restaurant. Market segmentation is heavily related to homogeneity.

Product

Your product is the sum total of all the tangibles and intangibles of need- or want-satisfying benefits; it includes the physical as well as the psychological product. This "P" asks what business you are in and what product you really sell. Although you might think that McDonald's is in the hamburger business, they are really in the safety and security business. Whether you eat at the golden arches in Minneapolis or Moscow, you know what you're going to get. There are no surprises; you feel safe in your food choices. Similarly, Disney World is really in the

entertainment business, not the theme park business. And what about Michelin? While they may sell tires, they are actually in the insurance business. Who can watch those cute babies riding around in a tire on television and not feel that, with Michelin, they are insuring the safety of their loved ones?

Position

Positioning requires that you look at how consumers classify and rank your product/brand relative to your competition. It asks the question "What image do you want to own in consumers' minds?" Positioning strategies have to be long term and related to your mission statement. It would, for example, be unrealistic for Taco Bell to want to "own" a fine dining position in consumers' minds when its mission centers on southwestern fast food at a low price.

According to Michael Porter (1985), a business can be positioned only on one of three criteria:

> *Price.* If your mission statement directs you to position on price, then the key is to be seen as either the least expensive or the most expensive. You can't get caught in the middle. Your pricing strategy may be middle-of-the-road, but if you position your brand on price, then you have to be at one extreme or the other. Wal-Mart positions itself on the pricing element. It wants to own the cheapest-place-in-town-to-buy-everyday-household-items position.

> *Segment.* You can also position yourself by the market niche you go after. The clearest example of this is a private club. Clubs are not out to be all things to all people. They go after a very narrow band of the market. Maybe it's golfers, or people who like to work out or drink imported beer. Whatever the product, an organization that narrows its focus to a special target market is really selling homogeneity, friendship, and exclusivity. Its physical product is only a vehicle for their real product.

> *Differentiation.* If you don't position yourself on price or market segment, then you have to position yourself on one of the other "Ps." You have to be known for some uniqueness. In my hometown, there was an ice cream store that sold "rainbow"

cones in "junior" and "senior" sizes. Their ice cream was like that in most other stores in the area—no better or no worse. But it was what they did with their ice cream that made the positioning difference. To make the rainbow cone, they would layer five (junior size) or seven (senior size) flavors of ice cream on a regular cone using a type of spatula scoop. When one flavor was put in, the next was laid along side of it, extending a little further out of the cone. This would continue until all the flavors were layered, resulting in a "rainbow" of color and flavor bands. People would drive for an hour just to get one of Walt's Rainbow Cones. Walt's positioned not on the ice cream, but what they did to the ice cream. You can also position on Place, like Appleby's neighborhood, or Promotion, as Absolut Vodka has done with its artful print ads.

Package

When you talk about a box of cereal or a bottle of perfume, the idea of packaging is obvious. What does the box look like? Although that's one way to look at packaging, in the expanded marketing paradigm, this "P" is more complex. There are really three levels of packaging that you can use to help market products. The first one is the actual product—the car, the clothing, the computer. The second level is the decor and ambiance of the store (or Web site) where it is sold. It includes color, texture, lighting, and sound, and also furniture design and any theme used. The third level includes all the symbols used to reinforce the brand's image—the company logo and signage, how the building looks, its landscaping, and surrounding neighborhood. Add to these the feel and look of your advertising, where you place your ads, how you get publicity, and how you generate public relations, and you'll have the total packaging "P."

Place

Place refers to the geographic location with respect to your target market(s), competition, employees, and distribution channels. It also includes relevant site characteristics such as convenient access to highways and exit ramps, proximity to other demand generators/attractions, restrictions

on site development, and natural scenic features. And in today's e-commerce world, it includes all the attributes of your Web site. How important is location? That depends on a lot of factors. But most of all it depends on what kind of a need your customer is trying to satisfy (i.e., where on Maslow's hierarchy that need falls). The more physiological the need, the more important is location; the more psychological the need, the less critical location becomes as a decision factor for consumers. Just remember that in today's fast-paced culture, distance is measured in terms of time, not in terms of miles. Think about place, then, relative to how long it takes people to make the purchase and whether it is worth their time and effort to do so.

Price

The pricing "P" is what a customer pays to get your product and is the single most tangible way for consumers to compare you with your competition. It establishes the all-important perceived "price-value" relationship for consumers, and it must deliver the financial return on capital for your business. What you ultimately decide to charge is really a marketing decision that is too often driven by accounting factors. You have to look at what you need/want for your ROI, the competitive influences on perceived value, and what the consumer is ready, willing, and able to pay. Since pricing is a marketing strategy in addition to a financial strategy, you have to take the decision out of just a balance sheet and put it into the consumers' minds. The bottom line in pricing is this: When your customers leave, will they feel that *you owe them* or that *they owe you?*

Promotion

Promotion addresses the question of how to best influence your customers to buy. Generally, promotion is thought of as advertising, special promotions, and direct sales. But in its broadest definition, it includes everything you do to influence people to come and then to influence their purchase choices once they are there. In other words, promotion includes *all* activities that are designed to influence consumers to choose your brand over those of your competitors. The overall goal of any promotion is to make a promise to the prospective guest—a promise that establishes an expectation higher than the competition's. In designing your promotional strategy, you must deliver on the promise and hopefully exceed customer expectations. This job falls to operations, reinforcing the belief that there is no way marketing can be separated from operations in today's competitive business environment. Marketing departments and advertising agencies can be very creative and, by design, are aggressive promoters. Sometimes, in their exuberance, they can make a promise and set an expectation level that can't be delivered. While the ultimate goal of your promotion is to make a promise to the guests, your promotion must be designed more specifically to break through the clutter of other promotional "noise" and drive revenues. Every day, consumers are bombarded with myriad messages to "buy me." Your message must be able to break through all that clutter in order to grab attention. This means that you have to be creative, develop a memorable message, and target the media channels that will hit your target markets.

Service Demand Performance

The final "P" represents the third function of marketing—that of servicing demand. Too many marketers see their job as simply getting customers to the door and operations as the folks who deal with the product, service, maintenance, accounting, staffing, scheduling, and other such functions. But it costs 6 to 10 times as much to get a new customer in the door as it does to get a current customer to return. If you fail to integrate operations into your marketing strategy, you'll end up with a big hole in your ROI. Consistently top service quality is the name of the game here. You can sell the sizzle but you also must be able to deliver it consistently. Once you're well positioned, it's hard for your competitors to knock you out of your market share unless you give a bad performance. Performance is the consistent delivery of the promise of the promotion. It's management getting the needed/desired

results through others. It's called operations. And it's the other side of the marketing coin.

—*Bonnie J. Knutson*

Bibliography

Harvey, M. G., Lusch, R. F., & Cavarkapa, B. (1996). A marketing mix for the 21st century. *Journal of Marketing Theory and Practice, 40,* 1–15.

Levitt, T. (1960, July–August). Marketing myopia. *Harvard Business Review, 38,* 45–56.

McCarthy, E. J. (1960). *Basic marketing.* Homewood, IL: Richard D. Irwin.

Porter, M. E. (1985). *Competitive advantage: Creating and sustaining superior performance.* New York: Free Press.

Ries, A., & Trout, J. (1986). *Positioning: The battle for your mind.* New York: McGraw-Hill.

Stevens, P. J. (1988). *Winning!!! Getting customers, keeping customers, and making money.* Okemos, MI: Hospitality.

MARKETPLACE OF IDEAS

John Milton's 1644 book, *Areopagitica,* in which he advocated a free and open discussion of ideas where "truth and falsehood grapple" so that truth could freely rise, has led to the "marketplace of ideas" metaphor as a measure of analysis for questions regarding First Amendment law. Open, public discussion and robust debate are critical components of a healthy democracy, and public relations professionals contribute to the information stream. As advocates for corporate interests, legislative issues, and social causes, public relations practitioners tell companies' and organizations' stories and communicate these entities' stances to the media and to the public. Public relations historian Scott M. Cutlip (1995) pointed out that public relations practitioners also engage in propaganda, as defined in the neutral sense: "Much of practitioners' endeavors are in propagating a doctrine, a cause, an institution, or an individual" (p. xi).

Indeed, public relations practitioners have the technical communication expertise, the access to myriad controlled media, and the contacts within media industries to serve as effective advocates, a role that renowned practitioner John W. Hill saw as a primary public relations duty. However, propagating a cause or being an advocate does not dictate the release of distorted, one-sided information. On the contrary, ethics scholar David Martinson (2003) suggests that the notion of "substantial completeness" be applied, meaning that public relations practitioners should supply information to "the point at which a reasonable reader's requirements for information are satisfied" so that people can make informed decisions (Wilcox, 2001, p. 110).

Likewise, as communication facilitators and liaisons, or "boundary spanners," practitioners also bring the views of various publics back to organizations and corporate management. Such "symmetrical two-way communication" processes, in which an organization communicates cooperatively with its publics—both giving and receiving information via dialogue—stands in stark contrast to mere publicity, or one-way communication. Although not always realistic to implement, the two-way symmetrical communication model is considered by many modern public relations practitioners to be the ideal. Not only does a two-way communication model ensure that entities consider their publics' wants, needs, and concerns for strategic and competitive reasons, but for companies and organizations to thrive, they ultimately must operate by public consent, as legendary corporate practitioner Arthur W. Page contended during his time with AT&T.

Many public relations professionals have declared their noble intentions to

> increase public knowledge and understanding by promoting expression and debate in the competitive marketplace of ideas . . . providing a voice in the public forum for every point of view, including the views of those—such as the homeless and powerless—who would not otherwise be heard because of limited media attention. (Cutlip, Center & Broom, 2000, p. 25)

However, some scholars argue differently. They contend that the voices of sophisticated communicators, often acting on behalf of powerful corporate elites, have much greater access to media and thus to the "marketplace" than the poor or disenfranchised; therefore, true debate cannot occur. Walter Lippmann, author of the 1922 classic *Public Opinion,* expressed similar concerns about society.

However, said David L. Martinson (2003), "professionals" are by definition dedicated to serving the common good and public interest. Therefore, he reasoned that public relations practitioners need to be more attentive to bringing about mutual understanding. Two-way symmetrical communication aids in such understanding, thereby indirectly bringing myriad views to the marketplace.

Regardless of First Amendment principles, there are public relations exceptions to the free marketplace analogy. Commercial speech—traditionally meaning advertising—is not legally protected. Issues of consumer health and protection stemming from false and misleading advertising supersede a company's right to say whatever it wishes. However, the recent *Kasky v. Nike* case calls the definition of "commercial speech" into question. Nike's appeal of a California Supreme Court ruling was dismissed by the U.S. Supreme Court in June 2003 by a 6-3 vote. Therefore, the case will go forward in California. The legal issue revolves around the contention by California consumer activist Marc Kasky that Nike misled consumers about the company's overseas labor practices in a publicity campaign including letters to editors and news releases. The case could ultimately cause companies and organizations to become more reticent, thus causing the "ideas marketplace" to shrink.

The Nike case underscores the public relations profession's credibility problem. Too common among the general public are notions of practitioners distorting the truth as expert "spin doctors," impressions that good corporate acts are insincere because their actions are "just public relations," and the idea that public relations spokespersons are hired liars. Although many public relations practitioners follow and espouse professional codes of ethics, honesty, public good, and stakeholder access—ideals that most recognize as not only noble, but as the better alternative for long-term business success—many do not.

Front groups are a case in point. Although they contribute to the marketplace of ideas, they may be deceptive and ultimately counterproductive to the public relations profession's credibility. With names that give the impression of grassroots organizations, front groups are funded by industries or special interest groups with specific public policy agendas. Lobbying by such front groups, called "stealth lobbying," keeps confidential the identity of a campaign's sponsoring organization. Such tactics, condemned by many practitioners and the Public Relations Society of America, seek to misrepresent and unduly influence and thereby compromise the free-marketplace concept.

—Diana L. Knott

See also Commercial speech; Hill, John Wiley; Page, Arthur W.; Public Relations Society of America; Spin

Bibliography

Callison, C. (2003). *The good, the bad and the ugly of how the general public views PR practitioners.* Paper presented at the Association for Education in Journalism and Mass Communication Annual Convention, July–August 2003, Kansas City, Missouri.

Cutlip, S. M. (1995). *Public relations history: From the 17th to the 20th century. The antecedents.* Hillsdale, NJ: Lawrence Erlbaum.

Cutlip, S. M., Center, A. H., & Broom, G. M. (2000). *Effective public relations* (8th ed.). Upper Saddle River, NJ: Prentice Hall.

Gillmor, D. M., Barron, J. A., & Simon, T. F. (1998). *Mass communication: Cases and comment* (6th ed.). Belmont, CA: Wadsworth.

Martinson, D. L. (1998). A question of distributive and social justice: Public relations practitioners and the marketplace of ideas. *Journal of Mass Media Ethics, 13*(3), 141–151.

Martinson, D. L. (2003). *Utilizing John Rawls' "A theory of justice" to examine the social utility of contemporary public relations.* Paper presented at the Association for Education in Journalism and Mass Communication Annual Convention, July–August 2003, Kansas City, Missouri.

Wilcox, D. L. (2001). *Public relations writing and media techniques* (4th ed.). New York: Longman.

MATERIAL INFORMATION

Investors desire information that will help them to decide whether to buy, hold, or sell the stock of any publicly traded company. Material information is any detail about a publicly traded company's plans, operations, or business conditions that would help a prudent investor decide whether to buy, sell, or hold shares of stock in the company.

Material is a key term in investor relations. The Securities and Exchange Commission (SEC) requires publicly traded companies to disclose all material information. Various investor relations tools are used to accomplish this task, especially since the SEC also requires that such notice be made in a public manner so that all interested investors have the same opportunity to obtain and use the information. Thus, disclosure of material information must be open, broad, and timely.

In reference to *timely*, the SEC offers two broad standards. One is that some investors should not have the opportunity to get the information before it is made available to all investors. Also, the information must be shared so that it is most relevant to stock transactions because it is not out of date.

Companies get into trouble when their sense of what information is material or relevant to stock transactions differs from that of its investors. They can incur the wrath of the SEC and investors if this information is not available when it is most relevant to those persons wanting to make stock transactions.

Material information comes in many forms. One obvious kind of information is the likelihood that the corporation will produce a profit or suffer a loss. A major change in senior personnel or the health of a senior executive could be material. It is often believed that key executives have a major influence on the business. Thus, the condition of these personnel is material.

If a company is suffering a substantial lawsuit, a dramatic change in the market, the arrival or loss of a major competitor, or implementation of a new process, that information is likely to be material. If an agriculture company has operations that are likely to be affected by the weather (drought or excessive rain, for instance), that is material.

The SEC uses rules and regulations to define what is material. Investigations are launched and audits are performed to increase the likelihood that material information is properly revealed in a timely fashion. For this reason, an ostensibly independent auditing firm to ensure objective compliance with SEC expectations audits the books of each publicly traded company.

Regulations, statutory law, and case law constitute a huge body of expert guidelines that are to be applied by executive management in conjunction with legal counsel and auditing firms to ensure that prudent stock traders get information they need and deserve.

—Robert L. Heath

See also Investor relations; Securities and Exchange Commission

MATRIXING/MATRIX MANAGEMENT

Starting in the mid-1990s, Hill & Knowlton's management addressed how to restore excitement, growth, and profitability to one of the oldest and best-known brands in the public relations industry. Ultimately the answer to that challenge was to embrace matrix management, which replaces a silo approach to account management with a management philosophy and organizational strategy that builds teams relevant to each account based on the most relevant expertise.

One of the steps in meeting this challenge was to ask, "How we can bring value to clients?" This question could not be answered without recognizing that it might require an end to the silo approach. A silo approach to managing client accounts assumes that one account manager with his or her team is the only resource made available to the client.

The silo approach had lots of problems. Clients were denied the broad talent, intellect, and experience of the firm—which should be one of the fundamental reasons they would hire Hill & Knowlton versus a local boutique. Clients were not getting full access to global resources and specialist skills. Growth was artificially restrained by the talent and experience of the local office. And staff didn't have the professional opportunity to interact with other offices and skills to encourage their own growth and development.

The matrix management style has some clear strengths. It provides clear fiscal accountability. It facilitates a hands-on training and mentoring environment for public relations people. It delivers local accountability for clients and accounting clarity for billing.

The challenge was preserving the historic strengths of geographic management while unlocking the potential for clients, agency people, and the firm. The solution was matrix management.

Matrix management, as introduced at Hill & Knowlton in the United States in 1996, was designed to deliver greater value for clients, staff, and the firm. It was a management tool to compensate for the weaknesses of local profit and loss (P&L) management by unlocking our potential.

MATRIX MANAGEMENT DELIVERS VALUE

There is no doubt that matrix management has delivered results.

- U.S. growth dramatically improved for Hill & Knowlton in the late 1990s and into the early 2000s.
- Profitability recovered quickly.
- Offerings of specialist client services exploded. Clients could be offered more specialist skills more easily than ever before.
- New business was won that would have been lost under the old local-only approach.
- The firm attracted better talent than ever. People were excited by the openness and devotion to clients that a matrix system provides.

The success of matrix management at Hill & Knowlton is clear. It added a lot of value for the firm and its clients. As a result of the initial success, each of the company's regions—Europe, Asia, Canada, and Latin America—now employs a version of matrix management to improve client service and the performance of staffs around the world. Matrix management is now the standard, so that any Hill & Knowlton client anywhere in the world can benefit from the best-teams and best-talent approach.

IMPLEMENTING THE CHANGES

Moving from a purely local management system to a matrix management system is a huge undertaking.

Never underestimate the amount of planning, work, and follow-up that it takes. It is enormous. Hill & Knowlton had to retrain its entire U.S. workforce; develop a new orientation for recruiting and training that got people off to the right start; plan and implement systems to support matrix management; and change the culture at the company to support this new work environment. Even clients had to understand what the "new" Hill & Knowlton was all about.

There were six key steps in successfully implementing the transformation to matrix management.

First, we needed to better understand our clients. We talked with lots of clients. We looked at their business challenges. We looked at their needs today and how those needs might grow in the future. We did a candid appraisal of our own alignment to be able to provide for those needs. Any additional service we might provide for a client deepened the relationship, both financially and functionally. Any service that we failed to provide simply left the door open for a competitor to come in and dazzle the client. We were also candid about how happy clients were with our service, and the answer was clear: not happy enough. In our business, a marginally happy client is one that we are about to lose.

Second, we had to assess our own skills and offerings. Were we staffed to provide what clients really needed, both today and in the near future? In many cases, we were disappointed. Although we had bright, talented generalists in our offices, we lacked the specialist talent that our clients need. To illustrate the challenge with a comparison, a specialist heart surgeon that opens 150 chests a week will develop tremendous professional skills that a once-a-week general-practice surgeon in a small town could never master. Although we still needed some small-town practitioners who were close to clients, we also needed the big-city talent of specialist leaders who could help organize our efforts to deliver more for clients.

One crucial step was to recruit a number of practice leaders in key areas who could be our leaders and organize our specialist skills for the firm. We identified several key practices that our clients would need: corporate, financial, consumer, health

care, media, public affairs, and technology. These practices covered our most critical areas for client services in the United States. Each would be an intellectual and motivational leader who could win client assignments, train our staff as specialists, and deliver greater client service. Their challenge was to create a brand within a brand, building a strong and determined point of view about our approach to client needs in each key practice area.

Third, we began rolling out our new leadership system, which included both practice heads to deliver the specialist skills and talent that our clients need and strong local-office general managers who knew the local marketplace and provided the strength in key local markets in the United States. The next key step was to review the local staff in each office and organize them into specialist practice areas to match our national practice approach to client service.

This effort required a massive human resource effort in creating new job descriptions for local general managers and practice leaders—and the rules of engagement on how they would work together. Absolute authority ended, and we moved into a system of collaborative decision making.

Fourth, we had to focus again on clients. The motivation for matrix management was really the clients—to bring more value to them. We had to work to align this new system with our clients and their needs.

As we mobilized and developed practice approaches, we had to go out with road shows and meetings to help clients understand how we might provide even more help and better solutions and results for them. We used these meetings to better understand their priorities and what they needed from us. Practice leaders helped us to diagnose client problems and opportunities and worked with local managers to develop the talent that we needed to respond to those opportunities.

The matrix system also opened the door for multiple-office and even global solutions. We focused on where we could find the best talent within Hill & Knowlton for what they needed, regardless of where they were based. We were freed from the shackles of looking for local-only solutions to any problems. Multi-office, best-teams, best-talent approaches to solving client problems were what we preached and practiced.

One of the key ways to ensure that this approach would work was to build an incentive system that supported it. That was the important step 5 in our transition. Key practice leaders and local managers had management objectives and bonus incentives that were built around the combination of personal goals and collaboration. Teamwork was rewarded and incentivized, while "piggish" behavior resulted in a personal and financial cost to the individual. It was one of the critically important symbolic ways that we assured our people that we were really serious about this new direction for the company.

We had lots of bumps in the road, but people really pitched in and got excited about making it work. It was invigorating for our staff, who felt as if they were suddenly opened to new training and development opportunities beyond the locale of the their home office.

Sixth, we knew that we had to track our performance. I named a head of client services for the U.S. company to develop a system of measuring, tracking, and reacting to service needs for all of our major clients. We built an annual tracking system with a client service review. That assessment of what we did well and what we did not was shared with practice leaders, general managers, and client service teams. We had a transparent look, completed by an independent reviewer and with candid client feedback about our strengths and weaknesses.

Each client service review was a goldmine of valuable client insight. We knew what was going well that we needed to protect. We knew where we fell short, and quickly moved to fix that. Fixing a problem can do wonders to improve a client relationship. It helps clients to understand that we're really in it for them and not just ourselves. What was really interesting, though, is that the most valuable part of the client service audit was the knowledge gained about other needs of the client. It told us exactly how and where to approach clients with new offerings from Hill & Knowlton that could expand the relationship and provide a value added for the client.

LOOKING BACK

One of the lessons for us was the importance of occasionally standing back and viewing our business anew. Although local P&Ls fit the business in the early days, it is no longer the best approach today. Although former Democratic House Speaker Tip O'Neill is right in saying that all politics is local, it's not the case for public relations. We had grown from a more modest cottage industry of hometown, locally focused companies to sprawling, diverse, complex mega-corporations with complex global needs and challenges. Our management structure had to grow with our clients. While many major companies developed their own matrix management approaches, we had to realize that it was the best system for us, too, if we were to keep pace with their increasingly complex professional public relations needs. Matrix management allowed us to get more talent to the table for our clients while retaining the great strengths and fiscal controls of local P&Ls.

—*Tom Hoog*

See also Account manager/account management; Client/agency relationships; Management theory; Public relations agency

MEAN AND MEDIAN

The mean is the arithmetic average of a group of numbers. Its relative ease of calculation—any spreadsheet program will compute a mean—and widely understood definition make it a common point of reference in many types of research. More important than its common use is its role in characterizing a data set. In a normally distributed data set, the mean represents the population parameter, or the typical response (found under "measures of central tendency" in statistics programs). Public relations researchers and practitioners often focus on the "average person's opinion" when investigating attitudes or planning campaigns. For example, on a five-point Likert item (1: strongly agree to 5: strongly disagree), one may report that the mean response was 2.2, which corresponds to agreement, but not strong agreement. The tendency to report that "68 percent of the respondents agreed or strongly agreed" with a statement should be avoided, as it lacks the overall precision of the mean and can mask a large portion who disagree with the statement.

In addition, using the mean provides a precise benchmark from which to measure progress. In research or campaign planning, measuring opinion change from time 1 to time 2, for example, is important for improving our knowledge of the impact and effectiveness of public relations activities and for the accountability of programs. As a campaign objective, with the initial measure of 2.2 one can set a precise target of, say, 1.4 for improved agreement with a statement after the communication campaign. Measurement with the same statement at both times allows direct comparison and evaluation of change.

The mean is also important as the basis for the calculation of numerous inferential statistics. T-tests and ANOVAs, which measure differences between groups, both assume an accurate mean in the computations. Very often we need to know if, for example, gender (a t-test) or education level (an ANOVA) makes a difference in what people think about a topic or how they react to a message. Questions attempting to measure such opinions or attitudes should always be formulated in a manner that provides an accurate mean. Aside from their inability to measure a range of opinions, "yes/no" questions do not allow the calculation of a mean; only response percentages can be reported from these questions (yes/no questions can be used, however, as the grouping variable in a t-test).

The median is another measure of central tendency. When all responses to an item are placed in numeric order, the median is the number that is the midpoint of the list. If the list has an even number of entries, the median is calculated by averaging the two numbers that fall to either side of the midpoint. In a normally distributed data set, the median and mean will be approximately the same. However, the median is useful as a measure of central tendency when the mean is either inflated by large responses

or deflated by small ones. For example, in examining the income figures within an organization of 50 people, very high salaries among 6 executives could inflate the mean income in such a way that makes it look like the company pays its employees better than it does.

Generally speaking, the fewer numbers there are in a data set, the more impact extreme values will have. Examining the distribution of the data points and the difference between the median and mean should indicate which number is the more accurate reflection of the typical response in a data set.

—*Maribeth S. Metzler*

MEASURING/MEASURES

Respected and successful public relations scholars and practitioners alike acknowledge the important role measurement plays in communication effectiveness and management. Essential to communication practitioners who employ one-way, two-way, asymmetrical, and symmetrical communication functions, research informs the decision-making processes in successful organizations. Measurement can be used to offer both insight and foresight and is often used to shape strategic initiatives based on the needs of publics. Measuring organizational communication is often broadly categorized as informal, formal, quasi-formal, or mixed. The two paradigms of research include quantitative and qualitative. No method is better than the other; rather, they are complementary.

Contemporary discussions of public relations research are rooted in the late 19th-century debates about whether or not researchers could or should borrow investigative methods from the physical sciences to understand the human and social world. Anchored in the foundation that the physical world was mastered intellectually and materially to a greater extent than the social world, positivist theorists, including Auguste Comte, John Stuart Mill, and Emile Durkheim, worked in the empiricist tradition established by John Locke, Isaac Newton, and others. Conversely, constructivist or naturalistic theorists were loosely labeled idealists. These scholars, including Wilhelm Dilthey, Heinrich Rickert, and Max Weber, found their philosophical origins in a Kantian tradition.

Within these broadly defined paradigms, communication research seeks to explain, describe, or explore the phenomenon chosen for study. Composed of both theories and methods, paradigms help us understand phenomena by advancing assumptions, asserting how research should be conducted, and defining legitimate problems, solutions, and criteria of "proof."

Measurement is generally the assigning of either words (qualitative) or numbers (quantitative) to a phenomenon. A qualitative study explores a specific program, event, situation, person, or group, and it usually applies only to the specific matter being studied; the results cannot be generalized. Those projects that seek to learn about regularities are usually deemed quantitative.

The different research paradigms hold different assumptions, which include ontological, epistemological, axiological, rhetorical, and methodological approaches.

The ontological assumption asks, "What is reality?" For the quantitative researcher, reality is objective, independent of the researcher, and can usually be measured objectively as well. Reality for the qualitative researcher can be constructed only by those involved in the research, whether it is the researcher, those people being investigated, or the reader(s) interpreting the study.

For a quantitative study, the epistemological supposition—or the relationship of the researcher to those or that being studied—is that the researcher maintains distance and is left independent of the research subject(s). This is why researchers try to control for bias, to select a systematic sample, and to be as "objective" as possible when analyzing the data. This is much different in qualitative research, where the researcher will interact with those they study.

Researchers from both camps claim objectivity, but mean different things. The quantitative approach takes *objective* to mean what is outside us or in the world of facts, independent of the knower—seeing the world free from one's own personal place or situation. To the qualitative researcher, objectivity means that how one views the world is based on one's knowledge and experiences of the world and place in it. According to the norms of qualitative research, then, the researcher is not separate from the research process.

Verification is a process that occurs throughout data collection, analysis, and report writing. Standards that need to be applied to *all* research projects include the need for research questions to drive the data collection and analysis rather than the other way around, data collection and analysis techniques being competently applied, researchers' assumptions being made explicit, and the study overall being warranted and having value, both for informing and for improving practice. But is *validity* even a word used by qualitative researchers? Some researchers use quantitative terminology, such as *external validity*, *reliability,* and *objectivity,* to facilitate the acceptance of qualitative research in a quantitative world. Instead of using the term *validity*, one could use *credibility* or *verification* by constructing standards of structural corroboration (relating multiple types of data to support or contradict the interpretation), consensual validation (seeking opinions of others), and referential adequacy (criticism).

The discussion of credibility in measuring has an impact on the axiological assumptions of the two paradigms. The researcher's values are kept out of a quantitative study, but become imperative to the value-laden nature of a qualitative study. Detaching oneself from the study is seen as failure to understand the subject by a qualitative researcher. That which is a limitation to a quantitative researcher is essential to a qualitative one.

Thus, the language differs between qualitative and quantitative research. Another aspect is that a quantitative researcher will use only impersonal and formal words, including words that have been formally accepted, such as *relationship, comparison,* and *within-group.* Some qualitative researchers have constructed a language different from the quantitative vernacular to reflect the nature of the research, including terms such as *understanding*, *discover*, and *meaning*. This differentiation extends to the writing of qualitative reports, in which the language is personal, informal, and based on definitions determined in the study.

Quantitative and qualitative research both follow specific procedures, which include a statement or definition of the problem, a review of prior related research, a research design, data gathering and data analysis, and an interpretive phase that results in conclusions and recommendations. However, the process of study is different. Quantitative measuring uses a deductive logic by testing theories and hypotheses in a cause-and-effect order. The concepts, variables, and hypotheses are set before the study begins and remain throughout the study. Communication practitioners who use quantitative methods are usually looking to develop generalizations that might predict, explain, or clarify how publics respond to organizations and their communication efforts. The data are measured with numbers and analyzed with statistical procedures.

Qualitative research is an inductive process. The researcher might identify several lines of inquiry before beginning the study. Most often, however, categorical data emerge as the study progresses. The emerging data provide "rich" information about that which is being studied, such as people's attitudes, opinions, and reactions. When studying people, qualitative researchers note verbal and nonverbal cues as data. The data are analyzed systematically and continuously throughout the research process using either traditional pen and paper or word processing and qualitative data analysis software. The research process continues until saturation is achieved. Saturation occurs when no new data are brought forth.

A research situationalist is a communicator who understands that both research approaches have value. Certain methods are appropriate for specific situations. Quantitative surveys might provide representative information that can be elaborated through qualitative data collection in in-depth interviews. Survey research allows one to test hypotheses generated through a pre-test and focus groups. Again, the approaches are complementary.

If time, money, and expertise are available, a communicator might employ what is called mixed- or multiple-method research. There are three different purposes for using multiple-method design. First, the goal may be triangulation, which seeks a convergence of findings. Second, one might look for bracketing, which pursues a range of estimates of the correct answer—or triangulation with a confidence interval. And third, one might seek complementarity, where different methods are used to assess different components or phenomena, to assess identified threats to validity, or to enhance the interpretability of different assessments of the same phenomenon.

Using different types of methods helps to guard against and correct for inherent methodological biases. Used together, the different methods paint different pictures and allow for more confidence in the decisions made from the research process. For example, visiting sawmill workers in the field improves the realism of employee surveys by providing an empirically grounded framework for survey research, and surveys may correspondingly improve on fieldwork's realism.

Combining measurement techniques might provide a fuller picture, but most likely will not give a more "objective" one. Different methods come from different theoretical traditions, so combining them adds range and depth, but not necessarily accuracy. Combining theories and methods carefully and purposefully should be done to add breadth and depth to analysis, but not to provide the "objective" truth.

Public relations research can be exploratory, descriptive, or explanatory. Exploratory research is done when little is known about an issue, a public, or an event. Most often, a case study or field study, including observation, and focus group and/or individual interviewing are used to gather information. A descriptive study looks for specific descriptions of events, conditions, circumstances, processes, and relationships in order to document and analyze them. Data collection techniques include but are not limited to observation, participant observation, in-depth interviewing, document and content analysis, and survey questionnaires. Explanatory or predictive research looks for explanations or causal relationships by using experiments and quasi-experiments (although uncommon, but successful when employed, in organizational settings), survey questionnaires and polls, content analysis, message indexes, and Web page counters.

Measurement in public relations should be both formative and evaluative. Formative research assists the effective communications manager to plan and implement strategic communication programs by determining what the current situation "looks like." Analysis and assessment of public opinion, the environment, and communication programs can assist in predicting a public's behavior. Used appropriately, formative research facilitates two-way, symmetrical communication efforts by allowing the communicator and the publics to communicate with one another. In addition, implementing formative research throughout a one-way, asymmetrical communication program allows for strategy reformulation.

Evaluative research is composed of tools that can help determine the effectiveness of a communication plan, program, or initiative. The conclusions that emerge from evaluative research are often used to communicate with others on an organization's management team. If conceived properly, a communication plan will include goals and objectives that reflect those of the organization. The evaluative research can determine to what degree the communication program met those objectives and will provide insight into where efforts might be focused in the future.

How does a communicator choose which method to employ? First, one must ask which assumptions hold to the views, experience, and comfort levels of the communicator, the research consultant (if one is employed), and those who will use the research. Does the communicator have qualitative research expertise? Is there an in-house data analysis department? What will hosting focus groups communicate to the audience? Does the leader of the organization want to see bottom-line dollar figures? The amount of time and money available will influence information gathering and analysis techniques types. Research can be expensive. However, if research is not implemented at the conception stage of a

communication program, and if it is not continued throughout the process as well as after, the cost of poor communication can be catastrophic.

As with any good strategic communication plan, a measurement program begins with identifying goals and objectives. These will reflect the goals and objectives of those who can use the research. At this stage of the measurement process, the researcher identifies the audiences, issues, or events that will be the focus of interrogation. When defining audiences, a communications practitioner is cognizant of both audience demographics and preferred communication methods. Designing an e-mail survey for employees who spend most of their day on fishing boats, for example, is not as logical as planning to conduct face-to-face surveys through an independent third party.

Ethical considerations are equally important in considering who will be the subject of measurement. Under most circumstances, people should remain anonymous and their responses confidential. If there is the possibility that this might not happen, it is the responsibility and obligation of the researcher to notify the participant. The researcher should also ensure that participation in the research project is voluntary.

Linking the research to other organizational measurables—such as behavioral expectations, levels of satisfaction, sales, projections, and productivity—also occurs in the preliminary planning of the research project.

Conducting a secondary research review will contextualize the problem or opportunity for the communicator, and may further determine the need for research. In public relations research, a review of the secondary research includes any of the organization's previous studies. It may also include projects that have been produced by government agencies and professional associations. Historical documents, databases, libraries, and the Internet also contain valuable information that can inform an organization's research plan. A communicator might find that someone else has already collected the information that is needed.

The goals and objectives of the research are the most important element in deciding whether to employ quantitative, qualitative, or mixed-method measurement.

If public relations practitioners want to make generalizations about a population, they employ quantitative research using a random sample. For example, if an external communications practitioner of XYZ not-for-profit wants to better understand how many residents in the community of Smithton support the organization's efforts, quantitative measurement is most likely the best choice. Quantitative measures provide information about numbers. A sufficiently large, random sample must be drawn from all residents in order for the communicator to assume confidently that the residents of Smithton support or do not support the organization. If the communicator is interested in tracking how the media respond to the organization and believes this might be indicative of how the residents feel, she might conduct a systematic content analysis. More likely, the measurement tool would be a telephone, face-to-face, or mail survey. Because surveys can give neither in-depth detail about the citizen's perceptions nor information that illuminates how the people interpret the activities of XYZ, the communicator might decide to use focus groups. If XYZ is applying for government funding to produce a community newsletter and needs to provide broad and detailed information in its application, the communicator might choose to use both quantitative and qualitative methods. This research project could then be used as a benchmark study. In the future, XYZ might want to determine if perceptions of the organization have changed after citizens began receiving the newsletter. Using similar questions, sampling techniques, and measures, XYZ can respond accordingly.

—*DeNel Rehberg Sedo*

See also Qualitative research; Quantitative research; Reliability; Symbolic interactionism theory; Validity

Bibliography

Daymon, C., & Holloway, I. (2002). *Qualitative research methods in public relations and marketing communications*. London and New York: Routledge.

Grunig, L. A., Grunig, J. E., & Dozier, D. M. (2002). *Excellent public relations and effective organizations: A study of communication management in three countries*. Mahwah, N.J.: Lawrence Erlbaum.

Heath, R. L. (1994). *Management of corporate communication: From interpersonal contacts to external affairs*. Hillsdale, NJ: Lawrence Erlbaum.

Jablin, F. M., & Putnam, L. (2001). *The new handbook of organizational communication: Advances in theory, research, and methods*. Thousand Oaks, CA: Sage.

Marshall, C., & Rossman, G. B. (1995). *Designing qualitative research*. Thousand Oaks, CA: Sage.

Reagan, J. (2002). *Communication research primer: Measuring and evaluating organizational communication*. San Francisco: IABC Research Foundation.

Salwen, M.. B., & Stacks, D. W. (1996). *An integrated approach to communication theory and research*. Mahwah, NJ: Lawrence Erlbaum.

Stacks, D. W. (2002). *Primer of public relations research*. New York: Guilford Press.

Weick, K. E. (1995). *Sensemaking in organizations*. Thousand Oaks, CA: Sage.

MEDIA CALLS

Media calls are telephone exchanges between reporters and sources. Telephone calls are basic media relations tools, along with correspondence, e-mails, faxes, and personal visits.

Receiving calls. Public relations practitioners welcome telephone inquiries from reporters and editors and routinely include telephone numbers on news releases and in story queries. The telephone remains the most widely used reporting tool for most journalists seeking quick answers and direct access to news sources.

Reporters call public relations representatives to obtain background information, verify information, obtain quotes, and arrange to speak to organizational experts. These impromptu conversations provide important opportunities to obtain unsolicited coverage.

Knowledgeable personnel should be available to speak to reporters in the hours following the release of announcements, especially if release happens late in the day when writers are on deadline. Failure to respond in a timely manner can lead to errors or omission from coverage.

Being responsive to unsolicited calls is an important way to build media relationships. Reporters and editors tend to seek out helpful sources and recommend them to colleagues.

Placing calls. Professional courtesy suggests that media calls always should be returned, but careful thought should be given to making unsolicited calls. Calls that *alert* reporters about *significant* breaking news stories, such as a pending announcement or industrial accident, are obviously welcomed. *Introductory* calls to reporters assigned to beats are also usually appropriate. However, *follow-up* calls inquiring whether a reporter or editor received a particular routine news story only annoy busy reporters and should be avoided.

Practitioners wishing to "pitch" stories to media sometimes make *cold calls* to assignment editors or reporters. Although this technique can work when a relationship already exists between the source and journalist, most editors and reporters will tell unknown callers to send them materials in advance, after which a follow-up call is appropriate. If used, cold pitches must be simple and compelling and should telegraph the idea in the first several sentences of the conversation.

Telephone calls are frequently employed to place guests on radio and television programs. Talent coordinators and producers almost always demand to see materials in advance but will then negotiate details by phone. Thereafter, arrangements should be confirmed in writing.

MEDIA CALL ETIQUETTE

Observe these commonsense rules:

- Always return queries promptly.
- When arranging for others to respond, make sure they understand the journalist's deadline and call back within an agreed-upon time frame.
- Avoid placing unsolicited calls while a reporter is on deadline.
- If callers sound suspicious for any reason, ask for a number and call back. This technique can help screen imposters.
- Include special instructions to media callers on office and home voicemail messages.

- Call journalists on their personal cell phones or at home only when you have permission to do so.
- Leave all appropriate numbers (office, home, cell phone, etc.) when leaving telephone messages for media personnel.
- Never speculate. If you don't know the answer to a telephone query, offer to call the person back.
- Always speak on the record, especially with unknown reporters.
- Don't avoid returning telephone calls. In an effort to demonstrate balanced reporting, journalists often tell audiences that repeated telephones inquiries were not returned. Avoid appearing evasive.
- Be succinct and be quotable.
- If you cannot respond to a particular question, say so. Declining comment for cause is better than saying "no comment."

—Kirk Hallahan

MEDIA CONFERENCES

Media or news conferences are held when an organization has important information to share that will affect the public. At the organization's request, the media gather at a designated date, time, and place to hear the information. Media conferences may be held to announce good news, address complex issues, or respond to a crisis situation.

The following criteria should be considered before deciding to hold a media conference:

1. Is the information newsworthy?

2. Is the information too complex for a media release alone?

3. Is it important that reporters have access to the information at the same time?

4. Is there visual value to the announcement?

5. Will reporters be allowed to ask questions?

If the answer is yes to *all* of the above, a media conference may be in order. If the answer is no to *any* of the above, holding a media conference may be a mistake. Reporters will not appreciate attending an event that they will consider a waste of time.

FORMAT

Upon arrival, reporters should be given media kits containing information that will assist them in developing their stories. Media conferences usually begin by welcoming the media and introducing the speaker(s) who will make the announcement, followed by a question-and-answer session. They should start on time and be brief. Satellite news conferences are used to make announcements to a large number of media in different geographic locations.

PLANNING A CONFERENCE

Select a site for the media conference that will accommodate the media and their equipment and, if possible, reflect the topic. For example, a beach might be the setting for announcing an environmental cleanup project. Be mindful of reporters' deadlines when picking a date and time.

Select the most appropriate person to make the announcement and respond to the media. Anticipate all questions that may be asked, not just those pertaining to the announcement, and prepare the speaker with answers.

Invite the media. Most often this is accomplished through a media or news advisory that contains only the necessary details for the conference—the topic; the date, time, and place; and contact information. Providing too much information will decrease the chances the media will cover the event, because they will already have the story.

Use visual elements. Television reporters and newspaper photographers will want more than "talking heads" as subjects. In addition, the name and logo of the organization should be prominently placed.

Prepare a media kit. This typically consists of a media release based on the announcement and other helpful background information, such as speaker biographies, organizational fact sheets, or graphics.

—Ann R. Carden

See also Communication technologies; News and newsworthy; Press kit

Bibliography

Smith, R. D. (2003). *Becoming a public relations writer* (2nd ed.). Mahwah, NJ: Lawrence Erlbaum.

Wilcox, D.L., Cameron, G. T., Ault, P. H., & Agee, W. K. (2003). *Public relations strategies and tactics* (7th ed.). Boston: Allyn & Bacon.

Zappala, J. M., & Carden, A. R. (2004). *Public relations worktext* (2nd ed.). Mahwah, NJ: Lawrence Erlbaum.

MEDIA EFFECTS

Scholars have long studied the impact mass communications have on individuals and society. Results of these studies tend to indicate both that Western societies have a dependency on mass media and that this dependency is not so complete as to make viewers and listeners thoughtlessly accept whatever messages they receive. To explain media effects, rejected models of media effects will be explained and current models of media dependency will be analyzed.

One early model of media effects was known as the "hypodermic" model. Much as a doctor's needle injects a patient with some drug, this theory held that audiences passively view whatever content major media outlets make available to them. Theoretically, having viewed set content would lead an audience member to behave in a predictable manner. However, several problems are associated with this theory. First, the proliferation of media outlets and the option of turning the television off make focusing audience attention on a single message exceedingly difficult. Second, this theory does not account for the tendency of audience members to respond to messages based on their own beliefs and values rather than on what they see on television.

A similar theory is known as the "magic bullet" theory. This argues that a media message will directly impact an audience. In other words, if an individual sees an advertisement for soft drink X, he or she will necessarily respond favorably to that soft drink and will likely buy it. Researchers have generally been unable to support such a conclusion. Although explanations vary, it is likely that this effect fails for similar reasons as the failure of the hypodermic effect. People have experiences other than what they see on television, and advertisements do not automatically overcome these experiences. Although a magic bullet can be properly aimed to hit its target, a direct effect from the simple presence of an ad is unlikely.

Although the hypodermic and magic bullet models of media effects have been widely rejected, media dependency theory offers some explanation of the ways in which media impact society. Developed by Sandra Ball-Rokeach and Melvin DeFleur, media dependency theory explains the growth of the media as well as the increased reliance many individuals have on various mass media forms. This theory holds that reliance on media is linked to the three factors of media, audience, and society. In this case, *media* refers to the number and type of information outlets that are available. In contemporary society, radio, television, print news sources, and the Internet are all viable ways in which people can receive information. This makes the task of selecting a medium more difficult, because audience members have many alternatives to which they might turn. At the same time, the sheer number of media options makes it more likely that there is some media option that will appeal to an individual audience member.

Audience refers to the degree to which a person or group of people depend on various media forms for information. Some audiences have a greater need or perceived need for information, and each audience will have different preferences about the precise forum from which they prefer to receive information.

Finally, *society* refers to all of the social factors that surround a need for information. When a nation is at war, its citizens are likely to have a greater perceived need for information than when the leading news stories are about more limited issues. Additionally, a person's place within a social structure will affect his or her need to access information. Together, these three factors indicate that the more someone relies on a particular form of media, the more that media outlet will influence the person's thoughts, feelings, and actions. People will rely more on media when their existing social networks do not fulfill all of their needs.

In 1996, DeFleur and Everette Dennis modified this work and coined the phrase *media information dependency theory*. Their theory has five major propositions. First, people in every society need information to make everyday decisions about politics, food, shelter, dating, and a wide array of other subjects. Second, people in traditional societies tend to pursue similar ways of life and rely on interpersonal methods for transmitting information. Third, contemporary urban-industrial societies are composed of a wide diversity of people from different backgrounds and groups. Fourth, increased social differences in industrial society cause people to have fewer effective interpersonal communication channels from which to obtain information. Fifth, people in urban-industrial society rely on the media to gain information that is typically unavailable to them from the interpersonal networks prevalent in traditional societies. In short, one of the reasons that so many people rely on the media—and thus give the media relatively great power to influence them—is that television or other mass media outlets may be the best available instrument for gaining the information needed to conduct everyday affairs.

Scholarly debate about media effects is ongoing. However, some theories have been rejected. There is neither a "hypodermic" nor a "magic bullet" effect where people simply absorb all media information presented to them. Rather, the effect of media correlates with how dependent people are on it. In contemporary urban society, many people rely on mass media to gain common information, which allows those media channels to serve a gatekeeping function that helps determine the issues that will be on the public agenda.

—*William Forrest Harlow*

See also Agenda-setting theory

Bibliography

Ball-Rokeach, S. J., & DeFleur, M. L. (1976). A dependency model of mass media effects. *Communication Research, 3,* 3–21.

Carroll, C. E., & McCombs, M. (2003). Agenda-setting effects of business news on the public's images and opinions about major corporations. *Corporate Reputation Review, 6*(1), 36–46.

DeFleur, M. L., & Dennis, E. E. (1996). *Understanding mass communication.* Boston: Houghton Mifflin.

McCombs, M. E., & Shaw, D. L. (1972). The agenda-setting function of the mass media. *Public Opinion Quarterly, 36,* 176–185.

MEDIA MIX STRATEGIES

Communicators often use formal mass media channels to develop and maintain relationships with key audiences. Primarily the domain of advertisers and media buyers, media mix strategies involve weighing the advantages and disadvantages of each medium against budget considerations. Media mix strategies also play a role in public relations work. Like advertisers, practitioners are challenged to develop unique messages that cut through media clutter.

Although buying media generally is not a public relations practitioner's responsibility, it is important to understand each medium's operations and needs when putting together information for media representatives. Furthermore, practitioners must consider their organization's overall communications objectives and internal resources and the advantages and limitations of each medium—as well as stakeholder media use behaviors, evolving technologies, and implications of media ownership and management change. Specific communication tasks best carried out by using mass media include placing press releases and public service announcements or advocacy advertisements, staging press conferences, offering interviews, coordinating product placements for films and TV, and organizing special events.

Designing messages and developing media mix strategies involve at least five important decisions. First, the practitioner should review the communication objectives established for the organization and for key public relationships in terms of credibility perceptions, timing, information opportunities, reach effectiveness, motivation, and cost per contact. Funding and staffing resources also must be factored in. Second, selecting media that complement a message requires an understanding of the pros and cons of each mass medium.

Among print media, newspapers are the most immediate and credible information source. Newspapers offer sections tailored to readers' demographic and psychographic needs, are geographically flexible, and lend local flavor. Newspapers' limitations are passivity, shrinking circulations, and low interest among young readers. Magazines target highly selective audiences and lend prestige appeal, produce demographic and geographic editions, and have a long shelf life with pass-along value. Disadvantages include lack of immediacy and long lead times. Direct mail is highly selective and relatively easy to personalize and measure, yet can be costly.

Electronic media such as television, radio, and the Internet are immediate and active—and attract both selective and mass audiences. Network television is beneficial for developing product or service image, and cable television has high penetration for higher-income households. Radio offers good demographic and geographic selectivity and is especially beneficial for targeting mobile populations. On the downside, transmission quality wavers, and messages are fleeting and cluttered. The Internet is an important, cost-effective, global communication vehicle among practitioners, yet stakeholders are concerned about privacy issues, content overload, and unwelcome solicitations.

A third consideration involved in developing media mix strategies is learning stakeholders' media use behaviors. For example, "surfing and scanning" interrupts message flow, sheer abundance of media content competes for attention, and traditional demographic and psychographic data often are inadequate in anticipating audiences' media habits. Fourth, new technologies seem to develop overnight, and practitioners quickly must learn how to use them. Finally, media ownership issues such as splintering and mergers affect change in media routines, personnel, and content.

Indeed, a number of variables are involved in practitioners' construction of viable media mix strategies designed to grow and enhance relationships with key publics. Such media mix decisions are a cornerstone of effective communication campaigns.

—*Donnalyn Pompper*

See also Advertising; Marketing; Media networks; Practice; Press kit

Bibliography

Burnett, J., & Moriarty, S. (1998). *Introduction to marketing communications: An integrated approach.* Upper Saddle River, NJ: Prentice Hall.

Duncan, T., & Moriarty, S. E. (1997). The IM audit: Testing the fabric of integration. *IMC Research Journal, 3*(1), 3–10.

Ogden, J. R. (1998). *Developing a creative and innovative integrated marketing communication plan: A working model.* Upper Saddle River, NJ: Prentice Hall.

MEDIA NETWORKS

One of the traditions of public relations is that it conducts much of its communication activity through "other people's media." Advertising buys time and space. Public relations typically uses "free time or space" in which it places news, stories, and comments through news reports, for instance.

Media, as discussed in public relations, come in two sizes. One is the mass media, which consist of complex networks of news gathering and dissemination, as well as entertainment programming and editorial commentary. Magazines, newspapers, and television are the traditional venues through which news, commentary, and entertainment reaches readers, listeners, and viewers. Public relations practitioners also use "their own media." Pamphlets and reports are key examples of media tools that practitioners use to disseminate information and commentary. In this sense, media are print and electronic networks that can be used to reach mass audiences.

Second, media networks are narrowcast information systems, consisting of multiple-output devices fed and controlled by a centralized source. Message recipients have no way to engage in direct feedback.

The output devices are usually display devices: Jumbotrons, video monitors, LCD and plasma displays, and so on. The centralized source is usually a computer-controlled audiovisual switching system, with source information stored and played backed in either analog or digital format. Videocassettes, compact discs (CDs), CD-ROMs, digital video discs (DVDs), DVD-ROMs, and computer hard drives are the storage media typically encountered.

Message content is dependent on venue or environment. Media networks are used in sports stadiums and arenas, office buildings, shopping malls, and individual retail spaces. Technological convergence is allowing the addition of billboards to the media network landscape.

Messages do not have to be homogeneous. It is possible to run several different messages simultaneously. A common example involves advertising in an athletic shoe store. Usually, there are several clusters of video monitors, with each cluster narrowcasting a different advertisement on each monitor in the cluster. Advertisements are usually repeated across the clusters, meaning that one monitor in each cluster is running the same advertisements.

Media networks are not simply a new way to advertise. Media networks can play a critical role in an office/business environment. It may be something as simple as a running stock ticker that includes the company's stock price along with the company's competitors'. Above the ticker could be copies of relevant business stories. An organization can go further with the media network and include messages from the CEO or minutes from meetings. Companies often use a media network to function as a message board, notifying employees of policy changes, upcoming events, or meetings. It is possible to have many of the functions of a company newsletter moved onto a media network.

Media networks provide the public relations practitioner with a unique opportunity. Narrowcasting allows for a fairly high level of customization and refinement of the message. There are three principles to keep in mind in considering the use of a media network for message delivery.

First, understand the limitations of the storage, playback, and output devices. For example, hard drive space is cheap and plentiful, making it easy to store large, high-quality audio and images. However, if the venue is a sports arena, the speaker systems are typically not that good, the acoustics of the space are horrible, and the output quality of a Jumbotron is well below television quality.

Second, message delivery is reliant on a electromechanical system with limited human oversight. Media systems lend themselves to a "set it and forget it" mentality. To function optimally, tape machines need to be cleaned on a regular basis, for example. If the message includes a lot of static (nonmoving) graphics that have long presentation times, those graphics will "burn in" to the display devices. Picture quality will degrade, and the effectiveness of the message will be diminished. Durability of the storage media is also a consideration. Videotapes wear out;

CDs and DVDs can get scratched; hard drives can fail. Some media systems do not have the actual media stored on site. Rather, they have the content beamed in via satellite. Satellite delivery has a whole extra set of potential problems and concerns, reception quality being only one.

The third idea is double-edged. Many media networks are "always on," meaning they are automated and run 24 hours a day, 365 days a year. That means that even though a message is narrowcast, potential exposure is maximized. That exposure is where the downside is found. Although the message may be a "hit" the first or second time it is encountered, what about the hundredth time? If the media network is located in a retail space or shopping mall, the people that work there will easily be exposed to the message dozens of time a day, several days a week. The result can be a backlash, involving everything from sabotage of the equipment (simply turning it off) to outright destruction of the data.

Whether damage is accidental-on-purpose or simply the result of wear-and-tear, the rapidity with which worn-out media (and messages) can be replaced must be taken into consideration. If it will take several weeks to get replacements sent out, consider budgeting for extra copies to hold in reserve as needed.

—Michael Nagy

See also Network theory

MEDIA RELATIONS

Sound media relations practices were critical to public relations campaigns long before most people even knew what a "public relations campaign" was. Mary "Mother" Jones used good media relations techniques when she traveled to Philadelphia in the summer of 1903 to support the textile workers' strike against the mill owners and to help focus attention on the tragedy of child labor. Mother Jones and the union organized a "March of the Mill Children" from Philadelphia to President Roosevelt's summer home on Long Island to dramatize the problem.

The marchers held press conferences, made press tours (Mother Jones and the children visited journalists to tell their story), made speeches, granted interviews, pitched feature stories to journalists, and put writers in contact with sources.

Modern media relations experts—whether in agencies, groups, corporations, or not-for-profit organizations—use these techniques, plus a few others:

- Distribute videos to Web sites and broadcast outlets.
- Ask journalists periodically about their information needs.
- Make sure journalists' names are on listservs (messages sent by electronic mail to keep interested individuals informed about an organization's activities).
- Prepare media packets (collections of leader profiles; information about the organization, group, service, or product; statistics; reports; news clippings; and similar materials).

Another modern activity—preparing managers to interact with journalists in interviews or news conferences—is a tad controversial, but it helps spokespersons to communicate more effectively. And it helps journalists because sources are prepared; they frequently bring along media packets to help journalists do their jobs.

Ethical practitioners are committed to keeping the media informed for a couple of reasons: (1) Practitioners can reach some of their publics only through the media. This is less true today, when professionals use the Internet in some instances to communicate directly with publics, than it was in 1903, when the newspaper was the only game in town. But still, some messages can be conveyed most effectively through the mass media. (2) Journalists are going to write about newsworthy groups, organizations, and individuals no matter what. They want to talk to the principals involved in newsworthy activities, because principles of objective journalism demand that, but the stories are going to be written with or without input from those involved. Good practitioners understand that it is far better to have input than not.

PROVIDE SOUND INFORMATION

The overarching principle in effective media relations is that practitioners provide accurate, relevant, fair, timely, complete information. This means in part that practitioners cannot put their organizations' interests above the public's interest when those interests conflict and then lie about what they've done. The best practitioners try to ensure that their organizations' interests are consistent with the public's interest because they think that's the right thing to do, and failure to do so nearly always leads to unfortunate consequences.

Practitioners who are compelled to put organizational interests above the public interest can experience extreme dissonance when those interests conflict, and they are unlikely to have good relations with the news media. Ironically, a practitioner who seems to put the public interest first can run into difficulty within his or her organization, for some organization men and women might charge that the practitioner is more concerned about journalism's needs than about the organization's needs. The ethical practitioner tries to educate the doubters about the realities of the media world.

One reality is that an organization or group cannot establish effective media relations if it is not credible, and it's extraordinarily difficult to recover lost credibility. If an organization is caught misleading the public a single time and never does it again, it will be a long time before that organization is perceived as credible. Many Americans still will not believe the tobacco and asbestos industries. The media will ignore messages disseminated by low-credibility groups, organizations, or individuals, or they will subject the messages to intense scrutiny and, frequently, substantial revision.

The Pentagon ran into a firestorm of criticism when it considered a proposal to plant news, some false or misleading, in international news media. The goal was to "de-position" (discredit) unapproved governments and to promote the United States. The plan was to have credible third parties who had no apparent connection to the U.S. government distribute "news" to friendly and unfriendly foreign media. The plan was attacked by numerous journalists, and the Pentagon's credibility was damaged severely—just for considering the plan. To their credit, many military public affairs officers opposed the proposal.

Contrast the Pentagon's boneheaded plan to the response of Odwalla Corp. when one of its products was contaminated with *E. coli* bacteria. Public health officials in Vancouver, British Columbia, and the states of Washington and California were struggling with several ill patients when a 16-month-old Denver girl died of complications from *E. coli* poisoning. Odwalla's apple juice turned out to be the common thread. Within 24 hours of notification of the problem, Odwalla recalled all the beverages and was cooperating with the media and public health agencies. Odwalla publicly acknowledged that juice from one of its plants tested positive for *E. coli*, created a Web site to respond to questions, announced procedures for ensuring plants were sanitary, and created an advisory council to discover ways to improve product safety. Odwalla should not have distributed the tainted juice in the first place, and it did pay a fine. However, in reacting to the crisis honestly and openly, it protected its credibility.

Public relations practitioners must be committed to ethical communication if they are to serve their clients well. Beyond that, they need to master several skills.

WRITE AND SPEAK CAREFULLY

Practitioners must be able to write and to speak well. It should go without saying—but it can't—that professionals must master language elements such as grammar, punctuation, spelling, and style. A practitioner simply cannot afford to write or speak a sentence like this one: The soldier picked up their rifle and moved on. The attempt to avoid sexist language is admirable, but the grammatical error is unforgivable. Nor should a practitioner write "412 West Elm Street" for a newspaper. That is a gross violation of virtually every newspaper's style. How can an editor who judges a news release have respect for a writer when the release contains errors? And how can he or she respect an organization that would employ such a writer?

Good writing must be reflected in everything, written and verbal, that a practitioner produces.

Some writers seem to think good grammar, spelling, and punctuation are unimportant in electronic mail. They are wrong, for a practitioner is judged harshly when he or she sends messages that contain grammatical and spelling errors or that fail to capitalize words properly (the most common error). Writers even need to write grocery lists carefully if they are to avoid bad habits.

A practitioner who wants to establish good relations with the media also must understand what the media need. In "olden times"—before the mid-1980s or so—many practitioners were reformed journalists, and they knew exactly what an editor wanted in a release, news conference, or interview. Practitioners no longer are drawn primarily from the ranks of journalists, and they sometimes have trouble deciphering editors' needs. Too often, a practitioner will distribute, by mail, fax, or electronic mail, releases that contain no news, or schedule news conferences that are of no interest to most audiences. This is poor practice because it damages credibility by making a practitioner seem unprofessional.

Effective practitioners produce copy that is similar to that published or aired by the target media. This means making sure their stories contain timely news that is of interest or importance to many people. It is helpful if the stories contain news values in addition to timeliness that editors use to evaluate information for stories. These include conflict (verbal or physical), prominence (well-known personalities, places, or issues), magnitude (large numbers of deaths or dollars), consequence (many lives affected), and proximity (local events, persons, or issues).

Practitioners who write news releases, arrange news conferences or media interviews with their bosses, or pitch feature ideas need to make sure the information they want to distribute contains at least some of these news values. And they need to understand that a message that would interest one medium's editor and audience might not interest another's. A release frequently is written multiple times to ensure that each medium gets a version tailored to its needs. Editors have a right to feel insulted when they get releases that are of no interest to their audiences.

The news also needs to be written in standard journalistic format. For print and online publications, that means writing in the inverted pyramid format, with the most interesting and important information at the top and the least interesting and important at the bottom. Writing for broadcast is a little different because one writes for the ear, rather than the eye, but the principles are the same. A broadcast journalist typically writes a label, which is comparable to a newspaper headline, that is read by an anchorperson. Then the writer produces a lead that he or she reads on the air. Rather than end with the least important information, a broadcast journalist typically reiterates the news. The other important difference is that broadcast stories typically are much shorter than print or online stories. Practitioners must keep these differences in mind when writing for broadcast.

Writing a lead is one of the hardest tasks facing any writer. It is doubly hard for a news writer—whether a journalist or public relations practitioner—because he or she must capture the heart of the story, package it in an interesting way, and produce a lead of 10–30 words. This is one of the great creative challenges, and most communication professionals must meet the challenge several times a day.

There obviously is too little space to address the fundamentals of writing the rest of a release, but a model that Michael Ryan uses at the University of Houston may be helpful. The model assumes two phrases in each paragraph and one sentence per paragraph:

- Paragraph 1: Heart of the news event or issue, followed by an attribution
- Paragraph 2: Background information needed for a reader or listener to understand the heart of the news in paragraph 1, followed by an attribution if needed
- Paragraph 3: A direct quotation that amplifies, but does not repeat, material in paragraph 1, followed by an attribution
- Paragraph 4—last: New information presented in each sentence, following by attributions or background material

This model requires that the most important and interesting information in each sentence be placed at the beginning of the sentence. When background information is not required, paragraph 2 is dropped.

Most broadcast writers would alter the model slightly so that sentences begin with attributions, and they typically would put a label above paragraph 1 as a lead-in.

Practitioners also need to work with those who supply visuals for media editors. They should not presume to tell photographers what to do, but practitioners certainly might make suggestions. A photographer who needs to take the picture of a CEO for a business publication's cover story might like to know about an interesting backdrop on a production line, for example. When a practitioner supplies photographs or video, he or she needs to be sure the people in those pictures have signed releases and that there are no copyright restrictions.

Many practitioners are not numerate (they fear numbers), but they have to get over this problem, for they likely will deal with numbers constantly and they will pass those numbers on to journalists. A good practitioner will check all numbers and will try to package those numbers in attractive graphs and charts that editors can use without change. This will ensure the numbers are accurate and that they can be interpreted easily by an organization's publics.

COMMUNICATION DURING CRISIS

Even the best relationships with journalists are tested during times of crisis, when confusion and chaos are most pronounced. The difficulty is that journalists want information *now,* and practitioners often just don't have it. They certainly don't have time to get the usual approvals from all departments to release information. Here are a few things organizations should *not* do during a crisis: release unverified information, for the information might be inaccurate; intentionally mislead or withhold information; fail to express concern; and fail to prepare for the worst that could happen.

Organizations can respond best to crises if they have anticipated the crisis and developed a plan. If an organization manufactures fireworks, for example, the practitioner needs to develop a plan for keeping the media informed in the event of an explosion. The plan might outline contingencies if nobody is injured, if some are injured, and if some are killed. Each person's job, from the CEO to the janitor, is specified under various conditions so that everyone knows what to do in the event of catastrophe. A list of the information (e.g., time of accident, number of injuries, cause, damage estimate) that must be disseminated is critical.

Rumors tend to complicate crisis communication, for they spread quickly among people who are under stress. Someone must be assigned to track rumors, to find out what people are saying about a catastrophe, and to seek the truth. When the truth is established, a spokesperson must pass the information along to the news media so the rumors can be squelched or confirmed quickly.

TALKING BACK

Most practitioners avoid "talking back" to the news media. If they don't like a story published in the local newspaper, they might wad up the story and slam it into the trash basket. Then they forget it. A practitioner must have cordial relations with local media representatives, and complaints about media coverage or lack of coverage are not conducive to good relations. Nobody wants to have his or her work criticized, and nobody wants to be in trouble with the boss.

However, some practitioners have become bolder in the last decade or so, partly because government regulations require that the printed record be accurate. Practitioners are extraordinarily careful about what they write because everything can end up in the record—and the record can get an organization into trouble. If a newspaper article is substantially incorrect, it can lead to many problems later on. It may be worth risking a damaged relationship just to correct the record.

Some practitioners talk back also because they believe they are just as responsible as journalists for protecting the public's right to know, and they don't want the public to know inaccurate information. Nor do they want important channels of communication polluted with inaccurate and distorted information. If they have the facts on their side, and they are not just expressing contrary opinions, they should correct substantive errors.

—Michael Ryan

Bibliography

Newsom, D., Scott, A., & Turk, J. V. (1993). *This is PR: The realities of public relations.* Belmont, CA: Wadsworth.

Rampton, S., & Stauber, J. (2001). *Trust us, we're experts: How industry manipulates science and gambles with your future.* New York: Jeremy P. Tarcher/Putnam.

Ryan, M. (1995). Models help writers produce publishable releases. *Public Relations Quarterly, 40*(2), 25–27.

Ryan, M. (2002, February 21). Pentagon shouldn't add to litter of disinformation. *Houston Chronicle,* p. 29A.

Sallot, L. M., Steinfatt, T. M., & Salwen, M. B. (1998). Journalists' and public relations practitioners' news values: Perceptions and cross-perceptions. *Journalism & Mass Communication Quarterly, 75*(2), 366–377.

Seib, P., & Fitzpatrick, K. R. (1995). *Public relations ethics.* Fort Worth: Harcourt Brace.

Thomsen, S. R., & Rawson, B. (1998). Purifying a tainted corporate image: Odwalla's Response to an *E. coli* poisoning. *Public Relations Quarterly, 43*(3), 35–46.

MEDIA RELEASE

A media release, also know as a press release, is one of the most frequently used tactics or tools in the public relations practice. A media release can be either a news release or feature release. News releases present hard news and feature releases offer human-interest stories. The most commonly distributed release is a news release. Although publicity is a strategy used by many public relations practitioners, those who specialize in working with the media are called publicists and media relations specialists.

Releases are sent to a media gatekeeper, such as a print journalist or television producer who determines the stories that appear in a publication or on a broadcast. The most common form of media release is the news release, which conveys information that is considered newsworthy and is written in an inverted pyramid format. The inverted pyramid format begins with a clothesline lead of information, including the elements of who, what, when, where, how, and why. Next, facts and details are developed in the body of the release, supporting the lead sentence. The release generally concludes with related, but less significant, information on the topic. Some practitioners place a boilerplate at the end of the release, which is a paragraph describing the organization releasing the information.

A feature release, on the other hand, presents a more attention-getting lead and develops a clear and logical story with a definite conclusion. A feature release is a human-interest story. Unlike a news release, feature releases tell a story, begin with a catchy opening called a hook, and offer a conclusion or ending to the story.

Public relations practitioners write and distribute three types of releases. An *advance story* announces something that will happen, such as a change in management or an upcoming event. A *cover release* reports something that actually happened, such as a sizable donation to a nonprofit organization, a community clean-up event, or a major management decision. *Follow-up releases* report the news after an event, such as the quarterly sales of a new product, the results of a research study, or the effect of policy changes. Releases have many uses. They can announce something (hires, mergers, price changes, layoffs), offer spot news (road closings, strike, school cancellations), give a reaction to something (charges against an organization, industry trends, new laws), and tell bad news (faculty products, recalls, apologies).

The factors that determine news include timeliness (or currency), impact (or something of far-reaching consequence), prominence of individuals or events, proximity and local tie-in, conflict, and novelty or uniqueness.

Some media gatekeepers receive over a hundred releases in one day, and many are thrown away or not seen. Therefore, a carefully crafted news release is essential. Releases should have a strong newsworthy angle, be accurate, contain well-researched facts, present information that is truthful and balanced, and strive for objectivity. Most important, releases should be tailored to the media gatekeeper and editorial environment of the targeted publication or show. They are often used as a trigger for publicity or media coverage. Some releases are accompanied by a pitch letter and may be part of a press kit of other media-related materials.

Public relations specialists adhere to specific formats when developing news or feature releases. Ideally, releases should be no more than two double-spaced pages. Most are labeled "for immediate release," meaning that the media outlet is free to release the information upon receipt. Releases are printed on organizational letterhead, have a contact name and number at the top, and include a dateline. Although public relations practitioners should pay special attention to the style of the publication they are targeting, many use the writing style of the Associated Press and include page slugs and end marks in news releases. Releases may be e-mailed, faxed, mailed or hand delivered, depending on the preferences of the media gatekeeper receiving the release. Some public relations practitioners distribute their releases through public relations news bureaus, such as Business Wire and PR Newswire. Most also post their releases on their organizational Web site.

Some media gatekeepers at weekly newspapers, regional publications, and specialty papers print releases with few changes; however, journalists at larger publications such as metropolitan newspapers seldom use a release in its original form. Rather, they will use only some of the information. In such cases, public relations practitioners use the release as a catalyst in which to persuade a gatekeeper to cover a particular story. Editors of trade publications, for instance, will use product information releases in a product update column.

—Emma Daugherty Phillingane

See also Clip (news clip) and clipping services; Feature; Media calls; Publicity

Bibliography

Aronson, M., & Spetner, D. (1993). *The public relations writer's handbook.* New York: Lexington Books.

Bivins, T. (1995). *Handbook for public relations writing.* Lincolnwood, IL: NTC Business Books.

Bivins, T. H. (1999). Public relations writing: The essentials of style and format. Lincolnwood, IL: NTC/Contemporary.

Diggs-Brown, B., & Glou, J. L. G. (2004). *The PR style guide: Formats for public relations practice.* Belmont, CA: Wadsworth.

Goff, C. F. (1989). *The publicity process.* Ames: Iowa State University Press.

Loeffler, R. H. (1993). *A guide to preparing cost-effective press releases.* New York: Haworth Press.

Newsom, D., & Carrell, B. (2001). *Public relations writing: Form & style.* Belmont, CA: Wadsworth.

Wilcox, D. L., Cameron, G. T., Ault, P. H., & Agee, W. K. (2003). *Public relations strategies and tactics.* Boston: Allyn & Bacon.

MENTORING

The term *mentor* has been used to describe relationships between apprentices and masters within trade guilds, but most recently it is used to describe relationships between professionals and protégés.

Mentoring can benefit both mentor and mentee. Mentors who actively recruit less experienced talent have the advantage of contacting quality pre-professionals early, and mentees get experience and begin to build a network. Mentors also learn valuable training and leadership skills while enacting their role and can experience greater job satisfaction.

Various studies have been conducted to learn more about the concept of mentoring. In the *Journal of Human Counseling,* Tsedal Beyene, M. Anglin, William Sanchez and Mary Ballou (2002) reported a study titled "Mentoring and Relational Mutuality: Protégés' Perspectives," where they studied the responses of the mentees after their experience in a mentoring program. One hundred and thirty-three students were questioned—they had diverse backgrounds and represented 35 different majors.

The researchers' definition of mentoring was a relationship in which both mentor and mentee derive knowledge and skills, as well as emotional support. Mentees look to their mentors to model professional behavior and to learn the often unwritten rules of an organization. The results were fairly consistent—almost everyone agreed with this definition, and most agreed that the mentor became a role model to them. The majority of the participants were not intimidated about questioning their mentors, and almost three-fourths agreed that the relationship was a success. The main qualities that the mentees described for an ideal mentor were "nurturing, knowledgeable, listening, a friend, trustworthy, open-minded, a role model, approachable, helpful, encouraging, initiating, loyal, patient, non-judgmental, should share similar interests, and should have a positive attitude and a sense of humor" (Beyene, et al., 2002, pp. 87–102).

Today mentoring is one of the most important tools in equipping professionals for the future. A mentor influences the life of another (mentee) by guiding and motivating him or her in the right direction outside the normal manager-subordinate relationship. These relationships help mentees reach the next level in their professional careers. Mentoring encompasses wisdom, loyalty, motivation, and trust. This role is not a one-time function; it is an ongoing process that lasts until the goal of the mentee has been accomplished. Because of this, mentors monitor their mentees on a regular basis to assess their development. When applied properly, mentoring is a win-win situation for everyone involved.

The public relations profession knows that mentoring is important. This is why the profession has made many successful efforts to implement mentoring programs in the field.

Because public relations plays a vital role in organizations, mentoring professionals and providing them with the right tools for success is essential. Because the public relations field is changing at a rapid rate, there is a great need to keep the employees up to date and committed to their organization and to the profession.

Some PRSA chapters have set up internal mentoring programs. These programs give new practitioners a chance to be guided by older, more experienced professionals. This is a chance for the experienced professional to show how things work. This guidance prepares the mentee to take on the upper-level positions of his or her superior in that organization or elsewhere. These investments show that organizations value their employees and will do whatever it takes to see them succeed.

A mentor has the opportunity to increase his or her professionalism and the professionalism of others through counseling and hands-on experience. This gives mentors a chance to sharpen their managerial skills while playing a significant role in the growth and career path of another. PRSA chapters have set up mentoring programs to help members enhance their skills and knowledge regarding the field.

Nationally, PRSA has also set in place the College of Fellows Mentoring Program. This program makes it possible for all levels of public relations practitioners to share knowledge and business expertise. This program also counsels one along his or her career path and in decision making. Members

of PRSA who are chosen to be mentors have over 20 years of experience. The mentors are carefully elected by the college because they "demonstrate superior capability as a practitioner, exhibit personal and professional qualities that serve as a role model for other practitioners, and have advanced the state of the profession" (PRSA, 2003, n.p.).

Paul Schrodt, Carol Stringer Cawyer, and Renee Sanders (2003) stated in their recent research that individuals with mentors receive more promotions, have higher incomes, and report more career satisfaction and mobility than those who do not participate in the mentor-mentee relationship. This, then, is one avenue for improving the quality of work life for organizational members.

Lynn Appelbaum (2000) stated that mentoring offers something longer lasting than the superficial payoffs such as free meals and gym memberships, which some organizations offer. Mentoring offers an environment that makes mentees feel accepted and supported on both personal and professional levels. This creates stronger corporate culture, teamwork, and better use of resources. It also connects employers to organizations outside of their own. Mentors set the foundation for career paths. These relationships are excellent avenues for expanding networks and giving timely advice about one's future.

—*Brenda J. Wrigley*

Bibliography

Appelbaum, L. (2000). Mentoring: A strategy to recruit and retain top PR professionals. *Public Relations Strategist, 6*(3), 18–20.

Beyene, T., Anglin, M., Sanchez, W., & Ballou, M. (2002). Mentoring and relational mutuality: Proteges' perspectives. *Journal of Humanistic Counseling, Education and Development, 41*, 87–102.

Burlew, L. (1991). Multiple mentor model: A conceptual framework. *Journal of Career Development, 17*, 213–220.

Public Relations Society of America. (2003). *College of Fellows: Register for a College of Fellows Mentor.* Retrieved August 28, 2003, from http://www.prsa.org/_Advance/cofellows/mentor_register.asp?ident=c013

Schrodt, P., Stringer Cawyer, C., & Sanders, R. (2003). An examination of academic mentoring behaviors and new faculty members' satisfaction with socialization and tenure and promotion processes. *Communication Education, 52*, 17–29.

MINORITIES IN PUBLIC RELATIONS

In recent decades, organizations have been urged to recruit minorities and those who are sensitive to cultural diversity. According to the United States Equal Employment Opportunity Commission (EEOC), more minorities hold professional jobs in private and government arenas than ever before. However, numbers of minority public relations practitioners still lag significantly behind those of Anglo practitioners. Ironically, many perceive that minority groups are doing especially well due to federal legislation. But in reality, anti–affirmative action sentiments continue to gain momentum.

Anglo males dominate senior-level management in the United States, and organizational theorists suggest that management culture is shaped by a Eurocentric, patriarchal bias that becomes normalized. For example, much of our trade literature and public relations research similarly contextualizes the status of "minorities" and "women." Perhaps this is because Anglo males once dominated the field. The terms *minorities* and *ethnicities*, as used here, refer to non-Anglos of both genders. Ethnicity is socially defined, based on cultural, psychological, or biological characteristics. The U.S. Bureau of the Census categorizes major race groups as Caucasian, African American, Hispanic, Asian and Pacific Islander, and Native American.

Back in the early 1980s, M. J. Layton (1980) wrote of one early critic of "minority issues" in public relations who called the field "the last of the lily-white professions" (p. 64). Two decades later, the U.S. Bureau of the Census reported that the public relations industry remains predominantly white (89.4 percent), followed by 4.5 percent black, 2.8 percent Hispanic, and 2.1 percent Asian. The trade publication *Public Relations Quarterly* also reports that very few Arab Americans and Native Americans work in public relations. Opportunities for minorities seemed boundless 20 years ago, when an estimated 4,000 of the 70,000

U.S. practitioners were minorities. Yet African American practitioners dropped from 7 percent to 6 percent by the 1990s even though the number of total practitioners had grown to 150,000.

Further underscoring this gap are comparative salary, status, and higher-education figures. According to *PR Week*'s 2002 Salary Survey, ethnic minorities are paid "considerably less" than their white counterparts, on average: blacks 36 percent less, Hispanics 31 percent less, and Asians 9 percent less. The U.S. Department of Labor reported in 1999 that among public relations managers, the mean annual wage is $56,770. White women's weekly earnings are 37.4 percent higher than those of Hispanic women—and women generally earn a little more than half (63 percent) as much as men. This means that Anglo males significantly out-earn all other demographic groups.

In terms of status, a culturally diverse senior-level management is an anomaly in the United States, particularly in the public relations industry. Numbers of minorities working in senior public relations management are dismally low. Hispanics comprise only 4.2 percent of managers in marketing, advertising, and public relations. Overall, statistics fail to correlate with the ethnic diversity of the larger U.S. population—82.2 percent white, 12.8 percent black, 11.8 percent Hispanic, and 4.1 percent Asian.

Even though level of education frequently has been invoked as a rationale for low numbers of minorities working in public relations, *PR Week* survey findings suggested that 29 percent of black and Asian respondents had earned graduate degrees—compared with 24 percent of whites surveyed. Thus, it seems that ethnic minorities in the United States are outnumbered and underrepresented in public relations management *in spite of* graduate degrees.

Indeed, the public relations industry has been criticized for lack of advancement and inequitable salaries among minorities. Overall, the profession has demonstrated low recognition of diversity, a poor record of educating for diversity, and underrepresented diverse populations. Some firms suggest that they find hiring minorities difficult because they receive so few applications from them. Because organizational theorists have noted that culture (shared values, beliefs, meanings, understanding) affects workplace processes, it is no surprise that multicultural perspectives rarely gain access to executive offices. Organizations tend to "play it safe" by ignoring class relations and attempting to "control" diversity.

Well aware of these trends, PRSA established a task force several years ago. Also, some public relations firms have worked to stimulate recruitment of minorities and fund scholarships to place minority students as interns. Furthermore, Larissa A. Grunig, a prominent senior public relations researcher, shared her vision to inspire new generations with heterogeneous chronicles of public relations history. Unfortunately, few public relations textbooks cover minorities' contributions in any great detail. Most offer only a few paragraphs.

A "handful of minorities" joined the public relations field in the late 1940s, but it wasn't until the civil rights era that "significant numbers" pursued public relations careers. Joseph Varney Baker became the first African American man to launch a public relations consulting firm, serve as a PRSA president, and earn accredited public relations (APR) status. The Rev. Barbara Harris, the first African American *woman* in public relations, began her career at Baker's firm and became its president in 1958. Recorded historical mentions of Hispanic, Native American, Asian American, or other minority practitioners are nearly nonexistent.

Beyond the public relations workplace, academic studies of minorities in public relations are few—whereas advice on *how to market to ethnic minorities* abounds. Moreover, all-black, all-Hispanic, all-Asian agencies have emerged in recent years. Some full-service agencies even have added "Hispanic public relations" (HPR) to their rosters. Of course, building relationships between organizations and key publics is fundamental to the definition of "public relations." Public relations researchers have called targeting the Hispanic market "important," "desirable," and a means "to increase company revenue." Practitioners are cautioned, however,

to beware of market tendencies to commodify ethnicity, a move that reinforces hegemony.

Characterized as "the most prolific scholar analyzing multicultural trends in public relations," Marilyn Kern-Foxworth has conducted surveys to examine the technician-manager role/salary dichotomy between whites and "women of color," the institutional constraints manifested by race, and minority representation in public relations textbooks. Time and again she concluded that minorities are underrepresented and underpaid.

A few studies have probed the relationship between race and career advancement. Those "people of color" who *are* employed as public relations practitioners often are pigeonholed into servicing "ethnic" projects—whether they really want to or not. Many minority practitioners reported being underutilized in their organizations, and overlooked when organizations assign or hire public relations practitioners. Paradoxically, one researcher concluded that stereotyping and pigeonholing hold back minority practitioners, and another found that most (85 percent) of the African American public relations practitioners she surveyed denied being pigeonholed.

Even though, as James E. Grunig (1992) wrote, "Excellence Theory" has contributed much to our understanding of the best way to "do public relations in an ideal situation" (p. 12) and serves as the dominant paradigm in public relations research, it makes no explicit mention of ethnic diversity. In other words, this normative theory offers no provision for exposing discrimination as an impediment to excellence. Donnalyn Pompper (2004) has argued that it is an integral two-way symmetrical model component because communication is more likely to be excellent when ethnic diversity is supported. Organizational effectiveness depends on as much diversity within an organization as outside it, and ensuring ethnic diversity is a public relations responsibility.

Indeed, much more work is yet to be done in examining the experiences of minority practitioners in public relations organizations. Unfortunately, much of our early research involved data sets with underrepresented minorities. Also, ethnicity variables have been homogenized and ethnic identities obscured—as in studies of "minorities," "multiculturalism," and "people of color." Finally, ethnicity variables have not been probed in studies of sexual harassment.

It is predicted that blacks, Hispanics, Asians, and other minority group members will make up 47 percent of the U.S. workforce by 2050 and that the number of men will grow at a slower rate than the number of women. Furthermore, numbers of Hispanic, black, and Asian workers will continue to grow well into 2010—while the number of white workers will fall below 2000 levels. Hence, it may be forecast that greater numbers of ethnic minorities will be available for recruitment as public relations practitioners.

—Donnalyn Pompper

See also Baker, Joseph Varney; Demographics; Excellence theory; National Black Public Relations Society (NBPRS); Practice

Bibliography

Grunig, J. (1992). Communication, public relations, and effective organizations: An overview of the book. In. J. Grunig (Ed.), *Excellence in public relations and communication management* (pp. 1–28). Hillsdale, NJ: Lawrence Erlbaum.

Kern-Foxworth, M. (1989a). An assessment of minority female roles and status in public relations: Trying to unlock the acrylic vault and assimilate into the velvet ghetto. In E. L. Toth & C. G. Cline (Eds.), *Beyond the velvet ghetto* (pp. 241–286). San Francisco: International Association of Business Communicators Research Foundation.

Kern-Foxworth, M. (1989b). Public relations books fail to show women in context. *Journalism Educator, 44*(3), 31–36.

Kern-Foxworth, M. (1989c). Status and roles of minority female practitioners. *Public Relations Review, 15*(3), 39–47.

Kern-Foxworth, M., Gandy, O., Hines, B., & Miller, D. A. (1994). Assessing the managerial roles of black female public relations practitioners using individual and organizational discriminants. *Journal of Black Studies, 24*(4), 416–434.

Layton, M. J. (1980, April). Blacks in public relations: A growing presence. *Public Relations Journal, 36*(4), 64–67.

Len-Rios, M. E. (2002). Latino professionals in public relations. *Public Relations Quarterly, 47*(1), 22–26.

Pompper, D. (2004). Linking ethnic diversity & two-way symmetry: Modeling female African-American practitioners' roles. *Journal of Public Relations Research, 16*(3), 295–325.

U.S. Department of Labor, Bureau of Labor Statistics. (2003). *Occupational outlook handbook.* Retrieved June 4, 2003, from http://www.bls.gov/oco/oc02003.htm

MISSION AND VISION STATEMENTS

Mission and vision statements delineate the goals, purposes, and values of an organization. Vision statements provide a broad guideline of future organizational goals; mission statements define the scope of the organization, differentiate it from competitors, and give a summary of why the organization exists. A good mission statement communicates to internal and external publics the strategy of the organization, the framework that will be used in attempting to achieve goals, and the norms and values of the organization.

The terms *mission statement* and *vision statement* are closely related, but there are distinctions between the two. The vision statement represents a desired future goal that identifies general priorities for the organization. Mission statements normally communicate the strategy of the organization in a more practical sense with regard to goal attainment. A general rule of thumb is that the vision statement defines where an organization is going and a mission statement gives basic information about how it is going to get there.

VISION STATEMENTS

A shared vision is an integral part of an organization. If all members of an organization share a well-defined goal, the organization can make more strategic and targeted management and operational decisions than it could without a clearly specified vision. A vision spells out a target for change and the desired long-term goal state.

Often vision statements will include elements of organizational culture such as values, philosophy, the role of the organization in relation to society and in relation to publics, and any other factors that might provide overall guidance and direction in shaping the organization. Although vision statements are sometimes critiqued as nebulous and vague, they can be an invaluable tool for determining long-term organizational priorities that must be addressed in defining the mission of an organization. Vision statements are also essential tools of organizational leadership, particularly in light of managing change. A leader creates vision to "provide a way for people to develop commitment, a common goal around which people can rally, and a way . . . to feel successful" (Nadler & Tushman, 1989, p. 105).

Although a vision statement is intentionally vague, it gives the employees of the organization an indication of what the company will strive to attain in the future, the values that it holds and advocates, and the areas of the business that will be most competitively focused on in the future. A good vision statement should allow all employees to answer the question "Where is this organization going?" in a similar manner, and it helps to define the purpose and culture of a company. For instance, an organization whose vision focuses on providing the highest-quality product would have different strategic emphases than one focusing on the most innovative new designs, or one with the most inexpensive merchandise. The vision statement indicates what core competencies the organization and its employees should reward.

A vision statement is usually created at the highest level of the organization by the CEO or another senior executive in a leadership position. A danger here is that simply creating a vision statement at the top of the organization and expecting others to follow it defeats the ownership and responsibility that are fostered when many participants work at crafting the vision statement. Conducting research with internal publics—such as labor and management—and creating a diverse group of representatives from internal stakeholders to work on the vision statement is the preferred method for crafting an organizational vision. This method results in a "shared vision" of what employees at all levels of the organization desire for the future, and develops participatory ownership and commitment to that vision across the organization. Research shows that these factors create higher levels of job satisfaction and productivity, as well as lower job turnover, making for a more efficacious organization.

MISSION STATEMENTS

Many disciplines discuss the topic of mission statements: organization theory, business management, sociology, communication, and related fields. There is little agreement among scholars on how to define mission statements or what elements a mission statement should include. Mission statements are used as tools to convey goals, organizational structure and strategy, legitimacy, values, participation and ownership among employees, leadership, responsibility to the community, ethical priorities, and commitment to publics and stakeholders.

Mission statements provide a foundation for business that encourages focus on an organization's strengths. The focus fostered by a clear and authoritative mission statement can provide a competitive advantage for an organization by allowing its members to remain strategic, both intellectually and in resource allocation. Without a clearly defined mission statement, an organization can flounder and make decisions that are well intended but do not emphasize its competitive strengths. By building on what it does well, an organization can reinvest in its strengths and become less dependent on the areas in which it is weaker, giving it an advantage in the competitive marketplace.

Mission statements provide a strong, intentional consistency with regard to organizational behavior. They often outline the hierarchy of priorities in an organization, and can be used to direct management decision making. The consistency provided by a clear organizational mission allows the formation of long-term relationships with publics and stakeholders. These groups know what to expect from such an organization and come to trust and rely upon the organization as one dedicated to a clear mission, enhancing the credibility of the organization.

Mission statements are more practical and short term than vision statements. The mission statement endorses a clear purpose for the organization and answers the question "Why are we here?" or "How are we different from our competitors?" Common elements of mission statements include key goals, management strategy, ethical values, relationships with publics and stakeholders, organizational structure, and so on. Many mission statements spell out an organization's competitive advantage and how it will be used to create a benefit to the organization, such as "By being the most cost-efficient manufacturer of this product, we will pass on savings to the customer, and therefore gain a majority of new sales in this market."

There may be little standardization of content among mission statements, but top-performing organizations almost always subscribe to exemplary statements of vision and mission. Although such statements vary considerably across industries and among organizations, a clear vision for the future and a thoroughly articulated mission statement are vital to the overall success of an organization.

—Shannon A. Bowen

See also Excellence theory; Management theory; Systems theory

Bibliography

Bowen, S. A. (2002). Elite executives in issues management: The role of ethical paradigms in decision making. *Journal of Public Affairs, 2*(4), 270–283.

Fairhurst, G. T. (2001). Dualisms in leadership research. In F. M. Jablin & L. L. Putnam (Eds.), *The new handbook of organizational communication: Advances in theory, research, and methods* (pp. 379–439). Thousand Oaks, CA: Sage.

Grunig, L. A., Grunig, J. E., & Dozier, D. M. (2002). *Excellent public relations and effective organizations: A study of communication management in three countries.* Mahwah, NJ: Lawrence Erlbaum.

Heath, R. L. (1994). *Management of corporate communication: From interpersonal contacts to external affairs.* Hillsdale, NJ: Lawrence Erlbaum.

Mazza, C. (1999). *Claim, intent, and persuasion: Organizational legitimacy and the rhetoric of corporate mission statements.* Boston: Kluwer Academic.

Mintzberg, H. (1983). *Power in and around organizations.* Englewood Cliffs, NJ: Prentice Hall.

Murphy, P. E. (1998). *Eighty exemplary ethics statements.* South Bend, IN: University of Notre Dame Press.

Nadler, D. A., & Tushman, M. L. (1989). Leadership for organizational change. In A. M. Mohrman, S. A. Mohrman, G. E. Ledford, T. G. Cummings, & E. E. Lawler (Eds.), *Large-scale organizational change.* San Francisco: Jossey-Bass.

Robbins, S. P. (1990). *Organization theory: Structure, design, and applications* (3rd ed.). Englewood Cliffs, NJ: Prentice Hall.

Siebold, D. R., & Shea, B. C. (2001). Participation and decision making. In F. M. Jablin & L. L. Putnam (Eds.), *The new handbook of organizational communication: Advances in theory, research, and methods* (pp. 664–703). Thousand Oaks, CA: Sage.

MODERNITY AND POSTMODERNITY

Modernity and postmodernity are difficult to define—the former because it covers an extended time period filled with massive changes, and the latter because it attempts to make sense of the present's shifting phenomena in the presence of disillusionment with modernity's versions of order and rationality. Both can be described as historical periods with sets of general characteristics. Anything beyond that is subject to dispute. Since the stakes are the nature of contemporary reality, linked with unfolding futures, the disputes will not be solved by scholarly decision or resolved by easy consensus. In general, supporters of postmodernity tend to see modernity as finished, to consider its demise as a positive event, and to position the present as uncertain, fragmented, and distinctly different from the stage of modernity that preceded it. Opponents of the idea of postmodernity tend to see it as a passing, or past, fad and view the present as late modernity, continuous with modernity itself rather than marking any distinctive rupture.

In the public relations literature, only Margaret E. Duffy's trenchant critique in 2000 of the existing linear orthodoxy in textbook histories registered awareness of the importance of the treatment of time in modernity-postmodernity differences. Her work implicated public relations education in the use of instrumental communication as part of a totalizing process and established the field's need for a postmodern informed historiography. However, subsequent public relations writings have not addressed the contested modernity-postmodernity periodization.

Outside the field, although there is limited agreement on the specific opening and closing dates, the two periods have been most strongly distinguished through chronology. The start of modernity has been traced back as far as the scientific revolution of the 17th century and as recently as the early 20th century. From both points, modernity's meta-narrative—or overarching theoretical story that offers universal explanations and validations—was one of progress.

Modernity's meta-narrative begins as a universal emancipation movement liberating people from ignorance, political tyranny, religious authority, and superstition, as well as mastering nature through science in order to relieve famine and supply basic necessities. Its methods involved the spread of bureaucratizing, centralizing, rationalizing, and Western practices everywhere. Later modernity extends those ideals and practices to 20th-century industrialization through functionalist scientific management involving Taylorism, the Ford Motor Company's assembly line, and the mass production of standardized goods with associated economies of scale. Its liberation component, albeit within a command and control framework, initiated comparable moves toward individual freedom through industrialization with improved living standards, paid employment, and parliamentary democracy.

Accounts of postmodernity put its start somewhere between the 1940s, and the atomic bomb, and the 1970s, and the oil crisis. Postmodernity is characterized as more democratic, more fragmented, and more mediated, as well as multiethnic, postcolonial, post-Fordist, postindustrial, and, in terms of knowledge, poststructural. Although less based in material production, it adds value through a new economy of intangibles by managing meanings, brands, and perceptions in ways that combine niche markets with dispersed global production, global sales, and flexible global workforces. Within public relations, George Cheney and George N. Dionisopoulos (1989) crystallized the contextual shift from modern material production to postmodern symbol production in 1989 by focusing on the management of meaning. They acknowledged how communication becomes constitutive so that "we must recognise organizational processes (even material ones) for how we know them—*through, with,* and *in* symbols" (p. 138). They also drew attention to the ethical challenge attendant on that acknowledgment by calling for an extension of the speech repertoire of the privileged to include the voices of the less powerful.

As its name suggests, postmodernity is connected to modernity and comes after it. From that vantage point postmodernity lists its predecessor's failures by observing how, without ending world hunger, the modernist road to freedom led to concentration camps, ethnic cleansing, and mass unemployment. Postmodernity offers three critiques: first, modernity's ethnocentric implication in colonialism, and the resultant lack of any sense of its cultural and economic values relative to other cultures; second, modernity's susceptibility to epistemological instability, that is, the ways in which things can be known and referenced once language is rejected as a mirror of reality for representing natural objects, and accepted as partly constituting or co-creating the world; and third, modernity's failure to reflect critically its own process and products, including environmental degradation and global inequities, when knowledge can no longer be innocent or separated from power.

For the first critique, postmodernists relativized the concept of the single and universal truth of the white Western male—with its Cartesian cognitive bias, restricted emotional range, and narrowly economic version of what constituted progress—using perspectives from other cultures. Ghandi, for example, when asked what he thought of Western civilization, relativized the ideas from an Indian perspective by replying that he thought it would be a good idea. For the second, postmodernists cast doubt on modernity's claim to offer a rationally objective mapping of reality. One destabilizing technique postmodernists deploy is word play, which frequently complicates and ironizes traditionally serious matters while simultaneously illustrating the serious point of language's irrational instability in playful fashion, as with the example of the pun in the next sentence on "partially," which allows two conflicting meanings—both "partly" and "biased in part"—to operate on the same word at the same time. Postmodernists also illustrate how referencing, or representing, the world requires multiple maps that can be based on sometimes arbitrary symbols and partially shaped by the standpoint of the cartographers and their technologies. Australian Aborigines, who inhabited their land long before the arrival of European explorers, reject the traditional verity of history and geography books that "Captain Cook discovered Australia," and map their territorial homeland through oral traditions called songlines rather than cartographic conventions called gridlines. For the third critique, postmodernists demanded increased reflexivity, or self-questioning about whether, for example, in the face of widening global industrialization with ever-depleting natural energy, food, and mineral resources, the final project of modernity might mean the end of nature through nuclear warfare or environmental catastrophe.

Derina R. Holtzhausen's 2002 writings on public relations and postmodernity echo Cheney and Dionisopoulos's 1989 call for inclusive discourse to restore the words and stories of people excluded, exploited, or marginalized within modernity. In expounding these postmodern values, she conflates them with critical theory while overlooking the fact that the majority of critical theorists condemn postmodernity. They describe it as, at worst, an amoral celebration of a commodified, consumerist, and unjust status quo, and, at best, as a subversion of exploitative modernity, but only at a level of theory irrelevant to any real world challenge. Holtzhausen's associated call for public relations practitioners to become organizational pro-democracy activists similarly runs counter to her own admission of the field's continuing dominance by modernist values, such as administrative control from the center, rationalized economic goals, and hierarchic workplaces: "The focus on public relations as a management function has possibly made the biggest contribution to establish public relations as a serious field of study" (Holtzhausen, 2002a, p. 254).

With such gains, why would the field split with modernity? Even prior to that kind of consideration, Elizabeth Toth (2002) stated bluntly that, despite her declared affinities with it, "postmodernism must

have a 'cash value' for public relations" (p. 243). The adherence to modernity's managerial functionalism is clear and the only short-term gain is for mainstream academic and applied public relations to seek status by being associated with the new, and therefore avoid looking outdated, without tampering with the old. Accordingly, despite Holtzhausen's (2002a) considered opinion that the "management and *Excellence* foci in public relations have become metanarratives that have drowned other, equally valid, discourses" (p. 258), her assessment has been contradicted by the latest *Excellence* book's assertion that two-way symmetric communication is "decidedly postmodern" (L. A. Grunig, J. E. Grunig, & Dozier, 2002, p. 328) and a force for democratic activism.

Even within instrumental rationalism, issues remain for public relations. If postmodernity marks a significant historical rupture, and public relations remains so deeply implicated in modernity, then the field risks cutting itself off from the methods of understanding, and the economic and geopolitical realities, of a changing world order. There are signs that the shift of power away from the West signaled by the 1970s oil crisis, and updated by Chinese expansion, will accelerate in contexts polarized by post-9/11 events. With corporations increasingly led by market demand rather than producer desire, the Third World, with more than 90 percent of the globe's population, will become the main economic driver of the 21st century. Despite its inconsistencies, postmodernity offers insights into those transitional arrangements, and public relations would do well to explore them by tackling Cheney and Christensen's (2001) still relevant postmodern question, "What would a non-Western, nonmanagerial, and nonrationalist form of public relations look like?" (p. 182).

—*David McKie*

Bibliography

Cheney, G., & Christensen, L. (2001). Public relations as contested terrain: A critical response. In R. L. Heath (Ed.), *Handbook of public relations* (pp. 167–182). Thousand Oaks, CA: Sage.

Cheney, G., & Dionisopoulos, G. N. (1989). Public relations? No, relations with publics: A rhetorical-organizational approach to contemporary corporate communications. In C. Botan & V. Hazleton (Eds.), *Public relations theory* (pp. 135–157). Hillsdale, NJ: Lawrence Erlbaum.

Duffy, M. E. (2000). There's no two-way symmetric about it: A postmodern examination of public relations textbooks. *Critical Studies in Mass Communication, 17,* 294–315.

Grunig, L.A., Grunig, J. E., & Dozier, D. (2002). *Excellent public relations and effective organizations: A study of communication management in three countries.* Mahwah, NJ: Lawrence Erlbaum.

Holtzhausen, D. R. (2002a). Towards a postmodern research agenda for public relations. *Public Relations Review, 28,* 251–264.

Holtzhausen, D. R. (2002b). Postmodern values in public relations. *Journal of Public Relations, 12,* 93–114.

Toth, E. L. (2002). Postmodernism for modernist public relations: The cash value and application of critical research in public relations. *Journal of Public Relations, 28,* 243–250.

MORAL DEVELOPMENT

Lawrence Kohlberg (1927–1987) was an eminent American psychologist who studied moral development. His *levels of moral development* describe the strata through which human beings progress in their understanding and their reasoning of whether actions are right or wrong. As we age, our understanding of moral behavior and the reasons for acting morally increase in depth and complexity. At some point in early to middle adulthood, that growth slows or stops for most individuals. Most people then operate on a primary level of moral development, but might advance or regress to another level situationally. Kohlberg's levels of moral development are generally excellent classification devices, but are understood as theoretical models, or simplifications, of a complex interplay of variables that describe moral conscience. Kohlberg's work helps us comprehend ethics in both theory and practice, and its application to public relations helps us understand the choices and levels of moral development found among public relations practitioners.

Kohlberg's empirical studies on the moral development of individuals spanned decades and examined the moral decision making of young children through older adults. His research incorporated many factors such as socialization and cultural norms, but it concentrated on identifying the moral reasoning that accounted for individuals' choices. Kohlberg's extensive research resulted in his identifying three major levels of moral development, each subdivided into two developmental stages. The first level of moral development is the *preconventional,* the second level is the *conventional,* and the third level is the *postconventional* or *autonomous.*

In the *preconventional* stage of moral development, also called level I, Kohlberg addressed the learning of infants and children who are not yet moral. In the first stage of level I, the infant or child reacts to punishment. He or she does not have the reasoning ability to understand why not to do something, but reacts instead to avoid the punishment that comes along with undertaking an action. In this way the child seeks only to avoid negative repercussions of behavior rather than to act morally. For example, what keeps a child from throwing food is not the understanding that it would be an irresponsible action, but the desire to avoid being scolded or otherwise punished for the action. In the second stage of the preconventional level, this understanding is coupled with the desire to earn praise and receive rewards for behavior. The child undertakes an action in order to receive positive reinforcement, or praise and rewards, rather than because he or she understands the nature of the action itself as good. Through this process, children are socialized into learning the norms of good and bad behavior. However, they have not yet developed a sense of morality in understanding that certain actions are morally worthy and others are morally unacceptable. Nor have they developed the analytical reasoning ability required for a higher-level moral analysis of behavior. In the preconventional level, children are simply pursuing the self-interest involved in avoiding punishment and seeking rewards.

Level II is defined as the *conventional* level of moral development. In the conventional level, moral agents make decisions based on conformity to expected roles and norms of behavior. Most adults operate at the conventional level of moral development and generally accept its tenets without questioning their validity. The first stage of level II was termed by Kohlberg "good boy/nice girl morality," in which the moral agent is motivated to act through role conformity. The socialization process allows us to understand how a "good boy or nice girl" is supposed to act in our society, thereby producing norms of expected behavior. The pressure to conform to the role of a good girl or nice boy is strong and leads the decision maker to desire to make decisions that are socially acceptable, meaning that others find those decisions morally permissible. For instance, a high school student might undertake the philanthropic activities of peer and referent groups in order to be perceived as a "well-rounded high school student." In the first stage of level II, the person reacts to the expectations of peers and parents as the primary agents of socialization.

The second stage of level II is the "law and order" stage, in which moral agents learn what is expected of them and how they are "supposed" to act. In this stage, individuals also want to conform to the role of a good citizen. The norms and laws that govern society act as indicators of moral worth of an action and are used by the person to decide how he or she should behave. For instance, if murder and stealing are illegal, then the individual concludes that these actions must be morally wrong. The pressure toward the role conformity of a good citizen is enough to prevent most agents from engaging in the behaviors society has deemed illegal, and therefore—in this view—immoral. The role conformity brought about in the first stage of level II is generally learned from peer groups; in the second stage it includes those norms but also incorporates the laws of one's society.

Kohlberg's final level of moral development is level III, the *postconventianal, autonomous,* or *principled* level. In this level, the moral agent operates by self-accepted moral principles that can be justified through analysis and argument. These moral principles are accepted not because society says they are right, but because the individual has examined and understands the moral argument.

Kohlberg acknowledged that most people never reach the third level of moral development, but, interestingly, some adults do.

Kohlberg divided level III into two stages. The first stage is the "contract and individual rights" stage, in which the primary moral concern is the rights of the individual. As R. T. De George (1999) wrote, "We speak of, and understand, morality based on the rights of individuals and the agreements made between consenting adults" (p. 36). Kohlberg argued that issues of fairness and justice for the individual are of primary concern in this stage. Most interestingly, the second stage of level III is "rationality," the apex of moral development according to Kohlberg. In this stage, people do not simply accept the moral standards of society, but question their justification rationally against moral norms and principles. This final stage of moral development incorporates a universal view of actions, in that they are judged to be right or wrong by the agent regardless of specific cultural norms that might change over time or by location. Incorporating the Kantian concept of duty, Kohlberg argued that agents at this level of development do not act in accordance with moral law out of compulsion or conformity, but because they understand the moral principle involved and why it is binding on them. This duty to follow the moral law is self-imposed by each individual, rather than externally imposed by parents, peers, or lawmakers. At this level of moral development, the desire to take the morally right action outweighs concerns of prudence, constraint, or even self-interest.

Calling this postconventional stage "autonomous," Kohlberg argued that agents are able to provide a rational defense of moral arguments. He evoked the argument for moral rationality espoused centuries earlier by Kant. Autonomy is the one true method of moral decision making, according to Kant, because "a moral agent is an agent who can act autonomously, that is, as a law unto himself or herself, on the basis of objective maxims of his or her reason alone" (Sullivan, 1989, p. 48). These objective maxims are the moral principles based on rational analysis and justification that cause this stage of moral development to differ from all others in significant ways. The rational, autonomous analysis of moral principles called for in this stage is a higher-order cognitive ability than is seen in the other levels of development. The postconventional level is of most interest to those who teach and study moral decision making because it allows the agent to conduct a thorough, rational analysis of ethical decisions and dilemmas. When a dilemma is encountered, the individual responds not by seeking the refuge of group or role conformity, or seeking the other-based guidance of rules and laws, but by conducting a logical assessment of the reasons why some actions are right and others are wrong. Once rational and principled reasons are determined, the agent can articulate and defend a moral decision based on the principles used to reach that conclusion.

Other scholars have been deeply influenced by Kohlberg's seminal work on moral development. For instance, philosopher Henry David Aiken (1978) identified three stages of moral discourse that are remarkably similar to Kohlberg's levels of moral development: (1) a pre-rational, reactive, emotion-based state; (2) a conformity or rule obedience state, and (3) a level of ethical reflection. These states of discourse mirror the levels of moral development Kohlberg identified and serve to reinforce their validity and contribution to our understanding of moral growth. Carol Gilligan (1982) argued that Kohlberg's levels did not sufficiently take gender differences into account and that female moral development is centered more on the value of relationships than is male moral development. However, the critical finding is that both males and females can reach the final stage of level III, the highest level of moral development, based on autonomous reasoning and examination of moral principles.

Scholars have used Kohlberg's levels of moral development to study the ethical choices of public relations practitioners as well as to argue the moral worth of public relations as a societal discourse.

—Shannon A. Bowen

See also Decision theory; Deontology; Ethics of public relations; Moral philosophy

Bibiliography

Aiken, H. D. (1978). *Reason and conduct: New bearings in moral philosophy.* Westport, CT: Greenwood.

De George, R. T. (1995). *Business ethics* (4th ed.). Englewood Cliffs, NJ: Prentice Hall.

De George, R. T. (1999). *Business ethics* (5th ed.). Englewood Cliffs, NJ: Prentice Hall.

Gilligan, C. (1982). *In a different voice: Psychological theory and women's development.* Cambridge, MA: Harvard University Press.

Kohlberg, L. (1969). Stage and sequence: The cognitive developmental approach to socialization. In D. A. Goslin (Ed.), *Handbook of socialization theory of research* (pp. 347–480). Chicago: Rand McNally.

Kohlberg, L. (1984). *The psychology of moral development: The nature and validity of moral stages.* New York: Harper & Row.

Kohlberg, L., & Candee, D. (1984). The relationship of moral judgment to moral action. In W. M. Kurtines & L. Gewirtz (Eds.), *Morality, moral behavior, and moral development* (pp. 52–73). New York: Wiley.

Sullivan, R. J. (1989). *Immanuel Kant's moral theory.* Cambridge, UK: Cambridge University Press.

MORAL PHILOSOPHY

Moral philosophy intersects public relations in the areas of ethical decision making, issues management, and corporate responsibility. In modern society, corporations are faced with a mandate to be good corporate citizens: to behave in the public interest as well as their own interests. Employing moral philosophy contributes to organizational effectiveness by aligning the interests of the company with those of its publics.

Moral philosophy is defined as the theoretical study of ethics. Philosophers study the composition of moral principles and expound on their justification using many methods of analysis. These methods of analysis can range from the weighing of consequences to the use of various tests, including concepts such as duty, fairness, justice, equality, and right. Philosophers concerned with defining moral principles ask such questions as "What is universally good?" and "What is the role of intention in determining the morality of an action?"

To varying extents within each philosophical school, moral philosophy attempts to base ethical decisions on rationality rather than on other decision-making bases such as faith. Although much of Western moral philosophy might have roots in the Judeo-Christian tradition, philosophy attempts to separate nonrational decision-making factors such as faith, prejudice, belief, and bias from the logical principles of the philosophy being applied. In seeking to determine moral principles, moral philosophers attempt to look beyond the cultural and religious norms that tell us certain acts are right or wrong, moral or immoral, and seek truths that span time and location. Such truths are called moral principles.

For instance, a generally accepted moral principle is that lying is wrong. Philosophers can arrive at this principle through a multitude of moral tests. Through a utilitarian test, lying is wrong because it produces more harm than good. Through deontology, it is wrong because lying does not uphold the dignity and respect of others and because we would not want to be lied to ourselves. Although these moral tests are simplifications of the actual philosophies they represent, they allow us to see the principle that lying is morally wrong. But what about lying to save the life of a potential murder victim? What is the morality of those who lied to Nazi soldiers in order to save the lives of Jews? Moral philosophy takes on such difficult questions of moral obligation, intention, consequences, duty, fairness, responsibility, and justice and provides consistent methods for solving such dilemmas.

There are three broad purposes or types of conceptual approaches that moral philosophy can take: meta-ethics, defining what constitutes ethics; normative ethics, determining what rules or principles should guide ethical decisions; and applied ethics, the application of normative rules to specific ethical dilemmas. Normative ethics is the most prominent type of moral philosophy. Normative moral principles are of interest to public relations because they can guide the decision making of public relations practitioners in a multiplicity of situations.

Moral philosophy studies ethics, the *application* of moral principles to decision making. Ethics assumes that an objective morality does exist and attempts to discover the rules, values, and principles that govern—or should govern—behavior. Ethics provides logical decision-making methods based on moral principles of right and wrong, whereas moral philosophy deals with the more abstract questions about what actually constitutes moral character, norms, values, and beliefs across societies.

We can divide moral philosophy into two primary approaches to ethical decision making, realizing that there are many interpretations and competing views within each paradigm. These two broad approaches are consequentialism and non-consequentialism. These types of ethical reasoning are diametrically opposed, as they hold differing values that dictate the parameters used to define what each considers an ethical decision.

Consequentialism instructs that the ethical decision is the one with the most favorable consequences. The morality of the decision is judged by the expected outcome of the decision (utility) rather than the decision itself. The "utility" of a decision is what it produces in terms of the outcome of implementing the decision. Utility can be measured in numerous ways, such as bringing the greatest amount of good, happiness, favorable consequences, or pleasure to the greatest number of people. Consequentialism expects the decision maker to be able to predict the potential outcomes of numerous decision alternatives and then choose among those alternatives to produce the greatest positive consequence. This paradigm is similar to a cost-benefit analysis. It looks not at a moral principle applied to the dilemma, but at the consequences of the decision.

Consequentialism dictates that the most ethical decision is the decision that produces the greatest utility. Therefore, the moral aspects of the decision come into play after the decision is made or in weighing the consequences of different options. The most prominent school of consequentialist thought is utilitarianism. Although there are varying forms of utilitarianism (hedonistic, eudaimonistic, and ideal, further subdivided into act and rule utilitarianism), the moral decision in this paradigm is that which has an outcome of creating the greatest utility or good for the greatest number of people affected by the outcome of the decision.

The second broad approach to ethics is the non-consequentialist approach. This view asserts that the worth of a decision should be judged by the moral principle applied, not by the resulting consequences of the decision. This view holds that duty is the basic moral requirement and exists independently of consequences. Arguments about justice, responsibility, fairness, and duty are generally appealing to the moral norms and principles used in non-consequentialist decision making. In this view, doing the morally right thing to uphold one's duty is the primary decision-making factor, and the consequences of an ethical decision are a secondary concern. When an ethical decision is made based on sound moral principles (such as "lying is wrong"), the decision is deemed ethical. The consequences of making a decision are not ignored, but they are not the primary decision making factor. Non-consequentialist philosophers do take the consequences of decision alternatives into account, but they do not allow the outcome of various alternatives to *determine* the moral principle used to make the decision. Deontology, as developed by Immanuel Kant, and the Rawlsian theory of justice, are common forms of non-consequentialist ethics.

In deontology, the decision maker must decide the ethical course of action by reason alone, basing his or her moral judgment on autonomous rationality, with the overall imperative of performing her or his moral duty. Kant's categorical imperative, a test of universal reversibility, is employed to ensure that the decision is based on a generalizable moral principle that is applicable across situations, times, and cultures. The categorical imperative asks the decision maker to place himself or herself on the receiving end of a decision as a test of its fairness and acceptability. Deontology requires a rigorous analysis of motives and intention to guard against bias or self-interest in favor of an objective vantage. Finally, deontology demands that people be treated as ends in themselves, with moral principles that maintain the dignity and respect of all involved supporting ethical decisions.

To allow consequences to dictate moral principle would violate deontology's guard against bias by allowing the outcome of a decision to affect the moral principle used to make the decision. In the words of one senior public relations practitioner, "If you do the right thing, the consequences take care of themselves" (Bowen, 2002, p. 280). Deontology argues that the consequentialist reasoning of "If I do X, then Y will happen" can be easily mutated to serve selfish interests or even to justify unethical behavior. By basing the decision entirely on moral reasoning according to categorical principle, deontology attempts to offer a method of analysis that rules out all considerations except the moral intention of doing the right thing.

Why use moral philosophy in public relations? Moral philosophy gives people standards, language, and tools for rational analysis with which to reduce the difficulty of articulating and defending moral judgments. What factors make one decision more ethical than another? Is there an intrinsic moral good that we can judge in ethical decisions, or is it up to every individual to define what is good for himself or herself alone? Furthermore, if moral standards are in conflict, whose standards should prevail? Only through moral philosophy can we conduct a rational and modestly objective analysis of such dilemmas. This analysis provides an excellent tool for the public relations practitioner to use when facing differing demands from the organization or client, the dominant coalition, publics, stakeholders, the media, and activists.

—*Shannon A. Bowen*

See also Decision theory; Deontology; Ethics of public relations; Utilitarianism

Bibliography

Bowen, S. A. (2002). Elite executives in issues management: The role of ethical paradigms in decision making. *Journal of Public Affairs, 2*(4), 270–283.

Day, L. A. (1997). *Ethics in media communications: Cases and controversies* (2nd ed.). Belmont, CA: Wadsworth.

De George, R. T. (1999). *Business ethics* (5th ed.). Englewood Cliffs, NJ: Prentice Hall.

Flew, A. (1979). *A dictionary of philosophy* (2nd ed.). New York: St. Martin's Press.

Kant, I. (1964). *Groundwork of the metaphysic of morals* (H. J. Paton, Trans.). New York: Harper & Row. (Originally published 1785)

Mill, J. S. (1957). *Utilitarianism.* New York: Liberal Arts Press. (Originally published 1861)

Rawls, J. (1971). *A theory of justice.* Cambridge, MA: Harvard University Press.

MOTIVATION THEORY

Although the term *theory* is used in motivation theory, no single recognized theory of motivation exists. Rather, *motivation* is used as an umbrella term for a number of theories that describe factors, traits, or situations that result in people moving beyond awareness and attitudes into behaviors.

One of the earliest 20th-century psychologists to focus on motivation was Kurt Lewin, noted for his three decades of work at Stanford University, the University of Iowa, and the Massachusetts Institute of Technology. Lewin established the Research Center for Group Dynamics and thought of motives as goal-directed forces. This was new thinking amid the psychological theories that behavior was due to blind impulses within individuals. His resulting field theory stated that actions were influenced by environmental factors as well as psychological traits.

Abraham Maslow's 1954 *Hierarchy of Needs* further refined this idea of internal and external influences by identifying five sequential categories of needs that must be met for individuals to feel fulfilled. First, physiological needs such as hunger and thirst must be satisfied; second, individuals must feel safe; third, people must feel like they belong to some social group; fourth, individuals must experience some type of self-esteem; and fifth, only then can individuals work toward reaching their own potential, what Maslow called self-actualization.

Lewin and Maslow's work established the two basic domains of motivation: internal and external. Researchers in the next two decades attempted to identify variables and factors that fit into these two perspectives in a variety of different environmental settings from the workplace to advertising.

A number of workplace theories cite motivation as a key element in employee workplace behavior. Frederick Herzberg's 1959 *hygiene theory* contends that the external job environment, consisting of hygiene factors such as company policies, supervisor behavior, and salary, must be satisfactory before individuals will be motivated to pursue higher-order, internal motivators such as achievement, recognition, and job advancement.

Perhaps the most famous workplace motivation scenario is the serendipitous finding known as the Hawthorne effect. Researcher George Mayo, conducting human relations research at General Electric's Hawthorne Works, found that individuals' group motivation and resulting productivity increased or decreased according to factory light levels. He concluded that the levels of attention being paid to them directly affected individuals' motivation—in fact, that security, belonging, and recognition were stronger factors than physical comfort.

Douglas McGregor's 1957 X and Y theories also contributed to the motivational theory umbrella. Often used in management situations, theory X states that individuals have an inherent aversion to work and therefore must be externally motivated to do it. Theory Y provides the opposite view, that individuals naturally have a need to work and external forces have only to encourage and provide opportunities for this need to be satisfied. This suggests that understanding individuals' internal motivations is necessary to know what external motivators would be most effective in creating or reinforcing desired behaviors.

The media environment with its rich variety of technologies has its own set of motivational studies, most based on trying to identify the effects media have on human behavior. The 1930s Payne Fund Studies, a 13-study, three-year effort directed by the Motion Picture Research Council, studied the influence of movies on children. The resulting 10 volumes, with their findings on topics from sleep disturbances being linked to scary movies to the influence on moral standards of on-screen actors, were not conclusive in proving effects, but were revolutionary in even attempting to tackle such a complex subject.

Radio figured prominently in early media/motivation studies, with the *War of the Worlds* broadcast fiasco and Herta Herzog's study of women listening to radio serials. Actor Orson Wells was so convincing in his 1938 radio rendition of *War of the Worlds* that people panicked, some to the point of jumping out of windows. Herzog, under the direction of Paul Lazarsfeld and the Office of Radio Research, combined four studies of radio and women listeners to conclude that the women's personal characteristics motivated them to listen because of the satisfaction they received from listening. This developed into the *uses and gratifications perspective*, which has subsequently been studied in the context of television and Internet use.

When television entered mainstream American homes in the post–World War II era, researchers shifted attention to what people heard as well as what they saw. As with films, the research began with effects on children in the first major study of its kind, *Television in the Lives of Our Children.* Of most concern were the potential behavior effects, but as with most motivational research findings, no significant link between what children watched and what it motivated them to do was established. That did not stop the flood of television studies that ensued—the 1960s *Violence and the Media* study identified the two worlds individuals' experience—television versus real-life experiences—and concluded that violent television content motivated individual violent behavior. This inspired George Gerbner's longitudinal study of violence in the media, resulting in his cultivation theory. This theory states that if individuals see enough violence repeatedly on television, some individuals become socialized to believe and/or accept that behavior as reality while others are motivated to emulate it. In 1977, the Ronnie Zamora murder trial provided the ultimate legal test for motivation and violent television when Zamora's attorney based his client's defense on behavior motivated by violent television. Though the defense was novel, Zamora lost.

Not all motivation theories are linked exclusively to media, however. Other researchers studied real-life social situations to determine what motivated individuals to behave in different ways. In the 1960s Albert Bandura studied how people learn new behaviors. His famous experiment with the Bobo doll, where children watched a doll being punched and when left alone with the doll, punched

it as they had seen others do, led to modeling theory and its premise of individuals being motivated to emulate the behaviors of others.

During the same period, Leon Festinger was exploring how individuals were motivated to solve situations in which they received conflicting information. His cognitive dissonance theory states that when discrepancies exist between beliefs or actions, people are compelled to resolve the conflict so they can return to a state of equilibrium. His conclusion was that the change in behavior motivated people to make a change in their thought patterns.

Applying these social, cognitive, and behavioral perspectives is an accepted part of marketing and advertising practice as well as being used in the more traditional realms of television and radio programming. One of the advertising industry's first introductions to motivational research came during the 1940s and 1950s via Ernest Dichter, head of the Institute for Motivational Research. Dichter conducted in-depth interviews that relied on a psychoanalytical, Freudian-based interpretation of consumers' responses to identify feelings and emotions such as tension and guilt and to use them to develop sales psychology. This led to further research on consumers' self-images, attitudes, and behaviors, along with their environments, as factors that influence consumers' decisions and motivate their buying behavior; this work was, in effect, seeking a direct link between psychology and purchasing behavior.

Not everyone accepted the early motivational researchers' premise that discovering these psychological desires would motivate individuals into behavior. One of the strongest criticisms of motivational research is that the data could not predict which thoughts individuals would act on. The heavy reliance on qualitative research techniques was also constantly questioned by traditional marketing and business scholars, with the result that by the end of the 1950s, the idea of psychology's direct influence on consumer behavior was losing credibility. Motivational research, however, was not dead; in fact, it is credited as being the forerunner of modern-day psychographic research models. These approaches focus on sophisticated systems combining consumers' demographics with lifestyle behaviors; one of the best known is the Stanford Research Institute's (SRI) Values, Attitudes, and Lifestyles System (VALS). Based on a complex, weighted combination of environmental, demographic, and lifestyle variables, the VALS system and others like it attempt to create categories of consumers to whom targeted advertising and promotional messages can be sent to motivate purchasing behavior.

Although much study has been devoted to why people behave as they do, there is still no reliable, statistically significant research that can pinpoint specific, reliable factors in human behavior. Although specific internal or external factors can be studied in depth, putting all of these complex factors together to come up with one motivational theory has not been accomplished. The complexity of human beings with their internal differences and the myriad external factors affecting each individual make that a challenging task for future researchers.

—*Barbara J. DeSanto*

See also Cultivation theory; Psychographics; Uses and gratifications theory

Bibliography

DeFleur, M. L., and Ball-Rokeach, S. (1989). *Theories of mass communication* (5th ed.). New York: Longman.

Lowery, S. A. and DeFleur, M. L. (1995). *Milestones in mass communication research: Media effects* (3rd ed.). New York: Longman.

McQuail, D. (2000). *McQuail's mass communication theory* (4th ed.). London: Sage.

MUCKRAKERS (AND THE AGE OF PROGRESSIVISM)

Muckrakers were early investigative journalists who exposed corruption and abuse by the newly emerging giant corporations and local political machines. For public relations, the focus was on the negative exposure of the corporations headed by the legendary robber barons such as J. D. Rockefeller, William Vanderbilt, and J. P. Morgan. The corporate response to the muckrakers resulted in a growth spurt for public relations in the early 1900s. Muckrakers showed that the newly emerging mass media—newspapers and magazines—could turn public opinion and public policy against the seemingly all-powerful corporate giants. These corporate giants began hiring public relations practitioners to present their side in the court of public opinion.

Today, television still dominates the news media landscape and provides many forums for investigative journalism. Many of these stories lead to problems and even crises for organizations. A few examples include when CBS exposed the danger of the drug Rezulin, when ABC battled the grocery chain Food Lion over food safety, and when NBC challenged GM on truck safety. While this is often called muckraking, there is a significant difference between investigative reporters of today and yesteryear. Most of the muckrakers were part of a larger social movement to effect change during a very turbulent social time in United States history, the Progressive movement. It is instructive to begin any discussion of the muckrakers by presenting the social backdrop of progressivism.

The age of progressivism or the Progressive Era ran from 1895 to 1920 as a reaction to the changing social structure of the United States. This time period saw the rise of urbanization, industrialization, and immigration. Before 1930, the majority of the U.S. population lived in rural areas. In fact the United States had very few cities with populations more than 100,000. By 1930, the majority of the American people lived in urban areas, and there were 93 cities with populations of 100,000 or more. Suddenly small-town living was replaced by city living—with its related problems of sanitation and crime. The United States was adapting to a new way of living: urban life.

The rise of cities was accompanied by the shift from an agricultural to an industrial economy. People no longer worked in small shops or farms. They worked in large factories. The work was hard, as people often worked more than 12 hours a day in extremely unsafe working conditions with low wages. The cities provided a large pool of labor, so it was easy to replace workers who were injured or agitating for better working conditions.

Immigration was helping to further increase the number of people in the cities. However, immigration patterns were changing. Before 1890, most immigrants were from the United Kingdom, Germany, and Scandinavia—from northern Europe. After 1890, most of the immigrants were from southern and central Europe. These new immigrants were often exploited because they were different and lacked political power.

Cities such as Chicago became a breeding ground for discontent. Segments of the population lived and worked in terrible conditions while having little recourse to change it. There were fears in the United States that socialism would take roots among the discontented and result in revolution, perhaps violent, or wide-scale adoption of socialist principles. One sign was the effort to unionize the workers.

The Progressives wanted change as well but in an orderly fashion and done within the existing political structure. The Progressives wanted to avoid violent revolution and socialism. In fact, most of the Progressives were upper- and middle-class Americans who wanted to preserve much of the status quo. They wanted limited change that made life better for the discontented lower class but did not change the basic political, economic, and social structures that benefited the upper and middle classes. Of course, one segment of the Progressives wanted more sweeping reforms, but they were in the minority.

From this landscape emerged the muckrakers, journalists whose words often brought about social and political change. Many muckrakers were much more radical than the Progressives, many being socialists themselves. President Theodore Roosevelt provided the name *muckrakers*, but he did not mean it as a compliment. In the 17th-century religious allegory *Pilgrim's Progress,* there is a group of people who can only look down and rake the muck; they could not look up and see the celestial crowd. President Roosevelt created the nickname after David Graham Phillips wrote a piece critical of Roosevelt's political allies as part of an expose on the Senate. But ironically, the muckrakers helped make Theodore Roosevelt a crusading president by providing the public opinion needed to

American journalist and political philosopher Lincoln Steffens (1866–1936), who published many articles exposing urban political corruption. He was prominent among the writers Theodore Roosevelt called "muckrakers."
SOURCE: © Bettmann/CORBIS

support many of "his" reforms. Lincoln Steffens, a leading voice among muckrakers, told Roosevelt after the muckraker speech, "Well, you have put an end to all these journalistic investigations that have made you."

Some muckrakers were activists who used fiction to dramatize their causes, and others were journalists interested primarily in revealing the wrongdoings of corporations. Upton Sinclair and Ida Tarbell represent the two variations of muckrakers.

Upton Sinclair was the prototypical muckraker. He was a reformer with a burning pen. Sinclair was appalled by the living and working conditions of the meat packers in Chicago. As a center of transportation that connected the Midwest to the East, its huge stockyards and processing plants made Chicago the meat packing capital of the United States at this time. Bubbling Creek was so named because it bubbled with blood from the slaughtered animals. Only poor workers lived near the dirty and smelly packing plants. Sinclair lived among the workers in the area known as Packingtown for seven weeks. There he learned about the abusive labor practices and unsanitary meat packing facilities. The end product was his book titled *The Jungle.* The meat packers, such as Armour, were exploiting the workers. They worked hard for low wages in dangerous conditions. During his stay, there was even a strike that was suppressed by management. The book also described the unsanitary conditions in the packing houses, which included grinding rats, refuse, and the body parts of workers in with the meat.

Sinclair struggled to find a publisher. Originally the book was presented in serial format in the socialist publication *Appeal to Reason.* Six publishers rejected the manuscript before Sinclair decided to publish it himself. After receiving more than 900 orders, Doubleday decided to publish the book and sold more than 150,000 copies. Eventually Americans read about the abuses in the meat packing industry. Sinclair hoped people would be enraged by the abuse of the workers and demand reforms to help them. The public reaction was much different. People were outraged, but it was over the meat they ate, not the exploited workers. Sinclair noted that he aimed for the heart but hit the stomach.

Public opinion did force the U.S. government to take some action. President Roosevelt read *The Jungle* and helped push for meat packing reforms but made it clear that he did not care for the socialist ideas promoted in the book. The federal government passed the Pure Food Bill and Beef Inspection Act. The meat packing lobby managed to water down the reforms. The laws had very little effect on meat packing, and reformers, including Sinclair, considered the measures to be failures. In the end the laws were largely symbolic—designed to reassure people that meat was safe. Such changes were common in the Progressive Era as people wanted limited change, and you cannot get much more limited than a change that simply makes people feel

better. The symbolic changes were designed to keep people quiet, not to make serious changes. The news media today are still doing stories on food safety, sanitation issues, and problems in meat packing.

The Progressive Era did see significant changes that improved the lives of workers. Child labor laws were developed, worker compensation programs were instituted, and measures were passed to hold employers liable for harm to workers. The environment also benefited as Niagara Falls was saved from corporate exploitation, and policies were developed for the conservation of natural resources.

Ida Tarbell was a journalist who decided to write about the abuses of corporations, but not be an activist for reform. Tarbell was a well-known biographer at the time, having published books on Napoleon and Abraham Lincoln. *McClure's* magazine agreed to let her write a piece on the history of Standard Oil, the monopoly created by J. D. Rockefeller. Tarbell's father had been part of the Pennsylvania oil industry that had been ruined by Rockefeller's questionable business practices. Although *McClure's* was known as a muckraking magazine, Tarbell's style was careful historical research and documentation. Tarbell researched the project for over five years. Here documentation came from court records of lawsuits against Standard Oil. She supplemented this data through interviews with current and former Standard Oil executives, government regulators, competitors, academics, and antitrust lawyers. In the end, Tarbell crafted an objective story based on public documents. She created a paper trail to document her work. Other investigative journalists of the time would often use gossip that led to inaccuracies in their stories. Moreover, there was no call for action as was common in reform pieces of the day, and she allowed Standard Oil officials to respond to earlier drafts.

The history of Standard Oil included ruining competitors by signing agreements with railroads that caused rates to be higher for competitors and by operating in New Jersey because New Jersey state laws helped companies get around the

Sherman Anti-Trust Act, a measure designed to prevent monopolies. The railroads were working with Rockefeller and his associates. The railroad would charge other oil producers more for shipping than they charged Rockefeller and his group, giving them a price advantage. Furthermore, the railroads would give part of this excess charge back to Rockefeller and his friends. This unfair advantage allowed Rockefeller to put others out of business. In Pennsylvania, the scheme was run under the name South Improvement Company (SIC). The practice was eventually found to be illegal, and SIC was ordered disbanded. However, the damage had been done, and many small oil producers had been put out of business. Later, Rockefeller used threats of such a practice to win control over the oil production in Cleveland, Ohio.

Tarbell's research was published in a 16-part series published between November 1902 and October 1904 titled *The History of Standard Oil*. It later became an 814-page book, and in 1999 was listed as number 5 on the list of the 100 most important journalistic works of the 20th century. Here is an excerpt from *The History of Standard Oil*:

> Little by little as the public began to realize the compactness and harmony of the Standard organization, the ability of its members, the solidity of the qualities governing its operations, they began to forget its history—they began to accept the Standard's explanation that the critics were indeed "people with a private grievance," "moss-backs left behind in the march of progress." It looked more and more to the outsider as if henceforth Mr. Rockefeller was going to have things his own way, for who was there to interfere with him, to dispute his position? No one, save that back in Northwestern Pennsylvania, in scrubby little oil towns, around greasy derricks, in dingy shanties, by rusty deserted oil stills, men still talked of the iniquity of the railroad rebate, the injustice of restraint of trade, the dangers of monopoly; still rehearsed with tiresome persistency the evidence by which it had been proved that the Standard Oil Company was a revival of the South Improvement Company.

Tarbell's own father warned her against writing the piece because he feared Rockefeller would retaliate against her. Tarbell's characterization of

J. D. Rockefeller was scathing. She referred to him as money mad, hypocritical, and a living mummy. Standard Oil did fight back by launching a smear campaign against Ida Tarbell. The main messages were delivered in pamphlets that simply attacked Tarbell without addressing the issues her pieces had raised. This reaction by Standard Oil is public relations at its worst, a simple knee-jerk reaction designed to suppress discussion instead of airing the facts. President Theodore Roosevelt read the *History of Standard Oil* and used many of the insights to build a case against monopolies. Clearly, Tarbell had an idea of the corruption she would find before writing the series. However, she did not have the activist bent of writers like Upton Sinclair or Lincoln Steffens. Her desire to expose Standard Oil was derived from personal experience with the dangers of J. D. Rockefeller's business practices. Tarbell actually pioneered today's style of investigative journalism that seeks careful documentation of corporate abuses.

The work of Sinclair and Tarbell illustrated two emerging forces that corporations would now have to face: the mass media and public opinion. The mass media was a new phenomenon driven in part by the growth of cities. Publications could reach hundreds of thousands of the new urban population. This would have been impossible prior to urbanization. It was now much easier for a large segment of the population to become aware of problems. When people become aware of problems, they can choose to press for change. Public opinion, opinions shared by a significant percent of the population, began to emerge as a force. When people read *The Jungle* and learned they could be eating spoiled meat, they complained to politicians and demanded action. Stories in the mass media could help to shape public opinion, and public opinion could shape public policy—the agenda setting and agenda building effects. In turn, public policy could affect how a corporation operated and its level of profitability.

The robber barons could not afford to ignore the new mass media or to refrain from trying to influence public opinion. Corporations needed to speak to the new urban population. It is no coincidence that modern public relations was believed to have developed in 1906, right in the middle of the Progressive Era. Corporate leaders, such as J. D. Rockefeller, hired former journalists to help them work with the mass media and become a part of the struggle to shape public opinion. Silence by corporations was no longer golden; corporations had to respect the power of the mass media. For instance, the policy for train accidents changed from barring the mass media from the site to helping them tour the site. Corporations wanted to present their side of the story to the mass media. Some went too far by actually buying the support of editors and reporters, but the roots of modern-day media relations were beginning to emerge along with a concern for how stakeholders felt about the organization. Motivated more by profit than compassion, corporations were learning that the opinions of stakeholders did matter and should be taken into account.

Still, these early days of public relations did view stakeholders more as obstacles than as possible assets to an organization. During the Progressive Era, corporations were beginning to change and public relations was to be an integral part of that change. Public opinion mattered, so a corporation had to be sensitive to the opinions of stakeholders in its actions. Slowly a recognition was emerging that corporations must think beyond just making more money. Stakeholders such as the news media, workers, and activist groups were emerging as a force in public opinion that must be considered, not ignored, by corporations.

—W. Timothy Coombs

See also Publicity

Bibliography

Brasch, W. M. (1990). *Forerunners of revolution: Muckrakers and the American social conscience.* Lanham, MD: University Press of America.

Burson, G. *Progressive movement & the 1920s.* Retrieved May 20, 2003, from http://www.jmu.edu/madison/center/main-pages/teacher/curriculum/chap9.htm

Sinclair, U. (1906). *The jungle.* New York: Doubleday.

Tarbell, I. (1904). *The History of the Standard Oil Company.* New York: McClure, Phillips.

MULTIMEDIA

Multimedia is a combination of discrete technologies. In the simplest sense, multimedia means "many media working together as one." Although the technologies are not necessarily communication based, the result of the combination is a communication approach or channel not previously available.

An easy, low-tech example is a "multimedia slide show," which was considered cutting edge 30 or so years ago. Utilizing the earliest versions of multimedia, agencies—public relations and advertising—often showed clients samples of creative tactics by using multiple, synchronized 35-mm slide shows with audio accompaniment. A bank of slide projectors would be used in conjunction with an audio player. The audio recording would have an extra, unheard track of information, consisting of trigger pulses to cue and advance the various slide projectors. A good example of this approach using music and still images can be found in the film *The Parallax View*, where the lead character is shown an absolutely harrowing recruiting film.

The mid-1970s marked the beginning of an unsuccessful attempt at interactive television via multimedia. Warner Cable used computer technology to deliver the QUBE system to subscribers in Columbus, Ohio. With the use of a special set-top box, viewers could participate in electronic town hall meetings and surveys, play along with game shows, call plays in sports broadcasts, and even participate in mock voting during the Academy Awards. The system was prohibitively expensive to maintain and was dismantled in the early 1980s. However, the QUBE system was an important failure. The use and integration of computer technology at the system level was an important step in the enhancement of the mass communication process. The combining of television and computer technology is one signpost of a major change in society. Alvin Toffler introduces the idea of an information society in his 1980 book, *The Third Wave.* Toffler explained the transition under way as American society is moving from an age of industry to an age of information. Television, as a technology, has moved from an

Industrial Age invention to a conduit of the Information Age.

Moving into the Information Age has precipitated a shift from multimedia to convergence. Whereas it was once easy to distinguish between the various elements in a multimedia presentation, convergence makes the distinction impossible for both message creation and message delivery.

Message creation now involves the seamless use of a variety of audio and video material. The ability to digitize any source and "reformat" it for use in any delivery system makes, for example, distinctions between film and video one of effect, not affect.

Multimedia and convergence provide the public relations practitioner with unprecedented degrees of latitude and flexibility in both the creation and delivery of messages. The positive effect of flexibility in message creation and delivery has a negative effect on message control. Message creators should realize that convergence allows for a message to easily move from one mass medium to another. For example, internal memos show up on a Web site called www.internalmemos.com, allowing an audience to see a message that was never intended for them.

—*Michael Nagy*

Bibliography

Dyson, E., Gilder, G., Keyworth, G., & Toffler, A. (1994, August 22). *Cyberspace and the American dream: A magna carta for the information age* (Version 1.2). Retrieved May 11, 2004, from http://www.pff.org/publications/ecommerce/fi1.2magnacarta.html

Toffler, A. (1980) *The third wave*. New York: Bantam.

MUTUALLY BENEFICIAL RELATIONSHIPS

A mutually beneficial relationship (MBR) is a highly desirable, normative outcome of effective public relations. An MBR occurs when the stakeholders of each organization believe that the subject organization works to achieve a condition where it and all its stakeholders benefit appropriately because of the quality of their relationships. As a platitude, MBRs are asserted as the outcome goal of public relations, without much attention to how that end is achieved or what it actually entails. Such platitudes may mask the darker intent and ability of the focal organization to persuasively promote the conclusion that the relationship is more mutually beneficial than it truly is.

As a best-case scenario, the logic of MBR reasons that when people believe that organizations operate with their interests in mind, they support rather than oppose those organizations. Thus, they buy from businesses they believe give them full value for goods and services purchased. They support activist or other nonprofit groups that share values and hold similar goal-oriented commitments, such as ending specific childhood diseases. They believe in and support governmental agencies that act in their interest, in what can be seen as the public interest, where they are the "public."

Critics of this line of thinking simply doubt that businesses, for instance, ever hold stakeholder interests equal to their own. By this logic, executive managements create policies and engage in marketing that justifies their salaries and makes the business prosper, even though the relationship is tipped to favor the interest of the business and may even harm the health, safety, sense of fairness, or other aspects of well-being on the part of customers or other stakeholders. Thus the logic of MBR challenges public relations practitioners to truly understand and be in a management position to help the organization to know the expectations of its stakeholders that define their best interests.

MBRs assume that stakeholders hold varying standards of how each organization should operate. These standards are forged through societal dialogue voiced by many points of influence: industry, activist, government, media reporter, and such. Disagreement and intolerance are part of the dispute over the definition of what is mutually beneficial and whether the organization truly operates to that end. Critics hold different standards. Some are more intolerant of the actions and ethical choices of organizations than others. Thus, MBR is a normative goal that cannot be totally satisfied for all parties in any relationship. Each organization, regardless of its type, has a wide array of stakeholders. Each may have different expectations for the quality of the relationship and whether it is satisfied by what the organization does and says.

Relational theory discusses process variables that can foster or impede the creation of MBRs, but it does not address the difficult question of shared interests or the co-creation of meaning. Beyond the process, MBR is not meaningful if it is not a normative goal that challenges each organization to foster—through dialogue, collaborative decision making, strategic commitments, and corporate responsibility—a positive balance between its interests and those of its stakeholders. As it builds relationships with stakeholders, the organization advances the public interest and helps to elevate the quality community. In any full discussion of MBR, the sense of community is a focal point. What any organization does and says needs to be judged by whether it truly advances the essence of community among all of the stakeholders.

By the same token, appeals to community can be used asymmetrically to the beneficial interest of the organization rather than those of its stakeholders. Thus, a government ostensibly fighting international terrorism can appeal to community to defend its policies against its critics. It may, in this rhetorical stance, argue that any critic of its battle against international terrorists is actually a supporter of terrorism because it does not immediately and completely agree with and support the government policies. This rhetorical stance would in fact be asymmetrical and serve the mutual interest of the critics whose ideas may indeed ultimately add value to the fight against terrorism but do so in ways that disagree with the positions of the administration.

Although academics in the late 1990s began to show enthusiasm for the concept of MBR, it was not a new or novel concept. Substantial discussion by various practitioners and academics earlier in the 20th century sought to determine how organizations could create relationships. Both the International Association of Business Communicators and the Public Relations Society of America have featured relationship building as a part of effective public relations and strategic business communication.

In its Vision, Mission, and Structure statement, the International Association of Business Communicators (IABC) features relationships:

IABC specializes in helping people and organizations:

- Make business sense of communication
- Think strategically about communication
- Measure and clarify the value of communication
- Build better relationships with stakeholders (www.iabc.com)

The Public Relations Society of America (PRSA) has been committed to meeting the challenge of relationship building since at least 1982, when it adopted its current official statement on public relations. There it acknowledged the professional need to engage in collaborative decision making and corporate responsibility to bridge differences: "Public relations helps our complex, pluralistic society to reach decisions and function more effectively by contributing to mutual understanding among groups and institutions. It serves to bring private and public policies into harmony."

Reviewing the wide array of institutions that require effective public relations, the PRSA publication *Public Relations Tactics: The Blue Book,* noted that "these institutions must develop effective relationships with many different audiences or publics such as employees, members, customers, local communities, shareholders, and other institutions, and with society at large" (p. B2).

In their summary of the discipline published in 2000, Scott Cutlip, Allen Center, and Glen Broom observed that the trend in the United States was for public relations to be less focused on one-way, self-interested persuasion and more on mutuality, reciprocation, and the idea of "between." Based on this trend, these authors posed one of the most widely disseminated definitions: "Public relations is the management function that establishes and maintains mutually beneficial relationships between an organization and the publics on whom its success or failure depends" (2000, p. 6).

One of the leaders in the formation of public relations as a management discipline, John W. Hill, principal founder of Hill & Knowlton, featured the concept of relationship in his books published during the 1950s and 1960s. He credited Ivy Lee with an even earlier discussion of the term: "Public relationships, he [Lee] wrote, involved not simply 'saying' but '*doing*'—not just talk, but action" (1963, p. 16). Hill reasoned that organizations simply could not avoid considering and meeting the challenges of multiple relationships "because the corporation deals with employees, stockholders, customers, neighbors, government functionaries, and many others—with all of whom it has many relationships" (1958, p. 4). To build relationships, organizations must not only talk, but act in appropriate ways. Thus, public relations can never be limited to communication and is best when it is part of management decision making that allows the organization to position itself and operate in ways that strive to balance its interests with those of its stakeholders.

At one level, the effort to achieve MBR, Hill reasoned, was a matter of reputation management. Do the organization's stakeholders believe the organization worked in their interests? Does it have the reputation for such actions? If not, is the problem with its reputation one that could be corrected by communication, or does it also or primarily call for new and improved actions and policies? To this end, Hill asked managements to think about how strong their relationships were with all of their stakeholders:

Typical of the questions that need to be answered before a sound public relations program can be constructed for a corporation are these:

1. How sound and stable are its relations with employees—and what do employees think about the company?

2. How are relations with customers, distributors, dealers—and what do they think of the company?

3. How are relations with stockholders and the financial community—and what is the opinion in those quarters about the company?

4. How does the company stand with prevailing public opinion in the communities where its plants are located—and to what extent does it assume its share of community responsibility?

5. Does the company have any problems with governments—federal, state, or local—and are these legislative or otherwise?

6. Does management have adequate and effective ways of communicating in person or by other means with its employees and with all other groups with which it has relationships?

7. Are key personnel informed sufficiently about company affairs—are they able to explain and defend broad company policies to employees and others?

8. Is there a well-thought-out and workable plan for responding to the many appeals by worthy causes for company contributions?

9. Is there a plan for cooperating with educators in supplying them with factual material for school use as desired?

10. Are members of management sufficiently articulate in explaining their own business and the workings of the enterprise system when occasion demands—and is the company benefiting enough from leadership by management in public and industry affairs?

11. Are the company's achievements and products sufficiently known to its public and is there need for improving goodwill?

12. Are press relations good, bad, or indifferent? (1963, pp. 136–137)

Hill was a practical counselor as well as one who sought high moral ground as the rationale for his profession and its profession. He reasoned, as advice to executive managements,

Business managements are concerned with the problems of conducting their corporate or industry affairs in ways that they may feel are contributive to public progress. They must arrive at effective policies that go far beyond their economic and operating functions into the complex realms of social, governmental, and political relationships. The large majority push forward into these policy areas as a matter of choice. But in terms of the long-range survival of corporate enterprise, there is little choice involved; it is a matter of essentiality. (1963, p. 230)

A realist, Hill knew and counseled that organizations could not operate with autonomy as long as they merely operated in their own interest and expected others to tolerate that point of view.

Recent studies have examined the variables that seem most essential to fostering MBRs. This line of analysis is far from finished, but key factors are emerging. Leading concepts in this analysis seem to be these:

1. *Open:* Fosters two-way communication based on listening for and sharing valuable information, as well as being responsive, respectful, candid, and honest. One-way communication occurs when an organization "speaks" but does not listen to or acknowledge the merit in what other people and organizations "say."

2. *Trustworthy:* Builds trust by being reliable, non-exploitative, and dependable.

3. *Cooperative:* Engages in collaborative decision making that ensures that the needs/wants of the organization and its stakeholders are met.

4. *Aligned:* Shares interests, rewards, and goals with its stakeholders.

5. *Compatible views/opinions:* Fosters mutual understanding and agreement; co-creates meaning.

6. Commitment: Supports community by being involved in it, investing in it, and displaying commitment to it.

The analysis of relationships has been explored from many points of view. *Systems theory* gives the rationale that no part of a system can operate forever imbalanced against the other parts of a system. Stated otherwise, one part of a system cannot prosper at the disadvantage of the rest of the system. A *rhetorical* perspective reasons that the effort to define interests assumes the co-creation of meaning. Many voices come together to define what constitutes a mutually beneficial relationship. *Social exchange theory* encompasses both of these theories and advances to reason that the quality of each relationship is based on give-and-take.

Dramatism theory assumes that individuals engage in battles of merger and division seeking higher levels of identification through courtship. Ultimate identification leads to a sharing of symbolic action.

MBRs are challenging because although they feature a positive outcome, such may not be possible with all publics. Frankly, critics whose values may not truly be in the public interest or otherwise meet the highest ethical standard can confront excellent organizations with challenges over values. For instance, at various times in the history of U.S. industry, companies were criticized as being destructive to the public interest if they engaged in hiring practices that opposed prevailing values to discriminate against people of color. It may be debatable how those values would help or harm the public interest. Thus, the question remains as a situational challenge to the ethics of public relations counselors: What truly is the public interest? Is it the narrow self-interested preference of any critic, or is it something else, something higher? Can the organization define this interest, can the critic prevail with its definition of the public interest, or is some other standard to prevail?

The concept of relationship underpins an even higher notion of community, which always is normative. Building community can be a positive incentive to discover what is in the best interest of the organization and its stakeholders and to move toward, if not fully achieve, that balance. But the concept of community can become a tyranny that may be manipulatively used by one side against the other. At best, such a ploy is an opening salvo to define the interest of the community, as critics typically claim that the organization is harming and not benefiting the community. As it is ad hominem to simply claim that an organization offends the community, it is equally ethically questionable to argue that to challenge the organization is to harm the community. Both of these tactics have been used, for example, by environmental activists and the organizations they criticize. In such debates, publics must be allowed or assumed to define themselves and speak their mind. Theory does not adequately get at the essence of MBRs if it leads to the conclusion that the organization alone can know what is a public, whose ideas are best, and which discussants of an issue are legitimate.

The concept of MBR commits organizations to a process and outcome that goes beyond mere manufactured image or reputation by avowing to seek positive relationships with its customers or publics. Such approaches to relationship building can be manipulative and disingenuous. One challenge of MBRs is to avoid confusing being nice to customers with working for a mutuality of interest.

—*Robert L. Heath*

See also Community and community building; Dramatism and dramatism theory; Hill, John Wiley; International Association of Business Communicators (IABC); Lee, Ivy; Public interest; Public Relations Society of America; Rhetorical theory; Social exchange theory; Stakeholder theory; Symmetry; Systems theory

Bibliography

Broom, G. M., Casey, S., & Ritchey, J. (1997). Toward a concept and a theory of organization-public relationships. *Journal of Public Relations Research, 9*, 83–98.

Cutlip, S. M., Center, A. H., & Broom, G. M. (2000). *Effective public relations* (8th ed.). Englewood Cliffs, NJ: Prentice Hall.

Heath, Robert L. (Ed.). (2002). *Handbook of public relations.* Thousand Oaks, CA: Sage.

Hill, John W. (1958). *Corporate public relations: Arm of management.* New York: Harper & Brothers.

Hill, John W. (1963). *The making of a public relations man.* New York: David McKay.

International Association of Business Communicators. *Vision, mission, and structure statement.* Retrieved May 13, 2004, from www.iabc.com.

Public Relations Society of America. (2002). *Public relations tactics: The blue book.* New York: Author.

NARRATIVE THEORY

According to communication scholar Walter Fisher, humans naturally are storytellers. This view of *homo narrans*—storytelling humans—fueled narrative theory or what Fisher called the *narrative paradigm.* From this perspective, narration is seen as a fundamental quality of human nature. In other words, humans "experience and comprehend life as a series of ongoing narratives, as conflicts, characters, beginnings, middles, and ends" (Fisher, 1987, p. 24).

Communication follows story format, with characters engaged in a plot sequence. Further, Fisher asserted that communication is narrative and all people are tellers of stories. Thus, we should regard all communication as story, regardless of its form, because we interpret it and fit it into our life stories. From this vantage point, "there is no genre, including technical communication, that is not an episode in the story of life (a part of the 'conversation') and is not itself constituted by logos and mythos" (Fisher, 1985, p. 347).

Essentially, we make sense of our lives by composing stories, woven from discrete experiences into functioning wholes. That is, knowledge is narratively configured, and it is through continuous activities in story making and storytelling that we interpret our experiences and describe them to others. However, because we collaborate with others in co-creation and analysis, narratives do not simply reflect our internal views. Further, the processes of narrative construction and meaning making are not static; rather, several types of information processing and attribution are at work.

In essentially the same way that individuals come to understand and describe themselves to others through their stories, organizations create and re-create narrated identities. Organizations tell stories about who they are, what their work is, who their stakeholders are, and who their enemies are—all of these crafting a particular identity or identities. Blake Ashforth and Fred Mael (1996) suggested that an organization's identity is crafted from "unfolding and stylized narratives about the 'soul' or essence of the organization" (p. 21).

Organizational members and public relations practitioners who understand an organization's identity, its publics, its key stakeholders, and the internal and external challenges it faces are in preferred positions to serve as leaders and spokespersons, weaving narrative explanations and responses. That is, recognition of these factors is useful in collaborating with others in the co-creation of meaning.

STORY POWER AND QUALITY

Fisher believed that stories are powerful and more persuasive than other forms of reasoning (e.g., statistics). This position is elaborated in his 1987 book, *Human Communication as Narration: Toward a Philosophy of Reason, Value, and Action,* in part by comparing and contrasting the underpinnings of the narrative paradigm with those of the rational world paradigm. Despite their power, however, not all stories are equally commanding. People judge stories (and as storytelling creatures, we all are qualified to do so), finding some more compelling than others.

To assess the relative quality of stories, Fisher used narrative rationality, which involves two criteria: story coherence and story fidelity. Coherence assesses the degree to which the story makes sense (e.g., is internally consistent). Fidelity assesses the degree to which a story fits with our views and experiences. Weighing coherence and fidelity, James Baesler (1995) found both to be important but concluded that coherence plays a greater role in the overall persuasiveness of a story.

In life, we tell and are told numerous stories. Some of these stories we accept and integrate into our story, our understanding of the world. Others we cast aside. Through this process, we create and re-create our lives and our understanding of ourselves and the social world; thus, stories are central to human understanding and expression.

NARRATIVE AND PUBLIC RELATIONS PRACTICE

In *Human Communication as Narration,* Fisher applied narrative theory to specific rhetorical situations (e.g., Reagan's rhetoric) and showed the diverse application of the theory. Clearly, public relations theory and practice share an interest in the telling and interpretation of stories. For example, according to Barry Brummett (1995), public relations involves "the practice of telling and managing stories that are told about people, institutions, and groups" (p. 24).

"Organizations can adopt or seek to influence the narratives of society by what they say and do" (Heath, 2001, p. 42). From narrative theory, organizations are seen as "providing 'plots' that are always in the process of recreation rather than existing as settled scripts" (Fisher, 1987, p. 18). Thus,

organizations and public relations practitioners can use existing public views and opinions as resources or seek to change them through new narratives. They work with internal and external stakeholders in co-creating meaning through stories told, stories adopted, and stories remembered.

For example, in times of organizational crisis or stress, public relations practitioners ideally work to develop a narrative that explains the situation and that previews resolution and a positive future. Clearly, an organization's past is critical in shaping how its stories of explanation will likely be seen (e.g., a history littered with similar infractions vs. a clean slate and positive community relations). Also at these times, the consistency of messages delivered to the public is of key import—what Fisher called narrative coherence.

CRITICISMS OF FISHER'S NARRATIVE THEORY

Despite its numerous strengths (e.g., heuristic value, parsimony, highly democratic orientation with all humans serving as story producers and evaluators), several aspects of Fisher's narrative theory have been criticized. One area of criticism concerns the completeness of the theory's description. For example, Robert Rowland (1989) asserted not all communication is narrative, nor does it strive to be. For example, Rowland cited particular types of science fiction and fantasy narratives as not conforming to earthlings' expectations or experiences. Additionally, some types of communication may fall outside Fisher's discussion of the theory. For example, some scholars maintain that Fisher failed to explain how narrative can result in unique outcomes and to account for its potential negative consequences, such as encouraging hatred or violence. A second area of criticism counters the first by suggesting that the theory is overly broad—so expansive that it fails to describe or distinguish between differing forms or types of communication. A third area of critique by William Kirkwood (1992) suggested that the theory may be seen as reinforcing the status quo. For example, it focuses on existing and accepted values (i.e., narrative fidelity) and ignores means by which stories can encourage change, denying a "rhetoric of possibility." In other words, the perspective could be taken as encouraging tellers to tailor their stories to what hearers already know, believe, and value, rather than to offer new visions. Essentially, the focus may restrict tellers to fit their stories to extant views, rather than leading people, through story, to new vistas. Instead of countering Fisher's views, Kirkwood intended to supplement and extend them—examining how stories may create previously unimagined possibilities.

—*Joy L. Hart*

See also Co-creation of meaning theory; Discourse theory; Rhetorical theory; Symbolic interactionism theory

Bibliography:

Ashforth, B. E., & Mael, F. A. (1996). Organizational identity and strategy as a context for the individual. In J. A. C. Baum & J. E. Dutton (Eds.), *Advances in strategic management 1996: The embeddedness of strategy* (Vol. 13, pp. 19–64). Greenwich, CT: JAI.

Baesler, E. J. (1995). Construction and test of an empirical measure for narrative coherence and fidelity. *Communication Reports, 8,* 97–101.

Bardhan, N. R. (2002). Accounts from the field: A public relations perspective on global AIDS/HIV. *Journal of Health Communication, 7,* 221–244.

Brummett, B.. (1995). Scandalous rhetorics. In W. N. Elwood (Ed.), *Public relations inquiry as rhetorical criticism: Case studies of corporate discourse and social influence* (pp. 13–24). Westport, CT: Praeger.

Fisher, W. R. (1985). The narrative paradigm: An elaboration. *Communication Monographs, 52,* 347–367.

Fisher, W. R. (1987). *Human communication as narration: Toward a philosophy of reason, value, and action.* Columbia: University of South Carolina Press.

Heath, R. L. (2001). A rhetorical enactment rationale for public relations: The good organization communicating well. In R. L. Heath (Ed.), *Handbook of public relations* (pp. 31–50). Thousand Oaks, CA: Sage.

Kirkwood, W. (1992). Narrative and the rhetoric of possibility. *Communication Monographs, 59,* 30–47.

Rowland, R. C. (1989). On limiting the narrative paradigm: Three case studies. *Communication Monographs, 56,* 39–54.

Seeger, M. W., Sellnow, T. L., & Ulmer, R. R. (2001). Public relations and crisis communication: Organizing and chaos. In R. L. Heath (Ed.), *Handbook of public relations* (pp. 155–165). Thousand Oaks, CA: Sage.

NARROWCASTING/ BROADCASTING

Narrowcasting and broadcasting are two ways to disseminate mass-mediated messages. Narrowcasting indicates that some sort of strategic discretion is being used in the selection of an audience for a message. Broadcasting is the opposite; here the primary consideration is how to reach as large an audience as possible. The strategic decision of whether to narrowcast or broadcast a message can happen at several levels, and across types of messages and different mass media.

One example is television. The traditional broadcast started with three networks, each with its own channel. The object in creating programming was to appeal to the lowest common denominator. With the advent of cable television, narrowcasting became a possibility. The number of channels expanded from three to hundreds—and satellite systems push the channel options even further—with each channel representing new possibilities.

Although increasing the number of channels promotes audience fragmentation, it also promotes demographically better-defined audiences. Content providers can fine-tune (or target) their messages. Advertising and public relations firms are also to be considered. With audience demographics better defined now than ever before, advertisers and public relations firms reap the benefits of being able to further refine messages for a specific audience. Added to this is the existence of two strata in the spots that run between programs—local and national.

Television is not the only medium to consider. The term *narrowcasting* is increasingly associated with radio. The Internet provides massive bandwidth, with the potential of tens of thousands of channels of content, each of them—creativity willing—unique.

Another medium to consider is the magazine. Technology has made it much less expensive to enter the print magazine business. Some magazines exist only on the Internet, sidestepping the costs of ink and paper. As the capabilities of the Internet grow, television will go through the same upheavals that print and radio have experienced.

Narrowcasting does have its problems. As an audience is further defined, it shrinks in size. That drives up the cost of getting the message (program, public service announcement, or advertisement) out. A balance will always have to be struck between the size of the audience to be reached and the cost of a message for that audience.

—*Michael Nagy*

NATIONAL BLACK PUBLIC RELATIONS SOCIETY (NBPRS)

Almost 200 African American public relations specialists were on the membership roster when the Black Public Relations Society (BPRS, pronounced "beepers") was founded in 1983. On the south side of Chicago, five women who worked at Morgan Communications Group—Sharon Morgan, Paula Robinson, Linda Williams, Deana Balfour, and Trina Williams—shared a concern regarding the status of black professionals in public relations. It was a historic moment because it was the first meeting of the Black Public Relations Society of Chicago. The organization would be a pivotal factor in the development of black public relations practitioners for decades.

From that momentous day in 1983, presidents of the Chicago BPRS chapter made tremendous personal sacrifices to keep the organization on track. Those who led the charge included Sharon Morgan, Paula Robinson, Billy Davis, and Chelsey Burroughs. Wynona Redmond took the helm of the group in 1998, a year in which the organization was reorganized. Redmond subsequently passed the baton to Paul Davis, who was the group's leader in 2003. Others who played pivotal roles in the success of the chapter were Stephanie Banks, Morgan Carter, Jackie Marshall, Deana Balfour, Barbara Kensey, Robbie Smith, Lydia Brown-Muhammed, Rae Jones, Jennifer Shultz, and entrepreneurs such as Tom Burrell, Michelle Flowers, Eugene Morris, and Robert Dale. The chapter celebrated its 20th anniversary in grand style during fall 2003.

The formation of BPRS in Chicago laid the groundwork for the formation of other African American public relations groups. In Los Angeles, after an article in *Essence* magazine touted the success of the Chicago group, Californian Helen Goss envisioned a similar group and enlisted assistance from another well-known communicator, Pat Tobin. Thus, the second BPRS chapter was founded in Los Angeles, the Black Public Relations Society of California, Inc. The chapter was begun in 1983 by a group of public relations practitioners who recognized a need for an organization that would nurture and strengthen professional development, resource sharing, mutual support, and networking among African American professionals and students interested in the public relations profession. Major initiatives undertaken by the organization focused on career development, training, program enhancements, networking, and scholarships.

Within the first year of its inception, the California chapter of BPRS elected officers, obtained a nonprofit 501(c)(3) classification, hosted a networking breakfast meeting, and outlined plans for an annual student scholarship program. The organization designates itself as the only organization on the West Coast with the primary goal of meeting the professional needs of African Americans in public relations. One of the most successful programs of the group is the annual Spring Development Professional Seminar. Attended by practitioners and students, the seminar features some of the industry's most well-known, seasoned, and influential business people working in public relations.

In June, the organization hosts an annual luncheon where outstanding African Americans working in public relations are honored. Additionally, during the luncheon African American students majoring in public relations, journalism, or communications and attending accredited California universities and colleges are given scholarships. By 2001, the organization had awarded more than $25,000 in scholarships.

The accomplishments of the California contingent of BPRS created a springboard that greatly assisted African American public relations professionals by providing a forum for the exchange of ideas, job opportunities, and networking. Future plans for the organization include the identification of untapped areas where African American public relations specialists might seek employment, utilization of technology to strengthen networking and communication activities among members, the development of a speaker's bureau, and the creation of new jobs.

Following the creation of the Chicago and Los Angeles chapters, other chapters were formed in Atlanta, Philadelphia, New York, and Washington, DC.

Philadelphia attempted to form its own BPRS chapter for black practitioners in 1987. Pat Tobin, who had been instrumental in the formation of the Los Angeles BPRS chapter, was in attendance in Philadelphia to offer her advice when the black professionals met. Others in attendance included Arlethia Perry, Pennsylvania State University; Mattie Humphrey, WDAS Radio; Delsia Scott Afantehao, OIC; A. Bruce Crawley, First Pennsylvania Bank; Sam Presley, Lincoln University; and David Brown, Public Private Ventures. The effort did not materialize at that time, but the Philadelphia chapter of BPRS was finally created in 2000. In celebration of its third anniversary, the Philadelphia Chapter of BPRS (PBPRS) held an aggressive membership drive during May 2003. The organization's mantra is to provide communication resources and professional support to its members. The group offers scholarships to assist students of color who are interested in pursuing careers in the communications industry.

To increase the active participation and employment of blacks in the various communications disciplines, especially public relations, the Black Public Relations Society of Atlanta (BPRS/Atlanta) was formed in 1987. The chapter was founded with 32 members. The first president of the chapter was Charlotte Johnson Roy, vice president of A. Brown-Olmstead Associates. The impetus for the formation of the chapter came from Peggy Seats, an independent marketing and public relations consultant who had moved from Chicago to Atlanta, where BPRS was chartered in 1983.

As a benefit to its members, the Atlanta chapter of BPRS and the Georgia chapter of the Public Relations Society of America (PRSA) assembled a blue-ribbon panel to discuss the merits of advanced communications degrees, certifications, and accreditations in May 2003. Participants were provided with frank dialogue and critical analysis regarding continuing education and development. More specifically, discussions focused on the necessity of certification, accreditation, and licensing and whether or not such designations were essential in advancing careers and providing job security. During prior meetings the organization showcased executives from Fortune 100 companies and Atlanta-based agencies and organizations who discussed their experiences in the areas of business-to-consumer, nonprofit, real estate, entertainment, and corporate public relations.

Additionally, the organization has provided programming to its members pertinent to professional development techniques and career enhancement. Other seminars organized by the group gave communications experts an opportunity to share their expertise on topics such as networking, demonstrating the value of public relations to clients, maintaining working relationships with media outlets, and training BPRS members to hone and market their unique skills.

To assist its membership during economic downturns, a seminar titled "Preparing for the Future: An Economic Reality" was planned and panelists discussed strategies and tactics for maintaining economic health during bull and bear economies. More specifically, the participants addressed financial investments, career opportunities, tips for starting a small business, financing education, and technology.

In 1993, the Black Public Relations Society of Washington issued a letter to several entertainment institutions that outlined complaints about area hotels and restaurants that seldom used the services of black-owned public relations firms.

The Washington, DC, branch of BPRS took its complaints a little further when it considered filing a class-action suit against several businesses that they claimed regularly discriminated against multicultural public relations professionals. The organization asserted that the discriminatory practices had circumvented entry into business and kept ALANA (African, Latino, Asian, and Native American) public relations agencies from securing mainstream accounts. Ofield Dukes, one of the organizers of the Washington, DC, chapter, succinctly summarized the situation: "For the past two decades, minority PR professionals in Washington have been invisible. We have been overlooked by mainstream businesses."

The Black Public Relations Society of Greater New York has provided a platform for public relations and communications practitioners for several years. To assist its members with their career aspirations the society hosted "An Evening with PR Recruiters and Human Resources Experts: Tips on How to Get and Keep Your Public Relations Position in Today's Marketplace" in summer 1993. Additionally, to keep their members apprised of the latest information and strategies for handling crisis communications, the chapter invited crisis communications specialist and political consultant Judy Smith to share her insights in February 2003. Smith's public relations and law background gave her entry to many of the nation's most high-profile cases. These cases included the confirmation hearing of Supreme Court Justice Clarence Thomas, the scandal over President Bill Clinton and Monica Lewinsky, the 1991 Gulf War, and the Chandra Levy investigation.

An attempt to form a national BPRS organization was made in Atlanta in 1994. The impetus to achieve national status for public relations practitioners of color was spurred by an organization and conference that merged the four primary national journalism organizations composed of journalists of color in 1994. Unity '94, an organization composed of the National Association for Black Journalists, the National Association of Hispanic Journalists, the Asian American Journalists Association, and the Native American Journalists Association, decided to join forces to form an organization that would host a national conference every five years. A national meeting of public relations professionals of color was held simultaneously in Atlanta, but the conference failed to cement the formation of a national organization.

To strengthen their efforts and gain more visibility, the BPRS chapters in existence formed the National Black Public Relations Society in 1998. All of the chapters of BPRS were formed because its members felt that their needs were not being met by the mainstream public relations organizations in existence at that time. They were formed with a mission of providing resources, services, and social venues for practitioners working in public relations, public affairs, communications, media relations, community affairs, governmental affairs, and other affiliated service professions. More succinctly, the organization's stated mission is

to address the challenges and emphasize the opportunities for the multifaceted constituency that we serve. This organization began more than 10 years ago with the goal to recruit and retain professionals in the industry and reinforce the importance of our role as business strategists and communicators. (National Black Public Relations Society Web site, 2003, n.p.)

Education, expansion and empowerment are the "success triad" needed to outline targets. To keep pace with the future, members see their reach extended beyond domestic borders. The organization, composed of a cadre of role models for young, inexperienced, entry-level practitioners, also has designed programs to prepare future public relations professionals.

The annual conferences organized by the national organization have provided an opportunity for members and professionals in the communications disciplines to convene to share information and resources and to address hot topics that impact public relations activities. The conventions have addressed such timely issues as understanding convergence in the newsroom, maintaining a competitive edge, pitching to the national media, cause-related public relations, creative messaging, doing business with the federal government, and public relations and the entertainment industry. Student attendees have been given information pertinent to securing entry-level positions and selecting the right courses for the new millennium. Some specific topics for the student-oriented workshops have been "Internship Options: Discovering Your Career

Path" and "Masters and More: The Benefits of Furthering Your Education."

National conferences were held in 1999–2003. The 2001 conference was held in St. Paul, Minnesota, with the theme "Techniques & Technology." The fourth annual conference was held in Washington, DC, with the theme "Public Relations: Power, Influence and Change." For the 2003 conference held in New York, the theme was "Public Relations: Technology Driven, Diversity Focused," and Michele Flowers, president of Michele Flowers public relations, was named Public Relations Practitioner of the Year. The 2004 convention of the National Black Public Relations Society was slated for Chicago.

—*Marilyn Kern-Foxworth*

See also Baker, Joseph Varney; Demographics; Kaiser, Inez Y.; Kendrix, Moss; Minorities in public relations

Bibliography

Black Public Relations Society to be formed in Philadelphia. (1987, October 14). *Philadelphia Observer*, p. 4.

Black Public Relations Society of Atlanta Web site. Retrieved from www.bprsatlanta.org

Lee, G. (1993, February 15). Black PR firms charge bias. *Washington Post*, p. WB7.

National Black Public Relations Society Web site. Retrieved from www.nbprs.org/aboutmain.htm

Odom, M. Black public relations professionals form their own network. (1987, August 27). *Atlanta Intown Extra*, p. 12E.

NATIONAL INVESTOR RELATIONS INSTITUTE

The National Investor Relations Institute (NIRI) is an association established in 1969 to advance the practice of investor relations as well as the professional expertise and status of its members. A national association with local chapters across the United States, NIRI serves professionals whose responsibility is implementing investor relations programs in order to attract capital for their organizations. NIRI membership includes more than 5,000 investor relations consultants and corporate

Chairman of the Board of the General Electric Company, Ralph J. Cordiner (center), pounds the gavel here to open a meeting of share owners of the firm. Some 2,500 owners attended the 68th annual meeting of the firm. Flanking Cordiner are Robert Patton (left), President, and Ray H. Luebbe, Secretary. Cordiner established the first efforts at formalizing a company's communication program with shareholders in 1953

SOURCE: © Bettmann/CORBIS

officers from major publicly held companies as well as small and mid-sized companies.

According to NIRI, 45 percent of its members have financial backgrounds, 21 percent corporate communication, and 20 percent public relations. Forty-five percent of NIRI members have more than 10 years of experience in the practice of investor relations. Seventy-seven percent of NIRI members are executives of public companies, 14 percent are consultants, and the remainder are vendors or associate members. Fifty-six percent of member companies are listed on the New York Stock Exchange, and 37 percent are listed on NASDAQ. More than 40 percent of member companies have a market capitalization of $1.5 billion.

Advancing the practice and professionalism of investor relations remains one of NIRI's priorities. The association has gone so far as to advance a definition:

Investor relations is a strategic management responsibility that integrates finance, communication, marketing and securities law compliance to enable the most effective two-way communication between a company, the financial community, and other constituencies, which ultimately contributes to a company's securities achieving fair valuation. (National Investor Relations Institute, 2002–2004)

Investor relations had humble beginnings in public relations departments where there was a considerable lack of financial expertise and knowledge of the securities markets. Ralph Cordiner, chairman of General Electric Co. (GE), established the first efforts at formalizing a company's communication program with shareholders in 1953. At the same time, shareholder relations positions were being established at other major companies.

Through NIRI's originating chapter organization, the Investor Relations Association, much consideration and discussion went into naming the field, establishing standards of ethical conduct, and distinguishing the type of training needed for the profession. Other organizations, such as the Public Relations Society of America (PRSA) and the American Management Association (AMA), influenced investor relations with financial communication and management views concerning the practice.

From the first meeting in September 1968, Investor Relations Association leadership sought to form a national organization that could keep up with the changing pace of investor relations. In February 1969, NIRI charter members signed a constitution, and at a May meeting officers were elected. The published proceedings of NIRI's First Annual Conference in 1970 became a valuable reference and included topics on investment research, the role of investor relations in corporate responsibility, the future of the analyst profession, and disclosure.

NIRI's annual conferences, publications, seminars, and workshops continue to provide a comprehensive knowledge base for professional development. Executive alerts and white papers offer summaries and guidance on issues and regulations affecting the practice of investor relations. Local chapter meetings and events allow investor relations professionals to develop networking opportunities.

—*Rebecca G. Aguilar*

See also Investor relations; Public Relations Society of America

Bibliography

Mahoney, W. F. (1991). *Investor relations: Professional's guide to financial marketing and communications.* New York: New York Institute of Finance.

National Investor Relations Institute. (2002–2004). NIRI Web site. Available: http://www.niri.org.

NETWORK THEORY

Network theory is closely associated with systems theory. It is the vital part of systems theory that addresses the pathways of information flow within and between systems. Each pathway is a repeated or potential route for information to flow from person to person, organization to organization, person to organization, organization to person, and so on. Network theory features the central premise, vital to public relations, that people need and want information. How they obtain this information or feel the lack of the desired information can affect their attitude toward and knowledge about various topics that are relevant to the goodwill and success of each organization. People may experience either information underload, not having the information they want, or information overload, possessing too much information to process comfortably. One of the predictors of satisfaction is that people feel they have the information they want and know that others do as well. If all relevant parties appropriately share information and use it wisely and ethically, decisions can be made that bring harmony rather than friction between people and organizations.

For these reasons, network theory poses two challenges to public relations practitioners. They need to know what information key stakeholding/ stake-seeking publics want or need. Also, they need to understand and strategically operate in the networks by which the needed or desired information can get from one point to the desired audience. In that sense, communication management as a paradigm of public relations relates to the ability to facilitate information flow and decisions that arise from the shared information. Thus, network theory poses a challenge of getting information to people who want and need it, and practitioners need to know where this information is available and how it can be shared in the network. This challenge may require that practitioners create networks where none exist. In addition, they need to know how to facilitate and maintain existing networks.

Information theory, refined by systems theory, rests on many assumptions about the nature of information. Central to that analysis is the reality that what is information or informative depends on the judgment of the people who obtain and evaluate the information. Typically, such people feel various amounts of uncertainty. Uncertainty can be uncomfortable and thus motivates people to seek information, process it, and form useful attitudes.

At various turning points in their lives, people want to know something. They may want information about products, services, missions, visions, policies, community service, problems, solutions, and myriad other aspects of their lives. The amount of information in any or each message depends on the impact it has on each person's sense of uncertainty. Information, so conceptualized, is the impact each message has, as interpreted. The amount of information is measured by the degree to which individuals who receive it and evaluate it become more or less uncertain on some matter based on their interpretation of the information.

So conceived, organizations and individuals are information processors. Each system—organization or individual—takes in information, processes it, and outputs it in various forms. Thus, the three major functional elements of a network are input, processing or throughput, and output. Newspapers and other mass media are seen as parts of networks—systems. In fact, it is logical that networks such as NBC, CBS, and ABC would be called such. They are part of the news and entertainment industry, a system composed of many information networks. Each is in and of itself a network that gathers information (input), processes that information into news, and outputs the information to listeners and viewers.

One of the contributions of network theory is the concept of openness. According to B. A. Fisher (1982),

> openness is the free exchange of energy between the system and its environment. That is, to the extent that the boundaries are permeable and allow the exchange of information—what energy is to a physical system, information is to a social system—that system is said to be more nearly open than closed. (p. 199)

Information is to human systems what energy is to natural systems. Information is the energy of human systems. It fuels human systems because people can get and use information that helps them to make appropriate decisions and to reduce uncertainties.

Network theory provides the rationale needed to analyze the effectiveness of systems' abilities to obtain, process, and output information. Network analysis focuses attention on how well information flows throughout an organization, by taking various pathways. Each pathway is a pattern that can be charted as a network. Since information is the life force or energy of an organization, researchers want to know how information flows and influence is exerted.

A network is the pathway or pattern of repeated interactions by which information flows between individuals within a group and between groups in an organization. A network consists of person-to-person connections by which information is exchanged. Networks consist of people who interact. A set of pathways, such as information flow between accountants in the accounting department of a company, is a *micro-network*. In this sense, a micro-network is a system (or a subsystem). When micro-networks are put together, they form a *macro-network* (a system or a supra-system). To some extent, both types of network correspond to the organization chart, but information also flows through networks that do not correspond to formal organizational structure. If a macro-network is a system, its micro-networks are subsystems. Klaus Krippendorff wrote in 1977 that several types of networks can be identified: (a) *line*, in which one person contacts another, who contacts another, and so on (A → B → C → D), (b) *commune*, an open exchange in which everyone interacts with everyone else, (c) *hierarchy*, in which the network functions as an organization chart or layers of systems, and (d) *dictator*, or a super gatekeeper.

Networks exist because a number of people are involved with and responsible for the ease or difficulty of information flow. Networks also consist of the relationships between the people that make them work. At the most basic level, such relationships can be described or brought to life through process words such as "talks to," "coordinates with," or "reports to." In this way, analysis focuses not only on the number of people involved but also the strength or intensity of the relationship between them, which can be estimated by the frequency of contact and the degree of interdependence.

In this sense, public relations practitioners are often thought to be links or boundary spanners who help or impede the flow of information from the organization to key publics or from those publics to the organization. Thus, the success of practitioners leads to organizations being viewed as either more or less open. For this reason, when public relations people help stonewall an issue, they close the network and impede the flow of information. Conversely, they help the organization to be open to its publics by being responsive to their interests and serving as the first and best source of information on matters relevant to the organization.

Networks exhibit the property of symmetry, which describes the degree to which the direction or flow of information reveals balance rather than imbalance in a relationship. Relationships can be one-way or two-way, and they can be symmetrical (influence balanced) or asymmetrical (one party has more influence than the other). In a one-way asymmetrical relationship, for instance, one person provides information and influence for the other, but does not receive much if any in return. Two-way symmetrical relationships exhibit the most balance because influence and information flow freely between the two parties.

One of many characteristic of networks is transitivity, the ease with which information flows from one person to the next. Relevant to this analysis is the analogy between information flow and the flow of water within a system of pipes and valves. Each person can be a valve. He or she can open or close the valve. Such actions increase or impede the flow of information. Typical of a line network, person A communicates with person B, who communicates with C, who communicates with D. Person D depends on all of the others for information; for this reason, it may be difficult for A and D to communicate because they depend on B and C. If the information that A wants to get to D flows with relative ease, the system has high transitivity. If the information does not flow because one or more links are impediments, the system lacks transitivity. This characteristic can easily be seen in the organizational practice of routing communication; it also refers to the ease with which communication flows across each link in the chain of authority.

For many years, network theory, along with its companion theories, has offered insights into the study and practice of public relations. This line of analysis has also been vital to organizational communication theory and research. Some scholars see public relations as a subdiscipline beneath organizational communication for this reason. The logic is simple: To the extent that an organization functions as a system and part of many other systems, it does so as a source and conduit for the flow of information. Such flows are systemically superior when they are two-way. Thus, by this analysis, public relations serves networks, organizations, and individuals by obtaining, processing, and outputting information between organizations and individual publics.

—Robert L. Heath

See also Openness; Stakeholder theory; Symmetry; Systems theory; Two-way and one-way communication

Bibliography

Farace, R. V., Monge, P. R., & Russell, H. (1977). *Communicating and organizing.* Reading, MA: Addison-Wesley.

Farace, R. V., Stewart, J. P., & Taylor, J. A. (1978). Criteria for evaluation of organizational communication effectiveness: Review and synthesis. In B. D. Ruben (Ed.), *Communication yearbook 2* (pp. 271–292). New Brunswick, NJ: Transaction Books.

Fisher, B. A. (1978). Information systems theory and research: An overview. In B. D. Ruben, (Ed.), *Communication yearbook 2* (pp. 81–108). New Brunswick, NJ: Transaction Books.

Fisher, B. A. (1982). The pragmatic perspective of human communication: A view from system theory. In F. E. X. Dance (Ed.), *Human communication theory: Comparative essays* (pp. 192–219). New York: Harper & Row.

Krippendorff, K. (1977). Information systems theory and research: An overview. In B. D. Ruben (Ed.), *Communication yearbook 1* (pp. 149–171). New Brunswick, NJ: Transaction Books.

Monge, P. R. (1977). The systems perspective as a theoretical basis for the study of human communication. *Communication Quarterly, 25,* 19–29.

NEW BUSINESS DEVELOPMENT

New business development is critical to the livelihood of any public relations firm and involves a variety of methods designed to secure a steady stream of clients. Most clients hire firms on a project basis, although the project may extend anywhere from one to three years. Thus the firm, in order to meet overhead and payroll, must ensure that continued work is available. This stream of work is vital to firm stability as well as to growth of individual staff members, who are challenged by and learn from new opportunities. Although necessary, new business development should be the result of strategic planning for the public relations firm. Firms that wish to maintain a consistent size and to offer a set level and/or breadth of service may engage in lower-key business development than firms that have charted a planned growth pattern.

All public relations firms' strategic plans for new business development should include a consistent, daily, two-pronged approach: (1) provide only the highest quality of service to existing clients and (2) network. Often overlooked in the quest for new sources of income is the current client. Although the great majority of clients may contract for a specified length of time, an excellent success record with demonstrated results provides impetus for the client to renew a contract. Similarly, noting opportunities and looking ahead for the client may provide additional work. Critical to this line of business development is educating the client and evaluating the firm's work: The client must understand public relations and its capabilities and must see the results manifested through evaluation.

Providing a high quality of service may not lead to additional contracts from the client immediately, yet referrals are highly valued as clients search for prospective firms. Such referrals also come from networking, which should be defined broadly enough to cover even building bridges from unsuccessful pitches. Future work can also arise from media contacts whom clients may seek out and ask to identify firms by expertise and reputation. Relationships established through a variety of professional associations and personal contacts along with pro bono work also often lead to new business opportunities. Furthermore, networking can build a broad range of affiliates who may be called on as consultants for specialized new business pitches; with a broad range of experts available for hire, firms can more readily demonstrate their abilities to meet a broader variety of client needs.

Another critical element in any firm's strategic plan is promotions. So many firms do not include themselves as their clients when such awareness programs are vital to their own longevity. In addition to public relations–based publications, awards programs and pro bono work offer opportunities to promote the firm's expertise. Peer-recognized work also becomes material to highlight on Web sites.

Firms may also engage in entrepreneurial activities designed to showcase their expertise and successes. Such activities might include creating a newsletter that targets key executives in defined areas.

More active and aggressive new business development includes typical sales approaches such as cold calls and arranged meetings to discuss possible opportunities. Other active development opportunities come by responding to RFPs (requests for proposals) initiated by clients who are in the market for a public relations firm.

—*Pamela G. Bourland-Davis*

See also Account executive; Client; Public relations agency

Bibliography

Canfield, A. S. (1998). Building client relationships by the numbers. *Public Relations Strategist, 4*(4), 33–34.

Croft, A. (1996). *Managing a public relations firm for growth and profit.* New York: Haworth Press.

Croft, A. (2002). Surviving the recession by practicing the four "Ps" of agency prosperity: Positioning, promotion, productivity and profitability. *Public Relations Quarterly, 47*(2), 25–31.

NEW ZEALAND, PRACTICE OF PUBLIC RELATIONS IN

See Australia and New Zealand, practice of public relations in

NEWS AND NEWSWORTHY

News is intangible, a compilation of mediated messages assembled according to the norms and constraints of a major social institution composed of businesses and dictated by economic imperatives. A distinctive writing style and image portrayal process distinguish news from all other communication formats.

Perhaps it is easier to define news in negative terms—underscoring what it is *not.* News is neither an essay nor a term paper, neither a short story nor a novel with scenes, characters, plotline, or climax. It is more than just a recorded voice, photograph, or video clip. Indeed, there is little consensus as to how to definitively characterize "news" or "newsworthy." Scholars, historians, and critics continue to analyze journalism's role in society and the cultural implications of news work.

Journalism historian Robert Park (1940) suggested that news texts have replaced the town crier of yore who walked through the streets singing out the time of day, announcing births, and so forth. Today, news takes the shape of its sponsoring mass medium, and the form, content, and production of print and electronic news differ substantially. Whereas print news is passive and static one-way communication, television news is active with both words and visuals. Web-based news offers interactive, two-way communication. Indeed, reporters—or journalists—still circulate knowledge, making public property out of social and cultural assets and, as Gaye Tuchman (1978) wrote, "transform[ing] mere happenings into publicly discussable events" (p. 3). They make abundantly available to all information that otherwise would be inaccessible due to geographic challenges and resource shortages. In the process, the news fosters a sense of community, defines who we are, and suggests what is important.

Contemporary journalists are professionals who subscribe to democratic ideals and are bound by codes of ethics as defined by trade organizations such as the Society of Professional Journalists (SPJ). Even though journalism is not a licensed profession, it is a respected and legitimate one that adheres to standards of fairness, accuracy, and objectivity. Most journalists began their career by earning a college degree. Journalism students across the United States are trained both in the classroom and in the field as apprentices or interns who hone their craft and learn practical skills such as how to cover beats, cultivate sources, and navigate newsroom politics.

In the classroom, budding journalists develop a "nose for news"—shorthand for defining "newsworthiness"—and memorize and internalize important clues known as news values. For example, "impact," "importance," and "the unusual" define about 75 percent of all news stories. Similarly, a sociologist who studied newsroom cultures at CBS, NBC, *Newsweek,* and *Time* resolved that "enduring" news values such as "ethnocentrism" and "moderatism" enable journalists to decide what is news. "If it bleeds, it leads" is a popular newsworthiness barometer used by television news workers, who seem to attach importance to visual violence. About 100 years ago, legendary news editor Charles A. Dana simply defined newsworthiness in terms of novelty: "When a dog bites a man, that's not news. But if a man bites a dog, that's news." However, today's media scholars posit that news is the end product of a process that is far more complex than this.

Todd Gitlin (1980) performed a meta-analysis of published theories developed to explain news and newsworthiness. He discovered three striking patterns. First, journalist-centered theories consider news to be a product of professional news judgments and objectivity. As such, journalists consider themselves uniquely qualified to identify what is news based on their own conceptions of newsworthiness. Tuchman (1978) wrote that news workers "claim the right to interpret everyday occurrences to citizens and other professionals alike" (p. 5).

Second, *event-centered* news theories invoke a cadre of metaphors to define news. For example, news has been characterized as a "mirror" that journalists hold up to the real world so that they may offer the "reflection" to audiences. One theorist described the news media as *amplification stations,* staffed by news workers who select, order, and explain signals from the physical world. Yet other scholars have invoked "conduit" and "link" metaphors to describe journalists' liaison function between serving audiences and selecting happenings. Such imagery and metaphor use is not without criticism, however. Media scholars, including those at the Glasgow University Media Group and the University of Birmingham Centre for Contemporary Cultural Studies, have argued that "reality" is a slippery concept—virtually impossible to offer in a pure, objective way.

Third, *phenomenological* theories characterize news as that which is selected and packaged in a form that audiences readily accept as "the news." These theories emphasize the human agency of news and argue that it is socially constructed in a context of commercial imperatives. For example, Roger Fowler has argued persuasively that news is not *found* or even *gathered* so much as it is *made* and *produced.* In other words, news does not happen in a vacuum. Journalism is a practice with a definable milieu that culminates in a manufactured product shaped by a complex—yet artificial or subjective—process of selection, collection, organization, and dissemination of data. In contrast to event-centered theories, scholars who advance phenomenological theories of the news consider the making of news to be a process, one that should not be studied devoid of context and other variables that affect a journalist's interpretation of reality.

Beyond analyzing the work of reporters that average audiences can witness firsthand, some researchers have examined what editors do behind the scenes because they also determine what is news. Editors act as "gatekeepers," opening and closing the news gate, along with subjectively selecting, processing, and organizing information that will become news. Furthermore, editors and their reporters set the news "agenda" by influencing what people "think about." For example, findings from a study of how daily newspaper editors construct the front page suggest that ideological biases help them to sift through a census of potential newsworthy happenings and issues and to pull out the important ones.

Indeed, defining "news" and determining what exactly is "newsworthy" is a highly subjective process that carries with it major social responsibility.

—*Donnalyn Pompper*

See also Agenda-setting theory; Framing theory; Gatekeepers; Media relations

Bibliography

Gans, H. (1979). Deciding what's news. New York: Pantheon.

Gitlin, T. (1980). *The whole world is watching: Mass media in the making & unmaking of the new left.* Berkeley: University of California Press.

Kerbel, M. (2000). *If it bleeds, it leads.* Boulder, CO: Westview Press.

Combs, M., & Shaw, D. (1993). The evolution of agenda-setting research: Twenty-five years in the marketplace of ideas. *Journal of Communication, 43*(2), 58–67.

Mencher, M. (2003). *News reporting and writing* (9th ed.). Columbus, OH: McGraw-Hill.

Park, R. (1940). News as a form of knowledge. *American Journal of Sociology, 45*(5), 669–686.

Tuchman, G. (1978). *Making news.* New York: Free Press.

White, D. M. (1950). The "gatekeeper": A case study in the selection of news. *Journalism Quarterly, 27*(4), 383–390.

NEWS SERVICES

News services now encompass what were once separate, but related, links in the information channels. News services include organizations such as the Associated Press, clipping services, and U.S. Newswire. Generally speaking, news services provide unfiltered news information. These services gather information from many sources and then make it available to newspapers, broadcast news organizations, and magazines for a fee. Because of their linking role in the information dissemination process, news services are targeted by public relations practitioners for media relations. Practitioners target their media releases to news services that may pick up the story and disseminate it to their clients. Thus, news services allow practitioners a means to reach a larger pool of news outlets.

The Associated Press (AP) started out as an organization for pooling information (text and photos) among member newspapers. If there is a big story in New York City, a San Francisco newspaper would not have to worry about getting a reporter to New York City. Rather, the San Francisco paper would simply look for copy and photos from a New York City newspaper.

Internet technologies have made it easier for an organization like AP to exist. Instead of members having to rely on wire or broadcast technologies to move information, they simply go to the AP Web site and upload or download text and photos.

Clipping services have been in decline due to the increasing presence of the Internet. Clipping services were very handy in culling particular information. If a person was interested in articles on U.S. steel production across multiple media channels (say, newspapers, magazines, and non-professional journals), the clipping service did all the dirty work. They had subscriptions to a wide variety of publications and employed researchers to copy information from sources at public libraries. The service would then pull all of the elements together in one package and send out a hard copy. Later, clipping services would employ the latest wire and wireless technologies.

Clipping services may make a comeback. Although the Internet has made accessing various news channels easier, the number of news channels has grown by orders of magnitude. There is an interesting new take on the clipping service, called Google News. Google News can be found on the Internet at http://news.google.com. This site is currently in beta, meaning that it is functional but its form and ability are not finalized. Google is applying their search engine technology to the culling of news stories.

The last element included in news services is represented by U.S. Newswire, a public-interest news wire service. U.S. Newswire has a similar "look and feel" to services offered by an organization such as the Associated Press. However, it must be stressed that U.S. Newswire is not a news reporting organization. The types of organizations that use U.S. Newswire for distribution include the federal government, Congress, and cabinet-level agencies; political campaign organizations; foreign embassies; associations, unions, advocacy, and civic groups; universities, think tanks, and research organizations; and public relations, public affairs, and law firms. U.S. Newswire also provides content to media, public relations, and news services including America Online (AOL), and Yahoo! News. In 1999, U.S. Newswire merged with Medialink Worldwide, Inc. The Web address for U.S. Newswire is http://www. usnewswire.com/index.html.

—*Michael Nagy*

See also Media relations; Media release

NEWS STORY

The news story is the basic, fundamental content component of all news media—print, broadcast, or electronic. Each news story reflects the shared values among journalists that answer the question "What is news?" Further, the news story is identified and classified by its content and structure.

NEWS VALUES

The process of deciding which stories, among the almost infinite possibilities on any given day, will be *news stories* is not simple. Although there may be close-to-universal agreement among journalists and scholars that certain events (a terrorist bombing of an American embassy abroad, for example) are appropriate content for a news story, decisions regarding many other issues, people, and activities are less clear. What could make an important news story in Chicago, for example, may be of no interest to people in Miami. Of all the possible stories that any news organization selects on a given day, what predicts which stories will become today's news?

Since the earliest days of American journalism, there has been rather remarkable consistency among journalists as to what the criteria are for determining whether a story is newsworthy. These criteria are derived from the values, shared by journalists, that define "news." A review of several prominent news writing textbooks reveals these criteria. Although there is some variation in terminology, the criteria themselves are highly consistent.

Timeliness. Readers must understand why this news story is being told or presented to them at this time. Did the event happen today? Is this story timely because it is the anniversary of an important event?

Proximity. This criterion is why an important news story in Chicago may have no interest to audiences in Miami; there is not a local angle. People like and want to know what is happening close to them, in their own communities.

Prominence. Well-known people attract much attention. Sports stars, entertainers, and politicians are prime examples of prominent people around whom many news stories are constructed.

Impact or consequence. The number of people who are affected by an issue and how seriously it affects them contribute to the newsworthiness of a story. Hundreds of people being inconvenienced by a detour is likely news in a local community, as is the sending overseas into combat one or two local citizens.

Rarity or novelty. The winning of a lottery is an example of a story that is news because it is a once-in-a-lifetime happening for the recipient. Events that are strange or unique are often news simply because of their rarity.

Additional criteria that are advanced by some journalists include *conflict* and *human interest.*

NEWS CONTENT

Until the last two decades of the 20th century, the content of news stories was dominated by several topics, among them governmental issues, disasters, crime, and sports. Undeniably, many news stories still originate from courts, city halls, capital buildings, and arenas. Such stories are often classified as "hard" news; they will be covered regularly by journalists because of their inherent values. Yet there has been an "explosion of subject matter" (Brooks, Kennedy, Moen, & Ranly, 1992, p. 5) as Americans have begun demanding information on a wider range of topics, many relevant to the individual. Many stories about individual interests (entertainment and travel, new product introductions, and decorating, for example) are classified as "soft news"—that is, they do not necessarily conform to traditional news values, but they are still of interest to news consumers. This shift in content has greatly increased the opportunities for public relations practitioners to contribute news stories.

One of the largest topical areas evidencing this expanding content is health. Whether there is a new cancer treatment, an outbreak of the West Nile virus along the Gulf Coast, or a promising drug for preventing baldness, American news consumers want the information. In the 21st century, the range of subject matter for news stories is greater than it has ever been. Each story must still conform to one or more of the basic criteria, but the way newsrooms look at content itself is far more broad than it was even 20 years ago. At times the distinction between "hard news" and "soft news" blurs on some of these topics.

Regardless of the specific subject, content of the news story is traditionally identified as a series of answers to six simple one-word questions: who, what, when, where, why, and how? Although there are several ways to structure the story, a news story can always be written on the basis of the answers to the following questions: *Who is involved? What happened? When did it happen? Where did it happen? Whey did it happen? How did it happen?*

News Story Structure

There are many ways in which a news story may be organized, but the most standard construction consists of a beginning (the lead), a middle (the body), and an end (the conclusion). Of these, strong agreement exists among authors of news writing textbooks that the most important structural element is the lead. It is the first thing that is read or heard in a story, and as such it often determines if the reader, listener, or viewer will continue attending to the story.

There are many types of leads, but the most common is the *summary*. Answers to the six questions (who, what, when, where, why, and how) are provided in the first sentence of the story. The summary lead is most often found when the news story is written as an inverted pyramid. In this structure, all of the important information is presented immediately, with support or elaboration following.

Other types of leads may focus more on answering one of the six questions. When the most important element of the story is a person, the lead may emphasize his or her identity. These are labeled *immediate identification* ("Laura Bush . . .") and *delayed identification* ("An 11-year-old child was killed earlier today when. . . . Dead is . . ."). Another type of lead presents multiple content elements ("The Supreme Court today handed down a decision impacting affirmative action, refused to rule on a domestic abuse case from Indiana, and prepared for their first break of the year"). It is generally advisable to keep the lead simple and straightforward; thus, writers are urged to use multiple-content-element leads sparingly.

Leads may also be anecdotal or narrative; they may be grounded in a quotation; or they may ask a question, tease, or be mysterious. These more creative leads are most appropriate for human interest stories and are least likely to be found in hard news.

The body of the story provides elaboration and support; it often gives context, scope, and impact. Although there are numerous structures for the body (Rich, 1994, pp. 211–233), the most common is the inverted pyramid. In this structure a summary lead that answers the basic questions is most often used, followed by supporting information in descending order of importance. It often has no conclusion.

Public relations practitioners must understand news values, content of interest to various media, and structures of news stories in order to better serve both the media institutions that use provided content as well as the organizations/clients they represent in the media.

—*Ruthann Weaver Lariscy*

Bibliography

Brooks, B. S., Kennedy, G., Moen, D., & Ranly, D. (1992). *News reporting and writing* (4th ed.). New York: St. Martin's Press.

Hough, G. A., III. (1988). *News writing.* Boston: Houghton Mifflin.

Rich, C. (1994). *Writing and reporting news: A coaching method.* Belmont, CA: Wadsworth.

NEWSLETTER

A newsletter is a type of publication produced most often by public relations practitioners. Almost all organizations—nonprofit and profit-making alike—create and distribute newsletters to members of their key audiences. With the development of desktop publishing, newsletters have grown in popularity. Although they share similar traits with magazines and newspapers, newsletters are smaller, less formal publications that are directed toward a specific audience, such as employees, customers, members of the community, donors, or volunteers. Although newsletters fall under the realm of public relations tactics, they existed long before the birth of the practice. In 200 B.C.E., the Han dynasty in China published a daily newsletter. Many historians consider newsletters to be the forerunners of the modern newspaper. In fact, one of the first successful publications in America was called the *Boston News-Letter*.

To be successful, newsletters must have a narrow and clearly defined target audience and a specific objective, such as strengthening ties with volunteers, educating the community about local programs of interest to them, encouraging donors to keep giving money and resources to a nonprofit organization, and informing employees about company policies. Internal company newsletters are quite common and are called house organs. They are used to build employee morale, promote teamwork, recognize outstanding achievement, and instill company pride.

Effective newsletters must have an overall key message that is communicated throughout each issue. For instance, a school district distributes a newsletter to parents of the children enrolled in the school. The key message is that if parents get involved in their children's education, their children will become more successful in their studies, and the objective is to encourage parents to help their children with their nightly homework and take an interest in their children's learning. Appropriate stories in such a newsletter would be articles on strategies to help children with their homework, tips on getting kids motivated to do their homework, easy-to-understand statistics on how helping children with their studies improves performance, a list of free or low-cost tutoring services for parents unable to help their kids, and a profile of an actual student whose performance increased with his parents' attention. Although stories may vary from issue to issue, newsletters carry the same overall theme in each issue, and the style and layout remain consistent.

Newsletters are distributed to a specific target audience on a recurring basis. Many appear quarterly, and some are distributed weekly or monthly. Few are distributed biannually or yearly because frequency helps build the relationship between sender and recipient. Although few in number, some short-term newsletters may be distributed daily. For instance, booth sponsors in a trade show might receive a brief newsletter each day of the show, which keeps them up to date on the show's happenings.

No matter what the frequency of distribution, newsletter stories are typically short, informal news and feature stories, although newsletters will also include sidebars; a limited amount of calendar information; news briefs; letters to the editor; and bulleted information about programs, activities, or employee updates. Most newsletters are four to eight pages in 8½ × 11–inch format, although they can be larger or smaller—one page to larger, multipage documents.

The parts of a newsletter include a consistent grid, nameplate, table of contents, masthead, headers and/or footers, headlines, subheads, body copy, bylines, pull quotes, captions, and graphics. A grid is a pattern or plan for pages in the newsletter, which includes a set of rules that apply throughout the piece, such as the number of columns, space between the columns, and location of headers and/or footers. The nameplate, also called a flag or banner, includes the name of the publication; volume, issue, and date; and a brief subtitle that explains the editorial focus or intended audience of the newsletter. The masthead tells the name and address of the sponsoring organization, editorial staff, contact information, and frequency of the publication. A header or footer is the information, which may include the publication name and date, that appears either on the top or bottom (or both) of each page. Pull quotes are quotations from the body copy or a blurb from the article displayed in enlarged type and set back into the article as an attention-getting device.

—Emma Daugherty Phillingane

See also Brochure; Collateral

Bibliography

Morton, L. P. (2000). *Public relations publications: Designing for target publics.* Norman, OK: Sultan Communications.
Parker, R. C. (1990). *Newsletters from the desktop: Designing effective publications with your computer.* Chapel Hill, NC: Ventana Press.

NEWSOM, EARL

Earl Newsom may have learned his appreciation for the power of words by listening to his Methodist minister father. Named Edwin Earl Newsom, he was born in Wellman, Iowa, on December 13, 1897, to a family of teachers, ministers, and musicians. So Earl leaned the art of teaching as he acquired an appreciation for language. His long career began as a teacher, not as a newspaper man. He had become, by his death on April 11, 1973, one of several practitioners who shaped the course of American industry.

Newsom had a keen sense of business. He liked selling. With his brothers, he established Newsom Brothers Piano Company. This enterprise sold pianos and was profitable enough to fund the college education of several of the Newsom youths.

Newsom earned his baccalaureate degree from Oberlin College and used it to launch his teaching career. He honed his love for the power of language at Oberlin and set out to share that affection and knowledge of its intricacies with students. After a short teaching career, he elected to seek a Ph.D. in English from Columbia University. He took a teaching position in New York City to help support his family and fund his studies.

Along with his study of English, he developed a fascination with the topic of public opinion, which was receiving substantial academic attention. This attention also addressed the national phenomena of activism and nonprofit organizations. World War I had demonstrated the impact of public campaigns through the Creel Committee. The Red Cross and the Liberty Bond campaigns showed how appeals to the general public could foster philanthropy and community involvement to solve national problems by encouraging citizen participation.

Newsom was an enthusiastic student of public opinion. He had read Walter Lippmann's *Public Opinion* (1922) and Edward Bernays's *Crystallizing Public Opinion* (1923). These legendary books examined how public opinion forms and influences the destiny of a people. Bernays applied those principles to the practice of public relations.

He had also read Gustav LeBon's *The Crowd—A Study of the Public Mind*, which offered an unflattering look at the mindless willingness of the masses to follow a bold leader. Other books on this subject heightened his insight into the way people acquire information, are influenced through persuasive messages, and develop motives that lead them to make certain choices and express different preferences.

Love for the power and grace of language coupled with an interest in public opinion underpinned his practice of public relations. Newsom's break, as it were, came in 1925, when through one of his students he was offered a job in the promotion department of the *Literary Digest.* The fields of public relations and advertising were booming along with the economy. Promotion and publicity were lucrative lines of work as the nation lathered

itself into a financial frenzy in the years leading to the burst economic bubble, the Great Depression.

What might today be called publics, markets, audiences, or stakeholders came to be known to Newsom as the "crowd." People joined in common idea and purpose were the foundation of any society. That was true of government, the nonprofit sector, and, of course, business. Public opinion, the opinion of the public, was sovereign. Nothing could challenge it. Thus, influencing it led to power, influence, and success.

His next endeavor was to work for a publishing company. That endeavor was unsatisfying. He left and worked for an investment house, where he directed public relations and sales. Through his partnership with architect Norman Bel Geddes, he met Paul Garrett, director of public relations for General Motors. In later years, GM was a client of his.

Newsom's career trajectory took him through a variety of partnerships and professional associations. Along the way, he acquired a reputation for being an effective counselor. He brought sage advice to corporate and trade association clients. He earned a professional reputation for being able to assist his clients in their efforts to build favorable images, affect public policy relevant to their interests, and develop relationships. He was particularly skilled in finding the common themes and interests that could unite trade associations and forge solid relationships among the members.

Clients such as Atlantic Refining and the Tea Bureau were pleased by Newsom's services. They were quick to recommend him to other potential clients. Sound service to one client led to a friendly relationship with another. Thus, Atlantic Refining laid the basis for his work with the Tea Bureau. That professional association sparked a contract with the International Wool Association. In his client relationships, he was fiercely loyal, preferring to keep a client for each industry category even though a more lucrative contract might come along. By this business practice, he found that his loyalty was reciprocated. Out of the succession of corporate and trade association clients, he eventually came to work with Standard Oil Company, Ford Motor Company, Eli Lilly, Campbell Soup Company, and the International Paper Company. In the public sector, he counseled the President's Commission on International Information Activities and the Internal Revenue Service. In the nonprofit sector, his clients included Crusade for Freedom, the Free Europe Committee, and the Ford and Rockefeller foundations. His association with Standard Oil led John D. Rockefeller III to hire him to counsel on the creation of Colonial Williamsburg.

Compared with many of the other princes of public relations who were forging the profession, Newsom was less likely to build his professional service around press relations and mass communication. He saw positioning and relationship building as being more important than press attention.

His agency services reflected his strengths, featuring four lines of specialization. One was public relations planning and program development. A second was writing, but he went beyond effective press releases. He added tools and range to the sorts of services provided by agencies, including annual reports, backgrounders, issue position papers, books, and congressional hearings. A third service was assisting clients' efforts to build their in-house departments. That required assistance with defining the sorts of personnel needed and then locating and hiring the most qualified persons. It indicated an understanding of the total range of what public relations could do for an organization—the many functions it could serve. The fourth service was conducting research. The agency did not gather data, but designed and executed research projects for clients using the outsourced services of companies such as Elmo Roper. Such research was an extension and an application of Newsom's fascination with understanding and working in constructive ways with the public opinion necessary for clients to meet their business objectives. To augment his own research capabilities, Newsom hired research specialists. That was an innovation in public relations agency history.

Newsom's academic curiosity and belief that public relations was an intellectual activity attracted leading intellectuals to join his agency. Some of these associates left to join large businesses or trade associations. That professional association led to new business opportunities or continuing professional services. Some former associates left to start their own agencies. Although small compared with his clients' organizations, Newsom's agency was a place of learning and professional development. At the time of his death, he was a director of the Advisory Council of the Committee for Modern Courts, a life member of the Academy of Political Science, and a member of the executive committee of the National Institute of Social Sciences.

His practice was theory based (public opinion theory) and heavily oriented toward counseling. For these reasons, Newsom was a pioneer in what came to be called issues management. He believed that organizations receive only the respect they earn. He used sophisticated research to understand the opinions of key publics, the information they wanted, their performance expectations of organizations, the ways they received information, and the leaders who affected their opinions.

Newsom and his colleagues assisted Standard Oil of New Jersey in a series of issues. Any of these issues could lead to outcomes harmful to the company's efforts to achieve its mission. The list of issues was long, but some of the most important were key publics' concern over the company's relationship with I. G. Farben, the German industrial giant in the years leading up to WWII. Other issues centered on the concern about the company's size. Was it a cartel, a monopoly? Did it engage in unfair business practices? Should the federal government take aggressive steps on behalf of customers?

For Ford Motor Company, Newsom worked on issues related to the succession of Fords in the leadership of the company. He also took on the problem of the original Henry Ford's blatant anti-Semitism, which cost the company business and goodwill. New leadership needed new ideas and a strong business persona. Newsom's approach was to change the organization to make it more acceptable rather than to manufacture an image that drifted far from reality.

Newsom resembled Abraham Lincoln. Both had craggy faces and swarthy complexions. Newsom liked to quote Lincoln, especially the line about how you can't fool all of the people all of the time.

—Robert L. Heath

See also Annual financial report; Backgrounder; Bernays, Edward; Goodwill; Hearing; Issues management; Position and positioning; Publics; United States government and public relations

Bibliography

Cutlip, S. M. (1994). *The unseen power: Public relations, a history,* Hillsdale, NJ: Lawrence Erlbaum.

Ross, I. (1959). *Image merchants: The fabulous world of public relations.* New York: Doubleday.

NONGOVERNMENTAL ORGANIZATIONS (NGOS)

A nongovernmental organization (NGO) is a part of the voluntary sector in which individuals organize to accomplish a social goal. The concept of nongovernmental organizations emerged when many colonies and territories were seeking their independence from colonial powers. These organizations were created during the transition from colonial rule to self-rule. After independence, these organizations continued to work in solving local problems such as infant mortality, education, and illiteracy. The growth of NGOs reflects a shift away from the beliefs that government is the primary provider of services, that economic growth is the singular key to progress, and that leadership is a top-down process. NGOs are organized groups of individuals that are not yet institutionalized. However, some NGOs will become institutionalized as their efforts become indispensable to society.

Much like American not-for-profit organizations, NGOs are formed by and sustained by individuals with a specific goal or agenda. Why do people join NGOs? Individuals often feel that they have little power to influence their local community and have an even smaller chance of influencing larger, national issues. The creation of nongovernmental organizations that work to articulate citizen concerns helps to bring important social issues into the forefront of public discussion. To encourage citizens to reach out to NGOs, these organizations should use interpersonal communication, media relations, and strategic communication programs. It

is also important that these organizations extend beyond merely serving elite causes and niche publics and work toward the resolution of larger, national issues.

In the United States there is a social cause group for almost every issue. Groups organize to protect the environment, children, and animals, as well as to advocate for consumer safety, women's rights, and minority issues. In other nations of the world, especially in societies that have been dominated by repressive governments, there is no tradition of cause groups acting on behalf of social issues. Today, there is a continuing emergence of NGOs throughout the world. These grassroots organizations work on behalf of issues but are not part of the formal governmental structure. Indeed, NGOs provide services that governments fail to provide to their citizens. Many NGOs begin by serving local issues and then, if successful, often become national organizations.

Nongovernmental organizations are not limited by national boundaries. International nongovernmental organizations (INGOs) extend their humanitarian efforts to the political arena. In developed nations, international organizations that operate on behalf of larger social causes include Freedom Forum, Amnesty International, and Greenpeace. These watchdog groups are crucial because they provide an external perspective on the situation in a particular nation. In developing or postcrisis countries, the United Nations, the United States Agency for International Development (USAID), and the George Soros Open Society Institute provide financial and human resources to help facilitate development. These international organizations underwrite or fund local groups that work to achieve societal goals. INGOs are especially important during the initial stages of a civil society because they work directly with indigenous organizations and provide important training and activating of local civil society leaders.

NGOs have the same organizational needs as other groups. Once a group of like-minded people come together to identify and work on a problem, there are certain structural, legal, and financial imperatives that must be met before the group can begin to work toward its core mission. NGOs usually must register with a regional or national office. The registration process is necessary because it may give the group tax-exempt status and certain fundraising benefits. The group must be able to articulate a mission statement and create bylaws to govern the organization. Bylaws should spell out how leaders are selected, the different responsibilities of the various elected offices, the ways in which finances will be monitored, and how changes to the bylaws can be enacted. Additionally, it is important for groups to specify in advance of their petition for legal recognition that the organization has identified different types of donors, grants, and corporate resources that can be used to sustain the organization's mission. For instance, an NGO that specializes in prenatal care should begin conversations with different government agencies and corporations that specialize on this issue. Partnerships between NGOs, government, and corporations are crucial to meeting the needs of the NGOs' target publics.

NGOs must also strive for transparency in their operations. Many NGOs have various revenue sources (e.g., grants, donations) and should work to make their financial status and their accomplishments open to public inspection and scrutiny. NGOs that do not use their grants and donations to serve their missions should be held accountable for misusing their resources and abusing the public trust.

NGOs can benefit from the strategies and tactics of public relations. Because NGOs seek to inform, persuade, and change the attitudes and actions of others, they can employ many of the proven functions of strategic communication. For instance, many NGOs seek media attention to expand the reach of their message and to encourage both the public and their elected officials to think about a certain issue. NGOs should create positions such as "Public Affairs" or "Public Outreach Specialist." Moreover, NGOs should train multiple members of their organizations in what constitutes news and how to work with the media. Skills such as news release writing, planning and executing effective news conferences, and helping the media to write stories about social issues can be developed with some training.

NGOs can learn a lot about meeting the needs of their publics by remembering the basic tenets of effective relationship building. NGOs should follow the principles of strategic management. The leaders of NGOs, often not trained in business techniques, should learn about strategic planning and evaluation. NGOs usually direct several programs simultaneously and need to be able to see ways in which to create synergy between projects.

NGOs can be strategic in the management of their programs by creating specific and viable objectives that can be measured. With a little research, NGOs can create benchmarks of issues both before and during the outreach programs. By creating standards or benchmarks of performance and service, NGOs can monitor their progress, change their programs, and better serve their intended publics. Evaluation does not need to involve sophisticated quantitative analysis or national-level surveys. Rather, short surveys, focus groups, or interviews with people before, during, and after a program can help the NGO to meet its objectives.

Corporations may want to learn more about the NGOs that work in certain areas. Partnerships between NGOs and business organizations are a win-win situation for both parties. NGO-corporate relationships between computer companies, pharmaceutical companies, and health-related organizations can give corporations exposure to new regions and allow them to be good corporate citizens. Moreover, many corporations have philanthropic priorities and are always looking for new ways to partner with locally based organizations that can provide evidence of success.

NGOs provide invaluable services throughout the world. Unfortunately, many NGOs are not able to achieve their long-term goals because of poor planning or an overreliance on donations. In many parts of the world, especially during and after a crisis, there is a large amount of assistance available. This financial assistance is not limitless, however. In many crisis situations, donors leave when the crisis appears to be abating. The NGOs that were created during this time of crisis are often left with few or no financial resources when the donor dollars cease to be available. Therefore, NGOs need to become sustainable. Sustainability means that the NGOs use their strengths to create revenue-producing ventures within their organizations to help fund public-oriented projects. For instance, some NGOs have developed expertise in survey collection and data analysis. They can make money from this skill and offer their services for a fee to business and other organizations. Other NGOs have developed sophisticated understandings of desktop publishing and can help profit-driven organizations in creating high-quality advertisements and professional documents. Finally, some NGOs can provide training to newer NGOs in their own country and abroad for small fees and donations. All of these practices help the NGO to be sustainable so it can continue to exist and serve its core mission.

A strong NGO sector has been linked to the development of civil society and democracy throughout the world. NGOs are an important part of any society's development and have much to offer their publics. But NGOs, just like other types of organizations, need to communicate with their members, the media, and their publics to be effective in their core missions.

—Maureen Taylor

Members of nongovernmental organizations (NGOs) wave fliers during a protest outside the conference room of the opening session of the World Trade Organization (WTO) conference in Doha on November 9, 2001.

SOURCE: © AFP/Corbis.

NONPROFIT ORGANIZATIONS

Nonprofit organizations comprise the sector of the ecomomy referred to as the nonprofit,voluntary, or third sector. Incorporated under state law as charitable or not-for-profit corporations, these organizations are distinguished from organizations that focus on either making a profit (the private sector) or serving as an arm of government (the governmental sector). The nonprofit organization must focus on making some portion of society better or preventing it from becoming worse. As a result, nonprofit organizations provide not only welfare services but also social, educational, and cultural services. This category of organization is also called not-for-profit.

The nonprofit sector has a significant impact not only on quality of life, but also on the economy. In 2000, over $200 billion in donations from individuals, corporations, bequests, and foundations were collected to serve a variety of community needs. This sector may be the fastest-growing sector in the United States economy, with over 1.6 million nonprofit organizations in existence. With their focus on issues such as education, culture, religion, social service, environment, and health, nonprofit organizations are an important part of both the economy and community life. Involvement in such organizations has long been characteristic of American culture. Researchers such as Harvard professor Robert Putman have suggested that the number or density of such organizations is predictive of a region's economic health, governmental efficiency, personal happiness, and faith in public institutions.

Statistics indicate that the number of nonprofit organizations continues to grow, with as many as 50,000 new charities created in recent years. Times of economic growth encourage the development of nonprofit organizations. Nonprofit organizations are developed within local communities to meet specific local needs such as an animal shelter or boosters to support the local marching band. They exist along with those organizations defined as regional or national, such as the American Lung Association. Included in the nonprofit sector are hospitals, schools, museums, homeless shelters, research centers, youth groups, symphony orchestras, houses of worship, and health organizations such as the American Cancer Society and the American Heart Association.

CHARACTERISTICS

State and federal laws specify the conditions under which an organization can be classified as charitable or nonprofit. These organizations must have the following four characteristics: they must be incorporated and must have a public purpose, their governance structure must preclude self-interest and private financial gain, they must be exempt from paying federal tax, and they must possess the special legal status that stipulates that gifts made to them are tax deductible. In order for that organization to be classified as tax exempt, to be eligible for tax deduction, or to be known as a 501(c)(3) organization, the United States Internal Revenue Service (IRS) Code specifies activities that are and are not permitted. Annual reports detailing the financial activity of the organization must be filed in order to maintain nonprofit status.

Although the majority of nonprofit organizations are funded through donations, sales of products can also help fund the organization, such as the annual cookie sale of the Girl Scouts. Although funding may come from major foundations, such as the Bill & Melinda Gates Foundation's support for improving health in the developing world, the United States government and state governments are also involved in funding the services of nonprofit organizations, often through grants for those specific services. Examples include local organizations such as legal services or safe visitation programs.

Traditionally, a separation has existed between governmental funding for services provided by nonprofit religious or faith-based organizations and those services provided by secular organizations, but even that division is disappearing. With increasing attempts to shift responsibility for public service and assistance from governmental programs to nonprofit organizations, recent attention has been directed toward enabling faith-based organizations to receive governmental funding for specific service programs.

With an increase in the number of nonprofit organizations, there has been an increase in competition for public attention, volunteers, and donation dollars. As a result, the public can expect numerous requests for donations every week. Because not all charities are honest and accountable to their donors, public understanding of nonprofits and analysis of their programs and appeals is essential.

Community Chest, later to become United Way, was begun in 1913 in Cleveland, Ohio. Serving as a type of gatekeeper for the community with numerous charities, Community Chest began with the goal of consolidating into a single appeal the needs of a specific community with the appropriate nonprofit organizations. Each United Way organization must meet the specific guidelines established by United Way. Each year as community needs grow and more nonprofit organizations become available, more organizations apply to be included as United Way organizations than United Way can handle. As a result, not every reputable program is part of United Way. And throughout the year each community experiences numerous additional appeals for funds.

An effective nonprofit organization will focus on gaining the appropriate public attention, public concern for its mission, conviction that the organization is bringing about effective change, and commitment to involvement and donations. These objectives are achievable through an effective public relations approach.

PUBLIC RELATIONS FUNCTION

The public relations function in most nonprofit organizations includes creating awareness and acceptance of the organization's mission; communicating effectively with key publics, including employees, volunteers, the community, those served by the organization, and the media; developing, maintaining, and monitoring the organization's issue area, organizational policy, and public policy relevant to the organization; and maintaining the organization's reputation with donors. This means that the communication function will include media relations, publicity, issues management, public affairs, speech writing, publications, promotional writing, and, at times, crisis management. Otis Baskin, Craig Aronoff, and Dan L. Lattimore (1997) argued that "public relations is the business of many not-for-profit organizations" (p. 368).

The nonprofit sector has been a starting place for a career in public relations for many individuals. Although starting salaries in the nonprofit sector may be somewhat lower than starting salaries in agencies or in corporate work, the sense of accomplishment through doing something good for the community as well as having the opportunity to work with interesting and successful volunteers has led to higher job satisfaction in this sector.

In their study of communicators and communication departments, David Dozier, Larissa A. Grunig, and James E. Grunig (1995) found that the communication departments in the nonprofit sector are about half the size of the departments in the corporate and governmental sectors. In addition, communicators in the not-for-profit organizations and professional trade associations are more likely to have attended graduate school and to hold advanced degrees. Responsibilities of communication professionals in the not-for-profit organizations include contributions to strategic planning as well as manager role knowledge.

Unfortunately, this level of public relations expertise does not exist throughout the nonprofit sector. In many social welfare agencies, insufficient funding to hire individuals with public relations expertise means little public relations activity may be present. As a result, even an awareness of the need or methods to inform the media of organizational news may be lacking.

The public relations function with nonprofit organizations includes several goals. The variety of goals demonstrates the need for a variety of public relations approaches. These range from the unidirectional publicity to a two-way symmetrical approach. Because one goal includes increasing public awareness of the organization, its mission, and its successes, publicity will play an important role for meeting some organizational needs. For example, fundraising programs such as Race for the Cure and the MS Walk-a-thon rely on publicity. Even the American Cancer Society's Great American Smokeout is based primarily on publicity. Visibility and name recognition are essential for new organizations but are also important to the continued success of older organizations. Both publicity approaches and news coverage can be an advantage in this area. However, the successful nonprofit organization must do more than create awareness—it must also make a difference. At one time nonprofit organizations assumed that they could accomplish the educational function of their organizational goals such as preventing or detecting heart disease, diabetes, or cancer by simply sending out messages. Success was demonstrated by the number of messages produced or the number of brochures distributed. Many organizations have revised their focus from the source of the message to the actions of the receiver of the message and now look to measure changes in that receiver. This could include not only the number of individuals having mammograms but also early versus late cancer detection rates.

Media relations is an important part of public relations for the nonprofit organization. Because the mission of nonprofit organizations focuses on issues important to the local community, there should be sufficient opportunity to find news the media should want to cover. Understanding the importance of establishing a strong relationship with the media is essential.

Volunteer recruitment and retention are an important public relations activity of the nonprofit organization. These individuals are characterized by their donation of time and service for the benefit of the organization without consideration of pay. As a result, volunteers have a special relationship with the organization. Orientation and training will probably be necessary. This can include training in effective communication skills such as writing news releases or public speaking. Two-way symmetrical communication is important as volunteers work with salaried employees to help set goals and objectives. The process increases volunteer commitment and satisfaction in the organization's accomplishments. Because volunteers must feel that donating their time is as important as giving money, positive relationships must be maintained with the volunteer group. Within this context, recognition of volunteers also becomes important. However, the organization must be alert to appropriate recognition that meets the needs and expectations of the volunteers. For example, some volunteers expect appreciation but are uncomfortable with gifts or too much publicity.

Employees present another focus in the public relations effort. A complicating factor in the nonprofit organization is when a large regional or national organization works to have a presence in the local community where a local office has limited staff and relatively little experience with the nonprofit organization but significant responsibilities in the local community. The responsibilities of developing and maintaining a good relationship with the organization's governing body as well as serving as leader for the local community call for effective public relations skills.

Nonprofit organizations are increasingly recognizing the necessity of effective relationships with governmental bodies. Accomplishing the goals of the nonprofit organization may necessitate petitions to local city councils for changes such as rezoning for homeless shelters or for smoking ordinances. Effective development and presentation of these petitions becomes another public relations function. Often these responsibilities extend to the state or federal level, where lobbying may be necessary to influence legislative understanding of proposed legislation on issues of concern to the nonprofit organization. Nonprofit organizations are permitted to lobby federal and state officials with communication on specific legislation and reflecting a view on that legislation. However, they are not permitted to participate in political campaigning. Because the IRS specifies which expenditures are allowable for a nonprofit organization, it is necessary that the organization stay current on the issue. The lobbying effort, however, remains an important public relations function for many nonprofit organizations.

The financial aspects of the nonprofit organization are part of the public relations concern. Fundraising in the form of requesting donations from the public is the most common financial base for the organization. Much of the communication activity of the nonprofit organization may be directed toward getting sufficient donations to enable the organization to accomplish its goals. Although many volunteers enjoy participating in fundraising activities because success is easy to measure, they also are aware of the amount of effort involved in securing those funds. As a result, stewardship is important. As part of the ongoing public relations effort, the organization must be sure that a significant amount of the income goes toward accomplishing the mission of the organization and not toward the fundraising activities themselves.

Because a return is expected from the donation in some kind of improvement in the public's welfare or general benefit, nonprofit organizations must maintain careful financial reports. These financial reports, somewhat similar to corporate annual reports, may be part of the public relations effort of the organization. However, analyses of the financial activity of major national nonprofit organizations by outside organizations compare organizations and enable the public to see whether or not specific organizations are spending donation dollars wisely. As the fundraising expenses, administrative expenses, and program spending are analyzed, the public is shown the efficiency of the dollars it has donated. Increasingly, the public is being educated to expect effective nonprofits to spend less than 25 percent of their capital on fundraising activities and more than 75 percent on program implementation. Nonprofit organizations are recognizing the wisdom in limiting staff size and eliminating expensive fundraising projects. From a public relations perspective, the organization must adapt to meet changing public awareness and expectations.

Grants from foundations or governmental agencies often provide significant funding for special projects of the nonprofit organization. Grant writing may become part of the communication activity of the organization. Because grant writing involves telling the story of the organization, public relations professionals in the nonprofit sector will wisely be prepared. Unfortunately, in times of economic downturn, available funds from grants tend to decrease.

Ideally, the nonprofit organization will manage issues effectively. Whether these issues include increasing public expectations of accountability in fundraising, the successful accomplishment of an organization's mission such as elimination of tuberculosis or polio, or insurance for volunteers, the successful nonprofit will adapt to the changes.

Unfortunately, even nonprofit organizations are susceptible to crisis situations. Sometimes these are major crises such as the one the United Way of America suffered when its leader was found guilty of fraud, conspiracy, and money laundering; that suffered by the American Red Cross when, in the weeks immediately following the New York Twin Towers disaster, it refused to share its computerized database of the victims; or that experienced by the Catholic Church in the sexual abuse scandals. In any event, a nonprofit organization is not immune. Effective public relations must be prepared to help lead the organization through these crises, rebuilding the organization's credibility and public confidence in it.

—Kathie A. Leeper

See also Fundraising; Publics

Bibliography

Baskin, O. W., Aronoff, C. E., & Lattimore, D. L. (1997). *Public relations: The profession and the practice* (4th ed.). Madison, WI : Brown & Benchmark.

Bonk, K., Griggs, H., Tynes, E. (1999). *The Jossey-Bass guide to strategic communications for nonprofits.* San Francisco: Jossey-Bass.

Cutlip, S. M., Center, A. H., & Broom, G. M. (2000). *Effective public relations* (8th ed., pp. 519–553). Upper Saddle River, NJ: Prentice Hall.

Dozier, D. M., Grunig, L. A., & Grunig, J. E. (1995). *Manager's guide to excellence in public relations and communication management.* Mahwah, NJ: Lawrence Erlbaum.

Ott, J. S. (2001). *The nature of the nonprofit sector.* Boulder, CO: Westview Press.

OBJECTIVES

Objectives are central to a strategic approach to public relations that is based on research. An objective specifies exactly what is desired from a public relations action. An objective is created from the information collected through formative/ background research. Evaluative research is used to determine whether or not the public relations action achieved the objective—whether it was a success or a failure. (Refer to "Formative research" for clarification on the connection between objectives and public relations research.)

Objectives are generally written using the word *to* and then an action verb such as *increase*, *reduce*, *earn*, or *convince*. An objective must be quantifiable; you must be able to measure it in some way. Moreover, the objective should specify the amount of desired change stated as a number or percentage. It is the specificity of an objective that creates the clear standard for judging success. The following objectives are measurable and specific: (a) "to increase attendance at the 2004 charity auction to 120" and (b) "to convince 60 percent of employees to support the restructuring proposal." A person can count the number of participants to determine if 120 people attended or use a survey to assess employee support for the restructuring program to see if it reaches 60 percent. Evaluation becomes possible because of the ability to measure an objective and compare it against a specific standard. Some experts recommend that an objective include a target date or deadline. This increases specificity by indicating the date for the desired change to be achieved. You need to decide what time frame is appropriate for your objective. For instance, the second objective could be rewritten as "to convince 60 percent of employees to support the restructuring proposal by the end of June."

There are many different types of objectives. One distinction is between *process* and *outcome* objectives. A process objective checks to determine if certain steps were taken in the preparation and execution of a public relations action. Sample process objectives include writing a news release, getting approval of Web pages, or securing a permit for a city park. Each of these actions can be converted to a full objective. "To send out a news release to 20 media outlets by July 7." "To receive management approval of the Web pages by October 13th." "To secure the permit for the park development fun run by March 11th." All three of these objectives are measurable; you have either completed the action or not, and each one has a set time for when the action should be completed. Process objectives address the question "Did we do what we were supposed to do?" A public relations action can fail because a certain action or step was not taken. Process objectives are a checklist for actions or steps that must be taken in your public relations action. This checklist is developed as part of the planning process and used to review the execution of the public relations action.

Outcome objectives are used to determine the success or failure of the public relations action. An outcome objective specifies what the public relations action hoped to achieve. A proper outcome objective often includes the target stakeholder(s) because public relations actions are focused on specific target stakeholder(s)—whom the message is designed to reach and affect. When appropriate, include a specific target stakeholder in the objective. The objective "to convince 60 percent of employees to support the restructuring proposal by the end of June" indicates employees would be the target. You would not include a target stakeholder if you were trying to reach a very general audience as in the objective "to increase attendance at the 2004 charity auction to 120."

Outcome objectives can be divided into three groups: (a) *knowledge*, (b) *attitude*, and (c) *behavioral*. Knowledge objectives center on learning: The target stakeholders know something after the public relations action that they did not know before the action. There are three types of knowledge objectives: (a) *exposure*, (b) *comprehension*, and (c) *retention*. Exposure means that the target stakeholder(s) has an opportunity to see or hear the public relations action. The public relations action appears in some media or location the target stakeholder uses, such as a newspaper, radio, or Web site. Comprehension is the ability of the target stakeholder(s) to understand the message. A message must be written in a fashion and in a language the target can understand. Retention means that the target stakeholder(s) remembers information about the public relations action. Ideally, the three informational objectives are related to one another. Stakeholders must be exposed to a message in order to comprehend it and must understand a message if they are to remember it properly.

Attitude objectives attempt to change how people think or feel. An attitude can be defined as an evaluation of some object. "I love turkey" or "I dislike traffic" are examples of attitudes. In each case an evaluation (*love* and *dislike*) is made of some object (*turkey* and *traffic*). For an outcome objective, a public relations practitioner is trying to change the attitude of some target stakeholder/audience. The public relations action should alter the target stakeholder's evaluation of a particular object. "At the end of the three-month campaign, current customers will have a 15 percent increase in the approval of IBM's customer service department." The target stakeholders in this objective would be current customers, and the object is IBM's customer service department. People should hold different attitudes after they encounter the public relations effort than before it. Reputation is a form of attitude and is a common focus of public relations actions.

A behavioral objective seeks to alter the way people act. Behavior change is the most difficult of the three outcome objectives. People are more likely to resist behavior change than to resist new information or even alter an attitude. People are creatures of habits, and we do not like to change those habits—our behaviors. In a behavioral objective, the public relations action is trying to change how a people act. The target stakeholder should act differently after the public relations effort than before it. "To have 15 percent more new donors give blood in 2004 than in 2003." This objective seeks to get more people (new donors) to give blood—change their behavior.

—*W. Timothy Coombs*

See also Benchmarking; Formative research; Goals, Qualitative research; Quantitative research; Research objectives; Reputation management

Bibliography

Austin, E. W., & Pinkleton, B. E. (2001). *Strategic public relations management: Planning and managing effective communication campaigns.* Mahwah, NJ: Lawrence Erlbaum.

Stack, D. W. (2002). *Primer of public relations research.* New York: Guilford Press.

OECKL, ALBERT

Albert Oeckl (1909–2001) was the most important figure of the post–World War II era of public relations in Germany. The obituaries on his death (April 23, 2001) reflected the mythically idealized position that Oeckl held. He became a living legend primarily through his national as well as international professional activities, but he is also widely known for his writings, public speeches, and teaching activities.

Oeckl was born December 27, 1909, in Nuremberg and studied law and national economy in Munich and Berlin. In 1934 he earned his doctorate with a dissertation, *German Employees and Their Living Conditions,* and worked initially as a junior lawyer. Although written under the national socialist government, his dissertation can, from our contemporary viewpoint, be regarded as a profound scientific work with no recognizable kowtowing to national socialist ideology.

Following his internship as a junior lawyer (1934–1935, in the Reichspropagandaministerium in the Munich state office), he began his vocational career in 1936 at IG Farben in Berlin, where he was later to be employed in the head office and the newly founded press office. As he pointed out himself, this was where and when he gained his first journalistic experience and where he learned about the basics of then-current public relations of an international company.

During the war he worked, among other positions, in the news service for the supreme command of the Wehrmacht (OKW, or German Armed Forces) and in the Reichsamt (the German "empire office") for economic development under Carl Krauch. A recent dissertation at Leipzig University (by Christian Mattke) has shed light on Oeckl's career until 1945. Press relations and monitoring as well as support service for visitors were Oeckl's first duties at IG Farben. He was also responsible for an address card index, which might have triggered the idea for his *Taschenbuch des öffentlichen Lebens* ("Pocket Book of Public Life," published in 1950).

On May 1, 1933, he joined the NSDAP (Hitler's ruling national socialist party until 1945); however, he never held a ranking office in the party, nor did he have any national socialist grade. After the war, in 1947, an allied committee classified Oeckl as a *Mitläufer* (nominal member), a designation given to former members of the Nazi party who were considered not to pose a threat to the emerging democratic, capitalist society. With this classification Oeckl did not have to fear legal consequences stemming from his role during the war. However, he concealed his party membership publicly throughout his life.

Oeckl started his postwar career as the assistant of Dr. Rudolf Vogel, a member of the German Bundestag (German parliament) and of the Christian Democratic Party (CDU). From 1950 to 1959 Oeckl was director of the Public Relations Department of the Deutscher Industrie- und Handelstag (DIHT), the German Association of Chambers of Commerce and Industry. From 1959 on he was head of the public relations department of BASF, also a multinational corporation. From 1961 to 1967, Oeckl held the title of deputy director; from 1967 to 1974 his title was director. In 1974 he retired from his active career.

Oeckl had early ambitions regarding an academic career. He accepted the invitation to teach as a lecturer at the University of Heidelberg, where he gave lectures and seminars from 1960 until 1969. Later on he also taught at Augsburg University. From 1974 until 1978, after his retirement, he taught social psychology and public relations at the International University in Rome in the position of an extraordinary professorship. From this lectureship he earned the title of an honorary professor. This title strengthened his reputation in a discipline in which only few representatives held doctoral degrees. Hence, Oeckl was considered the academically legitimized voice to speak up for the majority of practitioners, to represent the whole professional field of public relations.

From 1950 onward, Oeckl annually published the *Taschenbuch des öffentlichen Lebens* ("Pocketbook of Public Life") and quickly became well known from it. It contains a systematic collection of addresses and can be found even today on nearly every editorial or public relations desk. In 1964 he published his first major book, *Das Handbuch der Public relations. Theorie und Praxis der Öffentlichkeitsarbeit in Deutschland und der Welt* (*Handbook of Public Relations: Theory and Practice of Öffentlichkeitsarbeit [Public Relations] in Germany and the World*). A revised version of this handbook was published in 1976, under the title *PR-Praxis. Der Schlüssel zur Öffentlichkeitsarbeit* (*PR Practice: The Key to Öffentlichkeitsarbeit*). At that time, these books—as well as Oeckl's various lectures and articles—played an important role in the professional field. Even today, they are important historical sources for academic public relations research. Oeckl defined *Öffentlichkeitsarbeit* (the German equivalent of public relations) as "working *with* the public, working *for* the public and working *in* the public (sphere)" (1976, p. 34). Another definition he gave was "*Öffentlichkeitsarbeit* is the conscious, planned and continuous endeavor . . . to build and maintain mutual understanding in public" (1964, p. 43). This definition, which is very similar to the definition crafted by the British Institute of Public Relations during the 1960s, contains a society-oriented understanding of public relations with symmetrical presuppositions. This understanding also underlies the formula Oeckl coined later: "PR = Information + Adaptation + Integration" (Oeckl, 1976, p. 19).

Although Oeckl—due to demands on his time—never developed a scientific theory that was empirically testable, he created a kind of *normative practitioner theory*. This theory, based on many years of professional experience, is aligned to relevant scientific literature, particularly writings of communication research. It not only provides definitive dividing lines between public relations and other concepts of public communication such as advertising, propaganda, and publicity, but one of the core elements of this practitioner theory is a set of normative guidelines (how-to rules) that express ways to act, to behave as a public relations practitioner. For Oeckl, primary requirements in public relations are "truth, clarity (lucidity), as well as the unity of word and deed" (1964, p. 47). Alongside these demands, sociability, open behavior, integrity, and modesty are characteristics that he considers

important professional values. During the 1960s, Oeckl informed younger professionals about the basic management method, the Four-Phase Model of PR Management: (a) analyses, (b) programming/strategy building, (c) taking action/communicating, and (d) evaluation (1964, pp. 343ff.). Most important for Oeckl's understanding of public relations was his regard for it as a separate and high-level management (staff) function in all kinds of organizations, not as a subdiscipline of marketing, or as pure publicity or propaganda.

Oeckl assumed and informed the profession that he had coined the German equivalent of the term public relations, *Öffentlichkeitsarbeit*, in 1950 by translating the American term *public relations*. New research has shown, however, that this term had been used much earlier in a discussion of the press organizations of the Protestant Church (*Evangelische Pressverbände*) as early as 1917. Presumably, by 1950 the term had fallen into oblivion. But during the 1950s and 1960s the German term made an excellent resurgence. Today, notably, state institutions (ministries, municipal press departments) and nonprofit organizations use the term *Öffentlichkeitsarbeit*, whereas private companies and public relations agencies widely prefer the English term *public relations* or *PR*. In recent years, the term *communication management* is used more and more.

Predominantly due to his political organization activities, in which he drew upon his—for that time—profound number of publications and lectures, Oeckl acquired the reputation of Germany's "PR-Nestor." He was a co-founder of the Deutsche Public Relations Gesellschaft (DPRG) (German Public Relations Association) in 1958 and officiated as second president between 1961 and 1967, following Carl Hundhausen. In 1986 the DPRG awarded him the honorary president title, and a junior award for academic theses has his name. Also important were Oeckl's international organization activities: Since 1965 he served as Confédération Européenne des Relations Publiques (CERP) vice president, and in 1967 the International Public Relations Association (IPRA) voted Oeckl its first German president. Through his activities in these functions, an important early impetus was given to the academization of the vocational public relations field, from which came ideas for an academically based public relations education at universities and standards for ethical codes.

On the occasion of his 90th birthday, in 1999, CERP president Thomas Achelis presented a *festschrift* ("PR Builds Bridges") to Oeckl, with essays contributed by well-known German, European, and American public relations practitioners, scientists, and organizational representatives that mirror the reputation Albert Oeckl had reached in the international public relations community.

Oeckl played a similar role for Germany to that of Edward L. Bernays for the professional field of American public relations: founding father, influential and symbolic figure for the whole professional field, and representative of a modern concept of the practice. Preconditions for Bernays's and Oeckl's reputations as founding fathers were their outstanding professional achievements and the capability to present themselves and to produce their own images in an outstanding way.

In Germany Oeckl represents the highest standard of the public relations practitioner, carefully considering and reflecting the practice of his profession with a high—and academically based—reputation due to his teaching, his writings, and his positions. In the history of public relations in German-speaking areas, Oeckl can be considered the most important figure next to Carl Hundhausen. Although Hundhausen achieved more solid and greater academic recognition, he was not as outstanding in the practical field as Oeckl. Both of these giants in the profession represent a kind of professional continuity from the 1930s, the national socialist time, on to the Federal Republic of the 1950s and 1960s. Both credibly represent, on the other hand, the restart of postwar public relations in Germany, a profession that had to distinguish itself clearly from the propaganda of Nazi politics. For many years, until the end of the 1980s, Oeckl embodied German *Öffentlichkeitsarbeit* worldwide.

—*Günter Bentele*

See also Bernays, Edward; Promotion; Publicity; Symmetry

Bibliography

Oeckl, A. (1964). *Handbuch der Public relations: Theorie und Praxis der Öffentlichkeitsarbeit in Deutschland und der Welt* [Handbook of public relations: Theory and practice of public relations in Germany and the world]. München: Süddeutscher Verlag.

Oeckl, A. (1976). *PR-Praxis: Der Schlüssel zur Öffentlichkeitsarbeit* [PR practice: The key to public relations]. Düsseldorf: Econ.

Oeckl, A. (2004). *Taschenbuch des Öffentlichen Lebens* [Pocketbook of public life]. Bonn: Festland-Verlag. (First edition published 1950)

OFFICE OF WAR INFORMATION

See Davis, Elmer, and the Office of War Information

ONLINE PUBLIC RELATIONS

Online public relations involves the use of Internet technologies to manage communications and to establish and maintain mutually beneficial relationship between an organization and its key publics.

Organizations have adopted the Internet widely and integrated computer-based delivery into their mix of communications technologies. Particularly valuable is the Internet's ability to allow organizations and people around the world to exchange information on a 24/7 basis.

ONLINE PUBLIC RELATIONS TOOLS

Web sites

The World Wide Web is probably the most important Internet technology for PR practitioners, permitting organizations to display text, visual, and sound files using computer servers and browser software on personal computers. The Web provides the decentralized delivery of information using human-computer graphical interfaces to facilitate access.

Organizations use Web sites for a variety of marketing, human resource, and other management functions besides public relations. Among the most common applications for public relations are the following.

Online newsrooms allow journalists and others to access news releases and other press materials that can be downloaded quickly and easily and transferred directly to the news production systems of newspapers and magazines as well as radio and television stations. More than 90 percent of all reporters now use the Web as a basic research tool, although Web sites have not surpassed the telephone, personal contacts, and traditional news releases as the preferred source of information for reporters (Hachigian & Hallahan, 2003).

Investor relations sites provide a wide range of materials for analysts and investment professionals as well as individual and institutional investors. These materials previously were distributed only as hard copies: annual reports, quarterly reports, earnings information, government filings, analyst presentations and reports, fact books, and so forth.

Product promotion sites engage consumers and others in educational, informational, and entertainment activities. Food and household manufacturers, for example, now provide recipes and consumer tips online. Many production companies sponsor sites to promote movies, TV shows, books, and entertainment fare. Site content includes background information, downloadable photos and audio, streaming video, chat rooms and bulletin boards, and interactive games designed to illustrate key ideas and to promote involvement.

Education and advocacy sites are used by not-for-profit organizations to inform users about issues and engage in the social marketing of ideas. Many of the same techniques used in product promotion sites are adapted to the promotion of ideas (such as an appreciation of the arts) or causes (such as the eradication of social problems). Educational sites often include tutorials and learning materials as well as quizzes and tests that facilitate assessment of a user's learning or knowledge. Advocacy sites encourage public education in the same way, but encourage participation in public discussions and

debates. Unique features on advocacy sites include directories, maps, and other address information regarding where people can write public officials or file public comments. Also included are direct e-mail links and prototype texts that might be used.

Health sites are widely used to provide information on health and risk-related topics and to provide coping mechanisms for people affected by particular maladies. Users can include the sufferers of health problems, as well as family members, friends, and health care practitioners. *Telemedicine* includes the provision of diagnoses and advice by health professionals as well as the self-help activities by support groups and not-for-profit organizations concerned about particular health or safety issues.

Fundraising/development sites are used by not-for-profit organizations to build and maintain their support bases. Online fundraising has become an increasing important application of e-commerce technology. Visitors to sites of nonprofit organizations can become informed, but also involved by joining as members or by sending a financial contribution billed to a credit card.

Intranets and Extranets

Communication within organizations has been facilitated by the advent of *intranets,* or closed-system Web-based communications systems used to facilitate the distribution and sharing of information within an organization. In a similar way, extranets have enabled organizations to share data-based information with allied partners, including vendors and customers, using controlled-access (usually password-protected) Web-based information systems accessible to users outside the organization.

Although intranets are used primarily to manage internal operations, many traditional employee relations functions are now conducted online. These include the distribution of announcements, company newsletters, employee policies and procedures, benefits information, and performance recognition. Intranets are also being used to conduct employee suggestion programs, deliver special messages from management, register employees for organizational and social events, and provide access to various archived materials such as graphics standards and materials and historical records and photographs.

Extranets continue to be used by business organizations primarily to share research and development, production, distribution, and inventory control information. However, as extranets have expanded in use, many organizations have recognized the value of extranets for public relations purposes. News and information about developments and activities at an organization are important to employees of partner organizations. In addition, online relationship building efforts can cement allegiances and improve productivity.

Electronic mail (e-mail) can be used in a variety of ways for public relations purposes. Bulk or broadcast e-mails are used to distribute information about company developments to both internal and external publics, including the distribution of news and feature materials to the press. Individual e-mails can be used to communicate directly with members of key publics, such as managers, employees, customers, donors, or constituents.

Variations of the traditional text-based memoranda are including links that prompt users to go to a Web site for desired information or to access e-mail attachments, which can be in the form of word-processed or portable document format (pdf) documents. More advanced techniques include graphically designed e-mails, video e-mails, electronic newsletters, and e-zines.

People react negatively to unsolicited e-mails (spam). However, an acceptable alternative is to give prospective recipients the option to receive (opt in) or not receive (opt out) bulk e-mails. Such permission (sometimes termed *permission marketing*) enhances message effectiveness by targeting the message to people who have indicated an interest in the topic. Senders must be careful, however, to avoid distributing messages too frequently.

Discussion Groups, Chats, and Online Meetings

Organizations can tap the interactive potential of the Internet by participating in or by sponsoring opportunities for people to share ideas with others. These include *discussion groups,* also known as newsgroups or bulletin boards, where people can post messages that can be read later (asynchronously) by other discussion group members. Live *chats* use synchronous conferencing software to allow people to come together and interact in real time.

Variations on chats include *Webconferences* and *netmeetings,* where synchronous discussions are augmented by video (made possible by cameras on personal computers) or audio (where people use microphones attached to personal computers). This technology has permitted organizations to make online presentations (*Webcasts*) and to conduct seminars (*Webinars*) to inform and engage participants in remote locations.

Organization representatives can sign on to a wide range of discussion groups or chats online, where they can cull valuable insights about participants' opinions on key issues and can use both fora to articulate organizational viewpoints. An important ethical issue involves whether the organizational representative is clearly identified and all users understand his or her special interest.

Other Online Tools

Lesser-used tools include database file transfers, using file transfer protocol that enables the delivery of large volumes of data by an organization to an inquirer, who can then read, manipulate, and interpret the findings. Remote kiosks allow organizations to use online technology in public buildings and elsewhere so that occasional users can find answers to queries. CD-ROMs provide an alternative delivery mechanism to real-time online connections and enable users to access information in the same ways as the Web. Finally, wireless technology allows people to access Web-based content, e-mail, and other forms of online communication without access to a personal computer. Wireless technologies using cell phones and personal data assistants (PDAs) probably provide less functionality and somewhat limited information—but nonetheless will be important organizational communication tools in the future.

APPLICATIONS OF ONLINE PUBLIC RELATIONS

Organizations can use online public relations in a wide range of applications.

Research

The ability to monitor the Web and discussion groups and chat rooms has facilitated the ability of public relations professionals to scan the environment to identify emerging issues and then track particular concerns that might affect the organization. In addition to extant information available online (secondary data), organizations can use online technologies to collect primary data in the form of e-mail and Web surveys.

Information Distribution

E-mail and Web sites facilitate the dissemination of announcements and other information to targeted grounds, eliminating time lags created when organizations depend on the press or postal mail to distribute information. Information is available instantaneously and can be updated regularly as needed. The cost of delivered information can be lower, although many organizations use redundant systems to distribute information (printed and mailed materials, faxes, private wire services, and personal delivery).

Queries

Online technologies provide an ideal, low-cost, automated way for organizations to respond to routine, perfunctory questions, thus reducing the demand on staffs in offices at customer call centers. Although a large majority of queries can be addressed online, effective query management involves incisive anticipation of the most common topics of interest as well as mechanisms for handling the nonroutine, one-of-a-kind problems that might arise. Although many queries can be handled online, organizations must maintain other mechanisms to handle questions, such as telephone help lines and customer/consumer affairs correspondence functions.

Crisis Response

Online communications today play a critical role when organizations are faced with extraordinary events that create uncertainty or disrupt routine operations. People often flood Web sites and e-mail boxes seeking information, and organizations must now include online communications as a critical, first-response component in crisis management plans. Both content and technical Webmasters have become members of crisis response teams in many organizations. Tactics include the creation of a special home page and increasing the system's capacity to process increased volume. Other standard techniques include creation of news and information update pages, activation of online resources to assist victims and others, and use of electronic bulletin boards for employees and others to share intelligence and express concerns.

Discussions and Debate

Organizations can use online technologies to encourage the sharing of ideas among key publics and thus further public debate on issues important to them. A growing number of organizations use their intranets (as well as groupware) to facilitate work on projects among staff organized in *virtual teams.* Intranet discussions groups are being used more widely to seek employee input on problems, including suggestions for improvements in productivity. The effect of this expanded participation is greater involvement and affinity with an organization.

Among external audiences, forward-thinking organizations are creating mechanisms for people to provide feedback on social issues and the organization's issue positions, consistent with notions of about the importance of dialogue and two-way communications. Beyond serving as valuable research findings, public access to comments allows others to crystallize, change, or reinforce their own opinions. Publication of public comments submitted to government agencies is another way online communication can facilitate democratic processes.

Relationship Building

If the ultimate purpose of public relations is to establish and maintain mutually beneficial relationships with key publics, online communications have the potential to help foster positive reputations (as a prerequisite to establishing positive relationships) and to foster interaction between an organization and key publics. Online relationship building is critical where a user's only contact with an organization might be via online communications, but also can contribute to the process where offline relationships exist. The inherent interactive features of Web communications, for example, lend themselves to *two-way symmetrical* or *dialogic* communications, although many organizations so far have failed to fully exploit these features (Taylor, Kent, & White, 2001).

MANAGING ONLINE PUBLIC RELATIONS

Public relations managers face a variety of managerial concerns as online communications become an integral part of an organization's public relations effort. These include determining who in the organization will control and manage site content, the consistent and proper branding of online communications (such as domain names), the maintenance of content quality, the usability or functionality of the system, and the integration of online and offline activities.

Also important is compliance with the changing laws and regulations that impact online public relations activities. New issues include: (a) the disclosure and enforcement of electronic information privacy policies, (b) the right of employers to eavesdrop or monitor employees' use of private e-mail and other organization-owned systems, (c) the right of government to access electronic records to prevent terrorism, (d) the acceptance of electronic signatures, and (e) regulatory requirements for the retention of electronic messages.

Online communications also raise new concerns related to misuse by others that results in threats or potential losses to an organization. These include (a) defamatory attacks on organizations in discussion groups or attack/complaint Web sites, (b) intrusions into systems by hackers who aim to disrupt service or destroy content, or (c) misuse of content by lurkers who wish to gain competitive intelligence or who might stalk organizational personnel (*cyberstalkers*). Public relations managers must also deal with rogues who purchase desirable Web site domain names to resell them to organizations for a premium price (*cybersquatters*) or simply to deceive potential visitors for personal gain by diverting traffic. Finally, public relations managers must be concerned with the *theft* of digital assets (copyrighted or trademarked content) that can be diluted in value by excessive or fraudulent use by others.

Public relations managers also face challenges in assessing the effectiveness of online communications vis-à-vis other communications tools. Metrics for measurement of traffic have been developed that allow organizations to count access (such as *hits* on a Web site page), but also unique users (unduplicated *reach*), frequency of use, length of visits, and so on. Registration systems and *cookies* technologies also allow organizations to identify visitors (and to tailor personalized information to them).

Online public relations can be measured based on traditional evaluative standards used in public relations, such as awareness and attitude change. However, valid and reliable measurement techniques need to be developed to assess how mere exposure leads to greater awareness and understanding of online content and how online content leads to persuasion. Fortunately, the interactive nature of online communications makes actions taken online relatively easy to measure. Organizations can count click-throughs to promoted messages, online messages sent, and orders submitted for more information or for products and services. But if actions are taken offline, evaluation becomes more elusive.

More than any other communication activity, online communicators must address the question of return on investment (ROI) or the financial return derived from online communications investments. ROI analysis is a common way for organizations to evaluate investments in technology. Public relations managers will be called upon to demonstrate the cost-effectiveness of online activities and the consequences if these activities are not undertaken.

—*Kirk Hallahan*

See also Communication technologies; Crisis communication; Dialogue; Excellence theory, Home page; Qualitative research; Quantitative research; Relationship management theory; Web site

Bibliography

Cozier, Z. R., & Witmer, D. F. (2001). The development of a structuration analysis of new publics in an electronic environment. In R. L. Heath (Ed.), *Handbook of public relations* (pp. 615–623). Thousand Oaks, CA: Sage.

Hachigian, D., & Hallahan, K. (2003). Perceptions of public relations Web sites by computer industry journalists. *Public Relations Review, 29,* 43–62.

Hallahan, K. (1994, Summer). Public relations and circumvention of the press. *Public Relations Quarterly, 32*(2), 17–19.

Hallahan, K. (2004). Online public relations. In H. Bidgoli (Ed.), *The Internet encyclopedia* (pp. 769–783). Hoboken, NJ: Wiley.

Hallahan, K. (2004). Protecting an organization's digital public relations assets. *Public Relations Review, 30*(3).

Holtz, S. (2002). *Public relations on the net* (2nd ed.). New York: AMACOM.

Horton, J. L. (2001). *Online public relations: A handbook for practitioners.* Westport, CT: Greenwood.

O'Keefe, S. (2002). *Complete guide to Internet publicity: Creating and launching successful online campaigns.* New York: Wiley.

Taylor, M., Kent, M. L., & White, W. J. (2001). How activist organizations are using the Internet to build relationships. *Public Relations Review, 27,* 263–284.

OP-ED

Op-ed refers to the page in a newspaper that is opposite the page on which editorials are published. (Editorials reflect a newspaper's official position on problems and issues.) Some newspapers devote only one page to editorials, letters to the editor, and commentary; editorials typically are to the left and op-ed contributions typically are to the right, although everything is on a single page.

The best newspapers have balanced editorial and op-ed pages. They publish a blend of editorials;

letters to the editor (typically, not all letters are published); commentary from local and nationally syndicated political columnists; and *public commentary* from individuals who do not work for the newspaper.

The best newspapers also ensure that a broad spectrum of opinion is reflected in their letters, syndicated columns, and public commentaries. (Editorials do not reflect a broad spectrum of opinion because they are the newspaper's official voice, which is likely to lean to the right or the left.) A good balance is sought on political, economic, social, and cultural issues. This does not mean that two conservative and two liberal items will be published each day. It does mean that, on balance, a good newspaper will publish ideas that reflect a wide range of opinions.

The public commentary sections of most newspapers are open to anyone, and public relations practitioners sometimes try to have their organization's views published there. The public affairs officer for a legislator who is sponsoring a controversial and widely discussed bill, for example, might pen a piece explaining the legislation and submit it to all the newspapers in the state (under the legislator's name) in hopes it will be published in some of them.

A corporate public relations practitioner might write a commentary about the steps a corporation is taking to preserve the environment as it attempts to develop land in an environmentally sensitive area. That would be distributed under the CEO's name. Or a practitioner at one of the ubiquitous think tanks might submit a commentary purporting to show that chlorofluorocarbons are not really a threat to the environment after all.

Unfortunately, newspapers do not screen commentaries as carefully as they do other stories. Some commentaries contain factual error, and some reflect partisan views that have little basis in fact. For this reason, public commentary sometimes carries little weight with some readers.

Some newspapers also are extraordinarily difficult to get into. The *Houston Chronicle,* for instance, publishes only 18 of the 400 or so submissions it receives each week. Some organizations follow the lead of Mobil Oil Corporation's Herbert Schmertz, who helped pioneer the use of the paid commentary (*advertorial*). Mobil wrote commentaries that looked like op-ed pieces and then paid to have them published in newspapers across the country. Such commentaries get published, but they are not op-ed pieces, and they may have less credibility than commentaries that survive the rigorous screening process.

—*Michael Ryan*

Bibliography

Rampton, S., & Stauber, J. (2001). *Trust us, we're experts! How industry manipulates science and gambles with your future*. New York: Jeremy P. Tarcher/Putnam.

OPENNESS

The concept of openness, in terms of public relations, may have internal and external interpretations. From an internal perspective, employees may feel positively about open communication feedback cycles and company newsletters advocating the open-door policies of management. From an external perspective, the media may have negative interpretations of openness if the company spokesperson is evasive during a crisis situation.

The concept of openness, in terms of public relations and organizational communication, is derived from systems theory. This theoretical framework is concerned with complex, interdependent organizations that operate within dynamic environments. With the multiple pressures that organizations face (mergers, economic considerations, media coverage, community obligations), openness helps companies see themselves as part of a dynamic web of interdependencies and relationships. Openness involves interaction with the environment, reciprocal exchanges within and outside of organizations. The existence of diverse environments across industries, companies, and governmental entities means that the same organizing principles and solutions cannot be applied in all situations. In short, various contextual and environmental factors need to be considered, and organizations need to have some degree of openness in order to prosper.

Public relations representatives may help organizations achieve openness with various stakeholders (i.e., community, media). Thus, they are critical organizational boundary spanners. Larissa A. Grunig, James E. Grunig, and D. M. Dozier argued in 2002 that the systems perspective emphasizes the coordination of internal and external contingencies. Organizations depend on resources from their environments, such as employees and clients. A company with an open system uses public relations representatives to gather information on how productive its relationships are with the community, customers, and other stakeholders. In contrast, they argued that organizations with closed systems do not actively seek new information but operate on past history or the preferences of managers. The closed organization clings to the status quo (i.e., how we've always done it), and managers tend to exhibit defensive behaviors such as resistance to change.

Openness is synonymous with the concept of organizational boundary spanning (OBS). The boundary spanner straddles the edge of an organization. This person has a viewpoint within and outside of organizations; he/she knows many details about the company as well as its clients. Public relations representatives are the liaisons, explaining the organization's actions to its stakeholders and interpreting the environment for the organization. Public relations people should have open feedback loops with the primary decision makers acting as the members of the dominant coalition—the executive team—in the organization. The boundary spanners can alert managers to problems and opportunities in the environment and help them respond to these changes.

If managers keep their systems open, they allow for the two-way flow of resources and communication between the organization and the environment. The information can be used to adapt to the environment, or managers may use the data to try and control the environment. Control may be accomplished through consolidation of resources or persuasive influence. In some cases this strategy may be appropriate, but eventually some adaptation is required.

According to J. E. Grunig (2000), symmetrical public relations (a balanced approach) values openness and collaboration. Organizations need exchange relationships with the environment. They can be negatively impacted when there is an unwillingness on the part of managers to incur costs that build collaborative relationships. However, they incur greater costs from negative publicity, strict regulation, and other issues that result from closed relationships. Grunig argues that organizations will be more effective if they incorporate values of openness and collaboration into their corporate cultures and decision-making processes.

From an internal culture perspective, openness within the organization may not necessarily lead to successful boundary spanning. However, cherishing this value at all levels of the company will probably lead to communal, collaborative external relationships with stakeholders. According to John J. Rodwell, René Kienzle, and Mark A. Shadur (1998), some organizational professionals argue that employees must be given information about the company, its activities, goals, and vision. Additionally, they must be allowed to have channels through which information can be delivered to management.

Openness is essential for many organizational processes, such as public relations. Through openness in the system, the communication conduit for many aspects of organizational life is strengthened. Rodwell, Kienzle, and Shadur wrote in 1998 that employee attitude surveys often suggest that communication is an area that needs attention. By establishing and maintaining open feedback loops in the organization, positive internal public relations is likely to flourish. Employee morale and organizational commitment may also be positively affected.

Deloris McGee Wanguri argued in 1996 that an environment that encourages discreet and consistent communicative openness is recommended for organizational boundary spanners. From the discretionary viewpoint, this alternative does not advocate the disclosure of privileged information or knowledge that is potentially harmful to any individual or to the company and its clients. In other words, too much openness is problematic for many organizational relationships. In many cases, good judgment

on how much information needs to be revealed is recommended. Additionally, consistency is essential so that trust and respect can develop in these relationships. If the stakeholder learns to trust the consistent communication behaviors of the boundary spanner, respect and continued openness will permeate the relational encounters.

Using sound judgment and prudence in selecting information to share can increase communication openness and enhance perceived equity in these public relationships. If the information is accurate and appropriate for the target stakeholders (e.g., customers probably don't need to know specific quarterly financial results), the benefits outweigh the risks. Communicative openness can lead to positive dynamics, such as increased discussion and understanding, enhanced preparation for change, improved communication, and perceptions of communicative equity. In terms of equity, the receiver perceives that the sender is being straightforward and direct. The receiver also perceives that the sender is using proper discretion and consistent communication patterns. Thus, the organizational relationship is balanced. These perceptions of balance are critical for public relations professionals. Although public relations' stature has improved in society, the associations with propaganda and "spin" have not entirely disappeared.

Open systems, by their nature, react to change. These reactions may involve negotiation and compromise. With these dynamics, the boundary spanners and the stakeholders establish rules and then maintain and adapt the rules as needed. Stakeholders will learn to trust the source credibility of the boundary spanner when openness is valued.

Candor is a means of achieving credibility, and it must be constantly engaged and reengaged. Companies must engage in active listening, a primary part of any open communication process, with their stakeholders and respond to their concerns. Solutions may not be readily available, but mutually acceptable alternatives may be negotiated when such candor is exercised.

Although potential barriers to the effectiveness of communication will always exist, openness is an important and useful public relations strategy. It is a strategy, however, that requires continuous adjustments to cultural, structural, and behavioral changes. The practitioner's adjustments are relevant for both the organization and its stakeholders. Through open exchange of information, all parties can learn to deal with the changes and their effects on the public relationships.

Ultimately, if the participants in these communication transactions do not trust and respect each other, if the stakeholders do not value the conditions under which the information is shared (i.e., media people recognizing possible spokesperson evasiveness), or if practitioners fail to use discretion in their communication, then the resulting relationships will be negatively affected and the recovery may take many years.

—*Brian C. Sowa*

Bibliography

Bivins, T. H. (1992). A systems model for ethical decision making in public relations. *Public Relations Review, 18,* 365–383.

Eisenberg, E. M., & Goodall, H. L. (2001). *Organizational communication: Balancing creativity and constraint.* Boston: Bedford/St. Martin's.

Grunig, J. E. (2000). Collectivism, collaboration, and societal corporatism as core professional values in public relations. *Journal of Public Relations Research, 12,* 23–48.

Grunig, L. A., Grunig, J. E., & Dozier, D. M. (2002). *Excellence in public relations and effective organizations: A study of communication management in three countries.* Mahwah, NJ: Lawrence Erlbaum.

Lattimore, D., Baskin, O., Heiman, S. T., Toth, E. L., & Van Leuven, J. K. (2004). *Public relations: The profession and the practice.* Boston: McGraw-Hill.

Rodwell, J. J., Kienzle, R., & Shadur, M. A. (1998). The relationships among work-related perceptions, employee attitudes, and employee performance: The integral role of communication. *Human Resource Management, 37,* 277–293.

Wanguri, D. M. (1996). Diversity, perceptions of equity, and communicative openness in the workplace. *Journal of Business Communication, 33,* 443–457.

OPPORTUNITY AND THREAT

The idea of opportunity and threat in crisis management is rooted in the oft-recounted observation that the Chinese character for crisis is made up of two seemingly contradictory symbols: one for opportunity, the other for threat. The implication is that managers should view crises not just as threats—to their bottom line, to their reputations, indeed, to their very survival—but also as opportunities—to redefine problems, to promote self-sacrifice, to reaffirm relationships with key constituents—as well as a vehicle by which to achieve strategic advantage.

OPPORTUNITY AND THREAT DEFINED

The line of reasoning for treating threat and opportunity together is rooted in the term *wei-ji,* the Chinese word for crisis. It is the term *wei* that means threat or danger, and the word *ji* means opportunity. In the pictograph that makes up the word in Chinese, the term for threat is placed at the top, and the word for opportunity is below it. The placement suggests that although the threat in a crisis is real and apparent, the opportunity, though present, is somewhat concealed. The implication, of course, is that wise crisis managers look beyond the threat to see where opportunities lie.

Threat

Threat is central to the concept of a crisis. In their survey of the literature of crisis management, Matthew Seeger, Timothy Sellnow, and Robert Ulmer (1998) wrote that a crisis is composed of three distinct notions: surprise, a short response time, and a threat. Among the threats that an organization faces are a diminished ability to accomplish conventional organizational objectives, as well as the real probability of organizational loss. Indeed, Karl Weick (1988) got at this critical component of threat when he defined crises as "low probability/high consequence events that threaten the most fundamental goals of the organization" (p. 305).

Organizations should plan for crises, viewing their likelihood as inevitable, given the variegated threats companies face. Such threats originate from both internal and external sources. Internally, threats take the form of serious accidents, product safety incidents, or corporate misdeeds by senior executives. Organizations face external threats as well; these threats can emanate from activists who challenge a company's environmental record or consumer terrorists—such as Tylenol tampering incidents—as well as natural disasters.

Opportunity

Whereas the threat in crisis situations is self-evident, the opportunity is not. Weick (1988) acknowledged this problem when he concedes that crisis "events defy interpretations and impose severe demands on sensemaking" (p. 305). Yet if crisis managers are to strategically rescue their organizations from a crisis, they need to develop a sense-making process by which novel opportunities are seen, or, using Weick's term, enacted. That is, they have to cognitively re-create the crisis situation by developing a different way of seeing, one that envisions the situation as one in which opportunities are present.

One such opportunity is definitional; crises provide organizational officials wide latitude in managing meanings. A crisis is powerful in that it breaks frames; old ways of viewing problems are rendered obsolete. This gives a crisis manager an opportunity to redefine a situation in a way that was impossible before, and with new definitions come new solutions for problems. In short, a crisis provides a face-saving way to change paths by providing cover for decision makers—a helpful vehicle by which to disentangle oneself from intractable problems. Crises also proffer *an excuse to act* to bring about desired outcomes—even though the justification may have little to do with the action.

Second, a crisis emboldens people not only to act but to do so in a way that is costly to them—in the expectation that the sacrifice will bring a better day. Crises provide short windows of opportunity by which people are more likely to sacrifice—or accept dramatic change—in order to bring about a long-term good.

Third, a crisis provides opportunities for organizations to demonstrate to key constituencies that their concern is for customers more than for the bottom line. That is, crises give companies an occasion to reinforce their reputation and their commitment to ethics. Even if they are at fault, by reacting to a crisis in a positive way, an organization can build goodwill.

Finally, crisis managers can use a threat to the industry as an opportunity to position a company for a strategic advantage. The case of Starkist Tuna is instructive. After years of being criticized by environmentalists for the fact that dolphins were caught in its tuna nets, the Heinz Corporation developed a new policy by which it would purchase tuna only from suppliers that could prove that their tuna was caught in a manner that was safe for dolphins. The company then put the label "dolphin-safe" on its tuna cans. The implication of the message was clear: Heinz cared about the environmental consequences of its actions; its competitors did not.

—*Keith Michael Hearit*

See also Apologia theory; Crisis and crisis management; Crisis communication

Bibliography

Bradford, J. L., & Garrett, D. E. (1995). The effectiveness of corporate communicative responses to accusations of unethical behavior. *Journal of Business Ethics, 14,* 875–892.

DeFrancis, J. (Ed.). (1999). *ABC Chinese-English dictionary.* Honolulu: University of Hawaii Press.

Fearn-Banks, K. (1996). *Crisis communications: A casebook approach.* Mahwah, New Jersey: Lawrence Erlbaum.

Hearit, K. M. (2001). Corporate apologia: When the organization speaks in defense of itself. In. R. L. Heath (Ed.), *Handbook of public relations* (pp. 501–512). Thousand Oaks, CA: Sage.

Seeger, M., Sellnow, T. L., & Ulmer, R. R. (1998). Communication, organization, and crisis. In B. R. Burleson (Ed.), *Communication yearbook 21* (pp. 231-275). Thousand Oaks, CA: Sage.

Weick, K. (1988). Enacted sensemaking in a crisis situation. *Journal of Management Studies, 25,* 305–317.

ORGANIZATIONAL IDENTITY AND PERSONA

Organizational identity and *persona* are terms that refer to the self or character a company strategically communicates to multiple audiences in order to achieve organizational goals. They are central concepts in the study and practice of public relations because these corporate personalities shape public acceptance. Just as individuals often play multiple roles and manage multiple identities—for example, people manage their work, home, and relational identities—organizations rely on this public relations function to increase connectedness with audiences. Managing organizational identity and persona involves creating and maintaining a selected public face while resolving contradictions that might arise as audiences interact with this organizational character. If a corporation creates and manages its identity and persona carefully, it can more successfully persuade the public to embrace the organization and its products, services, or policies.

To understand how corporations benefit from this identity management function, it is useful to take a closer look at the concept of organizational persona. Jill J. McMillan suggests that the term *persona* (from the Latin for mask) is beneficial in labeling organizational communication as symbolically constructed while noting that corporations have recognizable social presences with which audiences create relationships. Indeed, as Robert L. Heath (1993) pointed out, "the symbols of the organizations' personae become real in the minds of persons involved despite the fact that the organizations are only symbolic and artificial" (p. 148). In other words, the only way audiences can often *know* an organization is through its employment of these symbolic personae. As Cheney and McMillan (1990) observed, as members of an organizational society, people must converse with corporate rhetors along with individual speakers. Organizational personae form the basis for this conversation. If people accept an organization's use of symbols, they will be more likely to have an ongoing dialogue with a company and its services.

Organizations rarely possess only one persona, however, and it is the interaction of various personae that constitutes an organization's identity. In Western society, the idea that individuals possess qualities that differentiate themselves from each other gradually came to describe differences in organizations as well. Thus, we may think of an organization's

identity as that which is communicated through its various identifying emblems, logos, insignias, programs, and public actions. As Lars Thoger Christensen and George Cheney noted,

> Some corporations, for example, work to personalize their identities in various ways, including the use of visible representatives (such as Hollywood celebrities or CEOs) or characters (such as Xerox's monk-scribe of some years ago). Other organizations prefer, or even feel compelled, to "center" or "ground" themselves in key values or concerns. (1994, p. 224)

Nike, for example, relies on both of these approaches. Not only does its swoosh logo identify it, but its inner-city teen programs reflect its business personality. An organization's identity is not static, however. Savvy organizations recognize that audiences interact with these corporate selves and adjust these public faces as needed. A company that in the 1950s communicated the identity of responsible benefactor through its logos and the like might recognize the need to update its identity to one of technological innovator to meet current societal expectations. This ongoing need to assess organizational identity can lead to challenges and even paradoxes for companies.

Examining the ongoing process of a corporation's effort to maintain its organizational identity and persona with multiple audiences suggests how challenging careful identity management can be. If audiences identify or accept a given organizational persona, the organization will be able to meet its goals more easily. Instead of regulation and close scrutiny, for example, a chemical company that projects the persona of a concerned corporate citizen finds less public resistance. Audiences who feel the chemical company shares their concerns will in turn identify with the company. An important aspect embedded in the concept of organizational identity and persona, then, is the idea of identification. The more a person identifies, or relates, to an offered corporate persona, the less direct or forceful a company's persuasion needs to be.

An audience member might identify with one organizational persona, however, and not with its other personae. Theresa A. Russell-Loretz (1995) investigated this paradoxical nature of organizational identity and persona in Dow Chemical recruitment videos. She pointed out that organizations must balance the need to be unique from other organizations with the need to be the same, in order to be part of the cultural mainstream. Dow, like all organizations, must convey its unique corporate values for recruitment purposes while simultaneously informing employees and customers that it shares basic Western business practices and procedures with other corporations.

All corporations, as a cornerstone of a successful public relations foundation, must articulate and monitor their identities and personae. Without these recognizable corporate personalities, a corporation will be unable to stand out from other businesses and attract attention. The challenge facing all corporations, then, is how to create and maintain their images in a way that the public finds both acceptable and appealing.

—*Ashli A. Quesinberry*

See also Identification; Image; Legitimacy and legitimacy gap

Bibliography

Burke, K. (1969). *A rhetoric of motives.* Berkeley, CA: University of California Press.

Cheney, G. (1983). The rhetoric of identification and the study of organizational communication. *Quarterly Journal of Speech, 69*, 143–158.

Cheney, G., & McMillan, J. J. (1990). Organizational rhetoric and the practice of criticism. *Journal of Applied Communication Research, 18*, 93–113.

Christensen, L. T., & Cheney, G. (1994). Articulating identity in an organizational age. *Communication Yearbook, 17*, 222–235.

Heath, R. L. (1993). A rhetorical approach to zones of meaning and organizational prerogatives. *Public Relations Review, 19*, 141–155.

Russell-Loretz, T. A. (1995). Janus in the looking glass: The management of organizational identity in corporate recruitment videos. In W. N. Elwood (Ed.), *Public relations inquiry as rhetorical criticism: Case studies of corporate discourse and social influence* (pp. 156–172). Westport, CT: Praeger.

PAGE, ARTHUR W.

Arthur Wilson Page (1883–1960) is one of the most important pioneers of corporate public relations in United States history. As vice president and head of the Information Department at American Telephone and Telegraph from 1927 to 1947, Page—the first public relations person to achieve that rank—developed and institutionalized many of the strategies and tactics that are still commonly used in the practice, particularly in his use of research to guide policy. During World War II, he assisted with government public information activities and drafted the news release that announced the use of the first atomic bomb. After the war he spent a dozen years as an independent counselor. Unlike most public relations professionals, then or now, Page became a member of the boards of directors of AT&T, Continental Oil, and Chase National Bank. He was a trustee of the Metropolitan Museum of Art, the Carnegie Corporation, and the J. Pierpont Morgan Library and volunteered for countless other philanthropic organizations. He is still counted among the field's outstanding practitioners, and the Arthur W. Page Society, an organization for senior public relations and corporate communications executives, was founded in 1983 to promote his principled approach to public relations.

Arthur W. Page

SOURCE: Property of AT&T Archives. Reprinted with permission of AT&T.

BIRTH AND EDUCATION

Page was born on September 10, 1883, in Aberdeen, North Carolina, the second of four children of Willia

Alice Wilson Page and Walter Hines Page. Walter Page wrote for and edited several prestigious publications, including *Harper's* and the *Atlantic Monthly,* before founding the publishing house Doubleday, Page and Company, where he served as literary editor of *World's Work* magazine. The Pages were Methodists and Democrats, both of which young Arthur became as well.

Arthur Page was educated at the Cambridge (Massachusetts) Latin School from 1896 to 1899 and the Lawrenceville (New Jersey) School from 1899 to 1901, and he graduated from Harvard College in 1905. At Harvard he was a member of the Hasty Pudding, two literary societies, and a Southern Club that he had organized. Although his academic career culminated in an undistinguished "gentleman's C," he never stopped working on behalf of education, raising funds to educate African American teachers, serving on the Board of Overseers at Harvard, becoming a trustee at Columbia Teacher's College, and spearheading a corporate giving campaign for colleges and universities generally. He was honored with Doctor of Law degrees by Columbia University in 1954 and by Williams College in 1959.

EARLY CAREER

Page said he wanted to be an architect, but his father wanted him to go into the family business. While at Harvard, Arthur wrote for *The Advocate,* contributing almost all of the editorials published during his senior year, and he spent his summers at *World's Work,* proofreading and collecting pictures for the public affairs magazine. *World's Work* published 21 feature articles under Arthur's byline after he went there full-time in 1905.

Page began to assume more responsibility, both at home and at work. In 1911, he became managing editor. He married Mollie W. Hall of Milton, Massachusetts, on June 1, 1912. When his father went to London to serve as U.S. ambassador from 1913 to 1918, Arthur took charge of the magazine. Toward the end of World War I, Page went to France to help prepare propaganda for the Allied Expeditionary Force's Psychological Subsection.

This group created leaflets on such topics as the amount of food army regulations provided for prisoners. The army dropped millions of the leaflets by airplane during the last two or three months of the war in hopes of convincing German soldiers to surrender.

Page's father died in 1918; therefore, when Arthur returned to the United States in 1919, in addition to editing *World's Work,* he supervised other Doubleday, Page publications, including *Educational Review* and *Radio Broadcast.* He published his first book in 1920, on the part American troops played in Europe during World War I.

AMERICAN TELEPHONE & TELEGRAPH

By 1926 Page was ready to leave his family's business. He was the father of four children: Mollie (born in 1913), Walter Hines Page II (1915), Arthur W., Junior (1917), and John Hall (1920). He had plenty of writing and editing experience, as well as a strong background in business administration. And he was ready to leave because he no longer agreed with F. N. Doubleday's leadership in the family publishing house. In the meantime, AT&T's new president, Walter Gifford, was in search of a new publicity director. When Gifford and Page met, Page said he would take the job, but only if the company was serious about taking a socially responsible approach to informing the public. Gifford agreed, and Page joined AT&T as vice president on January 1, 1927.

Nine months later, Gifford and Page birthed their most important policy in a speech Gifford made before a meeting of the National Association of Railroad and Utilities Commissioners. Gifford's statement (apparently written by Page) was a credo that would guide Bell System decision making and public relations for the next 50 years. Gifford pointed out that AT&T's stock ownership was "widespread and diffused" and conceded that AT&T was a monopoly. The company's far-flung stockholders and consumers depended on Bell, giving the system serious obligations: "Obviously, the only sound policy that will meet these obligations is to continue to furnish the best possible telephone service at the lowest cost consistent with financial safety." He believed this long-term policy would succeed, stating, "Earnings must be sufficient to assure the best possible telephone service at all times and to assure the continued financial integrity of the business." He spoke also of the "spirit of service" that marked Bell's history, a tradition that continued with "scientists and experts devoted exclusively to seeking ways and means of making the service better and cheaper."

The Dallas speech was the embodiment of Page's approach to public relations. First, like the speech, Page always emphasized quality service. As a monopoly, AT&T was subject to public criticism and government regulation. Knowing that all corporations operated at public discretion, Page insisted that the public must be served; only truthful communication about beneficial activities could command public support. He also espoused a belief in the two-way function of public relations, contending that the public relations practitioner must act as the agent for the public inside the councils of the company and that public relations must be based on management's policies, if for no other reason than that public opinion could become law. Therefore, public relations had figured in the development of the financial policy, and the policy served as the foundation for AT&T's public relations. Finally, Page stressed the importance of character. The Information Department was not burdened with making money; rather, it was the custodian of the company's ideals. It owed it to the public to make sure management upheld the financial policy.

PUBLIC RELATIONS ACTIVITIES

Under Page's supervision, AT&T used advertising, publicity, motion pictures, speeches, employee magazines, brochures, international expositions, and other media to promote its services and improve its reputation. Roland Marchand (1998) describes AT&T, with its advertising agency N. W. Ayer, as an important innovator in institutional advertising, which aimed to imbue huge corporations with a soul. In 1927, the campaign ran in 446 periodicals with a total circulation of 44 million at a cost of about $1 million. A favorite publicity tactic was the "first call ceremony," which celebrated the opening of a new line or the use of some new technology developed at Bell Laboratories. Page's predecessor at AT&T, James Ellsworth, originated both of these tactics, but Page brought them closer in line with management policies and raised the company's ethical standards.

Although he headed AT&T's public relations, Page's influence extended to the rest of the Bell System as well. AT&T was essentially a holding company, while its Associated Companies (such as Wisconsin Bell or New England Telephone) and its own Long Lines division handled local and long-distance operations, respectively. Western Electric was the manufacturing division, and Bell Laboratories the research division. With Page's encouragement, these companies staffed Information Departments of their own, with as many as 400 public relations officers employed in AT&T subsidiaries by 1938.

Because of his desire to advocate for the public, Page relied on opinion research, but AT&T treated different publics differently. Page commissioned annual surveys to identify trends in public opinion and encouraged the Associated Companies to conduct research, too. Just before World War II, for example, New York Telephone found that its customers wanted the company to place memo pads in all public telephone booths. Therefore, by 1943 the company had supplied memo pads to more than 2,000 booths. Yet the Bell System did not treat its employees' opinions with the same regard. The companies used such tactics as employee stock plans, company unions, and medical benefits to keep workers happy, and the Information Department implemented attitude surveys, analysis of discussion in company union meetings, and interpersonal and mass communication information campaigns. But the companies did not take workers' desires into consideration when making management decisions. For example, Bell policy during the Great Depression was to lay off employees or cut their hours, whereas AT&T continued to pay its traditional $9 stockholders' dividend—despite the fact that earnings could not support it.

The Depression caused other problems for Page and AT&T. By the 1930s the system controlled the telecommunications industry. AT&T controlled the only significant long-distance network, Bell accounted for 80 percent of the telephones in the United States, and it owned more than 9,000 patents. Because of AT&T's dominance, Congress empowered the Federal Communications Commission (FCC) to investigate the telephone industry in 1935. Page was personally investigated because, in addition to being a vice president of AT&T, in 1927 he had been made president of Bell Securities, a subsidiary that sold stock to the public and Bell System employees. The FCC reported on its investigation in 1939, but it failed to spur public criticism or congressional action against the company—or Page.

When one of the commissioners, a Harvard economics instructor, wrote a book criticizing AT&T, Page responded with his own book, *The Bell Telephone System* (1941), a plainspoken, methodical defense of company policies and activities. Page explained the financial policy and how it affected the company's mission to serve, including the public relations function. Harper Brothers published 30,000 hardbound copies; R. R. Donnelley and Son sold nearly 150,000 more in paperback.

Arthur W. Page's book, The Bell Telephone System (1941), explained the company's financial policy and how it affected the company's mission to serve, including the public relations function. Nearly 200,000 copies of the book were sold in hardcover and in paperback.

SOURCE: Property of AT&T Archives. Reprinted with permission of AT&T.

AFTER AT&T

During World War II, Page served the U.S. government as well as AT&T. Although he declined an offer to become an assistant to Secretary of War Henry Stimson, he did agree to serve on the Joint Army and Navy Committee on Welfare and Recreation. While directing AT&T's Information Department, he was also the War Department's de facto public relations counsel. For example, in 1944 he went to England to help prepare the troops for D-Day; later he conducted a study of the War Department's Bureau of Public Relations, recommending sweeping changes, many of which were adopted by the army and the navy. He also counseled Secretary Stimson on the use of the atomic bomb, and he wrote the news release handed out by President Harry S. Truman's press secretary announcing its use in Hiroshima, Japan.

After the war, Page returned full-time to AT&T, but he retired in 1947 at the age of 63. Still, Page's work was hardly over. He opened a consulting agency and cultivated an impressive client list, including AT&T, Kennecott Copper, Prudential Insurance, International Telephone and Telegraph, Continental Oil, Chase National Bank, Consolidated Edison, and Champion Paper. Page did not want to build an agency—he hired only a secretary—but simply to advise management on public relations. He also continued to volunteer for numerous philanthropic organizations. The counsel he gave all of these clients was consistent with the approach he had implemented at AT&T.

One of Page's projects caused him to operate more circumspectly than usual. Beginning in 1950 he headed the Crusade for Freedom, the fundraising and publicity arm of Radio Free Europe (RFE) and Free Europe Press. Noel Griese (2001) reports that the crusade sent out millions of flyers, leaflets, brochures, handbills, and the like, raising more than $1 million in its first year—but its costs almost equaled that. In its second year, the crusade actually spent more than it collected. Yet public officials seemed not to mind. In fact, RFE was funded mostly by the Central Intelligence Agency. Griese concludes that the Crusade for Freedom was simply a propaganda front working to convince the public of the importance of fighting communism in Korea and around the world. Page supported the crusade because he truly believed in the importance of its cause.

Page also continued to offer public service, especially in the field of transportation. Having switched political affiliation to the Republican Party, he helped with Dwight D. Eisenhower's presidential election campaign. Ike then invited him to chair an advisory subcommittee to the Presidential Advisory Committee on Transport Policy and Organization. Page also took part in a study of the New York–New Jersey transit. A frequent rider of the Long Island Railroad, Page was named project director by the Metropolitan Rapid Transit Commission in September 1955. The committee proposed a rapid transit loop linking New Jersey's commuter railroad network with Manhattan's subway system by means of two underwater tunnels.

Page's family also kept him busy. His four children produced 17 grandchildren, who often visited him at his Long Island estate. In March 1960, Page went to the hospital for the first of two surgeries for diverticulitis, a disease of the intestines and bladder, and he recovered enough to return to work in May. However, he returned to the hospital in August, and he died on September 5, 1960, in New York City.

Arthur W. Page represented the pinnacle of public relations professionalism. He was among the first members of the "Wisemen," a group of such luminaries as Pendleton Dudley, John W. Hill, T. J. Ross, James Selvage, Paul Garrett, and J. Carlisle MacDonald. This group included only those public relations professionals who had access to policymaking by their clients or employers—the same group that populates the Page Society today.

—*Karen Miller Russell*

Bibliography

Griese, N. L. (2001). *Arthur W. Page: Public relations pioneer, patriot.* Atlanta: Anvil.

Marchand, R. (1998). *Creating the corporate soul: The rise of public relations and corporate imagery in American big business.* Berkeley: University of California Press.

Page, A. W. (1920). *Our 110 days' fighting.* Garden City, NY: Doubleday.

Page, A. W. (1941). *The Bell Telephone system.* New York: Harper.

Russell, K. M. *The politics of public relations: Arthur W. Page, AT&T, and strategic corporate communications.* (Manuscript in preparation)

PAMPHLET

A pamphlet is a printed piece of collateral material used for public relations, advertising, and marketing purposes. Also called a brochure, a pamphlet is a communication tool or tactic and a form of direct media (like fliers, newsletters, and posters), which reach audiences through distribution channels other than mass media (newspapers, magazines, radio, television). A pamphlet is generally considered a simple form of a brochure, but some designers and practitioners consider *pamphlet* and *brochure* synonymous terms.

Pamphlets are commonly distributed to a target audience interpersonally, in information racks, and through the mail in a standard business envelope or as a self-mailer. To be effective, pamphlets must be strategically sound, which means they need to be targeted toward a particular audience, convey an overall key message, and attempt to achieve a specific objective. Some of the most commonly used objectives in public relations include increasing awareness about a specific organization and educating the target audience about a specific service or product.

Every organization, whether corporate or nonprofit, needs pamphlets or brochures to convey key messages to particular target audiences. A pamphlet is a tactic with a specific objective. For example, pamphlets can be used to inform utility customers about a fee increase, explain sexual harassment polices to employees, or persuade community members to volunteer for a neighborhood cleanup.

Although not considered as elaborate as brochures, pamphlets are produced in a variety of styles, shapes, and sizes. One popular format is an 8½ × 11 inch sheet folded in half, making four printed panels. Another format often used in public relations is a simple two-fold, six-panel, 8½ × 11 pamphlet. Pamphlets need to be created with a unifying design throughout the entire publication, which can be conveyed through an appropriate choice of typeface, line rules, screens and tints, consistent clip art, and color schemes. Since pamphlets communicate information to a single reader at a hand-held distance, they also need to offer an orderly sequence of information. The information is presented in stages through panels, and a common design visually connects all of the panels and holds the reader's attention.

Pamphlets are commonly printed in one or two colors, usually black for the type and another color to highlight specific areas. Some public relations practitioners begin with a layout and copy for a pamphlet and then work with a designer or printer to develop the final printed piece. Other practitioners create the entire piece themselves using any number of desktop publishing programs, such as PageMaker, QuarkXpress, and Microsoft Publisher.

—Emma Daugherty Phillingane

See also Brochure; Collateral

Bibliography

Diggs-Brown, B., & Glou, J. L. G. (2004). *The PR style guide: Formats for public relations practice.* Belmont, CA: Wadsworth.

Williams, R., & Tollett, J. (2001). *Robin Williams design workshop.* Berkeley, CA: Peachpit Press.

PARENT/STUDENT NEWSLETTER

A parent/student newsletter is a highly popular public relations tactic in the communication plan of individual schools and school districts. Defined as a two-way asymmetric, segmented, public relations tactic, a parent/student newsletter is designed to not only communicate the key messages of a school or school district to its key publics, but to also give the key publics a glimpse of life inside the walls of the educational system.

To understand the dynamics of the parent/student newsletter, the first step would be to break down the definition and examine its three main components: *two-way asymmetric communication, segmented*

audience, and *tactic.* However, to achieve a complete definition, one must simultaneously examine the parent newsletter and the student newsletter as two separate entities. Although one publication can, and often does, serve two different publics, often they are two publications serving two different publics.

The characteristic of being segmented means that, unlike the local newspaper, which is sent to a mass audience, the parent/student newsletter is delivered to a targeted list of people who have a vested interest in the organization. For example, some school districts send their parent newsletter to all taxpayers, believing that only the taxpayer has an interest in what is happening in the school, whereas others send their newsletter to every household in the school district, believing that everyone in the community has a vested interest in the state of education. When looking at student newsletters, the mailing list may be segmented to include current students or to include recent graduates.

Newsletters have been referred to as being "moderately interactive" because the audience, having a vested interest in the information, tends to be willing to supply feedback in the form of letters, phone calls, or e-mails. However, the parent newsletter is a good example of a two-way asymmetric tactic because there is a two-way communication between sender and receiver but the communication has an imbalanced effect, with the school district's or individual school's main purpose being to persuade its key publics of the value of the institution. The well-written, proactive parent newsletter will act as the school district's voice when the local media are running unfavorable stories or editorials regarding a particular issue. Although contacts are made with community papers, the real substance of a district's public relations efforts is verbalized in a quality parent newsletter.

However, this may not be true of a student newsletter. A true student newsletter, although most likely edited by an adult faculty member, is written by students for students, and in this format would be an example of the public information model of public relations. The purpose of the student newsletter is to disseminate information regarding the activities in school, whether academic or extracurricular.

There is little research or persuasion that occurs, and the nature of the communication is one-way.

A tactic is a specific action that is taken to fulfill an objective. A parent/student newsletter is one of a number of tactics available to the public relations professional. In addition to a Web site, it is a standard tactic in a school district's or individual school's communication plan and can include articles on budgetary decisions, contract negotiations, extracurricular activities, curriculum changes/additions, and classroom/school highlights.

—Kristine A. Parkes

See also Newsletter; Web site

Bibliography

Wilson, L. J. (2000). *Strategic program planning for effective public relations campaigns.* Dubuque, IA: Kendall/Hunt.

PARKE, ISOBEL

Isobel Parke (1926–) is president and senior counsel of Jackson, Jackson, & Wagner, one of the most well-known consulting firms in the United States. Parke stands out in public relations history for her wide breadth of contributions to the field since the 1960s. She has helped to increase professionalism of the practice and champion undergraduate public relations education. In particular, she has contributed to the development of modern-day strategic environmental communication and coalition building. Her ability to balance her commitments to public relations as a democratic process, to educational issues, and to environmental concerns makes her a role model for today's young women entering public relations. "Even though we didn't consider ourselves feminists, per se, we wanted equal opportunity," Parke said of women like herself working in public relations 35 years ago, "and we were prepared to work for that" (Parke, personal communication, 2003).

Parke's first foray into the practice of public relations occurred when she was in her early thirties and had the opportunity to help organize and promote the New England Pavilion at the 1964 World's Fair in New York. She had met Miriam Jackson and Patrick Jackson through mutual acquaintances and began to work for Jackson, Jackson, & Wagner, which was responsible for organizing and marketing the exhibition. She helped collect objects that represented New England from museums and then promoted the items through the media to attract fair attendees. She learned to work with media through trial and error. (She once sent a *Boston Globe* reporter a promotional photograph in a large, thick, blue paper "mat" frame in response to him requesting a "matte" finished photograph.)

After the Fair, Parke moved with Patrick Jackson and Miriam Jackson, owners and operators of Jackson, Jackson, & Wagner, to a 1735 farmhouse in New Hampshire. They grew their own fruits and vegetables and raised pigs while working for mostly nonprofit organizations. Parke's first client was a financially challenged repertory company. Parke helped the organization increase its audience base, but she also found herself placating creditors and electric companies that wanted to shut down the organization.

In the 1960s, Parke spearheaded Jackson, Jackson, & Wagner's statewide effort to build an environmental coalition to change an article in New Hampshire's constitution that allowed corporations to clear forests for purposes of business development. Parke brought together garden clubs, parent-teacher associations, residents, environmental organizations, and local businesses and politicians. This coalition helped establish state limitations and restrictions on land use, and it became a model for advocacy campaigns for the environment. Parke continues to serve on the coalition to maintain the amendment for open space.

Parke has described herself as "the inner wheel" (Parke, personal communication, August 5, 2003) of Jackson, Jackson, & Wagner, a behind-the-scenes motivator for Patrick Jackson's vision of strategic management. Although most of Parke's initial clients were nonprofit organizations, she began working with corporations who were seeking to better understand citizen groups and environmental advocacy. Parke said, "The first responsibility of public relations is to consider the public good" (Parke, personal communication, August 5, 2003). For almost 40 years, Parke's expertise has been built on issue anticipation and analysis, community coalition building, strategic planning, and crisis containment. She has counseled environmental coalitions on land conservation, health-care organizations on mergers and restructuring, and the private school sector on crisis communication. She explained part of her work philosophy: "It's important to have a holistic grasp of the historical and societal issues before working on public relations solutions" (Parke, personal communication, August 5, 2003).

Parke has enhanced professional development for public relations as a management function through her service to the Public Relations Society of America (PRSA). Parke is an accredited member and fellow of PRSA, served as a director of PRSA's national board from 1986 to 1987, and served as national board secretary in 1988. She was a founding member of PRSA's Yankee Chapter, which constitutes members from Maine, New Hampshire, and Vermont. It was these activities in PRSA that led to her passion for public relations education.

In 1986, Parke was appointed PRSA board liaison to the Public Relations Student Society of America (PRSSA). She recalled, "At the time I had an 18 year old step-daughter. I had little confidence in dealing with several thousand teenagers all at once!" However, she agreed to the position and attended her first PRSSA board meeting. The students at the meeting were surprised to see her because professional liaisons rarely attended their meetings. However, Parke wanted to familiarize herself with the students as well as the organization. She recounts the moment when she walked into the board meeting: "Arriving a little late, I walked in and there was a wary silence. They asked, 'Who are you?' I said, 'I'm your board liaison.' After a moment, they brought me a chair and we got to work" (Parke, personal communication, August 5, 2003). For the next two years she helped PRSSA with decisions and strategies for the benefit of its student members.

Parke was a 2002 recipient of the David W. Ferguson Award presented by the PRSA Educators Academy, which honors practitioners who have made significant contributions to advancing the profession through their support of public relations education. She was also a member of PRSA's Educational Affairs Committee (1992–2002), represented PRSA on the Accrediting Council on Education in Journalism and Mass Communications (1997–2003), and has been a member of PRSA's Commission on Public Relations Education (1997–present).

Along with this active career in public relations, Parke built a reputation for public service in New Hampshire. She is the first woman president of the New Hampshire Timberland Owners Association and president of the Rockingham County Woodland Owners Association. She is a member of several other organizations, including the Rockingham County Visiting Nurse Association and Hospice, the SPACE Board of Directors and Legislation Committee, the Epping Conservation Committee, and the Seacoast Growers Association.

Parke is an award-winning conservationist and for almost 40 years has worked to preserve New Hampshire's land and timber industry. She has operated and cared for Tributary Farm since first moving there in 1964. The farm was originally 61 acres, but in 1992 Parke and Patrick Jackson purchased over 100 acres adjacent to the property to save the land from possible real estate development. In 2002, the New Hampshire Tree Farm Executive Committee named Parke the New Hampshire Outstanding Tree Farmer of the Year. To be eligible for the award, Parke had to meet specific objectives within 5 years that were set forth in an action plan written by her. Her objectives included improving the harvesting quality of mixed timber species, encouraging wildlife, and providing recreational enjoyment. Parke makes Tributary Farm an educational experience for college students who come to work and for kindergarten children who come to explore. She also frequently testifies before the New Hampshire legislature on a variety of forestry issues, such as licenses and use of wood-burning plants. She has won the John Hoar Award by the Rockingham County Woodland Owners Association and the Kendall Norcott Award, the highest recognition from the New Hampshire Timberland

Owners Association. Finally, Parke is president-elect for the Granite State Woodland Institute. She said, "With ownership of land comes the responsibility of good stewardship for the next generation" (Parke, personal communication, August 5, 2003).

Born in a country village called Sturminster Marshall in Dorset, England, Parke received her high school degree in Boston from the Winsor School. She returned to England for her master's in modern history from Oxford University. After graduation, she worked for 12 years as manager of education programs at Moor Park College, an experimental adult education college. She was married to Patrick Jackson from 1974 to 1994 and remained an integral partner in his life and work until his death in March 2001. Parke said that she gave Jackson "the partnership he needed to establish for our profession the vision and the challenge of behavioral public relations" (Parke, personal communication, August 5, 2003).

—*Linda Aldoory*

See also Public Relations Society of America; Public Relations Student Society of America

Bibliography

David W. Ferguson Award. (2002). Retrieved September 23, 2003, from lamar.colostate.edu/~pr/ferguson.htm

Jackson, Jackson, & Wagner. (2003). Web site. Retrieved September 23, 2003, from www.jjwpr.com

Lent, C. (2002). *Epping conservationist earns statewide award.* Retrieved September 23, 2003, from www.seacoastonline.com/2002news/exeter/04232002/news/1109.htm

PARKER, GEORGE

George Frederick Parker is important in the history of public relations primarily because he and Ivy Lee formed one of the early public relations firms, Parker & Lee, in late 1904 and he was publicity manager to President Grover Cleveland during three presidential campaigns.

Parker was a man with connections. He had a way with people in high places, particularly in politics and business. If he didn't know a person, he knew someone who did. There were only two degrees of separation between Parker and any person of significance. It was not that he did not have journalistic skills; he had quite a background in the newspaper business. It was just that his ability to never meet a stranger, to know and influence people, was his greatest gift and his real value.

Today, such people are negatively called "schmoozers" because they attend key cocktail parties and effectively work the room. Still, such people are often a valuable commodity to executing both simple and complex campaigns. Parker would have to be called a superschmoozer because of the powerful people in his circle of acquaintances and his ability to persuade and convince them to take the actions he suggested.

Parker was born in Indiana on December 30, 1847. He lived much of his young life in Iowa, where his father had a farm. His interest in politics and journalism was apparent when he, at 26, founded the *Indianola Tribune,* a Democratic Party weekly in Iowa. When he was 29, he sold the newspaper and, for some years, wrote for other newspapers and studied in Germany. He returned to the United States and worked for the Democratic National Committee on the 1880 campaign in Indiana. During those years, he met Grover Cleveland and worked for him in the Pennsylvania campaign for the successful presidential election of 1884. Cleveland and Parker, during the election, developed mutual respect and a friendship. Cleveland asked Parker to prepare the campaign book for the party for the 1888 election. This was a secret task that meant Parker had to move to Washington, D.C., and work in the White House. The book was actually a brag book about the accomplishments of the Democratic administration. After he completed the book, Parker was transferred to New York to the party's national headquarters to work in the publicity department. Cleveland lost to Benjamin Harrison, and Parker was unhappy at the loss and how the campaign was run; he vowed that Cleveland would win in 1892.

Parker accepted a position as editor of the *New York Saturday Globe,* and for the 4 years between the elections he began to build Cleveland's reputation.

Cleveland did not like publicity or the press and was not effective at building relationships with politicians. Some historians say he lost the election to Harrison because he "suffered more from the newspapers than any other president" (Pollard, 1947, p. 499).

Relationship building being Parker's forte, he wrote a speech for Cleveland to deliver in Boston. In those days, speeches were mailed to newspapers to print, since there were no television or radio broadcasts. Parker and Cleveland disagreed over the distribution of the speech. Cleveland, since he disliked and feared the press, wanted it to go out only 5 days in advance and only to a few carefully selected newspapers, whereas Parker wanted it to go out 7 days in advance and sent to newspapers all over the country. Parker won the argument, and the speech was positively received. In 1892, Cleveland won the most decisive presidential victory in the 20 preceding years, winning swing states as well as traditionally Republican states. It made the bond between Parker and Cleveland, now built on trust, even stronger. That same year, Parker selected, edited, and wrote the introduction for Cleveland's *The Writings and Speeches of Grover Cleveland.*

Cleveland never made Parker a member of his presidential or White House staff, but he kept him close. He did make him U.S. counsel in Birmingham, England, and Parker worked there until the Republicans and McKinley won the White House. Then, he returned to the United States to head the publicity for the National Democratic Committee for the 1904 election. Upon his return, he learned about a young man who had won praise working for the 1903 New York mayoral election, Ivy Ledbetter Lee, a former *New York Times* reporter. Parker asked Lee to work for the National Democratic Committee. They worked on the campaign for Alton Parker. During that time Parker introduced Lee to numerous important figures, and Lee was impressed. When the Republicans won with Theodore Roosevelt, Parker asked Lee to join him as partner in a new publicity firm, which became Parker & Lee.

The nation's third public relations agency, Parker & Lee had offices adjacent to the New York Stock Exchange in either late 1904 or early 1905. Parker was 57 and Lee was 26. The two never did get along well. Historians agree that it was partly their age and partly their working styles. Parker was definitely the boss, and Lee, young as he was, did not appreciate taking orders from Parker. Many historians also agree that they probably took separate clients.

Their first client was General Asphalt Company, whose investors were worried about its solvency. Lee took on the task of informing the company's publics of the facts. Parker had financier Thomas Fortune Ryan as a client. Ryan had made many millions on the New York streetcar and subway lines and had donated nearly half a million dollars to the Alton Parker presidential campaign when Parker was heading it. He wanted to be kept out of the news, and Parker was happy to comply.

No matter how they did their business, they managed to gain from the press a reputation of honest and responsible information dissemination. Their credo was "Accuracy, Authenticity, and Interest." *Editor and Publisher,* then very critical of public relations, praised them. Beginning in the Alton Parker campaign, their press releases were printed like newspaper stories in columns and disseminated on galley sheets. This made them easy to read, and newspaper editors could use them without having to retype them, especially since Parker and Lee, former newsmen themselves, wrote them in accurate, journalistic newspaper style, unlike many political publicity stories of the time.

Lee acquired the Pennsylvania Railroad as a client in 1906 and then left the firm and took a job as director of publicity for the railroad. It was after Lee departed that he wrote his destined-to-be-famous Declaration of Principles, but there is little doubt that the ideals he and Parker followed led him to write it. There is also little doubt that Parker introduced Lee to key people that helped make his career successful.

Parker continued to do political legwork for Grover Cleveland after his presidency. In 1905, when the Equitable Life Assurance Society wanted to bring trust and prestige to their company at a time when the muckrakers were writing inflammatory pieces about corruption in the insurance business, Parker convinced Cleveland to accept an unpaid position as head of Equitable's board of trustees. As an apparent reward, Parker was made secretary to the trustees, a salaried position he held until 1909, but there is no published evidence of the work he performed.

Parker, in 1908, formed a partnership, Parker & Bridge, with Charles A. Bridge, who had been a newspaper editor at the *New York Herald* and was also office manager for Parker & Lee. Little is known about their business, but it folded in 1913. Parker continued to work. He was secretary of press and publicity for the Committee of the Protestant Episcopal Church from 1913 until 1919 and had various other jobs as political and press counselor until he died in 1928 at 81. In death as in life, he made connections; financier Ryan was a pallbearer at his funeral.

—Kathleen Fearn-Banks

Bibliography

Cleveland, G. (1892). *The writings and speeches of Grover Cleveland.* New York: Cassell; Kraus Reprint, 1970.

Cutlip, S. M. (1995). *Public relations history: From the 17th to the 20th century. The antecedents.* Hillsdale, NJ: Lawrence Erlbaum.

Cutlip, S. M. (1994). *The unseen power: Public relations. A history.* Hillsdale, NJ: Lawrence Erlbaum.

Hiebert, R. E. (1966). *Courtier to the crowd: The story of Ivy Lee and the development of public relations.* Ames: Iowa State Press.

Pollard, J. (1947). *The president and the press.* New York: Macmillan.

PASTER, HOWARD G.

Howard G. Paster, a veteran Washington lobbyist and political strategist who became global chairman and CEO of Hill & Knowlton in 1994, achieved distinction in the public affairs realm for overseeing a dramatic turnaround at one of the world's largest communications consulting firms. In restoring the reputation of Hill & Knowlton, which had endured a period of intense controversy due to missteps by its previous leadership, Paster projected an ethic of rigorous integrity. While many other CEOs in the 1990s succumbed to the swaggering spirit of the decade's economic boom, Paster inspired his colleagues by emphasizing integrity, counseling patience, and insisting on professionalism.

Paster, born December 23, 1944, completed his undergraduate degree at Alfred State College in history and political science in 1966. Later, he earned an MS from the Columbia Graduate School of Journalism.

Paster came to Hill & Knowlton from the Clinton administration, where, as the director of the White House Office of Legislative Liaison and the president's chief lobbyist on Capitol Hill, he had succeeded in winning congressional approval of two dramatic measures: a comprehensive federal deficit-reduction package and the North American Free Trade Agreement. Those victories required all the skill that Paster had built up during a lifetime in politics: as an aide to Congressman Lester Wolff of New York and Senator Birch Bayh of Indiana, and as a lobbyist for the United Auto Workers and for Timmons & Company. The bruising political battles over deficit reduction and NAFTA were severe tests of the Clinton administration's tenacity, and Paster's success in achieving those economic-policy breakthroughs helped lay the foundation for the strong U.S. economy of the later 1990s.

Engineering a turnaround at Hill & Knowlton posed a corporate challenge every bit as complex as the political struggles Paster had known on Capitol Hill. In the late 1980s and early 1990s, the firm took on lobbying clients that many viewed as inappropriate. The firm's public embarrassment over its client selection had damaged both its public standing and its internal esprit de corps. Combined with the after-effects of the early-1990s recession—which had momentarily damaged the firm's flow of revenue and made it difficult to retain top talent—the situation posed a stern test of Hill & Knowlton's resilience.

With its morale shaken, the firm needed more than the routine corporate steps of cost-cutting and talent development. Paster knew that an entirely new corporate culture had to be instilled throughout the firm, as a fundamental step in overcoming the firm's reputation problem. Embodying a theory that

Hill & Knowlton would later impress on its corporate clients—the theory of "the CEO as standard-bearer"—Paster knew that integrity, to be (and to be perceived as) authentic, had to flow from the top down.

Starting with his early conversations with the firm's leaders, Paster closely vetted the roster of clients, ensuring that they could withstand the harshest scrutiny. He developed a new Code of Professional Conduct—prominently posted at every office throughout Hill & Knowlton's international network—and he insisted that all senior corporate leaders personally sign the document. He tirelessly traveled to meet with the firm's regional presidents and senior managers, inspiring them with his personal concern for sound ethical standards. By delivering ethics-focused speeches at a new series of leadership conferences and workshops—called "H&K Colleges"—in the United States and Europe, he ensured that integrity would be the hallmark of the firm's rising generation of talent.

Paster propelled his credo both internally through the management ranks and externally through steady reputation-building initiatives. He worked closely with the regional presidents within the worldwide firm to make sure they shared and would promote his vision of elevating the entire public relations profession's standards. And by encouraging his clients and colleagues to speak out forcefully on public concerns as well as professional matters, Paster raised the firm's visibility in the news media—in both mainstream publications and the trade press—and helped win recognition for Hill & Knowlton as an idealistic practitioner of public relations and public affairs strategies.

During almost a decade as Hill & Knowlton's global chairman (1994–2002) and CEO—before being chosen as executive vice president of the parent WPP Group, where he went on to oversee all of the holding company's public relations and public affairs agencies—Paster single-mindedly focused on restoring the firm's renown for integrity. His willpower and perseverance ensured that the firm again earned public recognition for having the highest standards of integrity and living up to the public-spirited legacy of John W. Hill—the creator of the modern-day public relations profession and the founder of Hill & Knowlton.

—*Tom Hoog*

PENNEY, PAT

In 1966, Patricia Penney Bennett (known professionally as Pat Penney) became the first women to chair the Public Relations Society of America's (PRSA) Counselor's Academy, and she was the only woman to lead PRSA's first special interest group during the group's first two decades of existence.

At the 1965 Denver PRSA conference, Penney was nominated to become vice chair of the then-fledgling, 5-year-old group. She was then designated to become chair the following year. Male chauvinism so pervaded the practice at the time that a Detroit counselor rose to block Penney's nomination because she was a woman. Following a raucous discussion, the assembled members voted down the challenge. Penney's nomination was a milestone event in women's efforts to acquire greater prominence in the field.

Penney had served in 1965 as the first woman president of PRSA's Los Angeles chapter. She later became PRSA's national secretary in 1969.

A 1948 journalism graduate of the University of Kansas, Penney began her public relations career in the publicity department of Jerry Fairbanks Production in Hollywood and later became assistant news bureau director at the California Institute of Technology. She later became account director at the Harry Bennett agency and manager of corporate accounts for Communications Counselors, a subsidiary of McCann-Erickson.

She became a business partner with Harry Bennett, whom she married, and was president of Penney & Bennett, Inc. in Los Angeles from 1960 to 1973. The firm was a leading consultant in the emerging field of investor relations. Its prestigious client list included Prudential Insurance Company and Union Bank of California.

Following a brief stint as vice president of corporate relations at Summit Health, Ltd., in 1976 Penney opened her own firm, Pat Penney Public Relations, which she operated until the time of her death. Clients included her former employer, Summit Health, and leading Los Angeles financial institutions, consulting firms, charities, and philanthropic organizations.

Penney was active in and received awards from a variety of professional, business, and civic groups. From 1974 to 1988, she taught public relations part-time at the University of Southern California School of Journalism (now Annenberg School of Communications), where a public relations scholarship is established in her memory.

—*Kirk Hallahan*

PERJURY

Put simply, perjury is the crime of lying under oath. Although in common law it was considered a misdemeanor, today perjury is usually classified as a felony under both state and federal statutes. Government bodies at all levels depend on the truthfulness of sworn testimony for decision making and proper functioning. By undermining the integrity of these governmental processes, perjury constitutes a serious offence against the state. Subordination of perjury, a related offense, occurs when one person convinces another to commit perjury.

To secure a conviction for perjury, a prosecutor must show that the defendant knowingly made a false statement of material fact while under oath. A person who gives untruthful testimony because of confusion or poor memory does not have the willful intent necessary for perjury. Furthermore, statements are considered "material" only if they could have affected the proceeding's outcome. For example, a witness to a traffic accident who lies about his or her annual income has probably not committed perjury because the false testimony does not pertain directly to an element of the offense. However, a defendant charged with federal income tax evasion would be guilty of perjury for giving the same false statement regarding his or her yearly earnings.

Although the law prohibits all citizens from committing perjury, public relations practitioners in particular must be scrupulously honest when engaged in lobbying activities or when otherwise testifying before government entities. As a criminal offense, perjury carries serious legal consequences. Perjury is also unethical under the Public Relations Society of America's *Member Code of Ethics* as adopted in 2000, which counsels practitioners not only to "adhere to the highest standards of accuracy and truth," but also to "maintain the integrity of relationships with . . . government officials" (2003, p. B16).

Alger Hiss's two perjury trials (1949 and 1950) are still considered among a handful of United States "trials of the century." Hiss, a seasoned government official whose professional experience ranged from secretary to Supreme Court justice Oliver Wendell Holmes and attorney with the New Deal to aiding the formation of the United Nations and serving as president of the Carnegie Endowment for International Peace, was charged by magazine editor and former Communist Party member Whittaker Chambers with supplying government documents to the Russians in the 1930s. Hiss denied the charges, and though the statute of limitations didn't allow for espionage charges to be filed, he was indicted on two counts of perjury in December 1948. A hung jury in 1949 forced a second trial in 1950, in which Hiss was found guilty and sentenced to a 5-year prison term. Although Hiss maintained his innocence until his death in 1996, Soviet files made public that same year provided evidence of Hiss's guilt, but controversy lingers.

Lobbyists found guilty of perjury have tarnished the profession's reputation. For example, public relations practitioner Michael K. Deaver, a former top White House aide to President Reagan, was convicted of perjury in 1988. After leaving government service in 1985, Deaver started a lobbying firm whose clients included foreign governments and major corporations. Within a year of his departure from the White House, Deaver was found guilty of lying to a federal grand jury and a congressional subcommittee about his contacts with Reagan

Senator Karl Mundt (R) of South Dakota, who was acting chairman of the House Un-American Activities Committee (HUAC) when the first testimony on the Alger Hiss–Whitaker Chambers investigation was heard, is shown in his office scanning the headlines that tell him of the jury's January 21, 1950, verdict in Hiss's second perjury trial. Chambers, a senior editor from Time *magazine and an admitted ex-communist, identified Hiss and several other federal officials to HUAC as having been members of a communist cell whose purpose had been to infiltrate the U.S. government. The conviction made Hiss liable to a maximum sentence of 10 years in prison and fines totaling $4,000.*

SOURCE: © Bettmann/CORBIS.

administration officials on his clients' behalf, in violation of the Federal Ethics in Government Act. Although Deaver faced a possible 15-year prison term, the court sentenced him to 3 years' probation and ordered him to pay a $100,000 fine and perform 1,500 hours of community service.

—Nicole B. Cásarez

See also Ethics of public relations; Lobbying; Public Relations Society of America

Bibliography

Hersh, A., & Lipschultz, J. (2003). Perjury. *American Criminal Law Review, 40,* 907–932.

Linder, D. (2003). *The trials of Alger Hiss: A chronology.* Available: http://www.law.umkc.edu/faculty/projects/ftrials/hiss/hisschronology.html

Pertman, A. (1988, September 14). Deaver is sentenced; gets suspended 3-year term, $100,000 fine. *Boston Globe,* p. A1.

Public Relations Society of America (2003). *Public relations tactics: The blue book.* New York: Author.

PERSONAL NEWS STORY

See Human interest

PERSPECTIVISM THEORY

The claim that "it is all subjective" is almost commonplace among individuals in the 21st century. This claim reinforces the assumption that one's knowledge is self-reflexive; that is, it both *affects* one's perceptions and talk and *is affected by* one's perceptions and talk. This is generally talked about as the "problem of knowledge" or the "epistemic problem" and is referenced by the question "how do you know what you know?" Often, beliefs are informed by family, friends, science, religion, social connections, and education level, among other things; ultimately, much of what is accepted as knowledge is based on a person's perception about what exists and about what is deemed "true." Often disagreements between people are explained as the differences between their individual perspectives. The theoretical names of this problem include, among other names, *perspectivism theory*, a term that encompasses multiple philosophical and theoretical concepts.

The rubric of perspectivism theory can be divided into two different epistemological camps: radical perspectivism and perspective realism. Radical perspectivism presumes that either there is nothing "out there" or that the only thing that matters is one's individually constructed meaning of what may or may not be "out there." Radical perspectivism assumes that meaning, reality, and knowledge are constructed through language and that they have no correspondence to anything that may exist apart from the knower. The Greek sophists introduced radical perspectivism into ancient philosophy, and Frederick Nietzsche popularized it for contemporary philosophy. Robert Scott (1967, 1976) and Barry Brummett (1976) introduced radical perspectivism into the study of human communication with their discussions about rhetoric-as-epistemic and the concept of intersubjectivism. The ancient sophists and Nietzsche argue that humans are essentially solipsistic and cannot know anything other than what is experienced and known in their own head.

Perspective realism, on the other hand, assumes that a knowable reality exists apart from the knower but that humans have a finite understanding of and differing views about that reality. Thus, differences exist because people have differing perspectives on reality, rather than that people have different realities. This may sound like semantic games, but the difference between the two statements is significant because the differences are still held together by what is deemed the common ground of the actual but never fully knowable reality. Perspective realism was introduced into ancient philosophy, it can be argued, by Isocrates and Aristotle and has been explained to a modernist audience by Evander Bradley McGilvary (1956). This concept was adapted to the study of communication by Richard Cherwitz and James W. Hikins (1986) when they introduced rhetorical perspectivism and philosophical realism to the study of human symbolic interaction. Cherwitz and Hikins incorporated McGilvary's ideas when they contended that differences in knowledge are analogous to the differences that two people would give when they describe the same mountain from two different sides. They are seeing the same physical object but describing it in two different ways because each has a perspective that is limited by the geographical view of the same object. Another example of perspective realism is Kenneth Burke's concept of "terministic screens." Burke (1966) argued that the language humans use helps them to both explain what is experienced and to determine what will be experienced. Burke does not go as far as the radical perspectivists to argue against the existence of a reality that is external to the knower, but he does contend that our "observations" are as much a result of the particular terminology in which the observations were made as they are of the

object observed. Thus, we are affected as much by the language we use as by an external reality.

What application does this have for the study of public relations? Here the possibilities are almost limitless. One simple possibility is the basic understanding of a public. Is a public (or a consumer group) something that is discovered, or is it something that is created? The radical perspectivists would argue that a public is only created by how one talks about it; the perspective realists would argue that there is a particular public that is "discovered" rather than created but that practitioners will differ in how they view or understand it because of the language they use to describe it and the various epistemological and historical backgrounds (i.e., perspectives) of those who are describing the public.

Similar distinctions apply to those who are on the receiving end of the public relations message. The radical perspectivists would argue that each individual recipient of a public relations message will understand the message in radically different ways because each audience member has a different reality and no one can exert any control over that "reality." The perspective realist would argue that even though each audience member may have a different perspective on the message or product or service that is presented, there is enough common ground from the external reality that impinges on each of them that all audience members will have something in common in how they understand a message. Thus, there is a difference between the audience members, but the difference is limited. If the ad is about shoes, the perspectives will differ but no one will be thinking about elephants in India.

—*Mark A. Gring*

Bibliography

Brummett, B. (1976). Some implications of "process" or "intersubjectivity": Postmodern rhetoric. *Philosophy and Rhetoric, 9,* 21–51.

Burke, K. (1966). *Language as symbolic action.* Berkeley: University of California Press.

Cherwitz, R. A., & Hikins, J. W. (1986). *Communication and knowledge: An investigation in rhetorical epistemology.* Columbia: University of South Carolina Press.

McGilvary, E. B. (1956). *Toward a perspective realism* (Vol. 5). La Salle, IL: Open Court.

Scott, R. L. (1967). On viewing rhetoric as epistemic. *Central States Speech Journal, 18,* 9–17.

Scott, R. L. (1976). On viewing rhetoric as epistemic: Ten years later. *Central States Speech Journal, 27,* 258–266.

PERSUASION THEORY

One of the main goals of public relations is to persuade an organization's target publics to adopt a certain attitude, opinion, or behavior. Whether a company is trying to increase its customer base, recruit employees, or enhance its image, the use of persuasion is key.

Persuasion is not a dirty word, although it is often confused with its "black sheep" cousin, *propaganda.* Whereas propaganda may use coercion, manipulation, and deception to convince people to think or act a certain way, persuasion does not try to take advantage of the public. Instead, people are presented with reasons why they should adopt an attitude, opinion, or behavior. It remains up to them whether they choose to accept these reasons and reevaluate their thinking.

The art of persuasion dates back thousands of years. It was Aristotle, however, who provided the basis for persuasive reasoning: ethos, logos, and pathos. To this day, these "modes of proof" are at the core of the public relations practice.

MODES OF PROOF

Aristotle described persuasion as an art of proving something true or false and identified three ways to offer such proof: through *ethos* (source credibility), *logos* (logical appeals) and *pathos* (emotional appeals).

Ethos

Ethos focuses on the credibility of the source delivering a message. Is the source considered to be ethical and believable? Source credibility directly impacts the effectiveness of an appeal. If a person delivering the message isn't believable, it doesn't matter what appeals are being used, so selecting an appropriate spokesperson is critical.

Ethos appeals are often made by using celebrity spokespeople, satisfied customers, and people who are perceived as peers to back a product or cause. Public relations practitioners should consider how their target public will perceive a spokesperson's integrity, expertise, reputation, and authority. Similarity to the audience and likability also are important characteristics, as can be physical attractiveness and charisma. For example, a musician popular with teenagers may be an appropriate spokesperson for that age group but would probably have little influence over senior citizens.

A public's opinion leaders may be good choices as message sources. Opinion leaders are respected people to whom others look for guidance. The balance (consonance) theory, which suggests that people consider their relationships with others when listening to and adopting information, provides support for using opinion leaders.

Logos

Logos refers to appeals based on logic and reason. These arguments usually consist of facts and figures, and they address an audience on a cognitive level. Public relations tactics aimed at educating a specific group of people most likely would focus on logos appeals. Such information would be communicated straightforwardly and objectively for the sole purpose of making that group of people aware of something.

Although strong factual information should be the foundation for any argument, facts and figures can't always stand alone because they lack inspiration and motivation.

Pathos

Pathos refers to arguments that are based on emotion—on arousing feelings such as fear, guilt, anger, humor, or compassion. Public relations practitioners use these appeals when their purpose is to motivate a group of people to think or do something in particular, such as buy a product or support a cause. Pathos appeals can be seen everywhere:

- A fundraising appeal to feed hungry children hopes to arouse compassion.

- A public service announcement about drunk driving targets guilt.
- A commercial for a home security alarm system seeks to arouse fear.
- An ad for diamonds focuses on love.

Pathos appeals are usually more effective when they are combined with logos appeals. For example, the fundraising appeal to feed hungry children cannot just focus on the faces of sad boys and girls; it must communicate how many children are in need, why they are in need, and what can be done to alleviate that need.

AUDIENCE SELF-INTEREST

Before developing a persuasive message, public relations practitioners must first determine which appeal or appeals to use to best reach their target public. This choice depends on the wants, interests, needs, concerns, and beliefs of the target public. Human beings share basic needs, such as food, shelter, and clothing. They also want many of the same things—success, love, and security. Interests and beliefs, however, vary among groups based on age, lifestyle, and other demographics.

The concepts of selective exposure and selective attention suggest that people only expose themselves and pay attention to information that is consistent with their self-interest; if they do not perceive that they are affected by information, they will selectively avoid it. For example, people shopping for a new car will be attracted to car ads more than people who are not in the market for a new vehicle.

Analyzing a target public to determine its wants, interests, and needs requires research, which may include examining census or marketing data; conducting polls, surveys, focus groups, or interviews; or evaluating lifestyles.

FRAMING MESSAGES

Once a target public's wants, interests, and needs are analyzed, a message can be written to address those wants, interests, and needs. Teenagers, who typically struggle to "belong," will be attracted to messages that promise to make them look "cool." Young professionals climbing the corporate ladder will be attracted to messages that promise success. Mothers will be attracted to messages that promise to make their children happy and healthy.

There are many persuasive techniques from which to choose, including testimonials and endorsements (ethos); surveys, examples, and other factual information (logos); and a variety of emotional appeals ranging from humor to fear to sex appeal (pathos). The key is to select the ones most appropriate for the target public based on the analysis that was conducted.

Take, for example, a target public consisting of parents of freshmen college students. They will be concerned about their child going away from home for the first time and will want to ensure his or her happiness and health. A college sending a message to these parents regarding the availability of refrigerators for dorm rooms may select from several persuasive tactics. If an ethos appeal is used, the message might be delivered by current students, who will share their stories about the necessity of a refrigerator. A logos appeal may focus on facts surrounding student lifestyles and offer statistics on how many freshmen usually have a refrigerator. A pathos appeal may stress how having access to a refrigerator will enable students to eat healthy foods, which would address a common concern of parents.

ETHICAL USE

Because there may sometimes be a fine line between persuasion and propaganda, public relations practitioners must understand the differences and implement persuasive tactics in an ethical manner.

One of the most important elements of persuasion is that the information must be true. Unlike propaganda, which distorts facts and exaggerates claims, persuasion should be based on information that an organization honestly believes to be true. If a company claims that a diet pill is responsible for its users losing 50 pounds in four weeks, that claim must be true; otherwise, the claim is deceptive.

Sources used to deliver persuasive messages must be sincere and relay genuine feelings and emotions, especially if one is giving a testimonial or endorsing a product.

There also is a difference between tailoring emotional appeals to an audience's self-interest, as is done in persuasion, and playing on emotional insecurities in an effort to manipulate the audience. Manipulation may benefit an organization, but it won't meet its public's needs. Extra care should be given when using fear or guilt appeals to make sure the severity of the appeal matches the interest of the public. The greater the target public perceives the fear, the more severe the appeal can be; moderate appeals should be used if the fear is perceived as moderate. Effective fear appeals tell the audience not only the degree and likelihood of harm, but also how to reduce the chances of the harm occurring.

Several values of the Member Code of Ethics developed by the Public Relations Society of America pertain to the ethical use of persuasion: honesty, or adhering to the highest standards of accuracy and truth; fairness, or focusing on free expression and supporting all opinions; and, advocacy, which stresses responsibility in supporting "informed debate."

—Ann R. Carden

See also Demographics; Motivation theory; Propaganda; Psychographics; Psychological processing; Public opinion and opinion leaders; Publics

Bibliography

Cutlip, S., Center, A., & Broom, G. (1999). *Effective public relations* (8th ed.). Upper Saddle River, NJ: Prentice Hall.

Hasling, J. (1997). *The audience, the message, the speaker* (6th ed.). New York: McGraw-Hill.

Smith, R. D. (2003). *Becoming a public relations writer* (2nd ed.). Mahwah, NJ: Lawrence Erlbaum.

Wilcox, D. L., Cameron, G. T., Ault, P. H., & Agee, W. K. (2003). *Public relations strategies and tactics* (7th ed.). Boston: Allyn & Bacon.

Wilson, L. (2000). *Strategic program planning for effective public relations campaigns* (3rd ed.). Dubuque, IA: Kendall/Hunt.

Zappala, J. M., & Carden, A. R. (2004). *Public relations work-text* (2nd ed.). Mahwah, NJ: Lawrence Erlbaum.

PERT CHART

For complex public relations projects, it is essential to have an effective planning tool. Large-scale projects consume a large chunk of a public relations department's budget as well as its human resources, so a practitioner wants to do everything possible to ensure that the project runs smoothly. Planning is an essential feature for large and/or complex public relations actions. Planning helps him or her deliver a quality product on time and on budget. The program evaluation and review technique (PERT), sometimes called the critical path method (CPM), is an excellent resource for planning and monitoring complex projects. The system originally was developed for tracking missile development programs for the United States government. The PERT Chart is much like the Gantt Chart (*see Gantt Chart*), but it presents information as a network chart rather than as a bar chart. Like the Gantt Chart, a PERT Chart requires a practitioner to identify all the tasks that must be completed, the time each task will take, and the sequence of the tasks.

PERT Charts are designed to help practitioners plan the time that a public relations action will take and track its progress. They provide a method for organizing, scheduling, and coordinating tasks. Planning experts argue that PERT Charts provide a better visual depiction of tasks and contingencies than Gantt Charts. However, since they require the user to learn certain terms and symbols, they can be more difficult to interpret than a Gantt Chart. There are advantages and disadvantages to each. In general, PERT Charts are more technical; numbered circles or boxes represent the tasks, and arrows connect tasks and indicate if tasks are sequential or concurrent. If an arrow runs between two tasks, such as between "conduct an interview with the CEO" and "write the story about the CEO," the tasks are sequential. Diverging arrows, such as for "select paper for newsletter" and "write newsletter stories," indicate that the tasks are concurrent.

PERT Charts also deal with external contingencies, or factors beyond the practitioner's control that can still affect the time a public relations project takes to be complete. For example, a practitioner hires a printing company to produce brochures for a product launch. The brochures must be shipped to the company. External contingencies include the ability of the printer to complete the brochure on time and to have the brochure shipment arrive on time. A strike or fire at the printing company could delay the completion of the brochure. Bad weather could delay the arrival of the shipment. Practitioners must consider the external contingencies when planning how long a project will take. The skilled practitioner builds in extra time as a hedge against external contingencies.

PERT Charts also use the terms *critical path* and *dummy activities*. The critical path is the longest path through the chart and indicates the maximum needed to complete the project. Let us assume a project will take 70 days to complete—it has a critical path of 70 days. The path is critical because any delay in a task on this path will delay the project. For instance, assume that tasks four and eight are on the critical path while three, five, and seven are not. (PERT Charts label tasks by number.) Slight delays in tasks three, five, or seven will not affect the completion date because they are scheduled to take less time (30 days) than the critical tasks (70 days). Clearly a very long delay in any tasks can disrupt a project, but any delay in a critical path task will delay a project's completion. A PERT Chart provides an easy way to identify the critical path for a project.

A dummy activity is a task that must be completed in sequence but requires virtually no resources or time to complete. It is still important, however, because failure to execute it would delay the project. For example, say that a brochure is drafted and e-mailed to a manager for review. The e-mail must be sent, but doing so uses only a brief amount of time and electricity. Dotted lines are used in a PERT Chart to illustrate such a dummy activity.

PERT Charts even have a formula for calculating the time of a project. First, the manager identifies the best-case scenario time (the quickest possible time to complete the project), the worst-case scenario time (the longest possible time it should take to complete the project), and the most likely time to complete the project. Those numbers are then entered into the following formula:

$$\{[\text{Best time} + (\text{Likely time}) \times 4] + \text{Worst time}\}/6$$

In addition to task and time, a PERT Chart can include responsibilities for tasks. People can be assigned to tasks so that it is clear who is responsible for what in a project. If there is a delay on a task, everyone knows whom to contact about that task.

As with a Gantt Chart, a PERT Chart is only as good as the thought process that went into the planning. It does not magically add overlooked tasks. However, seeing the public relations action may indicate to planners that something is missing. The PERT Chart is used to guide the execution of the action as well. The manager plots what tasks have been completed and the time it has taken. When these data are entered, it becomes easy to see if the project is on track or how far ahead or behind it might be. The PERT Chart also serves as a reminder so that tasks are not forgotten. A manager knows exactly what has been done and what still needs to be done. Finally, these charts are helpful for developing budgets: by knowing exactly what needs to be done, a practitioner can calculate the costs of the materials, personnel, and equipment needed to complete the project.

—*W. Timothy Coombs*

See also Gantt Chart; Process research

Bibliography

Davidson, J. (2000). *Project management: 10 minute guide.* Indianapolis, IN: Macmillan.

PHILANTHROPY

Philanthropy is a unique characteristic of American society, and public relations practitioners play an important role in preserving the tradition of giving and helping. Broadly defined, philanthropy is voluntary action for the public good, including voluntary giving, voluntary service, and voluntary association.

Our tradition of philanthropy was dramatically demonstrated in the aftermath of September 11, 2001. Within hours after the terrorist attacks, millions of dollars in unsolicited contributions began pouring into the offices of disaster-relief charities.

In just seven days, donations to such charities and to special funds established to aid victims, their families, and communities approached $250 million. By week three, gifts surpassed $750 million. One month after the tragedy, the total stood at $1 billion.

Gifts came from individuals, corporations, and foundations—the three types of donor publics. Listing just a few examples, Chicago firefighters standing on street corners collected $360,000 in one day; film, television, and recording stars generated an estimated $150 million in pledges during a two-hour telethon broadcast on 35 networks just 10 days after the terrorist attacks; the corporate foundation for Citigroup gave $15 million to establish a scholarship fund for all victims' children; the Coca-Cola Company, its foundation, and its bottling partners gave $12 million to be divided among several relief organizations; the Lilly Endowment, one of the five largest independent foundations, pledged $30 million to the American Red Cross, the Salvation Army, and the September 11 Fund; and the Ford Foundation gave $10 million.

About 140 charitable organizations, such as the Red Cross, were involved in collecting and distributing the financial assistance so generously given. These organizations are part of our country's nonprofit sector, which is composed of more than 1.4 million tax-exempt organizations that are neither businesses nor government agencies. Collectively, their mission is to provide "goods" not provided by the business sector, which is ruled by the marketplace, or by the government sector, which is ruled by the ballot box. The nonprofit sector, also known as the voluntary or third sector of the U.S. economy, is grounded in the First Amendment of the Constitution, which guarantees the right to form associations. Nonprofits are the operationalization of voluntary action and serve as a conduit for voluntary giving and service. For example, following the terrorist attacks of September 11, charity officials reported that offers of volunteer help, blood donations, and donated goods were so numerous that they far exceeded immediate needs. Relief organizations were inundated by volunteers. Across the United States, without being asked, people left families, jobs, and their own problems to travel to the disaster sites to do whatever they could.

As dramatic as this demonstration was, it should not be viewed as a surprising aberration. A historic and deeply rooted cultural belief in the United States is that our country's social needs, to the greatest possible extent, should be addressed by private voluntary action rather than by government. Americans also eschew a dominant role for churches in meeting social needs, which is prevalent in countries with one state religion. In other words, philanthropy is highly salient in U.S. society because it is linked to such core values as religious freedom, opposition to powerful government, and individualism.

In his book on the history of U.S. fundraising, the father of public relations education, the late Scott Cutlip (1965/1990), stated, "America's philanthropy is typically American—born of the cooperative and generous spirit bred on the frontier, required by the problems of large-scale industrialization and urbanization, [and] made possible by the enormous accumulation of capital wealth" (pp. 530–531).

Cutlip also reported another extraordinary demonstration of philanthropy that testifies to the tradition's longevity and contradicts claims that America's response to September 11 was unsurpassed in history. During World War I, the American Red Cross War Council raised $114 million in just eight day—an amount that when adjusted for inflation far surpasses the $129 million raised by the Red Cross in the same number of days following the 2001 terrorist attacks. President Woodrow Wilson had proclaimed June 18–25, 1917, as National Red Cross Week, and the amount of money given in that short time represented more than $1 for every man, woman, and child in the United States.

VOLUNTARY GIVING

America's tradition of philanthropy is the envy of other industrialized nations. Quite simply, individuals, corporations, and foundations in the United State characteristically give away money. In 2002, Americans gave a total of $241 billion, of which 84 percent came from individuals, 11 percent came from foundations, and 5 percent came from corporations (AAFRC Trust for Philanthropy, 2003). With only a few exceptions, giving has increased every year since studies measuring philanthropy began.

Americans give money for many reasons, but, fundamentally, they make gifts because giving is a customary, admired, and expected behavior in our society. According to *Independent Sector* in 2001, almost 90 percent of all U.S. households contribute to one or more charitable organizations each year, and the average gift per household is $1,620. Wealthy individuals adhere to a philanthropic standard that is unusual in the modern world. The standard was outlined more than a century ago by legendary philanthropist Andrew Carnegie, who proclaimed, "He who dies rich dies disgraced" (1989/1883, p. 108). Attesting to the standard's continued influence, Microsoft founder Bill Gates and his wife, Melissa, have given away more than $25 billion of their wealth since 2000.

Approximately 700,000 companies report charitable contributions on their income-tax return every year. On average, these companies give away about 1.2% of their pretax revenues. Independent foundations, unlike the other sources of gifts, are required by law to give away each year an amount equal to 5 percent of their financial assets. Their purpose is to provide support to charitable organizations through grants. There are approximately 50,000 independent foundations in the United States; their combined assets total more than $450 billion.

VOLUNTARY ASSOCIATION

The United States has a large and pervasive nonprofit sector consisting of 1.4 million nonprofit organizations, of which more than 900,000, or 63 percent, are charitable nonprofits, meaning that gifts to them are deductible from donors' taxable income. This third economic sector allows Americans to collectively promote causes that they believe are important and in society's best interest. The causes, represented by the missions or tax-exempt purposes of nonprofits, are diverse and wide ranging. They touch on almost all aspects of American life.

Naming just a few broad categories, nonprofits are engaged in arts and culture, education, health, human services, recreation, and religion.

The United States relies on nonprofits and the services they deliver more so than any other country in the world. Most major social action in the past, such as civil rights, women's rights, and environmental protection, began in the nonprofit sector. As a former president of Yale University asserted, the United States can be distinguished from all other societies by virtue of the workload it assigns to its third sector.

Our propensity for forming nonprofits was first noticed as distinctly American by Alexis de Tocqueville more than 170 years ago. As he noted, Americans of all ages and all conditions constantly form associations. De Tocqueville was convinced that this propensity was a significant factor in the vitality and success of American democracy. Contemporary scholars agree: The nonprofit sector fosters the pluralism on which democracy depends.

CHARITY VERSUS PHILANTHROPY

Scholars have identified two primary but distinctive thrusts in voluntary action: *compassion,* most closely associated with charity, or helping the poor and needy; and *community,* concern with civic improvement and social change, or philanthropy. Authorities agree that, today, charity primarily is carried out by government through welfare programs. Cutlip said the term *charity* was replaced by *philanthropy* after World War I. Philanthropy translates from its Greek origins to "love of humankind." It is an investment in civilization. In a contemporary context, charity is a part of philanthropy, but only a minor part.

The term *charitable organization* is a legal term; it does not refer to programs dealing with the poor. Rather, the term is used by lawyers to refer to organizations described in Section 501(c)(3) of the Internal Revenue Code as serving religious, charitable, scientific, testing for public safety, literary, or educational purposes. The greatest proportion of charitable organizations—and the bulk of the money given to them each year—have to do with purposes not defined as charity.

PUBLIC RELATIONS PRACTITIONERS

Public relations practitioners play a vital role in sustaining America's tradition of philanthropy. Many practitioners specialize in fundraising, or helping charitable organizations attract philanthropic dollars by managing their relationships with donor publics. Other public relations practitioners serve as corporate contributions officers, helping businesses make contributions that are mutually beneficial for the community and the company. Foundations rely on the public relations practitioners to disseminate information on their grant making and on solutions to societal problems that their grants have helped solve. Many public relations firms serve nonprofit clients or advise businesses on their philanthropic giving.

Overall, public relations people in all three economic sectors utilize philanthropy to help their organizations succeed and survive. They represent diverse pluralistic voices in the marketplace of ideas and encourage interaction, thereby strengthening our democratic society.

—Kathleen S. Kelly

See also Fundraising; Nonprofit organizations; Public relations

Bibliography

American Association of Fundraising Counsel (AAFRC) Trust for Philanthropy. (2003). *Giving USA: The annual report on philanthropy for the year 2002.* Indianapolis, IN: Center on Philanthropy.

Carnegie, A. (1983). The gospel of wealth. In B. O'Connell (Ed.), *America's voluntary spirit* (pp. 97–108). New York: Foundation Center. (Original work published 1889)

Cutlip, S. M. (1990). *Fund raising in the United States: Its role in America's philanthropy.* New Brunswick, NJ: Transaction. (Original work published 1965)

de Tocqueville, A. (1966). *Democracy in America* (G. Lawrence, Trans.). New York: Harper & Row. (Original work published 1835)

Independent Sector. (2001). *Giving and volunteering in the United States 2001.* Washington, DC: Author.

Kelly, K. S. (1998). *Effective fund-raising management.* Mahwah, NJ: Lawrence Erlbaum.

Payton, R. L. (1988). *Philanthropy: Voluntary action for the public good.* New York: American Council on Education and Macmillan.

PHOTO-OP

One way for an organization to gain media attention is to create an opportunity for a news photographer to get a great shot. A picture can be a powerful message, and by having the right photograph picked up by media, an outstanding opportunity can be created. A photo opportunity (photo-op) is a planned act that will sum up the entire public relations campaign in a picture. When creating a photo opportunity to promote an event, it is essential to visualize how the event will be portrayed in pictures rather than words.

To get coverage of an event featuring a great photo-op, a news release or media alert is sent to media to notify them of the photo opportunity. The photo-op has a greater chance of getting noticed if the event is truly newsworthy. Notification of a photo-op spells out a unique visual for print and broadcast media outlets and should be formatted like a media release or media alert. It should be a condensed version of a news release limited to one page that spells out the details of the event and also intrigues its recipients. The alert should be formatted with headings like "who," "what," "when," "where," and "contact information." Special attention should be given to describing the visual appeal of the event.

Some examples of common photo-ops are a tree planting, a ribbon cutting, a signing ceremony, a plaque or check presentation, or a ground breaking for a new building. Although these examples may get media coverage, in order to truly attract media attention, a photo-op has to be creative. One must imagine the photo as it will appear on the local broadcast of the evening news or on the front page of the newspaper and make sure that it conveys the right message. The organization's logo should appear prominently in the photo. The logo will provide immediate identification with the organization or company and can appear on the podium, a backdrop behind the speaker, or even on a T-shirt or hat.

A single glance of the photo should reveal the entire thrust of the event, or the entire public relations campaign. A photo-op should be simple so as not to confuse the audience and the image. It is best to avoid a photo opportunity that is time sensitive.

An everlasting image will appear in newspapers and magazines for some time to come, but if a photo's timeliness is limited to one day, such as a Fourth of July celebration, its circulation will be greatly limited. The photo opportunity should also appeal to all media. One must imagine how the event will play out on television, in print, and on the Internet.

The appearance of a celebrity or other public figure will create intrigue and interest in the photo-op. A classic staged event to promote the film *The Seven Year Itch* was developed using special blowers installed in the grate underneath Marilyn Monroe's feet. Photographers captured the memorable planned image when her skirt "accidentally" flew up. This staged photo-op has everlasting appeal.

—Nancy Engelhardt Furlow

See also Media relations; Media release

Bibliography

Howard, C. M. (2000). *On deadline: Managing media relations.* Prospect Heights, IL: Waveland Press.

Kennerly, D. (1995). *Photo op: A Pulitzer prize-winning photographer covers events that shaped our times.* Austin: University of Texas Press.

Woods, J. V. J., & Gregg, S. (1999). *Media relations: Publicizing your efforts: Understanding the media and getting media exposure.* Columbia, MD: Enterprise Foundation.

PITCH LETTER

A pitch letter is a public relations sales tool. It is written to interest a media representative in a potential story idea and is tailored to a specific media outlet (unlike a news release, which may be distributed very broadly).

The most effective pitch letters draw on the writer's knowledge of the media outlet and the representative within it. First, a story must be pitched to the appropriate media outlet. Often this decision is fairly easy, since local media outlets are the targets for many public relations efforts. However, at other times broader audiences may be needed to achieve public relations objectives. For example, a paper mill in the Pacific Northwest has developed new effluent treatments that both reduce pollution control costs and greatly improve the quality of the water the plant discharges. The cost reduction aspects could be pitched to a trade journal to generate positive press with industry peers, and the water quality issue could be pitched to a sport fishing magazine to improve the company's image with those who fish. The key is to understand what the public relations objectives are for a story, and then pitch the angles to the right media outlets to achieve them.

Another important aspect of the media outlet is the editorial calendar. Some larger publications have special or themed issues planned months in advance. Being familiar with editorial calendars, available through certain media directories, will enable public relations practitioners to pitch stories that can result in very important placements.

Next, the story must be pitched to the appropriate person. There is no point in pitching a story about a company's community relations efforts to a news editor; such a story probably should be sent to the business or community editor (depending on the outlet). Pitching a story to the wrong person wastes time for both parties. On the local level, developing good working relationships with area media will make most of these choices fairly clear. On a broader scale, media directories should be used to pinpoint the best person at a specific outlet to send the pitch letter to. A pitch letter should never be addressed "Dear News Editor." Such a mistake typically ensures failure.

Finally, a story must be pitched in the appropriate manner. The letter should reveal the writer's understanding of the audience of the media outlet, the relevance of the story to that audience, and key points of interest. Assistance in arranging interviews and other information gathering should be offered. The point is to generate interest in the story with the media, not to write the story for them. As for tone, a hard sell is rarely, if ever, appropriate. The media value their independence and will not be told what stories they need to write. Beyond that, the choice between a straight business approach, creativity, or some mix is determined by appropriateness to both the topic and the outlet.

—Maribeth S. Metzler

PLANK, BETSY

Betsy Ann Plank is widely acknowledged as a pathfinder and legend in public relations. Her career, spanning more than 55 years, is filled with "firsts." Indeed, many in the field consider her public relations' First Lady.

Plank is the first woman to have served as president of the Public Relations Society of America (PSRA). She is the first and only person to be selected for three of PRSA's top individual awards: the Gold Anvil Award (1977) for being the outstanding U.S. professional, the Paul M. Lund Public Service Award (1989) for exemplary civic and community work, and the first Patrick Jackson Award (2001) for distinguished service to PRSA.

Plank is the first woman elected by readers of *Public Relations News* as Professional of the Year (1979) and also was named one of the World's 40 Outstanding Public Relations Leaders by the same publication in 1984. She was the first recipient of both the Arthur W. Page Society's Distinguished Service (formerly Lifetime Achievement) Award (2000) and PRSA Educators Academy's David W. Ferguson Award (1997) for exceptional contributions by a practitioner to public relations education.

In 2000, the Institute for Public Relations honored Plank with its highest award, the Alexander Hamilton Award, in recognition of her major contributions to the practice of public relations. In 2001, she was inducted into the Communication Hall of Fame at the University of Alabama, her alma mater. Five other universities similarly have recognized her as an outstanding public relations professional.

Despite all the accolades, Plank has refused to view her achievements as anything extraordinary. She stated,

> Mea culpa, I never had a plan! I simply seized opportunities as they came along and have been very blessed. I also credit my family—they always had expectations of excellence and hard work and were so supportive. I had the freedom to explore everything. There was no gender-bias there and, in retrospect, perhaps that accounts for my never recognizing any during a long career lifetime. (personal communication, October 23, 2002)

Plank was born on April 3, 1924, in Tusculoosa, Alabama. She attended her hometown university, the University of Alabama, where she earned a bachelor's degree in history, with English literature as a minor, in 1944. In later years, Plank liked to point out that there was no such thing as a public relations major when she attended college, and for that reason she became a leading advocate of public relations education.

Her career in public relations began by serendipity in 1947. At the time, she had moved to Chicago in search of continuing a career in radio broadcasting—without success. But then she met one of the city's only women executives, Duffy Schwartz, Midwest director of the Advertising Council, who became her first mentor. Schwartz recommended Plank for a temporary position at a public relations and fundraising agency serving nonprofit organizations and coached her in the unfamiliar field. After several months, Plank was offered a full-time position and worked at that agency and others throughout the 1950s.

In 1960, Plank joined Daniel J. Edelman, Inc. (now Edelman Public Relations Worldwide) and served as executive vice president until 1973. Plank then became director of public relations planning for AT&T before transferring to Illinois Bell (now SBC Communications Inc.), where she was the first woman to head a company department, directing external affairs and a staff of 102.

Plank spent more than 17 years with SBC and helped shape and articulate the company's response to the divestiture of the Bell System—what she considers the greatest challenge in her career. "We had a couple of years to break up the world's largest corporation and prepare it without a single missed step," she recalled ("Alabama Communication Hall of Fame," 2004, n.p.). There were many problems. It was fascinating to live through, challenging to prepare for and carry out, and almost twenty years later, "the telecommunications industry hasn't settled down yet" ("Alabama Communication Hall of Fame," 2004, n.p.).

Plank retired from corporate practice in 1990, but she continues to work as a public relations consultant through her Chicago-based firm, Betsy Plank Public Relations.

Much of Plank's energies throughout her career have been devoted to public relations education, with particular emphasis on the Public Relations Student Society of America (PRSSA). She admits that today students and their education are her most compelling interest and joy. She explained, "My professional life has given me a deep appreciation for colleges and universities preparing students for ethical practice in the evolving profession of public relations" (LaBresh, 2000, n.p.).

According to Plank, one of her proudest achievements occurred while she was president of PRSA. Not surprisingly, it reflected her confidence in the new PRSSA. Prior to 1973, a PRSA committee of "elders" had governed PRSSA. With Plank's strong advocacy, bylaws were amended to permit the student organization to govern itself. "It's a joy to have been part of such a watershed event in the history of PRSSA's remarkable and responsible leadership," she said (personal communication, October 23, 2002).

Plank served as the national advisor to PRSSA from 1981 until 1983. At the beginning of her tenure, she and Jon Riffel, often referred to as the "godfather" of PRSSA, established what is now known as Champions for PRSSA, a group of professionals who have special, ongoing interests in the student society, its members, and public relations education. In 1988, the Champions created annual PRSSA scholarships, which were later named for Plank. Since the program began, more than $65,000 in scholarships have been awarded.

In 1993, the student society honored Plank with its 25th Anniversary Award. Today, PRSSA has 243 chapters at colleges and universities across the nation, with more than 8,000 members, and Betsy Plank is widely known as the "godmother" of PRSSA.

Plank co-chaired the 1987 Commission on Undergraduate Public Relations Education, which developed guidelines for public relations curricula at U.S. colleges and universities, and is a member of the current commission, which deals with both undergraduate and graduate education. Plank was instrumental in establishing PRSA's Certification in Education in Public Relations (CEPR) program in

1989, which provides a review and endorsement process for undergraduate studies in public relations. She chairs the initiative to encourage university-based programs to seek formal certification.

Plank sees education and research as the most important developments in the future of public relations. She explained,

The hallmark of every respected profession is a formal program of study. Originally, few people in public relations were educated for it. Most came from newspapers or other media as I did, and concentrated primarily on publicity. Today, the field needs men and women who have studied for the practice, know its theory, principles, ethics, and expectations and who have a command of the skills and research required for it. (personal communication, October 23, 2002)

Plank emphasized that research is essential to assess the attitudes of an organization's constituencies and to evaluate the impact of public relations. "Research and education—both formal and life-long—are moving public relations to a stronger recognized position of professionalism" (personal communication, October 23, 2002).

To Plank, public relations is about building reputation and relationships. Although she was an early endorser of new technologies, she believes that interpersonal communication is key to effective practice. She stated:

Communications technology is a magic, wonderful tool, but simply a tool. It will never replace the human encounter, the willingness to listen and to address differences constructively. That requires understanding of human behavior, psychology and motivation—and that doesn't come with a keyboard! What is fundamental to public relations is how we help our clients relate and respond to their constituencies—employees, customers, owners, and the community at-large. (personal communication, October 23, 2002)

Plank also continues to believe that recent crises in the corporate sector, starting with the Enron scandal in 2001, present a wake-up call to organizations about their credibility, ethics, and need for transparency—all emphasizing the strategic importance of ethical public relations. She stated,

I foresee public relations addressing many more functions—all aspects of the organization's reputation and relationships. These crises provide a unique opportunity for public relations professionals to say to their clients, "We can help in restoring and reinforcing the organization's relationships of trust with its key stakeholders," and then to perform and position public relations in its strongest counseling and policy-making capacity. (personal communication, October 23, 2002)

Plank expressed gratitude for her chosen career:

I am so fortunate to be in a field that I love very much and of which I am very proud. This is a profession rooted in the history of this country, which was founded on the idea of people having an informed choice, participating in dialogue, reaching compromise and consensus. Public relations has played an essential role in that tradition and democratic process, which is now reaching people worldwide. (personal communication, October 23, 2002)

After more than 55 years in the practice, Betsy Plank continues to counsel clients and to pursue her passions for advancing public relations education and its students. She said, "In my lexicon, there is no such word as *retirement!*" (personal communication, October 23, 2002).

—*Kathleen S. Kelly and Cristina Proano Beazley*

See also Institute for Public Relations (IPR); Page, Arthur W.; Public Relations Society of America; Public Relations Student Society of America

Bibliography

Alabama Communication Hall of Fame. *Betsy Plank.* Retrieved January 10, 2004, from http://www.ccom.ua.edu/dean/halloffame/plank.html

LaBresh, B. (2000). Plank contributes scholarship, makes bequest for PR education in the College. *Communicator.* Retrieved January 10, 2004, from http://www.ccom.ua.edu/communicators00/stories/plankbequests.html

Plank, B. A. (1983, August). The new technology and its implications for the public relations profession. *IPR Review,* 7(2), 35–38.

Plank, B. A. (2000). *Extending the spirit of Arthur Page to those who will follow.* Retrieved January 12, 2004 from

http://www.awpagesociety.com/activities/distinguished_service/b_plank.asp

Plank, B. A. (2003). Footnotes on the commissions on public relations education and other legacies. In L. M. Sallot & B. J. DeSanto (Eds.), *Learning to teach: What you need to know to develop a successful career as a public relations educator* (3rd ed., pp. 27–32). New York: Public Relations Society of America Educators Academy.

Betsy A. Plank

SOURCE: Public Relations Society of America. Reprinted with permission.

POLITICAL ACTION COMMITTEES (PACs)

Political action committees, often called PACs, are an important aspect of American politics and the American electoral system. They exist legally so that corporations, trade unions, and other private groups can make donations to candidates for federal office—something that they cannot do directly. Many PACs represent special interest groups like the National Rifle Association of America; others represent large conservative or liberal coalitions. PACs in the United States have a long and at times controversial history.

They were invented by labor unions in 1943 as a loophole around federal campaign laws. The first PAC was organized by the Congress of Industrial Organizations (CIO) and was a model for later PACs. Corporations were not allowed to form PACs until the passage of the Federal Election Campaign Act of 1971 (FECA). By opening the door to corporate money being used to set up PACs, the FECA and its 1974 and 1976 amendments brought about a new and much larger role for trade associations and corporations in politics. Enormous growth in the number of PACs actively involved in politics soon followed, and today there are more corporate PACs than any other type. In 1974, there were 608 political action committees registered with the Federal Election Committee. At the close of 1995, there were more than 5,000 of them.

As the number of PACs has increased, so has the amount of PAC money spent in elections. In 1974, the 608 PACs contributed $12.5 million to congressional candidates. In the 1995–1996 election cycle, about 5,000 PACs gave $201.4 million to congressional candidates, most of them incumbents. This amount represented an increase of 12 percent from the 1993–1994 level and was more than one-third of the total money raised by these candidates. According to the Center for Responsive Politics, at the close of the 1998 election cycle, PACs contributed a total of $220 million to federal candidates.

PACs get their funds not from the sponsoring group's treasury, but from its members, employees, or shareholders. Most give the majority of the funds to congressional elections, in which they can contribute a maximum of $5,000 to a candidate for each campaign—the primary, runoff, and general election. However, some have conducted independent negative campaigns against candidates they oppose. An early example of this, which has served as a model for many others, was the $8.5 million campaign waged in 1988 by the National Security PAC that simply attacked presidential candidate Michael Dukakis on behalf of Republican George Bush.

PACs that work to raise money from people employed by a corporation or in a trade union are called "connected PACs." They rarely ask for donations but are legally free to do so. "Unconnected PACs," also called "independent PACs," raise money by targeting selected groups in society. The Supreme Court ruled in 1985 that there should be no limits on the spending of PACs on a candidate's behalf, provided that the expenditure is not made in collaboration with a candidate. The PAC must maintain legal independence. An individual's contribution to a PAC is limited to $5,000.

During a presidential campaign, PACs give to the parties to support the election campaign expenditures of the candidate. A PAC can contribute a maximum of $15,000 to a national party. It can, however, give much more to state and local parties. This amount is restricted in some states, but in others it is not. Pre–primary-election campaigns, or exploratory campaigns, are often financed by a PAC that was founded by a candidate. They may also be created by a "foundation"; donations to a foundation are tax-deductible, which makes them even more attractive to donors. The donations go to pay for an undeclared candidate's travel and politically related expenses that occur during a campaign.

The relationship between political parties and PACs is unusual because it is both symbiotic and parasitic. On one hand, it seems they are bound to be competitors. Both raise money from the limited pool of political givers, both try to elect candidates, and both strive for the attention of candidates and office holders. They do, however, have very different perspectives. PACs act on the basis of a narrow viewpoint, whereas parties operate from a broad-based vantage point. The success of narrow-based PACs comes partly at the expense of broad-based parties. As parties decline, PACs gain. On the symbiotic side of things, both parties work hard to nurture PACs and gain their money, and most PACs try to be used in a bipartisan way, usually to incumbents of each party.

So, which PAC spends the most money? The Association of Trial Lawyers of America beat out the American Federation of State, County, and

Municipal Employees union as the biggest spending PAC of 1997–98, spending $2,697,636. Five of the top 10 high-spending PACs are labor unions; these are national organizations and can pull together contributions from millions of members. The United Parcel Service PAC was the most generous PAC representing a single company, and the National Rifle Association was the top-spending single-issue PAC.

United States President Bill Clinton addresses the 54th annual meeting of the Association of Trial Lawyers of America (ATLA) while in Chicago, July 30, 2000. The ATLA is regularly one of the top-spending political action committees (PACs).

SOURCE: © Reuters NewMedia Inc./CORBIS

PAC funding of congressional elections has been heavily aimed at those already elected and seeking reelection. During the congressional elections of 1988, 1990, 1992, and 1994, FEC data show that Democratic incumbent senators received five times more funding from PACs than their Republican challengers. The Democrats received the majority of PAC money for as long as they had control of Congress, despite the fact that Republicans are usually viewed as more sympathetic to business. In 1994, however, the Republicans took the majority in both the House and Senate, and that all changed. The 1996 season revealed a reversal of PAC funds from the Democrats to the Republicans, especially from the business PACs. The Democrats regained some ground in 1998, receiving $4 million more from PACs than they did in 1996.

There are some congressional members who make a point of not accepting PAC money, but others heavily depend on it. In 1990, more than 80 percent of the financial support of nine members of the House came from PACs. The importance of this is obvious—if you have the financial backing to finance an election campaign, you have an advantage over a challenger who does not. This is deepened by the fact that contributions from PACs not spent on a campaign can be held until the next cycle, giving the incumbent a head start over a future challenger. The same is true in the Senate. In 1997, 30 senators elected in 1992 and standing for reelection in 1998 had already raised an average of $1.4 million per senator. The generally agreed-upon figure to be a good "start point" for senatorial elections is $5 million; those who already have 20 percent of that sum before the election starts have a distinct advantage. Since House members are elected only every two years, any House member seeking reelection is almost constantly seeking funds. Many House members spend more than $1 million during a campaign.

There are some in the United States who would like to see the amount of PAC money greatly reduced, fearing its potential influence on legislators. Even though records from PACs are made public and checked by the FEC and media members and the public are free to view them, some are still uneasy about the power of PACs and the legal dodging of limits placed on donations received. To some it seems that there is no motivation among the president, senators, and congressmen to alter a system that has benefited them so much. As public criticism rose during the 1990s, Congress considered several reform proposals, but no legislation was passed. The proposal that would have generated the most sweeping changes in campaign finance, the McCain-Feingold-Thomson Bill, failed by just six votes in 1996.

The future of the PAC donation system remains to be seen, but the current structure that appears to favor incumbents is holding strong in 2003.

—Ruthann Weaver Lariscy

Note: Special thanks to Amie Marsh-McCook for her contributions to this entry.

Bibliography

American Politics Index. (2002). *Political action committees* [online]. Available: http://www.historylearningsite.co.uk/

Center for Responsive Politics. (2003, June). *Top 50 PAC contributors* and *PAC contributions: The role of PACS* [online]. Available: http://www.opensecrets.org

Sabado, L. (1984). *PAC power: Inside the world of political action committees.* New York: W. W. Norton.

Sabado, L. (1990). PACS and parties. In M. L. Nugent & J. R. Johannes (Eds.), *Money, elections, and democracy: Reforming congressional campaign finance.* Boulder, CO: Westview Press.

POLITICAL SPEECH

Political speech is speech on issues of political and social importance. The First Amendment to the United States Constitution provides that the government cannot restrict an individual's right to speak regardless of what the government might think about that speech. The First Amendment originally referred only to Congress, but today it applies to all levels of government.

Scholars justify the First Amendment's protection of the right to freedom of expression in several ways. One of the primary justifications for protecting freedom of expression is self-governance. A working democracy depends on the ability of individuals to freely discuss politics without fear of being censured. Another justification is the attainment of truth. The idea is that truth will be found only if society is able to test concepts through open discussion. The freedom to criticize government is also seen as a stabilizing force in society. Unrest comes when individuals are not free to voice their displeasure and seek change. And finally, expression is seen as necessary for human self-fulfillment or self-realization. The ability to express oneself is what sets humans apart from animals, and therefore the right to freely express oneself is crucial to human dignity and integrity.

In determining whether government regulation of political speech is constitutional, the courts use the standard of strict scrutiny. That is, the government must establish that it has a compelling interest to protect through the regulation and that the regulation is narrowly tailored to achieve that interest. Because

of the importance of ensuring a robust public debate on political issues, some false political speech is permitted. For example, individuals can libel or defame political figures with impunity provided their statements were not made with actual malice—knowledge of falsity or reckless disregard of the truth. The purpose is to prevent speakers from being chilled by the threat of government censure.

Until 1978, corporations were not thought to have First Amendment rights because they cannot achieve self-fulfillment. Beginning in 1978, however, the U.S. Supreme Court came to recognize that corporations do contribute to public policy debates and that individuals have a First Amendment right to hear what corporations have to say on policy issues. The purpose of political speech by a corporation is not to promote a product or service, but rather to voice the corporation's views or position on a matter of public importance. Such speech falls within the realm of public relations.

The first case in which corporate political speech was recognized involved a Massachusetts law prohibiting a corporation from speaking on referendum proposals unless those proposals materially affected the corporation. The First National Bank of Boston challenged the law because it wanted to publicize its views on a proposed constitutional amendment that would have granted the state legislature the right to impose a graduated income tax on Massachusetts residents. First National opposed the amendment and sought to inform its customers of its position via a public relations campaign.

In denying the bank's claim, the lower court had said the issue was whether corporations had First Amendment rights. The court concluded they did not, but the Supreme Court disagreed. The Court said that the issue was not whether corporations had the same speech rights as natural persons, but whether the speech in question was protected by the First Amendment. In other words, the content of the speech determined the protection granted, not the nature of the speaker. Voters were entitled to hear First National's views on the topic; therefore, the bank's speech was protected by the First Amendment. The speech was not made less important because it came from a corporation rather than from an individual.

Two years later, the Court reinforced its protection of speech by a corporation, holding that the government could not restrict speech by a corporation simply because the speech might be offensive to some people. Nor can the government force a corporation to disseminate messages on political or social issues with which it disagrees, although the government can force a corporation to carry certain messages about its products, such as the Surgeon General's message on tobacco packaging.

Not everyone agrees that corporations should have First Amendment protection for political speech. These critics focus on corporate wealth and power, arguing that corporations have such power and influence that they distort the debate on public policy issues. Individuals need to be protected from that power and influence, it is believed. That position can be seen in the case of *Nike v. Kasky* (2003).

When Nike, the multinational athletic equipment manufacturer, became the subject of a public debate about the use of sweatshops overseas in the early 1990s, the corporation tried to restore its public image through a public relations campaign. An activist then sued Nike in California under the state's false advertising statute, claiming that statements made by Nike in the course of the public relations campaign were false and misleading. Nike argued that the statements constituted political speech, not commercial speech, and were therefore protected by the First Amendment. The trial court agreed, but the California Supreme Court held that the speech was indeed commercial speech because Nike hoped to reach consumers with its message. The court said that Nike was free to discuss the issue of overseas labor in the abstract, but it could not discuss its own practices unless it was truthful and nonmisleading. The U.S. Supreme Court declined to hear the case, leaving the California decision standing. The effect of the California decision is to reduce the sphere of corporate political speech. The emphasis is no longer on the right of individuals to hear the views of corporations, but rather on the speaker and the intended audience. So long as a court views the intended audience as consumers, corporations will have little or no political speech rights.

—*Karla K. Gower*

See also Commercial speech

Bibliography

First National Bank of Boston v. Bellotti, 435 U.S. 765 (1978).

Gower, K. K. (2003). *Legal and ethical restraints on public relations.* Prospect Heights, IL: Waveland Press.

Kasky v. Nike, Inc., 45 P.3d 243, 247–248 (Cal. 2002).

Moore, R., Farrar, R., & Collins, E. (1998). *Advertising and public relations law.* Mahwah, NJ: Lawrence Erlbaum.

Nike v. Kasky, No. 02–575 (S.C. June 26, 2003).

PORTFOLIO

A portfolio contains evidence of the accomplishments of a student or professional practitioner. Portfolios are especially valuable during a job interview because they offer evidence of the job candidate's proficiency in the practice. The evidence contained in a portfolio consists of samples of the person's work that reveal his or her knowledge, work ethic, skill, and creative talent.

Students who are studying public relations need to carefully develop a portfolio. Thus, they might write for their campus newspaper or get stories aired on the campus radio or television stations. Students should include in their portfolios all of the materials they produce as class projects; such projects can help demonstrate the skills they are honing to become an intern or entry-level employee. They are therefore wise to carefully participate in class projects and extracurricular activities with the intent of producing work that can augment their portfolios. They might write stories for the newsletter of their Public Relations Student Society of America chapter. They might create its Web site or otherwise contribute in some meaningful and identifiable way to that site. They might plan and help execute a fundraiser event. Or they can submit their work for various contests. PRSSA chapters often set aside days when students can meet with professionals to discuss materials that should be in portfolios or are in them already. Professionals can offer advice on how to augment the portfolio with materials they find most useful when they make hiring and promotion decisions.

Much like students, professionals should develop and carefully groom a portfolio. In contrast to a student's portfolio, a professional's portfolio contains some of the more important samples of that person's work. It can, for instance, include samples that earned awards. Organizations such as the Public Relations Society of America and the International Association of Business Communicators hold annual contests in which a wide array of public relations campaign strategies and tools are judged.

Internships are a vital part of a student's academic and professional preparation. They not only help the student learn the ropes of the profession by seeing what professionals do, but they also offer the student many opportunities to produce work that can be added to her or his portfolio. Any student who takes an internship is wise to negotiate the opportunities to do work that could be added to the portfolio.

A good portfolio fleshes out the student's or practitioner's professional life story. It tells what the person can do and demonstrates the skills the person possesses. At a crucial point in a career, it can mean the difference between getting a job or merely being a candidate.

—Robert L. Heath

See also International Association of Business Communicators (IABC); Internship; Public Relations Society of America; Public Relations Student Society of America

POSITION AND POSITIONING

A *position* is a stance a consumer takes regarding a product, service, or the nature of an organization relative to the competition. *Positioning* depends on how a consumer compares a product to the competitors' product. Hence, a consumer ultimately determines a product's position and plays a key role in marketers' positioning strategies.

One can take the example of a *luxury car.* Undoubtedly, a specific corporate image and specific product attributes or visuals would immediately come to mind. In sum, this is the position that *luxury car* occupies in the hearer's brain. More precisely, positioning is a process that marketers use to persuade consumers to think favorably about *their* particular brand, product, service, or organization. It is "the process of creating a perception in the consumer's mind," according to Kenneth Clow and Donald Baack (2002, p. 99). Given this example, a specific automobile marketing team's "positioning" will have been successful if the consumer thinks of *their automobile* rather than a competitor's model.

According to an integrated marketing communication (IMC) approach, all elements of the mix—advertising, public relations, personal selling, and so forth—generate synergistic energy that is used to build lasting relationships with key stakeholders. In this way, marketing is considered a *philosophy,* rather than simply a *function.* Hence, IMC campaigns that involve strategies designed to nurture relationships with consumers will be most successful in competing for a "share" of the consumer's mind—and thus increasing sales—since their brand is the one the consumer readily thinks of when deciding which product to buy amidst a sea of competitive brands. Moreover, effective positioning simplifies the process for consumers: they expend little mental energy on purchase decisions because they choose certain brands spontaneously.

All elements of the marketing mix are involved in the positioning process. For example, public relations practitioners use two-way communication between the organization and consumers and other key publics to develop solid relationships. Advertisers use one-way communication strategies involving slogans, taglines, themes, characters, images—all designed to generate awareness and promote key product attributes and benefits to the consumer. The sales team works one-on-one with vendors to stock the marketplace, place point-of-sales materials, create special end-aisle displays—and so on.

As simple as this process seems on the surface, the position-positioning dynamic is a deeply complex one. Essentially, a product's position is intangible, dynamic, and elusive. A competitor's sale price, new technologies, a negative news story, and numerous other variables can affect a consumer's perception. Furthermore, what marketers *think* they know about their products and consumers often is quite different from the reality. It is the marketer's job to discover which consumer perceptions should be built upon, maintained, or reinforced and which should be changed, displaced, or deemphasized.

Usually, reinforcing a position that reflects well on the organization is much easier than repositioning or reversing a consumer's negative view. Consumers' key beliefs and attitudes are paramount. For example, Johnson & Johnson's successful handling of the Tylenol product-tampering episodes in 1982 included reemphasizing hospitals' trust in administering Tylenol to patients. On the other hand, Winn-Dixie supermarkets has found that changing customers' negative perceptions of the stores' beef quality since the 1998 charges of past-due meat sales has been comparatively more challenging.

The first step in the positioning process is to develop a three-phase research plan. First, research is used to unlock the target market's existing perceptions. Since consumers ultimately determine a product's position, learning as much as possible about consumers demographically and psychographically—as well as how they use the product—can provide important clues about the existing position it holds in the their mind.

Second, researching key variables enables marketers to discover distinctive means by which to showcase a product to its best advantage—also known as creating a desired position. Basic approaches consider the consumer, competitors' strategies, social responsibility, and image strategies. Research enables marketers to assess consumers' reactions to tentative persuasive messages developed to affect a product's positioning. Of particular concern is how the messages play out relative to consumers' beliefs, attitudes, and product-use habits. Some marketers position their product using strategies such as problem-solution, country of origin, distributor location, distributor's service

capability, and low price. Here are some other approaches:

- Corporate image
- Product benefits/attributes: underscoring certain traits and characteristics
- Competitors: comparing with a competing brand
- Price-to-quality ratio: emphasizing this value relationship
- Product use: distinction from competition based on how a product is used
- Product class: identifying a hierarchical position within a category
- Cultural symbol: relating the product to a well-known symbol
- Distribution methods: associating product with reputable distributors who make products easily accessible for consumers
- Spokesperson: linking product with a celebrity
- Personality: relating a product to a certain lifestyle

Finally, marketers must consistently monitor the position that their products hold in consumers' minds and modify strategies accordingly. Key message development and communication over the long-term are crucial components of successful, well-researched positioning strategies. Expecting short-term promotional strategies to cement a desired product position constitutes a formula for failure. Moreover, positioning messages should be consistent across all segments of the marketing mix, and marketers should take care to create positioning strategies that competitors cannot duplicate easily.

Finally, positioning strategies also must be considered when developing market plans for international arenas in today's global marketplace. Again, research is key to discovering what is relevant to the consumer and how the product provides a benefit. A culture's heritage, traditions, and symbols cannot be overlooked. Given the strong emphasis on research, it is obvious that positioning is only as good as the research on which it is based.

—Donnalyn Pompper

See also Advertising; Marketing; Media networks; Two-way and one-way communication

Bibliography

Clow, K. E., & Baack, D. (2002). *Integrated advertising, promotion, and marketing communications.* Upper Saddle River, NJ: Prentice Hall.

Duncan, T. (2002). *IMC: Using advertising and promotion to build brands.* Madison, WI: McGraw-Hill/Irwin.

Morris, M. H., Pitt, L. F., & Honeycutt, E. D., Jr. (2001). *Business-to-business marketing: A strategic approach* (3rd ed.). Thousand Oaks, CA: Sage.

POSTCOLONIAL THEORY AND PUBLIC RELATIONS

Postcolonial theory is a relatively new lens through which to examine the academic discipline of public relations and other corporate and governmental practices. In essence, postcolonial theory offers the rationale for interventions that uncover traces of colonialist styles of thinking manifested in prevailing discourses on economy, society, culture, and politics.

Postcolonial is a way of theorizing challenges and resistances to dominant, often Western, theoretical and methodological perspectives. This interdisciplinary tool has been used extensively in literary criticism and cultural studies to critique the taken-for-granted worldviews of mainstream Euro-American writers, scholars, and thinkers. In recent years, postcolonial scholars have been trying to articulate radical new ways of understanding the world that challenge both overt and covert forms of economic, social, and cultural imperialism.

The postcolonial perspective gained currency in the domain of communication studies when *Communication Theory* brought out a special issue on the subject. In their introductory essay in this issue, Raka Shome and Radha Hegde pointed out that "there is a growing awareness of the limitations and parochialism of theory so steeped in Eurocentrism that it either ignores completely or oversimplifies the complexity of the 'rest' of the world" (2002, p. 260). Postcolonial theory plays a significant role in not only making sense of this complexity on the fluid matrix of a deterritorialized world but also in communicating this complexity.

In public relations literature, one of the earliest references to postcolonial theory is in a 1996 essay by Nancy Roth, Todd Hunt, Maria Stavropoulos, and Karen Babik, who, drawing on postcolonial scholar Edward Said (1978), talk about the need to address issues of relative power in the framing of universal ethical principles for the practice of public relations.

Power, which is central to postcolonial theory, is often neglected in the study of public relations. The discipline of public relations, of course, does acknowledge multiculturalism. But although the recognition of multiple identities, cultures, and ethnicities is a crucial first step in acknowledging demographic, ideological, and cultural diversities in the world, postcolonial scholars argue that global relationships and interactions have to be understood in terms of existing power differentials within and among nations, institutions, and organizations. For instance, one of the key postcolonial projects is to show how Western or West-trained policymakers seek to control power by legitimizing Western ways of thinking manifested in the Western paradigm of global management.

In the domain of public relations, there is an overwhelming emphasis on the communication of corporate goals. This communication is channeled through messages about a dominant, largely Western, model of economic growth and development. Such a model, postcolonialists argue, is often shaped more by powerful Western or West-based multinational corporations and their strategic publics in the market, trade, finance, and high technology sectors than by the needs and aspirations of a vast majority of the global population. In other words, publics that are not perceived to be "strategic" are marginalized or ignored.

A postcolonial examination of the predominantly Western paradigm of public relations is carried out by Debashish Munshi and David McKie, who postulated that the more common "homogenised worldview of public relations maintains old colonial legacies that support neo-colonial economic interests" (2001, p. 16). They pointed out, for example, that the Bhopal gas tragedy of 1984 in India, which claimed thousands of lives and maimed countless others, continues to be seen through the eyes of a major Western corporation (Union Carbide). Most mainstream public relations literature continues to depict the ways in which the company dealt with the crisis and maintained its line of communication with its shareholders and investors. The fundamental aim of the mainstream public relations approach in this case was to manage the impact the case had in the United States, where the corporation was based. The voice of the victims of the tragedy, akin to the marginalized subaltern publics of colonial historiography, is rarely heard in such depictions. Clearly, therefore, there is a significant power differential among a diverse range of publics.

The sustainability of public relations depends on addressing the issue of power differentials and acknowledging the existence of a multiplicity of publics. Postcolonial approaches provide an opportunity for public relations to look outside the dominant frame and effectively reach out to a broad range of publics instead of being limited to few elite publics. In a rapidly globalizing world with major demographic shifts, recognizing a broad spectrum of publics is not just a moral imperative for public relations scholars and practitioners but an economic and political one as well. In numerical terms alone, publics in the Third World, often a loose synonym for the non-Western "other," will have to be taken note of. After all, as Futurist David Mercer pointed out, "wealth increasingly depends upon market demand rather than supplier pressure, and—with more than 90 per cent of the world's population— the Third World will become the main economic driver in the Third Millennium" (1998, p. 15). In the interest of long-term equity, therefore, public relations scholars and practitioners would need to shed firmly entrenched paradigms rooted in the colonial era and work toward nurturing multiple relationships and recognizing a variety of worldviews.

—*Debashish Munshi*

Bibliography

Mercer, D. (1998). *Future revolutions: Unravelling the uncertainties of life and work in the 21st century.* London: Orion Business Books.

Munshi, D., & McKie, D. (2001). Different bodies of knowledge: Diversity and diversification in public relations. *Australian Journal of Communication, 28*(3), 11–22.

Roth, N., Hunt, T., Stavropoulos, M., & Babik, K. (1996). Can't we all just get along: Cultural variables in codes of ethics. *Public Relations Review, 22*(2), 151–161.

Said, E. (1978). *Orientalism.* New York: Vintage.

Shome, R., & Hegde, R. (2002). Postcolonial approaches to communication: Charting the terrain, engaging the intersections. *Communication Theory, 12*(3), 249–270.

An Indian protester uses a megaphone during a demonstration against the 1984 Bhopal gas tragedy in New Delhi on August 27, 2003. Scholars have pointed to the Bhopal tragedy as an example of postcolonialism because most mainstream public relations literature continues to depict how the company dealt with the crisis and maintained its line of communication with its shareholders and investors, while the voice of the victims of the tragedy is rarely heard.

SOURCE: © Reuters NewMedia Inc./CORBIS.

POWER RESOURCE MANAGEMENT THEORY

Power resource management theory is founded on the assumption that those who have control over resources (also known as stakes) have differing degrees of power over one or more of the following: decision-making processes, resource recognition and/or allocation, criteria building, interpretation of events or communication, agenda setting, issues management, and the like. In essence, there are as many resources as there are economic, political, and social contexts. Definitions of what might be considered resources and the values assigned to them are largely a phenomenon of social construction. Resource definitions and values can be frequently characterized as states instead of traits. Definitions of resources as well as assigned values can and often do change through ideological discussions or contests over what is or what should be.

Traditionally, however, public relations resources are those "things" that have the potential to accomplish organizational goals. In the arena of activism, for example, Robert L. Heath suggested that

> power resource management entails the ability to employ economic, political and social sanctions and rewards through means such as boycotts, strikes, embargoes, layoffs, lockouts, legislation, regulation, executive orders, police action, and judicial review . . . [It] assumes the ability of a group, a company, or a governmental agency to give or withhold rewards—stakes. (1997, p. 161)

Barry Barnes wrote that power resource management theory conceptualizes power as being "embedded in society as a whole" (1988, p. 61); however, not everyone or every organization has the discretion to use power. "The possession of power is the possession of discretion in the use of that power. When one person [or organization] is said to have more power than another it is a matter of the one having the discretion over a greater capacity for action than the other" (p. 61).

Considerations of power and the discretionary use of it in public relations can be interestingly contextualized among three levels of power. The first, and most traditional, conceptualization of power assumes that one has power over another to the extent that one can get the other to do something he or she (or it) would otherwise not do. This is the most obvious presence of power. Persuading members of a public to contribute to a new philanthropic effort or to adopt a specific interpretation of an organization's intended identity over an alternative one are examples of the first level of power.

The second level assumes that power comes from the mobilization of bias, meaning the ability to represent sectional interests as the interests of the masses within a given population; the definitions and values of a few are made to take precedence over the definitions and values held by the majority. For example, when public relations strategies and tactics are used to develop consensus around economic, political, or social issues (regardless of party lines) to favor one group of the public over others that have stakes in the outcome, they are being used for the mobilization of bias. It is important to note, however, that this process is rarely a conscious one in the minds of the majority participants.

The third level assumes that power, and the discretionary use of it, come from the ability of an individual or organization to engage in discursive practices resulting in the creation of a given population's wants and needs. At this level, the populations under study accept the construction of their wants and needs by parties other than themselves without question. The economic, political, and social norms by which a population operates and is governed are accepted as real and immutable, when in reality they are the results of the reification and institutionalization of the mobilization of bias. Public relations strategies and tactics can be and have been used in the institutionalization process. They also have been and can be used to challenge institutionalized norms, thereby bringing about change and new ideas.

From the standpoint of power resource management theory, then, power may be viewed as coming from the discretion, socially given, to determine and/or manage valued resources in complex ways within socially meaningful economic, political, and social arenas. To the extent that public relations is used to construct, add meaningful value to, and exercise discretion over resources, it is integral to power.

—*Tricia L. Hansen-Horn*

Bibliography

Bachratz, P., & Baratz, M. S. (1962). The two faces of power. *American Political Science Review, 56,* 947–952.

Barnes, B. (1988). *The nature of power.* Urbana: University of Illinois Press.

Blalock, H. M., Jr. (1989). *Power and conflict: Toward a general theory.* Newbury Park, CA: Sage.

Heath, R. L. (1997). *Strategic issues management: Organizations and public policy challenges.* Thousand Oaks, CA: Sage.

Lukes, S. (1974). *Power: A radical review.* London: Macmillan.

Ragins, B., & Sundstrom, E. (1989). Gender and power in organizations: A longitudinal perspective. *Psychological Bulletin, 105*(1), 51–88.

PR NEWSWIRE

Founded by Herbert Muschel, the originator of the *TV Guide,* PR Newswire has provided the technological means for public relations and investor relations practitioners to communicate with the media since 1954. Starting with a private teleprinter network to distribute news releases to journalists from public relations agencies and corporations, PR Newswire first delivered news releases to news sources in New York. Almost 50 years later, it has expanded into a global network using the latest communication technologies. Today, the company offers many multimedia tools, including Web-based conference calls, video news releases, Web sites, and cybercasting of press conferences, annual meetings, and events. PR Newswire serves as a communication bridge between public and investor relations practitioners and journalists. Its Web site caters to both journalists and communication professionals.

In March 2002, PR Newswire launched a special section tailored for journalists, who can use the company's services at no cost. PR Newswire's Web site allows journalists to locate sources for stories by sending e-mail queries to up to 10,000 public relations and news information officers in North America and Europe. In addition, the Web site allows journalists to conduct searches for news releases, as well as information about companies, and subscribe to e-mail alerts about various industries. The "Company Information Pages" section allows journalists to view news releases issued by a company, as well as biographical information about key people working for that company, product information, and white papers related to that company. The "Company Information Pages" section gives journalists access to photos, multimedia presentations, and tradeshows, and also a directory of contacts for each company.

Public relations and investor relations practitioners use PR Newswire to distribute news releases to the media for a fee. Practitioners can target the distribution of their releases to journalists by state, region in the United States, or country. The press releases are posted on PR Newswire's Web site and can be sent directly to journalists subscribing to PR Newswire's services. Practitioners can include pictures or multimedia presentations to accompany the news releases or can have them stand alone. For example, during the 9/11 attacks, the airlines posted press releases to PR Newswire within an hour of the terrorists crashing the planes into the World Trade Center. In addition, Southwest Airlines, although not one of the airlines involved in the attacks, included a video news release on PR Newswire's Web site about the precautions it was taking to ensure passenger safety to ease consumers' fears about flying again within a week of the attacks.

In addition to distributing news releases, practitioners can include information about their company or organization's experts for use by the media. When reporters need a source for a story, they can use PR Newswire's service called ProfNet (http://www.profnet.com). This service links journalists to experts from colleges and universities, corporations, government agencies, national laboratories, think tanks, scientific organizations, nonprofit organizations, and public relations agencies. The ProfNet database allows journalists to either post a query for experts or search a database. The information in these databases is compiled by and paid for by communication practitioners.

Practitioners can also monitor the impact of their communications through PR Newswire's eWatch service (http://www.ewatch.com). Since 1995, this service has monitored the Internet for information about or related to a communication practitioner's company or industry. For a fee, practitioners can keep a pulse on what consumers, businesses, and the media say about their products, company, and competitors. eWatch monitors more than 4,700 online newspapers, e-zines, broadcast sites, and portals. In addition, more than 66,000 Usenet and electronic mailing lists, as well as investor relations message boards, are monitored.

—*Cassandra Imfeld*

See also Investigative journalism; Investor relations; Media release

PR WATCH

Designed to educate and expose "manipulative and misleading" public relations practices, PR Watch (prwatch.org) is a Web site that posts information, articles, and book reviews about the public relations industry. The Web site is sponsored by the Center for Media and Democracy, a nonprofit public interest group dedicated to investigative reporting of the public relations industry and informing the public, journalists, and researchers about current public relations practices. The Center for Media and Democracy challenges public relations communicators' "spin" on issues and attempts to present accurate and unbiased accounts of the news. The organization has received widespread media attention, including coverage in *The New York Times, USA Today,* the *Wall Street Journal,* and the *Washington Post.*

Through its quarterly publication *PR Watch,* the Center for Media and Democracy tackles issues that it considers have become propagandized by the public relations industry. Since 1994 PR Watch has addressed public relations issues involving O. J. Simpson, Philip Morris, Mad Cow disease, breast implants, global warming, and terrorism. Each issue begins with an overview of the public relations industry's latest success in spinning news events, followed by in-depth articles that present different perspectives about news events initially "spun" by public relations practitioners. In addition to its quarterly publication, PR Watch also offers an e-mail newsletter titled *The Weekly Spin.* The free e-newsletter is a "compendium of current news tips about public relations, propaganda and media spin."

On its Web site, PR Watch pulls quotes from other media sources around the country that recognize the effect of public relations on current events in a section called Spin of the Day. The quotes pulled from media sources date back to 1994 and include publications such as the *Wall Street Journal, Salon.com, Editor & Publisher,* and *O'Dwyer's PR Daily.* In addition to posting the media's quotes about "spun" stories, the Spin of the Day section allows users to engage in discussion about the quotes and news stories. Called "Let's Talk About Flacks, Baby," Spin of the Day's discussion is an active and up-to-date forum for users and members of the media to discuss how public relations practitioners shape the news. Let's Talk About Flacks, Baby also allows users to discuss books written by the PR Watch editorial staff.

In addition to serving as a watchdog on current events, PR Watch monitors and reviews organizations in its Impropaganda Review section. This section of the Web site is dedicated to exposing industry front groups and anti-environmental think tanks. Impropaganda Review has examined organizations such as the American Council on Science and Health, the Center for Tobacco Research, and the Global Climate Coalition. Each in-depth review of these organizations provides a history of the organization, key personnel, and funding sources and a case study of how public relations practitioners use these organizations to advance their "propaganda" goals.

Although PR Watch is dedicated to providing journalists and researchers with information and examples of the public relations influence on the news, the site also includes links to several other Web sites, including public relations organizations, search engines, government institutions, and other activist Web sites.

—*Cassandra Imfeld*

See also Propaganda; Spin

PRACTICE

It is most practical, perhaps, to define public relations "practice" by explaining what a "practitioner" does and to compare and contrast this with the work of "academics." Both practitioners and academics have worked diligently to align perceptions of public relations work with those of other "professions" and to improve unflattering characterizations of public relations practice. On the other hand, practitioners and academics differ. Practitioners serve a strategic function as members of an organization's management team, whereas scholars teach in higher education settings and build public relations theory about conflict reduction.

Overall, the basic tenants of public relations practice have not changed significantly since Ivy Lee penned his *Declaration of Principles* in 1906; ethical practices, relationships, and mutual benefit take center stage. Unfortunately, public relations is considered all too frequently to be a *dis*honest means for spreading propaganda. Consequently, national and regional public relations trade organizations have organized to explain the profession's metamorphosis from mere press agentry or publicity to a reputable one that thrives on facilitating two-way communication flow between organizations and publics. Task forces continue to investigate means to advance the profession. For example, the governing body of the Public Relations Society of America (PRSA) formally adopted a definition of public relations that has been widely accepted: "Public relations helps an organization and its publics adapt mutually to each other."

According to the U.S. Bureau of Labor Statistics, the practice of public relations is one of the fastest-growing fields that does not require a graduate degree. Practitioners held about 122,000 jobs in 1998 (13,000 were self-employed), and the median salary range for practitioners was $53,000, according to the PRSA/IABC 2000 Salary Survey. G. M. Broom wrote that, nearly 20 years ago, the practice was a "traditionally male bastion" where only one in four (27 percent) PRSA members was a woman (1982, p. 17). Federally funded investigations, such as the Kerner Commission, recommended greater hiring of minorities and women in newsrooms and related fields such as public relations. Now, women account for about two-thirds of all public relations specialists in the United States. Practitioners work in "for-profit" settings (public relations agencies,

corporations, companies) and "not-for-profit" settings (government, education, fundraising, trade organizations). No state requires that practitioners be licensed.

A practitioner should have a solid understanding of our complex, pluralistic society and should possess good knowledge of human relations in order to manage change and to enable organizations to generate market share and income (funding, revenue, donations), to share ideas, and to affect behavior. Also, a practitioner acts as a "sponge"—soaking up popular culture, social trends, political policy issues, and other current debates. A foundation in psychology, sociology, political science, and the management sciences is vital to developing negotiation skills and cognitive complexity.

Several personality traits emerge among public relations practitioners. For example, they must thrive under pressure conditions, listen, be creative and inquisitive, and be good communicators. However, practitioners do more than write press releases, meet people, and smile in public. As managers, practitioners play an integrative role and must know how to conduct market research, identify stakeholders, interpret public opinion, counsel senior-level management, address public policy, set objectives, measure results, and manage resources.

The practitioner's day-to-day responsibilities are based on a long-term view of an organization's relationships with various groups, the ability to do multi-tasking, and a grasp of certain technical skills. For example, practitioners act as consultants and mediators, decision makers, and public speakers. They also get involved in the community, work closely with employees, participate in industry affairs, serve as a liaison between organizations and the media, organize special events, and anticipate and act in the wake of crises that threaten the organization's reputation. To excel in public relations, the practitioner should be able to write well for a variety of media (including speeches and reports), analyze and interpret public opinion, conduct research on an ongoing basis, and do planning, including setting objectives and measuring results. He or she should also have skills in graphic design, statistics, conceptual development, and technology.

Scott Cultip, Allen Center, and Glen Broom (2000) wrote that threats to successful public relations practice, called the "seven deadly sins in this (agency) business," were itemized by Robert Dilenschneider, former president and CEO of Hill & Knowlton and current chair of the Dilenschneider Group of New York and Chicago (p. 69):

1. Overpromising what cannot be delivered

2. Overselling public relations' capabilities

3. Underservicing by using junior staff, but promising senior staff attention

4. Emphasizing financial results over performance

5. Short-sightedness instead of long-term strategic thinking

6. Enabling encroachment by lawyers, financial officers, and others

7. Violating ethical standards

Finally, as in trade occupations of yore, practitioners serve as mentors to public relations student-apprentices and work with them side by side during relatively short periods of time called "internships." While "shadowing" practitioners, interns garner practical, hands-on knowledge beyond the classroom about how public relations works. Often, interns are asked to write press releases, update media lists, coordinate special event details, and perform office tasks such as filing and typing. These experiences serve students well when they are interviewing for full-time positions because they can share actual, practical examples of their work—including portfolios that showcase their skill sets.

Public relations scholars conduct research to further develop the public relations body of knowledge and to enhance public relations' image as an ethical profession, and in doing so they offer practitioners advice on how to be more successful. In recent decades, several academic journals have developed and published scholars' research findings: *Public Relations Review, Journal of Public Relations Research,* and *Public Relations Quarterly.* Public relations scholars set the tone for early theory building in the 1970s when they sought to define

and validate public relations by examining practitioners' roles. Other researchers have considered conflict reduction in terms of public relations practice models, gender and ethnicity workplace issues, international practice, measurement techniques, social issues/case studies, and more. Overall, public relations scholars draw from the theoretical perspectives of diverse social science fields to offer multidisciplinary perspectives.

Spheres of practitioners and academics formally overlap during annual meetings, such as the convention of the Association for Education in Journalism & Mass Communication (AEJMC) and the PRSA conference.

—Donnalyn Pompper

See also Code of ethics; Encroachment theory; Feminization theory; Internship; Lee, Ivy; Press agentry; Two-way and one-way communication

Bibliography

Broom, G. M. (1982). A comparison of sex roles in public relations. *Public Relations Review, 11*(4), 22–28.

Cutlip, S. M., Center, A. H., & Broom, G. M. (2000). *Effective public relations* (8th ed.). Upper Saddle River, NJ: Prentice Hall.

U. S. Bureau of Labor Statistics. (2000). Unpublished data from the Current Population Survey, 2000 annual averages, "Occupation and Industry package," table 2, tabulated by the Bureau of Labor Statistics, Division of Labor Force Statistics.

U.S. Department of Commerce. (1998). *Statistical abstract of the United States, 1998: The national data book* (117th ed.). Washington, DC: Government Printing Office.

PRESIDENTIAL PRESS SECRETARIES

The modern-day White House press secretary's primary responsibility is to be the official spokesperson for the president of the United States and his or her administration. Additionally, the press secretary's responsibilities include meeting with the president and other senior administration officials, conducting press briefings, helping the president prepare for press conferences, handling press arrangements for presidential trips, fulfilling interview and information requests, writing and disseminating press releases, meeting with the press secretaries of various departments, and gathering information about the administration.

Historically, some White House press secretaries have also acted as policy advisers and speechwriters, have helped make personnel decisions, and have been a voice of reason in times of crisis. Depending on their relationship with the president, some press secretaries were even able to speak in a frank and direct manner with the president. Twenty-six individuals, 25 men and 1 woman, have served the president of the United States in the press secretary capacity.

It is widely accepted that George Ackerson was the first person whose sole responsibility was to handle press relations on behalf of the president. Although Ackerson did not hold the official title of *press secretary,* President Herbert Hoover employed Ackerson in that capacity from 1929 to 1931. The title given to Ackerson and the nine men who followed him in that position was *secretary to the president.* James Hagerty, who handled press relations for Dwight D. Eisenhower, was the last person to hold this title; in 1956, it was dropped by legislation. As a result, Hagerty was the first person to officially hold the title of *press secretary.*

In the early years, the press secretary and his or her assistant primarily dealt with Washington-based print reporters and radio. But as communication technologies have evolved, the press corps covering the president has grown. Subsequently, these changes in technology have forced the Press Office staff to grow as well. Now, the White House Press Office employs several people who handle issues that deal with specific areas of the administration and whose responsibility it is to convey the "official administration position" to the press.

The White House Press Office currently falls under the jurisdiction of the White House Office of Communications, which was established by Richard M. Nixon in 1969.

Stephen Early, who ran Franklin D. Roosevelt's press office, was the first press secretary to successfully handle the press, and his success helped define the role of the press secretary for years to come. Charlie Ross, who was one of Harry Truman's press secretaries, shared a unique relationship with Truman. They were boyhood friends growing up in Independence, Missouri; thus Ross was a true administration "insider." Perhaps the most successful press secretary was Hagerty. He is credited with expanding the role of the press secretary and adding the element of frankness to the post.

The following is a list of those individuals who have acted in the capacity of press secretary or have held that official title: George Ackerson (1929–1931), Theodore Joslin (1931–1933), Stephen T. Early (1933–1945), Jonathan Daniels (1945), J. Leonard Reinsch (1945), Charlie G. Ross (1945–1950), Stephen T. Early (1950), Joseph H. Short (1950–1952), Roger Tubby (1952–1953), Irving Perlmeter (1952), James C. Hagerty (1953–1961), Pierre Salinger (1961–1964), George E. Reedy (1964–1965), William D. Moyers (1965–1967), George E. Christian (1967–1969), Ronald L. Ziegler (1969–1974), Jerald F. terHorst (1974), Ronald H. Nessen (1974–1977), Joseph L. Powell (1977–1981), James Brady (1981), Larry Speakes (1981–1987), Marlin Fitzwater (1987–1993), Dee Dee Myers (1993–1994), Mike McCurry (1994–1998), Joe Lockhart (1998–2001), Ari Fleischer (2001–2003), and Scott McClellan (2003–).

—*Adam E. Horn*

Bibliography

Levy, L. W., & Fisher, L. (Eds.). (1994). *Encyclopedia of the American presidency* (Vols. 1–4). New York: Simon & Schuster.

Nelson, D. (2000). *Who speaks for the president: The White House press secretary from Cleveland to Clinton.* Syracuse, NY: Syracuse University Press.

PRESS AGENTRY

Press agentry is the practice of attracting the attention of the press through techniques that manufacture news, no matter how bizarre. Methods associated with press agentry include staged events, publicity stunts, faux rallies or gatherings, spinning, and hype. A common practice in the late 1800s and early 1900s, press agentry is not part of mainstream public relations. Rather, it is a practice primarily associated with major entertainment-related events, such as Hollywood premieres and boxing events. The goal of press agentry is to attract attention rather than gain understanding. Although press agentry is considered an old-fashioned reference, even today, the term *press agent* is sometimes used interchangeably with *publicist* in traditional Broadway theater and motion picture industries. Today's entertainment industries are populated with publicists rather than press agents. Publicists are individuals skilled in media relations who attempt to get the name of their clients or events in the media by carefully constructing messages that inform, educate, and persuade. Some are astute in branding and positioning strategies to further the careers and success of their clients. In contrast, press agents want attention—good or bad—in most any form.

Press agentry has been called persuasion for short-term advantage through the use of truth bending and even distortion, but it can also be simply the staging of provocative acts to get publicity and draw attention to an individual, event, or cause.

The evolution of public relations is often described by four models: press agentry/publicity, public information, two-way asymmetric communication, and two-way symmetric communication. The earliest, which is the press agentry/publicity model, is described as one-way communication in which truth is not an essential component. The most sophisticated form of practice is the two-way symmetric model, focusing on mutual understanding, mediation, and two-way balanced flow of information. Therefore, it is understandable that one of the earliest proponents of the press agentry/publicity model was Phineas Taylor (P. T.) Barnum, the famed American showman and promoter who put Gen. Tom Thumb on exhibit and launched a mobile circus featuring Jumbo the elephant and freak shows. Barnum was a master of press agentry. For instance, he wrote letters both praising and criticizing his circus show to newspapers under an assumed name.

In the early part of his career, Edward L. Bernays was a master of press agentry. He persuaded 10 debutantes to hold up Lucky Strike cigarettes, manufactured by his client, the American Tobacco Company, as "torches of freedom" while participating in New York's Easter parade. In 1929, Bernays staged a global news event by organizing the "Light's Golden Jubilee," a worldwide celebration commemorating the 50th anniversary of the electric light bulb for his client, General Electric. Bernays managed to secure several prominent individuals for the event, including carmaker Henry Ford, electricity scientist Thomas Edison, and President Herbert Hoover.

Henry Rogers, one of the founders of Rogers and Cowan, the largest and most successful West Coast entertainment publicity firm, became well known when he promoted an unknown contract player for Columbia Pictures named Rita Hayworth. He contacted *Look* magazine with a telegram from the Fashion Couturiers Association of America, a fictitious group, claiming that Hayworth was the best-dressed off-screen actress. *Look* magazine took the bait and put Hayworth on the cover and printed 10 pages of photographs.

—Emma Daugherty Phillingane

See also Barnum, P. T.; Bernays, Edward; Entertainment industry publicity/promotion; Promotion; Publicist; Publicity

Bibliography

Goff, C. F. (1989). *The publicity process.* Ames: Iowa State University Press.

Loeffler, R. H. (1993). *A guide to preparing cost-effective press releases.* New York: Haworth Press.

Wilcox, D. L., Cameron, G. T., Ault, P. H., & Agee, W. K. (2003). *Public relations strategies and tactics.* Boston: Allyn & Bacon.

PRESS KIT

A press kit is a package of information put together for a special event, such as a press conference, new product launch, or media preview event. Its use should be reserved for events that merit more extensive information than a standard news release can provide. Press kits are not used as an everyday public relations tool.

The focus of a press kit should always be information. The media should find the kit to be a helpful resource when reporting on the event. Materials that do not further this purpose should not be included in the kit. A growing criticism of press kits is that they include too many meaningless trinkets or outright gifts designed to influence the media. Members of the media recognize this ploy, and many outlets instruct their reporters not to accept such items. Maintaining the focus on information will enable a public relations practitioner to provide the media with helpful material and avoid the appearance of impropriety (and clutter).

The anchor piece in a press kit is the news release about the topic of the special event. Other written pieces should be included, as appropriate, in support of the news release. These can include additional news releases, fact sheets, backgrounders, biographies, photos with cutlines, and article reprints. Product samples should be included when they are the focus of the event, but not in excessive amounts.

Press kits are typically packaged in a two-pocket folder. The folder itself is usually specially printed for the event. This additional expense is another reason press kits are not used on a daily basis. The folder should look professional and carry through with the theme of the event, if one exists, or the branding of the organization. Inside, a business card insert cutout is fairly standard on one of the pockets. When the folder is lying open, the main news release should be the top item in the right pocket (where the eyes naturally go first), with a table of contents on top in the left pocket. Although not always included, a table of contents can be quite helpful, especially in a large press kit. It should list, in order, what is contained in each pocket. Again, the purpose is to assist the media in covering the story, and anything that furthers that purpose should be included.

As an example, say a small waterfront town sponsors an annual festival that regularly draws 100,000 visitors for the two-and-a-half-day event. The event includes a variety of nationally recognized music and entertainment artists, along with water events, family-oriented activities, and a large fireworks display. The event has been nationally recognized, and local media, including those from a nearby large city, always provide coverage. To facilitate continued good press and add to it, an annual media preview event is held. The press kit designed for this preview has the colorful festival logo on the cover and contains the primary news release about the festival, individual news releases about headline entertainment, a timetable of special media coverage opportunities such as the setup of the fireworks barge, a fact sheet covering festival history and records, and a reprint of the article that named the festival one of the top 100 in the nation. The media also receive advance copies of the full festival program with a timetable insert for each stage and all special events. Both the media preview event and the press kit are designed to stimulate media interest in the festival and facilitate coverage when it occurs. (This description is based on the author's experience with Harborfest in Oswego, New York.)

Press kits are provided to members of the media at the event for which they are designed. Those who can't attend the event should be sent a press kit immediately after the event concludes. Another option, and one that is growing in popularity, is to provide electronic press kits online through an organization's Web site. Many organizations have a button on their Web sites that is a direct link to what can be called their cyber newsroom. Although providing items such as an actual program (mentioned previously) and trinkets is not possible with this method, all standard written tools and photos can be placed on a Web site and accessed at the media's convenience. A distinct advantage here is that large amounts of information can easily be made available, whereas a traditional folder does have limited capacity. Those in the press who criticize press kit gifts as influence attempts might view this method of presentation as preferable, because the focus is strictly on the traditional information pieces. This method also lessens the expense associated with producing a press kit by eliminating the need for specially produced folders. Finally, with the increasing use of corporate Web sites by individuals to gather information, particularly in the area of investor relations, having these specialized groupings of information available to anyone who cares to look for them provides a nonmediated method of reaching important publics.

—*Maribeth S. Metzler*

PRIVATIZING PUBLIC OPINION (AND "PUBLICTIZING" PRIVATE OPINION)

Legions of books, articles, feature stories, and editorials have decried the influence that large companies' version of the free market system has on the public opinion of the United States. The proposition that runs through this analysis is that corporate industry has the dollars and incentive to create a public opinion that privileges the role and interests of large companies in society. One of the reasons critics and supporters make this connection is the legion of statements by public relations practitioners and theorists that feature the role of public opinion formation as the essence of public relations and advertising— the outcome of corporate communication.

Out of this discussion arose the concept of privatizing public opinion. On this topic, Michael J. Sproule reasoned: "Organizations try to privatize public space by privatizing public opinions; this is, skillfully (one-sidedly) turning opinion in directions favorable to the corporation" (1989, p. 264). Endless pounding of the public collective mentality by messages supplied by deep-pocket corporations has led members of the public to believe that what is good for industry is good for America. One recalls one of the highlights of American popular culture: "What is good for General Motors is good for America."

In a sense, this view of public opinion formation opts for what can be called a propaganda approach to the mass communication of messages that shape any society's collective mentality. This line of reasoning assumes that the meaning of society is skewed to the advantage of industry, the private sector against the larger interests of the people of society. What is deemed to be good commercially for industry is good for Americans. Thus, for instance, Detroit automobile manufacturers used publicity and promotion to create a culture of new car ownership. Each fall, with great fanfare, the new models would roll off the design and assembly lines. The new season of automobiles was headline news. It was featured in the newsreels at movie theaters and sufficiently important to *Life* magazine that an entire issue would be devoted to the display of status and freedom in the shape of the latest models. These were carefully positioned and differentiated so that they demarked class structure. Of even greater relevance, the "true American" bought a new car each year—to have the latest model to show status and patriotism. Less trendy or affluent Americans were supposed to buy a new car at least every three years. Americans owed their identity— and paycheck—to Detroit. It was the American way. Thus, public opinion was formed through advertising and public relations to the benefit of the automobile industry. Public opinion had been privatized.

The experience of people and their love for automobiles were played out, according to the critics of privatizing public opinion, by industry after industry. The citizen consumer was held hostage to the whims and dictates of what was thought to be right, proper, and patriotic by large industry. What industry did was right. To criticize industry was just un-American, perhaps anti-American and even communistic. It attacked the American way of life. Industry knew best. It defined a lifestyle and way of life that was the envy of the world.

The evolution of this theme started in the middle of the 19th century as large industry replaced local or regional businesses. To operate as they preferred, the robber barons needed a favorable public opinion. They needed to be perceived as operating in the public interest. Although the first half of the 20th century saw a great deal of contentiousness over this view, the role industry played in World War II and postwar prosperity clearly demonstrated to believers in this version of the American way that the public owed deference to industry. It helped a million soldiers win the war and brought an era of prosperity that slowly put the Great Depression aside as a nightmare that had interrupted the American Dream. By the end of the 1950s, America had achieved the age of deference. Industry ruled supreme. It produced the cornucopia of goods and services.

If industry had privatized public opinion, the activism that marked the last four decades of the 20th century in the United States worked to "publictize" private opinion. Activists argued that industry must truly serve the public interest. The public interest defined by citizen activists—publics and stakeholders—would now tell industry the standards by which it would operate.

Out of this shifted equation, we had civil rights, consumer rights, environmental rights, animal rights, and so forth. The era of activism indicted the corporate view of public opinion and condemned many of the operating principles as violating what was the essence of the true American way. Industry did not have a right to clear-cut timber, stripmine minerals, or pollute indiscriminately to produce the American lifestyle. Activists were alarmed, for instance, when certain rivers would change color, since they suspected that manufacturers were changing dye colors and discharging their waste into the environment. Discharge into the environment became offensive rather than necessary.

Out of this dynamic clash of interests came a new sense of what public relations must be. This era of the 1960s launched increased interest into what became an issues management approach to corporate positioning and public communication. Dialogue replaced monologue. The definition of the principles and premises of society now clearly allowed for all voices to be heard. The dynamics of regulation and legislation changed. The American public became increasingly asked to bear the costs of increased operating standards that did not sell the environment, for instance, in the name of progress.

A rhetorical view of public relations features the dialogue between factions. It sees efforts by industry to privatize public opinion as being challenged by activists who argue for views that would "publictize" the private opinions of company executives, who must now position their companies and industries to avoid clashes with politicized activists. Public relations plays a robust role for all sides in this grand debate.

—Robert L. Heath

See also Activism; Advertising; Age of deference (end of); Differentiation; Issues management; Position and positioning; Promotion; Propaganda; Public interest; Public opinion and opinion leaders; Publicity

Bibliography

Heath, R. L. (1997). *Strategic issues management.* Thousand Oaks, CA: Sage.

Heath, R. L. (2001). A rhetorical enactment rationale for public relations. In R. L. Heath (Ed.), *Handbook of public relations* (pp. 31–50). Thousand Oaks, CA: Sage.

Sproule, M. J. (1989). Organizational rhetoric and the public sphere. *Communication Studies, 40,* 258–265.

PRIZM AND VALS

See Segmentation

PROACTIVITY AND REACTIVITY

In the world of public relations, being proactive instead of reactive could determine whether an organization thrives or dies. Proactive public relations is associated with strategic planning, whereas reactive public relations consists of a piecemeal approach to addressing problems and opportunities.

There are numerous reasons an organization should involve public relations in its long-range planning:

- The goals of public relations are coordinated with the goals of the entire organization.
- Strategies and tactics can be carefully thought out and developed rather than haphazardly put together.
- Programs will feature a more positive, rather than defensive, approach.
- It's easier to formulate short-term, reactive plans when necessary—for example, in a crisis situation—if a long-term plan already exists.

Whether organizations lean toward proactive or reactive public relations may depend on three factors: whether the organization is an open or closed system, how top management views the public relations function, and the skills of the public relations practitioner.

OPEN VERSUS CLOSED SYSTEMS

The survival of any kind of system is based on how well the parts of that system work together. Organizations are no different; they are systems that consist of interdependent parts working toward a common goal—successfully achieving the mission of the organization. The degree to which these parts work together may be influenced by whether they work in an open or closed system. Although no organization can be totally open or completely closed, every organization leans toward one or the other.

The characteristics of an open system include honest, two-way communication cultivated by an atmosphere of trust. Open systems rely on feedback to adapt to changing situations and meet the expectations of their publics. Closed systems, on the other hand, foster an atmosphere of distrust that results in limited information being provided to key publics and little, if any, feedback. Closed systems risk the threat of dying because they are insensitive to their publics' needs and unwilling to change.

Characteristics associated with each system are often determined by the traits held by the senior management of an organization and, in particular, its chief executive officer.

THE VIEW FROM THE TOP

The proactive or reactive function of public relations depends on how it is viewed from the top. This perception may develop from the proximity of public relations to senior management on an organizational chart or from how the public relations department first came into being within the organization. Was the position created as a result of a crisis, because the CEO understood the value of public relations, or has the department just always "been there"?

Practitioners must also do their part to earn respect and maintain the support of management by engaging in honest relationships and keeping a track record of contributions to the organization's success. In addition to basic communication skills, public relations practitioners who possess knowledge of business and finance, problem solving, and research techniques are perceived as more strategic—and proactive—thinkers and are often given more opportunity to become part of the decision-making process.

A STRATEGIC FUNCTION

Within an organization's structure, public relations is most often a staff function, a position that provides counsel and advice to the line functions that produce profits. The practitioner's responsibilities once again depend on the organization and its senior management.

Practitioners working in an organization with characteristics of a closed system will focus more on implementing tactics—such as by sending out news releases or developing a brochure—that are independent of each other rather than part of an overall strategic plan. Such a reactive approach focuses on one-way communication and emphasizes the organization more than the publics it serves.

Organizations that lean toward a more open system provide a setting within which public relations practitioners can engage in a proactive approach that emphasizes strategic planning, features two-way communication, and focuses on the organization's publics.

REACTING TO CRISIS

Even in a proactive environment, crises may occur that require an organization to react. However, proactive organizations can weather storms more successfully simply because they have a reputation for being open and operating in their publics' best interest. In addition, their proactive nature has no doubt led them to prepare a crisis communication plan, which anticipates various crisis scenarios and ways to respond to them.

Two classic examples of proactive and reactive public relations during a crisis are the Tylenol scare of 1982 and the *Exxon Valdez* oil spill in 1989. When seven deaths in the Chicago area were traced back to cyanide-tainted Tylenol, Johnson & Johnson, the makers of the pain reliever, stopped production of the capsules and recalled all 31 million bottles on store shelves throughout the country, a loss of $100 million dollars. This short-term financial loss resulted in long-term financial gain, however, because of the proactive approach by Johnson & Johnson, which put the safety of its customers first.

Exxon took a reactive approach when its tanker *Valdez* ran aground in Alaska's Prince William Sound, spilling 11 million gallons of oil that altered the environment and killed an abundance of wildlife along 1,300 miles of shoreline. Exxon chose to be defensive about the accident rather than accept responsibility and, in doing so, appeared to only take actions when public outcry required it to do so. Exxon customers cut up their credit cards, the company's "most admired company" ranking dropped more than 100 places, and its $3 billion environmental cleanup received little notice.

—*Ann R. Carden*

See also Crisis communication; Exxon and the *Valdez* crisis; Management theory; Openness; Systems theory

Bibliography

Cutlip, S., Center, A., & Broom, G. (1999). *Effective public relations* (8th ed.). Upper Saddle River, NJ: Prentice Hall.

Smith, R. (2002). *Strategic planning for public relations.* Mahwah, NJ: Lawrence Erlbaum.

Wilcox, D. L., Cameron, G. T., Ault, P. H., & Agee, W. K. (2003). *Public relations strategies and tactics* (7th ed.). Boston: Allyn & Bacon.

Wilson, L. (2000). *Strategic program planning for effective public relations campaigns* (3rd ed.). Dubuque, IA: Kendall/Hunt.

PROCESS RESEARCH

Process research is the easiest of all forms of research a public relations practitioner encounters.

Process research keeps track of what tasks have been performed and which tasks still need to be performed in the public relations activity. One can think of process research as a checklist of things to do or a shopping list. If you go to the grocery store without your shopping list, the odds are great you will forget something. The same is true for public relations activities. If a practitioner fails to identify all the tasks to be completed, the odds are great of missing a task. Depending on the task, such an oversight could cause the entire public relations activity to fail.

Process research also involves creating and monitoring schedules. Scheduling includes identifying and organizing the various tasks practitioners will need to accomplish to complete the activity and when each task should be completed to remain on schedule. A schedule tells a public relations practitioner what needs to be done and when it must be finished. The first part of scheduling is identifying what needs to be done—the tasks. It is critical to think of all the tasks that need to be done. Forgetting a task can throw off the schedule. It is good to brainstorm as a team, since more minds are better than one. The second part of scheduling is arranging the tasks in the proper sequence. The practitioner must understand which tasks are dependent on others and which tasks need to be completed in a specific order. For example, a practitioner cannot lay out a newsletter until the stories are written and cannot send a new release to the media until the proper people have approved it. The third and final part of scheduling is determining how much time each task will take. The entries on PERT and Gantt Charts provide additional information about scheduling. In the end, the schedule provides a guide of what tasks the public relations department must perform, the order of those tasks, and how long each task should take to complete.

The schedule also serves as a checklist. As each task is completed, it is marked off the schedule. It is common to note completed tasks on both PERT and Gantt Charts. The key is not to forget a task. It is terrible to have a public relations activity fail because someone forgot to complete something. Even seemingly small tasks can cause failure. The inability to deliver material to a printer on time can delay the publishing of an important piece of the public relations effort or mean that it will arrive too late to be usable.

The danger with process research is that some practitioners confuse it with evaluative research. Saying you will send news releases to 15 media outlets and then sending them does not equate to success in a public relations effort. In doing this, you have not achieved an outcome objective; you have just completed a task and achieved a process objective. Claims of success can be greatly exaggerated when process research replaces evaluative research. If you wanted to determine if you had succeeded, you would study where the 15 news releases were used and what impact they had on target audiences. Process evaluation is a useful tool as long as it is not confused with or used to substitute for evaluative research.

There is a second, more advanced use of process research. In a public relations campaign that spans a long time period, such as four or more months, a practitioner may run checks to determine if the campaign is having the desired effect—if progress is being made toward achieving the objectives. If substantial financial and time commitments are being made to a campaign, a process check is advisable. If the test shows that the desired change is not occurring, there is time to make adjustments to tactics and/or messages. An example will help to clarify this point. MacCorp wants to establish itself as a leader in community development. It does a lot for the community, but the message does not seem to be reaching the residents of Niles, the town in which MacCorp is located. Research found that currently only 25 percent of residents view MacCorp as a leader in community development. Therefore, its public relations department has designed an 18-month public relations campaign to promote MacCorp's existing community relations efforts and to highlight three new initiatives designed to strengthen K-12 education in the community. The objective is: "After 18 months, 60 percent of the residents of Niles will view MacCorp as a leader in community development." The public relations department anticipates seeing some effects

after 6 months. At 6 months into the campaign, MacCorp's public relations department might do a survey to check on perceptions of its leadership in community development. If there is some movement in a positive direction, the public relations campaign would seem to be on track. If there is no change or a drop, aspects of the campaign might need to be redesigned to avoid a complete failure. For instance, the message may not be reaching the target, so different media options might be employed. Process research can be used to check on the progress of a public relations activity toward achieving its objective. Such a process check will cost time and money. However, it is a useful investment when an organization has already committed large amounts of both resources to a campaign.

—*W. Timothy Coombs*

See also Gantt Chart; PERT Chart; Public relations research

Bibliography

Cutlip, S. M., Center, A. H., & Broom, G. T. (2000). *Effective public relations* (8th ed.). Englewood Cliffs, NJ: Prentice Hall.

Pavlik, J. V. (1987). *Public relations: What research tells us.* Newbury Park, CA: Sage.

Stacks, D. W. (2002). *Primer of public relations research.* New York: Guilford Press.

PROFESSIONAL AND PROFESSIONALISM

Although there are challenges to the concepts of *professional* and *professionalism,* professions still dominate our world. They are seen as "both necessary and desirable for a decent society" (Freidson, 1994, p. 9). A survey of the literature on professionalism provides several justifications for that claim. Some arguments are that professions meet the societal need for expertise and credentialism, that professions provide a "crucial link between the individual's struggle for a fulfilling existence and the needs of the larger society," and that professions are a stabilizing force in society, protecting vulnerable people, social values, and providing quality service. Emile Durkheim, one of the first writers on professions, said that it is within "special groups" or professions that "morals may be evolved" and that it is professions' "business . . . to see they be observed" (1992, p. 7). This is especially true in areas where legal sanctions are not effective. Although everyone would agree that there have been moral slippages, many would argue that, as an ideal, professionalism is worth pursuing. Turning to the public relations field specifically, Doug Newsom, Judy Vanslyke Turk, and Dean Kruckeberg have suggested that "the best PR is evidence of an active social conscience" (2000, p. 3), and James E. Grunig and Todd T. Hunt (1984) have said that it is while acting as autonomous professionals that public relations practitioners could try to change the organization as well as the public.

Harold L. Wilensky, a sociologist, wrote that "any occupation wishing to exercise professional authority must find a technical basis for it, assert an exclusive jurisdiction, link both skill and jurisdiction to standards of training, and convince the public that its services are uniquely trustworthy" (1964, p. 138). He identified two criteria: the job must be technical and it must require adherence to "professional norms." Professional norms require that the practitioner "adhere to a service ideal—devotion to the client's interests more than personal or commercial profit should guide decisions when the two are in conflict" (p. 138). This concept of service entails a necessary level of professional autonomy. This is an example of the trait approach to defining professionalism and is how the concept has traditionally been defined.

In the 1950s Edward Bernays recommended licensing as a means of ensuring professionalism. There seems to be consensus in the public relations literature as to what it means to be a professional. J. E. Grunig and Hunt's 1984 text, *Managing Public Relations,* listed five characteristics of a professional: a set of professional values, membership in strong professional organizations, adherence to professional norms, an intellectual tradition or established body of knowledge, and technical skills

acquired through professional training. The set of professional values was explained as follows: "In particular, professionals believe that serving others is more important than their own economic gain. Professionals also strongly value autonomy. That is, they prefer the freedom to perform in the way they think is right to the rewards they may get to conforming to what others want" (1984, p. 66). Similar perspectives can be found in popular public relations textbooks. This approach fits into the traditional professional paradigm.

The values, professional norms, body of knowledge, and technical skills are taught and inculcated in a variety of educational forms, such as degree programs, internships, and on-the-job training. In addition, various professional organizations offer the possibility of both accreditation and continuing education. Among these organizations are the Public Relations Society of America, the International Association of Business Communicators, the Association for Education in Journalism and Mass Communication, the International Communication Association, the International Public Relations Association, and the Institute for Public Relations Research and Education. Suggestions that the field of public relations adopt some sort of mandatory accreditation process and licensing have been rejected.

Recently the traditional paradigm of professionalism has been challenged. Depending on the scholar one reads, the challenge seems to have started in the 1960s and has been most discussed in the field of sociology. The reasons for the challenge have varied, again according to which author one reads. Among the reasons given are that various professions have abused their power, that they have been slow to reform, and that because of their power, they have not been accountable and cost-effective. Various system changes, such as increased specialization and division of labor, were also given as reasons for the challenge. The paradigm shift has already been felt in the traditional professions of law and medicine. The change has decreased the autonomy of the professions and increased the call for accountability. It has been praised for reducing the anomaly of being beholden to both a client and to a nebulous public interest, and for reducing financial costs and hypocrisy. On the other hand, it has also been criticized as being the death knell of public spiritedness and as a way of changing the professions from "watchdogs" of the public interest into "lapdogs" of the business community (Zakaria, 2003, p. 226). This possible change in paradigms has been noted by several writers in the public relations field (Grunig, 2000; Pieczka & L'Etang, 2001) and is perhaps reflected in a change in the tone of the new PRSA Member Code of Ethics.

—Kathie A. Leeper and Roy V. Leeper

Bibliography

Boynton, L. A. (2002). Professionalism and social responsibility: Foundations of public relations ethics. In W. B. Gudykunst (Ed.), *Communication yearbook* (Vol. 26, pp. 230–265). Mahwah, NJ: Lawrence Erlbaum.

Durkheim, E. (1992). *Professional ethics and civic morals* (C. Brookfield, Trans.). London: Routledge.

Freidson, E. (1994). *Professionalism reborn: Theory, prophecy, and policy.* Chicago: University of Chicago Press.

Grunig, J. E. (2000). Collectivism, collaboration, and societal corporatism as core professional values in public relations. *Journal of Public Relations Research, 12*(1), 23–48.

Grunig, J. E., & Hunt, T. (1984). *Managing public relations.* New York: Holt, Rinehart & Winston.

Newsom, D., Turk, J. V., & Kruckeberg, D. (2000). *This is PR: The realities of public relations* (7th ed.). Belmont, CA: Wadsworth.

Pieczka, M., & L'Etang, J. (2001). Public relations and the question of professionalism. In R. L. Heath (Ed.), *Handbook of public relations* (pp. 223–235). Thousand Oaks, CA: Sage.

Sullivan, W. M. (1995). *Work and integrity: The crisis and promise of professionalism in America.* New York: HarperCollins.

Wilensky, H. L. (1964). The professionalism of everyone? *American Journal of Sociology, 70* (2), 137–158.

Zakaria, F. (2003). *The future of freedom: Illiberal democracy at home and abroad.* New York: W. W. Norton.

PROFNET

PR Newswire (http://www.prnewswire.com), a targeted news distribution and monitoring service, offers reporters free access to industry experts through ProfNet. Launched in 1992, ProfNet provides journalists with access to more than 3,000 corporations; 700 nonprofit organizations and hospitals; 100 government agencies, national laboratories, scientific associations, and think tanks; and 1,000 public relations agencies. ProfNet connects journalists and experts from around the world, including Europe, Africa, Asia, Australia, and Latin America.

Communication practitioners subscribe to ProfNet for a fee. Instead of making cold calls to reporters, practitioners can receive e-mail queries from journalists who are looking for expert sources or can send alerts to the media through ProfNet's "Leads and Round-Ups." ProfNet links reporters who need sources for their stories to practitioners who need media coverage of their organization. One of ProfNet's biggest success stories is Marist College, a small college in the Hudson River Valley in New York. By using ProfNet to pitch faculty and students, the college has repeatedly secured media coverage in *The New York Times, CNBC,* Fox's *Good Day,* the *Christian Science Monitor,* the *Los Angeles Times,* the *Chicago Tribune, Fortune, Forbes,* and *Good Morning America.* Despite its small size, the college has earned a national reputation of providing the media with experts on issues such as criminal justice, technology, and business.

Communication practitioners who quickly, accurately, and narrowly target their responses to journalists' e-mail queries are the most successful in securing media coverage. Journalists sending e-mail queries through ProfNet Search can designate whether their organizations' identities are visible to communication practitioners or cloaked (anonymous). Journalists often choose to cloak their e-mail queries if they work for highly competitive news organizations and do not want to tip off other journalists about a story they are pursuing. By cloaking their queries, they can reach practitioners without disclosing key information to their competitors. Cloaked queries only include generic descriptions of the journalist's news organization, such as "a national daily" or "a major women's magazine." Journalists designate the deadline for their responses and the means of communication to be used—e-mail, phone, or fax.

Communication practitioners responding to journalists' queries must adhere to strict guidelines. Practitioners must limit their responses to three paragraphs and must include basic contact information, such as name, title, phone numbers, and e-mail addresses, for the practitioner and source. Responses must also include the sources' credentials and how they are relevant to the journalists' query. Communication practitioners are not allowed to use contact information obtained through queries sent through ProfNet to create their own database or to send unsolicited e-mails to journalists. Practitioners who fail to adhere to ProfNet's strict guidelines can lose access to the service.

Practitioners who use ProfNet can also use its "Leads and Round-Ups" service for a fee. This service allows communication practitioners to proactively alert journalists about experts who can comment on timely news events. The "Leads and Round-Ups" service is not designed to announce news or pitch stories but rather to provide journalists with experts who can offer informed perspectives on current national and internal issues. Like responses to journalists' queries, these alerts must adhere to strict guidelines and contain certain information. In addition, ProfNet's editorial team screens these alerts and distributes the information to the media.

—*Cassandra Imfeld*

See also Practice

PROGRAM/ACTION PLANS

As part of the strategic planning process, a program/action plan is a tactical roadmap that links the goals and objectives developed during the preliminary precampaign planning process with the actual outcomes of the campaign. An effective program/action plan lists a series of tactics for operationalizing campaign strategies and clearly defines the specific steps, behaviors, and "actions" that are needed to effectively execute those tactics. Whereas the strategic planning process outlines specific goals and objectives for each targeted public, the program/action plan focuses on the tactics that will be used to reach those goals and objectives. Tactics are specific communication behaviors, vehicles, or tools that are used to operationalize the strategies and impact the target. Campaign communication tactics can come in many forms and can make use of both controlled and uncontrolled media. Examples are letters, meetings, press releases, press conferences, placed media messages (advertisements), posters, billboards, and protests. For each tactic, the action plan must clearly identify who is accountable for performing tasks, meeting timetables or schedules, deploying necessary resources, and staying within budget.

THE PLANNING PROCESS

Public relations students and practitioners are often familiar with the acronyms used to describe well-known public relations campaign planning processes. Acronyms such as Marston's (1979) RACE (Research, Action Planning, Communication, Evaluation) and Hendrix's (2001) ROPE (Research, Objectives, Programming, Evaluation) represent the series of steps that are needed to effectively plan, implement, and evaluate a campaign. The goal of these planning processes is to provide a methodical and systematic mechanism that helps the campaign planner understand the issue at hand, clearly identify publics, develop realistic and attainable goals and objectives, select appropriate and effective strategies and tactics, execute those strategies and tactics, and finally evaluate effectiveness. It therefore not only serves as a blueprint for the nature (such as the selection of channels and media), order, and timing of all of the tactics to be used during the campaign, but also clearly articulates the roles and responsibilities for those who are involved and the allocation of available material and budgetary resources.

APPLICATIONS

When developing program/action plans, the careful practitioner must remain focused on the larger picture: the desired outcomes of the campaign. To reach those objectives, the practitioner must clearly identify the decision makers who make up the publics that are or will be involved. Similarly, the practitioner must use current knowledge or research in determining what will influence the decision maker, factors and processes that will be used to arrive at a decision and take action, and finally how best to reach and impact that decision maker. These behaviors or "tactics" must be coordinated to maximize the effectiveness of the campaign strategies. Tactics are selected and prioritized by their ability to reach and affect the target public. Traditionally, at this stage the issues of channel selection and placement are addressed; that is, communication vehicles (a letter, press release, or advertisement) are selected for their ability to gain the target's attention and to persuade or motivate the target public. Finally, the effective campaign planner will also build in some redundancy to increase the "reach" of the campaign and to reinforce the impact of previous strategies and tactics. For example, if voters in a local referendum are the targeted public, letters to the voter (based on lists of registered voters) might be coupled with an ad campaign that uses print or broadcast ads or with an advocacy approach that targets newspaper articles on the referendum issue. Multiple tactics should be used to increase the reach of the campaign, to reinforce previous strategies, and to build resonance whenever time, material, and budgetary resources are available.

The effective program/action plan also clearly defines the roles and responsibilities for all involved in executing a particular tactic. This high level of specificity not only allows for the more efficient use of resources such as time and manpower, but is also important in the budgeting process. As part of the delineation of roles and responsibilities, the action plan should also clearly identify the parties that are to be held accountable for effective execution of the tactics. When individuals and groups know that they will be held accountable for the effective implementation and execution of tactics, the level of follow-through and the quality of work increase.

The scheduling and timing of tactics are also an important aspect of a program/action lan. An effective campaign consists of a series of coordinated tactics that are used to reach a set of goals and objectives. This means that tactics should be scheduled and implemented to maximize their effectiveness while minimizing the impact of competing effects such as distractions, possible distortion, or competing campaign messages. Moreover, careful attention needs to be given to the nature of the campaign, the complexity of the issues, and the levels of current knowledge and involvement of all key publics. Complex or unknown issues may take longer to develop than more well-known or simplistic issues.

For example, the importance of scheduling and timing can be demonstrated by examining the use of campaigns around American holiday seasons. Although some tactics can be "tied in" to holidays (such as MADD's use of New Year to maintain awareness of the ravages of drinking and driving), many campaigns should avoid holidays because their targeted publics are focusing elsewhere, as are the mass media who might be used to reach them. Careful scheduling and timing also can maximize the efficiency of resources such as budgets and staffing. For example, unless the campaign is using the political process or needs to impact public opinion during an election period, a campaign tactic used around an election period will not only get less attention from the media and key publics (who are focused on the candidates and other electoral issues), but will also cost more because of the increased market costs of buying media time and space.

Tactics should be scheduled in a way that maximizes the use of available manpower or staffing. Realistic timelines need to be developed to ensure that all necessary steps are completed to produce high-quality messages and to effectively implement tactics. Although last-minute work and tight deadlines can be used to deliver fast results, poor message quality and staff "burnout" may detract from long-term success. When determining staffing, one should also carefully examine the use of paid and unpaid campaign workers; although volunteers who are committed to an issue can often perform as well as paid personnel, they may lack expertise or professionalism and may be "less available" when faced with competing events or schedules.

Finally, effective action plans must carefully include realistic budgetary outlines for all tactics and may often include a small reserve to cover unforeseen costs, to target unexpected obstacles, or to counter messages and tactics used by competing organizations. The costs of all planning, production, and message placement, as well as postage and distribution, need to be factored into any budget. Similarly, the campaign professional builds the costs of interim or midcampaign evaluation into the planning process. Effective action plans can make use of preliminary research and formative evaluation, but they also should plan and budget resources for interim evaluations, especially when facing complex or emotional issues. The use of many levels of evaluation in a campaign can help to ensure that programming and tactics are achieving results and are on track to meet strategic goals and objectives.

—*Dean Kazoleas*

Bibliography

Hendrix, J. A. (2001). *Public relations cases* (5th ed.). Belmont, CA: Wadsworth.

Marston, J. E. (1979). *Modern public relations.* New York: McGraw-Hill.

PROMOTION

Promotion, a counterpart of publicity, is used by an organization to gain awareness, increase awareness, and foster positive thoughts and opinions about an organization, product, service, or issue. Whereas publicity is often aimed at achieving short-term awareness, promotion typically builds and changes audiences' and markets' views over time. Newson, Turk, and Kruckeberg defined promotion as going "beyond press agentry into opinion making. Promotion tries to garner support and endorsement for a person, product, institution or idea" (2004, p. 4).

Publicity and promotion are among the most important functions of public relations. Each employs typical and specialized strategies and tactics. Publicity tends to be limited to media relations, whereas promotion "involves special activities or events designed to create and stimulate interest in a person, product, organization or cause" (Newsom,

Turk, & Kruckeberg, 2004, p. 400). In this sense, publicity is probably often a subset of promotion.

Two masters of promotion are featured in this encyclopedia: P. T. Barnum and Samuel Insull. Both realized that they needed continuous strategic communication to build and advance a market and to develop a customer base for their businesses. Barnum continually used media messages and events to keep public attention focused on his circus and his display of unusual items, animals, and people. Thus, he might publicize the arrival of a huge elephant and feature its name: Jumbo. People were attracted to novelty, as they are today, but today people might tune in to television to see an elephant. In Barnum's day, they had to travel to see the elephant, and it had to be taken to them. As the elephant traveled across the country, Barnum worked to get media comments and reports, which he could use in the next town to attract crowds to his show. Ever the showman and promoter, Barnum even took advantage of Jumbo's death. When Jumbo was struck by a train and killed, Barnum used that tragedy as a photo opportunity. Images can be seen on the Web today of people standing around and sitting on the massive beast, which was eventually stuffed and put on display.

Another master promoter, Sam Insull, knew that the fledgling electricity industry would fail without customers. The more customers, the more likely it would succeed. His efforts then were no different from those used to promote automobile sales by gaining media attention for cross-country races. He promoted the virtues of electricity over gas to illuminate houses. To do this, he featured homes that had electricity and asked neighbors to stroll by them to see how wonderful this innovation was.

Promotion, like publicity, occurs in a competitive environment. Voices compete in a public bazaar against one another for market share, brand equity, and favorable evaluation. Publicity can arise because of what reporters or other critics say about an organization and its personnel, executives, mission/vision, policies, products, and services. This publicity can be positive or negative. Negative publicity needs to be addressed by various strategies. Some change strategies are communication based, and others may require improvements in the organization—in its personnel, plans, policies, products, or services.

Similarly, promotions by one company or industry typically meet counterpromotion whereby practitioners make claims seeking competitive advantage. Such promotions may be joined by an entire industry, such as carmakers, and then segmented into competing product claims by individual companies and product lines. Automobile companies have been legendary for their efforts to promote automobile and truck sales. For years, fall was the time when these companies launched their new products. Magazines as well as news features at movies covered the introduction of new models. To the uncritical eye, these promotional presentations seemed to express the objective opinion of reporters. The same techniques are used today. Print and electronic media outlets are essentially unfiltered conduits through which promotional claims flow to customers.

A central theme of automobile promotions is that the manufacturers are eternally bringing newer and better models to the customers, who are expected to demonstrate their pleasure by buying a new car every year or every three years at least. As the industry promoted itself, so did individual brand lines struggle for brand equity and market share.

Promotion is used to target specific customers or potential customers. Markets can be segmented by various demographics. Media, both print and electronic, develop to bring customers and vendors together. Thus, teen magazines and television programs are tailored to the youth market because of the news, commentary, and entertainment that appear there. Advertising and promotion then move in to help fill the space and time with messages that are tailored to the needs, wants, and preferences of the market. Promotion sustains a flow of messages to keep constant attention on products and services that may appeal to the members of the target market.

Some of the great promotional efforts include those for Disney characters, such as Mickey Mouse, and the Sesame Street characters. Companies may create museums featuring the heritage of the company, product, and industry. Customers and other interested individuals can be informed and impressed as they visit such facilities. Perhaps no company has done that better than Disney. The media also engage in marketing promotion, such as with award shows—the Grammys and the Academy Awards.

Promotions are often used in conjunction with several other public relations functions. Colleges and universities have for centuries used promotions based on athletic competition, student accomplishments, and faculty merit to foster student relations, alumni relations, donor relations, and perhaps even government relations. Excellence is a product and service with many faces, purposes, and ends. Companies also use new product promotion to attract new and continuing customers. Such promotions are vital to publicly traded companies' investor relations.

Promotions are one of the oldest forms of public relations. Antecedents of modern public relations stretch back to the dawn of various civilizations. One of the oldest continuing forms of promotion, for example, is the fair. County fairs and state fairs have outlived the rural dominance of farm production in the American economy. They are a part of rural culture that now attracts thousands of urban dwellers. Fairs of agricultural produce even occur in urban settings. They promote agriculture, agricultural products, and agricultural lifestyle and are a meeting place of vendors and customers. They give an opportunity for farm equipment and automobile companies to meet customers and explain innovations. Local young women are featured as fair queens. County fairs lead to state fairs, which lead to trade fairs and world fairs. All of these events promote myriad aspects of a culture.

Promotions and publicity are the most typical public relations functions in terms of expenditure, but perhaps the most controversial. The efforts of Bernays to promote the sale of Lucky Strike Greens to women has been one of the most critically discussed promotional campaigns. In this sense, promotion can be seen as unethical because it rests less on facts about a product and more on activities and events that may create impressions and false motivations regarding a product or service. One of the ethical questions focuses on the extent to which promotion reduces the target customer's ability to make an informed and rational choice about a product, issue, cause, or service.

Although fraught with ethical problems, however, promotion, along with publicity, is here to stay. It is a vital function of public relations.

—Robert L. Heath

See also Barnum, P. T.; Bernays, Edward.; Brand equity and branding, Insull, Samuel; Lucky Strike Green Campaign; Market share; Publicity; Target

Bibliography

Newsom, D., Turk, J. V. S., & Kruckeberg, D. (2004). *This is PR* (8th ed.). Belmont, CA: Wadsworth/Thomson Learning.

PROPAGANDA

The word *propaganda* comes from the Latin word meaning to propagate or to sow. In its most neutral sense it means to disseminate or promote particular ideas. Propaganda has been defined in many ways, most of which center on synonyms such as *lies, distortions, deceit, manipulation, psychological warfare, brainwashing*, and the more recent word *spin.*

Spin, in particular, emphasizes the frequent difficulty of differentiating public relations from propaganda in that it is associated with the manipulation of political and corporate information to affect the way in which news is presented. As a result, the term *spin doctors* is now often used as a synonym for professional public relations practitioners. Propaganda has been associated with mass communication, mass persuasion, mind control, and mass brainwashing. It has a history of being used to promote an ideology and way of life that benefits some to the disadvantage of others. Few examples are more notorious than the propaganda efforts of Hitler, which he claimed to have learned from the British and American propaganda machines during the First World War.

People often see tactics they don't like as "propaganda," whereas when they approve of mass media campaigns they call them "preaching of the truth." Modern practitioners of public relations and academics focus on the concepts of symbolic manipulation, cognitive manipulation, scientific mass persuasion, and asymmetry as defining attributes that separate propaganda and unethical public relations from ethical and responsible approaches to the profession.

Many scholars have grappled with a definition of the word *propaganda*. The French philosopher Jacques Ellul, in his book *Propaganda* (1965), suggested that it was an essential part of modern technologically advanced societies, and Michael Sproule (1994) suggested that it is "the work of a large organization, nation, or group to win over the public for special interests through a massive orchestration of attractive conclusions packaged to conceal both their persuasive purpose and lack of sound supporting reasons" (p. 8). The social psychologist Leonard W. Doob summarized these definitional difficulties in 1989 by suggesting that "a clear-cut definition of propaganda is neither possible nor desirable" (p. 375).

Garth Jowett and Victoria O'Donnell have created a definition that focuses on propaganda as a communication process, more specifically on the purpose of the process: "Propaganda is the deliberate, systematic attempt to shape perceptions, manipulate cognitions, and direct behavior to achieve a response that furthers the desired intent of the propagandist" (1999, p. 6). This definition stresses that propaganda is "willful, intentional, and premeditated" (1999, p. 6). Although it clearly establishes propaganda as a neutral technique, it also comes close to a definition of public relations held by some of its practitioners and many of its critics, thus emphasizing the difficulty in establishing a clearer differentiation between the two practices.

The relationship of propaganda to public relations has always been a contentious one. Both of these practices stem from a common desire to affect the attitudes and perceptions held by people, collectively defined as publics, crowds, citizens, or consumers, toward an infinite variety of subjects, in order to shift opinion and beliefs in a desired direction. Propaganda in particular has been defined in largely negative terms because of its close historical association with religion, warfare, and political practices. Public relations, thanks largely to the strenuous efforts of its own practitioners, has managed to establish itself as a legitimate activity that enhances the images and perceptions of a wide variety of institutions. However, the common ancestry of these two practices tends to blur the distinction between them, with the result that there is often confusion in the minds of the public as to what is propaganda and what is legitimate and ethical public relations.

Public relations emerged at the end of the 19th century as a means of utilizing the increasingly powerful mass communication media to further the objectives of American industry, as well as to shape the public perception of a wide range of institutions and influential individuals. It was not coincidental that public concern about the increasing significance of the media in modern life was brought into sharp focus at precisely the same time as part of the ongoing examination of the strengths and weaknesses of an increasingly urbanized and industrialized America. These critics, labeled as muckrakers by both their detractors and supporters, focused on issues that threatened the orderly development of a progressive democratic society. In 1905, the journalist Ray Stannard Baker published a series of five articles examining the scandalous business practices of the railroads. The first four essays were exposés of such things as excessive shipping rates and illegal rebates, but the final essay tackled a relatively new subject when it examined the manner in which the railroads were able to corrupt public opinion by using press agents and dubious financial relationships with newspapers and magazines. Baker's work was the initial foray for what was to be a series of exposés that examined how press agents, promoters, and the newly emerging practitioners of public relations were moving their influence outside of government and directly affecting and shaping public opinion.

Will Irwin in 1910 began his 15-part series for *Collier's* magazine, which examined the newspaper industry. As Michael Sproule indicated, "Irwin's ability to trace links between outside interests, newspaper content, and public opinion made his . . . [work] a cornerstone in the foundation of postwar propaganda consciousness" (1997, p. 24). Irwin meticulously detailed how newspaper editors

were being increasingly influenced by pressure from advertisers, including direct economic subsidies, as well as by privileged individuals with economic power. He rejected the notion of banning advertising, however, and hoped that the increasing professionalization of journalistic practices would do much to eliminate the current abuses.

In later years, George Creel, before he became head of the Committee for Public Information in the First World War, undertook a muckraking examination of the public relations practices of large charitable organizations, in particular the Rockefeller Foundation. Creel concluded that some gifts from these organizations did indeed affect the way in which information was presented to the public.

Walter Lippmann (1915), in one of his early essays, examined the role of public relations as used by American industry in the ongoing battle to establish a minimum wage. In recognition of the contentious role of press agentry and other publicity techniques, the Post Office Appropriation Act of 1912 mandated full disclosure of a magazine's and newspaper's ownership and also required that all material published for payment had to be labeled as an "advertisement."

These and other muckraking attempts to illuminate the increasing role of public relations practitioners in manipulating public opinion became what is now known as the Progressive propaganda critique. This early confusion between legitimate public relations practices and more directive propaganda activities was only natural considering their similar objectives. In the period after the First World War, the increasing professionalization of public relations required that this emerging industry clearly differentiate itself from the discredited propaganda techniques associated with the war effort. George Creel's (1920) infamous book, *How We Advertised America,* left a bitter taste in the mouths of Americans who felt that they had been manipulated into supporting what was ultimately an unsatisfactory victory. The result of the massive efforts to mobilize public opinion was to leave a legacy of suspicion and hostility in the mind of the public, and the concept of propaganda became an anathema.

In this atmosphere, pioneers of public relations Ivy L. Lee and Edward L. Bernays established themselves as public relations professionals, perhaps because both had a solid background in propaganda activities. Lee had worked for the Red Cross and in later life was associated with the propaganda activities of both Japan and Nazi Germany. Throughout his professional career he stressed that "the essential evil of propaganda is failure to disclose the source of information" and used this as the cornerstone of his ethics of publicity (Lee, 1925, quoted in Sproule, 1997, p. 55).

Edward L. Bernays published a book actually entitled *Propaganda* in 1928, and he was not ashamed to use the word *manipulation* in his writings. In his earlier work, *Crystallizing Public Opinion* (1923), Bernays had outlined his philosophy of public relations and acknowledged the need for the public to be informed by specialists occupying the middle ground between lack of knowledge and a stubborn tendency to hold fixed views. He noted that "the advocacy of what we believe in is education. The advocacy of what we don't believe in is propaganda" (p. 14). In *Propaganda* (1928) he fully acknowledged the need for propaganda activities in a modern society, suggesting that the best propaganda was that associated with socially sound objectives. In a series of popular articles and speeches in the interwar period, Bernays advocated the use of propaganda as an alternative to force and as a means of making known minority opinions to society as a whole.

Many students of Bernays's profession believe he was imbued with the sort of analysis that made his double uncle, Sigmund Freud, an international icon for revealing the mysteries of the human mind. Bernays was fascinated by the workings of the human mind and had ample opportunity to study his uncle's thoughts on people's desire for identification, love of tribalism, and need for leadership. Bernays became a student of mass psychology and loved to speculate on the ways that the opinions of large numbers of individuals could be shaped. He became legendary for his self-touted ability to mold public opinion. Although he later worked to divorce himself from the tobacco industry, he at first delighted in his success at promoting Lucky Strike Green packaging to women. To his credit, however, Bernays avoided developing a consulting relationship with Adolph Hitler and Joseph Goebbels, who had invited his counsel because they were familiar with his book on propaganda.

The culmination of the propaganda critique came with the establishment of the Institute for Propaganda Analysis (IPA) in 1937. The IPA, much to the consternation of its critics, saw its mandate as that of analyzing all forms of propaganda, and it did not limit itself to examining the increasingly ominous words emanating from foreign countries, particularly the fascist regimes in Italy, Germany, and Japan. It was only a matter of time before the institute tackled domestic propaganda as manifested in the manipulation of public opinion and attitudes by professionals directly engaged in this activity. During its short life it took on such contentious issues as the establishment of "suspect" research foundations devoted entirely to extolling the virtues of certain industries (a favorite tactic of Bernays), the role of public relations firms in opposing social legislation such as wage and tax reform, and the use of pre-prepared stories and photographs for distribution to newspapers and magazines that cast certain industries in a favorable light.

In an increasing atmosphere of international conflict, such activities as these did not endear the institute to its supporters, and eventually it was closed in January 1939, never to return after the war. This closing symbolized the demise of the propaganda critique, and it can be seen as a victory for the increasing professionalization of the public relations industry. Although the study of propaganda reached its zenith during the Second World War, it now concentrated on understanding the psychological processes of persuasion and the successful creation of specific targeted messages. The studies of propaganda techniques and strategies conducted for the United States government during this period serve as one foundation for the academic discipline of communication studies.

Many leading public relations practitioners, in addition to Lee and Bernays, had their tussle with the aura and ethics of propaganda. Two of the more influential, John W. Hill and Albert Oeckl, are worth considering to appreciate the efforts that practitioners have made to separate their profession and its strategies from the taint of propaganda.

John Hill drew what he thought to be a clear line between the ethical approach to public relations and the unethical approach to propaganda that tainted it and its practitioners:

> Public relations in its controversial usage is sometimes dubbed "propaganda." Actually propaganda was a "good" word until brought into disrepute when Hitler and the Communists began to pollute the airways with their "Big Lies," and made it a "bad" word. In a public relations battle in a free country it is important that there be no lies. Different interpretation of the facts is possible, and each side is entitled to present its views, leaving it to public opinion to decide which to accept.
>
> The purpose of public relations in its best sense is to inform and to keep minds open. The purpose of "propaganda" in the bad sense is to misinform and to keep minds closed.
>
> Business managements have every reason and right to communicate regularly with all segments of the public whose support they seek; and more, to work for better understanding of the private enterprise system. (1963, p. 6)

Relations between Hill and Bernays were always strained, for many reasons. Without doubt, one of those reasons was their views on the rationale for, and the strategic practice of, public relations. Hill aspired to the "journalistic" rather than "mass persuasion" tradition of public relations, which assumes a valued role for informing citizens who are capable of making informed decisions. For this reason, the virtue of public relations, he believed, was that it offered information for people's consideration.

Hill was serious in his systematic efforts to work through his rationale of public relations in contrast to propaganda, which he believed discredited both the practitioner and the client:

> I have no patience with those who try to attribute insidious and mysterious powers to public relations. Such ideas are wholly fanciful and without basis in fact. Quacks, charlatans, and so-called "hidden persuaders" may come and go in the field of public relations but their time is short and their achievements ephemeral.
>
> Nothing could be more absurd than to imagine that the so-called "corporate image" can be created by a clever use of words or by "slick" stunts. The ability of a specific business, or of business in general, to defend itself against its detractors and to project its worth to people begins with definitely existing policies and intrinsic values. The rightful purpose of public relations is openly to confirm, strengthen, and defend these values. Without integrity this cannot be accomplished. (Hill, 1963, pp. 161–162)

Bernays, in his own and others' minds, was a practitioner who believed in the value of the "clever stunt." Such was not the stuff of a practice claiming to add value to society, a goal worthy of a dignified profession.

Albert Oeckl is one of the most influential practitioners and academics on the development and evolution of the profession in Germany. He began his career as a junior lawyer in the Reichspropagandaministreium in Munich (1934–1935). However influenced he was by the works of Bernays and the legendary Goebbels, he matured to a view of public relations that featured working for the public, in the public interest, and in the public sphere. His view of public relations was that every message and strategic action must meet the ethical standard of contributing to the good of the community and serving its interest. He aspired to what has become featured as the symmetrical view of public relations.

Propaganda studies has seen a minor revival since the 1980s as political issues surrounding the study of the subject have become less contentious, thus allowing academics and others to examine the role and function of propaganda in modern society without fear of being criticized. In particular, the war in Vietnam and the two subsequent military campaigns against Iraq have provided an enormous opportunity to examine how public opinion can be manipulated and shaped. In very recent years, thanks largely to the emergence of the Internet, numerous sites have been established to examine precisely the interrelationship between public relations and what are deemed to be propaganda activities. The result of all this activity tends to show that there is indeed an aspect of public relations practice that comes dangerously close to meeting a definition of propaganda.

In the world dominated now by the large media conglomerates, the role of propaganda assumes a greater significance and is practiced increasingly with an unseen subtlety. It often blends seamlessly with legitimate public relations practices, and it is highly likely that this trend will continue into the foreseeable future. Despite this problem, leading practitioners and academics have seen sound reason to divorce public relations from propaganda. Such diligent efforts are slow to pay off; the goal, however, is important and worthy of the effort. This debate, perhaps beyond any other, is the fundamental pursuit of leading practitioners and professionals in public relations. That struggle is enduring, not fleeting.

—Garth S. Jowett and Robert L. Heath

See also Bernays, Edward; Committee on Public Information; Hill, John Wiley; Lucky Strikes Green Campaign; Oeckl, Albert; Spin; Symmetry;

Bibliography

Bernays, E. L. (1923). *Crystallizing public opinion.* New York: Boni & Liveright.

Bernays, E. L. (1928). *Propaganda.* New York: Liveright.

Creel, G. (1972). *How we advertised America.* New York: Arno. (First published 1920)

Cull, N. J., Culbert, D., & Welch, D. (2003). *Propaganda and mass persuasion: A historical analysis, 1500 to present.* Santa Barbara, CA: ABC-Clio.

Doob, L. W. (1989). Propaganda. In E. Barnouw, G. Gerbner, W. Schramm, T. L. Worth, and L. Gross (Eds.), *International encyclopedia of communications* (Vol. 3, pp. 374–378). New York: Oxford University Press.

Hill, J. W. (1963). *The making of a public relations man.* New York: David McKay.

Jowett, G. S., & O'Donnell, V. (1999). *Propaganda and persuasion* (3rd ed.). Thousand Oaks, CA: Sage.

Lee, I. L. (1925). *Publicity.* New York: Industries.

Lippmann, W. (1915, March 27). The campaign against sweating. *New Republic, 2*(21) (part 2), 1–8.

Sproule, J. M. (1994). *Channels of propaganda.* Bloomington, IN: Edinfo.

Sproule, J. M. (1997). *Propaganda and democracy: The American experience of media and mass persuasion.* Cambridge, UK: Cambridge University Press.

PSYCHOGRAPHICS

Psychographics are audience segmentation methods that discover actionable audience segments by examining individual psychological, sociological, and anthropological factors—such as motivations, attitudes, self-concept, and lifestyle—that influence a particular decision about a product, person, ideology, or medium.

Although researchers Russell Haley and Emanuel Demby both claimed to originate the term *psychographics* in 1965, rapidly expanding technological access to audience descriptors in the following decades delayed a settled understanding of the concept. To illustrate the confusion, Heath writes that such widely used research techniques as geodemographics, which is generally considered psychographics, is not psychographics, whereas much survey-based research that includes a measurable attitude, interest, opinion, or lifestyle question is psychographics. Gunter and Furnham conversely classify attitudes and opinions research as psychographics, but suggest that lifestyle research is not. Rebecca Piirto Heath in 1995 dismissed as psychographics research any qualitative techniques such as focus groups, projective techniques, in-depth interviewing, and emotional probing. Yet in a 1996 article, she labeled these so-called psycho-qualitative tools as an important and growing trend in psychographics. Increasingly, any distinctions have been further weakened by a near-total knowledge of the behavior of individual consumers available through giant databases. Traditionally, the four major classifications of psychographic studies focused on geodemographics, personal values, lifestyles, and life cycles.

GEODEMOGRAPHICS

Geodemographics, in its most simple form, is plotting the residential location of concentrations of particular audience characteristics—of high-income single men, for instance—so that communication efforts can be directed with more cost-effectiveness. As extended by proprietary systems such as PRIZM or ACORN, researchers overlaid demographic knowledge with further questions concerning consumer behavior and attitudes.

The oldest of the geodemographic methods, PRIZM, was introduced in 1974. PRIZM (Potential Rating Index for ZIP Markets) reduces U.S. Census block group statistics to six categories that the company asserts account for most statistical variance between neighborhoods: social rank, household composition, mobility, ethnicity, urbanization, and housing. The system then correlates these classifications with consumer purchase records to categorize an individual neighborhood of 250–550 households into one of 62 different consumer segments. The resulting segments are labeled with such names as Boomtown Singles (middle-income young singles who live in smaller cities), or Rustic Elders (low-income, older rural couples), and the company claims that they help communicators transform mailing lists of current customers into insights about what psychographic traits those customers have. That knowledge then allows marketers to know where additional similar customers could be found.

LIFE CYCLES/GENERATIONAL COHORTS

The generational cohort to which one belongs is another psychographic characteristic that aids professionals in more clearly defining their targeted publics. William Straus and Neil Howe have conducted extensive generational theory research. They define a generation as a cohort group whose length approximates the span of a phase of life and whose boundaries are fixed by peer personalities. Further, a generation is shaped by its "age location" (e.g., participation in epochal events that occur during one's course of life). Examples include the Great Depression, the Korean War, World Wars I and II, the Vietnam War, and, most recently, the September 11, 2001, terrorist attacks on the United States. During each stage of the life cycle, a set of collective behavioral traits and attitudes is produced. Straus and Howe refer to each generational cohort's traits and attitudes as its "peer personality." Attitudes of one generation affect how that person's children are raised and, later, how those children raise their offspring.

The Generational Influences Model offers a visual diagram of how the generation to which an individual belongs affects his or her behaviors in today's marketplace. This model is derived from 30+ years of research collected via the Yankelovich MONITOR, an annual study that tracks American's lifestyles and values. People possess individualized value systems that affect the way they interact and view the world around them. Our value systems are affected by an array of environmental conditions we experience as children. Members of a generation are linked through the shared life experiences of their formative years.

According to Yankelovich Market Research, a person's "life stage" represents how old an individual is, and, therefore, where that individual is situated in life—either physically or psychologically. "Current conditions" reflect events that affect what a person buys (e.g., layoffs, recessions, wars, political turmoil, technological innovations). Our "cohort experiences" represent habits that define and differentiate the generation to which we belong. These experiences serve as the "filters" through which a person interprets all subsequent life experiences. As the Generational Influences Model explains, our life stage and current social and economic conditions play dominant roles in forming our cohort experiences, which, in turn, influence our values and preferences, and therefore have an effect on our marketplace behaviors as consumers (see Figure 1).

In short, the Generational Influences Model explains that a person's life stage, in combination with current conditions, aids in the development of a generation's cohort experiences. The cohort experiences, in turn, aid in developing individual core values, which influence preferences; these preferences and values serve as guideposts for marketplace behaviors.

To put these concepts into more concrete terms, each generation has its own typology. The literature offers a plethora of labels and categories: the more mainstream, research-based cohorts include the "Matures" (born pre-1930–1945, which include the GI Generation, Depression, War Babies); the "Baby Boomers" (born 1946–1964); "Generation X" (born

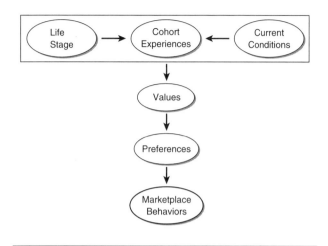

Figure 1   Generational influences.

SOURCE: Smith, Walker J. (1997). Reprinted with permission.

1965–1976); "Generation Y" (born 1977–1994); and "Millennials" (born after 1994).

PERSONAL VALUES

Values are central to peoples' lives, and because of their importance, values have been known to influence attitudes and behaviors. The study of human values has been cited as early as 1931 (e.g., Allport & Vernon's *A Study of Values*). Enjoying a history rich in empirical examination, values-related studies occur among an array of disciplines and within a variety of theoretical frameworks. However, until Milton Rokeach began conducting values research throughout the 1960s and 1970s, many of the previous studies that examined values included them as a subcategory of attitudes. Rokeach is credited for operationally defining and investigating values separate from those of attitudes.

Fundamentally, Rokeach's values theory is derived from consistency theory. As consistency theory explains, people are driven to reduce inconsistencies in order to regain cognitive balance in their lives. All consistency theories begin with the same premise: people are comfortable with consistency. Values theory explains that people are guided by a need for consistency and that inconsistency creates a pressure to change. Specifically, Rokeach defined a value as

an organized set of preferential standards that are used in making selections of objects and actions, resolving conflicts, invoking social sanctions, and coping with needs or claims for social and psychological defenses of choice made or proposed . . . A value is an enduring belief that a specific mode of conduct or end-state of existence is personally or socially preferable to an opposite or converse mode of conduct or end-state of existence. (1979, p. 5)

According to the values theory framework, values serve as standards that guide ongoing activities. Rokeach explained that values serve as general plans for resolving conflict and making decisions. Values also serve motivational functions and as the final analysis of conceptual tools we employ to maintain and enhance our self-esteem.

According to Rokeach, values are developed and learned by each person. They have dual purposes: they serve as cognitive representations of societal demands and as individual needs for morality and competence. Values transform these individual needs into shared goals and modes of behavior. Each person has a highly organized belief-attitudes-value system that guides behavior. These values are elaborately related to one's attitudes and behavior. Whereas values represent abstract ideals—positive or negative—that are not tied to any one specific object or situation, attitudes focus on specific objects and situations. Further, values are more stable over time than attitudes because they are more centrally connected to an individual's cognitive system. As a result, under some circumstances values serve as better predictors of an individual's behavior over extended periods of time than do attitudes; thus values represent an efficient, measurable set of variables more closely tied to motivation behavior than are demographic measures.

According to Rokeach, once a value is internalized, it becomes, unconsciously, a standard or criterion for guiding action, for developing and maintaining our attitudes toward objects and situations that are relevant to us to justify our own—or others'—actions and attitudes, for morally judging ourselves and others, and for comparing ourselves with others. In short, values are our "internal barometers." Put another way, values serve as that little voice inside our heads that guide many of our decisions and behaviors.

Lynn Kahle and his colleagues sought to develop a measure that corresponded with Rokeach's values and Abraham Maslow's hierachy of needs and provided a way to operationalize Maslow's work. Through extensive research, Kahle developed the List of Values (LOV), an instrument that encompasses a nine-value typology for use in conducting consumer-based research. Kahle notes that the LOV does not claim to provide an exhaustive inventory of every personal value. However, it does provide a useful instrument applicable for an array of social science studies.

These nine LOV indicators may be better represented at a more abstract level by "value domains" that reflect either an external or internal orientation based on an individual's *locus of control*. This concept explains the degree to which a person feels that the control of his or her world belongs to self (internal) at one extreme, or to fate (external), at the other extreme. *Internally oriented* values include self-fulfillment, self-respect, fun and enjoyment, excitement, sense of accomplishment, and warm relationships with others; *externally oriented* values include sense of belonging, sense of security, and being well respected. The external values imply a dependence on people or circumstances *outside* the individual's own control, whereas the internal values imply a more self-controlled independence on self.

One of the earliest commercially accessible psychographic systems using this conceptualization was VALS (Values and Lifestyles), built by Arnold Mitchell and provided to the market by SRI International. The version introduced in 1978 used Maslow's hierarchy of needs as its conceptual model, defining four major hierarchical groups: need-driven, outer-directed, inner-directed, and integrated, which roughly corresponded to Maslow's taxonomy. To counter significant criticisms, the company developed VALS2, which deviated from the original's orientation toward social hierarchy and instead focused on multiple personality attributes that were more closely focused on individual buying behavior.

Today, there are a variety of instruments available for studying personal values (e.g., Rokeach Value Scale, Schwartz Value Scale, AIO, and Value Tracking via Yankelovich MONITOR). However, the LOV appears to be one of the more mainstream measures used by academicians and practitioners because of its brevity and ease of administration, its availability for public use, its ability to incorporate demographic measures, and its repeated success across various industries (e.g., high degree of reliability and validity).

LIFESTYLES

Lifestyles research examines psychological self-concepts that can then be analyzed to determine future actions. Originally, these insights were limited to information primarily interpolated from demographic data or from self-reported survey data. For instance, a marketing company might have asserted that households that had a family income in the top 10 percentile of the nation pursued an "affluent" lifestyle. Yet some families might use their income to rent villas on the French Rivera, and other families to purchase heavy construction equipment for their businesses.

The advent of all-encompassing databases that capture lifestyle behaviors, such as individual consumer buying habits, recreational choices, and media behaviors, has transformed all types of psychographic research and also changed the focus of psychographic research applications. Inventory control systems using universal product code technology give retailers and researchers the capacity to track an individual's buying behaviors, and huge computer storage capacity gives marketers the power to integrate those data with public information like auto registrations, as well as home prices with media subscription and direct marketing purchases, to obtain true information about what individual consumers value and how each perceives his or her self.

This lifestyle research has provided information that, when overlaid on previous psychographic systems, provides further valuable insight into and refinement of consumer motivations. It has also shifted the segmentation philosophy of psychographics.

Life cycle and geodemographics research methods basically overlaid certain psychographic data onto broad swaths of consumers defined by geography, class, income, or sex. The new database lifestyle research allows individual consumers to signal their membership in a psychographic class by their combinations of behaviors. For instance, a cost-effective psychographic classification is more likely to be assembled from what in-line skaters read, such as health and fitness and weight loss magazines, than from their age, sex, or income.This focus on product-specific segmentation has permitted insights for marketers, advertisers, and public relations practitioners that earlier, broadly based psychographic systems did not generate.

—*Lisa T. Fall and William Thompson*

See also Demographics; Segmentation

Bibliography

Demby, E. H. (1994). Psychographics revisited: The birth of a technique. *Marketing Research, 6*(2), 26–29.

Gunter, B., & Furnham, A. (1992). *Consumer profiles: An introduction to psychographics.* New York: Routledge.

Heath, R. P. (1995, November). Psychographics: Q'est-ce que c'est? *American Demographics,* 72–79.

Heath, R. P. (1996, July). The frontiers of psychographics. *American Demographics,* 38–43.

Kahle, L. R. (1983). *Social values and social change: Adaptation to life in America.* New York: Praeger.

Kahle, L. R., & Chiagouris, L. (1997). *Values, lifestyles, and psychographics.* Mahwah, NJ. Lawrence Erlbaum.

Rokeach, M. (1979). *Understanding human values.* New York: Basic Books.

Smith, W. J. (1997). *Rocking the ages: The Yankelovich report on generational marketing.* New York: HarperCollins.

Straus, W., & Howe, N. (1991). *Generations: The history of America's future, 1584 to 2069.* New York: William Morrow.

PSYCHOLOGICAL PROCESSING

To the extent that public relations efforts attempt to influence the behavior of target audiences, practitioners must understand the psychological processes that underlie people's responses to messages on a given topic.

Psychologists generally differentiate between three aspects of the human mind that can influence learning and behavioral decision making: the cognitive, the affective, and the conative. Simply stated, cognitions deal with what people know—the information and thoughts stored in memory. Affect relates to people's physiological responses, including level of arousal, feelings, and emotions. Conation deals with both the unconscious (automatic) and conscious (reasoned and deliberative) inclination to take action. Behavioral decisions made in response to public relations efforts typically involve some combination of these three processes.

THE ROLE OF COGNITION

The acquisition of new knowledge can be examined from three principal perspectives. *Classical conditioning* suggests that people learn by making associations between objects, illustrated by Pavlov's early psychological studies in which he taught a dog to associate the ringing of a bell with being fed. *Operant or instrumental conditioning* focuses on altering people's knowledge or behavior by giving them rewards. *Social learning theory* stresses that people learn by observing others, accepting the behaviors of others as norms, and then modeling personal behavior after others.

Cognitive learning usually begins by *exposure* to a message. *Perception* of a message uses the human senses to collection new information and is followed by *comprehension,* which involves making sense of a message. *Understanding* involves reconciling new information with a person's extant knowledge stored in memory. Importantly, *remembering* information involves more than the simple passing through of a message into the brain. Instead, people analyze the information, focus on key parts, amplify on those parts, and make "mental notes" about information in a process known as *elaboration.*

Schemas

Cognition refers to the mental mechanisms that lead individuals to perceive, think about, and elaborate on public relations messages and appeals. Although practitioners tend to assume that members of target audiences will respond in similar ways to communications, this is not necessarily the case.

Rather, individuals are constantly building unique frameworks of knowledge, beliefs, and expectations based on their personal history, current circumstances, future plans, and interactions with others. These cognitive structures—representing the attributes and relationships among people, objects, and events—are known as *schemas.*

Schemas are believed to improve the efficiency of cognitive processing by allowing people to process information quickly. They also provide predictability about people and events by creating expectations about topics in people's minds. Schemas influence the types of messages that people notice (*attention schemas*), how they process information contained in the messages (*encoding schemas*), as well as how they retrieve information from memory (*retrieval schemas*). Other types of schemas include *event* or *script schemas,* which govern the sequence of events that people expect in particular settings, and *role schemas,* which govern the way people expect others to act in particular roles.

Stereotypes are one type of schema. Stereotypes, or *person schemas,* are based on the physical appearance and behavioral characteristics of other groups of people. According to social learning theory, people form stereotypes based on what they learn from parents, peer groups, and mass media. From these and other sources, people learn to separate others into different social categories based on age, gender, race, and other characteristics. Stereotypes can lead people to habitually look for a particular desirable or undesirable trait in another group. Although stereotypes can contribute to the efficient processing of public relations messages, they can thus produce biased judgments and behavior.

People vary in their use of schemas to assess public relations messages. In many cases, for example, people compare or screen new messages for relevance to information already stored in memory and focus on inconsistencies. Schemas involve assertions between related topics, so creative messages often involve making linkages between two seemingly unrelated sets of schemas. Examples are as simple as using similes or metaphors to make comparisons.

Research indicates that schemas congruent with existing attitudes toward a topic are more likely to be retrieved from memory than incongruent schemas. Also, schemas that are "primed" by exposure to specific messages are more readily accessible in memory and thus are more likely to influence subsequent behavior. Priming can occur even when people are unaware that they have been exposed to the priming messages. Effective message framing can facilitate the priming process by providing cues to what schemas should be evoked to process a particular message.

Schemas, once formed, are resistant to change and often produce self-confirming effects. However, public relations messages can and do lead to schema change under certain conditions. The *bookkeeping model* suggests that the slow accumulation of information over time can lead to gradual schema change. Under the *conversion model,* schema change is rapid and occurs when people are overwhelmed by new evidence. According to the *subtyping model,* people create schema subtypes based on exposure to new information in messages. Research indicates that subtyping is the typical mechanism by which schemas change.

Heuristics

Heuristics are a second type of cognitive mechanism that can produce rapid reactions to public relations messages. Heuristics are "mental shortcuts" or "rules of thumb" that people use in place of deliberate thinking when making decisions. People tend to use heuristics when they lack information or are overloaded with information, when they lack time to think carefully, when the decision is unimportant, and when the heuristic rule comes quickly to mind.

Like schemas, there are many types of heuristics. The *simulation heuristic* is used to make decisions based on a mental rehearsal of the sequence and outcome of events. The *representative heuristic* is used to categorize people based on a few traits that appear typical of that category. According to the *availability heuristic,* information that is more easily recalled from memory will be correspondingly more influential in making decisions. Amos Tversky and Daniel Kahneman (1974) confirmed that individuals use heuristics automatically and without awareness when making routine decisions.

The two leading persuasion process models—the Elaboration Likelihood Model and the Heuristic-Systematic Model—argue that heuristic cues (known as peripheral cues in the Elaboration Likelihood Model), can influence persuasion and are particularly important in cases when people are not motivated to pay attention to arguments.

Heuristics and schemas can increase the efficient processing and persuasiveness of public relations messages; however, they can also reduce accuracy, leading to errors in cognition. *Optimistic* or *negative bias* (the expectation of positive or negative outcomes) can influence the processing of messages, leading people to ignore or pay greater attention to negative messages concerning threats in the social environment. Errors can also occur when people rely on intuition or irrational assumptions when making decisions, or suppress thoughts that are inconsistent with behavioral intentions.

Cognitive Consistency and Dissonance

Social psychologists Fritz Heider (in 1946 and 1958) and Leon Festinger (in 1957) were among the first to argue that people strive toward consistency, balance, or consonance between mental representations of their beliefs, attitudes, and behaviors. Whereas Heider's balance theory primarily dealt with consistency among attitudes, Festinger's theory of cognitive dissonance showed that the consistency principle was relevant to a wide variety of cognitive elements, including behavior and behavioral decision making.

When beliefs, attitudes, behavior, and other elements are inconsistent with one another, people experience a negative affective state of discomfort or tension known as cognitive dissonance. The magnitude of dissonance tends to be greater when the belief, attitude, or behavior is more important or highly valued by the person, as well as when the belief, attitude, or behavior is proportionally more dissonant with other cognitive elements.

To reduce tension and maintain cognitive consistency, people try to bring their beliefs, attitudes, and behaviors into alignment with one another, typically by modifying the cognitive element that is easiest to change. Exposing target audiences to messages that are contrary to existing attitudes and beliefs can thus provide a motivational force for behavioral change. In general, people deal with inconsistency through avoidance, reactance (countering), or discounting (dismissing the importance of the fact or the credibility of the source).

THE ROLE OF AFFECT

Affect is a broad term that encompasses emotions, moods, feelings, and other affective states. Professor Susan McLeod (1991) differentiated among various forms of affect based on their stability and intensity. *Feelings* are typically associated with physical sensations, such as pleasure or pain. *Emotions* involve distinctive physical and affective reactions to particular attitude objects (people, issues, or events). Emotions can be dominant or secondary in a given situation and can stand alone or combine to form various emotional states. *Moods* are more general in nature and express the positive or negative way people feel at particular times. Because moods are less intense and more fleeting than emotions, they are easier to change in desirable ways.

Psychologists differ as to whether cognition and affect represent separate systems within humans; however, they generally recognize that people devote varying levels of both thought and emotion to information processing and behavioral decision making. Professor Kristie Fleckenstein conceptualized affect and cognition as states located at the opposite ends of an affective continuum, so that it becomes meaningful to think of affect and cognition as linked and expressible in degrees. Moods, feelings, and emotions cluster at the affective end of the continuum, attitudes at the midpoint, and evaluation (assessment of information according to previously stored criteria) at the cognitive end of the continuum.

The priority of cognitive or affective influences on learning and behavioral decision making is the subject of ongoing debate. Affect, psychologist Fredric Bartlett argued in 1932, is not simply a product of rational thought but often assumes primacy, initiating the formation of knowledge structures and serving as the basis for information encoding and retrieval. Conversely, people often employ cognitive techniques such as counterfactual thinking and thought suppression to regulate emotions, moods, and feelings. Thus, there is often close correspondence between cognitive and affective states and subsequent judgments and behavior.

Psychologists generally acknowledge that emotions, moods, and feelings can influence the way people process new information. Messages must arouse audiences in order for them to pay attention, and message creators can appeal to people's emotions to enhance message processing. The goal is to create sufficient levels of affective response—but not so much that people are overwhelmed so that they cease learning or become distracted. Thus, overly attractive spokespeople, highly graphic scenes of death or destruction, and excessive fear appeals can interfere with effective communication.

THE ROLE OF CONATION

A third aspect of the human mind relevant to public relations efforts is conation: the unconscious or conscious impulse, desire, inclination, or intention to take action. Until recently the study of conation has lagged behind that of cognition and affect, in part because the three domains are intertwined and often considered together when assessing human behavior. Isolating conation from other influences on behavioral decision making thus becomes difficult. Most psychologists agree, however, that conation is a separate and important element of human behavior and that decision making cannot be fully explained without taking conative factors into account.

In 1997, cognitive psychologists Richard Snow and Douglas Jackson placed conation between cognitive and affective domains, with motivation and volition constituting the conative domain. Motivation can involve achieving human *needs* (physiological, safety, social, esteem, self-actualization, etc.), *goals* (achieving particular outcomes), or *gratifications* (pleasure or satisfaction). Motivational factors provide the direction, energy, and persistence necessary to achieve change, while volition encompasses freedom of choice, the will to act, and self-regulation of behavioral effort.

Snow and Jackson envisioned motivation and volition as forming a sort of conative continuum or pathway by which individual wants, needs, and goals are transformed into intentions and actions. Other researchers are more inclined to interpret motivational factors from an affective perspective and volitional influences from a cognitive viewpoint. Conation—the inclination to take action—thus becomes the psychological "bridge" between affect, cognition, and behavioral change.

Conative behaviors in public relations generally deal with particular actions that are mutually beneficial for people and for organizations. The most obvious behaviors that practitioners try to influence in the for-profit and political arenas include buying, investing, working, donating, and voting. However, not-for-profit organizations help people to learn new skills, develop cultural or recreational activities, grow spiritually, engage in healthful habits, and avoid risky or antisocial behaviors.

INFLUENCING BEHAVIORS AND ATTITUDES

Influence in public relations involves altering a person's cognitive, affective, or conative behaviors. Most well-managed communications programs specify both organizational goals as well as behavioral change objectives that can help the organization achieve its desired outcomes. Although the behavioral objectives of many campaigns can be to merely increase a person's knowledge (awareness, recognition, or recall of a brand or key message point) or to generate affective response (emotional leaning toward a client's product, message, or organization), most programs specify conative actions as the desired outcome.

Traditional hierarchy of effects models suggest that behavioral change results from a person moving along a continuum from awareness to interest to desire to action (also known as the AIDA model). Variations of this notion emphasize awareness-comprehension-conviction-action and awareness-knowledge-liking-preference-conviction. Diffusion theory suggests a similar process that involves knowledge-persuasion-decision-implementation-confirmation. These models suggest that change begins with learning, after which people develop feelings and then act. More recent research suggests that in some instances the sequence is reversed. Research about low-involvement decisions suggests that people develop feelings toward topics, engage in minimal cognitive learning, and then act. Alternatively, forcing people to change their behavior can effect behavioral change. In this dissonance-radical behaviorism approach, people develop affective responses and then learn by observing their own behavior.

Both these approaches and most behavioral change models suggest that attitudes toward topics moderate a person's eventual behavior. An *attitude* is a predisposition toward a topic that combines both cognitive and affective dimensions—what a person knows and how he or she feels about it (likes it, is neutral, or dislikes it).

Various attitude theories, such as the theory of reasoned action and the theory of planned behavior, suggest that attitudes are reasonably good predictors of behaviors, provided that a person is able to engage in the requisite behaviors and that the person's goals do not change. Thus, many public relations campaigns have as their stated purpose to *crystallize attitudes* (shape or form predispositions about new topics), *reinforce existing attitudes,* or *change attitudes* (the most difficult outcome to achieve in a campaign).

Importantly, if an attitude is composed of both cognitive and affective dimensions, public relations campaign strategies essentially can influence attitudes in two ways: change what people know about a topic or change how they feel about a topic (i.e., increase their affective response or how important the topic is in their mind).

IMPLICATIONS FOR PUBLIC RELATIONS PRACTICE

The influence of public relations messages and appeals on learning and behavioral decision making depends greatly on the cognitive, affective, and conative states of the people exposed to the messages. Public relations efforts can be directed toward shaping, reinforcing, or changing the cognitive or affective processing of messages to achieve

the desired end result. When a target audience is knowledgeable and motivated to process messages, a well-reasoned argument, supported by factual evidence, may be effective in shaping attitudes and behavior. When audience members are unwilling to process messages logically, however, an emotional appeal may increase acceptance of the messages. Since people differ in their ability to put their thoughts and feelings into action, messages aimed at helping audience members develop conative attitudes and skills—the setting of goals, the development of plans, self-regulation of effort, and commitment to achieving desired results—also become critical in achieving behavior change.

—Cindy T. Christen and Kirk Hallahan

See also Attribution theory; Communication management; Diffusion of innovations theory; Involvement; Persuasion theory; Social construction of reality theory; Theory of reasoned action

Bibliography

Ajzen, I. (1985). From intentions to actions: A theory of planned behavior. In J. Kuhl & J. Beckman (Eds.), *Action-control: From cognition to behavior* (pp. 11–39). Heidelberg: Springer.

Ajzen, I., & Fishbein, M. (1980). *Understanding attitudes and predicting social behavior.* Englewood Cliffs, NJ: Prentice Hall.

Bandura, A. (1977). *Social learning theory.* Englewood Cliffs, NJ: Prentice-Hall.

Bandura, A. (2002). Social cognitive theory of mass communication. In J. Bryant & D. Zillman (Eds.), *Media effects: Advances in theory and research* (2nd ed., pp. 121–154). Mahwah, NJ: Lawrence Erlbaum.

Barry, T. (1987). The development of the hierarchy of effects: An historical perspective. In *Current issues and research in advertising* (Vol. 10, pp. 251–295). Ann Arbor: University of Michigan Graduate School of Business Administration.

Chaiken, S. (1980). Heuristic versus systematic information processing and the use of source versus message cues in persuasion. *Journal of Personality and Social Psychology, 39,* 752–766.

Chaiken, S., Liberman, A., & Eagly, A. H. (1989). Heuristic and systematic information processing within and beyond the persuasion context. In J. S. Ulemen & J. A. Bargh (Eds.), *Unintended thought* (pp. 212–252). New York: Guilford Press.

Colley, R. (1961). *Defining advertising goals for measured advertising results.* New York: Association of American Advertisers.

Festinger, L. (1957). *A theory of cognitive dissonance.* Evanston, IL: Row Peterson.

Heider, F. (1958). *The psychology of interpersonal relations.* New York: John Wiley & Sons.

Kelley, H. H. (1967). Attribution theory in social psychology. In *Nebraska Symposium on Motivation.* Lincoln: University of Nebraska Press.

Lavidge, R. C., & Steiner, G. A. (1961). A model for predictive measurements of advertising effectiveness. *Journal of Marketing, 25,* 59–62.

McLeod, S. H. (1991). The affective domain and the writing process: Working definitions. *Journal of Advanced Composition, 11,* 95–105.

Petty, R. E., & Cacioppo, J. T. (1986). *Communication and persuasion: Central and peripheral routes to attitude change.* New York: Springer-Verlag.

Petty, R. E., Priester, J. R., & Brinol, P. (2002). Mass media attitude change: Implications of the elaboration likelihood model of persuasion. In J. Bryant & D. Zillman (Eds.), *Media effects: Advances in theory and research* (2nd ed., pp. 155–194). Mahwah, NJ: Lawrence Erlbaum.

Ray, M. L. (1973). Communication and the hierarchy of effects. In P. Clarke (Ed.), *New models for communication research* (pp. 147–175). Beverly Hills, CA: Sage.

Rogers, E. M. (2003). *The diffusion of innovations* (5th ed.) New York: Free Press.

Snow, R. E., & Jackson, D. N. III. (1997). *Individual differences in conation: Selected constructs and measures* (Technical Report 447). Los Angeles: Center for the Study of Evaluation, University of California.

Tversky, A., & Kahneman, D. (1974). Judgment under uncertainty: Heuristics and biases. *Science, 185,* 1124–1131.

PUBLIC AFFAIRS

Public affairs is the management function responsible for interpreting an organization's external environment, or in the case of a corporation, its noncommercial environment, and managing an effective and appropriate response to that environment. The public affairs function in an organization or corporation typically includes the government relations area, and it frequently has responsibility for other activities in the political, public policy, and public perception arenas, such as issue management, internal and external communications, community relations, and philanthropy.

Historically, there has been considerable confusion over the definition of *public affairs* and how it differs or is distinguished from *public relations*. In the United States of the 21st century, one can find *public affairs* being used synonymously with *public relations* or as another name for government relations. And for a large number of organizations and corporations, *public affairs* is used as the name of the integrated department that includes all of the external, noncommercial activities.

Whereas the term *public relations* has been in common usage since the early 1900s, *public affairs* is of more recent vintage. Unfortunately, the exact origin and first use of *public affairs* are uncertain. However, an early use of the term was by Thomas Reid, who became the manager, public affairs of Ford Motor Company in the 1959–1960 time period. Use of public affairs has grown slowly in the corporate world. In 1970, only a small minority of the executives who participated in the Public Affairs Council had public affairs as part of their department's or their own title. By 2002, the Foundation for Public Affairs survey, *The State of Corporate Public Affairs,* indicated that although *public affairs* was the most common title used, it still was used by less than a third of the survey respondents. Clearly, there is no universal acceptance and use of the term.

PUBLIC AFFAIRS ACTIVITIES

Activities assigned to the public affairs department vary widely among corporations. Government relations, particularly at the federal level, is undoubtedly the oldest and most common activity in the public affairs function, with the first corporate Washington office being opened in 1901. The number of such offices grew modestly until the demands of the war effort on corporations during World War II resulted in a sharp increase. The growth of social activism in the 1960s, particularly the environmental and consumer movements, saw a significant expansion in staff and corporate resources directed at interpreting and responding to the ever increasing volume of laws and regulations flowing from Washington.

Likewise, the devolution of power from Washington to the states in the 1970s and 1980s saw a significant increase in corporate resources directed to state government relations. And the 1990s saw the need for corporations to become more actively involved in local government relations. In addition to this changing geographical orientation, corporations developed new programs to deal more effectively with their external environment, such as grassroots and grasstops programs, political action committees, public policy development and assessment, issue management systems, public interest group relations, and crisis management teams and systems. Subject matter experts were also added in such areas as the environment, consumer matters, and government regulations to deal with the growing number of external issues impacting the corporation.

The responsibilities of many public affairs departments also include the traditional public relations activities of corporate communications, media relations, community relations, charitable contributions, employee communications, and investor relations.

ORGANIZATIONAL STRUCTURES

Studies over the last ten years and more by the Public Affairs Council and the Foundation for Public Affairs indicate that about half of all corporations utilize an integrated public affairs organizational structure that includes the traditional public relations activities as well as government relations. The other half of the corporations house the government relations activities and public relations activities in separate departments. These studies have consistently revealed a consensus among senior corporate and public affairs management that an integrated public relations and government relations department is the most effective organizational structure for dealing with the corporation's external environment. The reasons generally cited for this view are that the issues facing a corporation in today's external environment are quite complex. To be effective in this environment requires multiple approaches, with the full range of the corporation's communications arsenal fully utilized. An integrated department allows a corporation to more quickly and effectively harness all of its internal resources and external activities and bring them to bear on an issue, thus increasing the chances of success. There are also substantial natural synergies between

government relations and public relations that are more easily captured in an integrated department.

The studies indicate that senior managers in those corporations that have separate government relations and public relations departments also recognize the benefits of an integrated approach and expect close cooperation between the government relations and public relations units.

—Woodrow Madden

Bibliography

Dennis, L. B. (1996). *Practical public affairs in an era of change.* Lanham, MD: Public Relations Society of America and University Press of America.

Dozier, D. (1995). *Manager's guide to excellence in public relations and communication management.* Mahwah, NJ: Lawrence Erlbaum.

Foundation for Public Affairs. (2002). *The state of corporate public affairs.* Washington, DC: Author.

Public Affairs Council. (1998). *Effective public affairs organizational structures.* Washington, DC: Author.

PUBLIC AFFAIRS COUNCIL

The Public Affairs Council, based in Washington, DC, is the leading professional society for public affairs executives in the United States. It provides state-of-the-art information, training, and other resources to its 500-plus organizational members and their employees to promote and support their effective participation in government, community, and public relations activities at all levels. For a profile of the Council, see Table 1. The council's corporate, association, and consultant members work together to enhance the value and professionalism of the public affairs practice and to provide thoughtful leadership as corporate citizens. For a profile of the membership composition, see Table 2 and for types of most active members, see Table 3.

Organizations join the Public Affairs Council to benefit from a variety of services, including *personalized information services* (council staff experts provide members with advice on public affairs best practices, political action committee [PAC] fundraising, grassroots advocacy, crisis communications, state government relations, and other public affairs topics); *education programs* (more than 30 conferences are sponsored annually, plus seminars and workshops, including the largest national conferences on PAC management, grassroots organizing, and corporate philanthropy; it also holds state government affairs workshops in five states each year, along with meetings for global public affairs executives, Washington lobbyists, issues managers, and others in the public affairs field); *strong advocacy for the public affairs profession* (the council supports the important role that public affairs plays in business strategy; council outreach efforts to business leaders, business schools, and the news media explain how public affairs contributes to an organization's bottom line); *customized benchmarking services* (members can compare themselves to "best-practice" companies or see how their staffing and budgets measure up to competitors); *communications* (council members receive *Impact,* the council's award-winning newsletter, which covers public affairs news and trends as well as intelligence on emerging public policy issues; members also receive the council's annual *Public Affairs Review* and the organization's twice-monthly electronic news service and gain access to the valuable best-practice information and databases in the council's Web site (www.pac.org.); and *unique connections to the public affairs community* (seminars, forums, online discussion groups, and board meetings facilitate idea sharing and the building of new relationships). For a summary of the Council's areas of expertise, see Table 4.

The council defines public affairs "as the management function that interprets and works to strengthen a corporation's business environment." It has been innovative in expanding the ways the business world responds to the rapid changes transforming politics and government at all levels in the United States and abroad. The record of the past half-century is dotted with milestones attesting to the creative approaches the Public Affairs Council has pioneered since it was created in 1954 as Effective Citizens Organization (ECO). Soon the ECO name gave way to Public Affairs Council, which seemed to the founders to better capture the mission of the fledgling organization. For example, political education for business leaders, today

universally accepted as a corporate imperative, was born in 1956 when the council launched a series of "practical politics workshops" for corporate executives at leading universities around the country. This effort at educating business leaders in practical politics would later be used as a pilot by other organizations intent on creating similar programs—the National Association of Manufacturers and the United States Chamber of Commerce among them.

The new council was the catalyst for the creation in the 1950s of the first corporate public affairs departments. In the tumultuous 1960s, it pressed the concept of "corporate social responsibility," along with state government relations programs, and, later, the ideas of grassroots political action, issues management, international risk assessment, and strategic planning, to name a few. Thousands of public affairs executives learned the basics of lobbying at council "clinics." The first conference to be held abroad on the growing phenomenon known as public affairs was conducted by the council in Brussels in 1972.

Early on the council took the lead in educating business in the most effective use of corporate political action committees (PACs). Today, it is the main source for companies around the United States seeking instruction in making their PACs more effective or in starting a political action committee from scratch.

Volunteerism, corporate community relations, and corporate philanthropy, all now "traditional" public affairs programs, owe their corporate acceptance to the council's continual efforts to expand the public affairs department's portfolio.

In recognition of the increasing importance that technology and new-century management practices have in advancing the professionalization of public affairs, the council early in the 1990s created the Center for Public Affairs Management. It deals specifically with management problems of public affairs executives in a quality-conscious, technology-minded corporate climate.

The council in the 2000s is pressing for a partnering of public affairs and public relations techniques to ensure maximum public policy and communications effectiveness.

Table 1   The Public Affairs Council, in Profile

Market

Public affairs professionals from the nation's key corporations (largely *Fortune* 500) and associations, plus their consultancies

Products

Member-tailored information, research, strategic intelligence, public affairs management, benchmarking and training in public affairs, lobbying, political action committee (PAC) management and grassroots management, and, of course, networking

Leadership

Members of the PAC's executive committee and board of directors drawn from the corporations, associations, and consultancies cited in "Products"

Formula for customer service and innovations in public affairs

Constant measurement of programs and services through management and financial reporting, benchmarking against competition, formal customer satisfaction surveys, and an overall sense of community for those in the public affairs profession

Partners and alliances

The Foundation for Public Affairs as events and needs warrant, national influential media, business, professional and other organizations; and outstanding experts from the many fields of public affairs

Headquarters team

Veterans from the key fields of public affairs

SOURCE: The Public Affairs Council. Reprinted with permission.

Table 2   Membership Composition

Fortune 500 corporations

    Emerging growth companies

    Associations

    Public affairs consultants

Industry sectors

    Manufacturing

    Utilities

    Retailing

    Transportation

    Financial services

    Health care

    Diversified service companies

SOURCE: The Public Affairs Council. Reprinted with permission.

Table 3   Most Active Members

Public affairs or corporate affairs vice presidents and senior vice presidents

International affairs executives

Grassroots and political action committee (PAC) managers

Corporate citizenship directors

Government relations directors

Media relations directors

Communications vice presidents and senior vice presidents

Senior Washington office executives

Legislative representatives

Community relations directors

SOURCE: Public Affairs Council (2003). Reprinted with permission.

Table 4 The Components of Public Affairs: The Public Affairs Council's Fields of Expertise

---

Advocacy
  Coalition building
  Grassroots programs
  Public interest/public policy groups

Corporate community involvement
  Community relations
  Corporate contributions
  Volunteerism

Corporate issues
  Crisis management
  Emerging issues

Government relations
  Local
  State
  Federal
  International

Politics
  Campaign finance
  PACs
  Political education
  Voter registration/get-out-the-vote efforts

Public affairs management
  Benchmarking
  Communication tools
  Maximizing external resources
  Organization and staffing
  Performance measurement and evaluation
  Professional ethics
  Public affairs competencies
  Staff training and development
  Strategic planning
  Effective use of technology

SOURCE: The Public Affairs Council. Reprinted with permission.

—*Wes Pedersen*

See also Community relations; Corporate social responsibility; Issues management; Lobbying; Nongovernmental organizations (NGOs); Philanthropy; Public affairs

Bibliography

Public Affairs Council. (2003). *Public affairs in the next 10 years.* Retrieved November 15, 2003, from http://www.pac.org/public/news/news_releases/news_080503.shtml

PUBLIC HEALTH CAMPAIGN

A public health campaign is an effort to persuade a defined public to engage in behaviors that will improve health or refrain from behaviors that are unhealthy. The communication elements of public health campaigns reflect four critical elements. First, campaigns are strategic and organized efforts. Second, they are typically designed to yield specific outcomes or results. Third, they normally focus on a large number of individuals. Fourth, they usually have specific beginning and ending dates. Public health campaigns typically follow seven steps: defining the problem, developing objectives, identifying target audiences, developing message strategies and tactics, selecting appropriate communication channels, implementing the campaign, and evaluating both the process and campaign outcomes.

DEFINE THE PROBLEM

The first step in any public health campaign is to assess and define the nature of the health problem. In 1999, Christopher Rissel and Neil Bracht outlined two basic forms of community health analysis. The *health planning approach,* sometimes referred to as the "trickle-down" approach, associates the concept of health with the absence of disease. Government agencies most often use the health planning approach. Through the routine collection of data, tracking the outbreak of diseases along with other, related information, including demographics, living habits, and environmental risks, epidemiologists and other health experts identify and prioritize health threats on a local, national, or international level. The *community development approach,* sometimes referred to as the "bubble up" approach, examines community health from a perspective that promotes individual and community empowerment. The broader concerns of educational, social, and economic vitality are factored into the analysis and any subsequent health intervention.

The U.S. Department of Health and Human Services' *Healthy People 2010: National Health Promotion and Disease Prevention Outcomes* reflects a health planning approach. Armed with statistics of current and emerging health threats, epidemiologists and other health experts devised this report. The *Healthy People 2010* report is one of the major engines driving the prioritization of specific efforts in current health services and research. For example, statistics continue to show that African Americans are dying from some forms of cancer at rates disproportionate to Caucasians, revealing the need for more effort in promoting earlier disease detection among this at-risk population. As a result, state and federal departments of health are placing special attention on this problem.

An example of the community development approach is the Adolescent Social Action Program (ASAP), a public health campaign aimed at youths living in high-risk areas in New Mexico. The ASAP program is a collaboration of the University of New Mexico, the university hospital, the county detention center, and schools and communities throughout the state. The campaign involves teaming youths in small groups with jail residents and rehabilitation patients to discuss such topics as violence and substance abuse. By using a listening-dialogue-action model the youths are able to examine the stories of the inmates and patients and then discuss how those stories are relevant to their own lives. After several weeks the focus turns toward the topic of leadership and community development. At the end of a seven-week curriculum, the youths typically enter one of two programs, a peer education program where they will work with younger elementary students, or a social action program in which they explore ways to change risky behaviors in their communities. In both programs they are encouraged to use their creativity in devising either an educational or action plan.

The U.S. Department of Health and Human Services' Healthy People 2010: National Health Promotion and Disease Prevention Outcomes is one of the major engines driving the prioritization of specific efforts in current health services and research.

SOURCE: U.S. Department of Health and Human Services. *Healthy People 2010: Understanding and Improving Health.* 2nd ed. Washington, DC: U.S. Government Printing Office, November 2000.

DEVELOP OBJECTIVES

Once specific problems are identified, development of specific goals and objectives is the next step in the public health campaign process. The *Healthy People 2010* report reflects broad-reaching goals for reducing disease and improving the overall health of the U.S. population by the year 2010. The two major themes of the report include increasing the quality and years of healthy life, and the elimination of racial and ethnic disparities in health status. Ten specific health indicators are identified in the report: physical activity, overweight and obesity, tobacco use, substance abuse, mental health, injury and violence, environmental quality, immunization, responsible sexual behavior, and access to health care.

These health indicators are supported by 21 specific measurable objectives that reflect the influence of behavioral and environmental factors and community health interventions. These 21 measures provide states and communities guidance in where to target public health campaigns and benchmarks for assessing the success of these campaigns. For example, the misuse of prescription medication can be a very dangerous health risk. One specific communication-related objective is to increase the proportion of patients who receive verbal counseling from prescribers and pharmacists about the appropriate use and potential risks of medications. The 1998 benchmark indicates that 24 percent of patients received verbal counseling from their caregiver, and only 14 percent of patients received verbal counseling from pharmacists. The target is to bring both percentages up to 95 percent, which would represent increases in the percentages of patients counseled by physicians and pharmacists of nearly 300 and 600 percent, respectively.

IDENTIFY TARGET AUDIENCES

Public health campaigns often involve segmentation of the community into a variety of dimensions that might include such factors as demographics (e.g., race, income level, and age) or psychographics (e.g., fear levels and readiness for change). Charles Salmon and Charles Atkin identified three basic types of target audiences in 2003. First is the focal audience whose health-related behavior is to be changed. The American Cancer Society's effort to persuade women age 50 and older to get annual mammograms is an example. The second audience is composed of those individuals who are capable of influencing focal audience members. An example is Partnership for a Drug-Free America's public service ads that urge parents to always ask their children where they are going and with whom. The third type of target audience is composed of individuals capable of altering the environment in ways that shape

individuals' health behavior. For example, over the past 10 years Mothers Against Drunk Driving has been successful in convincing lawmakers in many states to lower legal blood alcohol limits and stiffen penalties for alcohol-related infractions.

DEVELOPING STRATEGIES AND TACTICS

The effective use of strategies and tactics is key for a public health campaign's success. A sound foundation in social science theory is essential for a campaign to yield its full potential. A good example of a useful theory is Kim Witte's *extended parallel process model* (EPPM). Many health campaigns involve communicating some element of threat. The threat may come from continuing an unhealthy behavior or from not engaging in a healthy behavior, for example, continuing to smoke or not exercise. EPPM provides an explanation why some individuals react to a health message by going into a danger control response, which means taking action to control or eliminate the threat, while other individuals react to the same message by going into a fear control response, which means engaging in a process that controls fear rather than the threat. Often fear control responses are maladaptive and may involve message avoidance or erroneously rationalizing that one is not subject to a threat when in fact he or she is. Critical elements of the model include a person's perceived susceptibility to a health threat, the severity of the threat, the efficacy of responding to the health threat in a prescribed way, and a person's self-efficacy (i.e., his or her perceived ability to adopt the suggested behavior). The key is to tailor messages in a way that responds to each person's perceptions to promote danger control and minimize or eliminate fear control. The author is nearing completion of a four-year breast cancer screening promotion study that compares a tailored interactive computer program with a standard videotape program. Preliminary results indicate women receiving the EPPM tailored intervention are significantly more likely to get a mammogram than women who received the nontailored intervention, (40 percent vs. 27 percent).

SELECTING COMMUNICATION CHANNELS

Once message strategies and tactics are developed, communication channels must be selected to deliver this content. The two major types are mediated channels and interpersonal channels. Mediated channels include traditional media such as television, radio, and newspapers, as well as interactive media such as CD-ROM programs, Web sites, and computer games. Charles Atkin (1994) has identified several media features to consider in deciding which channels are appropriate for a particular campaign. These include *reach* (the proportion of the audience exposed to the message), *depth* (the ability to provide detailed information), *accessibility* (the ease of placing messages in the channel), *personalization* (the degree to which messages can be tailored to individual needs), *economy* (the cost of placing messages in a channel), *targetability* (the degree to which audience niches can be reached), and *participation* (the degree to which audience members are involved while processing a message).

Often, the audiences most in need of health information are the most difficult to reach. For example, low-socioeconomic-status populations can be hard to reach. People in these populations typically don't go to the doctor regularly and they tend not to read newspapers or magazines. They watch a lot of television, but don't consume much news or documentary programming. Creative solutions are necessary for reaching this at-risk group. One example is an outreach effort by the Association of Black Cardiologists (ABC) to combat hypertension, a leading cause of heart attacks and strokes. These cardiologists have trained barbers and beauty shop operators in low-income neighborhoods surrounding downtown Atlanta to take blood pressure readings and to provide information about heart disease. The effort has been so successful that the drug maker Novartis has awarded ABC $1.5 million to expand the program to five other states.

IMPLEMENTATION

Implementation of a public health campaign should occur only when the previous steps have been thoroughly developed. It is also important to understand the collaborative nature of many public health campaigns. As Timothy Edgar, Vicki Freimuth, and Sharon Hammond pointed out in 2003, few large-scale public health campaigns are implemented by a single organization. Often many partners such as foundations, state and local agencies, advocacy groups, researchers, pharmaceutical companies, health professionals, and private contractors work together to design and implement a campaign. These partnerships bring strengths to a project. Each organization has unique resources and expertise. For example, a foundation, government agency, or pharmaceutical company may provide the funding necessary to carry out a public health campaign. Researchers guide the scientific development in order to uncover new knowledge. A public relations firm develops and implements a publicity effort to inform the community about the health campaign and to recruit volunteers, and health professionals work with the campaign team to deliver care to patients and the resulting data to the research group. Although collaboration provides great benefits, it is important to realize that competing interests often characterize such partnerships. An understanding of group and organizational communication is critical in order to yield the most effective public health campaign.

CAMPAIGN EVALUATION

The final step is evaluation, although the process actually begins with the research conducted to determine needs before the start of a campaign, proceeds during the campaign to determine if benchmarks are being met, and continues after the conclusion of the campaign with the assessment of campaign outcomes. In 1999, Phyllis Pirie identified three basic types of evaluation. Evaluation for *accountability* seeks to determine if a campaign is worth the financial expenditure. Funding agencies and policymakers are particularly concerned with this. Evaluation for *program improvement* searches for ways to change activities for maximum benefit. This is a chief concern of campaign management and staff whose focus is on promoting the success of their campaign. Finally, evaluation for *generalizability* seeks to determine if a campaign could be mounted effectively in other locations. In addition to researchers, policymakers are particularly interested in generalizability in order to decide whether they should advocate the program on a wider scale.

Pirie noted that outcome evaluation can be effective only when careful needs and process evaluation are done. Otherwise, one cannot know for certain what is accounting for the outcome. On a community level, "pre-post test" evaluations are generally not as strong because there are so many variables outside the campaign that might influence outcome. Pirie argued that comparison of similar communities without a program is a more certain way of gauging campaign outcomes. A good example of this is the American Legacy Foundation's "Truth" campaign, a national tobacco counter-marketing effort launched in February 2000. The "Truth" campaign is based on the dramatic declines in youth tobacco that resulted from the Florida and Massachusetts antismoking campaigns, which have been much more successful than different approaches used in other states.

—Jeffrey K. Springston

See also Transtheoretical model of behavior change

Bibliography

Atkin, C. (1994). Designing persuasive health messages. In L. Sechrest, T. Backer, E. Rogers, T. Campbell, & M. Grady (Eds.), *Effective dissemination of clinical health information* (AHCPR Publication No. 95-0015, pp. 99–110). Rockville, MD: Public Health Service, Agency for Health Care Policy and Research.

Bauer, U. E., Johnson, T. M., Hopkins, R. S., & Brooks, R. G. (2000). Changes in youth cigarette use and intentions following implementation of a tobacco control program: Findings from the Florida Youth Tobacco Survey, 1998–2000. *Journal of the American Medical Association, 284*, 723–728.

Champion, V., & Springston, J. K. (1999–2003). *Community interventions for mammography screening* (National Cancer Institute Report No. R01 CA77736-01). Unpublished manuscript.

Edgar, T., Freimuth, V., & Hammond, S. L. (2003). Lessons learned from the field on prevention and health campaigns. In T. L. Thompson, A. M. Dorsey, K. I. Miller, & R. Parrott (Eds.), *Handbook of health communication* (pp. 625–636). Mahwah, NJ: Lawrence Erlbaum.

Farrelly, M. C., Healton, C. G., Davis, K. C., Messeri, P., Hersey, J. C., & Haviland, L. (2002). Getting to the truth: Evaluating tobacco countermarketing campaigns. *American Journal of Public Health, 92*, 901–907.

Guthrie, P. (2003, July 21). Shave, haircut, health screening: Barbers join the fight against hypertension. *Atlanta Journal Constitution*, p. 1A.

Minkler, M., & Wallerstein, N. (1997). Improving health through community organization and community building. In K. Glanz, F. M. Lewis, & B. K. Rimer (Eds.), *Health behaviour and health education: Theory, research and practice* (pp. 241–269). San Francisco: Jossey-Bass.

Pirie, P. L. (1999). Evaluating community health promotion programs: Basic questions and approaches. In N. Bracht (Ed.), *Health promotion at the community level* (pp. 127–134). Thousand Oaks, CA: Sage.

Prochaska, J., & DiClemente, C. C. (1983). Stages and processes of self change of smoking: Toward an integrative model. *Journal of Consulting and Clinical Psychology, 51*, 390–395.

Rissel, C., & Bracht, N. (1999). Social change theory: Applications to community health. In N. Bracht (Ed.), *Health promotion at the community level.* Thousand Oaks, CA: Sage.

Rogers, E., & Storey, D. (1987). Communication campaigns. In C. Berger & S. Chaffee (Eds.), *Handbook of communication science* (pp. 817–846). Newbury Park, CA: Sage.

Salmon, C., & Atkin, C. (2003). Using media campaigns for health promotion. In T. L. Thompson, A. M. Dorsey, K. I. Miller, & R. Parrott (Eds.), *Handbook of health communication* (pp. 449–472). Mahwah, NJ: Lawrence Erlbaum.

Siegel, M., & Biener, L. (2000). The impact of an antismoking media campaign on progression to established smoking: Results of a longitudinal youth study. *American Journal of Public Health, 90*, 380–386.

Witte, K. (1992). Putting the fear back into fear appeals: The extended parallel process model. *Communication Monographs, 59*, 329–429.

PUBLIC INTEREST

Public relations practitioners have always realized that their practice could serve or be at odds with the public interest. Realizing that, practitioners face two challenges. One is knowing what the public interest is and knowing how to serve it.

Considerations of what constitutes the public interest are central to discussions of the role of public relations in society and continues to challenge those who craft and implement codes of professional practice. Actual and proposed codes of ethics for public relations practitioners state that public relations should be practiced in the public interest. The Public Relations Society's Code of Ethics says, in part, "We are faithful to those we represent, while honoring our obligation to serve the public interest" (Public Relations Society of America, 2000, n.p.). Likewise, textbooks on public relations emphasize that the public relations profession shares with its clients a social responsibility. In fact, the "public interest, not personal reward, should be the primary consideration," according to *This Is PR* (Newsom, Turk, & Kruckeberg, 2000, p. 3).

There is no argument that public relations should serve the public interest. The challenges arise in defining and describing public relations practice in the public interest.

Earl Newsom quoted Walter Lippmann's somewhat unsatisfying definition of public interest, "the public interest may be presumed to be what men would choose if they saw clearly, thought rationally, acted disinterestedly and benevolently" (1971, p. 12).

In contrast to the challenge to be disinterested, public relations professionals are not disinterested; they are partisan. This and the persuasive functions of public relations to crystallize, change, and activate attitudes seem in conflict with Lippmann's definition of the public interest. Carried toward what can be called the propagandistic practice of public relations, a professional can aspire to shape attitudes to the interest of the client. Such efforts may be asymmetrical and work against the challenge of building mutually beneficial relationships.

Newsom, Ramsey, and Carell's 1992 survey of public relations practitioners revealed that practitioners feel responsible first to the client, second to the client's relevant publics, third to themselves, fourth to the public at large, and fifth to the media. The Public Relations Society of America (PRSA) Statement of Professional Values codifies that perception of responsibility: "We serve the public interest by acting as responsible advocates for those we represent."

D. L. Martinson (1995, 2000) focused on the repetition of day-to-day actions and decisions as the source of practice in the public interest. Repeated truth telling will become habit and serves the public interest, he said. He further advised that practitioners avoid excess in advocating for a client when the client's interests are in conflict with those of society. Loyalty to a client does not require violation of the rights of others.

Thomas H. Bivins (1993) questioned whether it is even possible for a public relations practitioner to discharge his or her duty as an advocate for a client while at the same time equally serving the public interest. He concluded that this responsibility may best reside at the macro level, the level of the profession, rather than at the level of the individual. Yet, every practitioner knows that the devil is often in the detail. That means that at the broadest level it is easy to understand and serve the public interest. But when a fact needs to be presented, its presentation can raise ethical questions, as can the word choice that accompanies the fact.

To help solve problems of this sort, Bivins, in 1993, proposed three paradigms under which public practitioners might serve the public interest. Once he had laid out these paradigms, he disputed the notion of whether public relations practice within those paradigms actually served the public interest. In paradigm I, the public interest is served by every individual acting in the best interest of the client. This principle erroneously presumes that all clients operate in the public interest. In paradigm II, the public relations practitioner balances work for paying clients with pro bono work for causes. The cause-related work, however, serves a special interest. In paradigm III, the public interest is served by ensuring that every client in need of professional public relations service can receive that service. This paradigm would make access to professional public relations services an obligation of the profession as a whole and not to the individual practitioner.

To extend his analysis of the role public relations plays in serving the public interest, Bivins offered a fourth paradigm that attempts to codify the obligation of the profession to serve the public interest. According to paradigm IV, "If public relations as a profession improves the quality of debate over issues important to the public, then the public interest will be served" (1993, p. 1). This might require pro bono work to ensure that multiple viewpoints are expressed. However, it does not require equal opportunity of all viewpoints to be expressed.

Scott Cutlip, Allen Center, and Glen Broom's classic 1985 textbook, *Effective Public Relations,* relies on the utilitarian definition of public interest as "serving the larger good over short-term private interests" (p. 482). They located responsibility for such service within the notion of corporate social responsibility, as did John W. Hill. According to Hill, "Big companies, if they are properly managed, have a keen sense of public responsibility . . . and make sure that each of their plants is a good neighbor in its respective community" (1958, p. 39).

As counselors to management, public relations practitioners help their employers and clients find ways of "identifying its own interest with the public interest," Hill (1958, p. 21) said. Corporate policies of maintaining the strength and welfare of the company in ways consistent with the community interest, building a labor force by providing the best possible working conditions and wages, and investing in the goodwill of those essential to the corporation's success contribute to the corporation's success. "Good corporate public relations depend, first upon sound policies truly in the public interest," Hill (1958, p. 163) reasoned. Hill defined the public interest as that which "promotes the general welfare, well-being, and security of the citizenry" (1958, p. 238).

The entire public relations industry suffers when practitioners represent bad clients. But, Hill admonished, "the better informed the people are, the more capable they are of judging where the public interest lies" (1963, p. 256). Thus, he would agree with Bivins that the role of public relations in the public interest lies, in part, in stimulating and participating in open, public debate of issues relevant to various publics' interest.

The responsibility for stimulating debate has become the core principle underscoring the 2000 revision of the PRSA Code of Ethics: "Protecting and advancing the free flow of accurate and truthful information is essential to serving the public interest and contributing to informed decision making in a democratic society. . . . We provide a voice in the marketplace of ideas, facts, and viewpoints to aid informed public debate" (Public Relations Society of America, 2000, n.p.).

—*Ann Preston*

See also Codes of ethics; Corporate social responsibility; Ethics of public relations; Mutually beneficial relationships; Propaganda; Publics

Bibliography

Bivins, T. H. (1993). *Public relations, professionalism, and the public interest.* Retrieved June 20, 2003, from the First Search database.

Cutlip, S. M., Center, A. H., & Broom, G. M. (1985). *Effective public relations.* Edgewood Cliffs, NJ: Prentice Hall.

Huang, Y. (2001). *Should a public relations code of ethics be enforced?* Retrieved September 8, 2003, from the First Search database.

Hill, J. W. (1958). *Corporate public relations: Arm of modern management.* New York: Harper & Brothers.

Hill, J. W. (1963). *The making of a public relations man.* New York: David McKay.

Martinson, D. L. (1995). *Client partiality and third parties: An ethical dilemma for public relations practitioners?* Retrieved June 20, 2003, from the First Search database.

Martinson, D. L. (2000). *Ethical decision making in public relations: What would Aristotle say?* Retrieved June 20, 2003, from the First Search database.

Newsom, E. (1971). A philosophy of corporate public relations: An interview with Earl Newsom. *Public Relations Quarterly, 16*(2).

Newsom, D., Turk, J. V., & Kruckeberg, D. (2000). *This is PR.* Belmont, CA: Wadsworth.

Public Relations Society of America. (2000). PRSA Member Code of Ethics.

PUBLIC OPINION AND OPINION LEADERS

Public opinion can be defined in many ways, but most researchers agree that public opinion is the collected views of select individuals interested in a particular subject. Very few issues will generate an opinion by the entire population; rather, those issues that someone has a personal interest in will be important to him and he will in turn seek the opinions of others as he tries to find more information about the issue. For example, a mother in a small town may not have an opinion on the quality of inner-city housing, but she may be extremely vocal on a local issue such as education.

Public opinion is extremely difficult to measure. This is partly because only a small number of people at any given time actually form an opinion on a particular issue. This is because the public tends to be passive. Rarely does an issue elicit opinion by every citizen; rather, a small vocal group is seen as representing the attitude of the general public when, actually, most people have no opinion on the issue. Additionally, one issue may elicit a response or attention from one portion of the public, whereas another issue may be the focal point for another group of citizens. Once a person who feels a personal connection to, or self-interest in, the issue forms an opinion, it is very difficult to change that opinion.

Public opinion can change over time in several ways. Events can trigger a rapid change in public opinion, such as the change in public opinion about President Clinton once the Lewinsky scandal broke. This was also the case for the quick rise in positive public opinion of President George W. Bush after the tragic events of September 11, 2001.

Mass media can shape public opinion in a number of ways. Through agenda setting, news reports shape public perception of issues by highlighting certain news stories and downplaying other current issues. Additionally, the way that news stories are framed or presented will influence public opinion on an issue. For example, how the media frame the debate on tax cuts or campaign finance reform will influence the public's perception of the issue.

Public opinion can change more gradually depending on the ebb and flow of public attitudes. As a result of the Iranian hostage crisis in 1979–1980, public support for an increase in defense spending surged during this time; but support gradually decreased as media reports of wasteful spending in the defense budget turned public opinion.

Change in public opinion can also be seen as evolutionary. Over time, American attitudes toward woman and minorities have evolved, leading to acceptance and support of minorities and women holding positions of political power. In both cases, opinion did not change rapidly, but rather gradually over time.

An opinion leader is someone who is viewed as influential and is respected. Opinion leaders help shape public opinion because people listen to what they say and they are seen as experts in certain areas. Opinion leaders form networks by talking to other individuals who share information and viewpoints on specific topics. Opinion leaders are highly interested in an issue and are better informed than the average person. They are avid consumers of mass media and are active in searching out information on the issue. Opinion leaders like to let their opinions be known.

Reaching opinion leaders is important in public relations because an opinion leader's view carries weight in the community. This is believed to be demonstrated through the two-step flow theory of communication. Sociologists Elihu Katz and Paul Lazersfeld studied the influences involved in choosing political candidates. These researchers found that while the mass media have minimal influence on which candidate a person selects, voters were most influenced by what they heard through personal communication with opinion leaders. This theory holds that public opinion is formed by people who are active and gain information on the issue, evaluate the information, form an opinion on the subject, and then express that opinion to others.

Opinion leaders act as catalysts for the formation of public opinion. Opinion leaders are described as being highly interested in the subject, better informed on the issue, avid consumers of media, early adopters of new ideas, and good organizers who can get people to take action. Opinion leaders are broken down into two groups—formal and informal. Formal opinion leaders include elected officials, heads of companies, celebrities, and so on. Informal opinion leaders are individuals with clout within the community who influence their peers and are seen as role models.

The term *opinion leader* suggests that the individual has influence over the public and is more than an informed peer. Opinion leaders must be active in attaining and sharing information about the issue to maintain their "leadership" role.

Opinion leaders existed long before mass media. Religious leaders, politicians, and great thinkers such as Aristotle used their knowledge and charisma to influence people on behalf of their causes. Today, however, opinion leaders are able to reach more of the public through print, broadcast, and, of course, the Internet.

—Nancy Engelhardt Furlow

See also Agenda-setting theory; Coalition building; Framing theory; Social construction of reality theory; Two-step flow theory

Bibliography

Chan, K. K., & Misra, S. (1990). Characteristics of the opinion leader: A new dimension. *Journal of Advertising, 19,* 53–61.

Haggerty, J. F. (2003). *In the court of public opinion: Winning your case with public relations.* Hoboken, NJ: Wiley.

Norrander, B., & Wilcox, C. (Eds.). (2002). *Understanding public opinion* (2nd ed.). Washington, DC: CQ Press.

Ries, A., & Ries, L. (2002). *The fall of advertising and the rise of PR.* New York: Harper Business.

Wilcox, D., Ault, P., Agee, W., & Cameron, G. (2000). *Public relations: Strategies and tactics* (6th ed.). New York: Addison-Wesley.

PUBLIC POLICY PLANNING

Public policy planning entails understanding the limitations and incentives provided by government policy that can affect the ability of organizations to operate so to achieve their mission and vision. Although public policy planning is vital to businesses, it is also relevant to decisions and actions taken by the executive managements of nonprofit organizations and government agencies.

In short, how any business operates is affected by market forces as well as government policies. Such policies are created and promulgated through legislation, regulation, and litigation. Legislatures create broad and specific rules that can affect how an organization generates revenue as well as the costs of doing business. Typically, regulators implement legislation. Litigation can stop, modify, mitigate, or create policies created by legislators and regulators. In the past three decades, the United States has witnessed many sweeping policies that have been created by litigation, perhaps the most important of which is the definition of consumer protection and failure to warn on the part of businesses. Cases in industries such as asbestos and tobacco have been won by arguments that convinced juries that businesses in these segments of the economy failed to warn persons who used or came into contact with these products of their health risks.

Traditionally, public relations has been the organizational discipline that has worked, along with legal counsel, to help organizations know, understand, adapt to, and change the public policies that affect their futures. At the end of the 19th century and during the first decades of the 20th century, for instance, public relations served industry to create a favorable public policy environment to support increasingly large and concentrated business organizations. Public relations helped industries to battle activists, legislators, regulators, presidents of the United States, and one another. The reason for this engagement was the need to have public policy that allowed or did not constrain business activities against the design of corporate leaders, some of whom are rightly called robber barons.

Two broad forces create the environment that affects business practices and policies: market forces (called the private sector) and public policy (the public sector) of the economy. How public policy influences—supports, facilitates, or impedes business practices—constitutes the political economy of a country.

In essence, the public policy arena helps define opportunities and constraints for business practices by suggesting legitimate and illegal means for generating revenue and managing costs of operations. Costs of operations tend to rise when activists successfully achieve higher levels of operating standards, such as consumer protection or air quality through lower emissions. Business plans must conform to the legislative, regulatory, and litigation constraints and opportunities that are created in what is the public interest.

Public policy planning, within this environment, consists of considering the constraints and opportunities created through government policy that can affect the strategic business plan that is developed by executive managements to achieve their business missions and visions. Until the early 1980s, business plans were often developed with little if any attention to the changing policies that could positively or adversely affect the future success of such plans.

The turbulent 1980s created a much different environment for executive managements in the United States. Strategic planning required a new sense of corporate leadership. Originally, if management wanted to create and implement a business plan, attention was largely limited to how it would position the organization vis-à-vis its competitors within an industry or across various industries. The questions were often reduced to "What will the market bear?" and "How can we position our business to succeed because it serves a niche or competes successfully for various reasons?" Much of the strategic planning in this era shifted from bureaucratic, to high uncertainty, and eventually to strategic responses to the prevailing changes in the public policy arena. The business response finally acknowledged the end to the era of deference.

Public relations and corporate legal counsel are often turned to in a reactionary response to public policy changes and increased constraints. The question or challenge posed by executive management is "What changes in policy can we make to allow us to operate as we wish." The assumption behind this question is that public policy that does not allow management its prerogatives is broken and must be fixed through, for instance, lobbying and other forms of government relations strategies and tactics. A more enlightened approach is to proactively adapt to public policy changes and work with advocates of change through collaborative decision making to truly serve the public interest.

The foundation of the public policy arena and the corresponding policy planning comes from the reality that businesses are artificial citizens. They are the creation of the state to serve some public interest. Thus, they operate at the pleasure of society as long as they serve the public interest. Businesses often lose sight of this reality and the subsequent demand that public relations in partnership with general counsel should engage in issues management. For this reason, the public relations discipline has argued that public policy challenges cannot be separated from the larger chore of strategic business planning. Some policies are truly in the public interest and the business must understand that. Other policies might not be, and they need to be opposed or changed. But this debate elevates above the interest of the company to that of the community served by that company.

Savvy public relations counsel through the 20th century in the United States cautioned business executives to never lose sight of their need to understand and operate in the public interest. As decades passed, businesses opted for a mentality that assumed that what was good for them was good for society. They turned the equation around and suffered a robust period of activism marked by the end of the era of deference.

Public policy planning by enlightened organizations begins with an honest and candid assessment of the prevailing standards of corporate responsibility and a proactive effort to "get right" with them. The organization cannot assume that society will bend to its needs. It must be responsive to the needs and interests of society. On this matter, societal values and expectations change. Public policy planning is best when it assumes this change will happen and can be understood and incorporated into the strategic business plan of the organization.

The public policy arena offers many opportunities for the strategic organization truly committed to effective public relations. Trend analysis supported by the expertise of public relations and corporate legal counsel can monitor and assess this trend, looking for advantages as well as threats to current operations and policies.

One trend is that changes that increase the cost of operations in one industry might offer business opportunity in another. Requirement of the chemical manufacturing and refining industry to do more to abate its impact on the environment can mean new or more business for companies that sell services and products to that end.

Another trend is that the cost of business can be shifted from one industry to another. If lower standards of automobile safety lead to increased numbers of fatalities and long-term disability injuries, the insurance industry can work with other interested parties, including consumer advocates, to raise automobile safety standards.

Activists often call for higher standards of operations. Trade associations can respond in several ways. One is to speak with a single voice to support or oppose various changes. The strength of such cases increases to the extent to which the debate is collaborative and truly in the public interest. Changes in policy can lead to higher operating costs, but they can also lead to reduced likelihood of onerous litigation settlements because the activist claims can be used to assess the standards of corporate responsibility.

Also, changes that are not reflective of fact, appropriate value, and sound policy can and should be opposed in the public interest. Thus, perfect rationale exists for the use of government relations, but the strength of the case increases if companies realize their mandate to operate in the public interest.

In similar ways, public policy planning can be used to foster the future of nonprofit and governmental agencies. The extent to which public policy gaps exist leading to community needs not met by business or government creates opportunity and challenge for the fundraising efforts of nonprofits. Some nonprofit organizations directly or indirectly engage in government relations to create and change regulations and legislation. Government agencies benefit by understanding public policy trends as they pitch their budget needs to Congress and other legislative bodies.

Public policy planning has become increasingly important to all sectors of the economy. Market forces alone do not offer challenge and opportunity. These market forces are shaped by public policy. For this reason public relations has played many roles in public policy planning.

—*Robert L. Heath*

See also Age of deference (end of); Executive management; Government relations; Issues management; Lobbying; Position and positioning

Bibliography

Heath, R. L. (1997). *Strategic issues management.* Thousand Oaks, CA: Sage.

Renfro, W. L. (1993). *Issues management in strategic planning.* Westport, CT: Quorum Books.

Sawaya, R. N., & Arrington, C. B. (1988). Linking corporate planning with strategic issues. In R. L. Heath (Ed.), *Strategic issues management: How organizations influence and respond to public interests and policies* (pp. 73–86). San Francisco, CA: Jossey-Bass.

PUBLIC RELATIONS

However old the practice of public relations is, its identity as we know it today became a serious professional practice in the latter part of the 19th century in the United States. The 20th century witnessed its development as a refined set of strategic best practices, an academic discipline to prepare future practitioners, and the subject for refinements through sophisticated scholarly investigation and discussion. Along the way, it never lost its fondness for knowing and following the best practices of effective professional practitioners.

In the opinion of some, public relations can be defined as the art of stealthy manipulation of public opinion, the manipulation of the opinions of consumers and politicians. It is viewed as spinning the truth to the selfish interest of some organization, issue advocate, person, or viewpoint. Journalists and other critics have referred to practitioners as *flacks,* meaning that the practitioners of this art deal with self-interested promotion of idea, set of facts, or points of view.

In contrast, public relations has been seen as a professional practice and academic discipline dedicated to fostering effective two-way communication between some organization or entity, such as an industry, and persons whose opinions can make or break the future success of the sponsor. Some discussants of the nature of public relations have advocated that instead of fostering sham relationships, senior practitioners are the consciences of their employers. They know better than other disciplines the moral standards by which their employers are judged. They advocate that first the organization must be good before it can be effective in its communication efforts. Practitioners recognize that the challenge of ethics is both broad and a matter of the devil is in the detail. Each word can pose ethical challenges as well as the formulation of the public relations policy of the organization.

Public relations is a set of management, supervisory, and technical functions that foster an organization's ability to strategically listen to, appreciate, and respond to those persons whose mutually beneficial relationships with the organization are necessary if it is to achieve its mission and vision.

Public relations practitioners are problem solvers. They are counselors who advise the organizational management on how to fit best into its environment. They are tacticians and technicians who design and craft communication tools such as media releases, employee newsletters, fundraising campaigns, publicity and promotion efforts, investor reports, and issue backgrounders and fact sheets.

No single definition of public relations exists. Throughout the plethora of definitions found runs a central theme. Public relations professionals communicate for and help to favorably position their clients to earn the favor of targeted markets, audiences, and publics. One of the earliest leaders of the practice, Ivy Lee, was characterized by his biographer as a "courtier to the crowd." His ideas, like those of many of his early successors, featured the democratic spirit that called on the practitioner to put accurate and credible information before the public that would—and could—then judge the worthiness of the case being made. In turn, judgment would be passed on the client of the practitioner. In this regard, public relations practitioners worked to bridge the relationship between the organization and the persons in society who could help or harm the organization. Ray Eldon Hiebert (1996) captured the essence of Lee's career: "His work was central to the entire problem of public communication in a complex and industrial environment"

(p. ix). Lee was compared to the likes of major figures of the American colonial period such as Sam Adams and Thomas Jefferson. "Like them, he understood the necessity for using words to get people to understand his point of view. Unlike them, however, he lived in an age when words could be used increasingly to maintain rather than prevent an excess of power" (1996, p. ix).

Public relations uses many forms, tools, and strategies of communication. One of the most typical is the media release or other tactical tools to attract reporters' attention to a service, product, organization, issue, and such. Attention, thus, is a vital goal behind the strategic use of public relations tools. Information and persuasion are part of the stock and trade of practitioners. In recent years, collaborative decision making and negotiation have become increasingly important. For these reasons, the rise of public relations in the past two centuries paralleled the growth and diversification of mass media. Today the practitioner may elect, or be required, to participate in any communication arena ranging from mass media to narrow and tailored messages presented, for instance, in a letter. The Web has become a vital tool and thorn in the heel of practitioners and clients.

Early on, the specter of the public, the audience, the judge and jury of approval, was the central theme of practitioners. None became more famous for his efforts to engineer consent than Edward Bernays. He believed that creating and responding to public opinion was the primary challenge facing practitioners on behalf of their clients. The challenge, as he framed it in 1923, was to respond to the public: "The public to-day demands information and expects also to be accepted as judge and jury in matters that have a wide public import" (1923, p. 34).

In the most mechanical definition of the discipline, it is viewed as the profession for placing information, as opposed to advertising, which uses paid access to the media to reach targeted audiences. In the worst sense, this view limits public relations to be defined as a stealth bomber that can get messages through the defenses of unwilling individuals who are manipulated by skilled spinners.

One of the legendary contributors to the definition of public relations is John W. Hill, the founding principal of Hill & Knowlton. At the time of his retirement in the late 1960s, his firm was the largest in the world. Hill believed that the practice of public relations operated in a climate of enlightened and rational public opinion. Public opinion, he thought, companies, governmental agencies, trade associations, and nonprofits operated in the climate of public opinion where they enjoyed the fruits of goodwill and suffered the consequences of its violation. They took their license to operate and prosper from their ability "to serve the needs or wants of people" (1958, p. viii).

Hill discussed public relations as a practice and as a condition. The practice focused attention on wise counseling and effective communication within the limits of the strength of the case that either side of a controversy could make as well as the ethical reputation of the organization. The objective of public relations as a practice was to create the condition of sound public relationships. Thus, he concluded, "Public relations bears directly upon the area of values associated with good will. Its task is not one of communications only, as some have supposed. Its roots reach to the very heart of corporate policy" (1958, p. ix). To this end, "Every corporation, group, or organization dealing with people has public relations, which may be good, bad, or indifferent" (1958, p. 163). The practice creates organized public relations that can affect the relationships an organization has with its publics. Thus, Hill reasoned, "I say 'organized' public relations advisedly. Every business, and for that matter, every activity with public overtones, has public relations whether or not it recognizes the fact, or whether or not it does anything about it" (1958, p. 259).

Communication could usefully increase understanding and allay misunderstanding. Thus, he advised, "Public relations is an outgrowth of our free society, in which the ideal of an enlightened and rational public opinion is brought ever closer as understanding increases between groups and individuals" (1958, p. vix). Unlike practitioners and other commentators who believe public relations is the skillful art or science of engineering consent, Hill cautioned,

It is not the work of public relations—let it always be emphasized—to outsmart the American public in helping management build profits. It is the job of public relations to help management find ways of identifying its own interests with the public interest—ways so clear that the profit earned by the company may be viewed as contributing to the progress of everybody in the American economy. (1958, p. 21)

The first step in public relations is to create sound policy that deserves the fruits of goodwill. On this point, Hill reasoned,

When corporate policy *is* sound, it serves the community interest and is deserving of the support of public opinion. But this is not to say that it will get this support merely because it deserves it. The people must be informed. Lacking correct information they may withhold their support. This is a job for public relations. (1958, pp. 54–55)

Hill believed that public relations served many functions that related to the organization's relationship with its key stakeholders. As counselors, practitioners must be sensitive to the conditions in which an organization currently operates. On this point, Hill offered tried advice:

It functions in the dissemination of information and facts when noncontroversial matters are involved. But when controversy exists, public relations may become the advocate before the bar of public opinion, seeking to win support through interpretation of facts and the power of persuasion. (1963, p. 6)

These many functions of public relations are like spokes in a wheel. One of the ways of thinking about each spoke is that it is a separate, definable function of public relations. Its uniqueness comes from the specific kind of problem it was developed to address with a specific kind of market, audience, or public. Government relations, for instance, is a function developed to support or oppose legislation and regulation. Investor relations builds relationships with investors. Publicity and promotion attract attention, inform understanding and shape opinions. Non-profits use publicity and promotion in tandem with fund raising. By the time Hill was sharing his experiences and philosophies, these functions had become well grounded in theory and best practices. They would be honed during the rest of the century.

Practitioners before and since the era of Hill have recognized that public relations is more than a communication function or discipline. It is a relationship building and repairing discipline that starts with the ability to understand the elements of the give and take, the exchange, between any organization and its stakeholders. An organization that is clever may be too clever. Hill advised, "Public confidence in the corporation as an institution must be earned and deserved. 'Smart publicity' will never replace sound management policies and acts in building a solid foundation of good will" (1958, p. 163). Thus, public relations practitioners need to serve as the corporate conscience, a concept explicitly stated by Hill nearly a half century ago:

> Good public relations has been called the corporate conscience—an indispensable attribute of modern and progressive business. By keeping its conscience alive and alert, through good conduct and effective communications, corporate enterprise will merit a continued vote of public confidence. (1958, p. 173)

Hill recognized the strategic advantage of thinking in terms of key publics, audiences, or stakeholders instead of broadly focusing attention on the opinions and the organization's relationship with the larger sense of all of the public. Thus, he indicated he had witnessed a move among practitioners from an interest in press relations to relationships with other audiences. The list included customers, employees, government, stockholders, neighbors in the locations where the company operated, educators, and others.

For several reasons, counseling requires perspectives that call on practitioners' understanding of people, the media, and ethics. What did Hill think constituted public relations counsel?

> Public relations counsel are not lawyers. They are not management engineers. They are not sales

specialists. . . . . Then on what do they counsel? Curiously enough the recommendations for which they are asked in one way or another may impinge on any of these fields. (1963, pp. 131–132)

What is required for a practitioner to be prepared to meet this challenge? Thus, he answered, "counseling on public relations calls for a variety of special experiences, abilities, and qualification. In my opinion the most important single element is integrity, which is a matter of character. Next to integrity I would rank judgment" (1963, pp. 131–132).

Counselors are expected to meet many challenges and exhibit many traits.

> The role of the counseling organization may be described as follows:
>
> 1. It provides objective counsel—advice uncolored by any subjective problems that may exist within the business.
>
> 2. It provides a diversity of experience in dealing with a multitude of public relations problems.
>
> 3. It gives client companies access to services, facilities, and the various specialists in phases of public relations, thus enabling the client to supplement its own staff operation.
>
> 4. It gives an outside viewpoint on probable public reactions to company policies and acts.
>
> 5. It underwrites with its own reputation the quality and continuity of the undertaking. (1963, pp. 135–136)

The counseling part of public relations counts a great deal for the outcome because

> public relations has no mystical power to work miracles. What is achieved in any worthwhile sense must be based on integrity, and on sound attitudes, policies and actions at the very top level of management. This makes public relations a management responsibility, and it is so considered by most advanced companies today. The old slogan—if it ever existed—'The public be damned' has given way to the eternal question in the ear of managements, 'What will people say?' This is bound to have a good effect upon the conduct of corporate affairs. (1963, pp. 259–260)

This democratic theme runs throughout public relations theory by persons such as Ivy Lee and John Hill. It suggests that the interests of its stakeholders must be known and considered by any organization wanting their goodwill. Without such goodwill, the organization might not fail, but it was bound not to flourish.

All of what the organization did became vital to the message it conveyed. Thus, Hill drew on the influence he received from Ivy Lee to conclude, "Public relationships, he wrote, involved not simply 'saying' but '*doing*'—not just talk, but action" (1963, p. 16). Organizations had to strive to demonstrate their commitment to truth and the desire for goodwill. They could not use words alone to achieve those ends.

If the organization did this, it could receive and enjoy the license to operate.

> It has been aptly said that business does not function by Divine Right, but only with the sanction of the people whose attitudes find expression through government. For this reason, enlightened managements of American industry have come to recognize the wisdom of conducting their affairs in ways that merit public approval. They are aware also of the value of communication as the next step in public relations, the aim of which is to build and hold goodwill and to help the business prosper. They know they should make their voice heard, listened to, and believed throughout the land. (1963, p. 263)

Luminaries such as those cited above recognize that public relations entails process and leads to the creation of meaning. In the 1940s, even before the writing of Hill, other pioneers sought to capture the essence of the discipline as they launched the era of modern texts in public relations, the teaching of the principles of public relations to undergraduates.

Soon to be lost under the influence of mass communication theory and systems theory, early authors featured the notion of relationship building. Authors who proudly announced the need to know, build, and repair relationships as the "new" essence of public relations may well have been turning the clock back to the 1940s. In that decade, Rex F. Harlow and Marvin M. Black featured that concept

in the revised edition of *Practical Public Relations,* published in 1952 under the auspices of the Public Relations Society of America. They believed that society required cooperation to function effectively. To public relations fell the responsibility of fostering cooperation. They defined public relations as "the art and science of getting along well with other people" (1952, p. 4). What they saw as the challenge of modern society was helping organizations deal with increasingly complex relationships. An organization must know and appreciate the needs and interests of its publics. It must adapt to those needs and interpret itself so the people understand how it is working to that end. To this end, professionals and the students who aspire to the calling need to understand the ethics and processes of relationship building.

At the same time Harlow and Black were carving up the definition of public relations, Scott Cutlip and Allen Center published *Effective Public Relations,* the college text that became the standard of academics and professionals. They noted the beehive of definitions and noted coatings other authors had put on that term. They were well aware of the counseling, technical, and relationship-building expectations voiced by other authors.

They knew public relations was often associated with hype, whitewash, ballyhoo, propaganda, and other ways to label shoddy manipulation. One of the contributions Cutlip and Center provided was a commitment to two-way communication. They defined public relations as

> the communication and interpretation of information and ideas from an institution TO its publics and the communication of information, ideas, and opinions FROM those publics to the institution, in a sincere effort to establish mutuality and thus achieve the harmonious adjustment of an institution to its community. (2000, p. 6)

Eventually, this same text offered the following definition: "Public relations is the management function that establishes and maintains mutually beneficial relationships between an organization and the publics on whom its success or failure depends" (2000, p. 6).

The Public Relations Society of America's Official Statement on Public Relations stated: "Public relations helps our complex, pluralistic society to reach decisions and function more effectively by contributing to mutual understanding among groups and institutions. It serves to bring private and public policies into harmony. To achieve their goals, these institutions must develop effective relationships with many different audiences or publics such as employees, members, customers, local communities, shareholders, and other institutions, and with society at large."

James E. Grunig and Todd Hunt (1984) defined public relations as the management of communication between an organization and its publics. This view was later expanded by arguing that organizations that are excellent practice public relations different than their counterparts do. Excellent organizations tend to be more willing to foster, maintain, and repair relationships. They work in the mutual interest of themselves and those persons whose interest and goodwill they need to succeed.

No single definition of public relations is totally satisfying. People who like public relations and believe it adds value to society define it in positive terms. Its detractors see it as hollow, shallow, spin, and manipulation. Leading practitioners and academics know the division of opinion exists. They recognize that winning people to the positive side is not a matter of proposing a definition but of building the practice on sound principles. Any definition of public relations proposed by its proponents therefore constitutes not merely a description of what they think the practice is. It also constitutes a challenge and mandate for how the profession should develop.

Central then to these positive definitions is the challenge to realize as a positive aspect of society that differences of opinions and choices exist. People can disagree. They can make choices. They can criticize companies, nonprofit organizations, and governmental agencies. They may not understand or know what they need to know to approve of these organizations. They may not be informed. They may be misinformed. So, one continuing challenge is that organizations must serve as the first and best source of information about themselves.

But public relations is not only about information. It deals with positioning the organization to deserve genuine goodwill because its interests are interlocked in a mutually beneficial way with its critics. That too is a daunting challenge because critics often do not want a mutually beneficial relationship that truly acknowledges the worth of the target of their dislike.

Public relations is about choice and evaluation. It deals with the fostering and adapting to preferences. It looks to understand and aspire to meet or exceed the value expectations of persons whose interest and support is needed.

The practice of public relations requires a hierarchy of skills, managerial, supervisory, and technical. It requires communication skills. But it is more than communication. Leading academics and practitioners reason that it seeks to build and draw upon integrity. To meet professional challenges and allay criticism, practitioners must foster trust, which is constantly tested by what they and their employers say and do. Thus, good public relations creates good public relations. Likewise, bad public relations fosters bad public relations. For these reasons, any operating and useful definition of public relations is normative. For this reason, any definition of public relations must acknowledge that its role and presence in society is judged by whether and how it adds value to the members of a society, however global.

—Robert L. Heath and
members of the Advisory Board

Bibliography

Bernays, E. L. (1923). *Crystallizing public opinion.* New York: Boni & Liveright.

Cutlip, S. M., & Center, A. H. (1952). *Effective public relations: Pathways to public favor.* Englewood Cliffs, NJ: Prentice Hall.

Cutlip, S. M., Center, A. H., & Broom, G. M. (2000). *Effective public relations* (8th ed.). Upper Saddle River, NJ: Prentice Hall.

Grunig, J. E., & Hunt, T. (1984). *Managing public relations.* New York: Holt, Rinehart and Winston.

Harlow, R. F., & Black, M. M. (1952). *Practical public relations.* New York: Harper & Brothers.

Hiebert, R. E. (1996). *Courtier to the crowd: The story of Ivy Lee and the development of public relations.* Ames, IA: Iowa State University Press.

Hill, J. W. (1958). *Corporate public relations: Arm of modern management.* New York: Harper & Brothers.

Hill, J. W. (1963). *The making of a public relations man.* New York: David McKay.

PUBLIC RELATIONS AGENCY

A public relations agency, or firm, is a company hired by another organization to provide certain services. Some 3,000 or more public relations counseling firms operate in the United States.

The hiring organization is referred to as the client. Under the best of circumstances, the firm helps improve the client's reputation and its relationships with its publics. The services can range from strategic and managerial—such as planning and implementing annual major campaigns and providing senior-level counseling—to the more tactical, such as generating news releases or printed promotional materials.

Increasingly, companies are turning to outside counsel even when they have internal public relations departments. Most of America's most-admired companies have a relationship with a public relations firm. Clients hire firms for different reasons. There might be a need for expertise that the client doesn't have, or there might simply be a staff shortage that an agency can help fill.

Some companies prefer to use the term *firm* to connote their emphasis on counseling and strategic planning and to differentiate from advertising agencies. Public relations is a management team concept that the term *agent* or *agency* doesn't imply. Many, though, use the terms interchangeably.

The Council of Public Relations Firms, a trade association representing large U.S. public relations firms, estimates that about 20,000 public relations practitioners work for public relations firms in the United States, and more than 40,000 worldwide. The larger companies, such as Hill & Knowlton, employ as many as 2,000 people worldwide. However, public relations is also a field in which independent practitioners, or freelancers, can thrive.

Several publications and organizations—including *O'Dwyers Directory of Public Relations Firms, PR Week,* and the Council of Public Relations Firms—track rankings of the top companies by revenue. Rankings can shift annually due to mergers and acquisitions and business factors, as well as ranking criteria and firms' willingness to disclose financial information. Some of the largest U.S. firms (based on global revenues) are BSMG Worldwide; Burson-Marsteller; Edelman Public Relations Worldwide; Fleishman-Hillard International Communications; GCI Group/APCO Worldwide; Golin/Harris International; Hill & Knowlton; Incepta (Citigate); Ketchum; Manning, Selvage & Lee; Ogilvy Public Relations Worldwide; Porter Novelli; Ruder Finn; and Weber Shandwick Worldwide. Fifty percent or more of public relations revenues are generated by the top 10 firms.

STRUCTURE/OPERATIONS

Account team

Typically, the agency will assign a specific team to work on the client's business or *account*. Titles vary within an agency, but there is usually an account supervisor or manager responsible for handling the account. Other account team members, such as the account executive, coordinator, and others, report to the supervisor.

Compensation

The client pays the firm for its work either by providing a retainer (a set monthly fee), an hourly rate, or a combination of these. Hourly rates vary for each person who works on the job, whether senior, mid, or junior level, intern, or administrative staff.

TRENDS

Growth

Government figures project rapid growth for public relations firms through 2010 as companies increasingly hire external consultants rather than hire full-time staff.

Jobs less centralized

The larger firms and most jobs tend to be concentrated in large cities, such as New York, Washington, DC, Chicago, Los Angeles, and San Francisco, where major media, corporations, and policymakers are headquartered. Many firms have local offices in other metropolitan areas. Clients often prefer that firms have offices in their locales, so many major firms will even open up an office to serve a large client.

Ownership

In recent years large advertising agencies and communications holding companies have acquired many of the top public relations firms. Examples are Omnicom Group Inc., which owns Fleishman-Hillard, Ketchum and Porter-Novelli; and London-based WPP Group PLC, which owns Hill & Knowlton Inc., Burson-Marsteller and Ogilvy Public Relations Worldwide, among others. In 2003, only one of the top 10 firms, Edelman, was still independent.

International focus

Public relations is becoming increasingly global. Numerous U.S. public relations firms have opened offices around the world or have merged with or acquired firms in other countries. Large European companies such as WPP Group PLC and Publicis have acquired medium and large U.S. firms to help increase their global presence.

Consolidation

Once it was common for major corporations to employ numerous public relations firms for different parts of their business, but now, many have cut down to a few or just one. For example, International Business Machines Corp. (IBM) and SAP AG, Europe's largest software producer, reduced their number of public relations firms from as many as 50 to 3 (IBM) and from 12 to 1 (SAP). On the other hand, hundreds of firms reported gaining new clients who had never before used public relations.

HISTORY

The practice of hiring a public relations agency dates back to the early 1900s, when the first publicity firms were established. These developed partially because companies began to realize they needed to respond to the "muckraking" activities that called for political and business reforms. The first known firm was The Publicity Bureau, founded in Boston in mid-1900. These firms were narrow in focus, chiefly providing media relations services such as disseminating press releases in an effort to get a client's name in the newspaper.

Ivy Ledbetter Lee established a cornerstone of modern-day public relations principles when he founded his firm, Parker & Lee, in 1906 and issued his famous Declaration of Principles. Lee declared that his company would not work in secret like other firms (such as The Publicity Bureau, which secretly operated news bureaus for the railroads). Instead, his firm would fully disclose its work on behalf of the client. He also stated that the firm would disclose information of value and interest to the public. These principles are now, in fact, important tenets of the Code of Professional Standards for the Practice of Public Relations of the Public Relations Society of America, the world's largest professional society for public relations practitioners.

Other important agency figures of the early 1900s included William Wolff Smith, George F. Parker (Lee's partner), Hamilton Wright, Pendleton Dudley, and Thomas R. Shipp.

World War I and the Committee on Public Information, or "Creel Committee" (1917–1918), provided training ground for numerous practitioners, including Carl S. Byoir and Edward L. Bernays. Other important counselors of the post-WWI period were Doris A. Fleischman (Bernays's wife); Harry A. Bruno; John W. Hill (of today's top-10 firm Hill & Knowlton); Edward D. Howard II of Cleveland; and Glenn C. Hayes of Chicago. Joseph Varney Baker opened the first minority-owned firm in Philadelphia in 1934, and the political campaign consultancy got its start in 1933 when Clem Whitaker and Leone Baxter opened their firm in San Francisco.

Post-World War II growth saw the establishment of firms such as Burson-Marsteller and Edelman. Earl Newsom became one of the practice's first independent counselors, advising companies such as the Ford Motor Company and paving the way for a new era in public relations firms.

—Catherine L. Hinrichsen

See also Baker, Joseph Varney; Baxter, Leone and Whitaker, Clem; Bernays, Edward; Byoir, Carl; Client; Dudley, Pendleton; Fleischman, Doris Elsa; Hill, John Wiley; Lee, Ivy; Muckrakers (and the Age of Progressivism); Parker, George; Public Relations Society of America; Publicity

Bibliography

Croft, A. C. (1996). *Managing a public relations firm for growth and profit.* Binghamton, NY: Haworth Press.

Cutlip, S. M. (1994). *The unseen power: Public relations, a history.* Hillsdale, NJ: Lawrence Erlbaum.

Hinrichsen, C. L. (2000). Best practices in the public relations agency business. In R. L. Heath (Ed.), *Handbook of public relations.* Thousand Oaks, CA: Sage.

O'Dwyer, J. (Ed.). (2003). *O'Dwyer's directory of public relations firms.* New York: J. R. O'Dwyer.

PUBLIC RELATIONS DEPARTMENT

A public relations department is the unit within an organization responsible for its public relations function, whether externally, internally, or both.

These departments were first established in the United States in the early 1900s. Today, more than 5,000 United States companies and 2,000 trade associations have public relations departments. Corporations, nonprofit organizations, religious groups, government agencies, and universities all engage in public relations activities. Even some public relations firms have their own public relations departments.

Some larger companies, such as AT&T, have employed as many as 800 people in their public relations departments, while others are a one-person operation. The department size is related to the size of the organization and perhaps the perceived importance of public relations within the organization. The trend, though, is toward smaller departments than in the past. Some might also oversee the activities of a public relations agency. Regardless of the size, the department is most effective when it has close access to senior management.

STRUCTURE

Organizational structures vary and largely depend upon how and why the department was first established. While some organizations have a stand-alone public relations department with its own senior executive, public relations is often a subgroup of marketing, sales, human resources, or a related department.

Most public relations counselors agree that ideally the public relations department director should either report directly to the CEO or have a close working relationship with that person. They believe the public relations staff should have a voice in shaping the company's mission and strategic planning, and serve as a counselor to senior management.

Public relations is the most common name and is used by about 30 percent of departments. Others include Corporate Communications, Public Affairs, and Community Relations. The U.S. government, which employs thousands of public relations people, tends instead to use titles such as public affairs or communications, because of a law prohibiting the hiring of "public relations" people.

Public relations might need to compete with different departments, such as advertising, for a share of the budget. However, a study of America's most respected companies found that the more a public relations function is designed, practiced, and evaluated against the organization's strategic business goals, the greater its support from top management for budget size and the greater its perceived contribution to the organization's success.

ADDRESSING PUBLICS

The public relations staff can demonstrate its value to senior management by participating in the organization's decision-making process and measuring its impact on its publics, rather than focusing too narrowly on tactics and communication output. The ability to anticipate and consider the perspectives of different publics is another way the public relations department brings value to the organization.

Examples of publics—also called stakeholders—can include employees, board of directors, shareholders, local residents, suppliers, government officials and regulators, financial analysts, customers/consumers, donors, volunteers, students, faculty, media, and others. The public relations department should conduct research among these publics to measure attitudes about the company and its programs and policies, and recommend to executives how best to address the needs of these varying publics. The ability of the department to establish long-term relationships with them is another measure of public relations' value to the organization.

UNDERSTANDING THE INDUSTRY

A successful public relations department, in addition to understanding communications and management, also understands the company's business and the industry in which it operates. Sometimes a lack of broad business experience and technical knowledge can hinder the staff's ability to effectively counsel management. The public relations department is more effective when it can use its in-depth knowledge of the organization and the industry to counsel leaders. It also gives inside staff an advantage over outside counsel.

USE OF OUTSIDE COUNSEL

In addition to the public relations department, an organization might also employ outside counsel, such as a professional public relations firm or freelancers, supervised by the inside staff. The department can often benefit from an outsider's perspective, and the firm usually offers expertise lacking among the in-house staff. Some leaders feel that the days of the traditional large in-house public relations department are coming to an end as companies increasingly downsize staff and turn to outside counsel. The ability to effectively manage outside counsel is another valuable service the public relations department can offer.

HISTORY

The history of public relations departments has contributed much to their relevancy today. In the early 1900s, publicity and public relations went through a boom period, and organizations began forming their own in-house functions. This is largely due to growing public pressure for corporations to begin acting in the public interest and be accountable to the public. Some of the earliest public relations departments were for nonprofit organizations, such as the YMCA, whose 1905 fundraising campaign was a forerunner of today's United Way drive.

Public relations pioneer Ivy Ledbetter Lee, recognized for his role as an early public relations counselor, was also instrumental in shaping public relations departments. He helped spur the growth of publicity departments and trained many corporate public relations managers.

In the 1930s, many businesses—including Bendix, Borden, Eastman Kodak, Eli Lilly, Ford, General Motors, Standard Oil, Pan American, and U.S. Steel—established public relations departments to help them regain public confidence that had been worn down by the Great Depression.

Paul Garrett was an early leader in corporate communications. His program for General Motors, which hired him to set up a corporate communications department in 1931, was a model for many corporations.

Another influential leader was Arthur W. Page, who became AT&T's first public relations vice president in 1927. Page was instrumental in defining the role of the public relations department within the company. When he was hired, he made it clear that he would not be a publicity man; rather, he would help shape policy. He also pointed out that the company's reputation would be determined by its performance: "All business in a democratic country begins with public permission and exists by public approval." Page was the first person with a public relations title to serve as an officer and member of the board of directors of a major corporation.

In honor of Page, senior public relations executives created the prestigious Arthur W. Page Society in 1983, to strengthen the management policy role of the chief corporate public relations officer.

Today, companies still turn to their public relations departments in times of economic downturn and prosperity alike, realizing that public trust and confidence are indispensable to the company's success.

—*Catherine L. Hinrichsen*

See also Lee, Ivy; Page, Arthur W.; Public relations agency

PUBLIC RELATIONS EDUCATION, HISTORY OF

As publicity and public relations boomed in the United States during the 1920s, colleges and universities began to offer courses that were the forerunners of modern public relations education. These courses came on the heels of the emergence of journalism as a separate field of study at universities, especially land-grant institutions in the Midwest.

The first public relations course was offered in 1920, only two years following World War I, at the University of Illinois by Josef F. Wright, the university's newly appointed publicity director. As would be the case later at other schools, there was little demand for Wright's "Publicity Methods" course, but Wright was motivated by a desire to bring prestige to his calling.

Indeed, many of the first courses in publicity were taught by college publicity directors such as Frank R. Elliott, who introduced a course in "Publicity" at Indiana University two years later. Eventually, however, regular faculty started teaching publicity. One notable example was Lawrence Murphy, who took over Wright's course at Illinois in 1927 and later became director of the journalism school at Minnesota.

The first course titled "Public Relations" was offered by Edward L. Bernays at New York University (NYU) in 1923. Bernays had just authored his seminal work, *Crystallizing Public Opinion.* He taught the one-semester courses two times in the Department of Journalism, then a part of NYU's School of Commerce, Accounting and Finance. James Melvin Lee, the department head and noted journalism historian, was skeptical but urged Bernays to proceed. Lee urged Bernays to attract working journalists by promoting the class in professional publications such as *Editor & Publisher* and *Printer's Ink.*

In the same year, NYU's School of Social Work also offered a course under the direction of Evart and Mary Swain, who had pioneered publicity and philanthropic fundraising at the Russell Sage Foundation. The course quickly became an established part of the social work curriculum and was augmented by other courses in writing and communication.

Other schools followed suit, including the University of Oregon, where a course in publicity was taught by public relations officer George Godfrey in 1927, and the University of Minnesota, where Thomas E. Steward taught a class in "Press Relations" in 1929. After two years, a course at the University of Washington taught by Byron Christian was suspended following a torrent of criticism from the state's newspaper editors and publisher organizations. By the late 1930s, courses were added at such diverse schools as American University, the University of Texas, and Wayne State University. Meanwhile, courses in public opinion had begun to be offered at schools such as Princeton.

Rex L. Harlow, a pioneer educator known as the father of public relations research, was on the faculty of Stanford University's School of Education when he began teaching a public relations course in 1939. This was the same year that Harlow organized the American Council on Public Relations (which later merged to create the Public Relations Society of America). Harlow was a recognized leader in practitioner education and crisscrossed the country giving workshops and seminars. He is credited with providing as many as 10,000 practitioners with their first formal introduction to the field.

At the same time, Kalman B. Druck, a young executive at the Carl Byoir firm who later formed his own major agency, taught a course at the City College of New York. Druck's class emphasized modern public relations principles—the importance of two-way communication, defining publics, and avenues for communication to and from key constituencies. The course later became a model for other classes after being described at length in an industry directory in 1945–1946. Ironically, the course could list only eight book titles as references.

During World War II, the first major in public relations was established at Bethany College, a small church school in West Virginia that continues to offer public relations today. Following the war, public relations education enjoyed a major growth spurt as colleges and universities hired staff to teach public relations methods. The most prominent program created during this period was at Boston University's School of Public Relations and Communications, founded in 1947. Most notable among the second-generation educators hired after World War II was Scott M. Cutlip, who was hired by the University of Wisconsin-Madison.

In 1946, one survey by Prof. Alfred McClung Lee found that at least 30 schools offered 47 different courses under public relations titles. By 1956, that number increased to at least 136, including 14 programs labeled as offering a major in public relations. The period also was marked by the first substantial output of books and articles on the booming craft, and recognition of the field as a unified profession under the aegis of the Publicity Society of America.

Throughout the 1960s and 1970s, educational offerings by colleges and universities continued to expand. The faint beginnings of legitimate research started to emerge from among more than a handful of teachers in the field. The first organization of teachers, the Council on Public Relations, was organized in 1956 as a unit of the Association for Education in Journalism. PRSA set up an Educational Advisory Council in 1959.

By the mid-1970s public relations education flourished as academic departments committed themselves to the professional training of practitioners. These included speech and communications departments in addition to journalism programs. In 1968 Prof. Walt Seifert of Ohio State University proposed creation of the Public Relations Student Society of America to encourage

students in public relations careers. Whereas traditionally public relations workers had been former newspaper or magazine writers or editors, public relations agencies and departments began to recruit young professionals directly from colleges.

Standards for instruction at both the undergraduate and the graduate levels became concerns of professional and educators alike, leading to the creation of several Commissions on Public Relations Education. The first Commission to promulgate guidelines for education was organized in 1975 by Scott M. Cutlip and J. Carroll Bateman, president of the Insurance Information Institute. Subsequent commissions updated their work in 1984 (under the direction of practitioner Betsy Ann Plank and Professor William Ehling) and in 1999 (led by consultant John Paluszek and educator Dean Kruckeberg). *A Design for Graduate Education in Public Relations* was completed in 1987.

Scholarly research in the field languished in the early years, in part because of the limited publications that accepted serious research on public relations topics. In 1975, *Public Relations Review* was launched under the editorship of Prof. Ray Eldon Hiebert of the University of Maryland, who continued to edit the publication during its first 30 years. Initial financial support was provided by the Foundation for Public Relations Research and Education (later organized as the PRSA Foundation).

In 1984–1985, Professors James E. and Larissa A. Grunig, also of the University of Maryland, launched a second journal that ran a brief stint. Their efforts were resurrected four years later by publication of a *Public Relations Research Annual* for three years, which was converted to the quarterly *Journal of Public Relations Research* in 1992. Codification of the field's literature was further advanced with PRSA's Body of Knowledge project in 1988 under the leadership of Professor James K. Van Leuven.

Several bibliographic studies chronicle the increased research productivity of educators in the field (Pasadeos & Renfro, 1992; Pasadeos, Renfro, & Hanily, 1999). Separately, a Delphi study sought to identify the most productive scholars in the field. Eight academics garnered 20 or more votes from

61 expert judges. The top vote-getters (in alphabetical order) were: Glen M. Broom, Scott M. Cutlip, David M. Dozier, James E. Grunig, Larissa A. Grunig, Robert L. Heath, Dean Kruckeberg, and Elizabeth L. Toth. Of these, James E. Grunig, Scott M. Cutlip, Robert L. Heath, and Glen M. Broom were identified as the most influential in a second round of analyses.

—Kirk Hallahan

See also Bateman, J. Carroll; Bernays, Edward.; Cutlip, Scott M.; Public Relations Society of America

Bibliography

Collins, E. L., & Zoch, L. M. (2002, August). *PR Educators: "The second generation": Measuring and achieving consensus.* Paper presented to Public Relations Division, Association for Education in Journalism and Mass Communication, Miami, Florida.

Cutlip, S. M. (1961, Summer). History of public relations education in the United States. *Journalism Quarterly, 38,* 363–370.

Pasadeos, Y., & Renfro, R. B. (1992). A bibliometric analysis of public relations research. *Journal of Public Relations Research, 4,* 167–187.

Pasadeos, Y., Renfro, B., & Hanily, M. A. (1999). Influential authors and works of the public relations scholarly literature: A network of recent research. *Journal of Public Relations Research, 11,* 29–52.

Public Relations Society of America. (1987). *A design for graduate education in public relations.* New York: Author.

Report of the 1999 Commission on Public Relations Education (2000). New York: PRSA. Retrieved February 2004 from http://lamar.colostate.edu/~aejmcpr/commission report99.htm

PUBLIC RELATIONS FIELD DYNAMICS (PRFD)

Public Relations Field Dynamics (PRFD) is a model that allows for the concurrent measurement and monitoring of multiple parties in a perceptual environment. PRFD is adapted from the study of small group communication and derived from Bales and Cohen's System for the Multiple Level Observation of Groups. At the center of PRFD is the notion of a fluid field encompassing all relevant actors. These actors (e.g., an organization and its publics) can be measured at one point in time or across the development of a controversial issue. A field theory like PRFD takes into account that every behavioral act takes place within the overall context of the interactive field.

Jeffrey Springston adapted the group system to macro-level applications vital to public relations. The dimensions in the PRFD system reflect (a) a friendly versus unfriendly relationship, (b) self-orientation versus community orientation, and a (c) low influence versus high influence capability. These three dimensions are essential to the study of public relations. Perceptions of friendly versus unfriendly behavior are relevant at all levels of interaction. This dimension taps fundamental notions of friend or foe.

The community versus self-orientation dimension reflects perceptions of how motivated an organization is to achieve either an integrative or distributive outcome in a given situation. This ties directly into perceptions of trust. Companies that are perceived to be more interested in the bottom line at the expense of the community have serious public image problems. One such example in recent times is the managed care industry, which has been accused by some as being more interested in costs than care. Members of the media are often particularly skeptical of an organization's community orientation. In general, the more an organization can demonstrate to the media and other publics that it has a genuine community orientation, the more successful the organization is in negotiating its position.

Finally, the influence dimension measures how much power or influence an actor is perceived to have in a given situation. Knowledge of this can help an organization determine which groups will be most attentive and involved in a public relations situation. For example, if a group perceives an organization to have a large influence on them, they will likely be more attentive to the organization than groups that perceive little organizational influence. Conversely, knowledge of how influential a public sees itself to be in relation to the organization provides insight into how likely that public is to exhibit active behavior, helping practitioners determine communication strategy.

PRFD allows organizations to identify allies, antagonists, and potential mediators. Combined, the three dimensions provide a powerful framework to map the entire field or public relations environment.

The system is graphically displayed placing the friendly-unfriendly dimension on the horizontal axis and the community versus self on the vertical axis. The influence dimension is represented by circle size—the more perceived influence, the larger the circle. Figure 1 displays three hypothetical actors in a relational field.

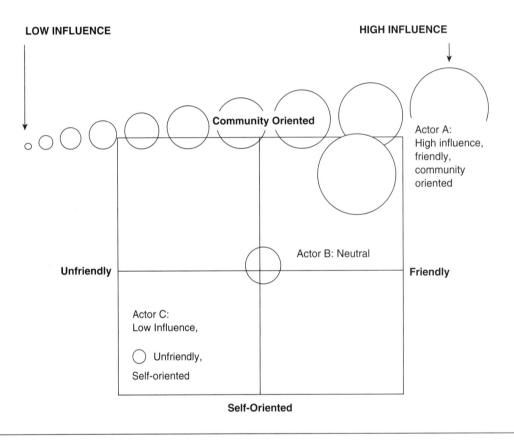

Figure 1   Field diagrams of the perceived relational landscape.

SOURCE: Springston, J. K., Keyton, J., Leichty, G. B., & Metzger, J. (1992). Field dynamics and public relations theory: Toward the management of multiple publics. *Journal of Public Relations Research, 4*(2), 81–101. Reprinted with permission.

Situating the three behavioral dimensions with field theory provides several advantages. First, the three dimensions are viewed as mutually exclusive. Thus, for any one interaction, behavior may be described as high influence, or as low influence, but not as both. Second, the dimensions are orthogonal. Placement on one dimension does not predict placement on other dimensions. Third, any specific placement on a dimension is not seen as inherently good or bad. Rather, the evaluation of behavior depends upon other interaction in the public relations field.

Fourth, Public Relations Field Dynamics allows behavior and perceptions to be tracked over time within a comparative framework. This is particularly useful to the study of issue negotiation, as it allows organizations to test alternative public relations strategies as issues develop and change over time. Fifth, PRFD is a system for viewing the impact of a public's or organization's internal dynamics on the larger interdependent field.

Another key strength of this system is its ability to map the relative degree of polarization and unification among the salient parties within a given environmental field. Polarization is the degree to which constituents are dissimilar in their opinions and perceptions; unification is the degree to which constituents are similar. Polarization and unification can occur on a single dimension, on two dimensions, or on all three. The more dimensions apparent in the polarization, the more difficulty publics will have in communicating with each other in ways that make "sense" to the other publics. For example, an organization that perceives itself as having high influence would likely use dominating rhetoric in an attempt to defeat a less influential organization. Such an attempt would likely be seen as confirmation that the dominant organization is not willing to listen to the voices of others. The more dimensions on which parties are polarized creates additional opportunity for public relations rhetoric to be outside the scope that can be understood or tolerated by another public.

One key component of the system is its ability to identify potential mediators in a given situation. As in any type of negotiation, organizations attempting to negotiate public relations issues with publics or other organizations are often confronted with environments in which some key publics are too polarized from the organization to enter into meaningful dialogue. In such cases, the most useful strategy may be to work with a mediator to establish productive contact. Almost any actor in a relational field can be a mediator, but those actors who are most likely to be acceptable to disparate parties are ones who are more friendly than unfriendly, who are more community-oriented than self-oriented, and who have greater influence in the relational landscape. Because a mediator is likely to be in a more neutral position than extreme ones held by other actors, the mediator can translate or interpret from one position to another in a way all involved parties can trust.

—*Jeffrey K. Springston*

Bibliography

Bales, R. F., & Cohen, S. P. (1979). *SYMLOG: System for the multiple level observation of groups.* New York: Free Press.

Springston, J. K. (1997). Application of public relations theory to breast cancer screening: A worksite study. In J. Biberman & A. Alkhafaji (Eds.), *Business research yearbook: Global business perspectives* (pp. 762–766). Slippery Rock, AR: IABD.

Springston, J. K. (1997). Assessing the group field. In J. Biberman & A. Alkhafaji (Eds.), *Business research yearbook: Global business perspectives* (pp. 767–771). Slippery Rock, AR: IABD.

Springston, J. K., & Keyton, J. (1996). Public relations field dynamics. In R. L. Heath (Ed.), *Handbook of public relations* (pp. 115–126). Thousand Oaks, CA: Sage.

Springston, J. K., Keyton, J., Leichty, G. B., & Metzger, J. (1992). Field dynamics and public relations theory: Toward the management of multiple publics. *Journal of Public Relations Research, 4*(2), 81–101.

PUBLIC RELATIONS RESEARCH

The topic of public relations research is vast. Consider that this volume has more than 20 entries that are directly related to research. This entry provides an overview to public relations research and indicates how it is utilized in the public relations process. The first half discusses research in general including the two basic approaches to research and some of the methods used in research. The second half explains the role of research in the practice of public relations and building the public relations body of knowledge.

Research involves the collection of data or information. Data are simply observations about the world around us. Research can be divided into two general approaches: qualitative and quantitative. Qualitative methods are descriptive and interpretive. Researchers collect data that provides descriptions of behaviors or events in a naturalistic setting—the data are collected in the "real world" rather than a laboratory. Researchers then interpret what the data mean. Different researchers can derive different interpretations from the same data. That is why qualitative methods are considered subjective; the data are open to multiple interpretations and all can be correct. Qualitative researchers are not trying to generalize their results beyond the sample they have studied. Their results only apply to the sample they studied.

Quantitative research is objective and reduces data to numbers. These numbers are then analyzed by using accepted statistical principles and statistical tests. The agreement on the statistical measures and principles makes the results objective. Multiple researchers looking at the same data analysis should reach the same basic conclusions. For example, a basic statistical test is the correlation. A correlation looks for relationships between two variables. It indicates if two things vary in a similar fashion. For instance, the value of one variable increases each time the value of a second variable increases. Each statistical test has an accepted level of significance, a point at which the finding is considered important. The level of significance in public relations research tends to be .05. That means the results have only a 5 in 100 chance of being an accident. (See the Statistical Analysis entry for a more detailed discussion). This means that if 10 researchers ran the same set of data and the correlation had a significance of only .10, all 10 would say there is no relationship. The reliance on numbers and statistics provides the agreement that makes quantitative research objective. Moreover, quantitative researchers are trying to generalize. They want to claim that the results should hold true for the general population and not just their sample. (*See* Experiment/experimental methods and Sampling for more information on generalizability.)

Researchers have a variety of methods for collecting data. Qualitative research might use surveys or experiments. Quantitative researchers might use case study or focus groups. Each of these methods has specific entries in this volume. The way you collect data reflects your general orientation to research and whether it is qualitative or quantitative.

The importance of research to public relations can be traced through its basic use in public relations—the importance practitioners place on research, and research's growing importance in training public relations practitioners. We can see how research fits into the practice of public relations by quickly reviewing four steps in the public relations process. Several similar four-step plans have been presented to describe the public relations process. Scott Cutlip, Allen Center, and Glen Broom's model is a commonly used one. Step one is situation analysis; the practitioner needs to understand what is happening in the situation. The

practitioner must understand what is happening before planning a response. Step two is strategy; the practitioner decides what should be said and done. This involves creating objectives, identifying target audiences, and creating messages. Step three is implementation; the practitioner decides how and when to deliver the messages. This concerns the selection of communication channels or media and the timing of the message. Step four is assessment; practitioners determine whether or not the objectives were achieved. The focus is on finding evidence of success or failure.

The situational analysis is formative research. Formative research (*see* Formative research for more details) provides the information needed to identify the problem or opportunity, identify target audiences, and develop objectives. The public relations process begins with research. Without this information or data, it is impossible to develop the strategy step. Implementation involves the use of process research. Process research tracks what the practitioner has done. Moreover, practitioners would research the various media options available before selecting the media to be used in a public relations action. Assessment is evaluative research. Evaluative research provides evidence of the practitioner's ability to meet the objectives. Research is used throughout the entire public relations process and is essential to the process.

Research is essential to building the body of knowledge for public relations. The body of knowledge is what we know about the practice. It includes theories and concepts that can be used to explain how public relations works. A growing body of knowledge should improve the practice of public relations by providing new insights into the profession and providing new ways of executing various aspects of public relations. Every profession needs a developed body of knowledge. Medicine, for example, draws upon a large body of medical research to fuel its development and growth. Research is essential to creating knowledge, in general, and for developing theory. Research helps us to understand various aspects of the public relations process—it builds knowledge about public relations. Theory must be tested to determine if it is valid. Theory can only be tested through research. Public relations research is applied. It tries to solve problems encountered by practitioners. In turn, this applied research generates new knowledge about public relations and theories of public relations. As research solves practitioner problems, the practice of public relations should become more effective. An illustration is the Jones and Chase model of issues management. The model improved the practice of issues management by making it more systematized and effective. New knowledge and theories about public relations improve the practice of public relations.

For years, public relations researchers were the ones exclaiming the value of public relations research. Practitioners nodded in agreement, but little was done to make research an essential part of the public relations practice. That trend has changed as practitioners now value and try to utilize research. The 1999 Commission on Public Relations Education and the Public Relations Society of America's Silver Anvil Awards stand as testimony to the respect research has gained among practitioners.

The Commission on Public Relations Education was composed of practitioners and educators. Their task was to decide the shape of public relations education for the next century. As a field evolves and changes, the training required to enter the field will change. The Commission sought to understand the current and future demands of the field. Those demands would provide the foundation for the curriculum used to train future public relations practitioners. Research emerged as one of the key skills needed by future practitioners. A significant change in the curriculum from the previous Commission report was the addition of a class dedicated to public relations research. Research was now recognized as a central job skill in public relations and a critical component of the public relations curriculum/training. Research had moved from the periphery to the core of the public relations practice and education.

The Public Relations Society of America (PRSA) is the largest professional organization of public relations practitioners in the United States. Each year PRSA sponsors the Silver Anvil competition. This competition recognizes the best work in the field and is one of the highest honors a public relations department or agency can achieve. Following the four-step process of public relations, each entry is judged on (1) research—collect information/data used to create objectives, target audiences, and key strategies; (2) planning—identify objectives, target audiences, and key strategies; (3) execution—explains the tactics used in the public relations effort; and (4) evaluation—assessment of outcomes to show whether or not an objective was achieved. Research is essential to earning one of public relations' highest honors. Formative research documents the research criteria, process research documents the execution criteria, and evaluative research documents success or failure to achieve an objective. Practitioners are reminded of research's value and the practice reaffirms its importance through the Silver Anvil Awards.

Research is establishing itself as a core element of public relations. That does not mean all practitioners embrace or even use it. If you review Silver Anvil Award entries, you will find lapses even in those public relations efforts seeking to be honored. However, public relations research is now a required element in a public relations curriculum. This means that future practitioners, coming from strong public relations programs, will have the skills and knowledge necessary to execute public relations research. As recently as the 1980s and 1990s, properly trained practitioners were not being provided with the research skills. As a result, research had been neglected out of a lack of skill. Lack of skill should not be a barrier with recent and future graduates.

Beyond developing knowledge and improving the practice, research has a bottom-line component. Public relations practitioners, like others in the business world, are becoming more accountable for their actions. Management wants to know what a unit is actually contributing to an organization or what an agency is providing to a client. Research provides hard evidence of what public relations is or is not contributing to an organization or client. Setting and achieving objectives is hard evidence of contributions. It is through research that objectives are formulated and evaluated. Public relations practitioners need to engage in proper research to establish their contributions to the organization or client. Performance reviews require the type of hard data research can provide. Documenting public relations' contributions through research can influence critical factors such as size of a budget, retaining a client, or retaining one's job. Research makes intellectual and practical contributions to the practice of public relations.

—*W. Timothy Coombs*

See also Experiment/experimental methods; Formative research; Process research; Qualitative research; Quantitative research; Sampling; Statistical analysis

Bibliography

Cutlip, S. M., Center, A. H., & Broom, G. T. (2000). *Effective public relations* (8th ed.). Englewood Cliffs, NJ: Prentice Hall.

Pavlik, J. V. (1987). *Public relations: What research tells us.* Newbury Park, CA: Sage.

Stacks, D. W. (2002). *Primer of public relations research.* New York: Guilford Press.

Stewart, T. D. (2002). *Principle of research in communication.* Boston: Allyn & Bacon.

PUBLIC RELATIONS SOCIETY OF AMERICA

Immediately following World War II, pent-up public demand for products and services ignited the American economy. The marketplace explosion also generated new needs for marketing publicity, public relations, and people who knew their way around a typewriter.

Earlier in the 20th century, the value of public relations had been established by such pioneers as Ivy Lee, John Hill, Edward Bernays, Arthur W. Page, and Rex Harlow. But few in the postwar population entering the field had knowledge of or experience in the practice. Facing a new environment that required wedding client objectives to public interests, many neophytes—as well as veterans—recognized the need for a national, collegial association in which they could share experience and make connections, establish standards of practice, and hone professional skills.

On August 7, 1947, at Chicago's Lake Shore Athletic Club, that "gleam in the eye" became reality with the formation of the Public Relations Society of America (PRSA). It was not a case of spontaneous generation. In 1936, the New York-based National Association of Public Relations Counsel (NAPRC) had held its first meeting. In 1969, the West Coast produced the American Council on Public Relations (ACPR). In 1944, Washington, DC, was the birthplace of the American Public Relations Association (APRA), and publicity clubs were up and running in a few major cities.

Convened at the Chicago table were six leaders from the ACPR and NAPRC. (APRA had declined the invitation and its merger with PRSA waited until 1961.) Six months later, the state of New York chartered the new national organization. It began with six chapters—Chicago, Detroit, Hawaii, Los Angeles, New York, and San Francisco—and President W. Howard Chase, also chairman of the executive committee, and Earl Ferris, chairman of the board of directors.

The first committees addressed eligibility, education, and professional standards. The *Public Relations Journal,* established in 1945 by ACPR, became the official publication of the new Society.

During November of 1948, PRSA held its first national conference in Chicago. In an October 1970 *Public Relations Journal* article, Rea Smith, acting executive director of the PRSA, recalled that two of the impressive speakers were Margaret Mead and S. I. Hayakawa.

From those ambitious beginnings in the late 1940s, PRSA has continued to track and contribute to the development of the contemporary profession and its growth in specialized areas of practice. The first special-interest section formed was the Counselors Academy in 1961. Today, that section roster includes 16 others: Association, Corporate, Counselors to Higher Education, the Educators Academy, Employee Communications, Environmental, Financial Communications, Food and Beverage, International, Independent Practitioners

Alliance, Military and National Security, Multicultural Communications, Public Affairs and Government, Strategic Social Responsibility, Technology, and Travel and Tourism.

Concern for ethical and professional standards has always been dominant on the Society's Agenda. In 1954, PRSA drafted a Code of Principles and a Code of Ethics. In 1960, it adopted a definitive Declaration of Principles, a Code of Standards, and enforcement procedures through Judicial Panels. From time to time, the Code has been revised, especially to keep pace with the requirements of the financial practice. PRSA's most critical—and embarrassing—ethical crisis occurred in 1956, when its president was charged by the Securities and Exchange Commission (SEC) with insider trading. Rather than undergo the Society's judicial process, he chose to resign his membership. President-elect John Felton promptly stepped into the position, becoming the only person to serve more than one term as president.

By the 1990s, it was apparent that the complex enforcement process rushed increasing litigation and change to the authority of a professional association. Thus, today, enforcement responsibility is vested in the board of directors, which may expel a member who is found guilty by a government authority or court of illegal behavior. The recent charge to the Board of Ethics and Professional Standards is to focus on raising the understanding of the code by all Society members.

Stressing both ethical and professional performance is PRSA's accreditation program, a written and oral examination of a member's knowledge, mastery of, and qualifications for public relations. Initially proposed in 1963 by the Counselors Academy solely for its members, the PRSA Assembly voted to extend the opportunity to all eligible members of the Society. Accredited members must now maintain and update their qualifications every three years. Now a major item in the Society's budget, the examination is periodically reviewed and revised, and by 2003, more than 4,000 members had earned the hallmark of Accredited in Public Relations (APR).

Organizations that partner in accreditation through the Universal Accreditation Board include the Agricultural Relations Council, the Florida Public Relations Association, Maine Public Relations Council, National School Public Relations Association, Religion Communicators Council, Society for Healthcare Strategy and Market Development, Southern Public Relations Federation, and Texas Public Relations Association.

Education for the increasing number of public relations students in U.S. colleges and universities became an ongoing PRSA priority in the 1960s. With more schools offering public relations studies, the Society established the Public Relations Student Society of America (PRSSA) in 1968 and in the following year chartered 17 schools for "alpha" PRSSA chapters, each sponsored by a PRSA chapter and having both faculty and professional advisors. By 2004, there were 243 PRSSA chapters with more than 8,000 members. Since 1973, PRSSA has been self-governing through a national committee of students, with guidance by professional and faculty advisors.

Annual conferences of PRSA and PRSSA are held simultaneously in the fall. Attended by 1,500 to 2,000 members and guests, the PRSA International Conference features leading authorities on major issues and more than 70 professional development sessions. While the two conferences have separate programs, there is much opportunity for interaction between professionals and students, who are invited to the Society's general sessions. PRSSA produced its own conference, with more than 1,000 students attending.

Paralleling PRSA's nurture of students has been Commissions on Public Relations Education—in 1975, 1987, 1999, and continuing—to research and recommend guidelines for formal education in public relations. Sponsored by PRSA and the Public Relations Division of the Association for Education in Journalism and Mass Communication, the commission also invites other professional and academic groups to participate. While researching and developing a report, the commission customarily meets at least three times annually and is co-chaired by a leading practitioner and educator. Research conducted by both the 1987 and 1999 commissions revealed surprising agreement among practitioners and educators about what should be taught in public relations studies. Both commissions recommended at least five courses in a public relations undergraduate program and that had become a standard for chartering a school for a PRSSA chapter.

PRSA also holds two seats on the Accrediting Council for Education in Journalism and Mass Communication, which reviews and accredits academic units where public relations is frequently taught. For public relations programs in these units or those housed in other units, PRSA offers a voluntary review and certification program administered by the Educational Affairs Committee.

To recognize and encourage exemplary performance, annual awards play a major role in PRSA. An inheritance from the APRA merger, the annual Silver Anvils honor outstanding public relations programs and the Bronze Anvils recognize outstanding tactics within a program or campaign. Awards to individuals include the Gold Anvil for an exceptional lifetime career and contributions to the profession; Outstanding Educator; the Paul Lund Community Service Award; the Patrick Jackson Award for Distinguished Service to PRSA; and the Public Relations Professional of the Year. The annual honorees receive their awards and recognition during the annual International Conference.

Another honor is membership in PRSA's College of Fellows. Founded in 1990, the college is a group of more than 300 accredited members distinguished by their careers, ethical performance, community service, and commitment to the profession. Each has been elected to the College and is expected to serve as a role model and mentor to other PRSA members and to aspiring students. Recently the College has encouraged Fellows to make gifts and bequests to public relations studies in colleges and universities of choice.

PRSA's foundation efforts have had a bumpy history and are now in a second reincarnation. Established in the mid-1950s, the Foundation for Public Relations Research and Education had its halcyon years in the early 1960s, when it sponsored a series of annual lecture-essays on the role of public relations in the early history of the United States and Canada. Written and presented by such noted historians as Dr. Allan Nevins, Dr. Eric

Goldman, and Dr. Ray Allen Billington, the published lectures endure as one of the most enlightening and proud records of the profession's heritage. Other major initiatives of that foundation included a fellowship program for educators, a scholarly journal (*Public Relations Review*), and a bibliography of public relations literature.

In the 1980s, however, an unfortunate controversy developed and that original foundation became the Institute for Public Relations, headquartered at the University of Florida. Subsequently, PRSA established another PRSA Foundation, responsible for student scholarships, research awards, and the Society's Body of Knowledge. In the 1990s, the Body of Knowledge began supporting the Communications Career Academies' program to interest bright high school students—primarily African Americans—in public relations careers. The foundation's curriculum of more than 50 lesson plans for that program is also available to PRSA chapters for their outreach to high schools throughout the country.

Recognizing that much of the PRSA's work, particularly in education and professional development, qualified for a 501(c)(3) status, the Society took that significant action in 2003–2004. As one result, the foundation board became advisory, reporting to the PRSA Board of Directors, and part of larger funding efforts to support cancer research, scholarships, and other programs of lifelong education.

After 47 years as the Society's publication of record, the *Public Relations Journal* was succeeded in 1995 by the *Public Relations Strategist,* a quarterly magazine addressing major trends and issues facing public relations and its clients and designed for readership by both public relations and business management. The year before, PRSA introduced *Tactics,* a monthly publication reporting immediate news of professional interest, practical counsel, ideas, and commentary.

PRSA's membership of more than 17,000 is organized through 18 districts and 116 chapters. Governance includes a representative national assembly of approximately 360 members and a 17-member board of directors. In addition to the president/CEO, president-elect, treasurer, secretary, and immediate past president, one board member represents each district and two are at-large members.

The PRSA staff of approximately 50 is responsible to Executive Director Catherine Bolton, APR. In 2004, the board approved relocation of the PRSA headquarters to 33 Maiden Lane, in Manhattan's financial district.

The makeup of PRSA's leadership has evolved over the years. In early years, most presidents came from the corporate sector, and increasingly, they have come from agency practice. In 1973, PRSA named its first woman president (the author) and by 2005, nine women will have been elected to head the Society. In the ranks of president, one has been of Hispanic heritage, one African American, and two have been educators. Many PRSSA alumni have served on the board, with two becoming president (in 2002 and 2004).

Despite that ascension to leadership by the new generation, an ongoing challenge is persuading the majority of PRSSA graduates to transition to the professional Society. Entry-level salaries often discourage joining and not enough employers yet sponsor membership and the professional opportunities it brings. If those alumni do join, they are often "lost" in a sea of seasoned veterans and become discouraged. Recognizing that problem, some PRSSA chapters are making special efforts to welcome and serve those younger members. In 2004, those efforts inspired a national group, New Professionals, to serve associate members—particularly PRSSA alumni—who seek mentoring and help in lubricating early career progress and participating in the Society. A month after the group's launch, more than 100 members enrolled and 40-plus senior members volunteered as mentors.

PRSA members have many opportunities to participate in leadership activities through numerous committees populating PRSA at chapter and national levels. The customary route to national positions is through chapter leadership.

Since 1980, PRSA objectives and goals have been driven by a strategic planning process, customarily with blueprints for action in five-year increments. The process has addressed issues from sophisticated communications technology to serve members

more effectively to a stronger role in international public relations.

International interests have early roots in PRSA. In 1952, three Society delegates attended the organizing meeting of the International Public Relations Association (IPRA). In 1961, PRSA joined the Inter-American Federation of Public Relations Associations and developed an ongoing liaison within the Canadian Public Relations Society (CPRS). In 1964, PRSA co-sponsored with CPRS and IPRA the Third World Congress in Public Relations held in Montreal. The Society has also co-sponsored two World Congresses in the United States. It now takes a leading role in the new Global Alliance of 60 professional associations throughout the world. Meeting semiannually, the Alliance agenda includes such subjects as ethical standards, professional development, and legislation.

In 2003, PRSA adopted the following three ongoing program priorities:

> Professional development—a concept of lifelong learning, embracing all of the Society's educational efforts, from academic to continuing education at every level. The latter includes such member services as seminars through meetings and the PRSA Web site, conferences, the Professional Resource Center, and publications.
>
> Diversity—seeking a membership which is more representative of American society, serving and being responsible to multicultural needs, and supporting client objectives related to diversity.
>
> Advocacy—spokesmanship for the profession and ethical practice to the public at large via media, speaking platforms, and coalitions with other public speaking groups; a vigilant "watch" for legislative and judicial actions which could have a negative impact on the practice.

In sum, they reflect the following pervasive professional concerns:

> Improving the capabilities of professionals and their prospects for moving up the ranks of management rather than being subordinate to such functions as marketing, advertising, and human resources.
>
> Persuading more minorities to enter the field, particularly as American society becomes more

diverse. Not only is this a "right thing to do," but professionals who understand and give voice to the culture of growing constituencies are essential to building productive relationships for clients.

Gaining respect for public relations, its role and value, remains an elusive goal and stubborn frustration. Its perception as a "soft," expendable function in cost-cutting crunches and client crises continues to be the profession's own public relations problem, and its problem to solve.

Going on 60, PRSA has become the world's largest association of public relations professionals. Even more significant, it is parent to the largest paraprofessional organization of students preparing for future practice. Beyond size alone, as the practice has grown, changed, and matured, so has PRSA. Both face escalating challenges to performance, ethical behavior, and trust. However, the fundamental mission of both remains the same—to foster responsible, constructive dialogue and relationships in a democratic society where decisions are shaped and made in the workplace and home, marketplace, and voting booth.

—Betsy Plank
Betsy Plank was the PRSA's first female president in 1973, and is the only person to win three of the organization's top individual awards—the Gold Anvil, the Paul Lund Community Service Award, and the Patrick Jackson Award for Distinguished Service to PRSA, and founded the PRSSA in 1968.

See also Plank, Betsy; Public Relations Student Society of America

PUBLIC RELATIONS STUDENT SOCIETY OF AMERICA

In retrospect, the late 1960s were curious, unlikely times for the Public Relations Society of America (PRSA) to launch a student organization.

Students were rebelling against the Vietnam War and constraints imposed by the "elder culture." Campus unrest—even riots—made daily headlines. Members of older generations were shocked at the "flower children," their penchant for drugs, indiscreet sex, and suggestive music, their protests, and their contempt for traditional American values.

None of that had been evident in the growing relationship between PRSA and its younger generation.

In the 1960s, education for public relations was beginning to flourish in U.S. colleges and universities, which recognized the practice as a burgeoning career field for their graduates. Increasing numbers of educators were highly respected and influential in PRSA and they championed student-professional encounters. There were public relations "clubs" at six schools: the universities of Florida, Southern California, Texas, and West Virginia, and at San Jose State College and Utica College.

As early as 1950, PRSA had considered a student organization, but didn't act on that vision until 15 years later. A rapid chronology then followed:

1965—President Ovid Davis invited students of the six clubs to attend PRSA's National Conference.

1966—President Robert Wolcott repeated the conference invitation.

April 1967—Board member Jon Riffel arranged for San Jose State's club members to meet with the Spring Assembly in Pebble Beach, California, and demonstrate how a professional-student relationship could work well.

In a statement to the Assembly, the Long-Range Planning Committee said "Perhaps our greatest concern for the future is the questions of where the next generation of practitioners will come from. Let public relations grow wild, without benefit of academic preparation, and a half century from now, it will be as forgotten as phrenology."

The Assembly unanimously approved a resolution by Professor Walter Siefert to form a committee to study creating a student organization and report to the Fall Assembly in Philadelphia.

Author's Note: The author thanks the Public Relations Society of America's staff and Professional Resource Center for their contributions to this entry.

President J. Carroll Bateman appointed a joint committee of PRSA and the Association for Education in Journalism (AEJ) to develop the report, with assistance by Dr. F. H. "Chris" Teahan , director of education (later vice president) of PRSA.

November 1967—The report to the Assembly recommended formation of the Public Relations Student Society of America (PRSSA). The vote was unanimous.

January 1968—President Edward P. VonderHaar appointed a committee of two practitioners, two educators, and two students and chaired by Jon Riffel. Its charge: develop plans for PRSSA and requirements for its chapters.

By year-end 1968—The Board had chartered 14 schools for PRSSA Chapters: the universities of Central Missouri, Florida, Houston, Kent State, Maryland, North Dakota, Northern Illinois, Ohio State, Southern California, Syracuse, Texas, and West Virginia, and San Jose State College and Utica College.

These and additional chapters thrived and grew. PRSSA organized them into districts, following the PRSA pattern. PRSSA agencies and "Pro-Am" program increased. So did internship opportunities. More students attended the PRSA National Conference and took advantage of internship opportunities. PRSSA launched a national publication, *Forum*. More students attended the PRSA National Conference. All were signals of an enthusiastic and productive relationship.

Nationally, a PRSA Committee on Student Organization governed PRSSA. It had two "token" students. By 1973, student leaders began to chafe at that junior role. At the 1973 PRSA Conference in Honolulu, they felt their muscle and persuaded the Board and Assembly to permit self-governance.

Students promptly elected their first national chair, Joan Patrick O'Connor of the University of Southern California, and other members of the National Committee: vice chair, editor, and nine district chairs. The PRSA Board appointed the faculty and professional advisors—but with limited voting privileges. Chris Teahan was administrator of the new national organization.

Another seminal action at the Honolulu conference was the introduction by the PRSA Education Committee of a PRSSA competition. Now known as the J. Carroll Bateman Case Study Competition, it has become the premier program in which chapter teams demonstrate their research, planning, and performance skills.

The downside of the student organization's rapid growth was the severe strain on the PRSA budget to support PRSSA. The National Committee recognized the program, took responsibility, and initiated national membership dues.

Students continued to attend the Society's annual conferences in the fall. In 1976, however, PRSA and the International Public Relations Association (IPRA) co-sponsored the Seventh World Congress of Public Relations in Boston. Scheduled in August, it served as the Society's Annual Conference. For students, the timing conflicted with summer jobs, school, and vacations.

Rather than skip a conference opportunity, the resourceful PRSSA President, Maureen Prater, risked producing a separate conference at her own school, the University of Dayton, in October. The venture was a success, attended by 300 students and professionals, and even eked out a minuscule profit. It also set a precedent. Since that time, PRSSA has produced its own national conferences, held simultaneous to the PRSA conference to take advantage of interaction with professionals. Today, more than 1,000 students customarily attend.

In 1981, the student organization claimed a unique group of advocates: the Champions for PRSSA. Designed to identify PRSA members and chapters having a special interest in students and their education, the Champions supplement the support provided by PRSA to PRSSA. Among the Champions' contributions are sponsoring annual PRSSA chapter awards for outstanding performance; producing a publication and videotape recounting PRSSA history; recognizing retiring National Advisors; sponsoring the annual scholarships for outstanding students; publishing a handbook of advice for getting and keeping entry-level jobs; and serving as speakers, judges, and counsel for PRSSA programs.

Several other PRSSA scholarships and awards also honor or have been established by individuals. They include the Altschul Internship Award, the Lawrence G. Foster Award, the Professor Sidney Gross Memorial Award, the Steven Pisinski Memorial Award, and the Gary Yoshimura Scholarship. An annual scholarship is also awarded by PRSA's Multicultural Section.

The role of the PRSSA administrator is key to PRSSA's continued performance. PRSSA leaders and members are on the scene for only a brief period of time—usually two years at the most—before they graduate and move on. Thus, their administrator provides essential continuity to the student organization. The first and longest serving was legendary—the late Chris Teahan, who, along with Jon Riffel, is a First Founding Father of PRSSA. After his retirement, Colleen McDonough served PRSSA, then was succeeded by Elaine Averick, who became the students' "Godmother" before she retired. Today's new Godmother-in-Progress is Janeen Garcia, wise counsel to PRSSA and broker of its relationships with PRSA.

In recent years, PRSSA changed its National Committee structure from geographic districts to program areas. There are now elected Vice Presidents for Chapter Development, Member Services, Professional Development, Public Relations, Regional Activities, and Internships/Job Services. A Webmaster position was also added to support and keep pace with PRSSA's increasing use of the Internet to communicate with and provide services to members. The PRSSA President makes annual reports to the PRSA Assembly and is a voting delegate.

Education has always been the driving force behind PRSSA's relationship with PRSA. Both educators and practitioners had long been concerned about preparing students for the profession that continues to grow in its scope and responsibilities. Students themselves recognize that this preparation spans academic study, practical experience, and mentoring.

PRSA's original provisions for chartering a school for a PRSSA chapter reflected those interests. PRSA Bylaws (Article XVI, Section 2) state its aim for PRSSA to "foster the students' understanding of current public relations theories and procedures, encourage them to the highest ideals and principles of the practice of public relations, instill in them a professional attitude."

Originally, PRSA's requirement for a school charter was the offering of at least two courses in public relations. In the mid-1970s, that provision obviously shortchanged preparation for the growing field. As a result, PRSA and the Public Relations Division of the Association for Education in Journalism decided to take a new look. They co-sponsored the First Commission on Public Relations Education, co-chaired by Scott Cutlip and J. Carroll Bateman. In its 1975 report, the Commission recommended four courses and outlined their content. The PRSA Assembly then adopted that standard for chartering a school.

The Second Commission went to work in the mid-1980s and was co-chaired by William Ehling and Betsy Plank. It had 25 members representing professional and academic groups. The Commission's 1987 report recommended 15 semester hours of public relations study—the equivalent of five courses—and their content. The PRSA Assembly then adopted that increased standard for school charters. At its next Assembly, PRSA also endorsed the five-course requirement, reaffirming its commitment to education.

Appointed in the late 1990s, the Third Commission was co-chaired by Dean Kruckeberg and John Paluszek and included 47 educators and practitioners. Its 1999 report, "A Port of Entry: Public Relations Education for the 21st Century," had worldwide distribution and impact. It confirmed the five-course standard, but emphasized that it was a bare minimum, with eight courses as the ideal undergraduate education in public relations. The Third Commission continues to monitor education and is responsible for future updates and recommendations.

Both the Second and Third Commissions began their work with extensive research among educators and practitioners, who expressed substantial—and unexpected—agreement on course content.

Initial predictions for the impact of the five-course requirement had been dire. Many schools would find it unacceptable and a threat to their curriculum authority and would abandon their charters. The predictions were wrong. Instead, schools qualifying for charters increased.

Oversight of adherence to that charter requirement is vested in PRSA's Educational Affairs Committee. Based on Commission reports, its recommendation for courses—or equivalent content—are Introduction to Public Relations, Writing and Production, Research, Supervised Public Relations Experience (e.g., internships), and Strategy and Implementation (i.e., Case Studies and Campaigns). The PRSA National Committee has oversight of other charter requirements: at least 10 members in good standing, a sponsoring PRSA chapter, and faculty and professional advisors who are PRSA members. The PRSA Board retains authority to grant or withdraw charters, based on recommendations of the PRSSA National Committee and the PRSA Educational Affairs Committee.

The educational underpinnings of PRSSA have given it integrity, unique statures, and respect as the world's largest paraprofessional public relations organization in schools of higher education.

One related issue remains thorny. While chartered schools are required to offer five public relations courses, there is no eligibility requirement for formal public relations study by PRSSA members. In practice, most have declared a major in public relations or are minoring in the discipline. The traditional rationale for open membership is to allow interested students from other areas of study—journalism, advertising, or business, for example—to be members so that they can become familiar with the role of public relations and bring that understanding to their future careers. Based on their interest or PRSSA experience, many of these students take an introductory course in public relations. Nevertheless, the debate about PRSSA eligibility continues and awaits future resolution.

Another stubborn issue of concern to both PRSSA and PRSA is how to encourage PRSSA graduates to transition to the professional Society, particularly to take advantage of its opportunities for professional development, contracts, and leadership. Estimates are that only 18 percent of graduates

become PRSA associate members. Recognizing that not all graduates enter the field, the stretch goal is 50 percent. Obstacles for achieving that include the prohibitive price of dues for entry-level workers, limited employer sponsorship, discomfort in transitioning from campus to an intimidating company of veteran professionals pursuing their own agendas, and difficulty in finding career mentors.

Both PRSA and PRSSA have launched strong efforts to address these problems. The student organization has mounted an ongoing campaign to promote the value of PRSA membership to early-career progress and to encourage students to aim for Associate membership immediately after graduation. The campaign is working—PRSA chapters are joining the effort. A few have already initiated successful programs to attract and serve young professionals. Spurred by those examples, in January 2004, PRSA formed a national New Professionals advocacy group. Co-chaired by Gail Liebl, past president of PRSA and past chair of the PRSA Technology Section, and Mary Beth West, PRSSA alumna and former PRSA Board member, the group's first announcement yielded an initial enrollment of more than 100, with more than 40 professionals volunteering as mentors.

Meanwhile, PRSA and the Champions co-sponsor Associate membership for graduates of the PRSSA National Committee. Beyond its deserved recognition of service to PRSSA, it assures that the senior Society will claim the proven leadership promise of these "best and brightest."

By 2004, PRSSA claimed 243 chapters, more than 8,000 members, and was still growing and going strong.

At the conclusion of his "Brief History of PRSSA," Chris Teahan posed a rhetorical question: "Given the knowns, is it a risk to predict that within the next few years one of these erstwhile 'kids' will be elected to the PRSA presidency and that future Grand Old Men and Women of Public Relations will be alumni of PRSSA?"

The first half of his prophecy came true in 2002 and 2004 when two PRSSA alumni—Joann Killeen and Del Galloway—became PRSA Presidents. As for becoming Grand Old Men and Women of Public Relations, that, too, will happen. Just wait and see.

—Betsy Plank founder of PRSSA

PUBLIC SECTOR

Simply, the public sector is that part of society that is not the private sector. Or, conversely, the private sector is that which is not inherently public. The private sector is generally thought about as private decisions and actions by individual and corporate persons. Thus, in contrast, the public sector is that which is not private, that which deserves to be done and thought because it is in the interest of all people—natural or artificial. In that balance between the public and private sectors, a crucial nexus is the point at which the private violates public expectations and public interests. Likewise, theorists are concerned at which point the public sector intrudes incorrectly into private activities, choices, and preferences. Knowing and managing this balance is one of the tasks of public relations practitioners and is, perhaps, the most profound rationale for the profession and its practice.

Public relations theory building over the past several decades has generated a considerable body of literature suggesting new perspectives and processes for public relations. A key concept in this theory building has been the questioning of the definition of *publics* and *the public* as they affect public relations in normative and positive theories and models. James E. Grunig has argued, "A positive model is a theory that describes and explains how public relations is practiced. A normative model explains how public relations should be practiced" (2001, p. 13). Perceptions about "publics" and "the public" in both types of empirically based and normative theories has a significant impact on the understanding of how public relations should be practiced and how public relations is practiced.

In an opening discussion in their textbook *This Is PR,* Doug Newsom, Judy Vanslyke Turk, and Dean Kruckeberg quoted Lucien Matrat's perspective on public relations. Matrat said,

Public relations, in the sense that we use the term, forms part of the strategy of management. Its function is twofold: to respond to the expectations of those whose behaviour, judgments and opinions can influence the operation and development of an enterprise and in turn to motivate them. (2004, p. 2)

Establishing public relations policies means, first, harmonizing the interests of an enterprise with the interests of those on whom its growth depends. The next step is putting these policies into practice. Newsom, Turk, and Kruckeberg moved the argument by quoting Matrat further: "This means developing a communication policy which can establish and maintain a relationship of mutual confidence with the firm's multiple publics" (2004, p. 2). This perspective on multiple publics is reflective of much of the scholarly definitions of public relations. Individually, these groups are defined as *publics.* Much of the research and practice has been focused on defining the precise nature of these groups (publics) and to effectively relate with them and to move away from the concept of *the public.* The dominance of the "publics" perspective is illustrated by Scott Cutlip when he stated "there is no such thing" as the general public (1994, p. 360).

In 2001, critical scholars Shirley Leitch and David Neilson took issue with the dominance of the perspective and deconstructed the basic theory of publics and presented a revised version of the concept. Leitch and Neilson deconstructed the concept that there is no general public by using the theoretical frameworks of Habermas (1962/1991). In Habermasian terms, there is "the public" and "the public sphere" (Leitch & Nielson, 2001, p. 130). From this perspective, "The public is made up of all the citizens of a nation. The public sphere, as distinct from the private sphere, is the ensemble of public spaces available for debate between citizens" (2001, p. 130). Leitch and Neilson suggested that these public spaces may be a community meeting or a public chat room on the Internet. Leitch and Neilson argued that public relations theory and model building that is centered on the concept of publics is heavily weighted in favor of organizations and attempts to abandon the concept of the democratic processes within society. This, they stated, is detrimental to society and also may be detrimental to the very organizations that marginalize or ignore the discussions among members of the society.

Leitch and Neilson indicated that the discussions that are held in the public sphere are the essence of a democratic society. They stated, "Democratic debate by the public within the many sites of the public sphere occurs in relation to, but distinct from the 'system.' The system includes both 'political subsystems' (state) and 'economic subsystems' (economy)" (2001, p. 130). They argued that in its ideal form the public sphere is the site where public opinion can form. The authors suggested that "through the democratic structures of society, public opinion places limits on and leads to reforms within the system." (2001, p. 130). Leitch and Neilson recognized that in practice the concept of public opinion is not unitary nor may it be easily interpreted. This, however, is one of the challenges of effective public relations research and strategies development because it is out of this public domain and public opinion that organizations often face serious challenges from groups that emerge from the discussion.

Many questions remain regarding how individuals form opinions in the public sphere. How do these individuals come to think in particular ways and then how do these individuals become part of larger groups holding similar positions? Robert L. Heath argued that the forming of opinions comes from the individual's interaction with the system in a particular situation. For example, an individual in a neighborhood may form an opinion in opposition to a governmental system that wishes to place a new prison in the individual's community. If other members of the community also share the feeling that they do not want the prison in their community, there is, in Heath's terms, a zone of meaning held by those individuals. That is, they share the same meaning for the issue. Heath suggested that the zones of meaning may apply to an issue, an event, or even an organization. Although the shared zone of meaning often results from opposition to issues, events, and organizations, the shared zone of meaning

may also be in support. An example of this may be support by parents for additional school crossing guards to ensure the safety of their children. This, of course, is the ideal situation for an organization that is supporting this action.

Although the discussion has focused on the zone of meaning being shared by a group, a zone of meaning may be held by an individual. This individual may be of concern to organizations within the system. An example of this may be the resident critic of the city council who represents only his or her views. When this zone of meaning becomes shared by others, the concern for organizations may be even greater.

The sharing of this zone of meaning may result in actions by the individuals holding the meaning. If the individuals join together in some form of united effort and action, they are called an activist group. This group may then move to attain the goals that reflect the zones of meaning shared by the members of the group. If these groups are effective, they may stop an activity that they oppose. An example of this is the community group suggested previously that wished to prevent the building of the prison. If they are effective they may be able to convince the legislature that there is a better place to build the prison. However, if an activist group shares a zone of meaning that the building of a new prison may be economically beneficial to their community, they may take actions to convince the governing body that their community is a better place to build the prison than some other community.

The organizational structures of these activist groups are problematic. As Leitch and Neilson have suggested, their perspectives and resulting action may not be unitary or easy to interpret. Individuals and groups that share concerns in a particular sphere may not be taking exactly the same path to alter the environment. As Leitch and Neilson reasoned, there are numerous voices and organizations in areas such as women's rights and the environment. Because there are significant differences of approach and action by the various activist individuals and groups, organizations wishing to form relationships must be cognizant of the differences within the activist groups.

The importance of the activist groups to organizations is that they, the activist groups, may come to control the social, political, or economic agenda within society. That is, the positions and perspectives that the activist group holds become the dominant viewpoint or opinion in the society. J. E. Grunig has argued that "indeed, many public relations practitioners believe their organization have lost control to activist group" (2001, p. 18). This loss of agenda setting to the activist individuals or groups may be severely detrimental to organizations that hold positions in opposition to those of the activist groups.

If the deconstruction of Leitch and Neilson and theoretical underpinnings of Heath, that there are zones of understanding in the public sphere, public relations theories and models must recognize and include the concepts of group development. This understanding must be included in the normative model and in the positive model. This should lead organizations into the concept of environmental scanning, that is, to monitor the environments of society to understand the various zones of meaning that may exist in the public sphere. As suggested by Hugh Culbertson, Dennis Jeffers, Donna Besser Stone, and Martin Terrell in 1993, the effective models must scan the social, economic, and political environments where an organization may exist.

—John Madsen

See also Privatizing public opinion (and "publicticizing" private opinion); Public opinion and opinion leaders; Public sphere discourse; Publics; Zones of meaning

Bibliography

Culbertson, H. M., Jeffers, D. W., Stone, D. B., & Terrell, M. (1993). *Social, political and economic contexts in public relations: Theory and cases.* Hillsdale, NJ: Lawrence Erlbaum.

Cutlip, S. M. (1994). *The unseen power: Public relations, a history.* Hillsdale, NJ: Lawrence Erlbaum.

Grunig, J. E. (2001). Two-way symmetrical public relations: Past, present and future. In R. L. Heath (Ed.), *Handbook of public relations* (pp. 11–30). Thousand Oaks, CA: Sage.

Habermas, J. (1991). *The structural transformation of a public sphere: An inquiry into a category of bourgeois society* (T. Burger & F. Lawrence, Trans.). Cambridge: MIT Press. (Original work published 1962)

Heath, R. L. (1994), *Management of corporate communication: From interpersonal contacts to external affairs.* Hillsdale, NJ: Lawrence Erlbaum.

Leitch, S., & Neilson, D. (2001). Bringing publics into public relations: New theoretical frameworks for the practice. In R. L. Heath (Ed.), *Handbook of public relations* (pp. 127–138). Thousand Oaks, CA: Sage.

Newsom, D., Vanslyke Turk, J., & Kruckeberg, D. (2004). *This Is PR* (8th ed.). Belmont, CA: Wadsworth/Thompson Learning.

PUBLIC SERVICE ANNOUNCEMENTS (PSAs)

Public service announcements (PSAs) are public relations tools used to broadcast announcements free of cost. The tradition of the Federal Communications Commission has been to expect television and radio broadcasting companies to demonstrate their community responsibility by providing free air space for important, noncommercial announcements. Because radio and television stations prosper through the sale of advertising time, they are reluctant to provide very much time and space for such announcements.

Such announcements have real value to nonprofit organizations, which can use them to notify members of the community of some event, such as a blood drive, or some need, such as limited available supplies of blood for transfusions. At times, companies can also qualify for free advertising time by being engaged in some community activity that the stations deem valuable enough to broadcast. Perhaps large and continuing commercial advertising time purchases qualify these businesses for free time for PSAs.

At various times, PSAs have been viewed as not worth the effort. All too often stations were only willing to run them at extraordinarily low viewer or listener times. Many of these ran in the late night and early morning when stations have a hard time getting advertisers to spend dollars to reach "nonexistent" viewers or listeners.

As times change, so has the future and fortune of PSAs. Many radio and television stations now partner with the more visible and worthy nonprofit organizations. For instance, on a monthly or quarterly basis, a station may take on a strategic partnership that serves to enhance the station's community image. It might promote the Salvation Army at Christmas. It might promote the March of Dimes or the American Heart Association (near Valentine's Day). The station tells of events, perhaps in the news segment, to publicize them. In this way, that version of a PSA actually has more clout that it would if run only as an "ad."

Radio and television stations may also agree to cover events, such as a charity fundraiser. They announce its day and build up to then. They cover the event and report on its success as a fundraiser. This is viewed as "soft news," which gives the image that the station cares about the community and serves the role of publicizing the event, the cause, and the nonprofit organization.

Radio and television stations often have a calendar of events. They may announce that periodically during a broadcast day. That tool helps nonprofit organizations to get out word to the listeners and viewers at no charge to the charity. In the broadcast of this information, the station can demonstrate that it is benefiting or serving its broadcast community.

With the advent of the Internet, radio and television stations can go one additional step in this community service. They can indicate that more information on an event or cause "can be found at our Web site." At the Web site, the station can link to the charity. The charity may also link back to the station, which is a way to repay it for its community service.

—*Robert L. Heath*

PUBLIC SPHERE (*ÖFFENTLICHKEIT*)

The term *public sphere* has been discussed for many years, especially in European countries. The term is relevant to the theory, teaching, and practice of public relations because it forces attention and gives substance to efforts to understand the form and content of the public arenas where practitioners do their work and academics conduct research.

Many writers have been interested in the implications of this term, including Immanuel Kant, Jean-Jacques Rousseau, John Locke, and John Stuart Mill in the 18th and 19th centuries, and Hannah Arendt and Joseph Schumpeter in the 20th century. Their discussion has dealt with the phenomena captured in terms such as *the public, publicité,* and *the public sphere.* Even earlier, the adjective "publicus" was used to designate a political order, or polity, in which the people were the carrier and the guarantor for the ruling law. During the 18th century, the German noun *Öffentlichkeit* (public sphere) developed out of the verb *öffentlich* (public). Since the 18th century, the term has much to do with claims for reasonable thinking in the tradition of the European Enlightenment.

In communication science and in public relations research, we can read much about *publics,* a term that refers to specific groups of individuals. In a similar way, public relations practitioners and academics sometimes discuss *the public* as some kind of totality of publics. In contrast to these terms, the term *public sphere* is discussed in sociology and is connected with sociological and political analyses. Today, primarily in a European perspective, we can find several traditions relevant to the use of the term. This discussion essentially distinguishes at least two important, different, and modern models of what is called the "public sphere." The first model is a *deliberative* or *discourse model*; the second can be called a *mirror model* or a *liberal model.* The first model is connected with the writings of Jürgen Habermas (1991), especially his classic book *The Structural Transformation of the Public Sphere* (*Strukturwandel der Öffentlichkeit*); the second model is based on the liberal theory of democracy (e.g., Ackerman, 1989) and systems theoretical approaches, especially writings of the German sociologist Niklas Luhmann (1990).

In 1962, the German sociologist and philosopher Jürgen Habermas (1991) published his book *The Structural Transformation of the Public Sphere,* which was translated into English and published in 1989. During the same year, a conference was organized by the American sociologist Craig Calhoun in which the Habermas approach was discussed extensively and critically. In this treatise, Habermas described the historical development and transformation of the public sphere beginning with ancient understandings and continuing with the representative public sphere in the Middle Ages, until modern understandings beginning with the 18th century.

On the basis of historical and semantic analyses (public vs. private; public vs. secret), he distinguished two distinct spheres: the private sphere and the public sphere. In the modern form, beginning with the bourgeois society, the "public sphere" first appears as a specific domain, a domain of social life in which such a thing as public opinion can be formed. The public sphere is open in principle to all citizens. A portion of the public sphere—so reasoned Habermas—is constituted in every conversation in which private persons come together to form a public. Citizens act as a public when they deal with matters of general interest. Public sphere

> is defined as the public of private individuals who join in the debate of issues bearing on state authority. Unlike the Greek conception, individuals are here to be formed primarily in the private realm, including the family. Moreover the private realm is understood as one of freedom that has to be defended against the domination of the state. (Calhoun, 1992, p. 7)

Later, Habermas defined the *public sphere* as a kind of network for the communication of contents or topics and opinions. Communication flows are filtered and synthesized in such a way that public communication is condensed to topics from which the specific public gathers and forms opinions. Public opinions are not representative in a statistical sense and are not the same as the aggregated individual opinions. The public sphere is characterized by a typical communication structure, which refers to the social space that is generated through communicative acting. For Habermas (1991), "public sphere" still is a central sociological concept like "act," "actor," or "group."

For Luhmann (1990), the public sphere also can be seen as a net of communication acts without being forced to connect further communication acts. The concept of the public sphere refers to social systems, not to psychic systems. Based on the distinction

between medium and form (Fritz Heider) Luhmann in his systems theoretical approach defined the "public sphere" as a kind of medium in which forms are continuously built and resolved through communication. In the view of Luhmann, it is—in contrast to Habermas—not necessary to combine the concept of the public sphere with implications of rationality or irrational elements of "mass psychology." Topics, and even more specifically issues, are continuously generated as "forms" of the public sphere. Luhmann proposed to use the mirror metaphor to designate the most important social function of the public sphere. The mirror public sphere is necessary for the political system, one of the functional systems of society, to observe not only the own face but also the observations of other actors (e.g., opponents and rivals). Like the market, public sphere—as a mirror—is an observation or perspective of observers and is to be suited or fitted for self-observation of the society and for building up certain expectation structures.

Both models, the discursive model of Habermas and the mirror model of Luhmann, are essentially normative. One critical argument concerning the Habermas model always has focused critical attention on the difficulty of separating (historical) descriptive from normative parts in his approach. One problem with both approaches is the difficulty of linking them with empirical studies that could generate arguments for testing the strength of one model or the other.

From these reasons, a new theory of the public sphere has been developed in the Social Science Research Center Berlin (Wissenschaftszentrum Berlin) starting in the early 1990s. Friedhelm Neidhardt, Jürgen Gerhards, and others have developed a modern theory of the public sphere, in critical discussion with Habermas and Luhmann, that describes the structures of modern public sphere yet positions them so that empirical studies can be connected with the model.

The public sphere in this perspective is defined as a "forum for communication," an open "communication system" that, in principle, is open for all actors who want to inform themselves about something, who want to communicate, or want to observe the communication of others. Certain "arenas" exist in this forum in which different actors inform other actors and communicate with each other. The most important actors are different types of "speakers" and the media. At the "gallery" of the arenas, a more or less great account of spectators is assembling, the *auditorium* (Publikum). The auditorium observes the arena communication in which speakers and the media, under certain conditions, come to a relative "consonance" on the basis of different opinions. In this case of consonance of opinions, the model speaks of "public opinion." Public opinion is the common opinion between the speakers and the media in the arena. Different from this public opinion are the aggregated opinions of the spectators in the gallery. It is an empirical question regarding which opinions of the spectators, both in kind and content, are the same as the public opinion (in the arenas).

Three *functions* of the public sphere are distinguished through the analysis of various theorists: the *transparency function* (open for all actors, for all topics of general importance), the *validation function* (arguments and positions should be open for changes through public discussion), and the *orientation function* (public communication generates public opinions that can be convincing in various ways and degrees by the audience). The model further distinguishes between types of arenas that occur on *different levels:* the first level is called the level of "Encounters." Communication that occurs in the bus, on the street, in railway stations, in waiting lines (queues), or at university campuses mark an elementary type of a "small" public sphere. Typical for that type of public sphere is the instability and the relative poorness of structures (not many structures of this type exist).

The second level is arenas of assembly. Assemblies normally are not only public, but also focused at topics or issues. In the history of the public sphere, the "freedom of assembly" was an important step in the struggle for civil rights. The freedom to have demonstrations is another institutionalized form of the freedom of assembly. In modern societies, the public sphere is essentially defined through mass media.

The third level of arenas and public sphere has primarily developed during the 19th century; freedom of the press is the historically first, institutionalized form of the mass media communication level. The three levels of arenas can be interpreted as three qualitatively different steps in the process of historical development and differentiation of an autonomous system of public sphere. On each level the capacity of information gathering and information processing of the system increases. At the same time, from level to level, a professionalization of communicator roles (journalism, public relations) can be observed along with a decrease of audience roles and audience activities.

Communicators ("speakers") and the (mass) media are the most important actors in the public arena on the third (mass media) level. The audience only plays the role of an observer, although some individuals from the audience can change and become actors in the arena. The reverse process is also possible. Peters (1994) and Neidhardt (1994) distinguish between four types of "speakers": *representatives, experts, advocates,* and *intellectuals.* Representatives represent organizations like private companies, political parties, associations, churches, and so on. They can act professionally (as responsible for the communication of the organization) in their main job or avocationally. *Advocates* don't have political power, but they speak for troubled persons or professions. Examples are foundation administrators, social workers, alcohol rehabilitation speakers, and so on. *Experts* and *Intellectuals* are also important actor groups for the modern public sphere. The "speakers," but also the media organizations, work with different specific end *strategies (attention* strategies, *selection* strategies, *persuasive* strategies, bottom-up, top-down strategies, etc.), which lead to certain *public communication patterns* like an *information* (communiqué) model and an *agitation* model, and so on.

This concept of the public sphere today is relevant not only for sociologists, but also for theoretical considerations of public relations activities of organizations. Holmström (1996, p. 149) argued that both the Habermas and the Luhmann theories represent two different worldviews. If that is true, a second problem arises: which of the two paradigms is most adequate in describing public relations phenomena. This line of questioning and the answers given depend on which aspect of the phenomenon one wishes to describe. The "arena model" of the public sphere seems to be convenient. It serves as a theoretical basis for public relations research not only because there are good possibilities of connecting this model with middle range public relations theories, but also because the results of empirical public relations and communication research can be combined with this theory.

—*Günter Bentele*

See also Public opinion and opinion leaders; Public sphere discourse; Publics

Bibliography

Calhoun, C. (Ed.). (1992). *Habermas and the public sphere.* Cambridge: MIT Press.

Gerhards, J., Neidhardt, F., & Rucht, D. (1998). *Zwischen Palaver und Diskurs. Strukturen öffentlicher Meinungs-bildung am Beispiel der deutschen Diskussion zur Abtreibung* [Between palaver and discourse. Structures of generating public opinions. The German discussion of abortion as an example]. Wiesbaden: Westdeutscher Verlag.

Habermas, J. (1991). *Strukturwandel der Öffentlichkeit.* Frankfurt A.M.: Suhrkamp (1st ed., 1962). (English translation 1989 under the title *The structural transformation of the public sphere.* Cambridge: MIT Press.)

Habermas, J. (1996). *Faktizität und Geltung. Beiträge zur Diskurstheorie des Rechts und des demokratischen Rechtsstaats* [Between facts and norms. Contribution to a discourse theory of law and democracy] (Trans. William Rehg). Cambridge: MIT Press.

Holmström, S. (1996). *An intersubjective and a social systemic public relations paradigm: Public relations interpreted from systems theory (Niklas Luhmann) in opposition to the critical tradition (Jürgen Habermas).* Unpublished doctoral dissertation, University of Roskilde, Denmark.

Hölscher, L. (1978). Öffentlichkeit [The public sphere]. In O. Brunner, C. Werner, & K. Reinhart (Eds.), *Geschichtliche Grundbegriffe* [Fundamental terms in the science of history] (pp. 413–467). Stuttgart: Klett-Cotta.

Luhmann, N. (1990). Gesellschaftliche Komplexität und öffentliche Meinung [Social complexity and public opin-ion]. In N.Luhmann (Ed.), *Soziologische Aufklärung* (Bd 5). Wiesbaden: Westdeutscher Verlag.

Neidhardt, F. (1994). Öffentlichkeit, Öffentliche Meinung, Soziale Bewegungen [Public sphere, public opinion, social movements]. In F. Neidhardt (Ed.), *Öffentlichkeit, Öffentliche Meinung, Soziale Bewegungen* [Public sphere, public opinion, social movements] (pp. 7–41). Kölner Zeitschrift für Soziologie und Sozialpsychologie, Sonderheft 34. Opladen: Westdeutscher Verlag.

PUBLIC SPHERE DISCOURSE

In 1962, Jürgen Habermas wrote the seminal *The Structural Transformation of the Public Sphere: An Inquiry into a Category of Bourgeois Society.* Since then, the concept of the public sphere has been the subject of much analysis and criticism, and the theory has undergone some minor revisions. The concept of the public sphere was presented by Habermas as both an empirical description and an ideal.

As conceived, the bourgeois public sphere was viewed as "the sphere of private people come together as a public" (Habermas, 1991b, p. 27). It was an arena in which there was equality among all of the participants in social discourse, where all top-ics were open for discussion, and was inclusive, at least in principle. Habermas conceded that, in fact, some potential participants were excluded, but argued that all had an equal chance to meet the criteria of education and property to be included.

The public sphere is a space where public opin-ion can be formed. The formation of public opinion "refers to the functions of criticism and control of organized state authority" (Habermas, 1991a, p. 399). The public sphere mediates between the realms of the private and the state, and the guaran-tees of the basic rights of citizens in the liberal state depend on the demarcation between the two. For such mediation to be effective, discourse in the public sphere must be critical and rational. Above all, such discourse must rise above simply aggre-gating individual interests and form a bridge between self-interest and the common good. (Habermas's writings on communication action and on discourse ethics, drawing on the works of George Herbert Mead and Lawrence Kohlberg, are an attempt to show how this can be done.) For this bridge to exist, society must institutionalize the "practices of rational public debate" (Habermas,

1992, p. 448). Habermas's last major work, *Between Facts and Norms* (1996), addresses the basic constitutional guarantees he sees as necessary structures. Among the structural guarantees are freedom of press and assembly. This recognizes the importance of communication institutions to achieving the functions of the public sphere.

In his empirical description of the evolution of the public sphere, Habermas saw it as a product of a particular epoch, arising first in Great Britain around 1700 and then in France (c. 1750) and Germany (c. 1800). The social precondition was a market economy that led to exchange relationships based on contract and parity of individuals before the law. Legitimation of the law became dependent on public opinion.

This seemingly ideal public sphere was transformed during the late 1800s. It became squeezed by the state taking over more and more functions of the private sphere and private interests assuming a more public character, thereby stressing self-interest at the expense of the common good. The communication industry changed by decreasing its political and news or information functions and becoming increasingly involved with turning the public sphere into an arena of consumption, both of products and of culture. As a result, Habermas wrote, we now have a public sphere "in appearance only" and the "sounding board of an educated stratum tutored in the public use of reason has been shattered" (1992, pp. 171–175).

This change came about, at least in part, because of the rise of the new media. In Habermas's analysis, public debate was supposed to achieve a consensus on what is in the best interest of all. But the rise of the new media expanded the public sphere to include those less educated and less oriented to a concern for the public interest. Conflicts based on self-interests emerged and the public sphere became an "arena of competing interests" as opposed to a search for the common good. When such private interests are taken into the public realm, the original relationship of the private and public realms dissolved. This expanded public sphere lost its public character and became more consumer oriented, focusing on tastes and preferences. It became a

public sphere in name only. In Habermas's words, "the pubic is split apart into minorities of specialists who put their reason to use nonpublicly and the great mass of consumers whose receptiveness is public but uncritical. Consequently, it completely lacks the form of communication specific to a public" (1992, p. 175). The media changed from "being a merchant of news to a dealer in pubic opinion," a purveyor of advertising and private interests. This change has been exacerbated by the increasing concentration in the media, which has come to dominate, and manipulate, the public sphere.

Specifically addressing the practice of public relations, Habermas wrote that "economic advertisement achieved an awareness of its political character only in the *practice of public relations*" (1992, p. 193, italics in original). He sees public relations techniques as dominating the public sphere. Whereas advertising is generally in the private sphere, "opinion management" lays claim to the public sphere by hiding its private agenda in the guise of interest in the public welfare (Habermas, 1992, p. 193). Habermas claimed that "public relations do not genuinely concern public opinion but opinion in the sense of reputation. The public sphere becomes the court *before* whose public prestige can be displayed—rather than *in* which public critical debate is carried on" (1992, pp. 200–201, italics in original). In sum, Habermas saw public relations as corrupting the public sphere.

Habermas's development of the concept of the public sphere has been subjected to several criticisms, among them that there were competing public spheres, not one, and that the exclusion of the role of women in his initial analysis was an omission. While defending his initial analysis, he conceded the validity of these and other criticisms. As a result, he revised his theory in several ways. The revisions were, first, that the rise of the social-welfare state has resulted in inappropriate bureaucratic and social intrusions into various spheres of activity that must be taken into account. Second, while Habermas defended his interpretation of the changing nature of the media infrastructure as moving from critical to manipulative, he suggested that the analysis was too simplistic and pessimistic.

Third, that the consensus formed in the public sphere may result in a tyranny of the majority, as opposed to being a constraint on power.

For Habermas, the public sphere provides a space for rational and critical debate. For this to happen, problems and issues must be identified and thematized, solutions developed, and the issues dramatized to the extent that they are taken up by the political structures. But he wrote that it is an open question whether "a public sphere dominated by mass media provides a realistic chance for the members of civil society" to bring about meaningful changes (1992, p. 455). It is also an open question as to whether the new interactive media can recreate the original concept of the public sphere.

Perhaps because of this pessimism, Habermas has turned his attention from the public sphere to discourse ethics. His concern and approach to ethics is mirrored in the discussion in recent public relations literature about different models of public relations (press agentry, two-way symmetrical, etc.) and the resulting ethical implications of those models. Habermas's indictment of public relations seems to be less applicable to public relations models based on interaction, transparency, and relationship building.

The concept of the public sphere, as developed by Habermas, is important for both the field of public relations and for our notion of a democratic civil society. A space where issues can be rationally discussed, critical opinions formed, and that is inclusive in scope is an ideal worth striving for and lends legitimacy to the system. It can be argued that such a civil society is, ultimately, in the best interest of any and all particularized private interests. At its best, public relations has a positive role to play in achieving that ideal.

—*Roy V. Leeper*

See also Critical theory; Public opinion and opinion leaders; Publics

Bibliography

Habermas, J. (1991a). The public sphere. In C. Mukerji & M. Schudson (Eds.), *Rethinking popular culture: Contemporary perspectives in cultural studies* (S. Nicholsen, Trans., pp. 398–404). Berkeley: University of California Press. (Original work published 1973)

Habermas, J. (1991b). *The structural transformation of the public sphere: An inquiry into a category of bourgeois society* (T. Burger & F. Lawrence, Trans.). Cambridge: MIT Press. (Original work published 1962)

Habermas, J. (1992). Further reflections on the public sphere. In C. Calhoun (Ed.), *Habermas and the public sphere* (T. Burger, Trans.). Cambridge: MIT Press.

Habermas, J. (1996). *Between facts and norms: Contributions to a discourse theory of law* (W. Rehg, Trans.). Cambridge: MIT Press. (Original work published 1992)

PUBLICIST

A publicist is an individual who generates publicity. The act of obtaining publicity is simply the dissemination of planned messages to targeted media in hopes of obtaining media coverage and thereby furthering the organization's interests. In most cases, the coverage is intentionally placed by an individual rather than a news reporter covering an assigned story for publication. Publicity can be sought by any individual, but those who specialize in it are called publicists. Many public relations practitioners, whose job title may not be that of a publicist, usually are involved in some activities that generate publicity. Although publicity may be a strategy used in a public relations program or campaign and is often confused with public relations, public relations is a much broader concept. Skilled publicists are experts in media relations, a sophisticated specialty that involves forming ongoing positive relationships with media gatekeepers.

Publicists act as conduits for information flowing from an organization to a public through the use of mass media so that the public will understand, sympathize with, and be favorably predisposed toward the organization. *Publicity* is a broad term that refers to the publication of news about an organization for which print space or broadcast time is not purchased, such as in the case of advertising. Unlike advertising, which is a controlled tactic, publicity is uncontrolled. Although a publicist can attempt to place a very different story than what actually appears in the media, news media in the form of stories as opposed to advertising appear to be a third-party endorsement by the media organization.

Much of the information in the media originates from public relations sources, particularly those in the role of publicist. Good publicists become a trusted source to media gatekeepers, earn a reputation of accessibility and honesty, and know their topics well. They are keen at what makes news and develop messages that are purposefully planned, executed, and distributed through selected media to further the particular interest of their organization or client. Publicists know when journalists are on deadline, thoroughly understand the editorial profile of the particular media they are targeting, and are familiar with the work of the journalists they are contacting.

Publicists write a variety of public relations tactics, including news releases, feature stories, backgrounders, position papers, biographies, fact sheets, and media advisories. They produce press kits, write pitch letters, and make pitch calls and work with many different media gatekeepers, including city editors, feature editors, section editors, assignment directors, radio news directors, and television producers. Moreover, publicists are astute at managing online newsrooms for their organizations and clients. They work with media directories, know the editorial calendars of publications that interest them, and subscribe to clipping services so they can track coverage.

In general, practitioners in the public relations practice use publicity as just one of the many tools in the communication step of the public relations process, but there are certain fields where publicists can be found in abundance. For instance, they are commonly found in government and entertainment-related industries. Publicists working primarily for government institutions or agencies are called public information officers. Publicity also plays a large part in entertainment. An entire field of journalists reports on the expansive world of entertainment to satisfy their public's interest. Publicists in the entertainment field focus their time on gaining coverage for their clients, attractions, or organization. They prepare press materials and pitch stories to media gatekeepers. They work with feature editors of metropolitan newspapers, associate editors of magazines, assignment editors of television news

shows, producers of television programs, news directors and program directors of radio stations, and a myriad of other journalists. A skilled publicist studies the work produced by a particular journalist and the editorial environment of the publication or show in an attempt to develop an interesting angle tailored for that particular media outlet.

Four models are widely accepted to describe the evolution of public relations: the press agentry or publicity model, the public information model, the two-way asymmetric model, and the two-way symmetric model. The earliest, which is the press agentry or publicity model, is described as one-way communication in which truth is not an essential component. The public information model focuses on publicity, however, to the extent that disseminating truthful information is central to the practice. The two-way asymmetrical model tries to persuade and relies on feedback from stakeholders. On the other hand, the two-way symmetric model is considered the most sophisticated form of practice because it focuses on mutual understanding, mediation, and two-way balanced flow of information.

Press agentry is closely associated with publicity in the entertainment world. Press agentry is the practice of attracting the attention of the press through techniques that manufacture news. Methods associated with press agentry include staged events, publicity stunts, faux rallies or gatherings, spinning, and hype. A common practice in the late 1800s and early 1900s, press agentry is not part of mainstream public relations. Rather, it is a practice primarily associated with major entertainment-related events, such as Hollywood premieres and boxing matches. The goal of press agentry is to attract attention rather than gain understanding. Even today, however, the term *press agent* is sometimes used interchangeably with *publicist* in traditional Broadway theater and motion picture industries. Today's entertainment industries are populated with publicists rather than press agents. Publicists are individuals skilled in media relations and they attempt to get the name of their clients or events in the media by carefully constructing messages that inform, educate, and persuade. Some are astute in branding and positioning strategies to aid the careers and success of their clients. On the other hand, press agents want attention—good or bad—in most any form.

Press agentry has been called persuasion for short-term advantage, through the use of truth bending and even distortion, but it can also be simply the staging of provocative acts to get publicity and draw attention to an individual, event, or cause. Therefore, it is understandable that one of the earliest proponents of press agentry was Phineas Taylor (P. T.) Barnum, the famed American showman and promoter who put Gen. Tom Thumb on exhibit and launched a mobile circus featuring Jumbo the elephant and freak shows. Barnum was a master of press agentry. For instance, he wrote letters both praising and criticizing his circus show to newspapers under an assumed name.

In the early part of his career, Edward L. Bernays indeed was a master of press agentry. He persuaded 10 debutantes to hold up Lucky Strike cigarettes, manufactured by his client, the American Tobacco Company, as "torches of freedom" while participating in New York's Easter parade. In 1929, Bernays staged a global news event by organizing the "Light's Golden Jubilee," a worldwide celebration commemorating the 50th anniversary of the electric light bulb for his client, General Electric. Bernays managed to secure several prominent individuals for the event, including carmaker Henry Ford, electricity scientist Thomas Edison, and President Herbert Hoover.

Henry Rogers, one of the founders of Rogers and Cowan, the largest and most successful West Coast entertainment publicity firm, became well known when he promoted an unknown contract player for Columbia Pictures named Rita Hayworth. He contacted *Look* magazine with a telegram from the Fashion Couturiers Association of America, a fictitious group, claiming that Hayworth was the best-dressed off-screen actress. *Look* magazine took the bait and put Hayworth on the cover and published 10 pages of photos.

—*Emma Daugherty Phillingane*

See also Bernays, Edward; Entertainment industry publicity/promotion; Lucky Strike Green Campaign; Media relations; Press agentry; Promotion; Publicity

Bibliography

Aronson, M., & Spetner, D. (1993). *The public relations writer's handbook.* New York: Lexington Books.
Bivins, T. (1995). *Handbook for public relations writing.* Lincolnwood, IL: NTC Business Books.
Bivins, T. H. (1999). *Public relations writing: The essentials of style and format.* Lincolnwood, IL: NTC/Contemporary Publishing Group.
Goff, C. F. (1989). *The publicity process.* Ames: Iowa State University Press.
Loeffler, R. H. (1993). *A guide to preparing cost-effective press releases.* New York: Haworth Press.
Newsom, D., & Carrell, B. (2001). *Public relations writing: Form & style.* Belmont, CA: Wadsworth.
Wilcox, D. L., Cameron, G. T., Ault, P. H., & Agee, W. K. (2003). *Public relations strategies and tactics.* Boston: Allyn & Bacon.

PUBLICITY

Publicity is one function of public relations that involves deliberately disseminating strategic messages through mass media outlets (such as newspaper, television, radio, or Internet), without payment to the media, to advance the particular interest of the publicity client. While publicity generally refers to information placed in the mass media, publicity can also involve placing information in a controlled medium such as an organizational publication or corporate report.

While publicity is a critical function of public relations, it is not synonymous with public relations. This is a common misperception among those who do not fully understand the role or scope of public relations, because publicity is among the most visible parts of public relations. Publicity is focused on the information dissemination aspect and is not generally considered a management function. Publicity is geared toward coverage obtained and does not play a role in setting policy or providing counsel at a top organizational level.

Generating publicity involves advancing the client's interest through target-media coverage of strategic messages and events. A good publicist has a comprehensive understanding of media outlets and appropriate content in those outlets and is able to carefully select the most appropriate outlets to obtain free coverage and be of interest to the client's target audience. Much of the success or failure in obtaining publicity hinges on the ability to understand what the media gatekeeper deems newsworthy.

Publicity is not always favorable, however. In the time of a crisis, negative publicity is also generated. It is a public relations practitioner's responsibility to provide the organization's side of the story in a way that accurately and favorable represents the client.

Some similarities between publicity and advertising do exist. For example, both use mass media as a channel to distribute messages. Format and context are different, however. Publicity appears in the mass media as a news or feature item or editorial content, and the source of the material is a public relations practitioner. One major advantage that publicity has over advertising is the added element of credibility because of the implicit third-party endorsement of the news medium. Information that has been deemed newsworthy by the media outlet is often perceived as more credible than a paid advertisement. Another advantage of publicity is the cost. There is no cost for the time or space in the mass medium; however, the publicist does incur some expenses for the time and energy associated with the publicity process.

A major disadvantage of publicity, however, is the lack of control over the message and delivery of the material. An editor may choose to print the written material precisely as it was written in the news release, or it may be altered dramatically, to paint a negative picture or include competitors. The information goes to a metaphorical media gatekeeper who has the responsibility of making the decision to let the information pass through to the mass media channel or not to use the information at all. Therefore, the information appearing in the media is uncontrolled.

Advertising is a result of time or space in the mass media outlet that has been purchased by the advertiser; the advertiser therefore has complete control of the message content as it will appear to readers, listeners, or viewers.

Publicity is one of the oldest forms of public relations. In fact, many public relations historians believe that the modern-day practice of public relations is an outgrowth of 19th and early 20th century publicity. Along with the development of industry in the late 19th century came technology advances that allowed communicators the opportunity to communicate to mass audiences without a fee. This gave rise to the growth of publicists who were well skilled in promotion for the sole purpose of making news. Many early publicists were so intent on generating free coverage in any way possible that they allowed accuracy and ethics to fall to the wayside. This gave the practice of press agentry a dubious distinction. Publicity and promotion are considered only a part of the public relations process today.

Publicity has come under fire for being ethically suspect due, in part, to the early days of press agentry, and also because material masked as "news" is often coming directly from a public relations practitioner. This makes several factors of special importance when generating publicity. Because public relations information is designed to assist in the news gathering process, it is important that all information released by the public relations practitioner is accurate and current. While the news story may or may not identify the source of the information, it is important that the publicist provide the source of the information on all publicity materials.

One common method for generating publicity is via research, polls, or surveys with an interesting and appropriate human interest angle for the media outlet. In fact, some research is designed for the sole purpose of generating publicity. Other tactics used to generate publicity include news releases often as part of a press kit, interviews (sometimes generated from an interview query letter) that require a well-prepared public relations spokesperson, coverage of an event resulting from a media advisory or media alert, video news releases (VNRs), and B-roll. Additionally, news articles that have appeared may be reproduced and used as part of a press kit. This is called a reprint.

Some guidelines to increase the odds of effectively generating publicity include the following:

Timeliness—News value of the information hinges in large part on how current the information is and the degree to which it can be incorporated into other current news angles. It is also crucial for the publicist to keep abreast of journalists' deadlines and lead times, so the information can be delivered at the most appropriate and useful time.

Newsworthiness—Material that is directly linked with a promotional event or sales element will not likely garner media attention. It is essential that the writer construct a logical link between an angle of interest to the gatekeeper and a favorable angle about the company or client.

Style—News editors prefer to receive information in journalistically approvable format. This often includes writing in AP style and inverted pyramid format. Materials that must be reorganized, rewritten, or edited are frequently disregarded in lieu of material that is already in the correct style.

Eliminating Errors—This includes spelling, grammar, and mechanics as well as facts, dates, figures, titles, and statistics. A public relations practitioner should always double check his or her copy before it is submitted to the journalist. Any errors will not only ruin chances of publication, but may also jeopardize future credibility.

Medium—Consider if the nature of the material is appropriate for a trade publication, or would it be better suited for an alternative-news weekly? Don't forget to carefully research and consider which specialized news outlets would be considered credible for the ultimate target audience of the message. It's also helpful to find out ahead of time how the journalist prefers to receive information (via facsimile, e-mail, phone call, or regular mail).

There are several common ways to measure publicity. Most organizations monitor common news outlets for publicity about the organization. However, this can be a daunting task, so press clipping services are often used. Press clipping services are available, usually for a monthly fee. Agencies that monitor thousands of news publications create press clip books, which contain copies of the relevant news stories as they appeared in the various media outlets. Press monitoring and clipping agencies are also able to verify that a VNR has appeared

in broadcast media and can monitor Internet content as well. Electronic versions of a clip book are now also available. Once the stories have been compiled into a press clip book, a content analysis of the type of coverage can be conducted. This gives the public relations practitioner a better idea of which key messages were commonly incorporated into the news stories and how favorable or unfavorable the coverage of the issue was.

Another way to help quantify the exposure garnered by the publicity is to calculate media impressions, which provide an estimate of the approximate number of individuals exposed to the news story or broadcast segment. To calculate an impression number, multiply each placement by the circulation or audience number of each hit. Public relations practitioners may also seek to quantify the value of publicity by determining and advertising equivalency number. Had the message appeared as a result of paid time or space in the medium (by estimating column inches or length of broadcast time, for example), how much would it have cost? Of course, this figure does not include the added element of credibity from the third-party endorsement of the news source and can be misleading.

—*Lisa Lyon*

Bibliography

Cutlip, S. M., Center, A. H., & Broom, G. M. (2000). *Effective public relations* (8th ed.). Upper Saddle River, NJ: Prentice Hall.

Newsom, D., VanSlyke Turk, J., & Kruckeberg, D. (2000) *This is PR: The realities of public relations* (7th ed.). Belmont, CA: Wadsworth.

Seitel, F. P. (2001). *The practice of public relations* (8th ed.). Upper Saddle River, NJ: Prentice Hall.

Wilcox, D. L., Cameron, G. T., Ault, P. H. & Agee, W. K. (2003). *Public relations: Strategies and tactics* (7th ed.) Boston: Allyn & Bacon.

PUBLICLY HELD COMPANIES

A publicly held company is one whose stock is owned and traded by the public. A company becomes publicly held through an initial public offering (IPO) of securities in compliance with the registration requirements of the Securities and Exchange Act of 1933 ("the 1933 Act") as well as applicable state laws. Companies "go public" to raise money for working capital, research and development, new business ventures, or debt retirement. Additionally, a corporation may become publicly held to improve shareholder liquidity, boost the firm's marketplace profile, or to improve its chances of attracting and retaining qualified personnel. On the other hand, an IPO is an expensive and time-consuming experience that subjects the company to state and federal filing and disclosure requirements, exposes management to increased personal liability for corporate actions, and results in a loss of corporate flexibility and control.

Public relations practitioners who represent organizations that intend to go public must be aware that Section 5(c) of the 1933 Act prohibits companies from offering stock before filing a detailed registration statement with the Securities and Exchange Commission (SEC). The 1933 Act defines an "offer" broadly as any "attempt or offer to dispose of, or solicitation of an offer to buy, a security or interest in a security, for value" (15 U.S.C. §77b[3]). A company that issues a press release about an intended public offering before a registration statement is filed, for example, is likely to have made an illegal offer to sell an unregistered security. Although public relations practitioners can continue to provide product-based information and engage in regular communication activities during this prefiling period, care must be taken to avoid what the SEC calls "conditioning the market" by generating publicity that arouses interest in the company's securities.

After the registration statement is filed, the SEC imposes a waiting period during which the company must refrain from advertising its shares or otherwise offering them for sale except pursuant to a preliminary prospectus that complies with the requirements of Section 10 of the 1933 Act. This "quiet period" is designed to give potential investors time to familiarize themselves with the detailed information disclosed in the registration process. After the SEC declares the registration statement effective, the registered securities can be bought and sold legally.

While the 1933 Act regulates primarily the initial issuance of securities, the Securities and Exchange Act of 1934 ("the 1934 Act") regulates the subsequent trading of those securities. Pursuant to the 1934 Act, most public companies must file annual, quarterly, and current reports with the SEC about their operations. Especially relevant for public relations practitioners are the 1934 Act requirements that public companies provide an annual report to shareholders and conduct a yearly shareholder meeting where shareholders elect the board of directors and vote on corporate policy proposals, including proposals submitted by shareholders. Shareholders who cannot attend the annual meeting can vote by proxy. Under the 1934 Act, shareholders must be furnished with proxy statements that disclose all-important facts about matters to be voted on at shareholders' meetings.

SEC Rule 10b-5 requires a public company to make full and timely public disclosure of all material information that could affect an investor's decision to purchase, sell, or hold the company's stock. Companies that knowingly make false or misleading statements of a material nature have committed securities fraud. Furthermore, any corporate insider (including public relations representatives) who knowingly disseminates a false or materially misleading press release or other corporate communication is also liable for fraud. Ignorance is no defense—public relations practitioners are expected to conduct a "reasonable investigation" to determine if statements made in corporate communications are, in fact, true. State "blue-sky" laws also prohibit fraud in connection with the sale of securities.

In 2000, the SEC adopted Regulation FD (Fair Disclosure), which provides that if a company intentionally discloses material nonpublic information to securities analysts or selected shareholders, it must also simultaneously release that information to the general public by means of an SEC filing, a press release, a teleconference, or a Webcast. According to the SEC, the rule is meant to eliminate a company's ability to give certain brokerage firms or institutional investors an unfair marketplace advantage by informing them of material information before communicating it to the investing public.

Rule 10b-5 also prohibits insider trading, which is the purchase or sale of company stock by corporate insiders who have access to material information that is not publicly available. Company officials, including public relations staffs, must refrain from purchasing stock in their own or anyone else's name until such inside information has been disseminated fully to the public. Furthermore, corporate insiders are also guilty of securities fraud if they "tip" family members or friends by passing them nonpublic material information to enable them to trade in the company's stock. In this situation, the "tippee" may also be liable for fraud.

In response to financial scandals such as Enron, Congress passed the Sarbanes-Oxley Act of 2002 ("the 2002 Act"), which imposes additional disclosure and certification requirements on public companies and their officers. Notably, the 2002 Act requires all public companies to have independent audit committees, to adopt a code of ethics for senior financial officers, and to include in each annual report an assessment of management's financial reporting practices. The chief executive and chief financial officers of public companies must personally certify the accuracy of the information contained in their annual and other financial reports. Furthermore, corporate attorneys must report evidence of material violations of federal securities laws to company officials, the audit committee, or the board of directors.

—*Nicole B. Cásarez*

See also Annual financial report; Investor relations; Material information; Securities and Exchange Commission

Bibliography

Davis, J. B. (2003) Sorting out Sarbanes-Oxley. *American Bar Association Journal, 89,* 44–49, 70.

Securities and Exchange Commission. (1999, May). *Q&A: Small businesses and the SEC.* Retrieved May 18, 2004, from http://www.sec.gov/info/smallbus/qasbsec.htm

Securities and Exchange Commission. (2000, August). *Final rule: Selective disclosure and insider trading.* Retrieved May 18, 2004, from http://www.sec.gov/rules/final/33-7881.htm

Securities and Exchange Commission. (2000, August). *The laws that govern the securities industry.* Retrieved May 18, 2004, from http://www.sec.gov/about/laws.shtml

PUBLICS

Publics are specific groups of people who are linked by a common interest or problem. In modern public relations, there is no such thing as a "general public." Strategic public relations manages relationships with key publics on whom the success of the organization depends. Such publics are more homogeneous and more easily identified than a nebulous, general public. Most organizations have a diverse set of publics derived from what an organization does and whom it affects. Some of these publics require constant and long-range relationships, whereas others exist as temporary and short-term relationships, as we discuss below.

Public relations is managed strategically when it is designed to build and maintain relationships with the publics most crucial to the success of the organization. The key to effective public relations is systematically identifying key publics and appropriately prioritizing these publics according to the situation. James E. Grunig and Fred Repper defined three stages in the strategic management of public relations: the stakeholder stage, the public stage, and the issue stage. Following this framework, publics can be identified in three ways: relationship to the organization (stakeholder stage), relationship to the situation (public stage), and relationship to the public relations strategy (issue stage).

RELATIONSHIP TO THE ORGANIZATION

Publics' relationships to the organization are usually identified with a stakeholder analysis. J. E. Grunig and Repper defined a stakeholder as "people who are linked to an organization because they and the organization have consequences on each other" (1992, p. 125). In the stakeholder stage, public relations should engage in environmental scanning, conduct research on stakeholders, and build and maintain relationships with key stakeholders. The first step in a stakeholder analysis is to identify publics based on the consequences they and the organization have on each other. One approach to identifying stakeholder publics is to consider how they are "linked" to the organization.

J. E. Grunig and Todd Hunt (1984) used a linkage model based on the work of Milton Esman (1972), William Evan (1976), and Talcott Parsons (1976) to identify stakeholder relationships to organizations. The resulting model has four linkages that identify stakeholder relationships to an organization: enabling linkages, functional linkages, diffused linkages, and normative linkages.

ENABLING AND FUNCTIONAL LINKAGES

Enabling linkages are those that allow organizations to exist, such as relationships with government regulators and legislators. Functional linkages are those that allow the organization to function, by providing the resources (such as labor and raw materials) for the company to exist and market products or services. Organizations must maintain frequent communication with enabling and functional linkages to develop healthy long-term relationships, because the stakeholders in these linkages can have immediate consequences on the organization. The enabling linkages identify stakeholders who have some control and authority over the organization, such as stockholders, board of directors, governmental legislators and agencies, and so on. These stakeholders enable an organization to have resources and autonomy to operate. When enabling relationships falter, the resources can be withdrawn and the autonomy of the organization restricted.

Applying systems theory, J. E. Grunig and Hunt divided the functional linkages into input linkages and output linkages. Employees, unions, suppliers, contractors, and others link themselves with an organization by what they provide to the creation of an organization's products or services. Consumers, corporate purchasers, outlets, and other individuals or agencies that use the organization's products or services comprise the output linkage. Functional stakeholders are essential to the day-to-day operations of any organization and necessitate an open flow of communication.

NORMATIVE AND DIFFUSED LINKAGES

Normative linkages are associations or groups with which the organization has a common interest. Diffused linkages are those in which the organization must respond to sporadic publics such as activists or special interest groups. Communication and interaction with the diffused and normative linkages are less frequent and tend to focus on short-term relationships or crises. Stakeholders with a normative linkage to an organization share similar values, goals, or problems. Many organizations belong to industrial or professional associations made up of competitors and peer institutions, or align themselves with political action committees to address common issues. The organizations that have the most systematic public relations programs with normative publics are the associations that represent the collective interests of their members.

Stakeholders belonging to the diffused linkage often identify themselves when the organization does something that affects them, in which case they would become an active public. These publics include members of the community, environmental groups, the media, voters, and other groups that organize to face a situation involving an organization. Diffused publics are usually situational and their relationship to the organization is often temporary. They attempt to affect the organization by working through members of the enabling or functional linkages. Appeals to governmental regulation and calls for boycotts represent such attempts.

Sometimes the organization identifies the publics needed to accomplish its goals and objectives (these are often the enabling and functional linkage publics). Sometimes the publics identify themselves (these often come from the diffused linkage). When publics begin to organize, public relations efforts move from the stakeholder stage to the public stage.

RELATIONSHIP TO THE SITUATION

Publics organize from among the ranks of stakeholders when they recognize a problem and decide to do something to seek redress. According to John Dewey (1927), a public is a group of people who face a similar problem, recognize the problem, and organize themselves to do something about the problem. Dewey explained a public as a group that evolves around a situation.

Building on the Dewey definition of a public, J. E. Grunig (1983) developed a situational theory of publics to segment them based on active or passive communication behavior. Those publics who do not face a problem are *nonpublics,* those who face the problem but do not recognize it as problematic are *latent publics,* those who recognize the problem are *aware publics,* and those who do something about the problem are *active publics.*

J. E. Grunig's variables that help predict whether a public will be a nonpublic, latent, aware, or active are: level of involvement, level of problem recognition, level of constraint recognition, and information seeking versus information processing behavior. Level of involvement is measured by the extent to which people connect themselves personally with the situation. However, people do not seek or process information unless they recognize the connection, which is the level of problem recognition. Whether people move beyond information processing to the information seeking behavior of active publics often depends on whether they think they can do something about the problem. Those who think that nothing can be done have high constraint recognition and are less compelled to become active in the resolution of the problem. Another consideration, referent criteria, is the guideline that people apply to new situations based on previous experiences with the issue or the organization involved.

By breaking down publics according to their perceived relationship to the issue, communication messages and strategies become clearer. Latent publics need more information about the issue to help them recognize the problem. Aware publics with high constraint recognition need information about how they can become involved and make a difference. Active publics seek information and are predisposed to act, so the strategy should focus on two-way communication strategies that involve the publics in the issue. (*See* Situational theory of publics for information on how these groups can be further segmented into all-issue, apathetic, single-issue, and hot-issue publics.)

RELATIONSHIP TO THE STRATEGY OR TACTIC

When publics have organized themselves around an issue, public relations management moves to the issue stage. In this stage, public relations managers engage in communication strategies such as issues management, public information campaigns, symmetrical negotiation, and crisis communication. As stated before, for any organization to accomplish its stated goals and objectives, it needs the participation and cooperation of its key stakeholders. Targeting the key publics for strategic public relations efforts is a critical step. According to Laurie J. Wilson (2000), there are three types of publics to consider when developing public relations strategies: target publics, intervening publics, and influentials.

The publics whose participation and cooperation are required to accomplish organizational goals are the target publics. To communicate effectively with these publics, an organization must understand them as much as possible. Target publics can be profiled by their demographics, lifestyles and values, media preferences, influentials, and self-interests. Effective strategies appeal to the self-interests of the target publics and reach them through the most appropriate channels. At the same time, knowing publics according to these characteristics will help an organization plan goals consistent with its publics' needs and interests.

The intervening publics pass information on to the target publics and act as opinion leaders. Sometimes these publics, such as the media, are erroneously identified as target publics. If an organization is satisfied when the message stops at a public, then it is a target public. If the expectation is that the message will be disseminated to others, it is an intervening public. In most cases the media are intervening publics. Other influentials can be important intervening publics, such as doctors who pass information on to patients and teachers who pass information on to students. The success of many campaigns is determined by the strength of relationships with intervening publics.

Influentials can be intervening publics, but they also affect the success of public relations efforts in other ways. Influentials can either support an organization's efforts or work against them. Members of some publics will turn to opinion leaders to verify or refute messages coming from organizations. The opinion of these personal sources is much more influential than the public relations messages alone. Therefore, successful campaigns must also consider how messages will be interpreted by influentials that act as either intervening or supporting publics.

STAKEHOLDERS, PUBLICS, AND MARKETS

There are subtle differences among the terms *stakeholder, public,* and *market.* Stakeholders are always connected to the organization by consequence, and smaller publics organize from this broader group in concern with a particular issue. Publics are different from markets in that publics usually arise and organize on their own and markets are created by the organization. Publics are usually more active than markets and often do not have an exchange-based relationship with the organization as markets do. Careful segmentation of publics can help a public relations program reach only those who care about the issue or message, at the appropriate information and education level to be understood, and can ultimately prevent waste of funds on publics who care little about the issue at hand. Employed symmetrically, the concept of publics is an essential element of building and maintaining relationships with those groups most vital to the organization.

—Brad L. Rawlins and Shannon A. Bowen

See also Situational theory of publics; Stakeholder theory; Symmetry

Bibliography

Cutlip, S. M., Center, A. H., & Broom, G. M. (2000). *Effective public relations* (8th ed.). Upper Saddle River, NJ: Prentice Hall.

Dewey, J. (1927). *The public and its problems.* Chicago: Swallow.

Esman, M. (1972). The elements of institution building. In J. W. Eaton (Ed.), *Institution building and development* (pp. 19–40). Beverly Hills: Sage.

Evan, W. (1976). An organization-set model of interorganizational relations. In W. M. Evan (Ed.), *Interorganizational relations* (pp. 78–90). New York: Penguin.

Grunig, J. E. (1983). Communication behaviors and attitudes of environmental publics: Two studies. *Journalism Monographs,* No. 81.

Grunig, J. E., & Hunt, T. (1984). *Managing public relations.* New York: Holt, Rinehart & Winston.

Grunig, J. E., & Repper, F. C. (1992). Strategic management, publics, and issues. In J. E. Grunig (Ed.), *Excellence in public relations and communication management* (pp. 117–157). Hillsdale, NJ: Lawrence Erlbaum.

Parsons, T. (1976). Three levels in the hierarchical structure of organizations. In W. M. Evan (Ed.), *Interorganizational relations* (pp. 69–78). New York: Penguin.

Wilson, L. (2000). *Strategic program planning for effective public relations campaigns* (3rd ed.). Dubuque, IA: Kendall/Hunt.

PUFFERY

Puffery is the use of unsubstantiated praise or vague or implied claims in advertising, publicity, and other forms of promotional communication. The claims are intended to enhance the attributes of the subject and often take the form of exaggerations (e.g., "whiter than white" and "miracle cleaner"), superlatives (e.g., "best," "ultimate," "tastiest," and "sexiest"), vague adjectives (e.g., "brilliant," "amazing," "exceptional," and "great"), or opinions, which may not be attributed to anyone. From a legal standpoint, a distinguishing characteristic of puffery is that it consists of statements of value or opinion, not of fact. The attributes claimed are impossible to measure, confirm, or deny because they are a matter of taste or individual judgment.

Puffery is associated with the early press-agentry tactics of public relations, such as P. T. Barnum's classic slogan to promote his circus, "the greatest show on earth." Although puffery continues to be an accepted and ubiquitous practice in advertising, its use in public relations is widely denounced within the field today. It is viewed as amateurish and ineffective because it sacrifices long-term credibility for short-term public attention. Many journalists will immediately disregard publicity pitches that rely on puffery rather than factual information.

The continued use of puffery in public relations contributes to a negative image of public relations practitioners as "flacks."

LEGAL AND ETHICAL IMPLICATIONS

The United States Federal Trade Commission (FTC) permits the use of puffery in promoting products, services, and ideas. Promotional materials, such as press kits, videos, brochures, and other collateral, are viewed as vehicles of commercial trade and subject to regulation by the FTC. Although there may appear to be a fine line between puffery and deceptive advertising, there are legal distinctions. U.S. courts have repeatedly upheld the legality of puffery. The courts' rationale is that it should be expected that "any seller will express a favorable opinion concerning what he has to sell; and when he praises it in general terms . . . buyers are expected to and do understand that they are not entitled to rely literally upon the words" (*Restatement of the Law of Torts* 48, 1965, para. 542). Guidelines created by the FTC to define deceptive advertising exclude puffery, noting, "The commission generally will not bring advertising cases based on subjective claims, such as taste, feel, appearance or smell" (*FTC Policy Statement on Deceptive Acts and Practices,* 1983).

Puffery becomes deceptive only when it falsely claims the substantive superiority of a product or service, and when it can be demonstrated that the false claim is likely to affect consumer choices. The law pertaining to false advertising under Section 43(a) of the Lanham Act requires that plaintiffs demonstrate that the ad or promotion is either literally false or that it is likely to mislead and confuse consumers. To prove that it is misleading, the plaintiff must introduce empirical evidence of the statement's impact on consumers. The bottom line: As long as claims are so vague or subjective that they cannot be directly tested or substantiated, they are considered puffery and are legal. Puffery cannot be false representation, because it does not include statements of fact.

In a 2001 case involving two U.S. pizza chains, Pizza Hut sued Papa John's, claiming its slogan, "Better Ingredients. Better Pizza," was false advertising. The Fifth Circuit Court ruled that the slogan was mere puffery, a vague expression of opinion. In addition, the court ruled that Pizza Hut provided insufficient evident to show that consumers purchased Papa John's pizza because they believed the company used better ingredients. However, Papa John's was ordered to stop making more specific claims about the superiority of its dough and sauce. Because these were material, measurable claims, they were not considered puffery and were unprotected if not substantiated.

There are other legal considerations related to puffery that should be of concern to public relations practitioners. Statements of puffery in advertising and promotional materials may unintentionally create express warranties that can leave a company vulnerable to consumer lawsuits. Agencies and individual practitioners may be legally liable if it can be shown that they participated in the production or dissemination of a statement that they knew, or should have known, was false or misleading. For publicly traded companies, puffery may present a potential conflict with securities laws that require companies to accurately report all information that might influence investors.

The Public Relations Society of America's Code of Professional Standards does not address puffery per se; however, its statement of professional values notes that "we adhere to the highest standards of accuracy and truth in advancing the interests of those we represent and in communicating with the public" (Public Relations Society of America, 2003, p. B16). Similarly, the American Association of Advertising Agencies' Creative Code states "we will not knowingly create advertising that contains false or misleading statements or exaggerations, visual or verbal, of claims insufficiently supported" (*Standards of Practice of the American Association of Advertising Agencies,* 1990).

Ivan Preston, a leading authority on the topic of puffery, as well other scholars and consumer advocates, have attacked puffery from ethical and legal standpoints and called for changes to address the legal loophole presented by puffery cases. Preston (1996) argued that puffery is, in fact, deceptive, because it causes consumers to more highly appraise the attributes of products and the importance of those attributes. Inflated expectations of the product's performance may in turn influence purchasing decisions. Targeting puffery to vulnerable populations, such as children or the elderly, raises particular ethical concerns.

AVOIDING PUFFERY IN PUBLIC RELATIONS WRITING

Public relations textbooks and the trade press discourage the use of puffery in public relations writing. Instead, media releases and other press materials should closely model the objective tone, factual substance, and concise characteristics of journalistic style. Adjectives praising a product or service and product claims should be substantiated or encapsulated in quotes from an identified source. Practitioners should also check for industry-specific guidelines for language use issued by the FTC, including those for the dietary supplement industry, Web site operators, home study courses, and environmental claims. Certain words, such as "new," "recyclable," and "biodegradable," may only be used if the product meets FTC guidelines for those words (Wilcox, Ault, Agee, & Cameron, 2001, p. 236).

—*Katherine N. Kinnick*

See also Barnum, P. T.; Press agentry; Spin

Bibliography

FTC Policy Statement on Deceptive Acts and Practices. (October 4, 1983). 4 Trade Reg. Rep. Paragraph 13,205 at 20,919.

Preston, I. L. (1996). *The great American blow-up: Puffery in advertising and selling* (2nd ed.). Madison: University of Wisconsin Press.

Public Relations Society of America. (2003). Member code of ethics. In *Public relations tactics/the blue book* (pp. B16–B18). New York: Author.

Restatement of the Law of Torts (2nd ed.). (1965). St. Paul, MN: American Law Institute.

Rotfeld, H. J., & Rotzoll, K. B. (1980). Is advertising puffery believed? *Journal of Advertising, 9*(3), 16–20.

Seib, P., & Fitzpatrick, K. (1995). *Public Relations Ethics.* Fort Worth, TX: Harcourt Brace.

Standards of Practice of the American Association of Advertising Agencies. (1990). Retrieved June 10, 2003, from http://www.aaaa.org/inside/standards.pdf

Wilcox, D. L., Ault, P. H., Agee, W. K., & Cameron, G. T. (2001). *Essentials of Public Relations.* New York: Longman.

PYRAMID STYLE

The pyramid style is used by journalists when writing news stories and public relations practitioners when writing media releases and other pieces. Using this format, the most important information goes at the top of the story and the least important information goes at the bottom.

In a media release, the pyramid begins with the "lead," the main purpose of the release that contains the news angle. This is followed by the five W's used by journalists—who, what, where, when, and why. At this point, usually a few sentences in length, the release should be able to stand on its own without additional details, if necessary. Supporting information comes next. Using this format, if the release is edited from the bottom, no critical information will be lost.

The pyramid style, also referred to as inverted pyramid style, may be used in other types of writing as well. For example, each entry in this encyclopedia is written in pyramid style. Just as an editor may read only the first few lines of a media release, readers of this book may not read each entry in its entirety. Therefore, each entry begins with a definition of the topic, an explanation of why it is important and basic information. The topic is then more fully discussed in subsequent paragraphs.

THE PYRAMID

Ronald D. Smith (2003) provided the following outline of the inverted pyramid used in public relations writing:

> *News lead.* This is the most important information. An editor should be able to read this first line or two and determine why the information is newsworthy—or why the media release should be thrown away.

Benefit statement. Once the newsworthy information has been clearly stated in the lead, the writer must show why the information is significant to the audience.

Secondary details. Any of the five W's not already mentioned come next. At this point, the audience should have all the information it needs to pursue the topic.

Background information. As the pyramid works its way to the bottom, it's time to add supporting information on the subject of the media release.

Action statement. The release closes with information on how the audience—not the media—can get more information on the topic.

Organizational identification. An optional component of the inverted pyramid is the organizational identification, a one- or two-line description of the organization's mission—what it does, why it exists. This should be consistent for every release regardless of the topic.

As mentioned earlier in this entry, reporters and public relations practitioners both write using the inverted pyramid format; however, benefit statements, action statements, and organizational identifications are exclusive to public relations and are not used by journalists when writing stories.

—*Ann R. Carden*

See also Media release

Bibliography

Smith, R. D. (2003). *Becoming a public relations writer* (2nd ed.). Mahwah, NJ: Lawrence Erlbaum.

Zappala, J. M., & Carden, A. R. (2004). *Public relations work-text* (2nd ed.). Mahwah, NJ: Lawrence Erlbaum.

QUALITATIVE RESEARCH

A large part of public relations research is found in the realm of qualitative research. Qualitative research—also called informal research methodology—is the gathering of information that is restricted to the setting in which it was obtained. Research employing a qualitative orientation includes data-gathering methodologies such as case study, historical and secondary, focus group, interviewing, and participant-observation. A sixth methodology often associated with qualitative research is content analysis, but its inclusion as a qualitative method has been questioned by its proponents, who argue that it is a quantitative method. Based on public relations use, it is considered an informal or qualitative method.

Many people misunderstand qualitative research. This usually stems from the assumption that *qualitative* means that numbers are not employed or assigned to the "data" gathered or that the research is devoid of theory. Qualitative research does employ numbers, and it is typically associated with *grounded theory*, or theory that arises from observations made in specific situations.

Data gathered using qualitative methods have a major restriction placed on their interpretation. The data are tied to the specific situation in which they were gathered. That is, the results cannot be generalized to a larger situation with any degree of confidence. This restriction is important, because misuse of qualitative research occurs most often either when data gathered for a case study are applied to a similar situation or when an interview is taken out of the context in which it was conducted and placed in a more general context.

Qualitative research does provide the researcher with several important advantages over its quantitative counterpart. First, the data are rich, in that they provide an in-depth understanding of a person, organization, event, or other research object. Second, the data gathered are not impersonal facts; they are value-based. John Hocking, Don Stacks, and Steven McDermott have argued that communication research asks four basic questions: what is it (definition), how much of it is observed (fact), how good is it (value), and what should be done (policy). All research methods address questions of definition, but qualitative methods are best at answering questions of value and policy (how well did the campaign do [value] and should we do it again [policy]), whereas quantitative methods are best at answering questions of fact and may address questions of value as population norms or normative expectations. Furthermore, whereas quantitative methods look at large numbers, qualitative methods look at small numbers; the quantitative survey may require 400 or more people to answer questions, whereas the interview may focus on only one person. What the survey provides is an understanding of what a large number of people think or will do and establishes norms; the interview examines significantly fewer people but provides a much fuller understanding of what each person thinks and why.

Third, qualitative methods provide an ex post facto understanding of the normative behaviors of larger groups. In this regard, qualitative research often expands upon what has been found in surveys and attempts to explain why the audience or public thought or behaved as it did. The key here is that the methods provide an explanation after the fact by choosing influential or appropriate people or messages. This, of course, means that qualitative methods cannot establish a cause-effect relationship, something only an experiment can do.

Fourth, qualitative methods work best when public relations requires environmental scanning or monitoring in relation to a specific public relations problem. Informal interviews, focus groups, content analyses, and participant-observation all establish expected behaviors from a day-to-day observation (or *ethnomethodology*); hence, these methods provide what Hickson noted as the daily activities of an ongoing organization or social unit. By focusing on daily events, researchers are informally looking for patterns that may or may not be followed, thus alerting them to possible problems.

QUALITATIVE METHODS

Qualitative methods are represented by at least six distinctly different ways of gathering information or data. Each differs from the others by the kind of information gathered and the amount of control that each provides the researcher. The first qualitative method, historical or secondary research, is found in almost all research methods, but is considered a qualitative method when the end result is the gathering of historical facts and figures (often this occurs during the definitional stage of a research project). Historical/secondary research can be broken into two complementary parts: strict data gathering and rhetorical analysis. Strict data gathering occurs when researchers examine extant documents found in libraries, databases, the media, and various industries to better understand a person, product, campaign, or industry. Thus, the historical or secondary method looks at primary (the actual reports or data), secondary (the data or reports as reported elsewhere, such as in the media or in books), or tertiary (reports of the published reports) sources. Rhetorical analysis takes that data and examines how it was used as a message by the messenger in specific situations or occasions. The key is that the information is extant; the research that produced it has already been published or presented in some fashion. All research methods—qualitative or quantitative—require historical/secondary research, but not all may include rhetorical analyses.

A second qualitative research method is the case study. The case study is an in-depth look at some person, organization, event, or campaign. It is specific to a particular problem, occasion, or opportunity, and the researcher controls what and how information is used in building the case. Case studies help in understanding why the particular object under study acted as it did or what lessons may be learned from its actions. Case studies are often used to establish business and public relations "best practices", examining how good business strategies or winning public relations campaigns operated. In some instances, looking at "worst practices" allows public relations practitioners to avoid pitfalls. As with all qualitative methods, however, the case study is unique and cannot be generalized to other cases, even if they are similar.

The interview is the third qualitative method employed in public relations. An interview provides in-depth information from an individual about themselves, events, or other things. The interview is controlled largely by interviewers, who have, through historical/secondary research, done background research on both the individual and the topic to be discussed. An interview schedule or questionnaire is then used to ensure that all relevant questions are answered and subsequent probe or extended questions are sometimes employed and the interviewee's responses are recorded for later analysis. In some instances, the interview of one person is the entire research project, such as an interview of the head of a leading public relations firm. Sometimes, several different interviews will be conducted—interviews with the heads of the top public relations firms, for example—to provide an understanding of a larger question. The key is that each interview is conducted separately from the others. Regardless of the number of interviews, the results are specific to those people interviewed at the specific time, place, and circumstances in which the interviewer found them.

Expanding the concept of interviews to a larger group of people "interviewed" at once is the underlying concept behind the focus group. The focus group method of research collects information from a group of participants who focus on a specific concern, concept, or product as led by a moderator. The moderator, like the interviewer, works from a set of prepared questions, but allows the participants to "tag" or expand on others' comments in the discussion. The focus group provides a variety of perspectives on the research object while maintaining group focus and cohesiveness through the moderator's direction. Focus groups typically consist of 5 to 15 members who meet at the same time in a room set up for the discussion. The discussion is usually recorded and transcribed for later analysis. Focus group research is also restricted in generalizing findings to larger audiences or the public due to the small number of participants and the fact that most members are volunteers, and thus do not represent a valid cross section of the larger group from which they are drawn.

Participant-observation is a qualitative method that is often overlooked in public relations research. Participant-observation requires that an individual become a part of a larger group—a company or a team, for example—and observe what occurs in daily interaction between members. As such, the researcher has no control over the group. The method's advantage is in the establishment of the group's norms or expected behaviors—its routines, rules for communication, and the roles that group members take on in different situations. Participant-observation takes a long time to conduct, but when approached from an informal basis it is something that all public relations people do

daily. Participant-observation may indicate the need for a larger research project based on whether the practitioner sees behavior that does not fit established norms. It is particularly effective as a method for gathering information when conducting an environmental scan or monitoring a problem.

The final qualitative method is content analysis. Although some question whether content analysis is a qualitative or a quantitative method, its use in public relations is most often seen as qualitative or informal. Content analysis provides a way to evaluate messages both objectively (by counting occurrences such as specific words, phrases, or graphics) or subjectively (by evaluating the themes or theses contained in messages). It approaches a quantitative, formal method in that certain rules for its conduct are established beforehand and the messages are then analyzed according to those rules. Because it works on messages that have already been uttered, written, presented, or published, it may fit better as a qualitative method; when used as a measurement instrument, however, it fits better as a quantitative method.

It should be noted that, within qualitative research, all methods may be employed. This is probably seen best in a case study in which extensive background (historical/secondary/rhetorical) research has been undertaken. To better understand what occurred in the case, interviews and focus groups may be conducted to obtain the points of view of the people involved with the case study. Participant-observation may have been employed, as the case may be something the researcher had actually been a part of and represents a reflective examination of what happened. Content analysis of important messages may provide insight into the communication strategies and tactics that were employed in the case. Employing multiple methods is called triangulation, and a good qualitative research study will use as many methods as possible to establish study validity.

—Don W. Stacks

See also Case study; Content analysis; Environmental scanning; Focus group; Interview as a research tool; Quantitative research; Theory-based practice

Bibliography

Hickson, M. (1974). Participant-observation technique in organizational research. *Journal of Business Communication, 11,* 37–42, 54.

Hocking, J., Stacks, D., & McDermott, S. (2003). *Communication Research* (3rd ed.). Boston: Allyn & Bacon.

Holsti, O. (1969). *Content analysis for the social sciences and humanities.* New York: Free Press.

Stacks, D. (Ed.). (2002). *Dictionary of public relations measurement and research.* Gainesville, FL: Institute for Public Relations.

Stacks, D. (2002). *Primer of public relations research.* New York: Guilford.

QUANTITATIVE RESEARCH

Quantitative research is almost always associated with the formal evaluation of numbers. That is, quantitative research is something that extends from the physical sciences to the social sciences and focuses on methods that follow certain prescribed rules for the gathering of, typically, numeric data. That said, it is important to understand that numbers by themselves have no meaning except the meaning that we establish in our theory. Quantitative research, then, focuses on research methods that allow researchers to say, with a certain degree of confidence, that something they systematically measured (via numbers) actually represents a larger number of people, or that something actually caused a change in something else.

The key to quantitative research is found in (1) measurement and (2) the collection of data in such a way that it can be reliably and validly interpreted when replicated by others. This, in turn, is found in the formal rules of quantitative research methods. These methods include survey research and experimental research, but arguments have been made to include content analysis as a formal, quantitative method. However, the majority of content-analytic studies focus on simple counts (Was a release picked up or not? Where or when was it reported?); thus, its use is more informal than formal. (It must be noted that thematic content analyses, which require a measurement item or scale for evaluation, may approach the formal nature of quantitative measurement.)

The key to any quantitative method is the gathering of data via some form of measurement. Measurement is the assigning of numbers to observations in a manner that has established validity and whose reliability can be assessed. All attempts at evaluating the attitudes, beliefs, or values of others requires the creation of some type of scale, a measure that focuses not on what is seen, but on what is unseen. Measurement scales attempt to identify how people will or have behaved, and why they behave in those ways. Once the data have been gathered, it is analyzed using statistical analysis. Because the responses to stimuli questions or experimental conditions are collected as numeric data, they are submitted to descriptive and/or inferential statistical analysis. This analysis collapses the individual responses to those of the group to which the individuals belong.

Quantitative research differs significantly from qualitative research in that quantitative research methods are not concerned with individual respondents per se. Users of quantitative research are more interested in how large numbers of subjects responded to stimuli. Thus, whereas qualitative methods provide rich data, quantitative methods provide normative data that can be parsed according to demographic or psychographic differences.

Part of quantitative research involves how data are collected. Because it is impossible to follow all members of a population around or ask them questions regarding their intentions to exhibit a behavior, quantitative research samples from a population in an effort to draw conclusions from the sampling. Public relations research often surveys respondents from some population to better understand how people feel or will behave. Some sampling techniques allow for conclusions that describe only those people who might have been available at the time of data collection. Other sampling techniques allow conclusions to be drawn about the larger population from which the sample was obtained. The former sampling techniques are called *nonprobability* (or *convenience*) sampling, whereas the latter are called *probability* sampling.

Sampling also occurs in experimental research. Experimental sampling is not concerned with generalizing to a larger population. Instead, it is employed to ensure that participants are chosen in such a way as to discount any possible biases that participants may bring with them to the experiment.

SURVEY

The dominant quantitative research method found in public relations is the survey or poll. Polls are distinguished from surveys by their length and the type of information that each attempts to obtain. Polls are very short—often comprising no more than 10 questions, including demographic or psychographic information—and last a few minutes at most. Surveys are longer, often taking over 15 minutes to complete, and attempt to delve into the reasoning behind why respondents think or act as they do. Both polls and surveys sample from a larger population.

When respondents are randomly selected from the population in such a way that any member could have participated in the study—a probability sample—the results can be generalized to that larger population. When respondents are selected due to availability or because of certain characteristics—a nonprobability sample—the results are limited in their ability to be generalized beyond those people surveyed or polled. Probability sampling allows researchers to estimate both how accurately they sampled the population and the potential for error in the measurement of respondents' answers. Nonprobability sampling, while allowing for estimates of measurement error, cannot establish sampling accuracy because the sample was not drawn at random.

There are two basic survey or poll types. The most common is the "snapshot," wherein one set of respondents is surveyed or polled once. When researchers are interested in what people think over time, a cross-sectional survey or poll is conducted. Cross-sectional surveys or polls measure from a population at various times and allow for comparison, and are often called "longitudinal" research designs. Cross-sectional designs are of three types: trend, in which different snapshots are taken from different samples over time; panel, in which the same sample is measured at various points in time; and the cohort-trend design, which follows different groups who share certain characteristics, such as age (e.g., a yearly survey of 18-year-olds of their views on voting).

Surveys or polls can be conducted in a variety of ways. Most commonly, respondents are asked questions over the telephone. Other ways of contacting people to gather survey or poll data include physical, person-to-person contact whereby a formal interview is conducted; the mail questionnaire, in which a questionnaire is printed and mailed to respondents; and the electronic (Internet or fax) method, in which questionnaires are sent to respondents via facsimile or on the Internet.

EXPERIMENTS

The experiment is rarely found in public relations research. Experiments typically test theoretical relationships between concepts and are the only way that a researcher can infer that something actually caused something else to occur. Experiments are highly controlled and contrived research projects that establish, in isolation, the impact of one variable (a concept or idea that has been defined in such a way as to be potentially observable or measured) on another. Experimental variables are either measured (the dependent variable) or manipulated (the independent variable) under highly controlled circumstances. It is this control that allows the researcher to say within a certain degree of confidence that the impact of changing the independent variable caused a change in the dependent variable. Further, because of the formal nature of experimental measurement, the dependent variable's reliability and validity can be established and compared to preestablished accepted norms.

The experiment also allows very sophisticated statistical analyses to be conducted. Because of the experiment's controlled nature, the direction of and confidence in the impact of one variable on another can be estimated and presented within those set acceptance levels (typically a 95 percent level of confidence that one variable caused a change in the other variable). Further, because the relationships between the variables have been theoretically established, the impact of several independent variables on one or more dependent variables can also be examined.

The experiment is a very powerful research method. Its very power, however, is also a limitation. Whereas a random survey of a sample allows researchers to generalize results to the larger population, the experiment's generalizability is almost nonexistent. The experiment's need for control makes findings difficult to extend to other contexts, but it does tell us that under the same circumstances a causal relationship will exist.

—Don W. Stacks

See also Experiment/experimental methods; Measuring/measures; Reliability; Sampling; Scales; Statistical analysis; Survey; Validity

Bibliography

Holsti, O. (1969). *Content analysis for the social sciences and humanities*. New York: Free Press.

Pavlik, J. (1987). *Public relations: What research tells us*. Newbury Park, CA: Sage.

Stacks, D. (Ed.). (2002). *Dictionary of public relations measurement and research*. Gainesville, FL: Institute for Public Relations.

Stacks, D. (2002). *Primer of public relations research*. New York: Guilford.

RACE AND CRISIS COMMUNICATION

Organizations face a wide range of potential crises ranging from rumors about the company, to environmental catastrophe, to product tampering and consumer death. By their nature, crises can be, to some degree, anticipated but not completely eliminated. All crises have the potential to inflict harm to the organizational image, but few are as potentially damaging as those involving race. Such crises have the potential to garner significant negative attention from the public, press, and important stakeholders.

Racially oriented crises have affected large companies such as Texaco, Denny's, and Cracker Barrel restaurants as well as smaller groups and organizations and even state and local governments. Although it is impossible to completely inoculate a company from racial crises, a thorough and annual review of practices and communications can identify potential for racial crises in areas such as hiring practice and procedures or customer relations. However, a racial crisis can erupt from a single statement or event.

Researcher Gail F. Baker (2001) has written that racial crises generally take one of three forms: actions, words, or symbols. Restaurants refusing to serve members of a particular ethnic population, or an organization with an apparent history of failure to hire or promote members from a particular population are two examples of activities that can and have resulted in racially oriented crises stemming from actions. Public or even private communication from a prominent member of an organization that includes racial slurs or other derogatory comments would be an example of words leading to a potential racial crisis. However, even a less prominent member of an organization (e.g., a mid-level manager) can create a similar crisis with the use of inappropriate words. In the heat of crisis escalation, if the organization does not separate itself from the individual, that person can be characterized as representative of the whole organization, thus fostering the crisis. Corporate or organizational symbols could include a logo, caricature, or design that is associated with the organization. Such symbols can, and have, led to crises requiring some form of change on the organization's part. A prominent example of such change was seen when high school, college, and professional teams across the nation changed their mascots from names or caricatures that might have been deemed offensive to some groups to images that moved away from potentially derogatory ethnic identification. For example, many teams formerly called "Redskins" were renamed with tribe names from their region.

When a racially oriented crisis occurs, organizations must respond quickly with the crisis response strategy that they deem appropriate. The full range of crisis strategies can come into play, from denial to capitulation. Organizations responding to racially oriented crises need to carefully measure the current level of attention to the alleged wrongdoing, the assessment of their own level of error, the type of response desired by affected publics and stakeholders, and the costs and appropriateness of those responses. Decision making, which includes all of those factors, will frequently not lead to an obvious decision on the appropriate steps to take, thus making the public relations or crisis manager's decision a difficult one.

*—David E. Williams
and Bolanle A. Olaniran*

See also Crisis and crisis management; Crisis communication; Exxon and the *Valdez* crisis

Bibliography

Baker, G. F. (2001). Race and reputation: Restoring image beyond the crisis. In R. L. Heath (Ed.), *Handbook of Public Relations* (pp. 513–520). Thousand Oaks, CA: Sage.

Coombs, W. T. (1995). Choosing the right words: The development of guidelines for the selection of the "appropriate" crisis-response strategies. *Management Communication Quarterly, 8,* 447–476.

Coombs, W. T. (1999). *Ongoing crisis communication: Planning, managing, and responding.* Thousand Oaks, CA: Sage.

RAILROAD INDUSTRY IN THE 19TH CENTURY

The railroad industry dramatically changed the United States during the 19th century. It gave rationale and lots of work to journalists and other writers who molded the practice of public relations. In that regard, the railroads helped spawn the public relations profession.

The relationship was synergistic. Public relations helped gain acceptance for this essential element of the U.S. infrastructure at a time when it met lots of resistance. It was noisy and spewed sparks. It scared people and farm animals. It was opposed because it competed with established modes of transportation. Public relations added to the ability of railroad entrepreneurs to gain legislative support for their innovation. Once the railroads were beginning their operation, they needed to expand. They would die without markets for their services. They used far-reaching promotion campaigns to attract riders and freight.

Before, during, and after the Civil War, vast regions of the East, Midwest, Southwest, and Far West began to open to farmers and merchants. Railroads followed and facilitated westward migration. Minerals, farm products, and other resources could now be moved over longer distances. All of this activity was a source of raw materials, labor, and markets for new industrial products, especially farm implements and other industrial equipment.

As it was introduced to the fledgling railroad industry, society was hesitant to adopt this industrial beast that shocked citizens' sensibilities of safety. The industry truly was unsafe. Engines could start fires along the lines. Employees worked at great risk, a problem that persisted into the 20th century. Newspaper editors and other concerned citizens alarmed citizens to the peril of this industrial monster.

By 1850 much of this opposition had waned. Events demonstrated the virtue of rail transportation. Towns welcomed the arrival of railroad service. Bands played. Politicians spoke. Local militia marched and displayed community enthusiasm for the trains that brought mail, relatives and friends, and freight.

The Civil War demonstrated the virtues of an efficient rail system. Without doubt, one of the advantages of the Union during the war was superior ability to move men and materials strategically and quickly. The Civil War also cost the lives and working ability of thousands of men in the prime of life. Immigrants were needed to open the new regions of the nation, exploit its resources, and supply industrial labor needs.

Public relations was a fledgling profession at the time. The broad array of newspapers served as a primary mass medium supplying information and appeals to a broad set of audiences. This medium, coupled with other forms of communication, became widely and enthusiastically applied to publicize and promote railroads and the countryside they opened to domestic and foreign laborers and families looking for a better future.

Railroads needed settlers. They were heavily subsidized by a federal government willing to give land, which could be sold to finance railroad construction and operation. To turn raw land into operating capital, the executives of the rail industry turned to professional communicators to get the word out that land was available. Opportunity awaited those who were bold. Bounty was to be had for the taking. This migration would sell land. Farmers would produce crops. They would need supplies and equipment. Towns would spring up like prairie flowers in spring. Vast fortunes would be made. States would be established. Minerals would be brought east to the manufacturing centers. The nation, and its citizens, would prosper. Popular culture would develop as legends abandoned facts. Even the motion picture industry, not even born, would use the West and railroads as the fodder of countless visions on the flickering screen. No longer was the western migration moving at the speed of plodding animals pulling wagons. The scream of the whistle time and again announced a new force firing the nation. This was a dream. But people needed to get the message and fall in love with the dream.

The publicity effort in one sense was simple. Newspaper persons were hired by railroad companies or thriving communities to write books and favorable news stories that would reach target audiences. Or newspaper persons were given free trips with ample adventure and boosterism conversations. Countless writers strained their thesauruses to find ever more glowing terms to fuel the migration. These messages were translated into languages of all of the people of Europe and even China, where labor was abundant and times were hard.

As is ever the case with companies, railroad companies needed to achieve name recognition. Regions and towns were made legendary by the names that became embedded in popular culture: Baltimore & Ohio; Southern Pacific; Northern Pacific; Great Northern; Burlington; Atchison, Topeka, and Sante Fe; Denver & Rio Grande; Illinois Central; Southern Pacific. The Southern Pacific knew that it needed markets to be viable. Even before its rails reached Los Angeles, its publicist, Charles Nordhoff, was hired. He was a reporter for the *New York Evening Post* who understood the Eastern press. He wrote *California for Health, Pleasure and Residence,* published in 1872, to attract a wide array of readers who identified with those motives.

Publicity was used to demonstrate to influential citizens the need for certain routes. Owners attracted investors and built relationships with legislators. These relationships often led to problematic business relationships. Perhaps the worst was the willingness of legislators to overlook the railroads' notorious lack of safety. Railroad operations killed or injured workers by the hundreds. Safety devices solved part of the problem, but labor relations were a constant source for the need of public relations.

As much as it needed continuing government relations, the industry fostered publicity and promotion. Techniques developed by the industry became the stock and trade for the profession. Investors needed to be assured that each company operated in ways that protected and promoted the interests of shareholders. Personal contacts were always important. Rail leaders wanted to be able to talk personally with legislators, newspaper people, investors, and influential local citizens. Favorable press was sought. Boosterism was the constant message set before this array of publics. The industry hired lobbyists. Prominent citizens from other walks of life could look forward to being paid for their opinions on extending railroad routes, as well as for their defense of rates and safety records.

Promotion required an endless string of favorable newspaper stories. Meetings and conventions were held. Some were staged events that in turn could be the subject of favorable news reports and editorials. Advertising was widely used. Newspapers that needed advertising dollars might be less willing to write harsh and accurate stories about the industry.

Secret press agents were widely employed. Reporters and editors were offered free passes. A trade association sponsoring the industry publication, *Railway Age,* established in 1880 a Bureau of Information. Executives were quite willing to commission and fund favorable books and articles. Railway staff might write such articles and then look for prominent citizens who would lend their names as authors. The objective was to get opinion leaders to support and promote the industry. Such leaders were co-opted to be "objective" spokespersons for the industry in an effort to attract support of other power elites. Local officials within a community—or even the governor—could often be relied on to participate in ground-breaking ceremonies.

Guidebooks and pamphlets were published in huge quantities. These publicity tools extolled the virtues of the West as the land of opportunity. Often quite shoddy in content as well as publication standards, these tools were often remarkable in their exaggeration. Wealth and health were standard themes. They featured opportunity to virtually every segment of the U.S. and European populations. They placed stories in European newspapers to attract investors, labor, and customers. They exploited chance circumstances. Having no role in the discovery of minerals in the West, they were quick to broadcast discoveries to lure passengers to gold fields and merchants to prey on miners. They hauled ore and supplied workers with food and dry goods. They made markets that they in turn served—the true mark of the entrepreneur.

To residents in crowded cities and disparate parts of the world, the vast expanse of the American West had huge appeal. Land offices were opened where people were likely to be looking for opportunity. Pamphlets were published in English, German, French, and the languages of Scandinavia and Eastern Europe. Letters from "success story" authors were placed in influential newspapers. These manufactured firsthand accounts were carried by emigrants as "contracts" of their new and bountiful future. To persons accustomed to thinking of land parcels in the few acres, dreams of vast and unclaimed acreages in the thousands were irresistible.

Without doubt one of the greatest publicity stunts of American culture occurred on May 10, 1869, at Promontory Point near Ogden, Utah. Dignitaries drove spikes of gold and silver to celebrate the creation of a transcontinental railroad by linking the Union Pacific and Central Pacific. Another burgeoning industry made the event even more dramatic. Telegraph wires were attached to the heads of the hammers and to spikes. Each time a hammer struck a spike that message was transmitted to awaiting news reporters, dignitaries, and the general citizen. This moment created a new word for the American vocabulary—transcontinental.

Practitioners, as the railroad industry demonstrated, were vital to gaining attention and creating meaning that became part of a culture. They helped to create a way of thinking and acting. They also engaged in defensive efforts to protect an industry challenged on safety issues by workers and by customers who fought for fair rates. Railroads helped to create the full range of activities associated with public relations.

—*Robert L. Heath*

See also Event; Government relations; Pamphlet; Promotion; Publicity; Trade associations (and Hill & Knowlton's role in)

Bibliography

Cutlip, S. M. (1995). *Public relations history: From the 17th to the 20th century.* Hillsdale, NJ: Lawrence Erlbaum.

Raucher, A. R. (1968). *Public relations and business: 1900–1929.* Baltimore, MD Johns Hopkins University Press.

REACH

Reach, as used in public relations, remains close to the general definition of the verb *to reach,* although in public relations it most often appears as a noun. As a verb, *reach* has been in the English language since the 16th century, according to the *Oxford English Dictionary* (OED), originally meaning to stretch out, extend, thrust, to touch or grasp, often by extending a part of the body (usually a hand). Today, according to *Webster's New Collegiate Dictionary*, *reach* also means to make an impression on, to communicate or, as a noun, the distance or extent of reaching or the ability to reach. This meaning comes closest to our usage in public relations as well as in marketing and advertising. Of course, today, reach goes far beyond the hand or voice.

In public relations, reach is useful as a measure. Reach refers to the number of connections a public relations program, campaign, or even press release achieves within the targeted audience. Reach may be defined to include the quality of connections. Many people who heard the campaign message that "seatbelts save lives" did not act. They were reached with the message but not motivated to act, to use seatbelts. To motivate the audience to "buckle up" took legislative clout in addition to the educational message.

Reach may also define the distance a public relations message travels as it connects. In today's global economy, public relations often must plan for global reach. A press release sent to and published by an energy trade publication in Houston, Texas, may be read in Melbourne, Australia, and Aberdeen, Scotland. Today's public relations message may require a global reach within a targeted segment of the world's population.

Whatever the distance, reach within a public relations campaign indicates the connectivity within the targeted audience. A press release announcing business news that is published in a daily newspaper may be read by many who are outside the target population and of no interest to the sending organization. Reach, to be useful, is defined within the target. The reach may be broken into levels. It may ripple out from the primary receiver. In the daily newspaper example, there is first the media that receive the release, narrowed to those that use it. Next are those who read the article and are a part of the targeted audience, then those who learn by word of mouth. Beyond those groups within the target audience, in keeping with the goals and objectives of the campaign, the reach of the message has minimal or no usefulness to the business. For instance, the popular AT&T advertising campaign slogan "Reach out and touch someone" is

still alive and well. In a Google search, it yielded 18,800 entries, long after the campaign was ended. Most have no mention of (or value to) AT&T at all.

The question arises: How do we identify the reach, how do we count it, how do we evaluate it? Instruments exist, but measuring public relations reach is far from an exact science, even today. Clippings count the media publishing press release information. Circulation numbers count those receiving (but not necessarily reading) the information. A direct mail letter reaches those on the mailing list, or if it doesn't and it went first class, subtracting letters returned from letters sent gives a close estimate but doesn't include letters received but not read. If the campaign asks the recipients to take a measurable action, the number who do so provides a qualitative reach figure to go along with the quantitative reach (those receiving the letter). These are simple instruments used only as an example.

To go full circle, to be useful in measuring the outcome reach must be an integral element for consideration and definition at the very beginning. Reach must be incorporated into the goals and objectives of a public relations effort. It must be a part of the plan.

—*Barbara Langham*

See also Campaign; Measuring/measures; Public relations research; Research goals; Research objectives

REGULATED MONOPOLIES

Regulated monopolies are organizations that are granted the legal right to operate in an environment where there is freedom from competition. The grant to operate in this manner is given by governmental agencies, and there is recognition that the monopoly is counter to traditional free-market theory and policy.

To offset the freedom from competition, the granting agencies may stipulate a variety of conditions that may include, but may not be limited to, the rates charged customers, the services that are to be rendered, the required amount of infrastructure building and maintenance, and the level of services that are required of the monopoly holder. Because of this unique arrangement, organizations operating regulated monopolies have need of business and public relations strategies to support their continued successful operations. Effective strategies must reflect the history and role of the regulated monopoly in the economic system.

The concept of the regulated monopoly in the United States began at the end of the 19th century and start of the 20th century. Prior to the late 19th century, the governmental philosophy at the federal, state, and local levels was generally one of laissez-faire—keep government out of regulation and let competition determine the provider of services. Government recognized the importance of competition, and in 1890 the Sherman Antitrust Act was passed to reduce monopolies and ensure competition. President Theodore Roosevelt used the act in the early part of the 20th century to attack the power of the industrial trusts. The growth of the industrial empires and the monopolies that they created and the resulting abuses of economic power became issues of public discussion. For example, unregulated railroads that had monopolies in certain areas of the United States could charge shipping rates that made it difficult for producers to maintain a profit for their ventures because shipping rates were set very high by the monopolistic rail carrier.

Much of the impetus for government action was the public discussion of the economic abuses by large monopolistic organizations caused by the writings of journalists called *muckrakers* by President Theodore Roosevelt while he was in office in New York. He later came to respect the writings of the muckrakers as they supported him as he sought to ensure competition in the American economic system. These writers and their publishers centered articles on the alleged economic and social hardships that the monopolistic organizations had created in society.

Out of this environment grew the regulated monopoly. The concept was used to ensure that essential services would be provided at reasonable economic cost, but the possibility for abuse was to be diminished by governmental control. Many of the controlled monopolies were created out a need for services, but where the cost of providing duplicate investments that would ensure competitive services was economically unfeasible. Examples of these monopolies were municipal water, sewer, and telephone systems, and electrical and gas systems. These services are often provided by corporations owned and operated by municipalities (municipal corporations). In many communities these vital services are provided by for-profit private corporations. The following discussions are premised on the idea that the regulated monopoly is a business entity that is privately owned or a corporation that is owned by stockholders. In most states municipal corporations as well as for-profit corporations are regulated by policies of a state board or regulatory commission. In some states these boards and regulatory commissions are elected; in others these boards and commissions are appointed, usually by the governor with confirmation of the appointees granted to the legislature, often the higher-ranking body if the legislature is bicameral.

The monopoly may be granted through license, contract, or franchise. In most states and communities the monopoly is granted for a period of time and must be renewed from time to time through a prescribed set of state regulations. These regulations, as noted earlier, may also indicate the rates, level of service, and other requirements. If rates are to be increased, or in some cases decreased, the rate change must be sought and received through the regulatory agency.

Public attitudes about regulated monopolies may change over time. Two examples may be considered. In the early part of the 20th century, much of the U.S. telephone system was controlled by regulated monopolies, especially AT&T. In the last quarter of the 20th century, the government and the courts moved strongly to end many of the monopolistic practices and to deregulate the industry. It was argued that technology made it economically possible to have competing providers. The argument was also made that competition would result in better service at lower cost. A similar, ongoing, and unresolved example is the public school system, which is, of course, a publicly owned and operated system.

Advocates of privatizing the public school systems argue that the public schools are a regulated monopoly and that competition would result in better schools at lower cost. Many same-thinking individuals suggest that all services provided by governmental regulated monopolies could better serve the society if privatized.

An organization that is a regulated monopoly must develop business and public relations strategies that will allow it to function effectively in the environment in which it exists. The strategic challenges for the regulated monopoly are similar in many ways to those of organizations operating in the private realm, but the regulated monopoly must recognize its unique place in the environment.

Key to the effectiveness of public relations strategies for the regulated monopoly is to recognize those publics that will influence its ability to function effectively. Among the publics that must be considered are the customers or clients, the regulators and policymakers, the activists concerned with the industry or service, the media, employees, and any of their organizations such as unions, suppliers, and political forces that may have dominion over the environment in which the regulated monopoly exists.

Perhaps the most intriguing challenge for the regulated monopoly is the building of relationships with the regulators. Individuals appointed to the boards or commissions that regulate the monopoly are usually selected through the political process and often represent the political and economic philosophy of the dominant political power. The person or persons appointed to such boards and commissions have the power to regulate, and, therefore, they are critical to success for the organization. Regulated monopolies must understand and become involved in the selection process of the regulatory boards or commissions. There may be many relationships that have to be built. If the individuals appointed are named by an executive, such as a governor, elected county executive, or mayor, it is imperative that the regulated monopoly attempt to build relationships with these executives. If an effective relationship has been built, the executive may consult with the organization before naming a new candidate or reappointing a seated member

seen as favorable to the organization. If individuals viewed as antagonistic to the regulated monopoly are nominated by an executive but must be confirmed by a legislative body, the public relations strategy may be to build relationships with the confirming body with the purpose of preventing the confirmation of the nominee. Should this strategy fail, the appointee may be more difficult to work with in the future, so the strategy is not without risk to the regulated organization. If the regulators are elected, the regulated organization may wish to recruit individuals to stand for election that are favorable to the management strategies of the regulated monopoly. During the course of the election campaigns, the regulated monopoly organization may work for the election of those favorable to its positions and work in opposition to those individuals opposed to its positions.

Once the regulatory agency is in place, keeping good relations with the agency is paramount for management and public relations strategy. Key to this is the recognition that the customers served by the regulated monopoly may be the organization's strongest allies, or may be the strongest antagonist if services are not provided to fulfill the needs and wants of the customers satisfactorily. Because many regulated monopolies provide essential services, their efforts are critical to the customers. If the services are not delivered effectively, significant opposition can be expected from the customers, and this can result in significant pressure on regulatory agencies to become more restrictive. This may be especially true in times of crisis, and effective public relations strategies must be prepared by the regulated organization in these situations.

An example of such a crisis was the failure of the electrical systems in the summer of 2003, when significant portions of the northeastern United States and much of southeastern Canada were plunged into darkness. At this time several activist individuals and groups issued statements critical of the electrical companies and their policies, and these statements were reported by the media. The media also sought out individuals and organizations that had been monitoring the electrical industry as part of their activist activities.

If regulated monopolistic organizations are to conduct effective public relations, they must have significant crisis plans in place, and they must also have strategies and policies to effectively counterbalance the activist individuals and organizations.

—John Madsen

See also Activism; Muckrakers (and the Age of Progressivism)

Bibliography

Levin, H. M. (Ed.). (2001). *Privatizing education.* Boulder, CO: Westview Press.

REINFORCEMENT THEORY

Reinforcement theory was proposed in 1960 by Joseph T. Klapper to challenge the dominant media effects theory, which had become popular during the middle decades of the 20th century. Reinforcement theory argued that the media do not have a dominant effect on readers', viewers', or listeners' attitudes, beliefs, and motives. The effect is limited or minimal, largely because people filter life experiences selectively. Klapper's work cannot be considered definitive, but it established criteria by which research on the effects of the media must be judged. He acknowledged that some mediated campaigns work wonderfully to reach audiences and form opinions in ways predicted by propaganda experts; however, in other cases campaigns are notorious failures, achieving very little if any effect on opinions and behavior. At best, reinforcement theory reasons, mass-mediated messages can situationally and functionally have varying effects, but for the most part the effects are limited because of myriad countervailing factors.

Prior to Klapper's work, researchers had sought to examine—and sometimes to prove—that media have dominant effects. Out of this research came the axiom "Scholars are interested in who says what through which media to effect changes in targeted audiences." The assumption of this propaganda research was that strategic effects would always occur. However, many studies conducted by the

time Klapper's 1960 book, *The Effects of Mass Communication,* was published had demonstrated that mediated messages were likely to be only partially effective, or even substantial failures, in achieving specific targeted goals.

In contrast to this body of scholarship and popular concern, simply stated, reinforcement theory reasoned that audiences of mass-mediated communication are likely to engage messages selectively and to have multiple influences, including interpersonal communication, that must be acknowledged to explain how much impact the media have on people's opinions. The theory reasons that changing opinions requires substantial cognitive effort. People do not change capriciously. They are exposed to a wide array of themes, arguments, and conclusions in the media to which they attend. They seem to consolidate or reinforce existing opinions rather than change them each time they are exposed to a new set of opinions presented through the media.

Reinforcement theory was developed to respond to the prevailing dominant media effects theory, which reasoned, in part based on the assumptions of propaganda research, that people are dramatically influenced by the messages they receive from the media. Television, for instance, was new and popular. Media scholars and critics wanted to believe that people passively watch lots of television and quickly adopt the ideas, news, and marketing that they see pouring out of their television screens. The essence of dominant effects theory describes mass-mediated messages as being a "magic bullet." The advertiser or program developer, according to this theory, loads the message into news or program content and fires the bullet into the minds of viewers, who accept it uncritically. For the better part of the 20th century, supporters of this line of analysis argued that the media have dominant effects. Others believe the media have moderate or minimal effects on the opinions of listeners, viewers, and readers.

The Effects of Mass Communication was a soundly based review of a substantial amount of social science research, which in essence concluded that people use the media selectively based on what they already know and believe, rather than passively accepting any and all of the ideas they receive through the media. Selectivity occurs at many points in the communication process. First, for instance, people choose to read, listen, and view some materials and not others. Since they can't consume all of what the media offer, they are selective. Children watch television shows tailored to them and are quickly bored by entertainment and news intended for adults. Likewise, adults select entertainment designed for their demographics and avoid that created for other demographics, including children's programming. Parents may watch programming with children but choose to do so for reasons other than sheer entertainment.

Klapper argued that five mediating factors or conditions need to be considered by investigators and media critics who seek to explore and explain media effects: (a) the clusters of predispositions that result in selective exposure (which messages to receive), selective perception, and selective retention; (b) the groups and their norms, which influence media use, predisposition, and impact; (c) the information, content, and predisposition that is disseminated via interpersonal communication; (d) opinion leadership; and (e) the nature and role of the mass media in a society with an operating disposition to freedom of speech.

People are selective in how they receive and interpret the content of media. Klapper argued, "By and large, people tend to expose themselves to those mass communications which are in accord with their existing attitudes and interests" (1960, p. 19). Liberals may watch the same news program as conservatives, but get completely different messages. People do not view in a purely neutral or objective fashion. They are not passive, at least when they have well-formed opinions and preferences. They filter what they see, hear, and read through the attitudes, beliefs, and values they possess prior to the media experience. Thus, for instance, if children or adults see ads for products such as beer or cigarettes, they will accept or reject the messages not only because of the intrinsic appeal of the message as presented, but also based on attitudes toward and knowledge about the product. People, according to this theory, are not merely sponges that take in messages like water. The messages are more likely to reinforce or be rejected based on what perceptual filters the viewer, reader, or listener brings to the experience. Thus, if a public relations practitioner uses promotion to increase the audience for a rock concert, that message conveyed through the media is likely to attract attention and be persuasive based on what audiences believed and preferred prior to receiving the information rather than due to the message as such. Fans of the group may be excited and even seek more information, whereas others might see it as uninteresting.

Selective retention or recall is another factor that, according to reinforcement theory, leads to minimal or limited effects. People do not recall all of what they see, hear, and read. What they "think they saw, read, or heard" may actually be what they wanted to "see, hear, or read" to reinforce existing opinions, preferences, and even stereotypes. For this reason, several people who encounter the same ad or promotional public relations message are likely to recall the message differently. The same can be said for responses to crises and issues. People with a favorable view of a company are likely to have a positive bias toward the reports on a crisis it is suffering. People who hate the company are likely to focus on the negative. Also, people are likely to recall news and promotional messages differently. We can even predict substantial amounts of distortion in this recall. Crucial facts that conflict with the person's preferred position on the matter may be forgotten, distorted, or discounted.

One of the most important factors in predicting media use and impact is the degree to which individuals find the content useful. In essence, people ask: Is it amusing? Does it help me form opinions that separate good outcomes from bad ones? Does it allow me to have deeper insight into which outcomes are good and for which reasons?

People also rely heavily on group norms—the persons with whom they identify most—for the formation of opinions. These norms have a telling effect on the likelihood that individuals will use mediated messages to change their opinions unless the group has or is tending to make a similar shift of opinion. Thus, if the message in the media conforms with group norms, the media can be thought to have dominant effects, but this is misleading because it ignores the greater influence of group norms. Group norms are a vital part of audience profiling through demographic profiles. Selectivity in this regard can be really sneaky. People tell one another what they saw, read, or heard in the mass media. Thus, the first person is likely to have given a selective interpretation of the message that is reinforced in impact because of the positive interpersonal connection between the two parties.

Since media reports often contain opinions of people who are opinion leaders, it may well be the effects of opinion leaders rather than the media per se that influence audience opinions. This can be true of news, especially when both sides are presented. People tend to favor one interpretation of the news, that of the person whom they see as an opinion leader. The same phenomena operate in advertising and promotion. Third-party opinion can be a major influence on the impact of news, promotion, and advertising.

Reinforcement theory advocates do not discount the possibility that media under specific circumstances can have a telling impact on the formation and/or conversion of opinions, but that is not the norm. Rather, people tend to use mediated messages, along with interpersonal influence, to reinforce rather than to dramatically change their opinions.

—*Robert L. Heath*

See also Advertising; Demographics; Promotion; Propaganda

Bibliography

Bryant, J., & Zillmann, D. (Eds.). (1986). *Perspectives on media effects.* Hillsdale, NJ: Lawrence Erlbaum.

Klapper, J. T. (1960). *The effects of mass communication.* New York: Free Press.

RELATIONSHIP MANAGEMENT THEORY

The term *relationship management* refers to the process of managing the relationships between an organization and its internal and external publics. In this context, John Ledingham (2003) defined an organization-public relationship as "the state which exists between an organization and its key publics in which the actions of either can impact the economic, social, cultural or political well-being of the other" (p. 184). Moreover, the concept recognizes relationships as the core focus of public relations.

The notion of relationship management represents a pivotal change in the nature and function of public relations. That change involves a rethinking of the role of communication message production and dissemination in public relations. Whereas earlier practitioners saw communication as the central function of public relations, today's public relations managers recognize the management of key relationships as the core function of public relations. Within that context, communication is envisioned as a strategic tool of public relations, with program evaluation centered on the impact of program initiatives on key relationships. That is, in today's practice, program success or failure is determined by the *quality* of organization-public relationships rather than the *quantity* of messages produced or the number of messages placed in the mass media.

The notion of relationships as the core concern of public relations emerged in the mid-1980s and has been the subject of a great deal of systematic inquiry over the past 20 years. The framework for *managing* relationships is the traditional management process of situational analysis, planning, program implementation, and impact evaluation. Further, relationships are seen as an exchange designed to support understanding and benefit both for an organization and interacting publics. Experience has shown that mutuality of understanding and benefit engenders long-term relationships, whereas initiatives designed primarily to benefit an organization—with public interest secondary—are not sustainable over time.

It also has been found that managing relationships in such a way as to generate mutual benefit results in positive public perceptions of an organization, perceptions that are manifest in support for an organization's public positions. Moreover, mutually beneficial relationships encourage loyalty toward an organization's product and/or services, providing a marketplace competitive advantage. Also, mutually beneficial relationships have been shown to protect an organization's market share in a competitive environment. Similarly, developing positive relationships with internal publics—such as employees—builds organizational morale, an important element in employee productivity. For the study and teaching of public relations, the so-called relational perspective provides an overarching framework for scholarly inquiry and for developing educational curricula.

It has been said that the emergence of relationship management as a foundation for public relations practice was spurred by four key developments:

1. *Recognition of the central role of relationships in public relations.* Recognition of the central role of relationships—rather than the organization, the public, or the communication process—provided a unifying concept for public relations and gave rise to a major shift in the core focus of the discipline.

2. *Reconceptualizing public relations as a management function.* The notion of managing organization-public relationships introduced managerial concepts and processes to a practice previously driven mainly by message production and dissemination. Reconceptualization focused attention on the need for public relations managers to be proficient in all aspects of the management process and to be accountable for public relations expenditures.

3. *Identification of components and types of organization-public relationships; their linkage to public attitudes, perceptions, knowledge, and behavior; and relationship measurement strategies.* Key dimensions of organization-public relationships were identified and linked to public perceptions, attitudes, and choice behavior. An organization-public relationship measurement scale was developed for use in predicting public loyalty, satisfaction, and behavior, providing the tools needed to access public relations value in terms of relationship quality.

4. *Construction of organization-public relationship models.* Models of the organization-public relationship were advanced, including a management process model and a multi-step developmental model, to provide greater insight into the "coming together" and the "coming apart" of organization-public relationships.

Research indicates that organization-public relationships mimic interpersonal relationships in terms of critical determinators of relationship quality. These include trust, openness, credibility, emotion, intimacy, similarity, immediacy, agreement, issue perception, and shared interests, as well as relational history (see Table 1). Moreover, organization-public relationships have been found to cluster into three relationship types—*interpersonal, professional,* and *community.* "In this context, *interpersonal relationship* refers to the personal interactions of organizational representatives and public members. *Professional relationship* refers to the delivery of professional services to public members, and *community relationship* is tied to perceptions that the organization supports the interests of the community. Also, relationships may be seen as communication driven (*symbolic*), or behavior driven (*programmatic*), underscoring the importance of both in developing long-term, mutually beneficial relationships.

A relationship management process model, SMARTS, is based on the four-step management model of (1) analyze, (2) plan, (3) implement, and (4) evaluate (Ledingham, 2003). The SMARTS model includes *scan* (environmental surveillance), *map* (setting goals and objectives), *act* (developing and pre-testing initiatives), *rollout* (putting programs in place), *track* (evaluating the success of the initiatives), and *steward* (monitoring and maintaining relationship quality). Moreover, a 10-step developmental model, based on an interpersonal relationship model, illustrates the "coming together" and the "coming apart" of an organization-public relationship.

In addition to managing relationships with internal and external publics, public relations practitioners working within an organization structure have learned the importance of developing relationships with senior management, the coalition that determines organizational policy and procedures. In that interaction, public relations practitioners are increasingly called upon to demonstrate the linkage

Table 1   Dimensions, Types, and Models of Organization–Public Relationships

			Dimensions, Types and Models of Organization-Public Relationships	
Dimensions	*Types*	*Models*	Relationship State: Indicators of and Contributors to	*Monitoring Strategies*
Trust	Symbolic	Org-pub model	Communication	Scanning
Openness	Behavioral	Expanded model	Frequency	Observation
Credibility	Personal	Developmental model	Complexity	Coorientational
Intimacy	Community	Professional model	Use	Measurement
Similarity		SMART model	Perceptions of:	
Immediacy		Phases model	Personal relationship	
Agreement			Professional relationship	
Accuracy			Community relationship	
Common interests			Problem agreement	
Relational history			Needs fulfillment	
			Goal sharing and reciprocity	
			Mutual legitimacy	
			Satisfaction and benefit	
			Consensus	
			Accuracy	
			Social exchange	
			Transactions	
			Submissiveness	
			Formalization and standardization	
			Symmetry and intensity	
			Duration, valance and content	
			Information resource and flow	

SOURCE: Ledingham, John A. (2003). Explicating Relationship Management as a General Theory of Public Relations, *Journal of Public Relations Research, 15*(2), 181–198. Reprinted with permission from Lawrence Erlbaum Associates, Inc.

between program initiatives and organization goals. Hence, the field is seeing increased exploration of relationship models and application of various relationship-measurement strategies.

The literature of public relations provides principles for public relations practitioners charged with managing organization-public relationships. Ten such principles are presented next:

1. The core focus of public relations is relationships.

2. Successful relationships involve benefit both for an organization and interacting publics.

3. Organization-public relationships are dynamic; that is, they change over time.

4. Relationships are driven by the needs and wants of organizations and publics, and relationship quality depends on perceptions of the degree to which expectations are fulfilled.

5. Effective management of organization-public relationships leads to increased understanding and benefit both for organizations and publics.

6. The success of an organization-public relationship is measured in terms of relationship quality, rather than message production or dissemination.

7. Communication is a strategic tool in managing relationships, but communication alone cannot sustain long-term relationships in the absence of organizational behavior.

8. Organization-public relationships are influenced by relational history, the nature of the interaction, the frequency of exchange, and reciprocity.

9. Organization-public relationships can be categorized by type (personal, professional, community), and whether they are symbolic (communication driven) or behavioral (program driven).

10. Relationship building is applicable in all aspects of public relations study and practice.

Note: Use of the term *organization-public relationships* is a convenience and is not intended to suggest greater importance in the relationship of an organization compared with a public.

—*John A. Ledingham*

Bibliography

Ledingham, J. A. (2000). Guidelines to building and maintaining organization-public relationships, *Public Relations Quarterly, 45*(3), 44–47.

Ledingham, J. A. (2001). Government and citizenry: Extending the relational perspective of public relations. *Public Relations Review, 27,* 285–295.

Ledingham, J. A. (2003). Explicating relationship management as a general theory of public relations, *Journal of Public Relations Research, 15*(2), 181–198.

Ledingham, J. A., & Bruning, S. D. (1998). Relationship management and public relations: Dimensions of an organization-public relationship. *Public Relations Review, 24,* 55–65.

Ledingham, J. A., & Bruning, S. D. (2000). Background and current trends in the study of relationship management. In J. A. Ledingham & S. D. Bruning (Eds.), *Public relations as relationship management: A relational approach to public relations* (pp. xi–xvii). Mahwah, NJ: Lawrence Erlbaum.

Thomlison, T. D. (2000). An interpersonal primer with implications for public relations. In J. A. Ledingham & S. D. Bruning (Eds.), *Public relations as relationship management: A relational approach to public relations* (pp. 117–203). Mahwah, NJ: Lawrence Erlbaum.

RELIABILITY

Reliability is often defined as the dependability or consistency of the scores on a measurement scale or the coding of a content analysis. That is, something that is reliable is also dependable. It may not be accurate, but it is dependable—like a watch that keeps perfect time but is always five minutes late. In research terminology, however, reliability is something that can be measured and is found in establishing a measure's scale or, in the case of content analysis, coding dependability. Reliability requires two things. First, the measure that is being tested for reliability must be quantitative and it must be numeric. Second, there must be at least two items in a scale—two coders, or a single coder who recodes after a period of time. Based on these criteria, reliability may be established through statistical analysis. Which analysis is employed depends on the type of research conducted.

Reliability is often discussed as the difference between what we know and what we do not know. By this we mean that all measurement or coding has the potential for error. Some of that error is *systematic* and known; the rest is *random* and unknown. Reliability establishes the relationship between known and unknown error in a measure or coding. *Excellent* reliability is one that accounts for more than 90 percent of the systematic error; 80–90 percent reliability is typically referred to as *good*; and reliability below 80 percent is worrisome. Numerous reliability statistics are used, and they differ according to what the research is seeking to measure.

TYPES OF RELIABILITY

As noted, we can establish reliability for both scores on measurement scales (attitudinal or general knowledge tests) and content analysis coding. All statistical reliability tests provide indices that range from 0 to 100, either as a *correlation* or as a percentage-of-agreement score. Further, the type of data acquired dictates which specific tests are employed. In general, data can be defined as being either categorical (i.e., the data represent frequency counts and percents of specified categories, such as yes or no, male or female, good or bad) or continuous (i.e., the data represent responses on a continuum where the distance between one unit and the other is equal, such as age or income).

MEASUREMENT RELIABILITY

In traditional measurement a measure's reliability in general has been established by examining how people respond to the statement in a measure. If the measure represents an attempt to assess attitudes or beliefs, then reliability is established via statistical analysis for the appropriate type of data the measures yields. If the measure is to be used over time, a different type of reliability is employed—one that is more applied and typically relies on correlational analysis.

When creating an attitude measure or *scale,* the researcher attempts to predict how individuals feel or evaluate some abstract object, such as credibility or persuasiveness. Although there are many different types of attitudinal measures, public relations typically employs what is known as the *Likert-type scale,* which requires people to respond to a series of statements as to whether they (5) strongly agree, (4) agree, (3) neither agree nor disagree, (2) disagree, or (1) strongly disagree with each statement. The responses are then summed across items. This assumes the data are continuous in nature and the computed score represents the participants' evaluation on the item. Reliability for Likert-type scales is established using *coefficient alpha* statistics. A coefficient alpha of .80 or better is generally accepted as good to excellent, an alpha of .70 adequate, and an alpha less than .70 problematic. An example of this type of measure would be James E. Grunig and Linda Childers Hon's 1999 measure of relationships. A second attitudinal measure asks people to pick only the statements that they agree with. This type of measure yields categorical data, and its reliability is established statistically by the KR-20 statistic.

Once a measure has its internal reliability established, it is often tested to see whether it is reliable in comparison with other groups or populations. In some cases the same people are administered twice, with a period of time separating each administration. This is *test-retest reliability,* with scores between the two administrations correlated to see if the participants responded similarly in both administrations. In other cases, the measure would be split into two representative questionnaires, and different groups would receive one or the other questionnaire. This is *split half reliability,* and the correlation between the two groups establishes the measure's reliability.

CODER RELIABILITY

Coder reliability establishes how dependable the coding is in a content analysis. Content analysis codes messages for certain *units of analysis,* placing instances of each into predetermined categories. A unit of analysis might be viewer sex using the categories male and female. To ensure that the coding is accurate and dependable, coders individually place the content into the appropriate categories (or if there is only one coder, the material is coded twice after a sufficient time between codings) and the number of correct versus incorrect codes is established.

There are at least four different types of coding reliabilities that can be used in a content analysis. Most common is Oli R. Holsti's coding formula that identifies how many items have been coded and then calculates the number of coded items for each coder, yielding a reliability coefficient between 0.00 (totally unreliable) to 1.00 (totally reliable). However, Holsti's formula fails to take into account that the coders may have agreed by chance on their coding. Cohen's (1960) kappa basically computes the same formula as Holsti's formula but takes into account chance, and is found in a number of statistical computer packages. Both, however, fail to take into account that the coders may have agreed by chance on their coding. William A. Scott's pi index and Klaus Krippendorf's alpha attempt to take chance out of the equation. Because they are more difficult to calculate, they are reported less often.

RELATIONSHIP TO VALIDITY

As noted earlier, reliability establishes how dependable the scores on a measure or coder are. It does not, however, establish whether that measure or coder is actually reflecting what it should. This reflects a measure or coder's *validity.* Reliability is required before validity can be established; without accurate measurement, the validity of the measurement or coder cannot be assessed. Thus, reliability is an initial requirement of any form of measurement or coding scheme, but it may not actually be measuring or coding what the researcher wants.

—Don W. Stacks

See also Measuring/measures; Scales; Statistical analysis; Survey; Validity

Bibliography

Cohen, L. (1960). A coefficient for nominal scales. *Educational and Psychological Measurement, 20,* 37–46.

Cronbach, L. (1957). Coefficient alpha and the internal structure of tests. *Psychometrica, 16,* 15–41.

Grunig, J., & Hon, L. (1999). *Guidelines for measuring relations in public relations.* Gainesville, FL: Institute for Public Relations.

Holsti, O. (1969). *Content analysis for the social sciences and humanities.* New York: Free Press.

Hocking, J., Stacks, D., & McDermott, S. (2003). *Communication research* (3rd ed.). Boston: Allyn & Bacon.

Krippendorf, K. (1980). *Content analysis: An introduction to its methodology.* Beverly Hills, CA: Sage.

Likert, R. (1932). A technique for the measurement of attitudes. *Archives of Psychology, 40,* 1–55.

Scott, W. (1955). Reliability of content analysis: The case of nominal scale coding. *Public Opinion Quarterly, 17,* 321–325.

Stacks, D. (2002). *Primer of public relations research.* New York: Guilford Press.

Stacks, D. (Ed.). (2002). *Dictionary of public relations measurement and research.* Gainesville, FL: Institute for Public Relations.

REPUTATION MANAGEMENT

Reputation management is the strategic use of corporate resources to positively influence the attitudes, beliefs, opinions, and actions of multiple corporate stakeholders including consumers, employees, investors, and the media. *Fortune* magazine relies on eight attributes in the development of the annual list of America's Most Admired Companies: innovativeness, quality of management, employee talent, quality of product/services, long-term investment value, financial soundness, social responsibility, and use of corporate assets. This list illuminates the extent to which reputation management emanates from everything a corporation does and says, whether voluntary or involuntary. When managed properly, corporate reputation can improve an organization's ability to sell products and services, attract investors, hire talented personnel, and exert political influence. Although not a zero-sum game, reputation management relies on a corporation's ability to distinguish itself from its competitors in the hearts and minds of various publics, thereby enhancing its overall position in the marketplace.

Reputations are value judgments that evolve over time based primarily on the emotional, financial, social, and cultural attachment between an organization and various publics. A 1990 study by Charles Frombrun and Mark Shanley suggested that publics attribute corporate reputations on the basis of three main factors. First, publics look at how the organization is positioned in its industry by using market and accounting signals to indicate performance. Second, organizational signals regarding conformity to social norms are evaluated. And finally, organizational strategic positions are considered in the construction of corporate reputation. The depth and breadth of reputation construction underscores the importance of reputation management to the overall well-being of a corporation—a fact not lost on corporate executives. According to a recent study of CEOs by Hill & Knowlton USA and *Chief Executive* magazine, 96 percent of the CEOs surveyed consider corporate reputation a vital component of business success.

Good corporate reputations do not just happen. Rather, the corporate reputation must be managed and cultivated. Organizations reinforce the desired corporate reputation across all business functions, including internal and external communication activities. It is the vast nature of corporate communication that makes it simultaneously the most important and the most difficult component of reputation management. For many multinational corporations, the consistent communication of organizational values is one way to ensure consistency across business units and among various stakeholders. For reputation management to be successful, the communication of corporate values and goals needs to be in sync with the lived experiences of the organization's stakeholders. For example, the recent Philip Morris campaign promotes the company as a leader in philanthropic giving. The campaign is technically accurate; Philip Morris does contribute over $60 million annually to different charitable organizations. However, the idea of Philip Morris as a philanthropist is so far removed from the lived experiences of the majority of publics that the message may have low salience, or worse, further enhance public perception that Philip Morris is less than honest.

Corporations are increasingly aware of the salience of reputation and the difficulty in repairing a tarnished reputation. Nearly 20 years after the *Valdez* spill in Alaska, recent news articles about the Exxon-Mobil merger include reference to the incident. Conversely, Jim Hutton, Michael Goodman, Jill Alexander, and Christina Genest (2001), suggested that well-managed communication activities have the potential to convert peripheral stakeholders into reputation advocates for corporations. Consider the case of Microsoft and its antitrust suits. It can be argued using Frombrun and Shanley's (1990) criteria that Microsoft managed its business and corporate reputation in a manner that appealed to the American ideal of capitalism even for those publics that may not have had a direct connection to the situation.

Media outlets influence corporate reputation both in the quality and quantity of coverage of a corporation's actions, leadership, and financial performance. Craig E. Carroll and Maxwell McCombs (2003) relied on agenda setting to explain the role media has in influencing stakeholder perception of a corporation's reputation. Through the agenda-setting lens the ability of the media to give salience to a particular reputation becomes apparent. For example, in the late 1990s Enron's reputation as an innovative, influential, and generous corporation gained salience through the coverage it received in the media. Enron and former CEO Kenneth Lay were the focus of numerous television and print special editions touting the corporation's positive attributes. Critics contend that the salience of Enron's reputation may have delayed response to the growing evidence that corporate reality belied the corporate reputation.

In addition to traditional media outlets, the Internet has influenced reputation management by giving voice to the "other." Specifically, publics that are disgruntled with an organization can establish a Web site devoted to alternative readings of the corporate reputation. Among those corporations that have had Web sites devoted to damaging their reputation are United Airlines (untied.com), All-State insurance company (allstateinsurancesucks. com), and Nike (Saigon.com/~nike/).

Scandal, however, is not the only factor that influences the news coverage a corporation receives. Five other factors, as outlined by Carroll and McCombs (2003), may influence a corporate reputation and the extent to which it receives news coverage:

- The size and age of the organization
- The degree to which the corporation is involved in more than one business segment
- The proximity of the organization to a particular news source
- The placement of the news coverage
- The perceived level of elite or celebrity status given to the organization's CEO or others closely tied to the overall corporate reputation

—*Amy O'Connor*

Bibliography

Carroll, C. E., & McCombs, M. (2003). Agenda-setting effects of business news on the public's images and opinions about major corporations. *Corporate Reputation Review, 6*(1), 36–46.

Frombrun, C., & Shanley, M. (1990). What's in a name? Reputation building and corporate strategy. *Academy of Management Journal, 33,* 233–258.

Hutton, J. G., Goodman, M. B., Alexander, J. B., & Genest, C. M. (2001). Reputation management: The new face of corporate public relations? *Public Relations Review, 27*(3), 247–261.

Miller, L. (1999, January). Few CEOs held accountable for corporate reputation. *The Internal Auditor, 52,* 15–17.

Nakra, P. (2000). Corporate reputation management: "CRM" with a strategic twist? *Public Relations Quarterly, 45*(2), 35–42.

RESEARCH GOALS

Research in public relations includes both practitioners constructing and executing public relations actions and researchers in pursuit of knowledge. The "Goals" entry in this encyclopedia refers to strategic actions and choices made by practitioners to achieve specific campaign-driven outcomes. In that case, research should not just happen, but should be designed to reveal something that is relevant to understanding and solving the problem facing the public relations practitioner.

Research goals are what direct public relations researchers. Research goals guide the research study and are the general outcomes desired by the researcher. The general goal of public relations researchers is to create knowledge and build upon the public relations body of knowledge. Research goals can be divided into two types: applied and basic. The goals of applied research involve trying to solve some practical problem, such as what publics are most likely to communicate on an issue or which message strategy would be most persuasive for the target public. The goal is the practical application of the research results. In most cases, practitioners are pursuing applied research goals.

Basic research goals seek to develop theory. A theory is a systematic view of a phenomenon, which specifies the relationship between variables; it explains how things work by establishing relationships between concepts/variables. These relations must be tested to prove the value and accuracy of the theory. The goal of some research is to test aspects of a theory, such as proving that two variables are related as prescribed in a theory. The articles published in research journals often pursue basic research goals, and the reader must decide how to apply that knowledge to public relations situations. However, public relations research can pursue both goals in the same study. Public relations is applied in nature, so testing a theory will often provide answers to practical problems as well. Research designed to test situational crisis communication theory, for instance, provides insights into how best to communicate after a crisis occurs.

—*W. Timothy Coombs*

See also Campaign; Crisis communication; Goals; Research objectives

RESEARCH OBJECTIVES

Like practitioners, public relations researchers need to develop objectives to guide their research projects. A research objective works with the research goal and specifies what is to be studied. Research objectives can take the form of a research question or a hypothesis.

A research question is stated as a question that explores the relationship between two or more variables/concepts. Research studies abbreviate research questions as *RQ*. Here is a sample RQ from an actual study: "How do journalists perceive the role of information subsidies supplied by public relations practitioners in the construction of news?" (Curtin, 1999, p. 58). The example is an open-ended research question because it leaves the direction of the relationship open; it just indicates that a relationship does exist. The sample RQ simply looks to see what type of relationship exists between journalist perceptions and information subsidies. A closed-ended research question will specify the direction or form of the relationship. A closed-ended version of the earlier RQ might be "Do journalists perceive the role of information subsidies supplied by public relations practitioners in the construction of news negatively?" The revised RQ specifies that journalists will have a negative perception of information subsidies.

A hypothesis states a predicted relationship between two or more variables/concepts. Research studies abbreviate hypotheses as *H*. Here is a sample H from an actual study: "Respondents in the favorable relationship history condition will hold more positive organizational reputations than those in the unfavorable condition" (Coombs & Holladay, 2001, p. 326). The sample H is a one-tailed hypothesis because it states the direction or form of the relationship between the variables. There will be a positive relationship between relationship history and organizational reputation. A two-sided hypothesis states that a relationship will exist between two or more variables/concepts but does not indicate the form or direction of the relationship. A two-sided version of the earlier H might be "There is a relationship between the relationship history condition and organizational reputation." The revised H does not specify the direction of the relationship, but just indicates that a relationship exists.

Each research study you read should provide an RQ, H, or both. The study will be designed to answer the RQ and/or H while the text of the research report will focus on explaining the answers.

—*W. Timothy Coombs*

See also Objectives; Public relations research; Research goals

Bibliography

Coombs, W. T., & Holladay, S. J. (2001). An extended examination of the crisis situation: A fusion of the relational management and symbolic approaches. *Journal of Public Relations Research*, 13, 321–340.

Curtin, P. A. (1999). Reevaluating public relations information subsidies: Market-driven journalism and agenda-building theory and practice. *Journal of Public Relations Research*, 11, 29–52.

Stewart, T. D. (2002). *Principles of research in communication.* Boston: Allyn and Bacon.

RETURN ON INVESTMENT

Firms and individuals have a variety of alternatives for employing their scarce capital. Return on investment (ROI) is one of the many analytical methods individuals and firms employ to aid in the allocation of funds. Although there are many definitions of ROI depending on the context, a working definition can be the amount that an individual or firm earns on the capital invested.

From the viewpoint of the individual, ROI is often considered in the context of investing in a common stock. For example, if the investor buys 100 shares of XYZ Corp. at $20 per share and sells the same stock at $25 per share (ignoring commissions), the ROI is (25 – 20)/20, or a 25 percent ROI. The question of whether the 25 percent ROI on XYZ Corp is "good" depends on the benchmark to which the ROI is compared. The most common

benchmark to which common stock ROIs are measured is the S&P 500 Index (which measures the return of the 500 large stocks on an unmanaged basis). For example, if the S&P went up 30 percent during the same period of ownership, the XYZ ROI of 25 percent would be considered a poor relative ROI. Conversely, if XYZ Corp. stock went down 10 percent when the S&P 500 went down 15 percent, XYZ Corp. would be considered a good relative investment because it outperformed its benchmark.

From the viewpoint of the corporate financial manager, ROI is employed in the process of selecting among the various capital project investment opportunities available to the firm, such as building a new plant, launching a new product, entering new markets, and so forth. *Capital budgeting* is the process the manager employs to determine which project(s) a firm should undertake to maximize firm value and, hence, the firm's ROI to shareholders and creditors.

There are many methods to rank the attractiveness of a firm's capital projects, including payback period, internal rate of return, and net present value. In general terms, an investment to the firm has value if the return on investment is more than it costs the firm to acquire. How the ROI is calculated depends on the method employed by the manager. As a rule of thumb, the best measure of ROI in the capital budgeting context is the net present value method, which indicates that the projects that provide the highest positive net present value should be given the highest rank.

There is no magical ROI threshold that is appropriate for each security investment or capital budgeting project. Each investment must be evaluated according to its risk profile, the firm's cost of capital, and norms of the industry in which the firm operates. Moreover, it is necessary to evaluate the ROI over relatively long periods of time, say 5 to 10 years, to get a feel of how a firm deals with the ups and downs of the business cycle.

Public relations is one of many organizational functions that is called upon to enhance businesses' ROI. For this reason, strategies such as publicity and promotion are used to support marketing. Also, public relations can help reduce costs by successful crisis and issues management.

—*Henry Hardt*

See also Crisis and crisis management; Issues management; Promotion; Publicity

RHETORICAL THEORY

Messages and the meaning they produce are an essential result of public relations. Practitioners are in the message and meaning business. Among other concerns, public relations theory and professional best practices require a solid understanding of messages and the meaning they can create. Practitioners are paid to influence what people know, think, and do. The rhetorical heritage provides a long-standing and constantly developing body of strategic and critical insights to help practitioners be effective and ethical in the way they create messages and participate in the process by which society creates meaning.

Systems theory is useful for understanding and shaping the process of public relations, but it fails to help practitioners and scholars understand the messages that are strategically and ethically relevant to each task. For over 2,000 years in Western civilization, the rhetorical heritage has examined the nature of messages and the strategic challenges in addressing rhetorical problems that demand the formation of shared meaning. Critical studies complete the troika of leading approaches to public relations. Some lines of critical investigation grow from the rhetorical heritage. Other approaches to criticism draw heavily on social theory to investigate and critique the roles large organizations play in the discourse of society.

Rhetorical theory features the role information and fact play in shaping knowledge and opinions as well as motivating actions. It addresses the ways that evaluations are debated and confirmed or challenged through discourse. People compete in public debate to assert the strength of their ideas and their interpretations of facts. They know that others may disagree. They often respond because they disagree. This spirited debate is the essence of the rhetorical heritage that values the right and ability of people to get messages and make judgments accordingly.

Rhetoric, as a term, has fallen on hard times in the past four decades. During the antiwar and activist protest era of the 1960s, the cry of the agitator in response to any establishment statement was "That is pure rhetoric." Rhetoric, instead of signaling informed and reasoned discourse, came to be associated with sham and hollowness. Media reporters picked up this meaning of the term.

By this influence, many people acquired a narrow and limited understanding of rhetoric as deceptive and shallow statements made falsely in an effort to manipulate and control rather than to reveal or assess fact, value, and policy. It is associated with spin, vacuous statements, propaganda, and pandering to audiences' interests. Some may see it only as telling people what they want to know or are willing to accept, rather than relying on judgments of knowledge, truth, and reason.

Adhering to the best Western rhetorical heritage, academic programs in English and speech communication include courses in rhetoric and rhetorical studies. Studied and taught in that context, the term *rhetoric* refers to the strategic options of communication influence within ethical standards. It is the rationale for suasive discourse. As a discipline, it addresses the ways people persuasively assert and challenge fact, value, and policy. It recognizes that humans deal with their lives through words and other influential symbols. They create collective action by appealing to one another. They dispute, cajole, agree, identify, challenge, and confirm. All of this is the domain of rhetoric, the rationale for forging conclusions and influencing actions. Rhetorical theory explains how people co-create meaning through dialogue that can define and build mutually beneficial relationships.

Rhetoric is the rationale for effective discourse. It consists of a well-established body of strategic guidelines regarding how messages need to be proved, structured, framed, and worded. It is concerned with how each message needs to be designed to be informative and persuasive. Because rhetorical theory arises out of disputes and differences of opinion, it offers guidelines on how people can negotiate differences and work together in collaborative decision making. It informs, creates divisions, and bridges divisions. It motivates people to make one choice in preference to another. If people everywhere shared the same information, opinion, and motives, there would be no need for rhetoric.

At its best, rhetoric is founded on the substance of good reasons and can help make society better for all. At its worst, it can involve deception, manipulation, slander, character assassination, distortion, misinformation, and disinformation.

Champions for the rhetorical heritage believe that freedom of discourse is the answer to the misuse of the art. The best corrective for deception, for instance, is a demonstrated case that one side of a controversy is engaging in deception. Public discourse, the forum of rhetoric, allows for combatants to challenge, correct, and elevate the discourse of society.

Society, according to Kenneth Burke, is a marketplace of competing ideas. This marketplace requires rhetoric that addresses "the Scramble, the Wrangle of the Marketplace, the flurries and flare-ups of the Human Barnyard, Give and Take, the wavering line of pressure and counter pressure, the Logomachy, the onus of ownership, the War of Nerves, the War" (1969, p. 23). For society to function, actions of the people of society need to be coordinated. Cooperation, even competition, requires rhetoric to foster shared perspectives and ways of acting in concert. Each perspective is a way of thinking. It is based on a set of facts and an interpretation of those facts. Each perspective offers its unique way of viewing reality. The terms of the perspective focus attention in unique ways and feature some alternatives as being preferable to others. For instance, sports enthusiasts share a perspective in which athletic competition is entertaining. That perspective might clash with one that is based on the fine arts. We can easily imagine the perspective of a sports enthusiast leading to different motives compared with those by one who prefers the fine arts. One person, by this logic, would want to see a ball game rather than attend the opera or symphony. Family feuds come from competing perspectives. Religions constitute different perspectives. Perspectives are fostered and countered by marketing, advertising, and publicity. Some people want pickups, and others prefer sports cars. Some individuals support the unlimited possession of guns; others call for restraint, reflecting a different perspective. Activists—concerned citizens in a

community—might argue with school board officials to oppose cuts in spending for the arts while athletics remains fully funded. Thus, rhetoric gives voice to competing preferences.

Championing the role of rhetoric in society, Christopher Lentz reasoned, "Truth should prevail in a market-like struggle where superior ideas vanquish their inferiors and achieve audience acceptance" (1996, p. 1). A scholar of the rhetorical heritage, George Kennedy recognized the role ancient Greek and Roman societies played in its development. "In its origin and intention rhetoric was natural and good: it produced clarity, vigor, and beauty, and it rose logically from the conditions and qualities of the classical mind" (1963, p. 3).

Rhetoric is enlivened with facts, as well as values and policy recommendations. It deals with choice. Which is best, most correct, and preferable? Rather than featuring rhetoric as vacuous statements, Aristotle believed that the communicator is obliged to prove any point he or she asserts. Proofs of several kinds were the substance of rhetoric. These proofs were logical when they dealt with facts and reasoning. They featured emotions as part of human nature. They revealed the character of the speaker. In this way, an audience could assess the credibility of all speakers by considering the values on which they based their life and built their messages. The end to which all discourse should be aimed, Aristotle reasoned, was what was good for society. He worked to inspire people who used rhetoric to do so because it advanced the quality of society. Values and good reasons have been a classic ingredient of rhetorical discourse, along with a scrupulous interest in the soundness of arguments based on fact and flawless reasoning.

Ethics is a fundamental ingredient in rhetoric. Drawing from the work of Aristotle and other Greeks, a Roman teacher, Marcus Fabius Quintilian (1951), was firm: "My ideal orator, then, is the true philosopher, sound in morals and with full knowledge of speaking, always striving for the highest" (p. 20). He continued, "If a case is based on injustice, neither a good man [or woman] nor rhetoric has any place in it" (p. 106). Such advice should inspire organizations using public relations to seek first to be ethical as a prerequisite for sound communication. For more than 2,000 years, persons who have considered the nature and societal role of rhetoric have recognized the need to be ethical as a first step toward being an effective communicator. Any organization that does not aspire to the highest levels of corporate responsibility is likely to find that its actions discredit its statements. Actions speak, and speak louder than words.

Appeals to join one point of view, to make one choice in preference of another, is the rationale for rhetoric. People identify with one another as they share perspectives. Thus, perspectives become the basis of rhetorical appeals. Advocates reason that one perspective is superior to its competitors. They court others to agree, to see the world in a particular way, and to prefer some actions instead of others. Public relations uses identification in publicity. It informs, evaluates, and recommends. For instance, practitioners might publicize a baseball team, an amusement park, or a brand of exercise equipment.

Rhetoric entails appeals to make adjustments. Skilled communicators adapt ideas to people. They know that if ideas are too foreign, they will be rejected. Ideas change slowly. A nonprofit organization might, for this reason, ask that donors adapt to the ideals and mission of the organization by giving modest amounts of money to support its charity. The nature of its charity has to be adapted to the people, by demonstrating that it fits with their values and preferences. Rhetoric also asks that people adjust to ideas. They might not at first accept the rationale for giving, but over time they can be convinced that this charity makes the community a better place to live.

Where there is agreement, rhetoric is not needed. Its rationale comes from uncertainty, doubt, difference of motive, and difference of opinion. In ancient Greece and Rome, individuals spoke in public to advocate one point of view in contest with competing views. Today, in an increasingly global society, organizations tend to speak or otherwise communicate instead of people. Even when individual voices stand out, they do so because they speak for an institution, an organization, and even a nation. The newsworthiness of their case is not only where they agree with others, but also where they disagree. This is as true for the promotion of products as it is for the advocacy of going to war or seeking peace. The voice might be a publicist for a small company advocating the virtues of its product or the president of a mighty nation seeking support for some policy or course of action.

Rhetoric can emphasize difference. Public relations practitioners may communicate to differentiate one product or service from another. Activists offer publics a choice between one vision of the future versus another. They might ask audiences to support them for increased sanctions against drunk driving as a choice to save lives and reduce injuries.

Rhetorical statements create narratives that give meaning to person's lives. We can imagine that narrative is one of the most characteristic forms of rhetorical statement. From childhood, we are taught that stories begin with "once upon a time" and may end "happily ever after." They might also have tragic endings. Narrative gives form and substance to rhetorical statements. Reporters use the form and substance in news reports. If the report is a crisis, then responding organizations engage in the narrative so that society eventually learns the "story" to account for what happened, why it happened, and what will be done to prevent its recurrence. Events, a standard public relations tool, are designed to have narrative form and content. Practitioners want audiences to pay attention to see who is doing what, why, how, when, and where. One of the major publicity events each year in the United States is the Academy Awards ceremony. Prior to the big night—and following it—stories are told about actors and other artists to attract audiences to see who won, why they won, what they wore, how they reacted to victory or defeat, and where their movie will be playing next.

Large organizations and activists often engage in advocacy and counter-advocacy regarding narratives of the future. The focal question is whether certain products or services as well as operations will lead to a tragic end or a "happily ever after" outcome. This competition asks listeners, readers, and viewers to adopt one narrative, one vision of the future, and make choices based on that preference. Activists often use the rhetorical tactic of comparing a picture of a dire future to one that is better. They advocate changes to avoid the dire future and achieve the better one.

Society cannot function without rhetoric. When it is working at its best, rhetoric serves society in fostering enlightened choice. Its vitality originates from the reality that facts require interpretation, some values are better than others in making specific decisions, and policies always require contingency and expedience.

Each rhetorical statement is a strategic response to a rhetorical problem. A rhetorical problem is an exigency that must be addressed because it raises doubt on some matter relevant to the actions and choices made by an organization. This problem sets the conditions for an appropriate response. A crisis, for instance, might constitute a rhetorical problem. This problem is different depending on the cause of the crisis.

A rhetorical enactment view of public relations acknowledges that all of what each organization does and says becomes meaningful because of the interpretations—meaning—people place on those actions and statements. Markets, as well as publics, can be influenced by what the organization does and says—and by what it does not do or does not say.

Publics offer competing perspectives through their rhetorical efforts that challenge the views and actions of organizations. For instance, activists in a community might be concerned about soot emitted from a manufacturing facility. They may call for higher standards of environmental aesthetics as well as of public health and safety. These calls might include letters to opinion leaders, speeches and rallies, and lobbying efforts with appropriate regulators. Disgruntled customers vote with their feet—and credit cards. They support one business by making a purchase from it. At the same time, this choice makes a statement of a lack of support for competitors.

Rhetorical theory champions the spirit and principles of the First Amendment to the U.S. Constitution. The right to speak is testimony to the positive role that public discourse plays in society.

Rhetoric is a body of principles and strategies that strengthens the voice and enlivens the ideas of competing points of view. As it informs the way individuals communicate for themselves, it also is relevant to the practice of public relations. It offers strategies and challenges, but ultimately rests on the principle that to be effective each individual or organization needs first to be ethical, good.

—Robert L. Heath

See also Activism; Collaborative decision making; Critical theory; Event; Promotion; Propaganda; Publicity; Publics; Stakes; Systems theory

Bibliography

Burke, K. (1969). *A grammar of motives.* Berkeley: University of California Press.

Heath, R. L. (2001). A rhetorical enactment rationale for public relations. In R. L. Heath (Ed.), *Handbook of public relations* (pp. 31–50). Thousand Oaks, CA: Sage.

Kennedy, G. (1963). *The art of persuasion in Greece.* Princeton, NJ: Princeton University Press.

Lentz, C. S. (1996). The fairness in broadcasting doctrine and the Constitution: Forced one-stop shopping in the "marketplace of ideas." *University of Illinois Law Review, 271,* 1–39.

L'Etang, J., & Pieczka, M. (Eds.). *Critical perspectives in public relations.* London: International Thomson Business Press.

Nichols, M. H. (1963). *Rhetoric and criticism.* Baton Rouge: Louisiana State University Press.

Quintilian, M. F. (1951). *The institutio oratoria of Marcus Fabius Quintilianus* (C.E. Little, Trans.). Nashville, TN: George Peabody College for Teachers.

RISK COMMUNICATION

Risk communication is a community infrastructure, transactional communication process among individuals and organizations regarding the character, cause, degree, significance, uncertainty, control, and overall perception of a risk. Risk communication provides the opportunity to understand and appreciate stakeholders' concerns related to risks generated by organizations, engage in dialogue to address differences and concerns, carry out appropriate actions that can reduce perceived risks, and create a climate of participatory and effective discourse to reduce friction and increase harmony and mutuality.

The community infrastructure model of risk communication features building and sustaining relationships that foster discourse and the sharing of perceptions, and communication and action structures based on shared meanings across varied and multiple constituencies, issues, and levels of understanding. Risk assessors and communicators realize that each key public makes an idiosyncratic response to each risk based on its unique decision heuristic. Each concerned public has an inclination to engage in or at least support activism to exert public policy solutions to correct intolerable risk perceptions.

Risk communication public relations campaigns typically involve large organizations, such as manufacturing facilities or energy transportation lines, whose activities can pose a risk to key members of a community. Strategic risk communication contends that people in key communities need to understand the levels of risks that they suffer from working or living in proximity to risk sources, and that they can take measures that would reduce their risks by understanding the prevailing risk and collectively taking actions so that it is reduced to or does not exceed tolerable levels. Risk communication based on this shared, social relations–community infrastructural approach works to achieve a level of discourse that can treat the content issues of the risk—technical assessment—and the quality of the relationships, as well as the political dynamics of the participants.

Views on risk communication have evolved from at least three separate streams of thought to guide the way risks are calculated, evaluated, and controlled: (a) scientific positivism, whereby data and methodologies of scientists dominate community efforts to ascertain the degree of risk and subsequent communications about the risk on behalf of the community; (b) constructivism/relativism, which assumes that everyone's opinions have equal value so that no opinion is better or worse than anyone else's; and (c) dialogue, which through collaborative decision-making ensures that scientific opinion becomes integrated into policies that are vetted by key publics' values.

Risk communication began when, at least in the perception of key publics, private-sector and public-sector organizations failed to understand and exhibit appropriate levels of corporate responsibility by failing to achieve proper control of risks associated with their activities. For example, the U.S. government became deeply involved in chemical-related risk assessment and communication processes in response to the 1984 Bhopal chemical spill, which motivated elected representatives and citizens to question whether similar risks loomed near their homes or at their work locations. Addressing such concerns, federal legislators created the Emergency Planning and Community Right-to-Know Act of 1986, title 3 of the Superfund Amendments and Reauthorization Act of 1986 (SARA). Legislators believed SARA would create a communication apparatus and strategic business planning process to empower people regarding estimated risks and risk perceptions.

Codifying environmental risk communication, SARA requires chemical companies to inform citizens regarding the kinds and quantities of chemicals that are manufactured, stored, transported, and emitted in each community. SARA's underpinning assumption was that as companies report toxic data about the materials they produce, transport, and store, people could become informed of the level of risk in their neighborhood. The Environmental Protection Agency established risk communication as a means to open, responsible, informed, and reasonable scientific discussion of risks associated with personal health and safety practices involved in living and working in proximity to harmful activities and hazardous substances.

Risk communication, as a subdiscipline of public relations studies, grew out of such risk perception and risk management efforts. Initially, risk communication research and activities took on a source-oriented, linear approach to communication, characterized as an exchange of information about risk among interested parties. During this period, classified as the technical risk assessment period, industrial spokespersons were advised to appease or assuage publics' apprehension by being credible and clear. Risk communication progressed beyond a source-oriented approach to a more interactive risk perception and risk management approach, where communication is viewed as an interactive process of exchange of information and opinion among individuals, groups, and institutions.

The current version of risk communication features complex social relations operating within community infrastructures.

Risk communication requirements are a political response to popular demands. . . . The main product of risk communication is not information, but the quality of the social relationship it supports. Risk communication is not an end in itself; it is an enabling agent to facilitate the continual evolution of relationships. (Otway, 1992, p. 227)

Numerous researchers from a variety of academic and professional fields including public relations, risk management, psychology, rhetoric, political science, and sociology have developed a typology of infrastructural risk communication process variables. For example, Robert L. Heath and D. D. Abel introduced a model in 1996 that included variables such as uncertainty, trust, information seeking, and cognitive involvement. Other infrastructural risk communication process variables include control, cognitive involvement, credibility, dread, firsthand experience, knowledge, perceived economic benefit, support/opposition, trust, and uncertainty.

Uncertainty, for example, is a central variable in the risk perception and communication process. Risks by definition are matters of uncertainty. In this vein, Terrance L. Albrecht (1988) defined uncertainty as the lack of attributional confidence about cause-effect patterns. Publics want information to reduce their uncertainties about the subjects under consideration and about the people who are creating those uncertainties. Thus, uncertainty is a measure of confidence regarding (a) the ability to estimate a risk and its consequences and (b) the ability to communicate knowledgeably on the facts and issues surrounding any specific risk.

People often decide what levels of risk are acceptable on the basis not of technical data

analysis, but rather of a question of value, such as fairness. Although people in general may debate the perception of risk in value terms, experts remain examiners of the actual risk, though not entirely removed from value judgments. Perceived risk has a structure that differs from the structure of expert judgments about risk.

For community residents, risk messages can be confusing because they come from a variety of media sources (can labels, public meetings, newsletters, media, activist documents, etc.) that involve a multitude of parties and often reflect competing scientific conclusions. Experts and regulatory agencies often operate on the assumption that they and their audiences share a common framework for evaluating and interpreting risk information. This confusion also stems from the fact that prominent government officials take opposing viewpoints about environmental risk matters and participate in highly public debates about risk estimations.

Numerous views of risk communication, however, identify understanding as the final dependent variable. People may understand, for example, what a plant manager says about air particle emissions at a community refinery. Those people may not agree with the risk assessments because they are not satisfied that those assessments achieve or constitute the proper levels of risk. This line of reasoning makes explicit the fact that risk communication is not merely a scientific or knowledge-based activity.

One of the consistent findings of risk assessment studies is the recurring theme that risks are a trade-off of costs and rewards. If risks are perceived to be acceptably low and the rewards or benefits of taking the risks are perceived to be high, then one can predict that the risks will be tolerated. For example, Brian R. N. Baird (1986) found that judged benefits of a hazard were ranked first among other variables in correlation with risk tolerance. People tolerate higher risks from activities seen as beneficial, if benefits extend beyond economic to include personal and family variables such as basic needs, safety, security, and pleasure.

A second factor that predicts support is the perception of the likelihood of adverse events as a result of the risk. According to Howard Kunreuther, Douglas Easterling, William Desvousges and Paul Slovic (1990), support is sensitive to the perceived likelihood of adverse events such as accidents or catastrophes. When risks seem more likely and are expected to have adverse effects, they are less likely to be tolerated and more likely to be opposed.

—*Michael J. Palenchar*

See also Crisis communication; Issues management

Bibliography

Albrecht, T. L. (1988). Communication and personal control in empowering organizations. In J. A. Anderson (Ed.), *Communication yearbook* (Vol. 11, pp. 380–404). Newbury Park, CA: Sage.

Baird, B. (1986). Tolerance for environmental health risks: The influence of knowledge, benefits, voluntarism and environmental attitudes. *Risk Analysis, 6,* 425–435.

Heath, R. L., & Abel, D. D. (1996). Proactive response to citizen risk concerns: Increasing citizen's knowledge of emergency response practices. *Journal of Public Relations Research, 8,* 151–171.

Kunreuther, H., Easterling, D., Desvousges, W., & Slovic, P. (1990). Public attitudes toward siting a high-level nuclear waste repository in Nevada. *Risk Analysis, 10*(4), 469–484.

Otway, H. (1992). Public wisdom, expert fallibility: Toward a contextual theory of risk. In S. Krimsky & D. Golding (Eds.), *Social theories of risk* (pp. 215–228). Westport, CT: Praeger.

ROBERTS, ROSALEE A.

Rosalee A. Roberts (1943–) was president in 1992 of the Public Relations Society of America (PRSA), the first and only Nebraskan elected and the fourth woman president. As president, she initiated the Visioning Committee, designed to re-create a strategic planning process to create the new direction and focus for PRSA into the next century. Also, she supervised a KPMG Peat Marwick complete resource and governance review of internal and external activities for PRSA. She supervised the completion of the first Professional Progression Guide to enable members to track their professional progress in the public relations profession.

As PRSA president, Roberts chaired the National Task Force on the Study of Ethical Issues, designed to increase awareness of ethical issues among PRSA members and the public relations profession and to aid in encouraging participation of senior level public relations practitioners.

Roberts is president of Rosalee Roberts Public Relations, Omaha, Nebraska, a public relations/marketing firm handling strategic planning, issues management, risk communications, reputation management, community relations, and media relations.

From 1995 to 1998, she was vice president of community relations and development and Executive Director, Children's Hospital Foundation for Children's Healthcare Services, Omaha, Nebraska. In this position, Roberts experienced in 1997 the international media story of the 3-year-old Woracek twins, who wandered into subzero temperatures in the middle of the night of January 17, 1997. She received worldwide media attention because of the twin's stay and release from Children's Hospital in Omaha, taking all calls in the high-profile story while protecting the children's and parents' wishes for privacy.

Roberts began her public relations career in 1965 after graduating from college and breaking an ankle in Quebec, Canada, where she'd gone to learn French so that she could enter the Peace Corps. She worked from 1969 to 1973 as promotions and public affairs manager at KETV–Channel 7. Then she joined Bozell public relations, working there for 20 years to become a partner at Bozell Worldwide, Inc., handling local, regional, and national clients.

Roberts was named national volunteer of the year in 1997 by the Arthritis Foundation and served on the boards of the Better Business Bureau, Child Saving Institute, Keep Omaha Beautiful, the Nebraska Humane Society, and the Omaha Literacy Council. Other civic activities include All Our Kids, a nonprofit youth mentoring and scholarship organization, and the Literacy Center for the Midlands.

Roberts received 2000 certification, Senior Level Ten, Environmental Risk Communications, from the Center for Risk Communications at Columbia

Rosalee A. Roberts

University. In 1994, she was named to the College of Fellows of the Public Relations Society of America. In 2003, she chaired the subcommittee studying a PRSA foundation endowment for the PRSA College of Fellows.

Roberts has received numerous awards for her professional and civic activities, including being named Nebraska Citizen of Distinction by the governor of Nebraska, the Arthritis Foundation National Volunteer Award, many PRSA presidential citations, and Outstanding Woman of Distinction for Communications, YWCA.

—Elizabeth L. Toth

ROSS, THOMAS J. "TOMMY"

Thomas J. ("T.J." or "Tommy") Ross was one of the rare third-generation practitioners working in the 20th century. He was a partner in a New York City agency named Lee & Ross, with Ivy Lee. The firm began in 1904 as Parker and Lee, founded by George Parker. Lee started his career by joining Parker. Ross continued a practice that was decades old. Tommy Ross, as he was known to his friends, was one of the original members of the Wise Men, a professional association of senior practitioner counselors in New York City, started by John W. Hill in 1938.

Typical of many public relations pioneers, Ross began his career in newspapers. Ross joined the Ivy Lee firm in 1919 and almost immediately became one of the most important forces in the destiny of that firm. The importance of the assignments increased as he demonstrated how well he could add value to the interests of clients and to the agency's success. He became a partner in 1933. Ross had demonstrated his ability to work with difficult projects for major corporate clients in service to Walter Chrysler of Chrysler Corporation and the Pennsylvania Railroad.

Ross acquired part of his counseling style and client list from Lee. Like Lee, he was an excellent listener and earned the reputation of always answering clients' questions clearly and frankly. From Lee, he made client connections with major companies, such as the tobacco industry. Both would work for publicity, but they knew that it must be grounded in sound business policy. Counseling before action was wiser than trying to answer for mistakes in judgment.

Like Lee, Ross worked quietly on behalf of clients. Reporters knew who his clients were and whence news releases came for those clients. In that regard, the agency did not act in secrecy. But they wanted clients to get the credit for effective public relations, not the agency. Client satisfaction and return business was the goal, not glory for the agency. In that regard, Ross viewed public relations as a *staff* function, not one that would presume to manage the company. Public relations was intended to inform and guide management in making decisions and responding to difficult or strained relationships.

Ross was part of the counseling team that took primary interest in the American Tobacco

Corporation account, starting in 1927. Like other industrial enterprises, the tobacco industry was having a hard time accommodating to the changing public policy environment of business. This industry is legendary in the 20th century for its clashes with antitrust lawyers and public health critics.

Lee and George Washington Hill of American Tobacco were good friends. As Lee was becoming more interested in the philanthropy of his most affluent clients, Ross became the leading counselor in the firm on clients' business relationship problems. This was especially the case in working for the American Tobacco, Chrysler, and Pennsylvania Railroad accounts.

George Washington Hill was flamboyant. He would go to any length to gain publicity for himself and his company, which relied heavily on the profits from Lucky Strike cigarettes. Hill retained Lee and Ross as well as Edward Bernays on this account, believing if they were the best and he hired them both, they could not be working for the competition. This account began with the primary focus on selling cigarettes, but by the early 1950s it had the added burden of responding to growing criticism from the health care industry.

The Chrysler account focused on selling automobiles, but also required attention to periodic differences with labor unions. One of the major issues facing the railroad industry, and Pennsylvania Railroad, was the desire on the part of some critics to nationalize the industry.

For such clients, Lee and Ross began by focusing on the soundness of the policies and practices of the clients. They knew, and frankly advised their clients, that you cannot convince any segment of the general public to believe something and act against their own interests. Thus, policy must begin with an honest assessment of the connection, the relationship, between the interests of each public (or market) and the client organization.

Ross was one of several leading practitioners who served on an advisory panel to create the Commission on National Voluntary Health Agencies from 1959 to 1960. Also on this committee were Arthur Page, Lindsey Kimball, National Fund for Medical Education president S. Sloan Colt, Arthur S.

Flemming (Secretary of Health, Education, and Welfare), Marion B. Folsom (former Secretary of Health, Education, and Welfare), Eugene Holman (chairman of Standard Oil of New Jersey), James A. Linen (*Time* publisher), and Juan Trippe (president of Pan American Airlines). Membership on such panels, along with other prestigious members, suggests the important role public relations practitioners can play in formulating governmental agencies and policies in the public interest.

After Lee's death, his name was dropped from the agency's title, which changed to T. J. Ross & Associates. This change, on October 1, 1961, occurred at the request of Lee's widow because none of her sons was any longer associated with the firm. The agreement created between Lee and Ross committed to the principle that the firm would support either partner's widow, who would have an interest in its management.

Ross retired as chairman of the firm in 1971 and died on May 27, 1975. Eventually, the agency this legendary figure had helped Ivy Lee to create and sustain became part of Golin-Harris. As was true of the other princes of public relations, Lee and Ross had helped to position and reposition companies and industries that defined the gross national product for much of the 20th century. Their clients were in railroads, chemicals, tobacco, manufacturing, electricity, banking, oil, food products, and coal, to mention some of the more obvious interests. They also counseled foundations and the arts, such as the Metropolitan Opera Association. The practice was more than publicity and press agentry. It recognized the value of relationships and the public interest. Summing his views based on years of experience, L. L. Golden observed, "After a half-century of practice, one of Ross's definite views is that the best public relations must stem from corporate performance. It is the action of the corporation that gives it a good reputation, not what it says about itself" (1968, p. 73).

—Robert L. Heath

See also Bernays, Edward; Counseling; Hill, John Wiley; Lee, Ivy; Page, Arthur W.; Parker, George; Press agentry; Promotion; Public interest; Publicity

Bibliography

Cutlip, S. M. (1994). *The unseen power: Public Relations. A history.* Hillsdale, NJ: Lawrence Erlbaum.

Golden, L. L. (1968, December 14). Public Relations: After half a century. *Saturday Review, 51,* 73–74.

Griese, N. L. (2001). *Arthur W. Page: Publisher, public relations pioneer, patriot.* Atlanta, GA: Anvil.

Freeman, W. M. (1975, May 28), T. J. Ross is dead at 81: Public relations pioneer. *New York Times,* p. 44.

RULES THEORY

Rules theory addresses the cultural and societal prescriptions and proscriptions for behavior in communication contexts. Rules can be explicit or implicit. Scholars use rules theory to understand how individuals and groups achieve their goals through communication. In the practice of public relations, rules theory addresses the ways organizations must, must not, should, or should not communicate with their publics in order to achieve their goals. Specific communication goals are often specified as compliance-gaining; relationship formation, maintenance, or dissolution; persuasion; and consensus building. Although research on rules theory has accumulated in the disciplines of organizational communication, social psychology, and sociology, the application of rules theory to the area of public relations is in its early stages of development.

The origin of rules theory has been credited to the 1953, posthumous publication of philosopher Ludwig Wittgenstein's book *Philosophical Investigations.* The introduction of rules theory for communication often is attributed to Donald P. Cushman and Gordon C. Whiting (1972). Their approach was influenced by the symbolic interactionist perspective developed by George H. Mead and focused on how communication is used to accomplish goals and construct meaning.

In 1980, Susan B. Shimanoff's highly influential book *Communication Rules: Theory and Research* was published. Shimanoff's book was the first book to systematically synthesize previous definitions of rules, differentiate rules from other concepts, and offer methods for measuring rules and developing theory.

Although scholars may have different views on rules, most agree communication rules are invoked in situations where there is human communication—whether it is interpersonal, group, organizational, or mass communication. Rules are socially constructed and are distinguished by their strength, the perceived consequences of noncompliance, and their contextual range. Shimanoff wrote, "A rule is a followable prescription that indicates what behavior is obligated, preferred or prohibited in certain contexts" (1980, p. 57). In her work, Shimanoff noted that another characteristic of a rule is that it must be physically or otherwise followable.

Cushman (1977) has pointed out that for rules to be present, parties in communication must agree upon what constitutes the rules for communication. In addition, Cushman has noted that part of what makes rules contextual is that not only are they tied to specific situations, but they are also determined by the communicator's role (i.e., a police officer may address a kindergarten class or his fellow officers). Rules are not the same as norms, laws, habits, heuristics, and principles.

RULE STRENGTH

Rules generate their power from the perceived social consequences that serve as enforcements. This social force originates from an individual's knowledge, experience, and/or perception of the social judgment that will be made about him or her for following or not following a rule. The social judgments that result from adhering to or defying rules may result in some form of censure or approval. The degree of censure or approval corresponds to the strength of rule that was (un)heeded.

Shimanoff introduced three kinds of rules classified by their strength: prohibitive, obligatory, and preferred. She defined prohibitive rules as those that proscribe what one *must not* do (e.g., use discriminatory language in the workplace), whereas obligatory rules prescribed what one *must* do (e.g., provide a news release about financial earnings statements). These two types of rules were considered to have greater social force than the third rule she identified, preferred rules. Accordingly, preferred rules dictate what one *should* or *should not* do. The probability that judgments about the communicator will result from not honoring preferred rules is less certain than the probability that judgments will result if one defies an obligatory or prohibitive rule.

Cushman and Whiting also distinguished rule strength in their discussion of procedural rules, or rules about communication order and interaction. The authors use different terms to describe rules. For them, rules can be formal (more permanent) or informal (more flexible). The authors also proposed that rules must be able to be presented as "in context X, Y is required or permitted" (1972, p. 228). For example, when introduced to a colleague, it is generally required that one reply, "Very nice to meet you." Rules that are required are considered formal rules, and those that are permitted are perceived as more informal because the consequences of rule compliance, censure, or approval, are applied less rigorously. In her book, Shimanoff (1980) noted that she favored the use of the term preferred instead of permitted, because, she argued, the latter does not imply that sanctions or rewards are applied.

Shimanoff did note that rules also differ by their intensity: "The intensity of a rule is measured by the degree of its salience in a given situation: the less important a rule, the less likely deviations from that rule will be negatively sanctioned" (1980, p. 97). Here, she suggested that even among obligatory rules, some carry more weight in an evaluation than others (i.e., covering up corporate negligence and disregard for car passenger safety may be viewed as more severe than telling a reporter, "No comment").

Recent research treats rule strength as a continuum, where the strength of a particular rule is a point on a continuous scale, whereby the scores near the top of the scale are viewed as more obligatory or prohibitive and those rated on the middle of the scale are viewed as preferred. In this way, proscriptive and prescriptive obligatory rules can have the same strength, but the valence of that strength ranges from positive to negative. Rules with strength in the bottom quartile are deemed rules with very little strength or, in the case where

the rating is close to zero, not rules. This conception of rules unifies previous conceptualizations and allows for the comparison of strength among rules regardless of their valence.

COMPLIANCE

Rule compliance specifies whether rules are followed. Shimanoff suggested that rules can be either met or violated and indicated that rules for preferred behavior were "empowered by rewards rather than punishments, but smaller or fewer rewards may be viewed as a type of punishment" (1980, p. 94). For Shimanoff, rule violations were measured on a continuum and meeting rules was viewed as dichotomous.

It has been suggested that rule compliance be designated as a continuum. Rule violations occur when rules are not followed and lead to negative evaluations (i.e., the company does not take responsibility for the safety of its products, blames an employee, and is rated negatively). Rules are met when the individual follows the rule (i.e., the company takes responsibility for its product's defect). The new concept introduced is that of surpassing the rule. This happens when the rule is followed but also exceeds expectations in the positive direction (i.e., not only does the company accept responsibility, but it reimburses its customers for the cost of the product).

Figure 1 is a diagram of the continuum that visually demonstrates that rule compliance does vary and hence censure and approval, rewards and sanctions, also vary by strength.

Rule compliance

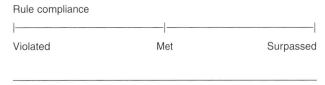

Figure 1   Rules compliance continuum

CONTEXTUAL RANGE

A rule's contextual range relates to the variety of situations in which a rule can be applied. Cushman and Whiting defined the range of rules as "the number of different contexts or circumstances in which the same action is applicable" (1972, p. 233). In other words, some rules are more generally applied across situations, whereas others are more restricted to use in specific circumstances.

An examination of rules theory at the interpersonal level has suggested that if there is co-orientation between communicators on rules (i.e., communicators understand and agree on the interpretation of rules), then communication symmetry is possible. Thus, communication becomes dialogic.

Other researchers have used rules theory in the context of relational communication, such as Web site rules for organizations providing customers with product information corrections, bylines for information sources, and promotional e-mail communications.

A recent exploratory study identified communication rules consumers held for interacting with both informational and e-commerce Web sites. It was found that there are different expectations depending on whether the Web site's main function is to provide information (e.g., news Web sites) or to sell products to consumers (e.g., e-commerce). This research indicates that at the level of person-to-organization communication, rules are dependant on the role of the individual (consumer vs. news reader) and on the role of the organization (e-commerce vs. informational site).

This line of research has implications for the concept of rule compliance and organizational roles. Typically, an online public's increased liking for an e-commerce organization occurs only when communication rules for online communication are surpassed. This suggests that meeting rules is not enough to improve organization-public relationships—surpassing expectations for communication rules is necessary.

Public health campaigns researchers are concerned with understanding group rules in order to increase the adoption of healthy behaviors within certain populations. Rajiv Rimal and Kevin Real's (2003) research is representative of this trend. They examined how perceived rules (they used the term injunctive *norms*) and group identity influenced

alcohol consumption by college students in order to determine how to develop messages to reduce alcohol consumption on campuses. They found that "those who perceived that society *dis*approves of consumption and simultaneously believe that most of their peers drink were themselves more likely to drink" (p. 197, italics in original). From this, a rule for the subgroup of consumers can be inferred: College students should not conform to societal expectations. This information can help those designing public health campaigns.

Barry Schlenker and Bruce Darby (1981) examined the social rules for providing apologies. They found that rules for apologies varied by how responsible the individuals felt the offender was for the accident and the severity of the resulting injury. The researchers learned that people expect more complete apologies when the consequences of an accident are more severe.

Research on rules from the interpersonal literature is particularly relevant for the areas of relational public relations and crisis management. In the 1980s, rules theory was applied to organizational communication to examine how rules affected communication within organizations. Since the 1980s, academics have studied communication between supervisors and employees, and displays of emotion in professional settings (nonverbal communication) and in employee selection.

Although rules theory is relatively new to public relations, it is used to (a) examine co-orientation to foster symmetrical communication, (b) determine how communication affects perceived relationships between individuals and an organization, and (c) identify and predict how messages will be received and effect behavior change.

—*Maria E. Len-Rios*

Bibliography

Cushman, D. P. (1977). The rules perspective as a theoretical basis for the study of human communication. *Communication Quarterly, 25*, 30–45.

Cushman, D. P., & Whiting, G. C. (1972). An approach to communication theory: Toward a consensus on rules. *The Journal of Communication, 22*, 217–238.

Len-Ríos, M. E. (2002). *Communication rules and corporate online communication.* Unpublished doctoral dissertation, University of Missouri, Columbia.

Len-Ríos, M. E. (2003). Consumer rules and orientations toward corporate Web sites: A pilot study. *Journal of Promotion Management, 9,* 125–143.

Len-Ríos, M. E., & Cameron, G. T. (2002, July). *Knowing what to say and when to say it: Rules for building relationships with online publics.* Paper presented at the annual meeting of the International Communication Association, Public Relations Division, Seoul, South Korea.

Rimal, R. N., & Real, K. (2003). Understanding the influence of perceived norms on behaviors. *Communication Theory, 32,* 184–203.

Schlenker, B. R., & Darby, B. W. (1981). The use of apologies in social predicaments. *Social Psychology Quarterly, 44,* 271–278.

Shimanoff, S. B. (1980). *Communication rules: Theory and research.* Beverly Hills, CA: Sage.

SAMPLING

Sampling refers to the process of selecting the people or the objects to be used in an analysis. Although sampling is most commonly associated with surveys, sampling also can be used to select messages for analysis. For example, a practitioner may be interested in examining a subset of the news stories that appeared about a product recall, a lawsuit, or a plant opening. Although this discussion will focus on sampling people, similar principles can be applied to sampling messages.

Researchers use sampling when they cannot survey everyone from the population of interest. A population refers to the group of people of interest. A census is when researchers are able to survey everyone from the population. However, typically this is not feasible. Researchers determine a sampling frame—a complete list of the membership of the population from which they will select their sample. The sampling frame is composed of the set of people that have a chance to be sampled. Researchers use a sampling method to obtain a sample, a subset of the population that is used to represent the population. A primary goal is to ensure that the sample closely matches the population so that one can generalize from the sample to the population. In other words, you want the sample to represent the population. This discussion briefly overviews basic concepts associated with sampling. Readers should consult additional references for more detailed information.

There are two categories of sampling methods: (a) probability (scientific) sampling and (b) non-probability (convenience or nonscientific) sampling. Probability sampling requires the use of a random selection of people to be included in the sample. Every member of the population has a known probability of being included in the sample. Probability sampling is preferred because it can provide more accurate, unbiased data and permits the calculation of the sampling error. Sampling error often is reported as the "margin of error" and reflects how confident the researcher can be in the accuracy of the results. Sampling error is calculated using a formula that assumes the random selection of cases to be included.

Sample size is a concern for researchers because it affects the accuracy of the sample. Statistics books provide tables indicating the sample size desired for a particular level of confidence in the accuracy of the results.

Commonly used strategies for probability sampling include simple random sampling, systematic sampling, and stratified sampling. Simple random sampling resembles drawing the sample from names put in a hat. Names of the members of the sampling frame are put into the hat and the desired number are drawn. Computer programs can be used to approximate pulling names from a hat.

A second sampling method is systematic random sampling. This method requires an unordered list of members of the sampling frame (e.g., members are not ordered by geographic region, age, or any other characteristic). A starting point is selected randomly (e.g., the 12th, 37th, or 101st name on the list) and every nth name (e.g., every 11th, 20th, or 35th name) is selected for inclusion in the sample.

A third method of random sampling is stratified sampling. It is called stratified because the people are organized (stratified) based upon some characteristic of interest, such as age, ethnicity, or sex. These stratification variables are selected because you believe they would make a difference in how people would respond to your survey. Then simple random sampling or systematic sampling is used to select a proportional representation from each strata of interest. For example, if your sampling frame is comprised of 70 percent women and 30 percent men, you may want to ensure that those proportions of women and men are evidenced in your final sample. This would enhance the precision of your sample.

Although random sampling methods are preferred, it may be impossible to meet the requirements for probability sampling. In this case researchers use non-probability sampling. However, it is important to note that non-probability sampling precludes calculation of sampling error, offers questionable generalizability, and is subject to bias in participant selection. Non-probability samples demonstrate bias because respondents are not selected randomly. Perhaps the survey participants differed from those who did not participate on important variables of interest, such as attitudes toward the organization or the campaign. Data obtained from the survey participants may not reflect the data that would have been obtained from a randomly selected sample. Researchers often turn to non-probability sampling when a complete sample frame is difficult to determine or cost considerations make probability sampling less attractive.

Convenience sampling, purposive sampling, and snowball sampling often are used. In convenience sampling, a sample is selected based upon being in the right place at the right time to be asked to participate. For example, people walking by a kiosk in a shopping mall might be asked to complete a survey. Or people waiting in line for an art exhibit might be asked to participate. Their availability and willingness to complete the survey are the basis for their inclusion in the sample.

Purposive sampling is used when researchers need to select participants who possess certain characteristics of interest. Characteristics might include having used a particular product, knowledge of a controversial issue, or a subscription to a local newspaper. For example, a researcher might be interested in the opinions of people who have seen a series of public service ads (PSAs) on television. The researcher does not want to include those who have not seen the PSAs since they would not be able to answer the survey questions. The researcher might attempt to recruit participants at community picnics, driver's license facilities, and high school football games. The researcher only asks those who have seen the PSAs to participate in the surveys.

In snowball (network) sampling, a person who has already participated in a survey might recruit others to participate through word-of-mouth referrals. Participants give researchers access to other potential participants who might be recruited by the researcher. This method is useful when organizations are reluctant to release the names of their members due to confidentiality issues (e.g., support groups for families of alcoholics) or when informal networks of people who are likely to be interested in or affected by the same issues need to be reached (e.g., dog owners who are concerned about or might be affected by a community action, such as dog owners using a dog park or participating in local events involving dogs). For example, a researcher might be interested in the attitudes of "soccer moms" toward the proposed building of a soccer field near a landfill. Because the city's soccer club organizers do not release the names of people involved in the club, the researcher contacts a few soccer moms who then provide the names of other soccer moms who could be contacted for participation in the survey.

—*Sherry J. Holladay*

See also Survey

Bibliography

Fowler, F. J. (2001). *Survey research methods* (3rd ed.). Thousand Oaks, CA: Sage.

Stacks, D. W. (2002). *Primer of public relations research.* New York: Guilford Press.

SANDBAGGING

Sandbagging is a term used to describe the efforts of an organization or an individual to avoid answering questions asked by reporters or key publics. Sometimes the response is as simple as "No comment." At the extreme, the response is couched in more complex terms, such as "We are establishing a commission to investigate. When we have found the facts, we will report them."

The term has military roots. For example, in the late 19th century it meant "to strike unexpectedly; to take by surprise." In the early 20th century, it meant "to intimidate, coerce, bully as by threats." This slang term further shows up as a verb in cooperation with "ghosting" and "goldbricking" when referenced as a Vietnam War slang term to mean "hiding out in the rear as if not seen."

This slang term also appears as part of mainstream gambling terminology—"to downplay or misrepresent one's ability in a game or activity in order to deceive (someone), especially in gambling." Further, various online dictionaries describe this term (verb) as follows: "to treat harshly or unfairly; to misinform, mislead—to give false or misleading information" and "to conceal or misrepresent one's true position, potential, or intent, especially in order to take advantage of." A person who carries out such behaviors is a "sandbagger" (noun). This term appears to also be framed as a propaganda technique when used in a political context.

—*Lisa T. Fall*

See also Spin

SCALES

The term *scales* may have multiple meanings to public relations practitioners. One use of the term denotes a particular measurement instrument such as a scale to measure reputation, credibility, or ethical climate. This use typically references an established measurement instrument developed by researchers, for which validity and reliability information is available.

Another use of the term describes a type of measure or scale, such as a Likert scale or Semantic Differential scale, which uses particular types of response options or answer scales. The scale refers to the way in which respondents record their answers.

Another use of the term is related to the previously mentioned use of answer scales and is synonymous with level of measurement or kinds of data to be analyzed. Practitioners may speak of answer scales that refer to how respondents record their responses to survey questions, which in turn produce certain types of data for analysis. Level of measurement is important because it dictates the types of statistical analyses that can be performed on the data.

In 2002, Don W. Stacks identified two types of attitude measures commonly used in public relations research: (a) Likert-type scales and (b) Semantic Differential scales. These scales can be adapted to examine attitudes toward a variety of things.

Likert-type scales use standardized response categories to record reactions to a series of statements reflecting issues of interest. Likert-type scales often provide five options for responses: (a) strongly agree, (b) agree, (c) neither agree nor disagree (neutral), (d) disagree, and (e) strongly disagree. Alternatively, the scale may be enlarged to seven categories by adding two options to the ends of the answer continuum: (f) very strongly agree; and (g) very strongly disagree. An advantage of the Likert-type scale is its consistent use of answer options that respondents find easy to complete. A practitioner might be interested in assessing community support for a proposed landfill to be built outside of town. The practitioner could write a series of statements reflecting issues related to the proposed landfill in order to gauge community sentiment. Statements might include (a) "The proposed landfill would provide jobs for the community," (b) "The proposed landfill would pose health hazards to community members," and (c) "The proposed landfill is necessary." A survey containing these items would be administered to a randomly selected sample of community residents. Respondents would record their reactions to the statements using the Likert-type scale options. The practitioner would analyze the data to obtain a clearer view of community attitudes toward various aspects of the issue.

The Semantic Differential scale consists of a series of items designed to assess the connotative meanings associated with a stimulus or attitude object, such as an organization, a person, a practice, a product, or a concept. The term *semantic* refers to meanings and *differential* reflects differences. A connotative meaning is a personal or emotional meaning, whereas a denotative meaning is the "dictionary meaning." Whereas there generally is high agreement on denotative meanings, this is not true for connotative meanings because they arise from personal experiences and perceptions. For example, the denotative meaning of "McDonald's" would relate to its being a fast-food restaurant. In contrast, the connotative meanings associated with McDonald's might vary widely and include meanings such as "fun," "playful," "convenient," "unhealthy," "inexpensive," and "tasty."

Practitioners often are concerned with connotative meanings because they reflect personal perceptions and these are important for understanding stakeholders. The stimulus used in research might be a person like "George W. Bush" or a well-known community leader. Alternatively, the stimulus might be a product like "genetically engineered food" or an organization like "A2Z Corporation." The different meanings reflected in the responses to items on the Semantic Differential scale can be compared to the meanings for other related stimuli, such as other restaurants, opposing political candidates, or different organizations.

The Semantic Differential scale consists of a series of bipolar (opposite) adjective pairs (good/bad, weak/strong) separated by a number of blanks or lines (usually seven) signifying response options. Respondents are asked to indicate their reactions to the stimulus by marking the blanks/options reflecting their connotative meanings on dimensions of interest. Traditionally, the three meaning dimensions used are evaluative (good/bad, valuable/worthless,

realistic/unrealistic), potency (weak/strong, large/small), and activity (active/passive, hot/cold, weak/strong). The reactions can be summed to provide a summary evaluation of the stimulus. The Semantic Differential scale's usefulness stems from its ability to discern connotative meanings and its ease of completion.

When the term *scale* is used to refer to level of measurement, it refers to the type of data to be used for analysis. There are four levels of measurement. The first level of measurement is called nominal. Nominal data represent unordered categories, names, or labels for a variable, such as sex (male or female), employment status (employed or unemployed), political party affiliation (Republican, Democrat, or Independent), or place of birth.

Ordinal-level measurement provides data that reflect the rank order of a variable on a single dimension. The options signal relationships to one another. However, there is no assumption of equal spacing between the options. For example, the answer options "good," "fair," and "poor" might be provided for a question about the respondent's assessment of the current employment opportunities in the community. In relation to the other two options, "good" is assumed to reflect a more positive assessment whereas "poor" reflects a more pessimistic assessment. However, it cannot be assumed that the "fair" option is truly halfway between the two options. "Fair" is only assumed to be more positive than "poor."

Interval-level measurement assumes equal distances or standard intervals between options. The Fahrenheit or Celsius temperature scales provide good examples from the sciences. Each degree represents a known interval. In research, true interval level measures are rare. Because statistical tests for interval-level measures often are more powerful and better known than tests for ordinal-level data, researchers tend to prefer interval-level data and analyses, and often treat ordinal-level data as interval-level data in their statistical analyses—a practice that is not without debate. For example, the commonly used Likert-type scale is technically an ordinal-level measure but is often treated as an interval-level measure. To elaborate, there is no standard interval or equal distance between "strongly agree" and "agree" or any of the other options. Although "strongly agree" is closer to "agree" (thus reflecting ordinal measurement), it technically is not correct to say that there are equal intervals between any of the options. However, in practice, researchers often act as if these do represent equal intervals.

Ratio-level measurement is considered the highest level of measurement and assumes a true zero point. A zero represents an absence of that variable. For instance, income, number of years of formal education, and number of purchases from a particular vendor represent ratio-level data because they potentially have zero as an option. Theoretically, respondents could report no income, no formal education, and no purchases from the vendor.

—Sherry J. Holladay

See also Measuring/measures

Bibliography

Stacks, D. W. (2002). *Primer of public relations research.* New York: Guilford Press.

SCAN

See Environmental scanning

SCHOONOVER, JEAN

Jean Way Schoonover (1920–) was president of Dudley-Anderson-Yutzy (D-A-Y), the first major public relations firm in New York City to be owned and managed by women.

D-A-Y traces its history to its founding by Pendleton Dudley in 1909. Schoonover and her sister Barbara Hunter purchased the firm from the original partners in 1970. It was acquired by Ogilvy & Mather in 1983.

Schoonover grew up in Westport on Lake Champlain, New York. She graduated with a B.A. from Cornell University in 1941, majoring in English and education. Her first jobs were as an English teacher and librarian at Castleton Union School in Hudson, New York, from 1941 to 1943.

Schoonover moved to New York City in 1943 in hopes of finding a job as a newspaper reporter. She worked as a ticket seller at Penn Station until she was finally hired as a reporter for *Food Field Reporter,* a biweekly trade paper for food industry executives. Schoonover interviewed Clarence Birdseye, who had sold his frozen food business to General Foods. Her story was noticed by George Anderson, a partner at D-A-Y, who hired Schoonover as an account executive in 1949.

Schoonover and Hunter purchased D-A-Y when it was ranked 15th among national public relations companies. They incorporated the company, with Schoonover as president and Hunter as executive vice president. When Schoonover signed the first paychecks, she discovered that the male executives were making $25,000 a year while she and Hunter were making $18,000. Later, Schoonover became chairman and CEO and Hunter became president of D-A-Y.

D-A-Y had the first home economics department and test kitchen in the agency business, with a staff of home economists developing recipes for food and wine accounts. Clients included Accent International, Florida Citrus Commission, Gelatine, Nestle Co., SuCrest Corporate, Taylor Wine Co., United Fresh Fruit & Vegetable Association, Wash 'n Dri, and Canaan Products, Inc.

Under the leadership of Schoonover, D-A-Y won a number of Public Relations Society of America Silver Anvil awards. On a budget of $25,000, D-A-Y handled the publicity for the bicentennial reenactment of the capture of Fort Ticonderoga from the British.

D-A-Y pulled off the public relations triumph of 1983 with the 100th birthday party for the Brooklyn Bridge. Over 2 million New Yorkers and tourists came out for the eight-block-long parade, and 1,200 journalists reported on the story around the world.

After a botulism incident occurred, D-A-Y helped the Tuna Research Foundation with counsel on acting responsibly and making changes to maintain customer confidence and product loyalty, containing the crisis that could have destroyed sales.

D-A-Y clients received help with the women's market through programs on Women as Economic Equals, in cooperation with *Ladies' Home Journal* and a credit card company. D-A-Y assisted AT&T with a conference titled Women in the Workforce.

Upon selling D-A-Y to Ogilvy & Mather in 1983, Schoonover managed D-A-Y, which eventually folded into O&M public relations offices, with offices in New York, Washington, Chicago, Atlanta, Houston, and Los Angeles. In 1988 Schoonover became vice chairman of the Ogilvy & Mather Public Relations Group and a senior vice president of Ogilvy & Mather U.S.

Schoonover retired in 1990. Since her retirement, she has spent her time in pro bono activities and serving on the board of directors of Bliss, Gouverneur & Associates, a New York public relations firm.

Schoonover volunteered her leadership as president of the YMCA of the City of New York from 1994 to 1998. She was president of the Women Executives in Public Relations in New York City from 1979 to 1980, and president of the Public Relations Society of New York in 1979. In 1987 through 1989, she was a member and vice chair of the Defense Advisory Committee on Women in the Services (DACOWITS). Her role was to report to commanding officers and the Department of Defense about military base conditions for women. She was on the Cornell University Board of Trustees from 1975 to 1980. She helped the International Women's Forum publicize "Why Women Lead" by Dr. Judy Rosner, featured in the 1990 issue of *Harvard Business Review.*

Schoonover has spoken to various groups, including a *Vital Speeches* selection, "Why Corporate America Fears Women," presented in 1974 to a seminar for life insurance executives.

Schoonover has won many awards for her achievements: (a) Advertising Woman of the Year Award (1972); (b) Matrix Award from Women in Communications (1976); (c) *Business Week's* Top 100 Corporate Women; (d) International Association of Women Business Owners Leadership Award; (e) National Association of Women Business Owners Entrepreneurial Woman Award; (f) National Headliner Award in Communications Inc. (1984);

(g) Big WEAL Award, Women's Equity Action League (1985); and (h) Achievement Award from the League of Women Voters of New York City (1997).

—Elizabeth L. Toth

Bibliography

Dudley-Anderson-Yutzy Public Relations. (1971, March 24). *Jack O'Dwyer's Newsletter,* p. 2.

Hartman, C. (1983, November). Selling the Brooklyn Bridge. *Inc.* (Reprint)

SEARCH ENGINE

A search engine refers to a tool used by computers to find information. Modern search engines typically employ graphic interfaces. The term *search engine* is closely associated with the tool used to search for information on the World Wide Web. Any graphic-search interface such as those used by universities and public libraries to search for books, magazines, multimedia documents, and so forth can be called a search engine. Without the search engine, it would not be possible to locate specific information from among the billions of unique Web pages that currently exist on the World Wide Web (Kent, 2001).

Search engines work by examining archival databases generated from the billions of Web sites currently accessible. Search engines use an assortment of indexing logics. Most search engines create indexes based on keywords, phrases, categories, and other heuristics. Many search engines also allow users to employ *real language*. Ask Jeeves, for example, lets users phrase their searches as actual questions rather than a collection of keywords. Other search engines, such as Google, employ networking logic, ranking pages by their connectedness to other Web sites. The more popular a page is, the more likely it is to rise to the top of Google's list.

When searching the Web, most search engines allow users to employ (a) Boolean logic (AND, OR, NOT), (b) phrase searches (surrounding words with quotation marks), (c) wildcard searches (replacing prefixes/suffixes with an *), and (d) nested searching (complex searches created by using parentheses and algebraic logic). Because search features vary from search engine to search engine, users are encouraged to learn the particular features supported by their preferred search engines.

Suggestions for effective Web searching include

1. Use multiple keywords—sometimes a dozen or more.

2. Search for phrases ("words in quotes"), especially with names, whenever possible.

3. Rare or unusual words such as *defenestrate* make it easier to narrow results.

4. Common works such as *computer* make it difficult to narrow results.

5. Order search terms from most important to least important.

6. Do not waste time searching through large lists of hits—more success will result by adding new search terms or rephrasing the search by adding quotation marks.

There are currently hundreds of search engines available for use on the World Wide Web. Notable search engines include AltaVista, Ask Jeeves, Google, Ixquick, Lycos, Mamma, and Yahoo.

—*Michael L. Kent*

Bibliography

Kent, M. L. (2000). Getting the most from your search engine. *Communication Teacher, 15*(1), 4–7.
Kent, M. L. (2001). Essential tips for searching the Web. *Public Relations Quarterly, 46*(1), 26–30.

SECURITIES AND EXCHANGE COMMISSION

The Securities and Exchange Commission (SEC) is the federal agency established to enforce the laws and rules governing United States securities markets. The SEC's primary functions involve the registration of securities and compliance with the rule of full disclosure—timely, relevant, and accurate information about a security and the issuing company that helps an investor make a buy, sell, or hold decision. The expertise of investor relations professionals depends in part on knowledge of the SEC and its regulations concerning securities and the publicly held companies that issue those securities. Investor relations professionals must also understand disclosure opportunities beyond filing requirements that could occur in releases, responses to rumors, and comments.

The SEC administers the Securities Act of 1933 and the Securities Exchange Act of 1934, along with a cohort of laws created to help protect investors. Those include the Trust Indenture Act, the Investment Company Act, the Investment Advisors Act, and the Public Utility Holding Act. These laws were written to prevent the kind of market collapse that culminated in the crash of October 1929.

Investors had no such protections in the boom of the 1920s when market manipulation and an absence of ethics, rules, and laws were prevalent. A highly speculative stock market and other weaknesses in the economy courted financial catastrophe and an ensuing depression. Congress held hearings to find ways to restore the public's faith in the securities markets. Participants in the hearings agreed that a corporation issuing a stock or bond must be fair and honest in disclosing to investors information about the company, the security, and level of investment risk, while brokers, dealers, and exchanges must be fair and honest in issuing securities to investors.

The Securities Act of 1933 established strong civil and criminal liabilities for omissions and distortions of facts concerning the issue of stocks or bonds. The Securities and Exchange Act of 1934 created the SEC and required stock exchanges to register with the five-member commission. The Trust Indenture Act of 1939 required that debt securities (such as bonds, debentures, and notes) not be offered for sale to the public unless a formal agreement (the trust indenture) between the issue and the bondholder conformed to standards of the act. The Investment Company Act of 1940 focused on compliance of disclosure of information about mutual funds and investment objectives as well as on investment company structures and operations. The

Investment Advisors Act of 1940 required that investment advisor firms or sole practitioners register with the SEC and conform to regulations. The act was amended in 1996 to limit registration to advisers with at least $25 million of assets. The Public Utility Holding Act of 1935 established regulation of interstate holding companies engaged in the electric utility business or in the retail distribution of natural gas.

The SEC is currently implementing the Sarbanes-Oxley Act of 2002, which will require corporate officers to certify company financial statements or be subject to criminal penalties. Among other provisions, the act has mandated creation of the new Public Company Accounting Oversight Board (PCAOB). The act was signed into law in the summer of 2002 in response to questionable accounting practices and poor internal controls that led to the failures of such high-profile public companies as Enron, WorldCom, and Global Crossing.

SEC commissioners are appointed by the president of the United States and a chairman is designated from among the five members. The SEC is organized into four divisions and 18 offices, headquartered in Washington, DC, with offices in New York and other regional locations across the United States. Approximately 3,100 analysts, accountants, lawyers, technical staff, and assistants work with commissioners to oversee the U.S. stock exchanges, broker-dealers, investment advisors, mutual funds, and public utility holding companies.

Publicly held companies meet certain filing requirements with the SEC, and the Division of Corporation Finance is charged with reviewing those documents, which include (a) registration statements for newly offered securities; (b) annual and quarterly filings (forms 10-K and 10-Q); (c) proxy materials sent to shareholders before an annual meeting; (d) annual reports to shareholders; and (e) filings related to tender offering filings, as well as mergers and acquisitions. Corporation Finance also works in conjunction with the Office of the Chief Accountant to monitor activities of the accounting profession, particularly the Financial Accounting Standards Board (FASB), that form generally accepted accounting principles (GAAP).

The Division of Market Regulation regulates broker-dealer firms and self-regulatory organizations (SROs), which include the stock exchanges and the National Association of Securities Dealers (NASD). This Division also oversees the Securities Investor Protection Corporation (SIPC) that insures customer accounts of member brokerage firms against the failure of those firms.

The Division of Investment Management oversees and regulates the $15 trillion investment management industry and administers the securities laws affecting investment companies (including mutual funds) and investment advisers.

The Division of Enforcement investigates possible violations of securities laws, recommends action, and negotiates settlements on behalf of the SEC. Typical violations include: (a) insider trading; (b) misrepresentation or omission of important information about securities; (c) manipulating the market prices of securities; (d) stealing customers' funds or securities; (e) violating broker-dealers' responsibility to treat customers fairly; and (f) sale of securities without proper registration.

—*Rebecca G. Aguilar*

See also Annual financial report; Investor relations

Bibliography

Mahoney, W. F. (1991). *Investor relations: The professional's guide to financial marketing and communications.* New York: New York Institute of Finance.

Securities and Exchange Commission. (2003, July). *The investor's advocate: How the SEC protects investors and maintains market integrity.* Available: www.sec.gov/about/whatwedo.shtml

Tyler, P. (1965). *Securities, exchanges and the SEC.* New York: H. W. Wilson.

SEGMENTATION

Segmentation is dividing an audience into smaller groups that are predicted to more likely react in a homogeneous manner to a particular motive in the reception of a message or product. As a public relations concept, segmentation helps practitioners focus actionable receivers' attention on specific messages most important to them, lowers total message distribution costs, encourages a broader spectrum of audiences to attend to a message, limits distracting or counterproductive messages being distributed to alternative audiences, and increases the perception of service from public relations practitioners to media gatekeepers.

Segmentation was initially formalized as a marketing concept by Wendell R. Smith in 1955. Although there are nearly an unlimited number of different segmentation possibilities, most authors group them into one of four broad categories: geographic, demographic, psychographic, and behavioral. Geographic segmentation differentiates between audiences that live in different geographic subdivisions, ranging from nation-states to individual neighborhoods or rural or urban environments. Demographic characteristics classify audiences based upon such personal qualities as age, sex, marital status, nationality, income, occupation, or education. Psychographic segmentation relies upon an individual's social status, personal lifestyle, or personality qualities to determine an actionable category. Finally, behavioral segments analyze an individual's product use, buying behavior, or media use patterns to form a segment.

Segmentation has been more often and more formally employed in advertising and marketing communication than in public relations, likely because of the research costs involved with establishing audience segments and the comparatively low-cost messages, compared with advertising media, of transmission media used for public relations. Public relations tacticians have discouraged "shotgunning" a single news release to numerous and diverse media. In some public relations writing, practitioners have urged media research to determine placement opportunities that hold concentrations of important audiences, and "story splitting" routines to discover aspects of public relations messages to share with different audiences, or to design events, products, or services that appeal to important audiences.

Although targeting public relations messages to specific audiences is a crude form of segmentation, marketing and advertising professionals have employed much more sophisticated models. Michel Wedel and Wagner Kamakura outlined a broad range of segmentation methods, notably focusing on tracking multiple identifiers for individuals within a universe of potential customers. Such multivariate statistics routinely uses cluster analysis, which mathematically groups similar people in clusters distinct from others within the sample; or conjoint analysis, which analyzes motive preferences for various combinations of attributes.

These models may pale in importance to further developments in segmentation in which individual consumers place themselves into their own segments. Inventory control systems, combined with the Internet, just-in-time manufacturing protocols, and new order-taking and shipping technology have integrated message transmission systems and message receiving systems so individuals can access messages that precisely meet their needs, and then create a precise product or service that matches their motives. As these systems further develop, public relations practitioners may need to turn their attention to developing media paths so that individual audience members can pursue information discovery that will lead to behaviors useful to their client organizations.

—*William Thompson*

See also Demographics; Psychographics

Bibliography

Wedel, M., & Kamakura, W. (2000). *Market segmentation: Conceptual and methodological foundations* (2nd ed.). Boston: Kluwer.

SEMIOTICS THEORY

One of the new trends in critical theory is the move to the application of structuralism and semiotics for finding meaning in media texts and campaign messages. The theories of structuralism and semiotics, incorporated into the body of knowledge known as critical theory, are closely related and operate on similar assumptions. These theories explore how language and communication have meanings based on underlying assumptions of the persons making meanings from messages.

These two theories explain that a kind of language, or structure, works at an unconscious, or deep, level of a person or a culture that nevertheless causes or prompts language and meaning at the conscious level. These became popular theories for critical scholars who were searching for additional ways to explain processing of meaning, ideology, and symbol use in all kinds of communication. Critical scholars turned to structuralism and semiotics theories that were being developed in linguistics and in anthropology and applied them to the understanding of media texts, campaign message texts, and other popular culture artifacts.

STRUCTURALISM

First, a look at structuralist theory as it developed in anthropology suggests that a deep structure in a culture, much like a hidden language speaking to the culture, gives rise to the surface structure of other language forms. Anthropologists argue that unconscious structures of myth, rituals, or symbols are unconscious or deep structures that all cultures have. These operate much like an ideology—an unconscious worldview that we follow but do not know that we follow—to shape each culture's beliefs, symbols, rituals, and language that are used to communicate to others and to oneself and to give meanings to oneself and others.

For example, research of campaigns from a structuralist perspective reveals hidden ideologies, rituals, symbols, and imbedded meanings in the messages. The tobacco wars between the tobacco industry and the antismoking activists, the pro-life and pro-choice campaigns on abortion, or the campaigns sponsored by those against breast implants and those who feel implants are representative of women's rights to their own bodies reveal ideologies such as civil rights, the right of a mother to control her own body, the right of the unborn fetus, patriarchy, feminism, and the religious right. All the campaign messages generated on both sides of each issue also divulge rituals such as the pleasurable act of smoking and the disgusting ritual of smoking, and symbols such as the humanity of the unborn fetus and a bloody coat hanger. A structuralist approach also allows a study of the various meanings that the

messages might contain, such as that human rights supersede personal rights, personal rights supersede medical risks, or a woman has the right to control her own body.

In these examples, the messages are mediated images that represent deep structures and the many ideologies of our capitalist, industrial, and personal-rights culture. Structuralist studies of all kinds of texts are of interest to critical scholars because they provide another system of uncovering meaning and explaining how individuals use and get meanings from media and campaign texts.

SEMIOTICS

Semiotics developed from linguistics but is very similar to the structuralist model of a deep, ideological, or unconscious structure that affects the conscious, surface level of communication and meaning. Linguistics names the underlying structure of language *langue,* that is, a set of rules the culture—unconsciously—follows to shape the everyday communication of the culture. The term *parole* is the name for this everyday communication, vocabulary, syntax, and grammar that a culture follows. In other words, each culture has its own unique langue and manifested parole that characterize that culture and that language. For example, a semiotic study of nightly news reports carried on network television can identify the words and visuals used to report on each story; these are the parole. Then the attempt to identify the underlying cultural ideologies and rules that govern and dictate the choice and the format of these messages represent the langue.

Semiotics provides a three-part model of meaning that can be used to uncover the imbedded and the obvious meanings of a text. Semiotics specifically means the study of signs, or things that represent something other than them. The semiotic model of meaning contains (a) an idea or object that is represented (known as the *signified*); (b) an image or word that represents it (known as the *signifier*); and (c) the combination of the signified and signifier that brings together the signifier and the signified to reveal the meaning of the object (known as the *sign*).

Any object, word, or message can be studied as a sign itself or for the signs that it contains. For semiotics an object or word that has meaning for a person is more than just the object or word. The object or word is pregnant with or full of meaning, understood according to the culture that contains it but also determined individually by the person who brings meaning to it. The semiotic model of meaning privileges culture or social context as the ultimate source of meaning for items that surround people in the social formation. For semiotics, any text in a culture possesses, first, the meanings that people in the society agree it contains and, second, the meanings that an individual who lives in the society is necessarily drawn to bring to the text.

Some examples can indicate the power of signs to deliver meanings. The Nike "swoosh" is an excellent example of the power of a sign. Nike has worked for years to establish their trademark swoosh as a sign of their company. In fact, the swoosh is so well known in our culture that this symbol used alone is enough to signify a Nike product to any individual. Examples of signs in all kinds of campaign communication reveal the power and importance words and visuals serve as signs that lead people to recall the organization that created them: the Budweiser Clydesdale horses, the unique lettering of the Pepsi or Coke logo, the donkey and elephant of the two political parties, or our national flag. The bottom line is that semiotics recognizes that symbols or cultural artifacts are more than just that; they are "meaning-full" artifacts that can represent significant meanings to people.

The theory of semiotics is informative because it is used to explain both how any cultural text is a conscious expression of meaning and cultural worldviews and how any text contains the underlying ideologies and language that give rise to these particular messages. Semiotics is used to study meanings as unconscious and conscious structures necessarily revealed in all kinds of texts. Any word or visual in a text has the potential to act as a sign representing the organization but delivering meanings because the word or visual is both a cultural sign and, from that, inevitably a personal sign for the person who lives in the culture.

APPLICATIONS

Semiotics has recently been applied to understanding campaign messages. Critical scholars who want to look closely at public relations, advertising, and marketing messages have initiated this relatively new line of research. This research attempts to uncover the underlying social pressures or cultural issues—the langue—that become expressed in commercial messages—the parole. Findings from the close critical textual analysis of campaign messages are very revealing.

Findings suggest that campaign messages not only advertise a product or present a corporate image as signifieds, but they inevitably signify social issues. For example, the widespread, underlying ideologies of patriarchy, of the physical ideal of women, of the organization's desired corporate image, and even ideologies that a person can buy happiness in a bottle of perfume or after-shave or buy a new identity through clothes or tennis shoe purchases are social and cultural assumptions that prompt, even dictate, the content of media messages.

Consider advertisements for a luxury, upscale product such as a Rolex watch or a Jaguar automobile. The very name *Rolex* signifies "expensive watch" and, further, means that any person observed wearing a Rolex most likely has disposable income and perhaps a lucrative job. The Rolex might be manufactured just as any other watch is, with perhaps a bit more care and with better-quality components. However, the name *Rolex* is a sign, and the word *Rolex* is also a sign, meaning luxurious and posh. The Rolex watch is more than just a watch; it is a watch with meanings attached to it as a sign. Advertisements for a Jaguar automobile also present upscale persons, huge and exclusive houses, perhaps situated in a country club setting; again, well-dressed persons, expensive houses, and country clubs are all signs that add to the desired sign and meaning of the Jaguar automobile as a luxury product for the very rich.

—Mary Anne Moffitt

See also Critical theory

Bibliography

Barthes, R. (1964). *Elements of semiology*. New York: Hill & Wang.

Goldman, R. (1992). *Reading ads socially*. New York: Routledge.

Goldman, R., & Papson, S. (1996). *Sign wars: The cluttered landscape of advertising*. New York: Guilford Press.

SITUATION ANALYSIS

A public relations situation can be described as the set of circumstances or problem an organization faces. A *situation analysis* is the detailed explanation of everything the communication professional can learn about the problem at hand. Ronald D. Smith wrote, "Without a clear and early statement of the situation to be addressed, you will not be able to conduct efficient research or define the goal of your communication program later in the planning process" (2002, p. 19).

The situation analysis makes it possible to develop hypotheses about causes of and solutions to the problem. Through research, the public relations practitioner can gain a thorough understanding of the organization's relevant publics, its environment (*see* Environmental scanning), and opportunities as well as challenges related to solving the problem. The situation analysis also helps identify the additional research needed in order to develop a successful plan. As Donald Parente (2000) wrote, the situation analysis should be organized, structured, detailed, and focused.

Why is situation analysis important to public relations practitioners? Public relations planning begins with a situation analysis—whether the planning is for a comprehensive public relations campaign or just one element, such as a writing project. Because the effectiveness of the plan correlates directly to the quality of information gathered in the research process, a thorough situation analysis is critical to a successful outcome of the project.

A situation analysis is also a key to successful decision making. Before a situation or problem can be addressed, the communication team and the organization's leadership must come to a shared understanding of the issue. The situation analysis should clarify the current situation and provide evidence to support any hypotheses.

A situation analysis can be useful as an initial step in crisis communication planning as well.

How do practitioners conduct a situation analysis? Situation analyses can be structured in a variety of ways, posing a myriad of questions about the current problem, the background of the organization, the organization's environment, and the significance of the situation. The situation analysis may also reveal gaps in existing information, pointing the way to the development of a plan for primary research.

Smith (2002) wrote that a traditional method of conducting a situation analysis drawn from the discipline of marketing is the SWOT analysis. Looking both inside and outside the organization, its strengths (S) and weaknesses (W) are analyzed, and its opportunities (O) and threats (T) are identified. Robert A. Sevier (1998) described strengths and weakness as internal/institutional, whereas opportunities and threats are typically external/environmental. Sevier cautioned that different audiences may place the same characteristic in opposite categories—one considering a characteristic to be a strength whereas another considers the same characteristic to be a weakness.

Another approach is to divide a situation analysis into categories of internal and external factors. Content of the internal factors that should be examined includes

1. *Mission*: Organization mission statement, charter, bylaws, structure

2. *History*: Descriptions of programs, services, products of the organization

3. *Resources*: Statistics on budget, staffing, sales, profits, stockholders

4. *Policies*: Policies and procedures related to the problem

5. *Position statements*: Opinion quotes from key executives regarding the problem

6. *Current plan*: Description of the current handling of the problem

7. *Stakeholders*: Description of the organization's current internal stakeholders

8. *Media*: Samples of internal communication tools such as newsletters and memos

Content of the external factors that should be examined includes

1. *Media*: Clippings, transcripts, and tapes of news media coverage of the organization and the problem situation; content analysis of news media coverage; lists of journalists covering related situations

2. *Supportive stakeholders*: Lists and background information on those who share the organization's positions on the situation

3. *Opposing stakeholders*: Lists and background information on those who oppose the organization's positions on the situation

4. *Public opinion research*: Information on public opinions related to the situation

5. *Events*: Lists of important dates or events related to the organization and the situation

6. *Regulatory bodies*: Lists of government agencies and others with power affecting the situation; copies of relevant legislation, pending bills and government publications

7. *Existing research*: Published research on topics related to the situation; relevant books, records, directories

Additional areas to consider in the situation analysis include the organization's culture, external communication tools (such as the annual report or Web site), emerging issues and trends in the organization's environment, history of the problem, consequences of the problem, opportunities for solutions, challenges or obstacles to solutions, publics that may not yet fit into the supportive or opposition categories, and the organization's competition.

A public relations audit may also be part of the analysis of internal factors. The audit may include examination of the organization's performance—the quality of goods or services as well as the viability of its causes and ideas. Structure may also be considered

in the audit. This includes review of the organization's mission as it relates to the problem, the role public relations plays within the decision-making body, and identification of resources (personnel, equipment, budget, time) that may be needed to address the situation. The final area of focus for the audit (Smith, 2002) is the public perception of the organization's visibility and reputation.

Information for the situation analysis can be gathered using both formal and informal methodologies. Secondary (or existing) research can be gathered from organizational records or libraries. Primary (or original) research may use focus groups, interviews, content analysis and surveys, for example.

The situation analysis should clarify all assumptions and back up assertions with evidence.

—Phyllis Vance Larsen

Bibliography

Austin, E. W., & Pinkleton, B. E. (2001). *Strategic public relations management: Planning and managing effective communication programs* (pp. 22–26). Mahwah, NJ: Lawrence Erlbaum.

Cutlip, S. M., Center, A. H., & Broom, G. M. (2000). *Effective public relations* (8th ed., pp. 347–351). Upper Saddle River, NJ: Prentice Hall.

Daugherty, E. (2003, Spring). Strategic planning in public relations: A matrix that ensures tactical soundness. *Public Relations Quarterly, 48*, 21–26.

Parente, D. (2000). *Advertising campaign strategy: A guide to marketing communication plans* (2nd ed., pp. 29–36). Fort Worth, TX: Dryden Press.

Sevier, R. A. (1998). *Integrated marketing for colleges, universities, and schools: A step-by-step planning guide* (pp. 129–141). Washington, DC: Council for Advancement & Support of Education.

Smith, R. D. (2002). *Strategic planning for public relations* (pp. 19–65). Mahwah, NJ: Lawrence Erlbaum.

SITUATION ETHICS

Situation ethics began in the 1940s and 1950s as a movement among Roman Catholic theologians who saw in the post–World War II environment a constellation of unique moral challenges that the traditions of law and casuistry were not equipped to address. Law and casuistry were tied to hierarchy and authority, and the experience of World War II showed how immoral following orders could be. So these theologians sought a way to listen for the voice of God in complex, particular circumstances. Spurning rules and paradigm cases as being too rigid, they argued that truly moral decision making was marked by deep personal responsibility and dialogue. But these theologians failed to persuade their superiors. In 1952, Pope Pius XII put an end to the movement among Roman Catholics by condemning situation ethics as dangerously subjective and relativistic.

Situation ethics returned as a Protestant debate in the 1960s. Popularized as "the new morality" by Episcopalian ethics professor Joseph Fletcher (1905–1991), this incarnation of situation ethics was championed as the golden mean between legalism at one extreme and licentiousness at the other. According to Fletcher, situationists are neither slaves to rules and regulations nor heedless of the needs of others. Rather, they follow only one rule, and that is to do the loving thing in every situation they face. Fletcher argued that no behavior is right or wrong intrinsically; more accurately, behaviors are right only if they lead to good consequences and wrong only if they cause harm. "The situationist enters into every decision-making situation fully armed with the ethical maxims of his community and its heritage, and he treats them with respect as illuminators of his problems," Fletcher wrote. "Just the same he is prepared in any situation to compromise them or set them aside *in the situation* if love seems better served by doing so" (1966, p. 26). Fletcher summarized his situation ethics in six propositions: "Love only is always good, love is the only norm, love and justice are the same, love is not liking, love justifies its means, and love decides there and then" (1966, p. 9).

In philosophical terms, situation ethics falls under the category of teleology, a way of justifying behavior according to consequences rather than principles (the ends justify the means). More specifically, it is a type of utilitarianism (the greatest amount of happiness for the greatest number of people). Because situation ethics came out of the Christian faith, it is sometimes referred to as *act-agapism*, referring to *agape*, the Greek word for selfless love used in the New Testament. In act-agapism, good emerges when the individual chooses the most loving course of action on a case-by-case basis.

Striking a responsive chord at a time when traditions were being questioned, situation ethics found a wide range of business applications. In *The Moral Crisis in Management,* Thomas Petit wrote, "The situational model . . . best fits the American manager's self-image of a tough-minded individual who demands freedom and is willing and able to be responsible in its exercise" (1967, p. 167). Fletcher himself applied situation ethics to business management, asking, "What, in the situation, is the most constructive decision to make, as measured by a primary concern for people, and not for profits alone nor only for . . . one company's sake?" (1967, p. 167). In an example of a clothing manufacturer who pays an illegal kickback to keep an essential order from a department store chain, Fletcher said that the manufacturer's bribe was the right thing to do in the circumstances. He broke a law certainly, but more importantly he kept his employees working and did not have to cut their pay. In this case, following the law would have devastated his employees and their families.

Applications of situation ethics to public relations followed. The most common example involved a company with a policy of full disclosure to the media being justified in deciding to withhold information that could harm an employee, a client, or the community. A more extreme application was put forth by Marquette University professor Steven Goldzwig, who argued that serious social change—he gave as an example the struggle against racial inequality—could at times justify "suggestion, innuendo, even misuse of facts." Desperate situations require desperate measures, argued Goldzwig, who said that demagoguery and techniques of propaganda may be "legitimate means of pursuing laudable social ends" (1989, p. 220).

The main attraction of situation ethics is its commonsense recognition that circumstances matter when making moral decisions. People generally follow the rules—they tell the truth and keep promises, for example—but they also understand that breaking the rules is occasionally warranted. Sometimes lies need to be told—to catch criminals, perhaps, or to protect national security—and sometimes a promise needs to be broken—if it was made in haste and keeping it would cause more harm than good. Situationism is often congruent with lived experience.

Another appeal of situation ethics is that it takes very seriously Immanuel Kant's philosophy that people should always be treated as ends in themselves, never as means to an end. Slavishly following rules, by contrast, can cause immense harm. "Always produce maximum profits" is a common rule that pleases Wall Street investors, but among other things leads to wages that are below subsistence, employment that does not provide for health care, and working conditions that endanger employees. Similarly, merely following the rules can keep companies out of legal trouble while they ignore concerns for employee welfare, public safety, and the environment. Situation ethics avoids these pitfalls by focusing on people rather than rules.

Despite these attractions, situation ethics has fallen out of favor. Its greatest weakness is that it grossly underestimates the value of moral rules. Understood in their broadest sense, moral rules are needed to sustain human community. People seldom or never need to decide whether to deceive, to cause pain, or to break a promise. Following moral rules maintains community; breaking moral rules destroys community. For this reason, following moral rules does not require justification. However, breaking moral rules always requires justification because it damages the basis of civilized society. Breaking moral rules introduces distrust, thus undermining the cooperation necessary for community.

Situation ethics has fallen out of favor for more practical reasons as well. It privileges individual judgment over conventional wisdom and assumes that the individual is capable of transcending his or her own self-interest and limited perspective when deciding to break a moral rule. For that matter, it assumes that the individual can calculate the potential harms and benefits of any particular action, as if the individual can peer into the future to see short-term and long-term effects of any particular act. It is even conceivable that maximizing the happiness of most people will cause harm to a few, thus creating what British philosopher and economist John Stuart Mill called "tyranny of the majority." Mostly, though, situation ethics ignores the fact that moral rules generally work, and work well. That is why certain practices achieved the status of moral rules.

To say that situation ethics has fallen out of favor is an understatement. The term is used today with utter scorn and contempt. Instead of meaning the application of *agape* in concrete circumstances, as Fletcher intended, situation ethics has come to refer to self-interest, rationalization, and a lack of professionalism. It now means immorality pretending to be good, an attempt to excuse unethical behavior. Canadian public relations specialist Nigel Atkin typified today's low regard for situation ethics when he defined it as "where you do that which is least painful, and hope that not many people find out about it" (1999, p. 349). Public relations practitioners have spent the last few decades writing and revising codes of ethics, looking for principles that can be applied locally, nationally, and even internationally. They are more likely than ever to reject the situationist claim that rules are meant to be broken. Instead, they are still searching for meaningful rules that their colleagues can agree to follow.

—*John P. Ferré*

See also Codes of ethics; Deontology; Ethics of public relations; Moral philosophy; Utilitarianism

Bibliography

Atkin, N. (1999, March 15). Transparency, dialogue and ethical decision-making. *Vital Speeches of the Day*, 347–351.

Fletcher, J. (1966). *Situation ethics: The new morality.* Philadelphia: Westminster.

Fletcher, J. (1967). *Moral responsibility: Situation ethics at work.* Philadelphia: Westminster.

Goldzwig, S. R. (1989, Fall). A social movement perspective on demagoguery: Achieving symbolic convergence. *Communication Studies, 40*, 202–228.

Petit, T. A. (1967). *The moral crisis in management.* New York: McGraw-Hill.

SITUATIONAL THEORY OF PUBLICS

James E. Grunig of the University of Maryland developed the situational theory of publics to put meaning into the term *public*, which is one of the two key words in the phrase *public relations*. Public relations practitioners often use the term *public* to refer to the mass population, which they also call the general public. At other times, they use the plural term *publics* to refer to the groups for which public relations programs are planned—especially journalists, employees, consumers, investors, governments, local communities, and members of associations and nonprofit groups. Practitioners also commonly use the terms *stakeholders* and *publics* interchangeably.

In contrast, J. E. Grunig distinguished between stakeholders and publics and used the two concepts to segment the general population into categories that help communication professionals identify strategic publics and to plan and evaluate public relations programs. He considered the term *general public* to be a contradiction in terms because a public is always a specialized group whose members have a reason to be interested in the activities and behaviors of organizations.

In its current state, the situational theory of publics is part of J. E. Grunig's theory of the role of public relations in strategic management. Following the lead of John Dewey, who wrote about publics in the 1920s and 1930s, Grunig theorized that publics arise when organizations make decisions that have consequences on people inside and outside the organization who were not involved in making that decision. In addition, publics often want consequences from organizational decisions that organizations might be reluctant to provide—such as lower prices, stable employment, or less pollution.

Grunig reserved the term *stakeholder* for general categories of people who are affected by the actual or potential consequences of strategic, or important, organizational decisions. Stakeholders are people who have something at risk when the organization makes decisions. Stakeholder categories generally are the focus of public relations programs, such as employee relations, community relations, investor relations, consumer relations, or government relations.

Within each of these stakeholder categories, however, the situational theory can be used to identify types of publics that differ in the extent to which they communicate actively, passively, or not at all about organizational decisions that affect them. Active publics, in turn, can develop into activist groups, or join or support activist groups. Active and activist publics make issues out of organizational consequences, and these issues may lead to crises. Thus the situational theory can be used to identify active publics in programs of environmental scanning, issues management, and crisis communication.

The situational theory is built from an explanation of why people communicate and when they are most likely to communicate. It uses the concepts of active and passive communication behavior to segment the general population into publics likely to communicate about one or more problems that are related to the consequences of organizational behaviors. The theory is situational because problems come and go and are relevant only to people who experience problematic situations related to organizational behaviors. As a result, publics arise and disappear as situations change, and organizations rarely, if ever, have a permanent set of publics.

In addition to explaining who an organization's publics are at a specific time, the situational theory also explains when communication programs are most likely to be effective—that is, to have effects on the short-term cognitions, attitudes, and behaviors of different publics and on the long-term relationships with these publics. Finally, the theory explains when publics develop from loose aggregations of individuals into organized activist groups. As a result, the situational theory provides a useful tool for strategically managing public relations programs—identifying publics, choosing realistic short- and long-term objectives for communication programs, and evaluating the outcomes of these programs.

The situational theory is similar to theories of market segmentation because it provides a method for segmenting the general population into groups relevant to public relations practitioners. Marketing theorists provide several criteria for choosing a concept for segmentation. Segments must be mutually exclusive, measurable, accessible, pertinent to an organization's mission, and large enough to be substantial. Most importantly, the people in market segments must have a differential response to marketing strategies.

In this sense, the situational theory of publics predicts the differential responses most important to public relations professionals: (a) responsiveness to problems and issues; (b) amount of and nature of communication behavior; (c) effects of communication on cognitions, attitudes, and behavior; (d) the extent and quality of organization-public relationships; and (e) the likelihood that publics will participate in collective behavior to pressure organizations.

The situational theory also helps to explain the nature of public opinion because it incorporates the assumption that two of the classic theorists of public opinion, John Dewey and Herbert Blumer, first made about publics: Publics arise around problems that affect them. Dewey also recognized the crucial role that publics play in American democracy: After recognizing that problems affect them, publics organize into issue groups to pressure organizations that cause the problems or to pressure government to constrain or regulate those organizations. The situational theory relates these classical theories of public opinion to public relations by showing that organizations need public relations because their behaviors create problems that create publics, which may evolve into activist groups that create issues and threaten the autonomy of organizations. The situational theory formalizes the classical conceptions of publics and provides concepts and variables for identifying and measuring publics and their opinions.

When the situational theory is expressed formally, it consists of two dependent variables (active and passive communication behavior) and three independent variables (problem recognition, constraint recognition, and level of involvement). The theory also specifies that active and passive communication behaviors lead to different cognitive, attitudinal, behavioral, and relational outcomes. The two dependent variables, active and passive communication behavior, also can be called information seeking and processing. Information seeking is premeditated—"the planned scanning of the environment for messages about a specified topic" (Clarke & Kline, 1974, p. 233). Information processing is message discovery—"the unplanned discovery of a message followed by continued processing of it" (p. 233).

The independent variables are situational variables because they measure the perceptions that people have of specific situations, especially situations that are problematic or that produce conflicts or issues. The three independent variables are defined as follows:

> *Problem recognition:* People detect that something should be done about a situation and stop to think about what to do.
>
> *Constraint recognition:* People perceive that there are obstacles in a situation that limit their ability to do anything about the situation.
>
> *Level of involvement:* The extent to which people connect themselves with a situation.

The theory states and research has confirmed that high problem recognition and low constraint recognition increase both active information seeking and passive information processing. Level of involvement increases information seeking, but it has less effect on information processing. Stated differently, people seldom seek information about situations that do not involve them. Yet, they will randomly process information about low-involvement situations, especially if they also recognize the situation as problematic. Because people participate more actively in information seeking than in information processing, information seeking and the independent variables that precede it produce communication effects more often than information processing. In particular, people communicating actively develop more organized cognitions, are more likely to have attitudes about a situation, more often engage in a behavior to do something about the situation, and are more likely to develop a relationship with an organization.

J. E. Grunig and Todd Hunt (1984) used combinations of the situational variables to define a range of publics (including nonpublics, latent publics, aware publics, and active publics) and to calculate the probability of communicating with and having effects on each type of public. Grunig described a large number of studies that have used the situational theory and described the kinds of publics identified in this research. These studies consistently have identified four kinds of publics: (a) *all-issue publics,* which are active on all problems measured in the study; (b) *apathetic publics,* which are inattentive to all of the problems; (c) *single-issue publics,* which are active on one or a small subset of the problems; and (d) *hot-issue publics,* which are active only on a single problem that involves nearly everyone in the population and that has received extensive media coverage. J. E. Grunig also included quantitative measures of the situational concepts and described the multivariate statistical techniques used to analyze survey data based on these measures.

—*James E. Grunig*

See also Activism; Crisis communication; Environmental scanning; Issues management; Public opinion and opinion leaders; Segmentation; Stakeholder theory; Strategies

Bibliography

Clarke, P., & Kline, F. G. (1974). Media effects reconsidered: Some new strategies for communication research. *Communication Research, 1,* 224–270.

Dewey, J. (1927). *The public and its problems.* Chicago: Swallow Press.

Grunig, J. E. (1989). Publics, audiences and market segments: Models of receivers of campaign messages. In C. T. Salmon (Ed.), *Information campaigns: Managing the process of social change* (pp. 197–226). Newbury Park, CA: Sage.

Grunig, J. E. (1997). A situational theory of publics: Conceptual history, recent challenges, and new research. In D. Moss, T. McManus, & D. Verčič (Eds.), *Public relations research: An international perspective* (pp. 3–46). Boston: International Thomson Business Press.

Grunig, J. E., & Hunt, T. (1984). *Managing public relations.* New York: Holt, Rinehart & Winston.

Grunig, J. E., & Repper, F. C. (1992). Strategic management, publics, and issues. In J. E. Grunig (Ed.), *Excellence in public relations and communication management* (pp. 117–158). Hillsdale, NJ: Lawrence Erlbaum.

SMITH, REA

Rea W. Smith, APR (1918–1981), served the Public Relations Society of America (PRSA) for 23 years— first as assistant to Shirley D. Smith, PRSA executive director, and her husband; then as vice president of administration in 1960; and finally as first woman executive vice president from 1975 to 1980.

In 1980, Smith became executive director of the Foundation for Public Relations Research and Education (now the Public Relations Foundation) until her death in 1981.

Her pioneering staff work for the national office of the PRSA included staff executive for judicial and grievance matters, for legal affairs, for committees on the development of PRSA's Code of Ethics, and for the Accreditation Boards, following the initiation of accreditation in 1962. She authored the organizational plan for establishing the International Accreditation Council, adopted in 1975.

Smith was born in Jamestown, New York, and began her career in public relations in the early 1940s. She was a TV talk show moderator and in Memphis, Tennessee, was one of the first women to produce political TV broadcasts. From 1946 to 1957, she and her husband were partners in Shirley D. Smith & Associates, a Memphis public relations firm.

Smith wrote many articles dealing with public relations and PRSA. She was treasurer of the Women Executives in Public Relations from 1971 to 1973, and a board member from 1977 to 1978.

—*Elizabeth L. Toth*

Bibliography

Smith, R. (1981, June). Foundation executive director, dies of heart attack, May 17. *PRSA National Newsletter, 9*(9), 1, 4.

SOCIAL CONSTRUCTION OF REALITY THEORY

The social construction of reality theory contends that reality is socially constructed and that the sociology of knowledge must scrutinize the manner in which this occurs. From this orientation, Peter L. Berger and Thomas Luckmann described reality as "a quality appertaining to phenomena that we recognized as having a being independent of our own volition" and knowledge as "the certainty that phenomena are real and that they possess specific characteristics" (1967, p. 1). In essence, people conceive their own distinctive social reality through contact and interaction with others.

Building on the work of Alfred Schutz, Berger and Luckmann argued that the reasonableness of knowledge in everyday life presents itself as a reality interpreted by individuals and subjectively meaningful to them as a rational and coherent perspective.

> The world of everyday life is not only taken for granted as reality by the ordinary members of society in the subjectively meaningful conduct of their lives. It is a world that originates in their thoughts and actions, and is maintained as real by these . . . the objectivations of subjective processes (and meanings) by which the intersubjective commonsense world is constructed. (1967, pp. 19–20)

For public relations scholars and practitioners, the social construction of reality theory raises questions about whether the differences between key stakeholders' realities may not be understood in relation to various differences between the two or more publics. Though not directly naming public relations, David R. Seibold and Brian H. Spitzberg argued that communication cannot be considered and realized without an appreciation for the interpretations communicators bring to symbolic discourse.

> Without attention to the ways in which actors represent and make sense of the phenomenal world, construe event associations, assess and process the actions of others, and interpret personal choices in order to initiate appropriate symbolic activity, the study of human communication is limited to mechanistic analysis. (1982, p. 87)

Language, as such, is the means by which people function on two levels: that of their individual thoughts, and the realization that others have similar meanings and interpretations. By concentrating on language and the subsequent symbolic meaning, public relations research can provide insight on relationships between words and issues, and between content and meaning, as well as by examining how interaction transpires regarding issues development.

Communication and public relations scholars examine the social construction of reality through the scrutiny of symbols and meaning within the substance of messages constructed and shared by organizations with key stakeholders. It is through these messages (symbols) that people create, manage, and share interpretations of reality through social interaction, which allows society to function by the sharing and giving of meaning to physical and social realities. Ultimately, this sharing provides a footing for cooperative behavior through social reality—the understanding each person has of what other people know.

A large amount of public relations research comes from the traditional theoretical position known as objectivism. This perspective operates on the assumption that awareness, knowledge, behavioral intentions, and behaviors are a given in nature, essentially uncontaminated by social factors.

On the other hand, a social constructionist orientation is a generally accepted and growing perspective in the field of public relations, arguing that public relations claims are subject to social interpretation and negotiation. From a rhetorical perspective to public relations, it is through dialogue that participants identify, create, and manage meaning by the rhetorical processes of statement and counterstatement. The study of public relations in this sense

> seeks to advance marketplace and public policy discourse by pursuing relational excellence in actions (organizational responsibility) and discourse that lead to the co-creation, co-management, or co-definition of meaning (zones of meaning) that reconcile strains and alienation and foster mutually beneficial relationships (Heath, 2001, p. 35)

From a public relations perspective that appreciates and incorporates social constructionist perspectives, steeped in rhetorical traditions, public relations can help individuals and groups from lay persons to decision makers understand, critique, and employ socially constructed, value-laden choices.

It was Berger and Luckmann's contention that the sociology of knowledge must concern itself with whatever passes for knowledge in a society, created by individuals and groups within that society, regardless of the ultimate validity or invalidity of such knowledge or the criteria used to evaluate such knowledge. This human knowledge, or perception, is identified, developed, rationalized, maintained, and altered in social situations. As if almost directly speaking to public relations scholars, they argued that "the sociology of knowledge must seek to understand the processes by which this is done in such a way that a taken-for-granted 'reality' congeals for the man in the street" (1967, p. 3).

Communication theories abound in public relations literature, and the concept of socially constructed knowledge and perceptions permeates the field's literature. A limited list of theories developed from this perspective include social cognition theory, social exchange theory, social identity theory, social judgment–involvement theory, social learning–social cognitive theory, social penetration theory, and the broader category of social theories of media effects.

For example, the relevance of mass communications studies to public relations is bound up with socially constructed realities; because mass communication is bound up with society, it is strongly influenced by the immediate circumstances of culture, history, and society. The forms of the symbolic environment, though socially constructed, are often reflected in and perceived through mass media.

Within risk communication studies, social constructionist concepts treat risk as social constructs that are determined by structural forces in society. Issues such as trust, control, and fairness among others are reconstructed from the beliefs and rationalities of people in society, and these social constructions reflect the interests and values of the individuals and the shared meaning of terms, cultural artifacts, and natural phenomena among groups. In a sense, what individuals and societies choose to call risky is largely determined by the social and cultural construction of perceptions, rather than some objective nature.

Within organizational studies, Eric H. Neilsen and M. V. H. Rao (1987) viewed organizational legitimacy as a complex process of a socially constructed reality, based on localized social norms and values. In the science/health communication field, numerous researchers have examined media coverage of scientific findings as partially socially constructed. Many researchers in the field of sociology of ignorance argue that scientists' claims regarding knowledge are either inherently social or at least partially subject to social processes.

Though not specifically coining this theory, aspects of social construction theory can be traced back to at least Plato's famous cave analogy, where the prisoners not only see shadows or reflections, but their knowledge of the people outside the cave is also created by shared perceptions. This shared, socially constructed perception is a result of their discourse about those shadows and reflections.

Building from the lead of philosophers and historians like Nietzsche, Dewey, Heidegger, Wittgenstein, Scheler, and Kuhn, social construction theorists generally accept the claim that knowledge is socially determined and constructed.

Earlier this century, Walter Lippmann discussed similar important aspects of the social construction of reality in describing how democracy works and the role of public opinion within the democratic system. Lippmann argued that "man is no Aristoletalian god contemplating all existence at one glance" but rather develops views of the world based on the "behavior of other human beings, in so far as that behavior crosses ours, is dependent upon us, or is interesting to us" (1922, p. 18). The individual and collective sense of reality is ultimately constructed by our experiences and relationships with others who also shape our experiences.

The social construction of reality theory argues against a purely objective sense of perception. Knowledge is not something that exists only in our heads and is learned from informative communication; rather, "the production of discourse . . . comes into being through social interaction, because discourse can be recognized as discourse only after it becomes part and parcel of the normative conventions that form the social communities in which we all must live and work" (Kent, 1993, p. 79).

—*Michael J. Palenchar*

See also Social exchange theory; Social movement theory

Bibliography

Berger, P. L., & Luckmann, T. (1967). *The social construction of reality: A treatise in the sociology of knowledge.* New York: Doubleday.

Heath, R. L. (2001). A rhetorical enactment rationale for public relations: The good organization communicating well. In R. L. Heath (Ed.), *Handbook of public relations* (pp. 31–59). Thousand Oaks, CA: Sage.

Heath, R. L., & Bryant, J. (1992). *Human communication theory and research: Concepts, contexts, and challenges.* Hillsdale, NJ: Lawrence Erlbaum.

Kent, T. (1993). Formalism, social construction, and the problem of interpretive authority. In N. R. Blyler & C. Thralls (Eds.), *Professional communication: The social perspective* (pp. 79–91). Newbury Park, CA: Sage.

Lippmann, W. (1922). *Public opinion.* New York: Macmillan.

Neilsen, E. H., & Rao, M. V. H. (1987). The strategy-legitimacy nexus: A thick description. *Academy of Management Review, 12*(3), 523–533.

Seibold, D. R., & Spitzberg, B. H. (1982). Attribution theory and research: Review and implications for communication. In B. Dervin & M. J. Voigt (Eds.), *Progress in the communication sciences* (Vol. 3, pp. 85–125). Norwood, NJ: Ablex.

SOCIAL EXCHANGE THEORY

Social exchange theory adapts microeconomic theory to a wide variety of exchanges between people and groups. Indeed, social exchange theory is not one theory but several theories that describe the emergent properties of social interaction. The most extensive application of social exchange has been in the area of interpersonal relationships. Social exchange theory has been invoked to explain how social relationships form, expand, and wither. More recently these theories have been used to characterize relationships between individual stakeholders and organizations.

Social exchange differs from economic exchange in that social exchange is relatively informal. It involves obligations that cannot be specified in advance; the exchange is less time bound than economic exchange. Unlike economic exchange, the elements of social exchange are quite varied and cannot be reduced to a single quantitative exchange rate. Social exchange requires one to trust others to honor their obligations. Relationships emerge out of tit-for-tat reciprocity in minor social transactions as both parties display their trustworthiness. Social exchange contrasts with economic exchange in that it tends to foster feelings of personal obligation and gratitude.

Simple social exchange models assume that rewards and costs drive relationship decisions. When relationship rewards exceed costs, a person moves to expand the exchange in a relationship. In contrast, when costs exceed rewards, the person will halt relationship advance or even terminate the relationship. In a mutually beneficial exchange, each party supplies the wants of the other party at lower cost to self than the value of the resources the other party provides. In such a model, mutual relationship satisfaction ensures relationship stability.

However, people often put up with less-than-satisfactory relationships. John Thibaut and Harold Kelley (1959) proposed two comparison standards to differentiate between relationship satisfaction and relationship stability. Relationship satisfaction increases when the balance of rewards and costs in the relationship exceeds the person's comparison level. The comparison level is based on the person's past experience or social observation. When the reward/cost balance falls beneath these expectations, the person will be dissatisfied with the relationship. Some people demand higher profits from their relationships than other people do. What is a satisfactory exchange to one person will be an unsatisfactory exchange to another person.

Relationship stability is determined by how the present relationship compares with the comparison level of alternatives—or the level of rewards that the person thinks she can obtain in other relationships. If the current relationship is perceived to be more profitable than the alternatives, the relationship should endure, independent of the person's relationship satisfaction. Combining these two standards, we can distinguish four kinds of relationships: (a) the *still-born relationship,* in which the association falls beneath the person's comparison level and available alternative relationships (i.e., low satisfaction and low perceived alternatives); (b) the *unstable relationship*, in which the relationship compares favorably with one's expectations but lags behind the perceived relationship alternatives (i.e., satisfied but attracted to other relationships); (c) the *malaised relationship*, in which a relationship compares unfavorably with the comparison level, but rates better than the alternatives; and (d) the *blissful relationship*, in which the target relationship exceeds one's expectations and the comparison level of alternatives.

One particularly useful version of social exchange theory is found in Caryl Rusbult's (1987) investment model. This model proposes that investments also serve to stabilize relationships. The greater the nontransferable investments a person has in a given relationship, the more stable the relationship is likely to be. In this formulation, relationship stability or commitment is a function of relationship satisfaction plus relationship investment minus perceived relationship alternatives. People sometimes find they have too much invested to quit a relationship or an enterprise. Therefore, they pour additional resources into the relationship to try to salvage their endangered investments. The investment model accommodates a variety of relationships such as employment and customer relationships.

The importance of relationship investment is illustrated in the tenets of relationship marketing. Relationship marketing advocates building a differentiated and unique relationship with each customer via the use of computer databases and information processing technologies. According to Don Peppers and Martha Rogers, the customer tells the firm what she wants; the firm then makes it and remembers the customer's preferences for the next time. The "learning relationship between a customer and an enterprise gets smarter and smarter with every individual interaction, defining in ever more detail the customer's own individual needs and tastes" (1997, p. 15). In theory this increasing degree of convenience represents a customer investment that will be lost if she deserts to a competitor. Peppers and Rogers wrote, "The learning relationship creates

what is, essentially, a barrier that makes it more difficult for a customer to be promiscuous than to be loyal" (1997, p. 16).

One can increase one's relationship influence by slowly expanding the other party's investments in a relationship. Increased dependency in a relationship increases the means of influence that the other party can exercise within that relationship. Resource dependency theories apply this principle to investigate the power dynamics of relationships. The balance of dependencies in a relationship determines the power the party has in the relationship. This is stated in the principle of least interest, which says that the person who has the least interest in the association (i.e., is less dependent upon the relationship) has the greatest influence over the trajectory of the relationship.

Social exchange theory also investigates how people respond when they experience relationship dissatisfaction. For instance, people develop power strategies to deal with relationship inequities. They may seek alternative sources of resources, reduce the other party's rewards, call for greater commitment on the other person's part; or try to enhance the perceived value of their own resources to the other party. In the worst case, they engage in sour grapes and devalue the other's resources for the self. Albert Hirschman (1991) developed the typology of exit, loyalty, and voice to explain how people in organizations responded to organizational decline. Caryl Rusbult and colleagues added the category of neglect to this model. Subsequent research has shown that people tend to exit relationships when they have low investments and perceive many alternatives. The options loyalty and voice are exercised when a person has high levels of investment in and satisfaction with a current relationship. Finally, the option of neglect is often exercised when satisfaction with the relationship is low, but the person perceives few alternatives.

The relationship management metaphor has gained popularity in marketing and public relations. However, the metaphor more readily applies to some organization-stakeholder relations than others. Wendy Zubava Ford (2001) investigated the expectations that customers have for interactions with service providers. Encounter-oriented customer exchanges focus on efficient service delivery. Different service providers offer identical services; hence the customer interacts with a role more than a person. In interactions with professionalized roles, customers expect relationship-oriented service. Here the offered services are adapted to the individual's preferences. The customer expects the service provider to discover the individual's needs and to construct an individualized plan to meet those needs. Ford found that a relationship orientation was positively related to personalized service communication.

Ellen Garbarino and Mark Johnson (1999) distinguished between low and high relationship-oriented organizational stakeholders. They found that trust, satisfaction, and commitment played different roles in predicting outcomes for these two groups. In addition, scholars have developed models that specify different kinds of relational processes for different kinds of organization-stakeholder ties. Dennis Arnett, Steven German, and Shelby Hunt (2003) developed a model of relationship marketing for nonprofits that took into account the individual's self-identification with the target institution. They found rather different predictors of stakeholder behavior depending upon whether the person had a low or a high relationship orientation toward the institution.

Social exchange theories continue to contribute to the study of organization-stakeholder relationships. For one, the metaphor that characterizes public relations as "relationship management" should acknowledge that not all long-term relationships are healthy or mutually satisfactory for the parties involved. Perspectives such as the investment model and resource dependency theory remind us that many relationships have dark sides. In summary, social exchange theory seems likely to continue as a helpful heuristic in exploring the ongoing interaction between individuals, organizations, and stakeholders.

—Greg Leichty

Bibliography

Arnett, D., German, S., & Hunt, S. (2003). The identity salience model of relationship marketing success: The case of nonprofit marketing. *Journal of Marketing, 67*(1), 89–105.

Ford, W. Z. (2001). Customer expectations for interactions with service providers: Relationship versus encounter orientation and personalized service communication. *Journal of Applied Communication Research, 29*(1), 1–29.

Garbarino, E., & Johnson, M. S. (1999, April). The different roles of satisfaction, trust, and commitment in customer relationships. *Journal of Marketing, 63*, 70–87.

Hirschman, A. O. (1991). *The rhetoric of reaction: Perversity, futility, and jeopardy.* Cambridge, MA: Belknap Press.

Peppers, D., & Rogers, M. (1997). *Enterprise one to one: Tools for competing in an interactive age.* New York: Doubleday.

Rusbult, C. E. (1987). Responses to dissatisfaction in close relationships: The exit-voice-loyalty-neglect model. In D. Perlman & S. Duck (Eds.), *Intimate relationships: Development, dynamics and deterioration* (pp. 209–238). Newbury Park, CA: Sage.

Thibaut, J., & Kelley, H. (1959). *The social psychology of groups.* New York: Wiley.

SOCIAL MOVEMENT THEORY

Charles J. Stewart, Craig Allen Smith, and Robert E. Denton, Jr. (1994) referred to the second half of the 20th century as "the age of the social movement in America" (p. 1). Though many definitions of social movements exist, Stewart et al. defined a *social movement* as "an organized, uninstitutionalized, and large collectivity that emerges to bring about or to resist a program of change in societal norms and values, operates primarily through persuasive strategies, and encounters opposition in a moral struggle" (1994, p. 17). They further defined persuasion as a "pervasive element" in a social movement. The focus on study of persuasive techniques and strategies has dominated the study of social movements and collectives by communication scholars.

Stewart et al. suggested that social movements, although not referred to by that name, were present in the American experience from the colonies forward. They argued that the American Revolution began as a social movement. Beginning public relations students learn from the history of public relations that public relations activities existed far before the naming of the discipline. Michael Pfau and Roxanne Parrott (1993) cited Cotton Mather's 1721–1722 efforts to persuade Boston citizens to inoculate against smallpox as one of the first social action campaigns in America. Public relations textbooks often cite examples from the American Revolution, such as Thomas Paine's *Common Sense* and the publication of *The Federalist Papers.* Scott M. Cutlip, Allen H. Center, and Glen M. Broom (1994) noted that "the tools and techniques of public relations have long been an important part of political weaponry. Sustained campaigns to move and manipulate political opinion go back to the Revolutionary War and the work of Samuel Adams and his cohorts" (p. 91). In 2001, Gabriel M. Vasquez and Maureen Taylor described the foundations stage of public relations and noted the work of J.A.R. Pimlott and Cutlip when making reference to the use of public relations efforts by American colonists who sparked the American Revolution. Cutlip et al. (1994) noted,

> Twentieth century developments in this field (public relations) are directly tied to the power struggles evoked by political reform movements. These movements, reflecting strong tides of protest against entrenched power groups, have been the catalytic agents for much of the growth of public relations practice, because the jockeying of political and economic groups for dominance created the need to muster public support. (p. 90)

Other social movements in American history included the temperance movement, the abolitionist movement and the women's rights movement. Just as the development of the mass media aided the emerging practice of public relations, so it aided the leaders of the social movements.

A discussion of social movements in a public relations encyclopedia must naturally turn to the influence of the research findings of other disciplines on public relations. In other words, what can public relations learn from research on social movements that has been done in communication, sociology, and other fields of study? Furthermore, what does that knowledge on social movements add to the body of knowledge in public relations?

Social movement study as a discipline is generally recognized as an outgrowth of collective behavior theory of the 1940s and 1950s. Sociologist

Herbert Blumer published his "Outline of Collective Behavior" in 1934. In this work, he provided guidelines for studying the formation of new forms of collective identity and for classifying crowd behavior. Blumer outlined a new way of classifying social movements as collective behavior.

Understanding the relationship between social movement theory and public relations requires an understanding of the relationship between rhetoric and public relations. Many authors have effectively made an argument for this link. Focusing on the dynamics of individual and organizational roles in social debate, William N. Elwood (1995) wrote,

> The individual and the organization both play important roles in the network of symbolic activity that is social life. The "individual" by participating in or associating with a variety of organizations is party to many kinds of "rhetorical situations" (and often multiple) exigencies through the use of persuasion. (p. 11)

Expanding on this observation, Elwood (1995) noted, "Thus the rhetorical situation applies to public relations inquiry" (p. 11).

The link between rhetorical analysis of individual speakers and rhetorical analysis of the organization's discourse has already been established in the literature. Elizabeth L. Toth and Robert L. Heath emphasized the need for a rhetorical perspective on public relations:

> Rhetoric has to do with relationships—how they are shaped—typically between organizations and individuals. Sometimes these relationships are constructive, based on fact, truth and cooperation. Sometimes they are destructive, resulting in a clash of base interests and narrow perspectives. (1992, p. xiii)

Pfau and Parrott (1993) clarified the relationship between the study of rhetoric and public relations campaigns in the preface to their book *Persuasive Communication Campaigns.*

Although there are textbooks that focus on persuasion, commercial advertising, political campaign communication, and social action campaigns, there is no book that attempts to integrate these areas. This omission is an unfortunate one, because what

Kenneth Boulding observed in very general terms to lead off this preface applies perfectly to the status of theorizing and research in influence: Much is presently known, but because scholars and practitioners focus their efforts in very specific fields, and because of inadequate communication across fields, there is duplication and wasted effort. Relationships between organizations and their stakeholder publics are certainly important to both social movement literature and public relations literature. An understanding of social movements or collective behavior is useful for the public relations practitioner because the actions taken by activists, as indicated above, often present themselves in the form of public relations issues or crises the organization must address. Study of social movements from a rhetorical perspective clearly demonstrates the ways public relations practitioners and academics can benefit from this additional knowledge base.

Public relations scholars have also examined organizational responses to the issues presented by social movements and activists through the study of issue management. Social movements and activist groups can result from the efforts of individuals who perceive situations facing them as undesirable and unite to collectively fight larger organizations and government.

Heath (1997) added to the knowledge on social movements and issue management by providing a five-stage model of activism. The five stages include strain (problem recognition), mobilization, confrontation, negotiation, and resolution. By this logic, public relations practitioners and issue managers who seek to monitor and respond to issues presented by social movements and activist groups can use the five-stage model to prepare a strategic response and monitor the development of various issues.

—Becky McDonald

See also Activism

Bibliography

Cutlip, S. M., Center, A. H., & Broom, G. M. (1994). *Effective public relations* (7th ed.). Upper Saddle River, NJ: Prentice Hall.

Elwood, W. N. (Ed.). (1995*). Public relations inquiry as rhetorical criticism: Case studies of corporate discourse and social influence.* Westport, CT: Praeger.

Heath, R. L. (1994). *Management of corporate communication: From interpersonal contacts to external affairs.* Hillsdale, NJ: Lawrence Erlbaum.

Heath, R. L. (1997). *Strategic issues management: Organizations and public policy changes.* Thousand Oaks, CA: Sage.

Heath, R. L. (2001). A rhetorical enactment rationale for public relations: The good organization communicating well. In R. L. Heath (Ed.), *Handbook of public relations* (pp. 31–50). Thousand Oaks, CA: Sage.

Leitch, S., & Nelson, D. (2001). Bringing publics into public relations: New theoretical frameworks for practice. In R. L. Heath (Ed.), *Handbook of public relations.* Thousand Oaks, CA: Sage.

Pfau, M., & Parrott, R. (1993). *Persuasive communication campaigns.* Boston: Allyn & Bacon.

Rice, R. E., & Atkin, C. K. (2001). *Public communication campaigns* (3rd ed.). Thousand Oaks, CA: Sage.

Stewart, C. J., Smith, C. A., & Denton, R. E., Jr. (1994). *Persuasion and social movements* (3rd ed.). Prospect Heights, IL: Waveland Press.

Toth, E. L., & Heath, R. L. (1992). *Rhetorical and critical approaches to public relations.* Hillsdale, NJ: Lawrence Erlbaum.

Vasquez, G. M., & Taylor, M. (2001). Public relations: An emerging social science enters the new millennium. In W. B. Gudykunst (Ed.), *Communication Yearbook 24* (pp. 319–342). Thousand Oaks, CA: Sage.

SOCIETY

All professions take and measure their contribution from their ability to add value to society. The history of the profession of public relations is inseparable from the changing nature of individual societies as well as the larger sense of what constitutes society. Legendary practitioners such as Ivy Lee, Edward Bernays, Earl Newsom, and John W. Hill recognized that their profession had to add value to society through their services to clients. They shaped what they believed was the ethics of their practice as well as the skills of their service by studying and dedicating to society. They may be faulted for failures, some of which are more clearly understood in retrospection, but no one can deny their concern. They took this responsibility seriously and thought in terms of it as they defined and added to the role of public relations in society.

They were not alone in this exploration and dedication. The Public Relations Society of America's "Official Statement on Public Relations" states,

> Public relations helps our complex, pluralistic society to reach decisions and function more effectively by contributing to mutual understanding among groups and institutions. It serves to bring private and public policies into harmony. . . . To achieve their goals, these institutions must develop effective relationships with many different audiences or publics such as employees, members, customers, local communities, shareholders, and other institutions, and with society at large. (Public Relations Society of America, 1997/1998, p. 2)

If we trace the antecedents of public relations broadly, we will find it at the very fabric of the evolution of ideas, policies, values, and organizations in every country, culture, and society. For instance, John W. Hill, principal founding partner of Hill & Knowlton, recognized the reality that public relations practitioners were needed to help organizations understand and meet their contract with society. They were the servants of society that gave them life. Hill advised, "Public relations is an outgrowth of our free society, in which the ideal of an enlightened and rational public opinion is brought ever closer as understanding increases between groups and individuals" (1958, p. vix). For Hill, the primary role of public relations was to "serve 'the public interest' {which} evolves from the properly combined energies and principles of all positive elements of our society" (1963, p. 256). Leaders in the profession have long recognized that their obligations, rights, responsibilities, and ethics derived from the societies where they operated.

Sensitivity to public relations' role in society has been a constant theme in published studies on the discipline. The early years of the *Public Relations Review* witnessed many articles that addressed that theme and the standards of corporate responsibility that must guide practitioners and their clients. In those treatises, service to society was a constant and serious theme. More recently, Ron Pearson (1992) examined in detail how critical standards surrounding the practice reflected different views of the role of business in society. Practitioners were in a position to adjust business to society or society to business. They could be the pawns of business or the servants of society. These were ethical and professional choices. Similar analysis underpinned Larissa A. Grunig's (1992) reasoning that public relations needs to add definable value to society if it is to have the status of a true and worthy profession. Central to its charge is the challenge facing it to raise the ethical standards of the organizations the practice represents. Studies of this kind by academics such as Roy Leeper in 2001, were accompanied by substantial investigation of the implications and challenges over the meaning of community and communitarianism.

Systems perspectives on public relations reason that an organization cannot long prosper or even survive if it is out of harmony with the interests of its publics and other organizations—with the larger society. A rhetorical perspective on public relations contends that dialogue is the essence of the struggle to achieve this balance of interests and perspectives. The fostering and vetting of ideas occurs in public through the process of statement and counter statement. However idealistic, this view of public relations assumes that public discourse refines ideas, vets facts and sharpens their interpretation, evaluates value priorities, and scrutinizes personal and sociopolitical policies and actions. Fundamental to this wrangle is the reality of social exchange whereby no organization is thought to be able to survive and thrive if its presence creates costs greater than its apparent benefits. One additional line of analysis, generically called *cultural/critical theory*, adds depth to these considerations by exploring the presence, causes, and remedies to alienation. For this reason, contemporary thought charges public relations theory with addressing the role and solution of alienation in society. To this end, and that of the other perspectives central to public relations theory, the fundamental concepts are balance and harmony.

Balance and harmony appear as central paradoxes on discussions of society. Authors for centuries have discussed the concept of society. It is a matter of eternal fascination to academics and practitioners of various kinds. The eternal question is not "Does each profession serve society?" but perhaps "How does society sustain each profession?"

One such curious mind led George Herbert Mead to explore this set of questions from the viewpoint of the behavioralist in 1934. He wanted to better understand and explain how individuals' experiences and relationships resulted from and formed their mind as well as their individual and collective sense of self. His analysis builds on the belief that individual awareness and normative behavior results from individual and collective dialectics of mind, self, and society:

> Our society is built up out of our social interests. Our social relations go to constitute the self. But when the immediate interests come in conflict with others we had not recognized, we tend to ignore the others and take into account only those which are immediate. The difficulty is to make ourselves recognize the other and wider interests, and then to bring them into some sort of rational relationship with the more immediate ones. (1934, pp. 388–389)

A society—composed of people and the organizations they create—learns from actions, reactions, mistakes and reevaluations based on the analysis of mistakes. As a profession, public relations can serve society by helping to solve these mistakes. Public relations can add value to organizations by making them good as a prerequisite for their being articulate.

Fundamental to the nature of society is the individual and collectives of individuals. Perhaps the ability to create collective behavior is a human trait that fosters survival, as perhaps today many might think that it endangers the species. To create society, humans need to foster a sense of mind, self, and society. Mind, as a collective entity, requires shared meaning. Without shared meaning, coordination of human activity as we know it is impossible. The key elements of information (facts and knowledge), evaluation (attitude and value), and action (based on choice) are the essential ingredients of rhetoric. Through symbols that allow discourse, people arrange society rather than merely enact it at a sensory level, which is more typical of other social animals. In the blending of collective interests, people must manifest and manage their self-interests.

Discourse allows the human species to recognize and balance interest, self, self-interest, and the interests of others. As Mary Douglas postulated, "Cultural theory is a way of thinking about culture that draws the social environment systematically into the picture of individual choices" (1992, p. xi). If individual choices could truly be independent, there would be no need for society as the essence of collective action characteristic of the human species. For her, "it is possible to write an objective account of how the ideas of the self (the ideal of it, of course, not the self itself) is [*sic*] treated in the normative debate which is the source and origin of culture" (p. xi). The rationale for society and culture grows from the awareness of and shared sense of danger. Danger is recognized as being antithetical to self, to self-interest, and to the interests of others. The rationale for society, by this account, is the collective management of risks. It entails enlightened choice making, a basic principle of rhetoric (Nichols, 1963).

As characterized by Douglas, the rationale for society and culture is the collective management of risk—joint problem recognition and problem solution. As she reasoned, "At the inception of any community a debate is opened about the future form of the society. This is an ongoing normative debate about values and beliefs about the world. It never stops" (1992, p. 43). So conceived, each profession plays a unique role in the collective management of risk. Out of this dialogue emerge idioms that express views of reality and preferences—norms.

In the search for security, words (symbols) count. Meaning defines interests, the balance of interests, risks, and the management of risks. Is this not the realm of public relations, not alone, but in conjunction with other professions? What is meaning? What meaning counts? What meaning is normatively preferable to balance competing interests? One of the best expressions of the logics that help discuss this view of society was made by the famed linguist Edward Sapir, who, in discussing the centrality of language and meaning to the human experience, observed,

> Human beings do not live in the objective world alone, not alone in the world of social activity as ordinarily understood, but are very much at the mercy of the particular language which has become the medium of expression for their society. We see and hear and otherwise experience very largely as we do because the language habits of our community predispose certain choices of interpretation. (quoted in Whorf, 1956, p. 134)

Society, by this view, can be conceptualized as a complex of cultures, each with its peculiar language culture. Interests are reflected, defined, challenged, and denied through language. Privilege and marginalization are challenges ever alive in society.

These polarities are basic to various competing philosophies of public relations for all of the understandable reasons. At times some organizations have used public relations to privilege their view of reality—their terministic screens (Burke, 1966). The concern over a propagandistic view of public relations focuses on the ability of some entities in society to use distortion, lies, misinformation, false reasoning, masked interests, blame shifting, and imbalanced relationships to benefit some interests at the disadvantage (marginalization) of others.

It is unrealistic to expect any profession to set things right. Many take their rationale from that challenge. None is solely responsible for creating divisions that are inappropriate to the greatest good of society. Likewise, none is solely responsible for correcting problems. But, as noted previously, the Public Relations Society of America asks a lot of its members and those dedicated to the profession. "Public relations helps our complex, pluralistic society to reach decisions and function more effectively by contributing to mutual understanding among groups and institutions. It serves to bring private and public policies into harmony" (Public Relations Society of America, 2004, para. 1). Definitions of professions are enriched by setting the challenge for themselves to serve society—the larger interests of humanity. Public relations (its practice and academic study) cannot be justified or studied appropriately independent of an

ongoing concern for its contributory role to the good of society. In this challenge, concerns about balanced interests offer rationale for a relationship approach to the discipline and challenge practitioners to think about the rationale and strategies needed to achieve mutually beneficial relationships.

—*Robert L. Heath*

See also Antecedents of modern public relations; Bernays, Edward; Hill, John Wiley; Lee, Ivy; Mutually beneficial relationships; Newsom, Earl

Bibliography

Burke, K. (1966). *Language as symbolic action.* Berkeley: University of California Press.

Douglas, M. (1992). *Risk and blame: Essays in cultural theory.* New York: Routledge.

Grunig, L. A. (1992). Toward the philosophy of public relations. In E. L. Toth & R. L. Heath (Eds.), *Theoretical and critical approaches to public relations* (pp. 65–91). Hillsdale, NJ: Lawrence Erlbaum.

Hill, J. W. (1958). *Corporate public relations: Arm of management.* New York: Harper.

Hill, J. W. (1963). *The making of a public relations man.* New York: David McKay.

Leeper, R. (2001). In search of a meta theory for public relations: An argument for communitarianism. In R. L. Heath (Ed.), *Handbook of public relations* (pp. 93–104). Thousand Oaks, CA: Sage.

Mead, G. H. (1934). *Mind, self, and society.* Chicago: University of Chicago.

Nichols, M. H. (1963). *Rhetoric and criticism.* Baton Rouge: Louisiana State University Press.

Pearson, R. (1992). Perspectives on public relations history. In E. Toth & R. Heath (Eds.), *Rhetorical and critical approaches to public relations* (pp. 111–130). Hillsdale, NJ: Lawrence Erlbaum.

Public Relations Society of America. (1997/1998). *Public relations tactics: The blue book.* New York: Author.

Public Relations Society of America. (2004). The public relations profession: About public relations. Retrieved from http://www.prsa.org/_Resources/Profession/index.asp?ident=prof1

Whorf, B. L. (1956). *Language, thought, and reality.* Cambridge: MIT Press.

SONNENBERG, BEN

The name of this legendary publicist/press agent is lost or blurred in modern discussions of public relations innovators. During his heyday in New York City, Ben Sonnenberg was larger than life. Image without substance, colorful, flashy, dapper, lavish, self-made, dominating, grandiose, glitter, aura, doer of favors, giver of gifts, ostentatious—these and many other similar phrases were used to describe his character and career. He was one of the princes of public relations who created an agency largely based on his personality. Like so many of these pioneers in the middle years of the 20th century, he left only a partial record of his work. No agency bears his name as his professional legacy. An oft-quoted line opens a feature story by Crosswell Bowen and George Clark on Sonnenberg in the February 1950 issue of *Harper's Magazine*: "Benjamin Sonnenberg may not be the richest or the most powerful man in his trade, but he is certainly the most successful in giving that impression" (p. 39). In that way, he became the prince to many merchant princes, individual leaders of government and commerce.

Born into crushing poverty in Brest Litovsk, Poland, on July 21, 1901, Sonnenberg came with his parents to New York City, where he became famous for creating legends for others through his publicity skills. He died on September 6, 1978, after having created a high lifestyle that included owning one of the most lavish mansions in New York City. In the judgment of Bowen and Clark, "Sonnenberg's role is conceived to stand out in bright, theatrical lights. His clothes, his house, his mode of transportation, eating habits, and manner of doing business all bear the unmistakable imprint of a character equipped to function in a lively and competitive field" (1950, p. 39). The side of the profession that appealed to Sonnenberg was press agentry aimed at getting high-profile recognition for his clients. He proclaimed that for a hefty fee he would see that his clients received "honorary degrees, the French Legion of Honor, and their pictures on the cover of *Time* magazine" (p. 39).

The walls of his lavish Park Avenue office were lined with framed magazine stories he had arranged to feature the professional reputation of his clients. Along with these stories were signed pictures of the powerful and famous: Franklin D. Roosevelt, Herbert Hoover, Fiorello La Guardia, "Wild Bill"

Donovan, Ely Culbertson, Prince Matchabelli, and Grand Duchess Marie of Russia. In the midst of this publicity clutter one could also find framed cover-page pictures of the barons of industry. A personality in his own right, Sonnenberg dealt in personae. He worked successfully to carve images for the rich and famous—for hefty annual fees.

Sonnenberg's lifestyle was not the result of his success. It was its foundation. He created personae for others. He did so for himself, as evidence of what he could accomplish for clients. His dress, mansion, bold mustache, and characteristic dress attracted attention—some of which was unflattering. The conservative John W. Hill slammed Sonnenberg's approach. Hill believed that he was not king of his agency, but one of many smart and ethical counselors who toiled to put information before the public to gain goodwill for clients. Second, the ostentatious lifestyle, perhaps most particularly his apparel, was Hill's target for the sharpest comment in private correspondence to Tommy Ross. Hill noted what he had learned about success in public relations from reading the *Harper's Magazine* piece: "After reading it I have decided to go in for elongated sideburns and a sailor suit" (private correspondence from John W. Hill to Tommy Ross, March 14, 1950).

Like others in his profession during the middle years of the 20th century, his goal was to attract clients who wanted to be recognized. His business clients wanted to become household names. They sought to be familiar and friendly parts of the lives of the American consumer who had turned away from business for many reasons, most particularly the damage done to business's reputation during the Depression. He spoke the language of business leaders and influential political leaders. He could build bonds of friendship and trust between them. Each sought the favor of the other. He not only believed that power of a society rested in hands of the few, but he also made that principle work handsomely for others who held a similar view of society, politics, and commerce.

He knew also that customers and community were important to his clients' interests. He convinced the leaders of the Texas Company (later Texaco and now

Chevron-Texaco) that clean restrooms attracted travelers, who also bought gasoline and other products. His love for theater sparked in him a mission that motivated his effort to convince the company to sponsor Metropolitan Opera broadcasts. That sponsorship is one of the longest and best signatures by an American company. Thousands have enjoyed an afternoon of opera because of his desire to define the persona of the company and build customer and community goodwill.

His professional counseling emphasis was more on image than issue. Rather than working an issue with the substance of sustained debate, he was more likely to work on the image of the client. His forte was creating justification for the actions and aspirations of his clients as the basis for achieving goodwill. Like others of his age, he believed that government and business policies stand before the court of public opinion. He thought that character was the essence of such debates. His client list included the barons of industry and the highest political leaders who wanted to be known and respected for their influence.

Each day he courted the favor of clients, prospects, and reporters. He thought a lunch without someone from those categories was a wasted opportunity. He courted the favor of the press. He wanted reporters to know him personally and to like doing favors for him. During the decades when leaders of major public relations firms were working to create professional associations to foster the ethics and style of the practice, Sonnenberg was one of several loner publicists and counselors who did not join in this professional leadership. He operated by his own standards and saw success as the ultimate ethic. He told Bowen and Clark, "I do what I do because it works" (1950, p. 49). By his own measure he was an adapter. He believed those who adapt to their culture and circumstances thrive; those who do not, perish. By that standard, this self-made millionaire was an adapter. He was larger than life—for himself and his clients.

—*Robert L. Heath*

See also Goodwill; Hill, John Wiley; Press agentry; Publicist

Bibliography

Bowen, C., & Clark, G. R. (1950). "Reputation of Sonnenberg," *Harper's, 200*(2), 39–49.

Cutlip, S. M. (1994). *The unseen power: Public relations, a history*. Hillsdale, NJ: Lawrence Erlbaum.

SOUND BITE

When a reporter interviews a subject for a news story, often only a small segment or a single quote from the actual interview will be used in the broadcast. These small segments are known as *sound bites*. A sound bite is a reference to the short comments that broadcast media use during news stories.

Although an interview with a reporter may last 30 minutes, what actually appears in the edited broadcast version will most likely be paired down to a 30-second (or less) sound bite. A sound bite is on average less than 10 seconds. Radio broadcasts tend to limit sound bites to only one sentence, a mere 8 to 10 words. Television sound bites are only one or two sentences in length, or about 25 words.

Because the length of a sound bite is so limited, it is important to have statements prepared in advance of an interview to increase chances of having the media use crucial portions of an interview. Once the prepared message has been delivered, it is important to stop talking. Answers to questions during the interview must be short and direct. Also, using clear and concise language as well as colorful and descriptive words will increase odds of the media using portions of an interview. By using short and direct responses and providing short sound bites, it is possible to have two short bites appear in one news segment.

For an effective sound bite, it is important to distill information into two or three key points. It is necessary to have a clear and concise message and corresponding key points to convey during an interview. By sticking to three key points or less, the audience is less likely to be confused and lose interest.

Unfortunately sometimes the sound bite may be taken out of context and be misleading. It is important that any spokesperson for an organization be prepared for an interview—have key messages already prepared that will make great sound bites and avoid using terminology that may be used out of context and sound negative. An interview subject who talks in sound bites is more likely to be included in the story since it facilitates editing and is short enough, and interesting enough, to fit the quick time frame of broadcast news.

—Nancy Engelhardt Furlow

See also Actuality; Interview as a communication tool; Media relations

Bibliography

Howard, C. M. (2002). Polishing your spokesperson for news media interviews. *Public Relations Quarterly, 47,* 18.

Ridgway, J. (1996). *Practical media relations.* Burlington, VT: Ashgate.

Segal, E. (2000.) *Getting your 15 minutes of fame—and more: A guide to guaranteeing your business success.* Hoboken, NJ: Wiley.

Woods, J., Veto, J., & Gregg, S. (1999). *Media relations: Publicizing your efforts: Understanding the media and getting media exposure.* Columbia, MD: Enterprise Foundation.

SOUTH AFRICA, PRACTICE OF PUBLIC RELATIONS IN

INTRODUCTION

Public relations in South Africa developed largely in isolation during the last 46 years. There is little contact with practitioners or educators in the rest of Africa, with the exception of the neighboring countries that are part of the Southern Africa Development Community (SADC).

The Republic of South Africa is considered the most advanced in sub-Saharan Africa with regard to public relations practice and education. Global standards are maintained, exemplified by two South Africans winning coveted public relations research awards in the United States in 2002. Ursula Ströh received attention for the best student paper for the International Association of Business Communicators (IABC) for her doctoral research titled "An Experimental Study on the Impact of Change Communication Management on Relationships

with Employees." Dr. Derina Holtzhausen (now living in the United States) won the Institute for Public Relations' Pathfinder Award for innovative research.

South African professional associations and their office bearers also excel in the global village. In June of 2003, a public relations consultant and past president of the IABC Southern Africa Chapter, Stephanie Griffiths, became the first non-American to be elected chairman of the IABC worldwide. Margaret Moscardi, executive director of Public Relations Institute of Southern Africa (PRISA), is on the executive board of the Global Alliance of Public Relations and Communication Management Associations (GA), and PRISA has been appointed the official secretariat of the GA.

It is not a well-known fact that in 1980 South Africa was the first country to research and evolve a body of knowledge for public relations, or that PRISA was the first public relations association in the world to obtain certification from the International Standards Organization (ISO), or that the first reader/text book on strategic public relations was produced in South Africa.

PUBLIC RELATIONS PRACTICE IN SOUTH AFRICA

Holtzhausen's research has indicated that top management's recognition of public relations as a strategic function is the most important change in public relations practice during the last decade. In another study, Benita Steyn found that chief executives expect the role of *strategist* from the most senior public relations practitioner, but the incumbent is not perceived to be performing that role.

The profound social and political changes in South Africa have forced practitioners to adapt to new realities, for example, more transparency, high levels of social responsibility, black empowerment, affirmative action, and cultural differences among publics. Learning how to balance First and Third World concerns, and adapting the Western model of public relations to African conditions are forcing practitioners to be more innovative.

A PRISA survey indicated that relations with employees and communities are now deemed more important by organizations compared with the previous emphasis on customers or the media. A greater emphasis on development and intercultural communication with previously ignored publics is also apparent. Technology is less of a factor in causing change in South Africa because key publics do not have access to technology.

There is increasing pressure from labor unions, the media, consumers, and society to be more socially responsible—a concept that, in the South Africa context, refers to the uplifting of previously disadvantaged communities. South Africa's King Report on corporate governance provides a unique opportunity for public relations practitioners to bring to top management's attention their expertise in building relationships with, and becoming more accountable to, organizational stakeholders and society.

GOVERNMENT COMMUNICATION

As a priority of the South African government, communication is driven centrally from the presidency by the Government Communication Information System (GCIS). The head of the GCIS sits in Cabinet and holds post-Cabinet briefings to communicate government's decisions on policy matters. The GCIS works closely with communication directorates in national departments and the latter, in turn, with their provincial counterparts to ensure consistency of government communication. Also in government, a focus on strengthening the strategic management of communication is observed.

The government places a premium on unmediated communication to the public, that is, direct dialogue between the Cabinet and the general public. In order to bring about an open and positive communication environment with all citizens, the GCIS has developed Government Information Centres and Multipurpose Community Centres. The main thrust has been to reverse the perceived media theme of "no service delivery" and "increasing poverty" to "The tide has turned! Build a people's contract for a better South Africa."

PROFESSIONAL ASSOCIATIONS IN SOUTH AFRICA

Public Relations Institute of Southern Africa

PRISA has been renamed the Institute of Public Relations and Communication Management. In terms of membership, PRISA is the third largest public relations institute in the world (after PRSA in the United States and IPR in Great Britain) and also one of the oldest. PRISA was formed in 1957 in Johannesburg and its official newsletter *Communika* launched in 1970. The first all-Africa public relations conference took place together with the Public Relations Society of Kenya and IPRA in 1975.

In 1980, student membership was introduced. A voluntary accreditation examination was introduced in 1987, with the United States, Canada, Great Britain, Australia, and New Zealand recognizing PRISA accreditation status. PRISA was a founder member of the Global Alliance in 2000. By 2002, PRISA membership stood at 1,300 practitioners with an additional 3,430 student members as well as 53 members in the Consultants Chapter.

International Association of Business Communicators

The first South Africans joined the International Association of Business Communicators (IABC) in 1967, and the Southern Africa chapter was formed in 1991 as part of the Europe/Africa Region. Pixie Malherbe, the first president, received the IABC Chairman's Award in 1994. The Sub-Saharan Africa Region, established in 2000/2001 as a developmental region, became the Africa Region in September 2003.

The majority of the 125 IABC members are in executive positions at large corporations. The Gauteng chapter has 95 members, the Western Cape 15, and the virtual chapter Ubuntu 15. Members forming part of Ubuntu are living in other African countries.

Other Communication Associations

South Africa Communication Association (SACOMM), founded in 1978, mainly serves the academic fraternity. UNITECH is the association for public relations and marketing professionals employed by universities and technikons (technical universities) and IMPRO, the Institute of Municipal Public Relations Officers.

SOUTH AFRICAN CONSULTANCIES

The largest consultancy (and the only one listed on the Johannesburg Securities Exchange) is Simeka TWS, with an income of R 20,8 million (2001 figures). It also has the largest turnover, namely R 75,9 million. Other large consultancies (in order of income) are Meropa Communications, Sasani Communications, Arcay Communications, Gilliam Gamsy International, Bairds Communications, Fleischman Hillard, Manning Selvage & Lee, Tin Can Communications, and Integrated Communications.

During the last three years, there has been an increasing demand for more strategically devised initiatives from the large public relations consultancies. *Perception* and *reputation management* have become the new buzzwords, which has led to a bigger emphasis on research, both qualitative and quantitative. This is often undertaken by research houses, such as Markinor, Research Surveys, Research International, and AskAfrica, to name a few.

The strategic skills base in the industry is lacking, however—most consultants have a journalism background, without the necessary tertiary education to be taken seriously in the business environment. All large agencies are currently investing in training and development to address this shortfall.

Several advertising agencies are restructuring to offer a total marketing mix solution (including public relations) to make up for the losses in advertising spending. Increasing competition and encroachment is also evident from management consulting and auditing firms, as well as market research institutions.

A trend that has emerged over the last five years is the strong focus on development communication, with large donor organizations allocating huge budgets to social marketing and development communication. Another trend is that government and corporate tenders now include very specific criteria with regard to black economic empowerment.

EDUCATION AND TRAINING

South Africa has extensive educational opportunities in public relations that compare well with the United States, widely accepted as the pacesetter in the field.

Universities

In 1960, the Potchefstroom University for Christian Higher Education (PU for CHE) launched the first *degree program* in journalism. Communication courses at South African universities followed in 1968.

At most South African universities (e.g., the Free State [UFS], Port Elizabeth [UPE], South Africa [UNISA], the Rand Afrikaans University [RAU], and PU for CHE), the subject field of public relations is positioned as part of the total communication training in the social sciences. It forms part of a degree in communication, journalism, media studies, communication management or business communication.

At PU for CHE, approximately 70 students graduate annually with a bachelor's degree in public relations. Since 2000, 15 students have obtained master's degrees and two students doctoral degrees in public relations. At UNISA (a distance education institution) around 500 receive bachelor's degrees each year. Since 2000, around six students have obtained master's degrees and three students doctoral degrees on public relations topics. In recent years, universities such as RAU, PU for CHE and UFS introduced structured (coursework) masters degrees in public relations.

The University of Pretoria (UP) specializes in Communication Management (Public Relations), taught as a separate management function within Economic and Management Sciences since 1993. Professor Gustav Puth (the "father of strategic communication" in South Africa) was responsible for this unique positioning, which resulted in an emphasis on the management and strategic perspective at UP, rather than the technician- or skills-oriented perspective common to the field. UP introduced its structured master's in Communication Management in 1995, converting it to a Web-based degree in 2002.

At UP around 45 students graduate each year with a Bachelor of Commerce degree. In addition, there are around 350 management students (majoring in marketing, human resources, tourism, business management, etc.) who enroll for Communication Management as a final (third) year subject each year. In total, sixteen master's students have graduated since 2000 and current enrollment stands at 36 (13 master's students for theses and 23 for coursework). Three doctoral students have graduated since 2000, with 12 students currently enrolled.

Technikons

SA technikons (technical universities) specialize in vocational training, the emphasis being on outcomes-based education/training. Curricula are determined at national level, resulting in highly homogenized public relations training. Technikons teaching public relations are Pretoria, Witwatersrand, Cape, Port Elizabeth, and Vaal Triangle, as well as the Durban Institute of Technology.

In total, the technikons had 555 first-year students enrolled in 2002 for the National Diploma in Public Relations Management. Together, they also had an enrollment of 89 B Tech degree (equivalent of an honors program) students, 15 M Tech (master's) students, and 1 D Tech (doctoral) student. The Technikon SA, a distance-learning facility, had 813 first-year enrollments and 46 B Tech students in 2002.

PRISA Education and Training Centre

The PRISA Education and Training Centre (PETC) is the outgrowth of a comprehensive education and training program that was launched by PRISA in 1964. The late Anna-Mari Honiball, doyen of informal public relations training in South Africa, was appointed the first Head of Education in 1989. At this time, PRISA offered the Basic Principles of Public Relations course (also licensed to colleges), as well as the Advanced Principles of Public Relations course. The first Public Relations

Management Course was offered in 1992. This was also the year that PRISA presented its first Educator of the Year Award. The first student conference, now an annual event, was held in 1999.

The three-year public relations diploma was implemented in 1997, becoming the first qualification outside Great Britain to be recognized by the IPR. PRISA has a license agreement with several commercial colleges in South Africa and neighboring countries as well as a number of technikons to offer some of its courses.

South African Public Relations Textbooks

1965: First South African public relations textbook, *Public Relations Practice in South Africa* (J. P. Malan and J. A. L'Estrange)

1982: *Handbook of Public Relations* (Chris Skinner and Llew Von Essen), plus various revised editions up to the present

1994: *Public Relations in South Africa: A Management Reader* (edited by Berendien Lubbe and Gustav Puth)

1995: *Public Relations, Development and Social Investment: A Southern African Perspective* (Gary Mersham, Ronél Rensburg, and Chris Skinner)

2000: *Corporate Communication Strategy* (Benita Steyn and Gustav Puth); *Introduction to Public Relations and Advertising* (edited by Danie du Plessis)

2002: *Effective Public Relations for Sub-Saharan Africa* (Scott Cutlip, Allen Center, Glen Broom, and Danie du Plessis); *Public Relations: A South African Perspective* (edited by Ronél Rensburg and Mike Cant); *Strategic Organisational Communication: Paradigms and Paradoxes* (edited by Sonja Verwey and F du Plooy Cilliers)

2003: Ronél Rensburg, "Public Relations in South Africa: From Rhetoric to Reality," in *The Global Public Relations Handbook* (edited by Dejan Verčić and Krishnamurthy Sriramesh)

United States textbooks are often prescribed but have become prohibitively expensive in recent years because of the exchange rate.

The Status of Academic Research in Public Relations in South Africa

Research in public relations is increasingly being conducted, although it is still in the embryonic stage. At South Africa technikons, the approach is pragmatic. Therefore, most academic research is conducted by university lecturers and their postgraduate students. At some institutions, however, theses and dissertations lack a clear definition of the field of public relations and often confuse it with marketing. In such instances, the main purpose of public relations is seen as serving the marketing function—the so-called integrated marketing communication (IMC) approach.

A notable exception is the University of Pretoria (UP), where a research program in strategic public relations was initiated in 1997. The findings of the landmark IABC *Excellence Study* was used to conceptualize research aimed at finding solutions to public relations problems in the local context. Phase 1 was completed by Retha Groenewald in 1998, establishing communication management training as a synthesis of public relations as well as organizational, management, and business communication—forming the theoretical foundation of UP's undergraduate training up to the present. Her quantitative study on the knowledge base of the public relations manager determined management, strategic communication, and management communication skills as being most important.

Phase 2 focused on the shared expectations between top management and the public relations department. In the first study, Estelle de Beer found that the perception of public relations managers was that senior management expected them to make a strategic contribution to organizational decision making. In the second study in phase 2, Steyn conceptualized and empirically verified the role of the public relations strategist, manager, and technician, according to the role expectations (normative) and the perceptions of role performance (positive) of 103 South African chief executives.

With completion of the UP *Excellence* project, the emphasis has shifted to the African Body of Knowledge (ABOK) project, currently being conducted by Gené van Heerden. Other focus areas are social responsibility, reputation, and change management.

The study field of communication management adheres to the proud tradition of UP as the leading research university in the country. For three consecutive years, PRISA has bestowed its Educator of the Year award on UP lecturers: Steyn in 1999 and 2001, and Ursula Ströh in 2000. Since 2000, lecturers at UP have produced 32 national and 16 international conference papers, as well as 15 articles in scholarly journals (14 national and 1 international).

Other public relations research that can hold its own internationally includes a doctoral dissertation by Professor Annelie Naudé from the PU for CHE in 2001. Her study addressed a void in public relations research by exploring the interactive use of the Internet, focusing specifically on its use by national government organizations (NGOs) in enhancing their development programs.

Expatriate Dr. Derina Holtzhausen conducted a study on the effects of political change on public relations practice in South Africa, as well as on public relations roles and models in the "new" South Africa—inter alia exploding the myth of the symmetrical/asymmetrical dichotomy in international settings.

Betsie Ferreira, a senior lecturer in public relations at Port Elizabeth Technikon, is currently completing her doctoral dissertation on vocationally oriented public relations education in globalized contexts in South African technikons.

Academic Journals Published in South Africa

In South Africa, academic communication journals are published by universities. *Communicare* (RAU) and *Communicatio* (UNISA) accept scholarly articles across the broad communication domain (e.g., public relations, organizational/development/marketing communication, and communication theory). *Equid Novi* (PU for CHE) focuses on journalism and *Communitas* (Free State) on community communication and information.

CONCLUSION

There is a vibrant public relations community at the southernmost tip of Africa, with regard to both practice and education. However, the field is still characterized by its search for identity, legitimacy, and professional recognition.

—Benita Steyn

Bibliography

Ferreira, B. (2003). *Vocationally oriented public relations education in globalized contexts: An analysis of technikon-level public relations education.* Doctoral dissertation, Rand Afrikaans University, Johannesburg, South Africa [provisional draft].

Holtzhausen, D. (2003). *The effects of political change on public relations practice in South Africa/Public relations models in the New South Africa/South African practitioner roles.* Retrieved September 18, 2003, from http://www.prisa.co.za

Naudé, A., Froneman, J., & Atwood, R. (in press). The use of the Internet by ten South African non-governmental organizations—A public relations perspective. *Public Relations Review, 30*(1).

Rensburg, R. (2003). Public relations in South Africa: From rhetoric to reality. In K. Sriramesh & D.Verčič (Eds.), *The global public relations handbook: Theory, research and practice.* Mahwah, NJ: Lawrence Erlbaum.

Steyn, B. (2003). Corporate communication strategy: A conceptualization. *Journal of Communication Management, 8*(2), 168–183.

Steyn, B. *Determining CEO satisfaction with the role played by the most senior corporate communication practitioner in an organization—A gap analysis.* Unpublished doctoral dissertation, University of Pretoria, South Africa. Manuscript in preparation.

SPEAKERS BUREAUS

A speakers bureau is a public relations tactic that provides individuals representing an organization the opportunity to speak about the organization's interests to other groups. The speakers bureau is composed of a pool of internal speakers that may include executives, employees, or volunteers who are made available upon request to other organizations. The speakers typically are provided without charge to civic and service organizations, business and professional organizations, and schools as a means of promoting the organization or its position on issues. Speakers bureaus are commonly operated by corporations, industry associations, health care organizations, and nonprofits.

Speakers bureaus have long been a standard tactic of community relations programs. Whereas some organizations have developed speakers bureaus primarily as a reactive response to help them more systematically handle frequent requests for speakers, other speakers bureau programs proactively seek out strategic opportunities to place organizational representatives in front of key constituencies or to position executives as "thought leaders" in high-profile fora.

As a form of direct communication, speakers bureaus offer a number of advantages over mass-mediated public relations tactics. Most important, the speakers bureau is a relationship-building tool. Knowledgeable, personable speakers help to put a human face on the organization and increase its credibility. The public speaking situation allows for interaction with the audience and immediate feedback, and allows the speaker to control the organization's message without filtering from the media. In addition, according to the 1980 publication *The Executive Speechmaker: A Systems Approach,* speakers bureaus demonstrate the organization's accessibility and desire to be a constructive participant in its community and industry.

A successful speakers bureau requires careful selection of participants. Although some organizations recruit participants simply by asking for volunteers, others invite specific individuals based on their credentials, relevant personal experiences, or known speaking skills. Because audiences prefer to hear firsthand accounts from those closest to a situation, the public relations representative may not always be the most appropriate choice for a speaker. CEOs who lack requisite speaking skills or personal warmth may not be good choices either.

A successful speakers bureau also requires adequate training and coaching of participants, research to identify desirable audiences and topics of interest to them, selection of key message points, and development of written scripts and speaking aids, which may include full text of speeches, speech outlines, audiovisual aids, and handouts. A speakers bureau may have several prepared presentation topics and corresponding speakers available to the public at any one time. These might include issue-oriented presentations (e.g., a presentation to announce a new venture, plant, program, or goal), a presentation designed to solicit donations or volunteers, and presentations adapted to specific groups (e.g., children, homeowners, non-English speakers, or senior citizens). Some shared "stock" content, such as an overview of the organization's mission, scope and operations, or references to an annual theme or slogan, may serve as unifying elements across the various types of speeches. Speakers bureaus can also be helpful in negatively charged situations to dispel misconceptions, explain organizational actions, gather support for a position, or bring legislative or regulatory roadblocks to light.

An obvious prerequisite for success is that external publics be made aware of the availability of a speakers bureau. The bureau should be promoted to appropriate groups and made accessible through the organization's Web site. Scheduled presentations should be publicized in appropriate internal and external media. In addition to seeking media coverage of the speech, many organizations multiply the value of speaking opportunities by "repackaging" their executives' speeches for use in op-ed pieces, internal publications, and Web sites. Finally, presentations should be evaluated through audience surveys or feedback from event organizers. Managing these tasks associated with large, proactive speakers bureaus may require full-time, professional-level staff.

It should be noted that the type of speakers bureau described here and considered to be a public relations tactic is distinct from for-profit talent agencies, which offer speakers for a fee, although some of these entities call themselves "speakers bureaus."

—*Katherine N. Kinnick*

Bibliography

Foundation for Public Relations Research and Education. (1980). *The executive speechmaker: A systems approach.* New York: Author.

Going outside the box for executive speaking opportunities. (1998, January 19). *PR News, 54*(2), 1.

Kinzey, R. E. (2000, August). Creating a speakers bureau for your nonprofit. *Public Relations Tactics, 7*(8), 20.

Lewton, K. (1998, April 16). Speakers bureau makes a comeback with a proactive twist. *Healthcare PR & Marketing News, 7*(8), 1.

Morris, F. E. (1989, Spring). Getting results from a corporate speakers bureau. *Public Relations Quarterly,* 14–15.

SPEECHWRITING

Speechwriting in its simplest form is the process of preparing a speech. It involves analysis of the audience and speaking situation; identification of a topic; development of arguments, appeals, and supporting materials; and ordering those materials in a systematic manner. Speechwriting in most corporate settings is much more complex, however, because the speech is often a statement of the organization's policy or position. Moreover, speeches remain one of the most important forms of communication employed by organizations. They are used to announce major policies and initiatives; restate positions; disseminate information; manage issues, image, and reputation; and persuade stakeholders to support the organization. Senior executives deliver speeches at annual meetings, to groups of employees, and to a wide variety of external stakeholders. Occasionally, CEOs take on celebrity status and may be called on to give speeches about social as well as general business issues to both domestic and international audiences.

The form of speeches prepared for executives vary from manuscripts to more general outlines or simple talking points. Although the nature of the speaking occasion will influence the formality of the speech, many executives favor manuscript speeches over outlines or talking points. Manuscripts allow for more precise language.

Corporate speechwriting usually involves a process of close collaboration of the executive speaker and a speechwriter or ghostwriter, and careful review of the speech by various aspects of departments of the organization. This process of speechwriting and review helps ensure that the speech is a corporate product and that it is fully vetted. Executive speeches are often reviewed by the public relations department, the legal department, and any other major divisions or departments discussed in the speech. This review process, although useful in ensuring that all statements are accurate and appropriate, sometimes reduces the quality of the messages. Professional speechwriters, for example, often complain that reviews by legal departments translate stirring prose into meaningless legalese. Mike Morrison, former speechwriter for Lee Iacocca, noted that the committee-written speech increasingly tends to be the norm in major corporations. Moreover, committee-written speeches often lack distinctiveness. Speechwriters often recommend, therefore, that these reviews be kept to a minimum.

Speechwriters also recommend that the writer get to know the speaker. This includes understanding the speaker's views on various issues, patterns of language use, pronunciation, interests, and backgrounds so that they may write more effectively in the speaker's voice.

Using a professional writer to prepare a speech for an executive is usually justified on three grounds. First, senior executives often do not have the time to research and prepare a speech. This lack of time is compounded by the fact that executives may give dozens of major speeches each year. Finally, executives rarely have the training or background to prepare a variety of successful addressees, tailored to a wide array of diverse audiences, focusing on a range of different topics. In essence, using a speechwriter improves the probability that an executive speech will have the desired effect. Despite these justifications, speechwriting does raise several ethical questions about honesty and authorship.

—Matthew W. Seeger,
Timothy L. Sellnow, and Robert R. Ulmer

See also Ghostwriting

Bibliography

Einhorn, L. (1981). The ghosts unmasked: A review of literature on speechwriting. *Communication Quarterly, 30,* 41–47.

Seeger, M. W. (1993). *"I gotta tell you": The speeches of Lee Iacocca.* Detroit, MI: Wayne State University Press.

Tarver, J. (1987). *The corporate speechwriter's handbook.* New York: Quorum.

SPIN

Public relations professionals have been called all kinds of names—sandbaggers, flacks, propaganda machines, spin doctors. Unfortunately, these labels connote a P. T. Barnum/Jerry McGuire approach to public relations management. Further, these negative names imply that the industry engages in promoting hype, puffery, and communication manipulation. These terms also suggest that press relations is the primary function for which public relations practitioners are responsible. And even more disturbing is the point that *spin doctor* has become a mainstream term used by the media to associate smoke-and-glass strategies with public relations professionals.

The reasons this black cloud of spin looms over the industry are as varied as the definitions used to describe public relations itself. Whereas some view public relations as a management function that promotes mutually beneficial relationships and encourages positive behavioral change, others advocate that their primary responsibility is to engage in image and reputation management. Still others believe that the public relations function is concerned mainly with media relations and publicity.

Why does this negative perception linger? An attempt to provide an exhaustive list of "how comes" would be an unproductive effort. The purpose of this entry is to provide an in-depth discussion that offers information from various viewpoints, enabling practitioners to make more clearly defined and educated decisions about how—and why—they plan to practice public relations.

ORIGINAL SPIN MODEL INTRODUCED

Today, when the term *spin doctor* is used in the same sentence with *public relations*, many professionals get chills up the spine. But the chills are immediately followed by feelings of frustration. Many questions regarding the spin doctor paradigm are still left unanswered: (a) From where does this negative stereotype stem? (b) What has caused this misperception to continue? (c) What can the public relations profession do to diminish such inaccuracies? (d) Is this model really becoming acceptable as a mainstream way of doing business among public relations practitioners?

Sumpter and Tankard originally identified the *spin model* as an alternative approach to other models being practiced in the public relations industry. After providing a thorough overview of what this model entails, they concluded

> The field of public relations needs to come to terms with the spin doctor phenomenon. A cursory review of some public textbooks suggests little discussion of the role, and, indeed, some rather drastic differences between spin doctoring and standard public relations activities. Do public relations practitioners want to distance themselves from the spin doctor phenomenon, as Bernays appears to be recommending? Do they want to claim the spin doctors as part of their field? Or do they want to select what is effective from the spin doctor repertoire and incorporate it into the traditional public relations model, while ignoring the rest? The spin doctor conception of truth, and ethics of spin doctors, would also seem to be topics of further discussion. (1994, p. 26)

Something of an ominous, conspiracy-like theory, the public relations spin model still prevails today—10 years after Sumpter and Tankard initially suggested that it existed. But now this model seems to be even more predominant than it did when the authors introduced it. Evidence lies not only in the profession but also in the plethora of literature written about spin.

Robert Dilenschneider, a well-known public relations practitioner, is an advocate of denouncing public relations' association with spin. "I think the time has come for public relations professionals to condemn spin and label spin doctors for what they are: purveyors of deception, manipulation, and misinformation. Spin is to public relations what pornography is to art" (1998).

OVERVIEW OF PUBLIC RELATIONS AND ITS HISTORICAL UNDERPINNINGS

During the early 20th century, public relations as a formal profession started with what James E. Grunig defined as the "press agentry/publicity model." This was the era when the "public be damned" and "closed systems" philosophy was embraced. Today the profession seeks to actively engage in what Grunig defined as the "two-way symmetrical model," where professionals focus on mutual understanding, mutual cooperation/accommodation, and relationship-building programming and strategizing.

Negative Perceptions Based on Historical Activities

There appears to be some "bad karma" among practitioners schooled in journalism programs and among journalists who have been ill-treated by public relations practitioners. This negativity also stems from the history/nature of deceitful, manipulative public relations activities practiced during the early part of the 20th century. There is also a notion that public relations practitioners are vying for the same space to which journalists believe they are entitled.

Lack of Clarity Regarding What Public Relations Practitioners Do

Public relations activities are very diverse. Some practitioners engage in publicity and promotional activities, and they utilize varying propaganda-type techniques (bandwagon, glittering generalities, etc.) and persuasive methods. Although this capacity determines how many public relations professionals have been depicted on television, in the newspaper, and in movies, these are *not* the only kinds of activities in which practitioners are involved. Public relations professionals are responsible for much more, including strategic planning and counseling, fundraising, researching, and developing and maintaining relationships between an organization and its key publics. This is just a range—not a cumulative list by any means. And public relations is practiced among a variety of disciplines, ranging from health care, government, entertainment, and travel/tourism to corporate, nonprofit, and financial institutions.

Lack of Consistent Viewpoints Across the Public Relations Profession

Some very successful public relations professionals promote themselves as prominent spin doctors and receive much publicity for it (e.g., Michael Sitrick, Howard Rubenstein, and John Scanlon). Other very successful public relations professionals publicly seek to deface spin doctor behavior and the term itself (e.g., Dilenschneider).

Lack of Consistent Viewpoints Regarding the Semantics of Spin

Spin has traditionally and historically been associated with political and governmental campaigns. In turn, these industries have been associated with the use of propaganda techniques. The term *propaganda* also has a negative connotation. So we should consider the way we engage in and discuss the concept of strategic persuasion. The term *motivation* has a much more positive connotation, and people seem more responsive to being *motivated* to do something than being *persuaded* to do so.

Varying Degrees of Ideologies Regarding Moral Judgment

There is also the issue of the varying viewpoints about moral judgments and individual ideologies. *Situationalists* reject moral rules and ask if the action (behavior) yields the best possible outcome in the given situation. *Subjectivists* reject moral rules and base moral judgments on personal feelings about the action (behavior) and the setting. *Absolutists* believe that actions (behaviors) are moral, provided they yield positive consequences through moral conformity to moral rules. *Exceptionists* believe that conformity to moral rules is desirable, but exceptions to these rules is often permissible. Therefore, a person's behavior depends on his or her individual ideologies about moral judgments.

Varying Degrees of Ideologies Regarding the First Amendment

Another factor that influences a person's behavior is based on his or her individual ideologies regarding the First Amendment. According to the *absolutist* view, the First Amendment means exactly what it says: "Congress shall make *no* law abridging the freedom of speech." As such, public relations practitioners can say whatever they want, providing it meets the criteria of the First Amendment. Conversely, the *balancing* approach sees the absolutist view as impractical and deems this categorical approach as artificial. Balancers believe that in every case the courts should weigh the individual's interest in free expression against the government's interest in restricting the speech in question. Thus, public relations practitioners need to think carefully about what they say, how they say it, and *who* it will affect.

Varying Ideologies Regarding Social Responsibility

A third factor that influences a person's behavior depends on his or her individual ideologies regarding social responsibility. Some practitioners believe that their primary responsibility is to their stockholders, who financially support the organization. Hence, these practitioners are interested foremost in supporting the "bottom line." Others believe that they are responsible to the greater community and society at large—not just their stockholders. Therefore, in some situations the bottom line is not the primary concern.

REASONS PUBLIC RELATIONS PROFESSIONALS ADVOCATE SPIN

- Every issue has two sides; hence, there are two viewpoints.
- Practitioners are responsible for advocating the viewpoint of the organization they represent, based on the fiduciary relationship/commitment between the organization and its stockholders.

- Truth is relative.
- Practitioners are merely utilizing framing and agenda-setting theories.
- Media positioning is one of the primary tasks of a public relations practitioner.
- Spinning has been around for centuries (e.g., J. E. Grunig's press agentry model, Edward Bernays's "engineering" of public opinion).
- It's really just the word that offends people—not the behavior per se.
- Society should be exposed to a "free marketplace of ideas."
- Spinning supports the absolutist view of the First Amendment.
- Spinning supports the absolutist view of moral judgment: Actions are moral provided they yield positive consequences through moral conformity to moral rules.
- Spinning supports socially responsible behavior.

REASONS PUBLIC RELATIONS PROFESSIONALS DENOUNCE SPIN

- Spinning is unethical because it misrepresents and distorts the truth.
- Spinning is a far cry from J. E. Grunig's two-way symmetrical model of public relations, which seeks to develop mutually beneficial relationships between an organization and its publics.
- Spinning is a form of propaganda that, when used deceitfully and manipulatively, does not fairly represent the information.
- The spin model suggests that public relations professionals are nothing more than "journalists in-residence" and "press agents" whose main goal and obligations are to "earn ink."
- The word *spin* has a negative connotation, and "perception is reality"; hence, some may view this negative word and its association with the behavior it represents as representative of the behavior of *all* public relations practitioners.
- The spin model violates the PRSA Code of Ethics. Public relations practitioners are obligated to uphold this conduct. By practicing spin-oriented public relations, practitioners are violating the code of ethics.
- The spin paradigm does not support socially responsible behavior.

IMPLICATIONS: WHAT PUBLIC RELATIONS PROFESSIONALS CAN DO

The word *spin* will never go away. However, by keeping the word alive via use in our everyday dialogue, we perpetuate its existence and give it power to survive. We should strive to diminish its use as a commonplace term among the media. We should also be committed to practicing ethical public relations. Further, we should never deceitfully manipulate a message to communicate half-truths. And we should discourage professionals who tout that they practice spin as their "duty" as public relations practitioners.

Finally, we should continue to educate people whenever we can about what public relations really is. We need to remind people that although publicity and promotional strategies are viable components of the communication mix, they are not the sole functions of public relations. Furthermore, instead of advocating propaganda as the foundation for these activities, we should broaden our thinking to that of *motivating* particular behaviors and influencing positive changes in our society.

—*Lisa T. Fall*

See also Propaganda

Bibliography

Dilenschneider, R. (1998). Spin doctors practice public relations quackery. *Wall Street Journal*. Retrieved May 2004 from Nexis database.

Dilenschneider, R. (1999). Spin. *Vital Speeches of the Day, 66*(4), 123–125.

Dilenschneider, R., & Kosmicki, R. (1998). *Spin: A high-risk strategy*. Paper presented at Bulldog Reporter and PR Newswire Media Relations '98 Conference, pp. 1–8. (Reprint)

Ewen, S. (1996). *PR! A social history of spin*. New York: Basic Books.

Grunig, J. E., White, J., Grunig, L. A., Dozier, D. M., Ehling, W. P., & Repper, F. C. (1992). *Excellence in public relations and communication management*. Hillsdale, NJ: Lawrence Erlbaum.

PRSA Code of Ethics. Retrieved May 2004 from http://www.prsa.org

PRWatch Web site. Retrieved May 2004 from http://www.prwatch.org

Sumpter, R., & Tankard, J. (1994). The spin doctor: An alternative model of public relations. *Public Relations Review, 20*(1), 19–27.

Prince Charles on a walkabout in Sheffield in 1998, with his Deputy Private Secretary Mark Bolland behind him (holding files). Described by the British newspapers as the prince's "spin doctor," Bolland left Charles's employ soon thereafter to set up his own public relations agency.

SOURCE: © Tim Graham/Corbis.

SPIRAL OF SILENCE THEORY

In a political election campaign, politicians are quick to criticize public opinion polls that show them to be trailing. They will argue that the poll is inaccurate, that the only poll that matters is on election day, or that they are picking up momentum in the race to gain votes. Although some have questioned why a politician would devote resources to proving that unfavorable polls were wrong rather than simply running a more effective campaign, "spiral of silence" theory offers some explanation of this phenomenon. This theory argues that any opinion that is perceived to be the opinion of a majority will hold disproportionate weight in influencing others. This effect happens, at least in part, because people who believe that their opinion is in the minority are less likely to express their opinion. The failure to express a minority point of view reinforces the unequal status of that opinion because there is no longer an advocate for it. This leads to a continuing spiral of silence. Politicians do not want people to think they are trailing in the polls because if that information were to become ingrained in the public mind, supporters of the trailing politician might quit

working as hard to bring about his or her election—thus ensuring the doom of that campaign. The spiral of silence is not limited to political campaigns, but to any issue where a person or group of people need others to support them or buy their product.

In 1965, Elisabeth Noelle-Neumann worked for the Allensbach Institute for Opinion Research in West Germany and had been monitoring public opinion about that fall's federal election. Several months before the election, she asked survey respondents two questions. First, she asked them to name the party for which they intended to vote in the upcoming election. Second, she asked them to name the party they believed would win the election. In early polling, the Christian Democrats and the Social Democrats (the two main parties in West Germany, and the two leading parties in the united Germany today) were roughly equal in responses to both questions, and those results held for about six months. That is, the same number of people intended to vote for each party, and the same number of people believed that each party was likely to win the election.

As the election neared, Noelle-Neumann noticed an interesting phenomenon. While the number of people intending to vote for each party held steady, the response to the other question changed. Although people still intended to vote in similar numbers, two months prior to the election four of five voters expected that the Christian Democrats would win the election. In the two weeks prior to the election, public opinion began to diverge and the Christian Democrats gained 5 percent in the polls (as the party for which someone actually intended to vote) and the Social Democrats lost approximately 5 percent. Actual voting behavior followed the voting behavior perceived and predicted for others, and the Christian Democrats won that election with a 9 percent advantage.

This theory, according to Noelle-Neumann, makes five separate assumptions (1991, p. 260):

1. Society threatens deviant individuals with isolation.

2. Individuals experience fear of isolation continuously.

3. This fear of isolation causes individuals to try to assess the climate of public opinion at all times.

4. The results of this estimate affect behavior in public, especially the open expression or concealment of opinions.

5. This assumption connects the preceding four. Taken together, they are considered responsible for the formation, defense, and alteration of public opinion.

Certainly this theory is not meant to apply to all people at all times. There will always be individuals who violate social trends and who care little about the opinions of others. Taken as a whole, however, these assumptions point to some powerful phenomena about human behavior. The first assumption indicates that an individual who has an opinion or who takes an action different from that of others will no longer remain part of the "in crowd." In the case of the German elections, people who supported the losing party would fit this profile. The second assumption indicates that most people want to be on the winning side or part of the popular group, and the third indicates that people continuously monitor those around them to gauge their opinions. In 1965, something happened in West Germany that caused people to start believing that the Christian Democrats were going to win the election. There are many possible explanations that would be very difficult to explore in retrospect—perhaps that party increased its advertising efforts, perhaps a Social Democratic candidate committed a gaffe, or perhaps Christian Democratic supporters became more vocal. It is important to note here that the actual change in public opinion was not real. Rather, people began to perceive that support in the election had changed.

Whatever the reason for the perceived shift in support, this led to the fourth assumption of the theory. When people began to believe that the Christian Democrats would win, those who supported them were emboldened to voice their support publicly. Meanwhile, those who supported the Social Democrats began to tone down their public support. Although they did not initially change their actual voting intentions, they were less likely to speak up at parties, attend rallies, donate money, display signs, or partake in the myriad other activities necessary for a political campaign to be successful. The interconnection of these four assumptions led to the fifth. When people believed that the Social Democrats were losing, they quit publicly supporting them. This led people to perceive even less support for the party, which led to a cycle of decreasing support. Eventually, this led to the aforementioned nine-point shift in public opinion that ultimately decided the election.

Two points are important to make here. First, "spiral of silence" theory does not completely explain public behavior. Examples abound of products that have been marketed as the "rebel" or otherwise atypical choice and of candidates who have run successful campaigns as "underdogs." However, the fact that the theory does not explain human behavior universally does not deny its value in cases where it does. Many studies have been conducted that demonstrate a shift in behaviors on some part of the public based on their perception of what the majority opinion was. Second, the spiral of silence applies well beyond the political realm. Although that classic example from Noelle-Neumann's work has been used here for the sake of clarity, applicability of the theory has been shown in a wide variety of public information campaigns.

Although much support had been found for this theory, it is not without its critics. One line of criticism has argued that people are more capable of deviating from majority opinion than this theory gives them credit for. In particular, assertiveness, knowledge, and the amount of time one spends interacting with media might influence the degree to which they are swayed by public opinion. Additionally, the argument has been advanced that there is no such thing as a unified public opinion. Since many societies are experiencing more nearly equal gender, racial, and social roles, public opinion may fragment along those lines. Therefore, it might be harder to claim that someone's behavior was the result of a dominant opinion that does not exist. Those responding to this criticism have argued that public opinion can still exist in subgroups and that some questions still lend themselves to opinion polling. For example, there are only so many presidential candidates for which one can vote, and surveys can assess what percentage of the public intends to vote for each one.

Continuing research in this theory will likely further explore the question of how attitudes change over time and how this influences the willingness to speak publicly on any issue. With that said, present research has demonstrated the effects of the spiral of silence across a number of areas of public opinion. People generally wish to avoid being socially ostracized for opinions and actions that deviate from the social norm, so they monitor the opinions of others. In some cases, this may cause people to fail to express opinions that they perceive as being in the minority. This, in turn, leads to decreased support for the position and even more silence.

—*William Forrest Harlow*

Bibliography

Larsora, D. L. (1991). Political outspokenness: Factors working against the spiral of silence. *Journalism and Mass Communication Quarterly, 68*, 131–140.

Noelle-Neumann, E. (1991). The theory of public opinion: The concept of the spiral of silence. *Communication Yearbook, 14*, 256–287.

Noelle-Neumann, E. (1993). *The spiral of silence* (2nd ed.). Chicago: University of Chicago Press.

Simpson, C. (1996). Elisabeth Noelle-Neumann's "spiral of silence" and the historical context of communication theory. *Journal of Communication, 46*, 149–173.

SPORTS PROMOTION

Sports promotion is an aspect of the public relations profession that relies heavily on publicity and promotion to foster the brand equity of teams, conferences, types of sports, and specific athletes. As professional, collegiate, and amateur sports functions assume an increasingly important role in society and culture, sports organizations and athletes face increasing scrutiny from media and society. A scan of the news on almost any day reveals events from the sports pages that are now making the front page, the business page, and the top of the broadcast instead of being covered only on the sports page. Consider these examples.

NBA star Kobe Bryant was accused in July 2003 of assaulting a Colorado woman during his visit there to have knee surgery. In a press conference, Bryant tearfully admitted to adultery, but denied the charge of felony sexual assault.

Iowa State University Head Basketball Coach Larry Eustachy resigned from the university in May 2003 after it was revealed that he partied with college-age students in Columbia, Missouri, into the early-morning hours on January 22, 2003. Photographs taken by a University of Missouri student showed the coach at a party that night near the college campus.

The National Association of Stock Car Auto Racing (NASCAR), the fastest-growing segment of auto racing and one of the fastest growing segments of sports in general, endured months of media scrutiny and public criticism after superstar Dale Earnhardt died in the final lap of the 2001 Daytona 500, the Super Bowl of NASCAR racing. NASCAR, a relatively insular organization not used to intense criticism and media scrutiny, faced the crisis after having just fired its public relations firm.

Chicago Cubs power hitter Sammy Sosa apologized to fans in June 2003 after admitting he used a corked bat during a game with the Tampa Bay Devil Rays. Sosa said he was not aware that he was using a corked bat; he said he mistakenly picked up a corked bat that he sometimes used during batting practice. Sosa was immediately ejected from the game after umpire crew chief Tim McClelland, who was working the plate, spotted the cork when Sosa's bat shattered. Sosa's other bats were confiscated by security personnel and immediately turned over to Major League Baseball.

In early 2002, a jury convicted Thomas Junta of manslaughter when he beat another father to death. Jurors found Thomas Junta guilty of involuntary manslaughter in the beating death of Michael Costin, 40, after a youth hockey practice attended by the sons of the two men in Reading, Massachusetts, on July 5, 2000.

Despite all the wealth generated in sports, problems exist when the millionaire and billionaire athletes go on strike to demand higher compensation. It is also problematic when athletes, both professional and collegiate, misbehave, causing negative publicity for themselves, their universities, and their sports franchises. Fans and taxpayers, already disturbed with the off-court antics of athletes, must contend with sports franchise owners who hold cities hostage by threatening to move the team if the local government does not build luxurious stadiums at taxpayers' expense. All of this can generate unwanted, negative publicity for an industry that has grown as big and profitable as sports and is avidly watched by the media and the fans.

Turn on the television any given weekend and you are likely to see hundreds of thousands of people crammed into stadiums, arenas, and racetracks to watch the sport of their choice. Be it the NFL, the Final Four, or the Masters golf tournament, fans are paying increasingly higher ticket prices to watch the Kurt Warners and Jeff Gordons of the world slam dunk, pass, and race their way to victories and championships. Many of these athletes are millionaires several times over, and they play the role of heroes to the throngs of young and old people who pay premium prices to watch them compete.

In addition to the dollars spent to attend sporting events, there are also millions of dollars spent each year on sports memorabilia—clothing, hats, collectibles, and so forth. David M. Carter and Darren Rovell wrote that sports "has become a massive industry all its own, one estimated to generate spending approaching $200 billion annually" (2003, p. xix).

Once considered a relaxing pastime, sports are now big business. Consider the following examples:

> Anschutz Soccer, Inc., the Major League Soccer investor group, announced it will pay a reported $40 to $50 million for the United States broadcasting rights to the 2006 and 2010 men's World Cups and the 2003 women's World Cup.

> Reebok signed an unprecedented lifetime endorsement contract with Philadelphia 76ers guard and NBA Most Valuable Player Allen Iverson. The contract extended an existing 10-year, $50 million deal for the remainder of Iverson's professional career.

> Duke Blue Devils basketball coach Mike Krzyzewski agreed to a lifetime contract that will keep him with the school through at least 2011, extending a run that has produced three NCAA championships, six ACC titles, and more than 500 victories. It also gives Krzyzewski the title of special assistant to the president, a position he says he intends to hold after retiring.

A business with the power and reach of sports calls for the expertise of persons trained in public relations and crisis communication. Though the job of sports information director has existed at the collegiate level for many years, all types of sports organizations from amateur to Olympic to professional are finding they have a greater need than ever for experienced people to meet the media and plan and implement the strategies needed to publicize and promote athletes and organizations. This job requires a person who understands the world of professional and collegiate sports and who is trained in news and sports writing, public relations, media relations, crisis communication, and ethics.

Often referred to as sports marketing or sports communication, it has become clear in recent years that the expertise of a skilled public relations person is needed in this area.

The marriage of public relations and sports is a natural one when one considers that sports, like other businesses, demands the expertise of a person trained in media, communication, and public relations skills. Carter and Rovell stated, "The sports business has become an extremely involved industry that now includes the same elements and applies the same business principles seen throughout the rest of big business" (2003, p. xix). Sports organizations, whether professional, collegiate, or amateur, deal with the same challenges faced by organization and corporation public relations practitioners: media relations, getting key messages to the appropriate target publics, ethics, building alliances with stakeholder groups, image, and crisis management, to name only a few.

Melvin Helitzer, author of one of the most comprehensive texts on sports promotion and publicity, described sports promotion as "make money or else," an objective at least as important as "win or else." In a comprehensive description of sports promotion across all levels (high school to professional sports), Helitzer wrote,

A major sports team—college or professional—must be as successful at the bank as they are at the stadium. This has been a mind-boggling development. For over 150 years sports were hobbies. They promoted exercise, fun and, in athletic competition, amateur purity. But in the past 50 years, sports have turned from lily white to professional green. . . . One day, college athletes—like Olympians—may redefine the word *amateur*. (1999, p. 1)

Steven A. Lesnik and Howard Schacter described the sports public relations job as "one of the youngest and fastest growing segments of the PR industry" (1997, p. 405). They identified two public relations tactics as crucial for this area: (a) achieve the communications objectives of a sports-related company or organization and (b) support and enhance a sports marketing activity executed by a company or organization.

In 1997, Nicholas Neupauer noted the absence of college courses or programs in the area of sports information or sports communication. He noted that in the 1960s, college sports information professionals belonged to the American College Public Relations Association (ACPRA). After the realization that a split was needed between the sports promotion people and the college public relations administrators, the College Sports Information Directors of America (CoSIDA) was founded in 1957. Today, CoSIDA is a vigorous membership association, and it is the premier organization for college sports information and communication professionals.

Neupauer argued that the public relations discipline is largely ignoring the emergence of sports information as a public relations specialization:

Token SID classes do pop up from time to time at institutions, appearing in the catalog as "special topics courses." But only a smattering of schools offer classes on a consistent basis. SID majors, minors, tracks, or concentrations are rare in undergraduate education. Even the PRSA ignored the field. In its "1987 Report of the Commission on Undergraduate Public Relations Education: A Design for Undergraduate Public Relations Education," the PRSA described the importance of PR specializations in publicity and media relations, community relations, employee relations, consumer relations, financial/shareholder relations, public affairs, fundraising and international public relations. But it overlooked 'sports information directing' as a PR specialization worthy of attention in undergraduate education. (1997, p. 35)

This seems unusual considering the dramatic growth of collegiate as well as professional sports. Neupauer urged public relations organizations such as PRSA to include sports information and sports communication in its discipline.

—*Becky McDonald*

See also Crisis communication; Promotion; Publicity

Bibliography

Carter, D. M., & Rovell, D. (2003). *On the ball: What you can learn about business from America's sports leaders.* Upper Saddle River, NJ: Prentice Hall.

Helitzer, M. (1999). *The dream job: Sports publicity, promotion and marketing* (3rd ed.). Athena, OH: University Sports Press.

Lesnik, S. A., & Schacter, H. (1997). A practical guide to sports marketing and public relations. In Clarke L. Caywood (Ed.), *The handbook of strategic public relations and integrated communications* (pp. 405–416). New York: McGraw-Hill.

Neupauer, N. (1997). Sports information: The most coveted, ignored profession. *Public Relations Strategist, 3*(3), 35–37.

STAKEHOLDER THEORY

Stakeholder theory provides a theoretical grounding for public relations practitioners to expand their understanding of how individuals, groups, and external organizations impact their organization. Stakeholders are important to public relations professionals because these groups are essentially the "public" in public relations. Stakeholders, in essence, are the audiences for organizational messages. Stakeholder theory is an outgrowth of general systems and resource dependence perspectives suggesting that organizations must forge links with stakeholders to acquire valuable resources or stakes and reduce uncertainty. One of the central tenets of stakeholder theory is that organizations should attend to the needs of a broader set of stakeholders that reaches beyond stockholders. From a public relations perspective, stakeholder theory seeks to identify and manage the diverse needs, values, and interests of various stakeholders and the potential communication tensions between these groups.

R. Edward Freeman (1984) was one of the first proponents of stakeholder management. He argued for considering stakeholders as part of the larger strategic planning process. In this case, organizations that develop strong instrumental links including communication channels with stakeholders are likely to hold a competitive advantage over organizations that do not. A key idea in his work is that organizations and stakeholders can and should mutually influence one another in an ongoing process of accommodation. Since organizations are dependent upon stakeholders for resources, these groups have the ability to withhold their resources if they disagree with the organization on important issues.

Much of the research on stakeholder theory discusses how narrowly or broadly organizations should define their stakeholders. Freeman defined *stakeholders* as any individual or group that impacts or is impacted by the actions of organizations. Researchers agree that stakeholders can be located both within and outside the organization. For instance, Robert L. Heath (1997) delineated activist publics, intra-industry players, inter-industry players, potential activist publics, customers, employees, legislators, regulators, judiciary, investors, neighbors, and the media as a loss of potential stakeholders. More recently some researchers have argued for non-human stakeholders, including wildlife and the environment. Certainly, after environmental disasters such as the Exxon *Valdez* and

Chernobyl, one can reasonably argue that these groups are impacted by organizations. However, organizations depending upon their industry or circumstances are going to have different potential stakeholders. For this reason, identifying stakeholders is a key issue for public relations practitioners.

STAKEHOLDER IDENTIFICATION

One of the difficulties associated with stakeholder theory is being able to identify stakeholders. Since organizations are such powerful forces in society, it is arguable that they have the ability to impact all of society. Public relations professionals are expected to narrow the potential stakeholder possibilities and prioritize key stakeholders for the organization. Ronald K. Mitchell, Bradley R. Agle, and Donna J. Wood (1997) suggested that stakeholder identification is a function of the stakeholder's power to influence the organization, the urgency of their claim, and the legitimacy of the relationship with the organization.

Certainly, the context in which the organization operates impacts stakeholder identification. For example, Thierry C. Pauchant and Ian I. Mitroff (1992) suggested that during crisis situations the organization may have different stakeholders than in normal business conditions. In addition, the communication needs of those stakeholders may be different depending upon the organization's situation. Once organizations identify key stakeholders, they should assess their relationship with each group and then work to build mutually beneficial relationships.

STAKEHOLDER ANALYSIS

Stakeholder analysis is an expansive process that involves the organization examining its operations, structure, history, and role in society. From the perspective of stakeholder theory, organizations must assess the strengths and weaknesses of their key stakeholder relationships. In doing so, public relations personnel should identify issues concerning which stakeholders approve or disapprove of the organization's activities and whether those issues are important to the stakeholder or not. These communication specialists should then work to understand the underlying business trends in their environment and work to create mutually beneficial relationships with these stakeholder groups over time. Freeman and D. R. Gilbert (1987) suggested four tactics for stakeholder analysis: first, identifying new stakeholders; second, formulating strategies with these stakeholders; third, integrating multiple stakeholder concerns; and fourth, searching for new stakeholder issues and concerns. Although these tactics are useful for public relations professionals, it is important to acknowledge that organizations must often deal with many stakeholders with competing demands and varying levels of power over the organization.

Stakeholder theory suggests that public communication is not about persuasion but rather "diminishing the difference between what it does and what its stakeholders expect it to do" (Heath, 1997, p. 119). Public relations practitioners, then, must be able to negotiate with multiple stakeholders and work to reduce differences with stakeholders when possible. M. B. E. Clarkson (1995) suggested four strategies to deal with stakeholders: reaction, defense, accommodation, and pro-action. Proactive responses include anticipating stakeholders' concerns and working to resolve issues in advance. Accommodation involves working to lessen the gap between the organization and stakeholders while still looking for concessions. Defense strategies involve the organization defending its own position and refusing to do more than is minimally required. Reaction strategies involve fighting against stakeholder issues or withdrawing and ignoring stakeholder issues. These strategies are often used to assess an organization's level of corporate social responsibility. In these cases, researchers often argue for more proactive strategies to communicating with stakeholders.

In this vein, some research argues for not only negotiating with stakeholders in a proactive manner but also developing reservoirs of goodwill with stakeholders that may benefit the organization long term. Robert R. Ulmer (2001) explained that Malden Mills, a textile manufacturing company, invested in primary stakeholders over time. The company benefited greatly from these investments after a 1995 fire almost destroyed the organization. This research suggests that organizations can benefit not only from seeking potential needs from stakeholders and resolving tensions between stakeholders, but also by investing in stakeholders that they believe are critical to their business ventures. These investments may not be immediately beneficial for the organization, but over time the organization may reap the rewards when it most needs them. Although stakeholders can be a source of rewards for organizations, they can also create tensions, particularly in terms of potential problems among stakeholder groups.

MULTIPLE STAKEHOLDERS

Because stakeholders can be a broad set of individuals or groups, it is important to realize that there can be great diversity in any particular organization's stakeholder group. As a result, public relations professionals should consider potential conflicts between stakeholder groups. In these cases, organizations may have stakeholders that have competing or contradictory demands on the organization. Ulmer and Timothy L. Sellnow argued (2000) that organizations have the option to interject strategic ambiguity into their stakeholder communication in order to meet the competing demands of stakeholders. However, they contend that organizations should be careful to use strategic ambiguity ethically. They provide two criteria for evaluating the ethicality of strategically ambiguous stakeholder communication. First, they suggest that communication with stakeholders should not privilege some groups over others by introducing biased or incomplete information. Second, communication that emphasizes competing interpretations should be based on information that is available, reasonably complete, and unbiased.

Organizational stakeholders play a key role in any organization's success. Public relations practitioners are instrumental in addressing stakeholder concerns. As boundary spanners, public relations professionals are often responsible for identifying stakeholders, seeking out potential stakeholder

issues, and managing potential tensions between stakeholder groups. Organizations that manage stakeholder issues effectively are likely to hold a competitive advantage over organizations that do not. As a result, public relations practitioners must take seriously the role of identifying and managing stakeholder issues, particularly given the competitive and dynamic business environment.

—Robert R. Ulmer, Matthew W. Seeger, and Timothy L. Sellnow

Bibliography

Clarkson, M. B. E. (1995). A stakeholder framework for analyzing and evaluating corporate social performance. *Academy of Management Review, 20*(1), 92–117.

Freeman, R. E. (1984). *Strategic management: A stakeholder approach.* Marshfield, MA: Pitman.

Freeman, R. E., & Gilbert, D. R. (1987). Managing stakeholder interests. In S. P. Sethi & C. M. Fable (Eds.), *Business and society: Dimensions of conflict and cooperation* (pp. 379–422). Lexington, MA: Lexington Books.

Heath, R. L. (1997). *Strategic issues management: Organizations and public policy challenges.* Thousand Oaks, CA: Sage.

Mitchell, R. K., Agle, B. R., & Wood, D. J. (1997). Toward a theory of stakeholder identification and salience: Defining the principle of who and what really counts. *Academy of Management Review, 22*(4), 853–886.

Pauchant, T. C., & Mitroff, I. I. (1992). *Transforming the crisis-prone organization.* San Francisco: Jossey-Bass.

Ulmer, R. R. (2001). Effective crisis management through established stakeholder relationships: Malden Mills as a case study. *Management Communication Quarterly, 14*(4), 590–615.

Ulmer, R. R., & Sellnow, T. L. (2000). Consistent questions of ambiguity in organizational crisis communication: Jack in the Box as a case study. *Journal of Business Ethics, 25*(2), 143–155.

STAKES

To sustain themselves, organizations "require a continuing provision of resources and continuing cycle of transactions with the environment from which these resources are derived" (Pfeffer, 1981, p. 101). The resources in these transactions can be characterized as the stakes in an ongoing negotiation process between an organization and its environment. Specifically, "a stake is anything—tangible or intangible, material or immaterial—that one person or group has that is of value to another person or group" (Heath, 1997, p. 28). Exchanging or withholding such stakes provides a means of influence among organizations and their stakeholders.

Typically, the exchange of stakes is interpreted as a ratio. In other words, did both parties derive approximately equal benefits from the exchange, or did one party acquire a considerable advantage from the transaction? Ideally, stakes are exchanged in a harmonious and collaborative manner that is perceived as just and beneficial to all parties. This harmonious exchange allows for the ongoing mutual accommodation among organizations and their stakeholders.

From a public relations perspective, organizations engage in strategic issues monitoring and analysis to develop an awareness of essential stakes, their availability, and their possible manipulation by external audiences. In addition to identifying desirable or essential stakes and groups, organizational analysis includes consideration of

> the willingness of stakeholders to grant or withhold their stakes. How willing are they to exchange them? What can be done to increase the chances they will be granted rather than withheld? What operations or policies increase favorable exchange? (Heath, 1997, p. 117)

The ability to control critical stakes reflects an organization's power base. As long as an organization, whether for profit or nonprofit, is dependent on another organization or group to function or thrive, it is dependent on negotiating the exchange of stakes.

Although stakes take many forms, each stake cannot and should not "be equally involved in all processes and decisions" (Donaldson & Preston, 1995, p. 67) within an organization. The stakes held by organizations and their relevant environments are prioritized according to three general criteria: (a) the perceived value of a given stake, (b) the willingness or ability of groups to grant or withhold those stakes that are perceived to have value, and (c) the scarcity or availability of a resource from multiple sources.

Stakes, whether tangible or intangible, are held on a voluntary or involuntary basis. Tangible stakes that are held on a voluntary basis involve the strategic acquisition or inherent possession of a desirable resource. For example, purchasing stock in a company is a strategic acquisition of a stake in a company. Owning land that is appealing to others for development or mineral rights is an example of a voluntary and tangible stake with value to other groups or organizations that may rise or fall in various circumstances. Tangible and involuntary stakes emerge when the actions of one group or organization have the potential to infringe on the comfort, safety, or values of another group. For example, the construction of a nuclear power plant may be advantageous to a power company and some of its customers. At the same time, however, the plant may put thousands of residents at an increased risk of health problems or, in the case of catastrophic failure, diminish property values and complicate future development in the area.

Tangible stakes can also be exchanged voluntarily or involuntarily within an organization. Employees may voluntarily exchange wages for job security in situations where the organizations face bankruptcy. For example, on several occasions airline companies have received wage concessions from their employees in order to continue operating. Conversely, employees can involuntarily and unwittingly lose their stake in an organization that falls victim to incompetence or unethical management. For example, Enron left its employees with neither their jobs nor their retirement funds after the company collapsed due to illegal and unethical behavior by its executives.

Intangible stakes flow largely from social resources. Relationships with media reporters, state and federal regulators, legislators, local government, activist groups, and local citizens, to name a few, are often influential in the success or failure of an organizational venture. In such cases, the acceptance or success of a proposed action by an organization may depend on how that action is perceived by the public. Hence, each of these relationships influences the outcome.

Government agencies can serve as allies of social activist groups or a concerned public that has a stake in an organization's activities. Public policy is a stake that can hinder or enhance an organization's viability. Therefore, if an organization fails to maintain credibility with an influential audience, the organization may eventually face policy changes that are detrimental to its future success. Policy stakes are of ongoing importance to organizations. Organizations that fail to monitor and participate consistently in policy issues may face diminished prosperity due to the emergence of an unfavorable public policy.

Reputation is also a determining factor in the exchange of stakes. Groups are most likely to exchange stakes willingly when they perceive a mutual interest between themselves and another relevant group or organization. From an instrumental perspective, if firms communicate on a "basis of mutual trust and cooperation, they will have a competitive advantage over firms that do not" (Jones & Wicks, 1999, p. 208).

Organizations face resistance from both industry competitors and special interest groups as they seek to acquire and exchange stakes. For example, activist groups often function as stake seekers, working to acquire stakes that are valued by targeted organizations in order to fortify their leverage for producing desired change or averting undesirable change. Simultaneously, industry competitors compete to acquire stakes that give them a competitive advantage. Thus, organizations must acquire and exchange stakes amidst a series of organizational relationships (Pfeffer & Salancik, 1978).

In a fundamental way, stakes are a vital focus of public relations activities. Public relations specialists seek to influence stakes and the ways in which stakeholders perceive, exchange, or modify stakes and their availability.

—Timothy L. Sellnow, Robert R. Ulmer, and
Matthew W. Seeger

See also Conflict resolution; Mutually beneficial relationships; Power resource management theory; Reputation management

Bibliography

Donaldson, T., & Preston, L. E. (1995). The stakeholder theory of corporation: Concepts, evidence, and implications. *Academy of Management Review, 20*, 65–91.

Frooman, J. (1999). Stakeholder influence strategies. *Academy of Management Review, 24,* 191–205.

Heath, R. L. (1997). *Strategic issues management: Organizations and public policy challenges.* Thousand Oaks, CA: Sage.

Jones, T. M., & Wicks, A. C. (1999). Convergent stakeholder theory. *Academy of Management Review, 24,* 206–221.

Mitchell, R. K., Agle, B. R., & Wood, D. J. (1997). Toward a theory of stakeholder identification and salience: Defining principle of who and what really count. *Academy of Management Review, 22,* 853–886.

Pfeffer, J. (1981). *Power in organizations.* Cambridge, MA: Ballinger.

Pfeffer, J., & Salancik, J. R. (1978). *The external control of organizations.* New York: Free Press.

Seeger, M. W., & Ulmer, R. R. (2001). Virtuous responses to organizational crisis: Aaron Feuerstein and Milt Cole. *Journal of Business Ethics, 31,* 369–376.

Ulmer, R. R., & Sellnow, T. L. (2000). Consistent questions of ambiguity in organizational crisis communication: Jack in the Box as a case study. *Journal of Business Ethics, 25,* 143–155.

STATISTICAL ANALYSIS

When using quantitative data, a researcher collects information in the form of numbers. *Statistical analysis* is used to make meaning of those numbers. Statistical analysis can be divided into two broad categories: descriptive statistics and inferential statistics. Descriptive statistics is used to summarize and simplify the data. Formative research frequently uses descriptive statistics to understand the current public relations situation by reporting what has been observed. Means, percentages, and frequencies (how many people responded a certain way) are commonly used in descriptive statistics. For instance, a survey can be used to collect data about the current community perceptions of the organization in terms of environmental responsibility, involvement in the community, and contributions to the community. The survey asks people to rate each of the three factors on a five-point scale using the options very unfavorable, unfavorable, neutral, favorable, and very favorable. Descriptive statistics would be used to identify how the community members perceive the organization. You could determine (a) what percentage of the community held a favorable, a neutral, or an unfavorable perception of the organization on these three factors; (b) the mean score of the community perceptions for each of the three factors; or (c) how often people rated the organization as (1) unfavorable, (2) unfavorable, (3) neutral, (4) favorable, and (5) very favorable (frequencies) on each of the three factors. Public relations practitioners are much more likely to use descriptive statistics than inferential statistics.

Inferential statistics allows a researcher to examine possible relationships between two or more variables. Researchers look at analyses of differences and analyses of relationships with inferential statistics. Evaluative research makes use of inferential statistics. Analyses of difference seek to determine if there is a statistically significant difference between two or more sets of data. Statistically significance is the degree of confidence you have that your results can be found in the larger population and not just in your sample. You need to establish that your results are not a result of chance/accident but more likely a true difference between variables. An example would be an organization testing two versions of a message designed to promote a new product. Two separate groups are exposed to each message and their recall of the message assessed. Inferential statistics, such as "t-test" or "chi-square," could be used to see if there is a significant difference between recall scores for the two messages. If one message scores significantly higher on recall, you would want to use that message. If the two messages scored the same, you could use either one or both of the messages. Correlation is used to uncover relationships between variables. A correlation indicates if two variables change together in a predicable manner. There is a positive correlation when the value of one variable increases as the value of the other variable increases; for example, ice cream sales tend to increase as the temperature rises. There is a negative correlation when the value of one variable increases while the value of the other variable decreases, and vice versa; for example, sales of new homes tend to drop as the lending interest rate rises. If an organization launches a reputation campaign, it expects a positive correlation between exposure to the reputation messages and stakeholders' evaluations of the organization's reputation. You could collect data to determine if there is a positive correlation between exposure to a reputational message and favorable perceptions of the organization. Again, you would need to determine if the relationship is statistically significant.

—*W. Timothy Coombs*

See also Formative research; Quantitative research

Bibliography

Austin, E. W., & Pinkleton, B. E. (2001). *Strategic public relations management: Planning and managing effective communication campaigns.* Mahwah, NJ: Lawrence Erlbaum.

Stack, D. W. (2002). *Primer of public relations research.* New York: Guilford Press.

STEWARDSHIP OF LARGE ORGANIZATIONS

Stewardship is one of many finely honed principles that public relations practitioners and academics use to understand the quality of the relationships between an organization and its various stakeholders and stake seekers. All too often the justifiable criticism of public relations efforts is that organizations ask customers and others to commit to support the interests of the organization. Stewardship reverses that equation. It is a concept used to constantly assess the quality of relationships. It is a management tool for challenging executives to respond to and support the interests of the individuals and groups whose lives the organization affects.

In the oldest sense of the word, a *steward* is someone entrusted with managing the interests of others. The term often refers in practice and in law to one individual (a steward) being in charge of land and animals for someone else. The steward is expected to follow the golden rule: Manage the affairs at hand for someone else as the steward would want to have his or her affairs managed by someone else. In this sense, the obligation to be a steward can range from the legal implications of being a steward all the way to merely doing so because it is the ethical or right thing to do. It obligates one entity to treat another's interests as though the interests of the second party are very important

to the first party. The term has long stood for balancing self-interests so that instead of one interest exploiting another, the stronger or obligated interest serves the other interest. In addition to having implications for legal service, the term is often used in a religious context. In the simplest sense, this application advises that we should love and care for others as we would want to be loved and cared for. In an era where sustainability is a global ethic, stewardship asks that people look to the interests not only of people and resources living today but also those who will be living in the future. We have obligations today to wisely manage resources to ensure their abundance in the future. For this reason, stewardship opposes selfishness.

In 2001, Kathleen Kelly critiqued one of the enduring models of public relations programming, suggesting that it was inadequate because it did not include stewardship. This critique is relevant to existing relationships or emerging ones of various kinds. It extends the logic captured in the ROPE method of public relations. This acronym refers to stages in public relations programming: Research, Objective setting, Planning and implementing, Evaluation. Kelly reasoned that this model was insufficient because it assumed that new challenges were the constant focus of public relations strategists. In the context of fundraising and development, for instance, they were looking to new donors rather than necessarily working to ensure that the current pool of donors were satisfied by the quality of their relationship with the organization engaging in public relations. Kelly suggested that ROPE should become ROPES by adding stewardship as the last step in the process, which is not linear but circular. As Kelly concluded, "stewardship completes the process and furnishes an essential loop back to the beginning of managing relationships" (2001, p. 280).

The concept of stewardship adds positive dimensions to the theory and practice of public relations. One of the reasons that issues management arose in the 1970s as a key dimension of the practice was to reorient the thinking of senior managements from a reactive approach to publics and push them to be more proactive. Stewardship challenges management to think constantly about what can be done to keep and foster existing goodwill rather than allow it to deteriorate to the point where corrective and restorative measures are needed.

As applied, this concept has helped organizations to rethink their approach to community relations. Instead of taking for granted the goodwill of residents where the company operates, the concept of stewardship challenges managements to ask themselves what they can do each day to ensure that if the community could vote, it would vote to keep the business operating in the community. Stewardship raises the standard of public relations ethics so that managements do not think only about how the community is benefited by the wages and taxes paid by the company. It suggests that instead of merely supporting little league teams for the value of having the company's name on the backs of the children at play, the company would want to ensure that the children also have a safe place to play and enjoy a wholesome experience. The challenge is to add value to the quality of life in the community.

Investor relations is constantly challenged to keep current investors while it seeks new investors willing to pay higher prices for the stocks. That keeps the stock value going in an upward rather than a downward trajectory. It also suggests that investors have a long-term reason to remain loyal to the company. Investor relations operates on the principle that investors loan money to privately traded companies. This money is traded for shares of stock, but the objective is to earn profits and dividends from the money loaned.

Stewardship has implications for planning. It asks managements to think about the elements that truly define and sustain relationships with their publics and customers (or donors) as being truly mutually beneficial. In fundraising, for instance, nonprofits ask that people contribute money to the organization so that the organization in turn can do something worthy for people in various states of need. The call could be to seek funding to cure childhood diseases or a specific disease such as breast cancer. The philanthropy might be not only to build a new wing on the museum to house special collections, but also to serve as an educational center to enrich the arts experience of children.

Stewardship has implications for communication. If standard elements of the communication relationship focus on understanding, agreement, and satisfaction, the organization can evaluate the extent to which these communication objectives are being achieved. Do people understand what we have to say? Do they agree with what we say? Are they satisfied by what they know and think about our organization, its mission, and contribution to the communities where it operates?

Stewardship has implications for public relations ethics. The most serious indictment against public relations ethics is the tendency to advance the interest of the organization at the expense of its publics. For instance, publicity can be a problem when the product or service publicized simply is not what it is touted to be. For instance, the public relation activities sells tickets and makes profits for the sponsors but does not leave customers feeling satisfied that they received good value for the money they paid. Companies that operate in communities in ways that degrade the quality of life in the community are not engaging in stewardship. If they appear at the edge of town (out of reach of the city taxation) and sell products at a price that runs local companies out of business, many critics reason that the company has not engaged in stewardship. Is the egg not lopsided if the money that would otherwise go to the community makes the shareholders of the company fabulously wealthy? Can that be evidence of stewardship?

Stewardship asks management to ask themselves what they can constantly do to earn the loyalty of publics and customers (donors). Stewardship rests on legal obligations as well as ethical standards that focus attention on the mutuality of interests the organization has with its publics. The challenge is not to ask, "What's in it for me?" but to ask, "What's in it for us?" As the organization works to foster its public relationships, it needs to learn to build from its base to expand and extend the quality of its relationships to position itself to be seen and known as committed to the interests of others. It is a steward of others' interests.

—Robert L. Heath and Kathleen S. Kelly

See also Community relations; Ethics of public relations; Goodwill; Investor relations; Issues management; Mutually beneficial relationships; Nonprofit organizations; Objectives; Philanthropy; Public relations research; Strategies

Bibliography

Kelly, K. S. (2001). Stewardship: The fifth step in the public relations process. In R. L. Heath (Ed.), *Handbook of public relations* (pp. 279–290). Thousand Oaks, CA: Sage.

STRAIGHT NEWS

News stories are carefully constructed to enlighten audiences and to uphold journalism's civic function as society's Fourth Estate or "watchdog." Generally, journalists choose one of three presentation forms when constructing news: straight (hard, spot) news, feature (soft) news, and editorial/opinion. Each category is distinctive in its purpose and process. Some reporters lament, however, that these traditional boundaries are evaporating in the wake of changing economics of the news business, new technologies, and growth of celebrity journalism.

Basically, straight news satisfies the public's "need to know" what happened or what was disclosed within the previous 24 hours. These are timely reports of local, national, and international events told with a sense of urgency. In a newspaper, the first page and front section generally run only straight news stories—issues in debate or events filled with conflict and action. In television news programs, the lead stories usually are straight news. Objectivity, fairness, and balance are hallmarks of straight news. It is intended simply to inform, whereas feature news entertains, and editorials and opinion columns offer analysis and point of view.

As for process, straight news is characteristically defined by universal journalistic conventions. First, the *inverted pyramid* style is the standard for straight news. This means that the first sentence of a newspaper straight news story is the most important part and the last sentence the least important. The inverted pyramid format is designed to help readers decide early on whether they have the time or inclination to read all the way through to the end. A well-written straight news story enables a reader to stop reading at any time after the first paragraph and still come away with a story's main point.

This preconception influences a reporter's selection of details to include in a straight news story, how points are organized within the story's body, and the tone used to tell the story. Journalists are trained to use the inverted pyramid as a template for writing straight news—and do so automatically without even thinking about it. Editors may confidently cut stories from the bottom up to make room on a page for breaking news. Furthermore, copy editors know to write straightforward, subject-verb headlines using traditional, conservative fonts for straight news stories. Creative imagery and clever wordplay generally are reserved for feature story headlines.

Second, straight news also is distinguished by use of a summary lead (or lede)—the first, fact-packed sentence that identifies the five W's and H (who, what, when, where, why, and how). Journalism scholar James Carey has suggested that all too often news stories fall short when it comes to the "why" and "how" because these story components usually require deeper explanation than space or time—both expensive commodities in journalism—will allow. By contrast, features usually begin with a delayed (or blind) lead in order to pique readers' curiosity.

Based on one fact set, the following are examples of three varieties of leads.

Editorial/op-ed lead

It's no secret that Americans grow more cynical and politically disengaged with every passing generation. Another Flag Day has come and gone with little fanfare. Whatever happened to patriotism and citizenship?

Feature (soft) news with delayed (blind) lead

Perhaps Flag Day has become the Rodney Dangerfield of national celebrations. June 14, anniversary of the official adoption of The Stars and Stripes, seems to get no respect.

Straight (hard) news with summary lead

Fewer than 10 percent of Americans are aware that Flag Day is an official national celebration, according to results of a Florida State University poll released today.

Following the lead, a straight news story's body economically itemizes details and supporting information about an issue or event. Marginally relevant details rarely are included in a straight news story. Considered the extreme opposite of creative writing, straight news involves only hard-working words; the writing is mostly devoid of adjectives and adverbs. Such stories offer short paragraphs (or grafs) of one or two clear, concise sentences. In short, a straight news journalist must remember to explain complex ideas, to use words that average readers are familiar with, and to use simple sentence structure.

Other important straight news characteristics include presenting at least two sides of a story, using officials or authorities as sources, and incorporating direct quotes. Gaye Tuchman categorically classified these individually and collectively self-validating, intermeshed traits as a "web of facticity" (1978, p. 82). She explained that reporters gather facts to differentiate what is known and how it is known. In the process of incorporating direct quotes into straight news stories, reporters hope to underscore their impartiality, maintain credibility, and avoid libel lawsuits. Several cultural critics have pointed out, however, that journalistic conventions promote a limited, preferred take on the news by favoring authorities' worldview and by marginalizing working-class and minority voices.

Offering a longitudinal perspective on the news business, 30-year veteran journalist Jim Lehrer has opined that "the old rules" no longer apply since the boundaries separating straight news, feature news, and editorials have become blurred—negatively affecting journalism's credibility and increasing audience confusion. For example, known for their straight news reports during the week, celebrity journalists such as George Stephanopoulos and Cokie Roberts increasingly appear on weekend television news programs as commentators or pundits and unabashedly unmask their opinions. Similarly, newsroom convergence with new technologies may mean a reduced number of news workers and may force those remaining to single-handedly manufacture all varieties of news products. Such trends threaten to discredit straight news reporters and their news organizations, as well as to increasingly confuse audiences.

Overall, straight news reporters

- Use the inverted pyramid style
- Write five-Ws-and-H summary leads
- Avoid injecting their opinions
- Minimize the number and complexity of words
- Explore both sides of a story
- Include direct quotes

—Donnalyn Pompper

See also Feature; Framing theory; News and newsworthy; News story; Pyramid style

Bibliography

Carey, J. W. (1986). Why and how? The dark continent of American journalism. In R. K. Manoff & M. Schudson (Eds.), *Reading the news* (pp. 146–196). New York: Pantheon Books.

Gitlin, T. (1980). *The whole world is watching: Mass media in the making & unmaking of the new left.* Berkeley: University of California Press.

Lehrer, J. (1999). Blurring the lines hurts journalism. *Nieman Reports, 53*(2). Available: www.nieman.harvard.edu/reports/99–2NRsummer99/Lehrer.html

Tuchman, G. (1978). *Making news.* New York: Free Press.

STRAIN

Strain refers to the feelings of some publics that a gap exists between what they believe exists and what they believe should exist. Awareness of such conditions can lead people to believe that problems exist. Strain was introduced into discussions of social movement and activism in 1963 by sociologist Neil Smelser to explain the motives that give individuals the incentive to engage in that kind of collective behavior. Strain, in this sense, results from a comparison of what is versus what should be, a perceived impairment. If, for instance, people recognize that homelessness exists and believe that it should not, they are experiencing strain. Robert L. Heath called strain "a product of problem recognition and outrage" (1997, p. 169).

Strain can also be viewed as problem recognition. It presses public relations practitioners to ask whether publics recognize that some problem exists that they believe needs correction or solution. Problem recognition is a key variable in situational theory. Heath wrote, "[Any] given day, hundreds of people—a potential constituent audience of public—feel discomfort about various aspects of their lives" (1997, p. 165). Examples of such problems may be loss of a job, product defects, sexual harassment, chronic illness caused by toxic chemicals, or corporate accounting scandals. "Awareness of such conditions," Heath noted, "can lead people to believe that problems exist" (1997, p. 165).

Interest in concepts such as strain increased during the 1960s in the United States, when social movements were pressing for change in every aspect of American life. That pressure led scholars and public relations practitioners to think more deeply about the dynamics that lead individuals to take collective action. Such collective action could change the power dynamics of society. It could lead to changes in public policy. These new forces against industrial autonomy led to the formation of issues management.

For public relations practitioners, awareness of activist organizations and the issues they address is necessary. A history of corporate and organization activity in the United States is sufficient to remind us that corporations have often suffered severe financial losses and challenges to their legitimacy when their boards were not responsive to or aware of the needs of stakeholder publics.

One of the leaders in understanding the dynamics of social movements, Hans Toch, (1965) defined a social movement as "an effort by a large number of people to solve collectively a problem they feel they have in common" (p. 5). Concern with the motives of change is the typical focal point addressed by students of social movement. They work to unlock the secret of the motivation people need to foster and lead a social movement. In this vein, Smelser (1968) defined collective behavior as being purposive, not random. It is socially oriented activity. Together, people attempt to reconstitute their sociocultural environment.

One of the functions of the activist group or activist organization is to frame the issue or problem in a new way so it is perceived as urgent by key publics. Often this reframing process results in a sustained social movement that is able to form alliances with like-minded organizations and to garner the funds needed to achieve policy formation or change. Heath (1997) noted that an activist group "takes a vital step toward the establishment of strain once it creates a perspective that, like a new pair of glasses, allows a key public to see its world in a different way" (p. 168).

One incentive leaders of activist social movements have to frame issues is the realization that a legitimate gap exists between what an organization does and what key publics expect or prefer it to do.

What types of conditions or problems motivate groups of people to organize and take action about an issue or problem? What conditions motivate these groups of people to seek policy change from government or financial compensation from an organization? The following example helps augment the discussion of strain. Homelessness in the United States became a visible problem in the 1980s. According to statistics supplied by the Department of Housing and Urban Development (HUD), the number of homeless people doubled from 1984 to 1987.

Data on food and shelter requests by the U.S. Conference of Mayors was first collected in 1986. Since then, the number of requests has increased every year despite the efforts of federal and state government to address them.

From Albuquerque, New Mexico, to Manchester, New Hampshire, the problems of the homeless are becoming more visible. Once confined to large cities, homeless populations now are expanding into less urban locations.

Illegal to Be Homeless: The Criminalization of Homelessness in the United States (2003) chronicles attempts made by the National Coalition for the

Homeless (NCH) and other activist groups to address the plight of the homeless. The report was published by the Civil Rights Work Group (CRWG) of the NCH and was based on survey data collected about homelessness and incarceration patterns and practices of local jurisdictions from 42 states. The NCH works with advocates for the homeless nationwide. According to the report, the NCH worked cooperatively with local and statewide coalitions, service providers, advocates, and homeless people to provide the data used in the report.

Smelser (1963, 1968) used a value-added approach to identify determinants of collective behavior. These are structural conduciveness, strain, the growth of a generalized belief, the need to mobilize people to action, and social control. Strain occurs when people compare their current situations or problems with what they believe should exist. Activist groups form to inform publics about the seriousness of the problem and to persuade legislative bodies and policymakers that action needs to be taken.

Strain is likely to be part of a larger sense of engagement by activists against some organization. Heath (1997) included strain as the first of five stages that describe the process of activism: strain (problem recognition), mobilization, confrontation, negotiation, and resolution.

Seeking social change, activists such as the NCH use communication strategies and channels to persuade other people to support their movement. Strategies used by NCH affiliates included challenges to laws and policies seeking to criminalize the homeless; grassroots efforts to raise public awareness of criminalization of the homeless; organizing efforts to challenge anti-homeless ordinances; voter registration drives for the homeless; educating and organizing homeless people to fight for their own civil rights; tracking data such as arrests, citations, fines, and harassment of homeless people; and efforts to establish liaisons with providers of housing and support services and members of the legal community.

Part of the challenge facing pubic relations practitioners is to monitor issues and perform situational analysis. This challenge requires them to assess the growth in numbers, the depth of incentives to fight, and the increasing or decreasing strength of activism. Heath noted that strain can be measured "by the number and kind of people who belong to a support group or support the issues it promotes" (1997, p. 167).

Work by Heath and others has resulted in the following observations about strain:

1. Strain is an effective step to help activist groups achieve organizational legitimacy or public acceptance.

2. The level of strain demonstrated by activists can be strong, moderate, or weak.

3. Organizations can monitor the existence of strain through an effective and active issues management program.

4. Organizations can respond to claims of strain by managing issues, symbols, and rewards.

5. Strain can manifest in explosive fashion.

6. Strain is the energy source of activists.

7. Strain is easier to achieve when activist groups persuade publics to recognize and identify with the problem.

8. Strain can be communicated through the use of emotions, reasoning, logic, facts, and statistics.

—*Becky McDonald*

See also Issues management; Legitimacy and legitimacy gap; Situational theory of publics

Bibliography

Grunig, J. E., & Hunt, T. (1984). *Managing public relations.* New York: Holt, Rinehart & Winston.

Heath, R. L. (1997). *Strategic issues management: Organizations and public policy challenges.* Thousand Oaks, CA: Sage.

National Coalition for the Homeless. (2003). *Illegal to be homeless: The criminalization of homelessness in the United States.* Washington, DC: U.S. Government Printing Office.

Smelser, N. J. (1963). *Theory of collective behavior.* New York: Free Press.

Smelser, N. J. (Ed.). (1968). *Essays in sociological explanation.* Englewood Cliffs, NJ: Prentice Hall.

Toch, H. (1965). *The social psychology of social movements.* Indianapolis, IN: Bobbs-Merrill.

STRATEGIC BUSINESS PLANNING

Strategic business planning entails setting policies and procedures (and budgeting for them) to accomplish goals and objectives relevant to the mission and vision of a business, government agency, or nonprofit organization. Regardless of the type of organization, planning is needed to set the course of the organization and then decide the means by which that course will be accomplished. In that regard, public relations planning should be a valued part of the strategic business planning process. Senior practitioners should be engaged in public relations planning to support the strategic business planning of their organization.

In analyzing the development of strategic thought in the business context, George S. Day and Robin Wensley identified a chronological sequence in the development of strategy approaches encompassing three broad eras: the Long-Range Planning Era (corresponding roughly with the 1960s), the Strategic Planning Era (1970s), and the Strategic Management Era (1980s).

In examining the different types of planning systems adopted by organizations, Frederick Gluck, Steven Kaufman, and A. Steven Walleck suggested that relatively few organizations other than large, multinational, diversified manufacturing companies have developed full-fledged strategic management systems despite their obvious advantages. They suggested that, in reality, most organizations do not go much beyond long-range planning systems.

Although strategy has been conceptualized from a number of different perspectives, undoubtedly the most commonly adopted perspective is the linear-planning perspective of strategy. From this perspective, strategy formulation has normally equated with the process of strategic planning, which has generally been depicted as a logical rational process directed toward achieving prestated organizational goals, and using prescribed tools and techniques to achieve these goals. This model strategy formulation

is typified by the work of Kenneth R. Andrews, who defined strategy as

> the pattern of decisions in a company that determines and reveals its objectives, purposes, or goals, produces the principal policies and plans for achieving those goals, and defines the range of business the company is to pursue, the kind of economic and human organisation it intends to be, and the nature of the economic and non economic contribution it intends to make to its shareholder, employees, customers and communities. (1987, p. 51)

Andrews separated the task of strategic decision making (the formulation of strategy) from its implementation. For Andrews, the implementation of strategy is seen primarily as an administrative function: Once the purpose of the company has been determined, the company's resources can be mobilized to accomplish it.

Similarly, Thomas L. Wheelen and J. David Hunger suggested a four-step process of strategic management that comprises the following elements:

1. *Environmental scanning:* Both internal and external to the organization.

2. *Strategy formulation:* Comprising the development of long-term plans for the management of environmental opportunities and threats, in the light of organizational strengths and weaknesses. This incorporates the definition of the corporate mission, the specification of objectives and the development of strategies and policy guidelines.

3. *Strategy implementation:* Comprising the process by which strategies and policies are put into action through the development of programs, budgets, and procedures.

4. *Evaluation and control:* Performance is measured and evaluated against target in order to take any necessary corrective action and resolve problems.

This view of the separation of strategy formulation from implementation has been challenged by other strategy scholars such as Henry Mintzberg and Andrew Pettigrew, who argued in 1992 that the separation of these elements in the process are not always so readily recognizable in practice. Moreover, formalized strategic planning models have come under increasing criticism on a number of grounds, not the least being the implied assumption of logical rational behavior on the part of those engaged in the planning process (e.g., Eisenhardt & Zabaracki, 1992). Perhaps one of the most persistent critics of the linear planning approach to strategy formation has been Henry Mintzberg, who labeled this approach the Design School model of strategy. Here Mintzberg draws the distinction between strategic planning and strategic thinking:

> Strategic planning is not strategic thinking. Indeed, strategic planning often spoils strategic thinking, causing managers to confuse real vision with the manipulation of numbers. . . . Strategic planning, as it has been practiced, has really been strategic programming, the articulation and elaboration of strategies, or visions, that already exist. (1994a, p. 107)

Mintzberg went on to argue that the strategy-making process should be about synthesis—"capturing what the manager learns from all sources . . . and then synthesizing that learning into a vision of the direction that the business should pursue" (1994a, p. 107). Mintzberg distinguished this from the analytical role of planners, who he suggests should make their contribution around the strategy planning process and not inside it—supplying the formal analyses or hard data that strategic thinking requires.

Mintzberg and James A. Waters have also questioned whether strategy should be thought of only in terms of an entirely intentional pattern of actions preconceived by management. Rather, they suggested that strategies may sometimes emerge in the form of a pattern in a stream of decisions and actions without any preconceived plan. Thus, Mintzberg and Waters distinguished between deliberate and emergent strategies—the former involving the existence of intentions that are then realized; the latter being where patterns develop in the absence of intentions, or despite them. In practice, however, Mintzberg and Waters acknowledged that it may be unrealistic to expect to find examples of purely emergent or purely deliberate strategies;

rather, these two forms of strategy making should be viewed as two extremes along a continuum of "real-world" strategies. Hence, they acknowledge that, in practice, strategy making may exhibit a combination of deliberate and emergent strategy-making tendencies.

Mintzberg's vociferous criticisms of the so-called Design School approach have been challenged by, among others, Igor Ansoff, who rebutted most of Mintzberg's criticisms of the Design School perspective and, in turn, highlighted a number of fundamental flaws in Mintzberg's own arguments, perhaps most notably claiming that Mintzberg's criticisms of planning are based on an outdated view of how planning systems have evolved since the 1960s. Moreover, Ansoff suggested that Mintzberg's own theories prescribe a world free of explicit strategy formulation and strategic managers. The debate between these two eminent scholars only serves to highlight the still contested nature of our understanding of strategy and strategic management processes.

In terms of public relations' contribution to the business planning process, the main role for public relations is generally argued to be that of intelligence gathering and stakeholder management in terms of public relations' boundary-spanning role. As Jon White and David M. Dozier suggested, "when organisations make decisions they do so based on a representation of both the organisation itself and the organisation's environment (1992, p. 92). Thus, at least in principle, public relations does have a potentially useful role to play in the process of business planning, bringing different stakeholder perspectives to the attention of senior management and thereby helping to ensure that management have a balanced view on the likely impact of policy decisions before committing themselves to any particular course of action.

—Daniel A. Moss

Bibliography

Andrews, K. R. (1987). *The concept of corporate strategy.* Burr Ridge, IL: Richard D. Irwin.

Ansoff, H. I. (1991, September). Critique of Henry Mintzberg's "The Design School": Reconsidering the basic premises of strategic management. *Strategic Management Journal, 449–461.*

Day, G. S., & Wensley, R. (1983, Fall). Marketing theory with a strategic orientation. *Journal of Marketing, 47, 79–89.*

Eisenhardt, K. M, & Zabaracki, M. J. (1992). Strategic decision-making. *Strategic Management Journal, 13, 17–37.*

Gluck, F., Kaufman, S., & Walleck, A. S. (1982). The four phases of strategic management. *Journal of Business Strategy, 2(3), 9–21.*

Mintzberg, H. (1990, March). The Design School: Reconsidering the basic premises of strategic management. *Strategic Management Journal, 171–195.*

Mintzberg, H. (1994a, January/February). The fall and rise of strategic planning. *Harvard Business Review, 107–114.*

Mintzberg, H. (1994b). *The fall and rise of strategic planning.* New York: Prentice Hall.

Mintzberg, H., & Waters, J. A. (1985). Of strategies, deliberate and emergent. *Strategic Management Journal, 257–272.*

Pettigrew, A. M. (1992). The character and significance of strategy process research. *Strategic Management Journal, 13, 5–16.*

Wheelen, T. L., & Hunger, J. D. (1993). *Strategic management and business policy* (4th ed.). New York: Addison-Wesley.

White, J., & Dozier, D. M. (1992). Public relations and management decision-making. In J. E. Grunig (Ed.), *Excellence in public relations and communications management* (pp. 91–108). Hillsdale, NJ: Lawrence Erlbaum.

STRATEGIC COMMUNICATION

See Communication management

STRATEGIC PARTNERSHIPS

Strategic partnerships are crafted through public relations to foster and promote mutually beneficial relationships. These partnerships occur, for instance, because a company wants to work on an issue that can best be approached through the formation of a strategic partnership with an issue-relevant, well-established, and resourceful nonprofit organization. For instance, if a company is trying hard to diversify its workforce, it might create a strategic partnership with a nonprofit organization, such as the Urban League, that seeks to promote job training and placement as part of its mission. In such partnerships, the company might provide funding for training—equipment and teachers. It might also encourage its skilled employees to serve as instructors. It might provide on-the-job training, internships, and other means for desirable employees to make the transition into the workforce. Both organizations benefit, as does the community and key citizens, who can increase their income and self-esteem. That, some might say, is the essence of public relations.

The 1970s brought many changes to public relations. Out of the effort to manage issues, companies realized that strategic partnerships were a useful public relations tool. One of the leaders in the development of a systematic approach to strategic partnerships was Mary Ann Pires, who wrote,

> Interestingly enough, the genesis of the business and interest-group factions is identical: the unique American political system. Among its hallmarks are the rejection of a powerful central state and the concept of individuals and voluntary organizations seeking to affect the political process. (1988, p. 185)

In this sense, strategic partnerships not only require a commitment to pro-activity, but also are one of the best ways to demonstrate that virtue. Strategic partnerships succeed if the various organizations can replace walls with bridges.

One tradition of activism is that it approaches targeted organizations with an agenda to change the organization. Pressures of that sort can lead to the building of walls to protect the organization against this kind of attack. Organizations don't like criticism. They often turn to public relations to meet (blunt) the challenge. An old saying of public relations practitioners is "When life deals you lemons, learn how to make lemonade." Strategic partnerships are lemonade.

Such partnerships can be sparked from either side of an issue but eventually must test both sides' patience. The two sides may approach a problem with different assumptions, tools, and resources. The search is for common ground, a meeting place of principle, and a joining of mission.

Going into strategic partnerships is not easy. Corporate management does not like to acknowledge that others can influence how they plan and operate. Special-interest organizations worry that attaching themselves to companies will lead to their being co-opted. Thus, the relationship has to build beyond friction, difference, and division. To that end, Pires advised (1988, p. 187),

- Strive for long-term relationships.
- Start by listening to what the groups have to say—to their needs, issue concerns, and so forth.
- Don't overpromise.
- Be prepared to give as well as get.
- Treat people decently, respecting confidences.

Dialogue and collaboration are the standard communication relationship. Patience is required. Sharing is a pre-supposition.

As we think of strategic partnerships, we may realize the difficulty in creating and sustaining any such relationship between a business and a special-interest group. Public relations, however, does not operate in an environment of organization and a single special interest. Companies have many stakeholding publics that may very well not agree with one another and may not support any other strategic partnership. This tangle of relationships can become a daunting snarl of competing and conflicting interests. A multiple public environment poses gargantuan challenges.

Many approaches to strategic partnerships exist. Today, companies may invite key activists to serve on the board of directors or participate in special decision-making or guidance panels. They may work together to create legislative and regulatory agendas and issue positions. Classic stories exist where a business, such as a company that sells building products, works collaboratively with an environmental group. They work together to set standards of corporate responsibility, join in doing battle in the legislative and regulatory arenas, and monitor the issues together. The activist group may endorse the company as "environmentally friendly," which may also have marketing and brand equity advantage. Such efforts can have a positive impact for both organizations and the community in which they have an interest. The company can reduce costs and increase profits. The interest group moves steadily toward its mission.

For either side in a strategic partnership, Pires offered sound advice forged on the anvil of experience (1988, pp. 193–197):

- Define your objectives.
- Know your issue.
- Build the alliance.
- Maintain flexibility.
- Treat people decently.
- Maintain your contacts.

Such advice may sound peculiar in the context of a discussion of public relations. This discipline and practice is often viewed as telling, even manipulating, rather than listening and cooperating. Creative strategic partnerships are in fact the essence of excellent public relations. They serve a mutual interest to the benefit of all parties.

However positive the presentation of strategic partnerships, one must not be a Pollyanna. They can fail. They can backfire. They can become dysfunctional. Good purpose and sound efforts can trip over personalities. Staging and posturing can offset every positive effort to work together.

Despite their liabilities, senior practitioners are likely to counsel clients on both sides to look for agreement and cooperation to each other's mutual benefit.

—Robert L. Heath

See also Activism; Collaborative decision making; Co-optation; Dialogue; Mission and vision statements; Mutually beneficial relationships; Nonprofit organizations

Bibliography

Pires, M. A. (1983). Texaco: Working with public interest groups. *Public Relations Journal, 39*(4), 16–19.

Pires, M. A. (1988). Building coalitions with external constituencies. In R. L. Heath (Ed.), *Strategic issues management: How organizations influence and respond to public interests and policies* (pp. 185–198). San Francisco: Jossey-Bass.

STRATEGIES

The original meaning of the word *strategy* is derived from the Greek word *strategos,* which referred to a role, namely, that of a general in command of an army. It later came to mean the "art of the general," comprising the skills necessary to undertake that role.

Although the origins of strategy can be traced back through history, the application of the concept of strategy in a business context is arguably a comparatively recent phenomenon. Cynthia A. Montgomery and Michael E. Porter (1991), for example, regarded the pioneering work in this field as occurring in the 1960s. In their opinion, management thinking was, at that time, oriented toward discrete business functions such as marketing, finance, and production, and there was a pressing need for the development of a more holistic view. The development of a "strategic perspective" was seen as the tool to accomplish this goal.

There are, in fact, almost as many different definitions of strategy as there are writers on the subject. In 1983, Donald C. Hambrick suggested two main reasons for this lack of consensus: first, strategy is a multi-dimensional concept; and second, strategy is situational and will consequently tend to vary by industry.

Rather than striving to identify a single comprehensive definition of strategy, which seems likely to remain elusive, various scholars have sought to identify those areas of broad agreement about what constitutes the basic dimensions of strategy. In 1991, Henry Mintzberg, recognizing the multifaceted nature of strategy, suggested five alternative yet related definitions of strategy, which he termed the five P's—strategy as a plan, a ploy, a pattern, a position, and a perspective. Examining each of these definitions of strategy leads to different implications for the content and the nature of the process of strategic decision making.

Strategy as a plan represents perhaps the most commonly accepted understanding of the term *strategy*. This definition implies that strategy represents "some sort of consciously intended course of action, a guideline (or set of guidelines) to deal with a situation" (Mintzberg, 1991, p.12). As a plan, strategy can be defined in general terms or can relate to a specific course of action. In the latter sense, Mintzberg suggested that strategy becomes a ploy—"a specific manoeuvre intended to outwit an opponent or competitor" (1991, p.13).

As a pattern, strategy encompasses not only the planning aspect of strategy, but also the resulting behavior, in terms of a stream of actions. Here, emphasis is placed on the fact that strategy is "consistency in behavior," whether or not it is intended. In other words, strategy is inferred from consistency of the organization's actions, which may or may not be consistent with a stated plan.

As a position, strategy is seen as a means of locating an organization in its environment. From this perspective, strategy "becomes the mediating force—or 'match'—between organisation and environment, that is, between the internal and external context (of the organisation)" (Mintzberg, 1991, p. 16). Mintzberg also maintained that this definition of strategy can be compatible with either (or all) of the other definitions in that a position can be preselected and aspired to through a plan (or ploy) and/or it can be reached (perhaps even found) through a pattern of behavior.

If this previous definition sets strategy primarily in its external context, strategy as a perspective looks within the organization and, indeed, within the head of the individual strategist. Under this definition the content of strategy consists not just of a chosen position, but of an ingrained way of perceiving the world which is shared by the members of an organization, and is shown through their intentions and/or by their actions. This definition implies above all that strategy is a *concept*—an abstraction that exists only in the minds of the interested parties.

Mintzberg emphasized that these various definitions of strategy should be seen as complementary, with each contributing to an overall understanding of the concept of strategy. Strategy as a plan introduces the idea of intention, emphasizing the role of conscious leadership; strategy as a pattern focuses on action, introducing the notion that strategies can emerge; the idea of strategy as a position introduces context, rooting strategy in the situation that the organization finds itself in, encouraging the consideration of competition and cooperation; and perspective emphasizes that strategy may be nothing more than a concept, and focuses attention on the question of how intentions diffuse through a group to become shared as norms and values and how patterns of behavior become deeply ingrained in the group.

A HIERARCHY OF STRATEGY PERSPECTIVES

A further useful distinction between differing forms of strategy and strategy making is offered by Ellen E. Chaffee, who in 1985 identified three distinct "clusters" of strategy definitions and approaches to strategy: (a) linear strategy, (b) adaptive strategy, and (c) interpretive strategy. Examining each of these three approaches or perspectives will reveal something of the contested nature of the current understanding of the concept of strategy.

The linear approach emphasizes the planning aspect of strategy. Strategy is seen as a form of methodical, directed, sequential planning that contributes to a rational decision-making process with the overall aim being the achievement of pre-stated goals. The adaptive approach, on the other hand, emphasizes the importance of strategy as a means by which organizations seek to respond to the changing nature of their environment.

Like the adaptive approach, the interpretive approach emphasizes the relationship between the organization and its environment. However, the interpretive approach emphasizes the idea of management holding a cognitive map—a world-view that colors how managers interpret the changes facing the organization and the responses they adopt to them. Therefore, strategy in the interpretive model is perhaps best thought of in terms of a set of orienting frames of reference that inform the way organizational stakeholders understand the organization and its environment.

Chaffee (1985) postulated a hierarchy of strategy models, based on the level of sophistication of the different strategy perspectives. Chaffee suggested that, at the simplest level, firms begin with linear strategies, moving on to adaptive approaches, and then ultimately to more sophisticated interpretive approaches to strategy. It is important to integrate each lower-level model with models that represent more complex systems because organizations exhibit properties of all levels of complexity.

Adaptive and interpretive models that ignore less complex strategy models ignore the foundations on which they must be built if they are to reflect organizational reality. Furthermore, a comprehensive interpretive strategy probably requires some planning, as would fit with a linear strategy, and some organizational change, as would fit with an adaptive strategy; and a viable adaptive strategy may well require some linear planning (1985, p. 96).

Such arguments emphasize the fact that different approaches to strategy and the process of strategic management may not be as mutually exclusive in real-world conditions as some theorists imply. Indeed, a recurring theme in the strategy literature is the need for the greater consideration of how many of the concepts proposed by strategic theorists can be operationalized.

LEVELS OF STRATEGY

In addition to these distinctions between these broad perspectives of strategy, writers such as Gerry Johnson and Kevan Scholes (1999) have pointed to the distinction between different levels of strategy: corporate, business, and functional/operational. Corporate strategies focus on decisions about the broad scope and direction of an organization's development. Business or competitive strategies focus on decisions about how best to compete in the markets in which an organization operates. Functional strategies are concerned with decisions about how each of the separate organizational functions (marketing, production, HRM, etc.) can in turn contribute to the achievement of higher-order strategies.

THE STRATEGIC POTENTIAL OF PUBLIC RELATIONS

As Jon White and David M. Dozier (1992) acknowledged, it is comparatively rare to find public relations included in the dominant coalition (the most senior level of decision making) and contribution to top management decision making. The main reason for this relative lack of representation at the most senior levels within organizations appears to be partly the lack of senior managerial experience and expertise amongst practitioners, many of whom may have comparatively little experience of the sort of issues that top management decision makers frequently have to tackle. Second, senior management personnel will generally have had very little exposure to public relations and tend to see it as a largely tactical function.

Returning to the various perspectives of strategy, it's clear that there is limited acknowledgment of the existence of these different perspectives of strategy within the public relations literature. Indeed, the vast majority of public relations studies have, by inference, assumed a largely linear perspective of strategy making. This may not be bad in itself, but it limits the scope for public relations to be recognized as able to contribute to the more sophisticated adaptive and interpretive strategic decision-making developments.

—Daniel A. Moss

Bibliography

Andrews, K. R. (1980). *The concept of corporate strategy.* Burr Ridge, IL: Richard D. Irwin.

Boulding, K. E. (1956). General systems theory—The skeleton of science. *Management Science, 2,* 197–208.

Chaffee, E. E. (1985). Three models of strategy. *Academy of Management Review, 10*(1), 89–98.

Hambrick, D. C. (1983). Some tests of the effectiveness and functional attributes of Miles and Snow's strategic types. *Academy of Management Journal, 26,* 5–25.

Johnson G., & Scholes, K. (1999). *Exploring corporate strategy* (5th ed.) London: Prentice Hall.

Mintzberg, H. (1991). Five P's for strategy. In H. Mintzberg & J. B. Quinn (Eds.), *The strategy process: Concepts, contexts, cases* (2nd ed., pp.12–19). Englewood Cliffs, NJ: Prentice Hall.

Mintzberg, H., & Waters, J. A. (1985). Of strategies, deliberate and emergent. *Strategic Management Journal, 6,* 257–272.

Montgomery, C .A., & Porter, M. E. (1991). *Strategy—seeking and securing competitive advantage.* Boston: Harvard Business School Press.

White, J., & Dozier, D. M. (1992). Management decision-making. In J. E. Grunig (Ed.), *Excellence in public relations and communication management* (pp. 91–108). Hillsdale, NJ: Lawrence Erlbaum.

STYLEBOOK

A stylebook is a handbook, or manual, used by professionals, academicians, and students, that contains rules/guidelines for how to produce publishable manuscripts. For example, the Associated Press *Stylebook* provides guidelines on the use of words/phrases, punctuation, copyrighted material, captioning photographs, writing newspaper copy for sports and business, and an assortment of other publishing rules.

Many professions use manuals of style, including the print and broadcast industries, publishing, law, and psychology. Stylebooks provide structure to publications, providing continuity of writing style and consistent usage of words, grammar, and citations. They may even prescribe fonts and other features.

In professional public relations contexts, the Associated Press *Stylebook* is perhaps the most valuable text for a practitioner interested in correctly applying the conventions of print publishing. The bulk of the stylebook consists of hundreds of definitions of commonly used words/phrases and how the Associated Press uses the words in publications.

The *Associated Press Stylebook and Briefing on Media Law with Internet Guide and Glossary* points out that the Associated Press's text contains instructions for the use of commonly confused words such as *because* and *since*, instructing writers to "use *because* to denote a specific cause-effect relationship: *He went because he was told. Since* is acceptable in a casual sense. . . . *They went to the game, since they had been given the tickets*" (2000, p. 28, italics in original). The stylebook also explains the Associated Press's idiosyncratic use of words such as *doctor* (a term typically reserved for medical doctors and dentists, and *not* used to refer to professors), *e-mail* (lowercase, with a hyphen), and *World Wide Web* (three words, all capitalized).

For public relations practitioners who produce broadcast copy or prepare messages for radio or television sources, there exists an assortment of broadcast stylebooks, such as Robert A. Papper's *Broadcast News Writing Stylebook.* As is the case with the Associated Press *Stylebook,* public relations professionals use broadcast stylebooks to create effective broadcast copy.

Other stylebooks of note to academicians or those interested in publishing in academic journals include the *Publication Manual of the American Psychological Association, The MLA Style Manual,* and *The Chicago Manual of Style.* All of these texts include lengthy sections on spelling and grammar, how to write well, how to organize manuscripts, proper citation of sources, and how to prepare manuscripts for publication in academic journals. Large agencies, corporations, and other organizations often craft their own stylebooks to increase uniformity of presentation, an important aspect of brand equity.

—*Michael L. Kent*

See also AP style

Bibliography

Achtert, W. S., & Gibaldi, J. (1985). *The MLA style manual.* New York: Modern Language Association of America.

Chicago manual of style (14th ed.). (1993). Chicago: University of Chicago Press.

Goldstein, N. (Ed.). (2000). *Associated Press stylebook and briefing on media law with Internet guide and glossary.* New York: Associated Press.

Papper, R. A. (1995). *Broadcast news writing stylebook.* Boston: Allyn & Bacon.

Publication manual of the American Psychological Association (5th ed.). (2001). Washington, DC: American Psychological Association.

SUBJECTIVE EXPECTED UTILITIES THEORY

Subjective expected utilities (SEU) theory is one of the oldest attempts to explain how people make decisions. The theory is based on the intuitively simple proposition that people make decisions to maximize positive outcomes and minimize negative ones. Persuasion theory pursues insights to understand how people make decisions. The assumption behind this line of inquiry is that once researchers and practitioners know how people make decisions, messages can be used to strategically influence the decisions people make. That premise, for instance, is the basic assumption underlying marketing communication, including promotion and publicity. It also has ethical implications that arise from the fear that practitioners can manipulate attitudes and behaviors.

SEU theory is closely connected to *learning theory* explanations of the process of persuasion. Learning theory reasons that people learn to make rewarding decisions, which are preferred to those with negative consequences. To that end, people acquire information they use to form attitudes and develop motivations that lead toward positive outcomes and away from negative ones. Advocates of learning theory know that people acquire attitudes through learning experiences rather than responding to motives based on innate drives. The assumptions of this theory are essentially timeless. Philosophy, the predecessor of persuasion theorists, has long argued that people seek positive outcomes and avoid negative ones. The problem, at times, with philosophical analysis of these choices is that people make decisions that are too narrow or short-sighted. Thus, for instance, although a decision might appear to maximize rewards at the moment, it leads to negative consequences for the long run. Consequently, children would rather play than do homework. Play leads to enjoyment, a positive outcome. However, if children only learn to play and do not study and acquire knowledge, they may be cut off from a lifetime of increased enjoyment.

For reasons such as this, SEU theory is alluring in its simplicity but devilishly difficult to use to make predictions that are subjected to careful research and thoughtful applications of strategic communication. For instance, we know that even though television advertising purveys a wide array of appealing products with promises of a nice and enjoyable life, not every viewer buys all of the available products. Therefore, we know intuitively that the fundamental premise of SEU theory is both true and too much of a generalization. People simply don't opt for all that is presented as positive. They make more complex decisions.

The term *subjective* in the theory suggests that individuals make calculations based on available data of what choices are best. The theory assumes that two individuals may make substantially or marginally different choices based on their individual subjective calculations of outcomes. In this sense, we know that individuals make decisions that are perceived and predicted to be best for them. People like to hold useful attitudes, those that foster satisfying decisions. For this reason, they acquire information and fine-tune the decision they make. They can even try out the decision, such as purchase a product or give to a charity, to see in their own judgment whether the choice is productive. We also know that people can differ substantially in what they find appealing. Some tastes, such as eating hot peppers, have to be acquired and cultivated. But, the underlying premise is that the choices, however cultivated, form attitudes that lead to motivations that have positive consequences.

Part of the *subjective expectation* implied by the theory to explain the formation decisions rests on the way people know and weigh the positive and negative elements of each decision. The assumption is that each individual acquires functional attitudes that sort decisions into relevance and priority. Thus, not all of the products or services that one sees in television advertising are relevant. Young people see products and services differently than their parents or grandparents do. Life insurance has little appeal to a child, whereas toys and amusement parks are appealing. SEU theory suggests that people sort decisions based on whether even making a decision is relevant because of the positive or negative consequences expected.

Just as *subjective* is a key term, so is *expected*. It is a calculated or estimated outcome. People learn attitudes and make judgments based on some amount of uncertainty. Consumers ask, "If I buy a cleaning product, will it really work?" One of the ethical (and even legal) challenges to product and service advertising focuses on the liability that can be incurred in asserting—often more by implication than by direct claim—that some product or service will lead to positive outcomes and have no negative consequences. First, we know that people often acquire and interpret data to lead to attitudes and motives they want to make. In many instances, it is not the acquisition and interpretation of data that lead to a choice, but, rather, the desire to make a choice motivates the information acquisition and analysis process. Humans are infinitely capable of rationalization where they calculate decisions they want to make rather than necessarily making the most "rational" ones. Regardless of the pathway to the decision, people do subjectively calculate how an attitude or a combination of attitudes will produce desirable outcomes.

One of the frustrating lines of analysis that SEU theory has tackled is understanding how people make decisions among relative positives or relative negatives. The fundamentals of the theory simplistically assume that people avoid the negative and prefer the positive. However, decisions often entail choosing among several positives. For instance, people are likely to encounter a plethora of automobile ads. When the time comes to buy a new automobile (or a used one), what drives that choice? First, we assume that individuals subjectively expect some to be more positive (based on various attitudes, such as cost, maintenance record, style, color, model, brand, or features) than others. Thus, even though people prefer positive outcomes, they calculate in idiosyncratic ways what is "best" for them at each decision point. To make such calculations, they often deal with substantial or quite shallow amounts of information. Their decision may reflect well-formed or poorly formed attitudes and reflect substantial or inadequate decision heuristics. Rather than being merely positive or negative, or most positive, the decision is likely to be much more complex or absolutely simple, such as buying by brand or copying a friend's choice. For instance, one person might study the choice for days, whereas another might make the choice on what seems to be a whim—even the pitch of a salesperson. Both believe the choice will lead to positives, but the complexity of the decision is often difficult to unlock through research and frustrating to persons who engage in marketing communication.

Another frustrating line of analysis is the reality that people often have to make decisions based not on variously positive choices but rather on which of several negative choices is least bad. That heuristic can be telling of the differences between some individuals' choices. People who engage in health communication often suggest that people undergo diagnosis and testing, which is uncomfortable, in order to reduce the likelihood of suffering a devastating medical outcome, such as severe surgery or death. In making such decisions, people again may turn to the considerations of time and relevance. Is the problem one that will happen far in the future, thus seeming to require no choice today? Is the problem one that will happen to me? For instance, men and women are differentially prone to some cancers. The practice of medical treatment often requires helping individuals to understand and sort through various treatment options. All the options may have negative aspects. The choices leading to cure, one hopes, are subjectively calculated to be the most efficacious with the least negative consequences. First, making such decisions assumes an often complex weighing of relative negatives in terms of treatments—the means to an end. Second, the decisions also may vary by what individual patients see as preferable outcomes—least negative. Thus, SEU theory has sought to help explain how people sort means and outcomes, especially those that are fraught with a disproportion of negative aspects.

SEU has been a powerful and productive line of research and practice. Promotion, publicity, and advertising tend to call attention to the positive elements of products and services. Promises are made or implied that good outcomes will occur and negative ones will not. This is a compelling logic of applied persuasion that seeks to know and use insights into human decision making, attitude formation, and behavior. Many other theories, such as information integration and reasoned action, have been developed to refine this line of inquiry.

The assumptions of SEU theory have substantial ethical consequences for public relations academics and practitioners. The knowledge that decision processes can be used to design public relations campaigns leads to the argument that scientific persuasion is asymmetrical and inherently unethical. This ethical concern needs to be kept current in academic and practitioner discussions. However, the ability of any campaign to manipulate many, if any at all, and for a long time may be more daunting than imagined, as counter campaigns and the complexities mentioned above complicate the ability of academics and practitioners to solve the puzzle of all of the confounding factors that shape individuals' decisions.

—Robert L. Heath

See also Information integration theory; Learning theory; Persuasion theory; Promotion; Publicity

SURVEY

Surveys are instruments that are used to collect data on a wide range of behavioral, attitudinal, and cognitive issues, including respondent perceptions, attitudes, beliefs, values, purchasing practices, and other behavioral intentions. Surveys consist of a series of questions about an issue of interest to the practitioner. Practitioners may use surveys to gauge stakeholders' opinions on an issue relevant to an organization's practices, determine the effectiveness of a campaign, measure the community's perceptions of risks associated with a new production process, or assess an organization's reputation.

Surveys typically involve securing responses from a subset of the population of interest (called a *sample*) to which the practitioners hope to generalize. Surveys are the most popular research methodology in public relations due to their relative ease of construction, administration, tabulation, and analysis. However, practitioners must be careful when constructing survey questions and deciding who should complete the surveys (sampling) and how (e.g., self-administered or administered by a trained interviewer). Practitioners must also decide whether their research design is cross-sectional or longitudinal.

As in all research, reliability (providing consistent measures in similar situations) and validity (responses correspond to what they are intended to measure) are concerns. The goal is to have the questions and response options mean the same thing to all respondents. Practitioners need to be able to attribute differences in answers to differences in respondents rather than to possible extraneous factors such as educational level, technical expertise, or interviewer style, which introduce error. Threats to reliability and validity can produce inaccurate results. For this reason, careful attention should be devoted to the words used in the questions and response options and how these are phrased. Technical jargon, ill-defined terms, words with multiple meanings, and loaded ("red flag") words can create problems related to the interpretation of and response to questions and the selection of answer options. When the possibility for misunderstanding exists, precise definitions should be provided.

Other problems occur when questions are too complex and ask for several pieces of information in a single question. This often occurs when two issues contained in a question are connected by *and*. For example, if respondents were asked to agree or disagree with the statement "XYZ Corporation is an asset to the community and provides needed employment for the community," they are being asked to respond to two issues (XYZ Corporation as an asset to community and as employer). Other problems arise when questions are leading and seem to suggest the desired response. For instance, the question "Is school violence the biggest problem facing our public schools today?" seems to suggest that yes is the desired response.

Finally, the method of survey administration may affect the reliability and validity of the results. There are two methods of survey administration. First, surveys may be self-administered through the use of a questionnaire that is mailed and returned, posted and returned via the Internet, or distributed to the desired sample in a particular setting and collected (e.g., distributed and collected at a town hall meeting, an information-giving session for employees, etc.). Respondents complete these surveys themselves. Error may arise from their failure to read questions thoroughly, their skimming through answer options, and their difficulty in recording responses. Additionally, there is no guarantee that the desired respondent completed the survey. Second, surveys may be administered by trained interviewers through face-to-face or telephone interviews. This method is more expensive due to the costs of training interviewers and compensating them for their work. However, training interviewers to be consistent in their behaviors increases the uniformity and accuracy of survey completion.

The survey instrument itself consists of a series of questions that may be closed-ended, open-ended, or a combination of both. Closed-ended questions ask respondents to select among the response alternatives provided. Closed questions necessitate anticipating all possible answer options in advance and including them on the instrument. The options must be exhaustive and mutually exclusive. Closed-ended questions are useful because they offer greater uniformity of responses and are more easily tabulated. The following is a closed-ended question: "How would you describe your political affiliation? Would you say you are a Republican, a Democrat, or an Independent?" Additionally, questions using the popular Likert-type scale response options, which range from "strongly disagree" to "strongly agree," are closed-ended questions.

Open-ended questions allow more freedom for the participants to respond. However, the responses are much more difficult to interpret. The following is an open-ended question: "What do you feel is the most important issue facing our community today?" The respondent (in the case of a self-administered survey) or interviewer must write down the response to this question. Answers may vary in length from single-word responses to rather lengthy descriptions of numerous issues. Once the data are collected, the responses must be coded (i.e., interpreted and categorized by the researcher) before they can be analyzed. This introduces an extra step and may create error when the researcher interprets the responses differently from what the participants intended, the respondents are not adept at expressing themselves, or the handwriting is illegible.

—*Sherry J. Holladay*

See also Reliability; Sampling; Validity

Bibliography

Fowler, F. J. (2001). *Survey research methods* (3rd ed.). Thousand Oaks, CA: Sage.

Stacks, D. W. (2002). *Primer of public relations research.* New York: Guilford Press.

SWEDEN, PRACTICE OF PUBLIC RELATIONS IN

The communication business in Sweden has grown rapidly during the last decade, though the growth has declined in the early 21st century due to a period of recession. Since 1995, the Swedish Public Relations Association has more than doubled its number of members to 4,500, making it the second largest association in Europe and, per capita, one of the largest associations in the world (the population of Sweden is 9 million people) (see Table 1).

The incentive to engage in public relations in Sweden is driven primarily, perhaps even exclusively, by the desire to add positively to the organizations' bottom line. They seem less motivated to view and use public relations as a means for building relationships. No evidence whatsoever shows that Swedish enterprises or public bodies have professional communication unless it affects the businesses. It has become more and more obvious to every professional communicator that you either work in-house or as a consultant.

Almost every second year since 1982, the Swedish Public Relations Association has conducted a member survey, of which the 2003 survey is the latest. The data show clear tendencies: internal communication and media relations are the two areas that will grow most during the coming years. Changing processes and ethics are other issues of great importance to association members, as are corporate branding and strategic planning. The intense debate regarding trust and confidence within the business community has further strengthened the focus on information and communication.

The position of the communication departments is strong in Sweden. In listed companies, 73 percent of the directors of the corporate communication are part of the CEO groups, whereas in public authorities the figure rises to 77 percent. This means that professional communication is part of the business decisions, and that the competence and skills of leading professional communicators must include business administration, production management, political science, behavior science, and management in general.

In the years 1998 to 2003, the Swedish Public Relations Association has arranged a management program called the Communication Executives Program for top senior professional communicators. Organized in tandem with the Stockholm School of Economics to fulfill the requirements heard from many CEOs both in the private and the public sector, this management program provides all the areas described above to give the professional communicator a better platform to have a seat in the CEO team.

In a telephone survey of 800 Swedish public relations executives by Research International 2000, 99 percent of respondents in the private and public sectors declared that they considered effective, professional communication a winning concept. The following areas were also considered of importance:

- Creating good relations with stakeholders and publics (88 percent)
- Advising executives (88 percent)
- Developing communication strategies (87 percent)
- Establishing credibility among stakeholders (84 percent)
- Image creation (83 percent)
- Crisis management (77 percent)

This study was the first of its kind in Sweden. The purpose was to obtain a clear picture of the values and attitudes toward professional communication held by the dominant coalitions.

Since 1995 the Swedish Public Relations Association has been a driving force and participant in the monitoring, measuring, and reporting of intangibles/intellectual capital. In 1996 the association published *Return on Communications* and has since been involved in different projects concerning the issue within the European Union, OECD, and Nordic Industrial Fund.

A PROFESSIONAL COMMUNICATOR CANNOT ABDICATE FROM CORPORATE BRANDING

For many years branding questions have been part of the work of the marketing people. Today the corporate brand is a matter of the board of directors. The value of the corporate brand is a main factor in considering merchants and acquisitions and must be maintained as well as other assets or intangibles. It also means that the head of corporate communication should be in charge of this area. A professional communicator cannot abdicate from his or her responsibility. The assignment of a communicator includes maintaining and developing the company's image and reputation. This means having a broad knowledge about the company business and its products and services, as well as an understanding of the business and product processes.

The need for integrated communication has increased as all companies or other organizations have realized that they must take into consideration all the stakeholders, such as the employee, the customers, the society, and the owners/shareholders. This work is neither new nor hocus-pocus. It is all about professional communication work.

SCRAP THE CODE OF ATHENS?

Ethics has become more and more important, and a committee within the Swedish Public Relations Association is working with professional ethical codes. It is about time to scrap the Code of Athens since professional communicators cannot use the code as a guideline to the daily work. The Code of Athens was written in the 1960s and is not applicable to the communication work of today or tomorrow. A member survey shows that members think it is important that the same code be used by both in-house communicators and consultants.

Public Relations Consultancies in Sweden (PRECIS) has developed a new standard, the Stockholm Charter, which has also become the standard of the International Communications Consultancy Organisation (ICCO).

Norms shall create identity and shall be able to communicate. They shall be consistent, reliable, guiding, and inspiring to a professional communicator. The norms shall guide and advise a communicator in different situations that can arise in his or her daily work. This issue is one of the priorities for the Swedish Public Relations Association during 2004.

PROFESSIONAL COMMUNICATION ENABLING BUSINESS CREATION AND ORGANIZATIONAL DEVELOPMENT

The professional area of communication is represented by professional communicators, many of whom are members of the Swedish Public Relations Association. For a number of years, this area has developed its own discourse with academic support from scholars such as Sven Windahl. The

knowledge and the theories in use have, however, to a great extent been developed by and for the practitioners themselves. As a result, professional communication is rather poorly represented in the academic context, particularly in the educational management programs. It can be assumed that this knowledge accumulation has mainly been following the path of the traditional perspective of the public relations discourse. This may have resulted in managerial measures focused on defensive actions with the objective to preserve and defend present values, in particular the organizational trust capital. This in itself is not negative but may result in decreasing effectiveness of professional communication measures as far as the pro-active creation of businesses and influencing organizational change are concerned.

With today's rapidly changing network community, organizations must keep a fast, steady pace in the development of structures, processes, and businesses. All managerial measures must take active part in this, regardless of whether the organization is business oriented. Research has shown that development of organizations tend to be path dependent. Development follows limited perspectives with the effect of unevenly allocating resources. As a result, organizations run a considerable risk of neglecting certain potential areas for development. This may later have negative consequences. This is true for the technology-driven development that dominated the organizational life up to the 1970s, as well as the stock market–driven development of today. Through short-sighted obedience to demands from the stock market, many companies have put themselves in situations where they have aroused unrealistic expectations and thereby jeopardized sustainable growth. It can therefore be assumed that there is a need for knowledge development in order to create the prerequisites for organizational development processes from an optimal system perspective.

Professional communication is not presently used to its full potential as far as participation in the development of businesses and organizations is concerned. It may certainly be advocated that the present focus of most communication measures on preservation of trust capital constitutes a foundation for further development. There are, however, reasons to believe that many organizations need to refine the trust capital further, rather than just preserving it. Professional communication has great potential for use in organizational and business development.

This program is intended to substantially contribute to the development of knowledge about how communication processes can be managed to enable effective participation in creating business and organizational change.

In cooperation with the Swedish Public Relations Association, Stockholm School of Economics has during the last five years conducted an executive educational program called the Communication Executives Program. This program has established a dialogue between the school and professional communication executives.

PURPOSE

The general purpose of this project, as stated above, can be divided into the following subpurposes:

To make an inventory of communication knowledge as it is manifest in the discourse of the practitioners and relate this to the knowledge present in the academic discourse, in particular, organizational theory, social cognition, and sociology.

To publish suggestions for theories and methodologies that can be applied to the role of communication processes in organizational change and business creation. Results will be published in academic as well as practitioners' contexts.

To initiate self-reinforcing research and knowledge development processes in this field by participating in the establishment of educational programs, and thereby making the area interesting and available for doctoral students, and creating the prerequisites for a professorship at the Stockholm School of Economics.

PROCESS

In order to meet the overall purpose of generating and establishing new knowledge in this field, a certain duration is required for a research program of this nature. There is, however, also a need to develop knowledge in the short term. The program will therefore have a duration of five years. All three subpurposes are expected to be fulfilled within this time frame.

Year 1: In the first year the program will conduct a large number of interviews and participant observations with professional communicators in order to create an empirical base for extraction of methodologies applied and theories in use in the discourse of practitioners, and relate that knowledge to the academic discourse. Publication of preliminary results will start after six months through the publication channels of the Swedish Public Relations Association. Research results will be published quarterly thereafter.

Year 2: During the second year the academic publishing of results will commence and educational programs in professional communication at graduate level will be established.

Year 3: In the third year the knowledge development will open up opportunities for doctoral students to enter the field.

Years 4 and 5: At the end of the program the accumulated knowledge will have reached the advanced stage of prerequisites for a professorship in this field at the Stockholm School of Economics. Furthermore, the accumulated knowledge will be synthesized into a final publication. Thereby the field will be established in the academic setting.

RESOURCES

During the whole length of the program one qualified research capability will be allocated full-time. The position will be held by Sven Hamrefors,

Author's Note: The author thanks Sven Hamrefors, assistant professor at Stockholm School of Economics, Sweden, for his contribution to this entry.

Table 1   Some Facts About the Swedish Public Relations Association

Number of members	4500 (70% women and 30% men)
The members represent:	
Private companies	35% (16% are listed companies)
Public sector	27% (of which, 7% are municipality, 4% are County Council, and 16% are National Government
Consultants	16%
Organizations	7%
Students	6%
Others	9%
SPRA turnover:	SEK 12 millions (Euro 1.2 millions)
Secretarial staff	6 persons
Accounting:	2 persons

SOURCE: Swedish Public Relations Association. Reprinted with permission.

assistant professor at Stockholm School of Economics, who is also the program director for the Communication Executives Program and has been since the start of that program. The total estimated cost for the program is SEK 6 million (Euro 600.000).

—*Margaretha Sjöberg*

See also Brand equity and branding; Codes of ethics; Counseling; Ethics of public relations; Internal communication

SYMBOLIC INTERACTIONISM THEORY

Symbolic interactionism theory offers to public relations students and practitioners a way in which to view communication as a social process, and also a research method framework to investigate that process. The theory is based on the assumption that people behave in certain ways because of their meaning making—interpretive—actions. The mind, self, and society work together to influence how people make meaning. With historical foundations in the social sciences, symbolic interactionism theory makes three assumptions about the communication process. The theory assumes communication occurs when people share meanings for symbols, such as words or pictures. Social interactionists, or those who study social interactionism theory, hold that people are created through communication. And there is an assumption that social or collective action can occur when communicators understand and negotiate the meanings of other people.

HISTORICAL FOUNDATION

The interdisciplinary development of symbolic interaction has changed the way individuals, groups, and society are analyzed. No longer is it exclusively believed that people can be reduced to being studied as objects or animals. Social interaction theorists assume people communicate through socially created and used symbols, including language. People assume roles based on symbols interpreted in their group(s) and interact through these roles. By way of roles, people create ideas of self and mind, and through interaction, society forms.

The beginnings of interactionism theory development are found in the works of the Scottish moral philosophers during the 1800s. Although these men disagreed on the fundamentals of the human mind, especially important to the emergence of symbolic interaction was their conviction that it is not possible to study individuals without considering human interaction. Their emphasis on communication and on the emotion of sympathy was the foundation for interactionists' view of society and the origin of self.

The ideas of the moral philosophers can be found in the works of William James and John Dewey, who influenced philosopher George Herbert Mead, often referred to as the most influential scholar of symbolic interactionism theory. The theories of Mead and Dewey are founded in an understanding of the individual within society. Charles Horton Cooley furthered the concept by considering the self from a sociological perspective. He used a critical framework of a group and underscored the role societies play in shaping an individual's motivation. Cooley conceptualized society as existing in the minds of the people within a social unit, making it real to those people. He argued that there are any number of different minds that exist through a melding and sharing of histories, expectations, and experiences.

The works and class notes of philosopher George Herbert Mead provided his students at the University of Chicago with enough material to posthumously publish three influential books in the 1930s. Of these three books, *Mind, Self, and Society* is most relevant to the public relations community. Mead's arguments coincide with those of other pragmatists of the time, but his work was the foundation for symbolic interaction, a unique form of interpretive research.

At the core of Mead's intersubjective thoughts lies his notion of mind. Mead's mind is symbolic. It emerges and develops through interaction with others. According to Mead, our thoughts and identity are in response to and develop as part of a social process. The self is an object that develops through awareness; it is determined through the roles other people take, and by interaction with others through symbols, including language. As humans we are able to think, and according to Mead, thinking is a reflective process that develops through our interactions with others and through our recognition of

ourselves from the viewpoint of others. Our reflective self is rooted in society, or in a "generalised other" (Prus, 1996, p. 53). This generalized other—a society, a community, a workplace—are people interacting with each other in a manner made possible through shared symbolic representations.

A student of Mead, Herbert Blumer, coined the term *symbolic interaction* in 1937. Elaborating on Cooley's method of sympathetic introspection, Blumer's main argument was that researchers must have intimate familiarity with the study's participants, and that the only way to achieve intimate familiarity with human group life is to interact with it while it is happening. Equally important to Blumer was the notion that all individual analysis must be examined as reflective and/or interactive units within a human group. In brief, Blumer contended that: (a) humans act based on the meanings held within themselves; (b) those meanings are a product of human interaction; and (c) the meanings are modified through an interpretive process. His theories provided the framework for ethnographic research for students in all social sciences.

Interpretive researchers study people as part of a group. People are investigated as active participants in interaction. The most common research methods are participant observation, observation, and open-ended interviews. Life is studied as it happens. Intersubjectivity is analyzed. Researchers question the meanings people attach to their situations and look at the ways people construct their interactions with others.

While interpretive research is regaining popularity after experiencing unpopularity in the academic community from the 1960s to the 1980s, it retains some of its original pitfalls. The research is time consuming and labor and emotionally intensive, making it an expensive research method. The data can be ambiguous, much more so than the data produced from a simple survey. It is also difficult to condense and present the data collected. Interpretive studies are neither as readily supported by funding agencies, nor as widely accepted within organizations, as are quantitative research projects. However, for those who want to address the *how* and *why* of communication efforts, symbolic interactionism theory provides a framework for investigative measures that take into account a more holistic view of an organization and its publics.

USING SYMBOLIC INTERACTION THEORY

Understanding symbolic interaction theory is useful in any communication scenario and at any stage of communication planning. Indeed, understanding the basic tenets of the theory can assist any communicator who wants to send a message, or anyone who is receiving one.

The theory is based on three premises: (a) people act toward things on the basis of the meanings they have for them; (b) the meaning of such things is derived from, or arises out of, social interaction; and (c) the meaning is negotiated through an interpretative process.

In contemporary public relations practices, a common goal is to communicate effectively with various people or groups of people. Symbolic interaction theory suggests that any one of these people or peoples make meaning through a process that is shaped by other people's meanings and meaning-making processes. That is, people respond to messages differently depending on their life histories, social circumstances, and knowledge, which are informed by other people and society (including the workplace). Important to the public relations scholar and practitioner is the acknowledgement that the sender of messages is an integral participant in the communication process. The messages or signs might be in the form of words, objects, or actions. According to this theory, whatever their form, people will make meaning through interpreting the signs and reacting according to the meanings they have created for those signs.

As an example, assume that an organization's internal communications professional wants to communicate to employees that the organization values its employees. Without investigating what "value" means to the employees, the communicator uses his own definition of value, which means an increase in salary. The communicator convinces the organizational leader to make increases to all employee salaries and announces the increase through a monthly newsletter. Because the communicator neither talked with the employees nor researched what "valuing employees" means to them and assumed that they would all share the same meaning, the communicator can expect that the employees will react in different, and possibly even negative, ways. At a minimum, employees will evaluate the signs (the increase in salary and the announcement in the newsletter). They will do this using their own meaning of "value," which will include all of their experiences and history within the organization and outside it. How the employees react will reflect the meanings they have attached to other such signs from within the organization, or even at a different workplace.

Continuing the example, assume that the employees do not agree that salary equals value. Instead, valuing employees means a simple thank-you for a job well done from the job supervisor. Without having investigated this meaning, the communicator would not know that his own meaning of value is different from that held by those with whom he wants to communicate.

Symbolic interactionism theory suggests that working to negotiate shared meanings is a process of clarification. Signs can be modified to further negotiate meanings. If there is not an opportunity to do this through dialogue or through other investigative methods, the communicator can attempt to assume the positions of those with whom he or she wants to communicate. By assuming social positions of others, communicators can better imagine and hence negotiate meaning. The process allows one to identify that one's own assumptions might not be similar to the intended receivers'.

—DeNel Rehberg Sedo

See also Measuring/measures

Bibliography

Blumer, H. (1969). *Symbolic interactionism: Perspective and method.* Englewood Cliffs, NJ: Prentice Hall.

Mead, G. H. (1934). *Mind, self, and society.* Chicago: University of Chicago.

Meltzer, B. N., Petras, J. W., & Reynolds, L. T. (1975). *Symbolic interactionism: Genesis, varieties and criticism.* London: Routledge & Kegan Paul.

Prus, R. C. (1996). Symbolic interaction and ethnographic research: Inter-subjectivity and the study of human lived experience. Albany: State University of New York Press.

Stryker, S. (1980). *Symbolic interactionism: A social structural version*. Menlo Park, CA.: Benjamin/Cummings.

SYMMETRY

The concept of symmetry in public relations was first explored by James E. Grunig in an attempt to relate Lee Thayer's (1968) concepts of synchronic and diachronic communication to the discipline. Grunig extended these concepts into four models of public relations and published a textbook explicating these models (Grunig & Hunt, 1984). The models are (a) press agentry/publicity, (b) public information, (c) two-way asymmetrical, and (d) two-way symmetrical. Symmetry is the concept upon which the two-way symmetrical model is based.

In public relations, symmetry means balance and implies a perfectly equal division. This division is conceptualized as that between an organization and a public, and the division can be thought of in terms of relationship-influencing factors, such as locus of control, power, and authority. In a symmetrical relationship, these factors are evenly held by the organization and its public or publics. Symmetry induces a symbiotic relationship between organization and public; the two are equal partners, interdependently sharing information in order to arrive at mutual understanding, which is the balance implied in the term.

However, symmetry is not static—it is a sliding scale in which the balance adjusts and readjusts toward equilibrium. These adjustments and counter-adjustments are made when an organization and its public vary approaches along a continuum from accommodation to competition, depending on how strongly each feels about the issue under discussion. Using negotiation tactics, an organization or public might give up some of what it wants in order to get more of what it wants on another issue or in the future. Symmetry is characterized by collaboration and compromise, as well as by using dialogue to understand all sides of the issue and arrive at enduring, long-term solutions.

Although this depiction of symmetry is theoretical, symmetry also occurs in the actual practice of public relations. The two-way symmetrical model is based on using social scientific research to understand the values, attitudes, and beliefs of publics. It is a two-way model because the communication is dialogical. The two-way asymmetrical model is also based on using social scientific research to understand publics. Here the models diverge as follows: The symmetrical model uses research for the purpose of understanding publics, adapting to their ideas when necessary; and the asymmetrical model uses research to understand how the beliefs of publics can be altered to favor the organization, without the organization actually changing. In the asymmetrical model, the balance is in favor of the organization conducting the research—publics can be persuaded to change their beliefs, but the organization does not do anything to change itself. In the symmetrical model, the balance is maintained through dialogue and mutual willingness to adapt to the other side; both publics and organization are willing to discuss, educate, collaborate, and incorporate meritorious ideas of the other into their own approach. Symmetrical and asymmetrical models of public relations can be used by any organization, including activist groups and publics outside an organization. However, using a symmetrical approach does not imply that an organization must accommodate whatever a public wishes or vice versa, but that each must work to understand the merits of the other view. J. E. Grunig explained, "The concept of symmetry directly implies a balance of the organization's and public's interests. Total accommodation of the public's interests would be as asymmetrical as unbridled advocacy of the organization's interests" (2001, p. 15). There are four primary benefits to using a symmetrical approach to the public relations function, as discussed next.

SYMMETRY AS RELATIONSHIP BUILDING AND MAINTENANCE

Using a two-way symmetrical approach, as opposed to any of the other three models of public relations, results in the building, strengthening, and maintenance of relationships with publics. As one-way models, neither press agentry nor public information incorporates the ideas of publics. The asymmetrical model researches the attitudes of publics, so that the organization can better persuade them to adopt the beliefs that are advantageous to it. Symmetry is actually a long-term, dialogical process that seeks to create and maintain relationships with publics. Through mutual understanding and collaboration, trust and credibility can be built between an organization and publics. Sometimes the publics can persuade the organization on an issue, and sometimes the organization will persuade publics on an issue. This give-and-take is the crux of symmetry.

Establishing symmetrical, pre-need relationships with strategic publics helps the organization in times of decision making and crisis. Publics are less likely to jump to hasty conclusions when they have a symmetrical relationship with the organization. Symmetrical relationships are more enduring than asymmetrical ones, in which one side will always feel as if it "lost" the issue and will become frustrated, often dissolving the relationship. Furthermore, activist groups are more likely to target organizations that do not discuss the issue of concern with them than organizations that show a willingness to listen, understand, and to varying extents incorporate their ideas. Even when little common ground can be found initially, a symmetrical relationship allows the possibility of continued dialogue and inventing options for mutual gain.

SYMMETRY AS A CONTRIBUTOR TO ORGANIZATIONAL EFFECTIVENESS

Although it is an idealistic and normative model, the symmetrical approach results *in practice* in satisfactory and beneficial relationships with publics. Building effective relationships with publics (such as government regulators, activist groups, investors, community publics, and so forth) is crucial to the long-term survival and profitability of an organization. J. E. Grunig wrote, "With the two-way symmetrical model, practitioners use research and dialogue to bring about symbiotic changes in the ideas, attitudes, and behaviors of both their

organization and publics" (2001, p. 12). These pro-active, symbiotic changes can often save the organization enormous sums of money that would have been spent on legal settlements, regulatory compliance, or damage control if a symmetrical model had not been employed.

A second major way that symmetry contributes to organizational effectiveness is by enhancing the organizational culture in a way that allows open communication inside the company. Simply stated, authoritarian systems operate on an asymmetrical worldview, whereas participative cultures operate on a symmetrical presupposition. Research has found that authoritarian cultures use one-way models of communication (press agentry and public information) and two-way asymmetrical communication to persuade employees along the lines that management desires.

A symmetrical worldview supports two-way communication inside the organization as well as with external publics. The presuppositions characteristic of the symmetrical worldview are interdependence, an open system, moving equilibrium, equality, autonomy, innovation, decentralization, responsibility, innovation, conflict resolution, and interest group liberalism. Dialogue is the basis of the symmetrical worldview and the symmetrical model of public relations, and facilitating a participative culture and information sharing inside the organization. Symmetrical internal communication helps to make an organization effective by increasing the satisfaction of employees and allowing long-term relationships with employee publics to be maintained.

SYMMETRY ENHANCES THE RESPONSIBILITY OF PUBLIC RELATIONS

Every organization has a core of decision makers, including the CEO and top officers, who determine organizational strategy. This group of five to eight influentials is termed the *dominant coalition*. The ideal situation is for the head of public relations to be a member of the dominant coalition so that the views of publics can be incorporated in strategic planning. However, when public relations is seen as a technical function, limited to communicating the will of management rather than having input into the decision making process, its input is often excluded from the dominant coalition. The use of a symmetrical approach is vital to public relations gaining a seat in the dominant coalition.

Through symmetrical relationships, the public relations function performs a boundary-spanning role. Public relations thereby holds the knowledge of publics outside the organization that other departments do not, and this information is of great value in strategic decision making. Public relations counsel can convey the attitudes, values, and beliefs of a given public to management for consideration in strategic planning. In this manner, the public's ideas can be incorporated into organizational policy, or the organization can be aware that it should pro-actively prepare for dissent from that public. The organization has taken the public into account and planned for contingencies, avoiding surprises that can cost the organization in litigation, negative press, and loss of credibility. Information gained through symmetrical dialogue is valuable in strategic planning. This information can earn public relations access to the dominant coalition and increase the responsibility of the communication function in the organization.

SYMMETRY IS INHERENTLY ETHICAL

Scholars such as Jürgen Habermas (1984) and Ron Pearson (1989) asserted that organizations have a moral obligation to engage in dialogue with publics. J. E. and Larissa A. Grunig used symmetry as a way of satisfying that obligation. They espoused the idea that "public relations will be inherently ethical if it follows the principles of the two-way symmetrical model" (1996, p. 40). Symmetry is based on dialogue and is therefore an ethical form of communication.

Symmetrical public relations provides a means through which publics and organizations can debate the merits of issues and determine the best course of action through discussion, negotiation, and collaboration. When public relations is based on a symmetrical worldview, it performs an idealistic social role. Public relations acts as the grease on the wheels of society, developing mutual understanding through dialogue and informed debate.

—Shannon A. Bowen

See also Ethics of public relations; Excellence theory

Bibliography

Grunig, J. E. (1976). Organizations and public relations: Testing a communication theory. *Journalism Monographs, 46.*

Grunig, J. E. (1984). Organizations, environments, and models of public relations. *Public Relations Research and Education, 1*(1), 6–29.

Grunig, J. E. (1989). Symmetrical presuppositions as a framework for public relations theory. In C. H. Botan & V. J. Hazleton (Eds.), *Public relations theory* (pp. 17–44). Hillsdale, NJ: Lawrence Erlbaum.

Grunig, J. E. (2001). Two-way symmetrical public relations: Past, present, and future. In R. L. Heath (Ed.), *Handbook of public relations* (pp. 11–30). Thousand Oaks, CA: Sage.

Grunig, J. E., & Grunig, L. A. (1996, May). *Implications of symmetry for a theory of ethics and social responsibility in public relations.* Paper presented at the meeting of the International Communication Association, Chicago.

Grunig, J. E., & Hunt, T. (1984). *Managing public relations.* New York: Holt, Rinehart & Winston.

Grunig, J. E., & White, J. (1992). The effect of worldviews on public relations theory and practice. In J. E. Grunig (Ed.), *Excellence in public relations and communication management* (pp. 31–64). Hillsdale, NJ: Lawrence Erlbaum.

Habermas, J. (1984). *The theory of communicative action: Reason and the rationalization of society* (T. McCarthy, Trans., Vol. 1). Boston: Beacon Press.

Pearson, R. (1989). Beyond ethical relativism in public relations: Coorientation, rules, and the idea of communication symmetry. In J. E. Grunig & L. A. Grunig (Eds.), *Public relations research annual* (Vol. 1, pp. 67–86). Hillsdale, NJ: Lawrence Erlbaum.

Thayer, L. (1968). *Communication and communication systems.* Homewood, IL: Irwin.

SYSTEMS THEORY

Systems theory was developed to understand the dynamics of natural and human phenomena. The system is a basic unit of analysis. Theory addresses the nature of each system as part of its environment that consists of other systems. The key concern of proponents of systems theory is to understand how well or poorly each system functions within its dynamic relationship with other systems.

Most definitions of public relations imply that communication plays a strong role in the interdependence of the public relations practitioner, the organization, and its stakeholders. This interdependence is equated to Daniel Katz and Robert Kahn's *open system* rather than a *closed-system* perspective. Presented in 1966, the open system stems from the 1940s and 1950s and is based on the biological approach of Ludwig von Bertlanffy, who emphasized the interconnectedness of all the parts of a body. Each human or social system, like each physical organism, is surrounded by permeable boundaries. Organizations in open systems are dependent on other organizations or groups in their environment. They cannot depend only on internal processes and interaction as in a closed system. Organizations also must interact with other groups in their environments.

In 1986, Gerald Goldhaber described a systems loop, the loop being input from the environment, throughput, and output with feedback coming back on the loop to be reinput into the organization. This feedback represents the effects of other organizations or groups of the organization and leads it to adapt or change to coexist better with its environment. Organizations representative of closed systems believe they are independent of environmental influences. To succeed and survive, however, in an increasingly turbulent environment that cannot be ignored, organizations are dependent on or have to cope with factors in their environment. Public relations is one of the primary links in sustaining this interdependence, both internally and externally, to the organization.

Factors in the environment that affect an organization also result in decisions that have inescapable consequences for the relationships the organization has with its stakeholders. Relationships exist whether acknowledged or not. That is where public relations contributes to an organization's existence.

The strategic skill used by public relations practitioners to manage these relationships between an organization and its stakeholders is *boundary spanning*. This is the process by which the practitioner scans stakeholders in the organization's environment useful for it to adapt to that environment. Boundary spanners are individuals within the organization who frequently interact with the organization's environment and who gather, select, and relay information from the environment to decision makers of an organization. That interaction with the environment can be on a formal or informal basis. These stakeholders serve in a microsystem with public relations that could be referred to as a *public relations system*.

Many scholars in public relations purport that research and theorizing in public relations is strongly influenced by systems theory and that systems theory could be considered a meta-theory for public relations. Systems theory tenets are evident in many studies of public relations and implied in others. It was in 1976 when both Bell and Bell and separately James E. Grunig first incorporated systems theory in public relations. Probably the most extensive development of systems theory in public relations was Larissa A. Grunig's (a.k.a. "Schneider") doctoral dissertation of 1985. She concluded in the structural-functionalist tradition that structure and organizational constraints control the flow of information from within the organization and from it to its external stakeholders. However, functionalism alone is insufficient to justify systems theory as a meta-theory in public relations.

CRITIQUES AND RESPONSES

Other scholars in public relations also have addressed perceived weaknesses in the extent and possible consequences of systems theory. In his discussion of the pluralist paradigm in public relations, Timothy Coombs said in 1993 that for the pluralist paradigm, where power is equalized in the policy-making process, systems theory failed to address power advantages of corporations. This power advantage is particularly acute in considering public relations assisting an organization to achieve its goals by aligning itself with others in the environment. Public relations remains an advocate for an organization. This viewpoint will be addressed later in the discussion of organizations pursuing their own *self-interests*.

Others also have criticized systems theory when discussing organizational power. Pamela Creedon agreed with L. A. Grunig in that the functionalist perspective implied by systems theory inhibits the examination of the "foundation of institutional values or norms that determine an organization's response changes in its environment" (1993, p. 160). In essence the systems approach emphasizes the need of the organization over the needs of the entire system structure and that there is a sought-after degree of control. Organizational advocacy does not necessarily include mutual understanding, dialogue, or reaching consensus with stakeholders.

These critiques and possible responses essentially can be distilled into the Jürgen Habermas's school of interpersonal or intersubjective common interests among interdependent systems, and Niklas Luhmann's school of independent social systems where there is no difference between public and private interests. Habermas's objective is the social integration of society, the breakdown of system boundaries, whereas Luhmann's objective is for inner-systemic integration and the maintenance of system boundaries. The Habermas school of thought could be equated somewhat to the critical and ethical perspectives in public relations. In 1990, Ron Pearson examined systems theory and public relations with an ethical view to take functionalism one step further. Functionalism maintains a balance of a system as a whole, to maintain homeostasis with other elements of its environment. Pearson put forward the concept of interdependencies as a way of ethically balancing the connections among stakeholders. This focus on interdependencies ultimately leads to ethical and power-balanced relationships as the organization attempts to continually maintain and adapt to its environment. It is within this interdependence where both strategic and ethical considerations are present. The major difference in functionalism and systems theory, according to Pearson, is that functionalism usually emphasizes structure, output, and performance in contrast to systems theory, which emphasizes input, throughput, and output. With input, systems theory lends itself more to the interdependence, ethical side of the argument. This type of input should be that

which supports change on both sides of the equation, that of the organization and that of the stakeholder(s) in a symmetrical manner. According to Habermas's theories, it is unethical to enter a system representing particular interests or self-interests. Luhmann's theories promote just the opposite view since no perspective for society, as a whole system, exists in actuality.

INTERESTS AND SELF-INTERESTS

Common interests and *self-interests* have been referred to but not specifically addressed yet. Interests from the conflict resolution literature can be defined as those underlying, broader, and more abstract values that individuals and organizations may have in common. Self-interests, from the public relations literature, are not selfish interests but those interests that have intrinsic value for the survival of an entity (e.g., quality of life, needs of family and friends, and even economic well-being). These self-interests motivate individuals and organizations to act and to change behavior. Taken one step further, *enlightened self-interests* in the long-term assist relationships to be mutually satisfactory. Enlightened self-interests meld the intersubjective and social ends of systems theory thought because positive relationships in the long term means adapting, adjusting, and changing to other stakeholders in the environment. There are inevitable effects in a public relations system of one stakeholder on another. This is inherently ethical because stakeholders have a constraining effect; they have consequences for each other. One of the tenets of the social systems perspective is that organizations and systems fundamentally differ and tend toward independence, yet political and economic system restraints and the self-governing restraints of a system's interconnectedness lead to a system becoming interdependent. The basic survival of an organization in the long term depends on the relationship of self-interests and enlightened self-interests between it and its stakeholders.

Self-interests are just that—values owned exclusively by an individual organization. Thus, there can never be total consensus among individuals or organizations. It is not so much a matter of finding consensus or common ground or complete resolution of any conflict. It is a matter of settling issues in overlapping areas of self-interests. This is enlightened self-interest. Individual or public trust is not an issue because in the regulated systems of modern society, organizations cannot avoid dealing with other stakeholders. There is a pattern of interdependence, pursuing self-interests of both parties so that both do well. This also relates to mixed motives in public relations where situations and issues are not resolved at the extremes in a pure asymmetrical or symmetrical manner, but there are trade-offs, compromises, and so forth that lead to both parties being mutually satisfied in their self-interests—those self-interests not being identical.

J. E. Grunig's *Excellence in Public Relations and Communication Management* in 1992 advocated two-way symmetrical communication as an ethical but interpersonal and strategic form of communication. The practice, however, of strategic communication in systems theory would be deemed unethical in Habermasian thought. But strategic communications would be judged highly ethical according to Luhmann where self-interests can overlap; the system self-enforces ethical or reciprocal behavior to coexist in the same system. It allows autonomy and interaction to exist side by side in a complementary manner.

Stakeholder relations or public relations practice in systems theory then becomes a question of conflicts among different stakeholders or systems by means of regulation, law, economics, and self-interests. The objective is sustainability through mutual self-regulation, self-restriction, and adjustment in a society of continuous conflicts and disagreements. This is inevitable because systems, organizations, on down to individuals are separate entities biologically, but also in frames of reference or perspective—again self-interests. The public relations manager acts as a system's representative in a

particular self-interest or enlightened self-interest. Mutual understanding in symmetrical communications becomes a type of awareness where stakeholders understand the self-interests of each other in the relationship—not the type that totally reconciles the different stakeholders, but the type that allows them to complement one another in a sustainable relationship.

—*Kenneth D. Plowman*

See also Publics; Relationship management theory; Stakeholder theory; Symmetry; Two-way and one-way communication

Bibliography

Coombs, W. T. (1993). Philosophical underpinnings: Ramifications of a pluralist paradigm. *Public Relations Review, 19*, 111–119.

Creedon, P. (1993). Acknowledging the infrasystem: A critical feminist analysis of systems theory. *Public Relations Review, 19*, 157–166.

Goldhaber, G. M. (1986). *Organizational communication* (4th ed.). Dubuque, IA: Wm. C. Brown.

Grunig, J. E. (Ed.). (1992). *Excellence in public relations and communication management*. Hillsdale, NJ: Lawrence Erlbaum.

Grunig (a.k.a. "Schneider"), L. A. (1985). *Organizational structure, environmental niches, and public relations: The Hage-Hull typology of organizations as predictor of communications behavior*. Unpublished doctoral dissertation, University of Maryland, College Park.

Habermas, J. (1991). *The structural transformation of the public sphere: An inquiry into a category of bourgeois society* (English trans.). Cambridge: MIT Press.

Holmstrom, S. (1998). *An intersubjective and social systemic public relations paradigm*. Unpublished doctoral dissertation. University of Roskilde, Denmark.

Katz, D., & Kahn, R. L. (1966). *The social psychology of organizations*. New York: Wiley.

Luhmann, N. (1995). *Social systems* (English trans.). Palo Alto, CA: Stanford University Press.

Pearson, R. (1990). Ethical values or strategic values: The two faces of systems theory in public relations. In L. A. Grunig & J. E. Grunig (Eds.), *Public relations research annual* (Vol. 2, pp. 219–234). Hillsdale, NJ: Lawrence Erlbaum.

TACTICS

Tactics are the tools that practitioners use to perform strategies that are formulated by managers, including public relations managers. Usually the most comprehensive part of a communications plan, tactics are the tools of implementation. While objectives, goals, and strategies outline what practitioners wish to accomplish with their public relations endeavors, tactics are what implement it. Addressing the application aspect of public relations, tactics allow you to customize your plan to address specific target publics and markets. They are selected to achieve specific objectives. Most often plotted out in outline form in a communications plan, tactics provide a tool kit with which to carry out the plan and achieve the intended goals. A good analogy is to view tactics as the engineers in the field who carry out the research and planning done by the scientists in their laboratories. Thus, after a solid foundation of research, planning, and identifying goals and objectives, public relations practitioners can then enter the execution stage with the implementation of tactics.

In sum, tactics are what practitioners do and strategies are how they think. As is true of every profession, public relations requires an understanding and application of a variety of unique tools. Tactics are the tools by which strategic public relations programs

and plans as well as other planning options are implemented.

Tactics are part of a hierarchy of elements that define the public relations profession. One can argue that at the top of the pyramid of strategic elements of the profession are the ethical choices, management philosophies, public relations program, and strategic business planning options that drive public relations counseling. No savvy organization that engages in strategic communication, issues management, and public relations positioning does so by accident or whim. This level of analysis requires careful assessment of the strains and challenges that must be addressed as any organization seeks to build, maintain, and repair mutually beneficial relationships with its stakeholders or stake seekers. These may be publics interested in issue positions or customers, donors, or beneficiaries of the organization.

Whether an organization is large or small, it is likely to engage in some or many public relations functions. Functions are the broad headings that group types of activities use to address specific public relations needs. The list of functions is comparatively shorter than a list of tactics and includes employee relations, customer relations, investor relations, student relations, government relations, donor relations, member relations, and such. In large sophisticated organizations one or more persons may be in charge of one or two specific functions. In smaller organizations, several specific functions may be grouped together more tightly.

Strategic business and public relations plans are executed through functions that require the use of various strategic options. Strategies are the choices practitioners make regarding how to accomplish the ends specified in the strategic plan and enacted through functions. Strategies often also focus on outcomes to be achieved. One strategy is to attract attention, another is to inform. A third is to persuade, which could entail seeking to create favorable opinions, changing opinions, or adapting to the opinions that prevail on some matter. Persuasion can include efforts designed toward motivation. Strategies are employed during crisis response. Strategies are the essence of communication. They typically are independent variables leading to desirable dependent variables that are necessary to create, maintain, and repair mutually beneficial relationships.

The following list of tactics suggests the many tools practitioners use to reach out to and work with their customers, audiences, and publics:

- Media releases
- Lobbying
- Media kits
- News alerts
- Press conferences
- Product (service) releases and stories
- Feature releases and stories
- Employee newsletters and other forms of employee communication
- Customer hotlines
- How-to releases and events
- Expert columns (such as those in newspapers that promote real estate, fashion, cooking, and automobiles)
- Events
- Road shows/media tours/trade shows/product shows
- Videos, books, booklets, catalogs, and pamphlets
- Briefings and backgrounders
- Samples and coupons
- Web sites
- Intranet sites

- Position papers
- Placed and commissioned articles
- Sponsored books and editorials
- Negotiation and collaborative decision making
- Newsletters
- Executive comments
- Speakers bureaus

This long list is more illustrative than definitive. It demonstrates many of the tools that can be used by practitioners as they perform their practice. Practitioners are expected to be expert in the use of these tools based on strategies to be accomplished and functions to be performed in support of public relations programs.

There are several things to consider in choosing your tactics, such as the development of media materials, media distribution lists, and plans for media relations, as well as consideration of internal audiences, event coordination, collateral, partnership opportunities, sponsorship possibilities, and, in some cases, even advertising support when available.

Media materials may include news releases, fact sheets, biographies, visuals, and story angle lists. If media kits are to be used, these materials are the ones most commonly included in them. Good supplemental tools include B-roll (preferably on Beta video format), PSA (public service announcement) scripts, pitch letters, media advisories, trend alerts, and media drops.

In developing media lists, the identification of intended targets is essential. Generally, separate lists will be customized for trade and consumer audiences. Broadcast and print media must all be considered for maximizing message dissemination, whether to reach an international, national, regional, or local market.

Media relations tactics should then include initial distribution of materials, editorial calendar development, comprehensive follow-up, and media monitoring. Follow-up will include fielding media inquiries that may include expert or spokesperson interviews, providing additional information, editorial contribution to existing articles, feature coverage, op-ed pieces, bylined articles, case studies, and press conferences. Proactive strategies to consider are media tours, backgrounding sessions, executive interviews, and analyst relations. Currently, interactive opportunities also must be considered that include Web sites (as both targets and sources of information about your initiative), blast e-mails, online press-rooms, cyber events, and listservs. Community relations often take a grassroots approach with local speaking opportunities, sponsorships, lobbying, activist groups, and public service announcements.

For events, both interior and exterior audiences must be considered. Events for interior audiences may include incentive events, retreats, quarterly meetings, internal galas, press conferences, product launches, and holiday parties. Exterior event possibilities include trade shows, launch parties, grand openings, ribbon cuttings, shareholder meetings, road shows, guerilla marketing, press conferences, IPOs (initial public offerings of stock), community events, CEO roundtables, educational seminars, and free service giveaways.

Collateral may include marketing or sales pieces, such as brochures, product information sheets, capabilities kits, product displays, video loops, point-of-sale materials, product shots, direct mail pieces, newsletters, annual reports, electronic business cards, interactive CD-ROMs, invitations, event signage, high-resolution logos, trade show throw-away materials, booth graphics, and giveaways. Although usually included under media materials development, items such as press kit folders or containers, media drop materials, and video or audio samples are sometimes listed under collateral items, depending upon whose role it is to conceptualize and develop.

If advertising tactics are to be considered in a communications plan, it is often in the context of how these placements run in tandem with or can supplement the public relations efforts. Possible advertising outlets include print, radio, television, outdoor, Internet, transit, on-site, Yellow Pages, and on-hold telephone recordings.

With so many possibilities to keep track of, timelines are essential in assigning goals for implementing the tactics. You can see how the goals, objectives, strategies, targets, and reach all come into play in real terms with tactics, as they are the approach and tools by which you achieve the rest.

Scholars and senior practitioners who discuss the activities that define the practice often distinguish between the managerial activities of practitioners and their tactics or technician activities. According to this analysis, persons who are new to the profession tend to spend most of their time engaging in what are called "tactician activities" rather than managerial decision making. Some persons prefer to remain primarily in the role of tactician, whereas others aspire to move into more managerial activities.

The division between strategy and tactics guided, at least somewhat, the editorial design of the two professional publications of the Public Relations Society of America (PRSA). One, *The Public Relations Strategist,* features articles that discuss general policy and planning content. An issue might center on the strategies of activists and the challenges they pose to public relations practitioners. Articles in the *Strategist* might present the thoughts on business, the economy, public policy, or public relations planning by leaders in those fields. The journal might look at trends such as the challenges and advances facing practitioners in specific countries, for instance Russia as it developed more of a financial-commercial business model in place of the old state-control economy.

The other publication, called *Public Relations Tactics,* addresses best practices in the design and use of tactics. One long-running feature of *Tactics* was the column by Bill Adams, who invited practitioners to "Ask the Professor" questions about specific tactics. This might include the best way to capture the news interest of local reporters. It might feature the best approach for addressing employee concerns during a crisis. An issue might note the characteristics and techniques of effective public relations writing. It could offer advice on events or ways to be assertive during a television show interview. A feature in *Tactics* might single out the advantages and challenges of achieving Accredited Public Relations (APR) status. The advice in *Tactics* is practical, that is, something practitioners could do each day to strengthen their professional skills.

Further evidence of the strata of skills and challenges of public relations practitioners is the discussion presented in *Public Relations Career*

Guide, published by the PRSA Foundation in 1993. This publication addressed the typical activities of public relations executives, directors, managers, supervisors, and technicians. All levels perform tactical duties, but the proportion of a day devoted to such duties declined as a person ascended the ladder toward management. The proportion of each day's activities devoted to technical and craft skills declined as the practitioner matured, but at no level of the practice was the individual unlikely to need proficiency in these vital skills of the profession. Tactics define the profession. They are the tools of the trade.

—Lisa K. Merkl and Robert L. Heath

See also APR; Functions of public relations; Public Relations Society of America; Stakeholder theory; Strategies

Bibliography

PRSA Foundation (1993). *Public relations professional career guide.* New York: Author.

TAG

A tag or tagline is a short descriptive phrase used in public relations, advertising, and marketing to convey a key message. *Tagline* and *slogan* are terms that are often used interchangeably. Taglines are clever words, phrases, or sentences that appear at the end of an advertisement or other communication tool to summarize the message in a highly memorable way. If the tagline is repeated from advertisement to advertisement, it is generally called a slogan. The word *slogan* comes from the Gaelic expression for "battle cry," and slogans and taglines are the battle cry for a company, nonprofit organization, and brand. Therefore, taglines can be attached to a profit-making institution, a nonprofit organization, or a particular brand that is produced by an organization.

In the case of a particular brand, taglines play an important part in branding strategies and become a unifying theme in a campaign, which is a series of ads or collateral under some kind of thematic umbrella. A tagline summarizes the promise of the brand or how the brand wants to be positioned in the marketplace. In the case of a tagline for an organization, it becomes incorporated into a corporate identification system, which consists of a tagline, a logo, and an organization's name. In either case, taglines sum up the theme for an organization's unique positioning in the market or a brand's benefits in a short, easily remembered message.

Effective taglines are short, simple, and memorable and differentiate the company or product from its competitors. They are designed to be repeated, provide quick and easy identification of the organization or product, create a lasting impression, and ensure continuity. Frequently, taglines appear at the end of an ad as the final phrase, but they are usually incorporated throughout the materials produced by the organization or brand.

To write an effective tagline, a clear understanding of the organization's or brand's mission, unique characteristics, and competitive differences is needed. Some well-known taglines include "Microsoft: Where do you want to go today?"; "Visa: It's everywhere you want to be"; "L'Oreal: Because I'm worth it"; "AT&T: Reach out and touch someone"; "Nike: Just do it"; "Bounty: The quicker picker-upper"; and "Yellow Pages: Let your fingers do the walking."

—Emma Daugherty Phillingane

See also Advertising; Graphics; Logo

Bibliography

Arens, W. I. (2002). *Contemporary advertising.* Boston: McGraw-Hill Irwin.
Bendinger, B. (2001). *Advertising: The business of brands.* Chicago: Copy Workshop.
Cohen, D. (1988). *Advertising.* Glenview, IL: Scott, Foresman.

TARGET

The term *target* is used both as a noun and as a verb. As a noun, a target consists of specific individuals or groups that an organization wants to reach with its messages. Used that way, it would be appropriate to say that adult, 25-year-and-older, female customers of middle income would be a target for an integrated communication message about a specific product or service. As a verb, *target* means to set sights on that group or individual the organization wants to reach. Used as a verb, it would be appropriate for a political campaign advisor to say, "We will target young voters with college educations with X message."

The term target is widely used in marketing, advertising, and public relations. It draws on a military, recreation, or hunting context where a shooter aims at a target. The goal is to strategically hit the intended mark. As a preliminary step to some other outcome, an organization might work to get a specific message to a target. A nonprofit organization might do that by using carefully selected channels to reach potential donors or volunteers who are sympathetic to the mission and cause of the organization.

Target is generally defined by goals and objectives, with various tactics used to reach the intended target audiences. Practitioners should always strategically choose their targets to achieve their desired results, keeping in mind that reaching target audiences is also a way to measure someone's goals and objectives. Some ways to evaluate the level of success in a campaign or communications initiative is to measure both quantitative outcomes, such as garnering media coverage or generating inquiries, as well as more qualitative gauges, such as increasing business, selling products, receiving service requests, changing audience behaviors, and altering perceptions of intended target groups.

The most basic communication model features a source, message, channel, and receiver. Typically, the source has no reason to reach everyone in a population. For instance, in a marketing scenario, there is no reason to try to get a product presentation before people who are unlikely or never customers. Thus, targeting is one way of increasing communication efficiency: putting the right message in front of the right market at the right time. Thus, the source designs a message that is crafted to appeal to the target audience. Then the source works to get that message through one or more channels that increase the likelihood that the target will see, read, view, and respond to the message.

Targets are defined in some way. Definitions may feature demographics such as age, gender, marital status, income, or religious affiliation. Targets may feature psychographics that depend on values, beliefs, lifestyles, and attitudes. A target may also be defined by featuring sociographics such as employment, identifications, affiliations, and cause relatedness.

Targets are determined in a marketing communication context based on the return on investment that appears to be achievable by getting a specific message to a particular, definable market—group or groups of customers—at a particular time. For instance, if a computer manufacturer had a specific product aimed at college students, those students, as well as the parents of those students, could constitute a target market. The company might advertise and use promotions in campus newspapers and magazines to reach students. They might link to Web sites that are popular with students. They might target reporters whose messages can feature promotional activities and materials in magazines, newspapers, radio, and television that are frequently used by college students. The company also might target administrators on college campuses. Thus, we can think of student customers as primary targets, which are targets that can receive a message directly through media channels, and as secondary targets, which are targets that can be reached through other targeted audiences. These targeted audiences might buy a computer for a student or they might pass the message to the student that a specific brand of computer was for sale at a special price for college students.

Targets can be defined through public relations and marketing research. Sampling techniques can be used to segment larger populations into subpopulations based on some demographic, sociographic, or psychographic profile.

Broadcasting messages to targeted audiences works on the mass dissemination of information into media outlets where the target market or public may encounter the message. If the target population is 5 percent of a larger audience, the message might be designed and featured so that it could attract the targeted market's attention among many other messages. One of the challenges of public relations is to get messages to targets, often by passing them through other audiences and communication vehicles, and hence relating to the old maxim of reaching media that influence the intended target audiences in which the attempt is made to elicit some behavioral change or action. In a magazine, for instance, among the stories that many readers of the magazine might encounter, the organization would target placement and message appeal to increase the likelihood that the individuals in the intended market would stop to read the news item about the product or service; likewise for that target to listen to or watch a broadcast news segment.

A broadcast occurs when many channels are used or the channel reaches many audiences, most of which are not targeted. In contrast, a narrow cast results when a channel reaches only the intended or targeted audience. An employee newsletter is a narrowcast channel intended to reach employees of targets of messages especially designed for them. So, too, would be the annual financial report of a publicly traded company when it reaches intended or current shareholders of the company's stock.

Much of what has been said previously focuses on markets and audiences targeted with messages designed to sell products and services. Obviously, employees would be a public, but not a market. Activists would be a public. A company might target a message on some issue of concern to be received by the activists. So, too, the company might target persons and groups who are likely to agree with the company and take its side on an issue. During a crisis, one of the challenges is to prepare clear, informative, and credible messages that are targeted to a wide array of audiences. The crisis is the central theme, but the target audience may vary and the message must be tailored to each audience.

Ultimately, both an intended audience whose behavior you wish to somehow influence and media must be thoroughly considered when reviewing the checklist of who to target. Decisions on who to target stem from what must be accomplished and why, which are key considerations in determining how to approach a target. For instance, goals to increase awareness of a product, service, or situation, driving traffic to a corporation or entity, increasing business or sales, educating various publics about important topics or services, and reinforcing brand image are likely the most common goals and objectives. A typical outline of who to target might then read: current and potential customers, third parties who guide those primary customers, employees who double as influencers but who are also customers, potential partner organizations, and the ever-present and crucial media that influence the above.

This last component of securing coverage in targeted media to publicize the cause, initiative, or campaign is critical and where careful selection of media distribution lists becomes key. As previously noted, most public relations plans, after listing the intended targets, include the seemingly generic phrase of "media that influence the above" to complete a campaign's list of targets. This is actually a crucial ingredient in any communications plan that helps define the types of media targets likely to be reached with the coverage of the targeted media outlets—print or electronic.

The identification of intended targets is a key determinant in developing media lists. Generally, separate lists will be customized for trade and consumer audiences, with broadcast, print, and electronic media all being considered for maximizing message dissemination. Although trade outlets (usually publications and Web sites) deal with specific industries, consumer media are mainstream in nature, providing messages appropriate for the "common man." Keeping this in mind, news releases must also be customized to reach these various targets. For instance, although the introduction of a new motor oil would require a media release to garner mainstream coverage (outside of only paid advertising) to get the public to buy it, a more strategic approach would be to first target trade audiences through automotive publications, for example, to reach the technicians and mechanics who can influence or recommend what brand their customers should use. Similarly, a hospital system may want to tailor various releases to highlight certain information that would be pertinent to targets that patronize particular facilities, taking into account demographics such as socioeconomic status and ethnicity that likely will vary depending upon the location of the different hospitals. A third example presents itself with community relations, targeting different editions or zones of a major metropolitan newspaper or calling attention to members of a neighborhood or area of town who fall within a community newspaper's delivery area.

All the possible options and variations of a target audience should be considered, because media are also broken down by such demographics as ethnicity, age, and socioeconomic status. This line of thought should be continued when trying to determine market scope as well. Location of target audience base will factor in when deciding among international, national, regional, or local markets. It will probably be a combination of more than just one, with some international targets even being found locally. For example, several large urban areas, such as Houston, Los Angeles, and New York City, have myriad subcultures that follow news outlets apart from the major television networks and dominant daily newspapers. Most experienced public relations professionals have a collection of media lists that range from the obvious mainstream news desks to Hispanic, African American, and Asian programming and publications, as well as society lists, parent and child publications, newsletters for the elderly, women's magazines, and medical target media.

In considering targets, it also is important to consider the types of mediums that most likely appeal to specific groups. Again, age, socioeconomic status, and cultural mores often help determine whether a particular target audience would be more prone to respond to television, radio, newspapers, magazines, or electronic outlets.

So, while public relations practitioners initially identify desired target audiences, they most often reach those targets by procuring placement in the media. And, ultimately, measuring impressions and reach help to evaluate the success of a campaign in not just reaching but also influencing those target audiences to act in a certain way that helps achieve an organization's goals and objectives.

—*Robert L. Heath and Lisa K. Merkl*

See also Advertising; Goals; Impressions; Investor relations; Marketing; Narrowcasting/broadcasting; Objectives; Promotion; Publicity; Reach; Strategies; Tactics

THEORY OF REASONED ACTION

Theory of reasoned action contributes to the understanding of persuasion theory and human motivation by explaining how actions are the product of behavioral intentions to act in one way rather than some other. Persuasion theory is a broad approach to explain the cognitive and behavioral aspects of human choice and behavior. That body of academic thought features the choices people make as voluntary actions that reflect in various ways behavioral intention. The logic of this aspect of persuasion theory is that persons, through self-persuasion or the influence of others, make choices and act as a reflection of their behavioral intentions.

Martin Fishbein and Icek Ajzen are credited with the theory of reasoned action as an extension of their information integration theory, which builds upon principles and predictions of subjective expected utilities theory. This body of persuasion theory features human behavior and choice as voluntary. Accordingly, behavior is neither the product of drives nor independent of individual volition. As such, this body of theory and research approaches human actions as the product of reasoning where many factors impinge on choices. As such, the theory of reasoned action sees human behavior as multifaceted, and therefore not easily manipulated by any single influence. It focuses on people as decision makers and wants to understand the dynamics of such decisions.

The theory of reasoned action postulates that behavioral intention to act one way or another is the result of two factors. The first is an individual's attitude toward the behavior. The second is based on the perception of what the targeted individual thinks important others would want him or her to do. Thus, persons consider what opinion leaders, of various kinds, think is the preferred behavior.

As explained by information integration theory, an attitude toward a behavior is the sum of all of any person's beliefs about the behavior and the evaluations (positive or negative) of the behavior. For instance, a person might believe that brushing one's teeth (a) reduces the likelihood of dental decay, (b) brightens one's smile, and (c) cleans one's breath. Thus, the attitude toward the behavior is the product of three beliefs. Next, the theory would ask whether the person sees these beliefs as having a positive or negative evaluation. Advertisers and dentists would like to assume that all three beliefs carry positive evaluations. Thus, if they looked at the intention of one person, they can conclude that he or she has a positive attitude toward the behavior of brushing teeth. Marketers of toothpaste and toothbrushes would see this attitude as positive toward their campaign objectives. Also, dentists who want to reduce damage to teeth as part of a constructive program of dental hygiene will also see this attitude toward behavior as supporting their efforts.

The second part of the theory rests on each individual's perceptions of what important others would prefer that person to do. This means simply that people consider what others think is good or bad behavior as part of their efforts to form intentions to act one way or another. People, through social connections, think about what others think is best, right, or proper. They take such considerations into count when deciding what to do. What's more, not everyone's opinions count the same amount to the person making the decision. Parents quickly realize the impact their children's friends have on decisions. Adolescent claims that "everyone has X or is doing Y" is important to their children's decision. "What will people think if I X" suggests the conversational importance of others' preferences as part of various decisions. People want to please, or at least not displease, certain people more than others by what they do. Thoughts of this kind influence the choices they make. These thoughts of what others think, expect, and prefer are called subjective norms. In conversation and through other means of forming intentions, people learn and refine the subjective norms they use to make choices.

Theorists note that behavioral intentions are a product of seeking positives and avoiding negatives. A negative outcome, based on the example above, would be to have tooth decay. Most people, one assumes, do not think of that as a positive health outcome. A positive outcome would be brighter teeth or fresher breath. One imagines that yellowed teeth and stale breath are not viewed positively.

In terms of subjective norms, adolescents are likely to view peers as important others. What mom or dad thinks about brushing teeth has less to do with their children's perception of being seen as acceptable than do friends. Moreover, fresh breath and whiter teeth are likely to be more salient beliefs than is tooth decay for dating-age individuals. In contrast, business colleagues may see these as positives but not for romantic but business and career reasons.

Thus, this theory helps communicators and marketers to understand what behavioral incentives people hold central to their decisions. If people think positively of fresh breath, dental hygiene, and white teeth, is it manipulative to feature toothpaste and toothbrushes as being able to deliver these positive outcomes? At least it seems ethical if the products will actually deliver on the marketers' product feature claims. As such, this theory is an extension of its distant ancestor, learning theory, which postulates that people learn attitudes and behaviors as ways of solving problems needed to seek rewards and avoid negative outcomes.

Publicity and promotion campaigns often draw on the principles of this theory in support of marketing and advertising efforts. Fundraising, for instance, can invite people to support the symphony or feed needy children. If someone does not have a positive attitude toward either charitable outcome, the fundraiser is going to be unsuccessful. Their efforts might be enhanced if they tell the targeted person that some influential opinion leader supports the benefits. For this reason, fundraising may enlist the visible participation of a celebrity. But if the person who is targeted wants to spend that part of his or her budget on a trip with friends, the campaign is likely to be unsuccessful. For this reason, the theory offers predictions that are more likely to help segment markets than to offer ways to effect easy and dramatic changes in attitude, belief, and behavior.

Nevertheless, changes in behavioral intentions can and do occur, as explained by the theory. Three options are possible to account for these changes. One is the formation of a positive attitude toward the behavior where previously there was a neutral or negative attitude toward the behavior. One can imagine how a series of messages relevant to needy children might, over time, lead to the formation of an attitude supportive of charitable giving to that cause for persons who did not originally have that attitude. They might also become aware of subjective norms they had not known or attended to previously. Also, they may reorient the weights and influences of various important persons to form a new subjective norm. For instance, if many friends voice commitment to supporting needy children, the targeted person might well adopt a similar norm. And the person can redefine the complex of relationships between norms, attitudes, and influencers.

This theory is maturing to a new level called the *theory of planned behavior.* It reasons that one more concept must be added to increase the predictability of the theory. To this end, the theory of planned behavior adds the concept of perceived behavioral control. Simply, this variable is a measure of individuals' perception of the ease or difficulty of performing the target behavior. Similar to the work of other researchers and theorists, this theory postulates that individuals' intentions are coupled to their perceived self-efficacy in accomplishing the action. It is easy to imagine, for instance, someone writing a check for a contribution to serve needy children. Such action does not, in and of itself, require much of a sense of self-efficacy. A more complex but predictive use of this variable is to imagine that the targeted individual will likely estimate how much efficacy his or her contribution will have in conjunction with those of others. Simply stated, the theory analyzes how much efficacy the person perceives is necessary to take meaningful action. Can the charitable action be accomplished and will it do any good? For this reason, one can imagine, that fundraisers include in promotional presentations

evidence that shows how charitable contributions accomplish a collective goal, such as helping needy children.

The theory of reasoned action offers many options for practitioners and theorists who want to help explain the dynamics of human volition, the choices people make that can be influenced by public relations.

—*Robert L. Heath*

See also Advertising; Fundraising; Information integration theory; Marketing; Persuasion theory; Subjective expected utilities theory

Bibliography

Ajzen, I. (1985). From intentions to actions: A theory of planned behavior. In J. Kuhl & J. Beckmann (Eds.), *Action control: From cognition to behavior* (pp. 11–39). Berlin: Springer-Verlag.

Ajzen, I. (1991). The theory of planned behavior. *Organizational Behavior and Human Decision Processes, 50,* 179–211.

Ajzen, I., & Fishbein, M. (1980). *Understanding attitudes and predicting social behavior.* Englewood Cliffs, NJ: Prentice Hall.

O'Keefe, D. J. (2002). *Persuasion theory & research.* Thousand Oaks, CA: Sage.

THEORY-BASED PRACTICE

Theory-based practice is public relations practice guided by theoretic generalizations that shed light on the situation at hand; it is thought to be more effective than public relations conducted by intuition or habit, as in the "we do it this way because we have always done it this way" approach. Theory can be defined as any symbolic generalization culled from empirical evidence that is interpreted and is used to describe, explain, understand, predict, and control phenomena under study or consideration. Theory lends a perspective, or way of looking at a situation, that helps determine understanding and the best course of action to address the situation. Different interpretations of a symbolic generalization are likely to stimulate a proliferation of additional theories. Also, different members of a community—such as the public relations profession—are likely to formulate and employ different but possibly related theories. There is no one theory that belongs to a particular community, just as there is no one shared worldview from which theory derives, although similar language pertaining to theory might be shared. Theories are seldom static; on the contrary, theories tend to be dynamic, growing entities that cannot be fully understood if they are divorced from the dynamics of their development.

In traditional science, predictions in the form of hypotheses are derived from theory and can be tested. Theory is flexible, and different methodologies and units of analysis can be used to test it. Such testing of hypotheses may result in the identification of relevant variables or attributes and the development of models of relationships between or among these variables. A common result of testing a theory is a revised or new theory that determines refined or new applications for practice. According to Stephen Littlejohn (2002), theory development is a continual process or formulating and testing sets of concepts believed to explain how things operate.

Generalizations—or theories—useful to public relations can come from many different fields and bodies of knowledge, most often in the social sciences, such as psychology, sociology, and communication, including rhetoric and persuasion. Some critics of public relations have questioned whether the field is worthy of scholarship and theory-building efforts, and other critics charge that public relations merely applied theories developed in and by other disciplines. Some supporters of public relations counter that productive theory development is essential for public relations research—or, for that matter, any academic discipline—to be called a science.

M. A. Ferguson (1984) wrote that working from the assumption that theory is not an explanation based on supposition or conjecture but that theory is a way to understand events and to predict research findings supporting the theory, it can be argued that practitioners who question the value of theory in practice have two choices: they can make decisions in their practice of public relations based on intuition or conjecture—essentially, "flying by the seat of their pants"; or they can make their decisions based on generalizations culled from empirical evidence in a scientific approach to practice.

An example of a predominant theory of public relations is "excellence theory." Proposed by James E. Grunig and Todd Hunt in their 1984 book *Managing Public Relations,* the theory basically suggests that there are four types or models of public relations—press agentry or publicity, public information, one-way asymmetric persuasion, and two-way symmetric communication—and that public relations practitioners who practice the two-way symmetric model for the organization they are representing are more likely to practice "excellent" public relations. This theory has proven to be very heuristic, in that it has spawned considerable additional research, both by the theory's original authors as well as by dozens of other public relations scholars. Another example is "contingency theory," which, according to Amanda Cancel, Glen Cameron, Lynne Sallot, and Henry Mitoork (1997), suggests that public relations practitioners decide their courses of action depending on the widely varying attributes of each situation in public relations practice, and that the situations range on a continuum from total advocacy on behalf of the organization being represented, at one end, to accommodation of the organization's publics, at the other end.

A good theory goes beyond description to explain the interrelationships of variables and to predict likely effects and outcomes. In general, theories are broader conceptualizations than models that delineate or map connections between variables in a theory. For example, the RACE acronym—research, action planning, communication, evaluation—popularly thought to summarize the process of public relations practice, is considered by scholars to be a model rather than a theory. There are also types of theories; "normative" theory is often described as the ideal that may be aspired to in practice, while "positive" theory may be prescribed for practical application, and "grounded" theory may explain common, everyday occurrences. Paradigms are a system or setup of theoretical beliefs.

Scholars in communication-related disciplines such as public relations have been encouraged to build theories of the "middle range" that would yield hypotheses about a limited range of phenomena that could be rigorously tested. These middle-range theories were thought to be superior to speculative "grand" theories and to limited, isolated empirical generalizations, such as those concerning effects of fear appeals on attitude change. Likewise, according to R. T. Craig (1993), isolated empirical generalizations or "sets of laws" were thought to be inferior to conceptually integrated middle-range theories because they lack organizing and heuristic advantages. However, according to Thomas Kuhn (1970) and Fred Suppe (1977), given that an individual's personal background—including knowledge, beliefs, intellectual capacity, training, and experience—can be relevant in interpreting a theory, the idea that a group of scholars must share a worldview, as traditionally required by science, is being challenged. It seems more likely that groups of scientists in a particular community share the same or similar language about a theory rather than share identical interpretations about a theory. Additionally, as Craig wrote, because of increasing interdisciplinary discourse, such as that stimulated by postmodernism, deconstruction, critical/cultural, and other influences, it has been argued that theory can be better conceived as practical, historically situated discourse rather than the more traditional scientific view of theory-as-knowledge.

Mark McElreath and John Blamphin (1994) wrote that, in the 1980s and 1990s, a series of Delphi studies were conducted involving dozens of leading public relations scholars and practitioners to identify contemporary priority research questions in public relations with the result that gaps in the Public Relations Society of America's Body of Knowledge were identified. The studies concluded that more sophisticated theories are available to understand the managing of public relations and should be used, including development of more systems-based contingency and situational theories; symbolic interaction theories; theories regarding legal and public policy issues, feminist concepts of equity and nurturing, ethics, and conflict resolution;

and multicultural general systems theories among increasingly differentiated publics.

In a recent investigation of the status of theory building by public relations scholars Lynne Sallot, Lisa Lyon, Carolina Acosta-Alzuru, and Karyn Jones (2003), nearly 750 abstracts or articles published in *Public Relations Review, Journal of Public Relations Research,* and its predecessor, *Public Relations Research Annual,* since their inceptions through the year 2000, were subjected to content analysis. According to M. A. Ferguson (1984), nearly 20 percent of articles analyzed were found to have contributed to theory development in public relations compared to only 4 percent of abstracts studied in an earlier analysis of *Public Relations Review* from its inception to 1984. From her analysis, Ferguson concluded that there were three overall foci of research conducted in public relations from 1975 to 1984 that lent themselves to productive theory development: *social responsibility and ethics, social issues and issues management,* and *public relationships.* She predicted that the area of public relationships offered the best opportunity for theory development in public relations.

However, the more recent study by Sallot, Lyon, Acosta-Alzuru, and Jones (2003) found that no dominant theoretical paradigms per se have yet emerged in public relations. Excellence theory is arguably the closest public relations comes, at this time, to having a paradigm, but only accounted for 13 percent of articles that developed theory. Theory building about public relationships was next most prevalent, followed by ethics and social responsibility, crisis response, critical-cultural, feminism and diversity, and international topics. Such growth in theory development in the academic publishing about public relations is thought to reflect increased application of theory in public relations practice. Joep Cornelissen, after considering how practitioners interpret, reframe, and adapt theories to practice, suggested in 2000 a "translation model" of theory application based on the premise that scientific knowledge is seldom used in unaltered form in practice. This and other interdisciplinary influences are expected to continue to contribute to ever more theory building in public relations, as evidenced in part by the range of topics covered in Robert L. Heath's (2001) *Handbook of Public Relations* and in this *Encyclopedia of Public Relations.*

—*Lynne M. Sallot*

See also Best practices

Bibliography

Cancel, A. E., Cameron, G. T., Sallot, L. M., & Mitrook, M. A. (1997). It depends: A contingency theory of accommodation in public relations. *Journal of Public Relations Research, 9*(1), 31–63.

Cornelissen, J. P. (2000). Toward an understanding of the use of academic theories in public relations practice. *Public Relations Review, 26*(3), 315–326.

Craig, R. T. (1993). Why are there so many communication theories? *Journal of Communication, 43*(3), 26–33.

Ferguson, M. A. (1984, August). *Building theory in public relations: Interorganizational relationships as a public relations paradigm.* Paper presented to the Public Relations Division at the annual conference of the Association for Education in Journalism and Mass Communication, Gainesville, Florida.

Grunig, J. E., & Hunt, T. (1984). *Managing public relations.* New York: Holt, Rinehart & Winston.

Heath, R. L. (Ed.). (2001). *Handbook of public relations.* Thousand Oaks, CA: Sage.

Kuhn, T. S. (1970). *The structure of scientific revolutions* (2nd ed.). Chicago: University of Chicago Press.

Littlejohn, S. W. (2002). *Theories of human communication.* Belmont, CA: Wadsworth/Thomson Learning.

McElreath, M., & Blamphin, J. (1994). Partial answers to priority research questions—and gaps—found in PRSA's body of knowledge. *Journal of Public Relations Research, 6*(2), 69–104.

Sallot, L. M., Lyon, L. J., Acosta-Alzuru, C., & Jones, K. O. (2003). From aardvark to zebra: A new millennium analysis of theory development in public relations academic journals. *Journal of Public Relations Research, 15*(1), 27–89.

Suppe, F. (Ed.). (1977). *The structure of scientific theories* (2nd ed.). Urbana: University of Illinois Press.

THIRD-PARTY ENDORSEMENT

For more than a half-century, public relations practitioners have touted *implied third-party endorsements* effects as a rationale for obtaining exposure for clients in the news and entertainment portions of mass media.

Conventional wisdom in the field argued that media organizations implicitly expressed their approval of organizations, products, services, candidates, or causes whenever they devoted coverage to them. Importantly, no specific recommendation or explicitly positive comments were required. The mere fact that the media covered a particular topic was sufficient justification to suggest an endorsement effect.

Two kinds of implied endorsements are particularly important for public relations professionals: publicity endorsements and product placement endorsements.

PUBLICITY ENDORSEMENTS.

Claims about third-party endorsement effects were first invoked most frequently when practitioners and clients compared the relative benefits of publicity (coverage in the editorial portions of the press) to paid advertising. Mass media researchers during the middle of the 20th century generally agreed the news media were a powerful force that could confer status, legitimacy and credibility on the topics they covered. In the same vein, research had consistently shown that people distrusted advertising and avoided, resisted or counter-argued with claims that appeared as advertising.

Research in 1980s and 1990s challenged claims about publicity's third-party endorsement effects and the superiority of news versus advertising. More than a dozen experimental tests were published where identical messages were either labeled as news or advertising, or presented in editorial versus advertising formats.

Studies directly comparing groups exposed to one format versus the other suggested a clear preference among participants for information presented in editorial formats. But the results were not consistent when commonly used experimental measures of message impact were analyzed: topic recognition or recall, message learning, attitude change or behavioral intent.

Kirk Hallahan contended that the differences previously attributed to third-party endorsements effects could be explained by (1) people's strong dislike for advertising compared with news, and (2) different cognitive processing rules that are invoked based on the content class (news versus advertising) in which a message appears.

Because news values stress the importance of impartiality and balance in coverage, media audiences expect the language and tone of news to avoid excessively laudatory claims, which is why people might be more accepting of messages presented as news versus advertising. Journalists are expected to be impartial—to *tell*, not to *sell*. However, if the language used in news is excessively laudatory, the credibility of the source can be compromised. When it sounds like a journalist is a confederate of a product promoter, any advantage associated with publicity versus advertising is diminished dramatically.

Similarly, when a person is highly involved in a topic, Hallahan found that content class made little difference. Indeed, people who are actively seeking information were open to obtaining information from a wide range of sources. Although people understand that the purpose of ads is to show products in a highly favorable light, individuals who are highly involved in seeking information or in making a judgment will disregard the source and will pay attention to ads. Audiences know that advertisers are knowledgeable—they must simply be wary about misrepresentations or omitted facts. Some evidence also suggests that today's young people are more open to obtaining information from many sources, and might not be as predisposed to news as prior generations.

PRODUCT PLACEMENT ENDORSEMENTS

Product placements represent a separate form of implied media endorsement that has gained popularity as organizations seek exposure in the entertainment media.

Product placements involve the conspicuous use of a company's product, facility, or name in television shows, motion pictures, or other entertainment fare. The client's product, logo, or sign is often incidental to the action being depicted. So branded products are used as props in natural ways that call little attention to themselves.

One benefit derived from product placements involves additional exposure for the brand or idea. Evidence is inconclusive about whether audiences believe any endorsement is implied. To be most effective, products must be an integral part of the action, such as E.T.'s penchant for "Reese's Pieces" in the 1982 movie blockbuster *E.T.: The Extra-Terrestrial*.

For many years, automobile companies maintained offices in Hollywood to provide cars free of charge for use in movies and TV productions. Scenes of a star behind the wheel suggested that the featured model of car was exciting and glamorous. However, it is doubtful that viewers actually thought the actor drove the same car in real life. Today client organizations continue to seek product placement opportunities and employ agents in Hollywood to routinely screen scripts for possible promotional opportunities and other product tie-ins.

In the same way, many destination resorts, theme parks, and cruise ship lines encourage production companies to use their sites as settings for movies and TV shows. Many states and larger municipalities also court movie and TV production companies to shoot on location—for both the benefits derived by the local economy and for the potential worldwide exposure. Other organizations—ranging from the U.S. military to various special interest groups—maintain offices in Hollywood that work with producers of entertainment fare so their activities or issues can be incorporated in entertainment shows and will be presented in a favorable light.

Such placements are important forms of implied media endorsement even though no direct recommendation or promotional message appears. Although many consumers have become aware of commercialization of product placements, many others have not—or simply forget later that a commercial "plug" is involved. Meanwhile, vestiges of these powerful images can linger in the audience's memory.

—*Kirk Hallahan*

See also Advertising; Endorsement; Involvement; Publicity

Bibliography

Hallahan, K. (1999a). Content class as a contextual cue in the processing of publicity versus advertising. *Journal of Public Relations Research, 11,* 293–320.

Hallahan, K. (1999b). No, Virginia—It's not true what they say about publicity's third-party endorsement effect. *Public Relations Review, 25,* 331–350.

TRADE ASSOCIATIONS (AND HILL & KNOWLTON'S ROLE IN)

Trade associations have played a major role in the history and practice of public relations because they offer to their sponsoring corporate members an opportunity to pool financial and intellectual resources to work together to set industry standards, to engage in research and policy formation, and to set intra-industry standards of performance without violating antitrust guidelines.

Trade associations are formal organizations constituted by members of a specific industry, such as the chemical manufacturers, or industrial function, such as the National Association of Manufacturers. These formal associations can create a joint stonewall of opposition against all threats experienced by the members. Or, in a more ethical and proactive mode, these associations help the member organizations to set operating standards, lobby public policy issues, develop and communicate issue positions, implement standards of corporate responsibility, and cooperate on behalf of the public interest. Such associations must not set prices or otherwise create a monopoly that would breach antitrust and fair practices legislation. Thus, the focus of trade associations is more on public policy and reputational matters than on marketing strategies and pricing.

Trade associations grew in popularity and power as similar industries matured to realize that although they had to maintain competition, they were faced with similar challenges such a strikes, regulation, legislation, and public criticism. Leaders in the trade association movement realized the virtue of setting standards of ethical performance and holding members to these standards to reduce

the likelihood that their actions would lead to a legitimacy gap. Mutual interests led to mutual aid, but such initiatives could not be seen as dominating the public policy forum. One primary virtue of a sound trade association is its ability to speak for an industry or function with a single voice. Another is to set high, self-imposed, and self-policed standards of operation.

Under the leadership of John Hill, Hill & Knowlton became one of the major agencies working for an impressive array of trade associations. Hill & Knowlton believed it could serve an industry best by counseling it in its entirety instead of merely serving one member. On many occasions, Hill & Knowlton served an individual client's needs and interests by also working for the industry. No clearer case of this practice exists than its long-term counseling and communication activity for the steel industry through the American Iron and Steel Institute (AISI).

Hill did not innovate the concept of a trade association, but he and his agency leaders raised the art of public relations service to industries to a high level. Ivy Lee was one of the pioneers in this regard, working for the Anthracite Coal Operators during a hotly contested labor strike. On Lee's advice, the American Petroleum Institute (API) was formed in 1919. API's influence continues nearly a century later as petroleum policy continues to evolve. Pendleton Dudley provided professional service to the American Meatpackers Association, which was formed (1906) to deal with issues raised by muckrakers such as Upton Sinclair in *The Jungle.* Carl Byoir served the interest of the Eastern Railroads against Pennsylvania truckers, which in turn had the professional services of David Charnay's Allied Public Relations Associates. Lee & Ross, the firm of Ivy Lee (sustained after his death) and Tommy Ross worked for the Copper and Brass Research Association (42 major copper companies) and the Cotton Textile Institute.

However influential these agencies were, none was more central to the U. S. economy than was Hill & Knowlton. The cornerstone account of Hill & Knowlton's trade association business was the iron and steel industry (AISI). That gave Hill the incentive, during the Great Depression, to open an office in New York City that became the center of his agency as it eventually achieved national and international status. Hill believed that industry needed a voice. He was a conservative on economic matters, believing that basic big industries were the foundation of the American economy. In Hill's opinion, the relationship between these industries and the markets and publics they affected, however, was not one sided. He believed that industry could not operate without the permission and support of its constituencies. This support, he realized and counseled, must be earned; it could not be assumed or taken for granted. Communication was vital to the relationship in order to foster support and understanding. Counseling could position each industry so that it operated in the public interest. It had to earn its right to operate by serving society, which in turn had the right to understand and approve of the industry's actions and policies.

The AISI was formed in 1908 as an evolution from a long-term loose association of iron masters originating in 1855. Five principal purposes formed the rationale for the Institute. It was designed to promote the interest of the industry, a purpose that was obvious. To do so, it was intended to gather statistics and monitor issues. The institute engaged in investigations and research. Based on this information, it created a forum for information exchange and discussion on matters that affected the industry. It promoted the use of iron and steel. As it matured, in some part due to counseling by Hill & Knowlton, the Institute sought to increase understanding of the role that steel, iron, and profits played in the economy. It fought socialization and nationalization and lauded the fact that steelworkers were the best paid laborers, a fact used during strike talks. The institute applauded its workplace safety record. It worked to make the steel industry a good neighbor, a vital part of each community where it operated. Finally, it championed its technological innovation to make America the steel and iron capital of the world. Policy battles, such as environmentalism, would demonstrate that some of its claims were overstated by the changing standards of time, but each era brings new challenges

to industry trade associations and their public relations practitioners.

In addition to counseling, Hill & Knowlton assisted with the industry's corporate image advertising campaign. This effort featured the positive role steel played in the American economy. Hill & Knowlton drafted, obtained executive approval, and issued press releases for the industry at key moments. It worked for expansion of the industry's *and* individual companies' community relations programs. It prepared and published *Steel Bulletins and Steelways,* which was a trade publication that reached 100,000 readers. Hill & Knowlton provided monitoring efforts to scan, identify, analyze, and track issues, such as efforts to nationalize the industry, the effects of inflation on pricing, and the relationship between the industry and its labor unions. Hill & Knowlton received and interpreted clippings that were useful in its media relations program for the industry. It supported the industry's lobbying efforts by assisting in the development of issue position, monitoring opinion, and working with key legislators.

In addition to steel and iron, Hill & Knowlton served as the agency of record for the Licensed Beverage Industries, Aerospace Industries Association of America, Aircraft Industries Association, American Petroleum Institute, Newsprint Information Committee, Pharmaceutical Manufacturers Association, The Savings Banks Association of the State of New York, Tobacco Industry Research Committee, Tobacco Institute, Natural Gas and Oil Resources Committee, American Forest Products Industries, Manufacturing Chemists' Association, Can Manufacturers Institute, Copper and Brass Research Association, National Association of Manufacturers, Glassware Institute of America, American Bakers Association, American Butter Institute, Anthracite Institute, Association of General and Surety Companies, National Fertilizer Association, National Air Council, National Machine Tool Builders Association, National Retail Dry Goods Association, Outdoor Advertising Association, Shipbuilders Council of America, Association of Soap and Glycerine Producers, Sunglass Institute, and Wine Institute. This list is offered to suggest the abundance of trade associations, these being but a few. Of more importance, these trade associations suggest the influential position in the economy of the United States held by Hill & Knowlton during John Hill's days of the 1940s to 1960s.

One of the standing rules of Hill's practice was that he would not allow his firm to represent front groups, those whose names and identities do not give publics the opportunity to know the true identity and motives of the client. Thus, for instance, if his firm were representing the steel, tobacco, chemical, or aviation industry interests, Hill believed that any reporter or member of a public had a right to know the identity of the client.

Often trade associations bring together a variety of interests, some of which may have various conflicts. For instance, the composition of the Licensed Beverage Industries (LBI) included distillers, rectifiers, importers, wholesalers, package stores, and taverns. Among the issues addressed by the association were bootlegging, import tariffs and fees, state-owned package stores, monopoly package stores, and uniform product quality. Key publics included schools and ministers, as well as state and federal legislators looking for opportunities to raise "sin taxes." Product advertising using romantic circumstances and alluring images were topics for corporate responsibility. The industry joined forces with law officials to fight bootlegging not only because of the tax issue (favored by the states) but also on the basis of product safety (an industry issue). In these ways, the association found ways of operating in the public interest while fostering the interest of the industry.

That equation was vitally important for Hill's agency. Hill's leadership was evident in the culture of Hill & Knowlton. He was an economic conservative. He believed in the free enterprise system, but argued in his books and to his clients that the public interest must guide the positioning and communication policies of each industry. Each side must never assume that they deserve the goodwill of key publics. They must earn that goodwill, the opportunity for public relations counseling. They must communicate to achieve mutual understanding with their key publics, the opportunity for public relations communication in all of its forms.

One of the problems of representing trade associations is managing the delicate balance between the industries' needs and preferences against those of its markets and key publics. The LBI is an excellent example of how the tax issue could not be carried to an extreme without endangering the public interest on another measure. Legislators could look to the industry as a source of tax revenue. But as the cost of legal alcohol rose, so did the incentive to buy from bootleggers. Thus, the taxing authorities as well as the industry could lose revenue and the public could be motivated to engage in illegal behavior that could also cause health problems from the consumption of unsafe alcohol. Alcohol abuse was a potent aspect of the work of the industry. In the 1950s, the industry was concerned about the public policy implications of alcoholism, sales to minors, and drunk driving. Hill & Knowlton worked to help the industry adopt a responsible drinking mentality and to get its side of these issues out to key publics, especially opinion makers.

Tobacco became one of Hill & Knowlton's most longtime clients as well as perhaps its most controversial. Some of that controversy continues to date on the assumption that the scientific rebuttal campaign style initiated by Hill & Knowlton and the industry in the 1950s kept people from fully knowing what health hazards might be associated with cigarettes especially. Hill & Knowlton was brought into client relationship with the industry in late 1953. The objective was to get balanced media coverage to combat what the industry believed were irresponsible and unscientific claims about the health hazards of the use of its products. For more than 15 years, Hill & Knowlton worked with the industry, in part to change its positioning on matters such as responsible use of the product, as well as on the battle for sound science in policy making regarding restrictions on cigarette advertising such as warning labels.

Hill & Knowlton was frequently at odds with labor, large and small. For instance, it worked for the steel and the shipbuilders industries against laborers' claims. Such issues were never clear-cut. What is a fair wage, especially given the profitability of an industry and its role in the national economy? Hill & Knowlton recognized the potential voice of labor in newspapers and other venues. One of the assumptions Hill & Knowlton made was that the public needed to be aware of the wages of labor and the profits of the industry. Fair wages is not a given. It is contestable. Hill & Knowlton served its industrial clients to help give their view visibility so the public could decide where to throw its weight and support.

No matter how lofty the client, Hill and his agency never lost sight of the fact that public relations must appeal to the public. Hill never doubted that the public was the sovereign entity in society. A client's case was only as good as its ability to convince a public that deserved the truth supplied through open communication. If the case could not be made, then the public had spoken. Industry must constantly reposition and redefine itself to keep pace with changes in public preferences and expectations. These fundamental principles were championed by John Hill and made known to Hill & Knowlton clients as a condition of contract. Never would John Hill or his senior colleagues at Hill & Knowlton believe they could engineer consent. Consent was a challenge to be earned by sound policies and effective communication.

Business was the business of America. That principle was firmly embossed on the mind of senior management of Hill & Knowlton from the 1940s to 1960s when Hill's role with the agency ended. But Hill reminded his colleagues that good business was right and deserved the strongest public relations. He knew that public relations was more than communication. It was relationship building. He recognized that without the proper relationships, even the strongest and most powerful industry could fail or at least suffer from public rebuke.

These points are evident in his agency's work for the Manufacturing Chemists' Association in the 1950s. The industry had relationship problems. Without reducing those problems, its lobbying efforts would be hampered. It had to address problems, some of which persist to this date: air and water pollution, tariffs, community relationships, safety, need for recognition for the role the industry plays in the economy and the American lifestyle,

the industry as an attractive place to work, and the understanding of the industry's contribution to a stronger economy, public health, and better living.

Hill knew that industries needed to meet the expectations of the persons whom they touched and served. He advocated continual communication to get the point across from the industry's point of view. He learned by long experience that industry must listen to its critics and make strategic and honest changes. Operating with a pro-industry bias a mile wide, Hill worked to foster the innovation and dynamic changes of trade associations that could reposition an industry and give it a single voice. The client list amassed by his agency during his maturing years demonstrates from only one practitioner's agency the centrality of public relations to trade association relationship building for the good of the public interest and private enterprise.

Hill was explicit and succinct in his counsel to corporations and trade associations.

A corporation or an industry may find itself faced by unfavorable public opinion because people are unaware of the facts. The way is then open for the corporation to attempt to change the public attitude and to win people to its point of view. On the other hand it may be wise to change an unpopular policy, making a frank acknowledgement of need for change. Such declaration of honest intent will usually meet with public approval. (1958, p. 39)

—*Robert L. Heath*

See also Byoir, Carl; Hill, John Wiley; Lee, Ivy; Legitimacy and legitimacy gap

Bibliography

Cutlip, S. M. (1994). *The unseen power: Public relations, a history.* Hillsdale, NJ: Lawrence Erlbaum.

Hill, John W. (1958). *Corporate public relations: Arm of management.* New York: Harper & Brothers.

TRANSTHEORETICAL MODEL OF BEHAVIOR CHANGE

One of the more ambitious and useful models for promoting social and individual change comes from the work of James Prochaska, Carlo DiClemente, and their colleagues (1983, 1984, 1992, 1997). Through their review of some 200 theoretical approaches and paradigms, Prochaska and others have identified a set of principles and concepts common or integral to most change efforts. The resulting "transtheoretical" model therefore is an interdisciplinary amalgamation of many theories and philosophies of change, a distillation of best practices derived from disparate schools of thought and tested in a variety of settings and topics.

Undergirding this model is a set of assumptions. First, change does not occur in a single step, but rather through a series of (often nonlinear) stages that range from an initial state of lack of awareness to an eventual state of compliance. According to the model, individuals move through these stages while engaging in (or being subjected to) one or more processes of change. Transition from one stage to the next occurs as a result of shifts in an individual's "decisional balance," which can be, and often is, influenced by communication. As a result, this model is highly relevant to public relations professionals engaged in efforts to influence individuals' cognitions and attitudes and behaviors in a variety of contexts.

STAGES OF CHANGE

The transtheoretical model, sometimes referred to as the "stages of change" model, is best known for describing the transition process that individuals undergo when engaging in behavioral change. Through a series of questions in a standard protocol, researchers develop segments that correspond to the various stages in the change process. In the *precontemplation* stage, individuals do not recognize a need to change and often lack awareness of the problem or issue that may be adversely affecting them. Occasionally, individuals in this initial stage are aware of the problem but are unwilling to discuss it. Denial, rationalization, and fear of admitting failure are common characteristics of individuals in this stage.

In the next stage, *contemplation,* individuals recognize the existence of a problem, but are often waiting for a "magic moment" or simply engaging in wishful thinking. In this stage, which can last for days or years, individuals often think, discuss, and seek information about the problem and its various remedies.

At a certain point, contemplators become increasingly confident about the prospects of change and begin to focus their information search on the best course of action to take. In what is called a *preparation* stage, individuals may set a timetable for change, start turning away from old behaviors, and prepare for the inevitable adjustment that awaits once they commit to change.

The briefest stage, ironically, is the actual *action* stage, which occurs when an individual actually modifies her or his life by sacrificing old ways of thinking and behaving in favor of new ones.

Once the individual has actually attempted change, one of two things can occur (and often both do). First, the individual may engage in *maintenance* of the new behavior, which involves both an internal commitment as well as a resistance to external pressures in the form of peers and family members and unexpected situations that tend to trigger old behaviors. Alternatively, the individual may engage in *recycling* and relapse into those old behaviors. Sometimes this happens from the inherent difficulty in the proposed change, or perhaps from the realization that the costs of change (time, money, friends, and prestige) are simply too high.

Each stage can be characterized by differences in an individual's decisional balance, that is, the relative importance placed on the *pros* (perceived advantages) and *cons* (perceived disadvantages) of change, and in self-efficacy, that is, an individual's degree of confidence that she or he possesses the requisite skill, knowledge, and perseverance to change. In terms of decisional balance, "cons" inevitably exceed "pros" in the precontemplation stage, as the need for changing comfortable behavioral patterns may not even be recognized; cons and pros are fairly equivalent in contemplation; and pros must exceed cons for an individual to reach preparation. In terms of self-efficacy, confidence tends to be low in early stages of change, but must be very high if an individual is to reach the maintenance stage and remain committed to some new behavior.

APPLICATIONS

The transtheoretical model has numerous applications to public relations campaigns. First, most individuals are in the precontemplation stage for many issues and social problems, and yet many campaigns are designed for individuals in later stages (such as preparation). At best, this discontinuity can result in inefficient and wasted communication; at worst, it can result in boomerang effects and resentment from individuals who are not psychologically prepared for, or predisposed to, change but are being prodded to do so. Campaigns targeting precontemplators should raise awareness of a problem, trigger some initial consideration of pros and cons of change, and provide testimonials from others who have undergone change. Contemplators, on the other hand, typically are not suffering from an awareness deficit but rather lack of motivation. Communication efforts targeting these individuals should use emotional appeals and tip the decisional balance toward the advantages of change. For individuals in the preparation stage, the most useful information focuses on specific actions to be taken, that is, specific strategies for coping with the imminent change. Boosting individuals' self-efficacy is particularly important, as confidence is needed to take the next step of action. Once the new behavior is attempted, campaign messages targeting the segment of those who have changed should reinforce the new behavior and educate about ways of preventing recycling. If recycling does occur, campaign messages should focus on ways of restoring self-confidence and motivation, something that often requires interpersonal channels to have an impact.

The various mechanisms for conveying the previous campaign messages and achieving the previous effects are described by Prochaska and colleagues as *processes of change*. In the parlance of public relations, these processes constitute strategies for moving individuals from one stage to the next. In general, these processes involve changing the way individuals think or feel about an issue or problem or altering actual behaviors in an attempt to move individuals from one stage to the next. For example, campaign planners can design messages to increase awareness of an issue or problem among precontemplators ("consciousness raising") or to arouse emotions and motivate individuals to change ("dramatic relief"). Alternatively, campaign planners can alter physical environments in attempts to promote new patterns of behavior ("stimulus control") or offer new behavioral practices to replace old ones ("counter conditioning").

The transtheoretical model has attracted a great deal of attention from academics and professionals alike, many of whom have applied and tested it in different countries, with different issues and social problems, and with different population segments. It offers many new avenues for research and program planning to public relations professionals.

—Charles T. Salmon and Aileen Webb

Bibliography

Prochaska, J. O., & DiClemente, C. C. (1983). Stages and processes of self-change of smoking: Toward an integrative model of change. *Journal of Consulting and Clinical Psychology, 51,* 390–395.

Prochaska, J. O., & DiClemente, C. C. (1984). *The transtheoretical approach: Crossing traditional boundaries of therapy.* Homewood, IL: Dow Jones Irwin.

Prochaska, J. O., DiClemente, C. C., & Norcross, J. C. (1992). In search of how people change. *American Psychologist, 47*(9), 1102–1114.

Prochaska, J. O., & Velicer, W. F. (1997). The transtheoretical model of health behavior change. *American Journal of Health Promotion, 12,* 38–48.

TRAVEL AND TOURISM PUBLIC RELATIONS

With travel and tourism continuing among the top three global economic engines, the need for and opportunities in public relations in the travel and tourism industry continue to grow. Despite grim forecasts about the effects on tourism of faltering economies, terrorism, political instabilities, crime, and disease, in 2002 almost 715 million international tourist arrivals were registered, according to the United Nations–affiliated World Tourism Organization (WTO). This represents an increase of 22 million compared with 2001 and marks the first time that the number of international tourist arrivals has exceeded 700 million. By comparison, in 1956, when WTO first published statistics, there were 50 million worldwide international arrivals. Taking into account additional economic contributions of domestic travel, tourism in general continues to withstand tremendous challenges and remains robust overall in many nations' economies. The growth of travel and tourism public relations parallels the industry.

Eric Cohen (1972) wrote that, historically, it appears the words *tourist* and *tourism* were derived as a subcategory of traveler, historically separate from categories of travelers such as warriors, crusaders, or pilgrims. Linked to travels of English gentlemen on tour as part of their education and entertainment, the word *tourist* first appeared in English, with the *Oxford English Dictionary* dating the word *tourist* from 1800 and the word *tourism* from 1811. The word appeared as *touriste* in the French Robert dictionary in 1816 and *tourisme* in 1841, both derived from English.

A multilayered, overlapping, and interlocking distribution system of sellers and buyers of travel products makes travel and tourism big business for public relations. Travel suppliers—which include destination tourism-and-convention entities; hotels, resorts, and others providing accommodations; transportation conveyors, such as cruise lines and ships, airlines, trains, and motor coach operators; sightseeing tour operators and other ground infrastructures such as local car rental agencies, taxis, attractions, restaurants, duty-free shops, and souvenir retailers—are all travel sellers. At the other end of the travel selling-buying continuum is the traveling public, the ultimate buyers and consumers of travel products. In between are travel wholesalers and consolidators, who buy and package travel products from suppliers and then sell travel packages to retail travel agents or direct to ultimate consumer travelers, and retail travel agents, who buy travel products either directly from suppliers or from travel wholesalers or consolidators and then sell the travel products to ultimate consumer travelers.

Public relations practitioners may represent and act on behalf of any of the travel sellers—suppliers, wholesalers, or travel agents—with the purpose of building relationships with any of the travel buyers—wholesalers, travel agents, or consumers—in a bid to generate awareness, disseminate information, and attract brand preference and loyalty for the travel products represented.

Travel sellers may have public relations representation "in house" or may contract for representation with an independent firm specializing in travel and tourism public relations; it is not uncommon for travel sellers to have both in-house and external independent public relations counsel simultaneously.

Media relations with the travel industry press as well as with the consumer travel press constitute an essential element of travel and tourism public relations. Numerous publications, such as the industry newspaper *Travel Weekly* and industry magazines *Travel Agent, Meetings and Conventions,* and *Conference & Incentive Travel,* are widely read by travel sellers and must be serviced regularly with information about travel clients; typically such information is supplied by public relations practitioners. Similarly, the consumer travel media widely read by the traveling public, such as *Conde Nast Traveler, Travel & Leisure,* travel sections of major consumer newspapers such as the *New York Times* and specialty publications such as *Diversion,* the magazine for physicians who travel often for pleasure, are "motivated" by public relations practitioners to "cover" their clients.

A traditional tool used by practitioners in travel and tourism public relations in conducting media relations is the working press trip or "junket" whereby travel journalists either individually or in groups experience the sellers' travel product as a consumer tourist would but at free or reduced costs arranged by the practitioner. In recent years, many media outlets have sharply restricted journalists' acceptance of free travel and other gifts, to some degree curtailing the effectiveness of press trips in exposing journalists firsthand to travel products. However, many freelance travel writers and travel industry journalists still participate in press trips. Practitioners are well advised to follow the guidelines for media relations issued by the Society of American Travel Writers (SATW) and may join SATW as associate members to maximize their media relations efforts.

In addition, there are countless industry associations of benefit to travel sellers, such as the American Society of Retail Travel Agents, the Travel Industry Association, the Meeting Planners Association, the American Hotel Association, the International Air Transport Association, the Caribbean Tourism Organization, and the Caribbean Hotel Association, to name only a few. Travel suppliers such as resorts, hotels, and airlines may offer free or discounted travel to retail travel agents and meeting planners in familiarization or "fam" trips, for which public relations practitioners provide publicity in industry media and other support. Some travel industry associations have annual conferences and trade shows for travel sellers and buyers, including consumers, such as the International Adventure Travel & Outdoor Sport Show, for which practitioners may produce and provide support communications ranging from brochures to promotional giveaways. Destination entities, such as the Canadian Tourism Commission and the British Tourist Authority, may sponsor traveling seminars and receptions for retail travel agents, for which practitioners may produce and provide support communications ranging from publicity to newsletters and brochures, travel posters, films, and videos.

Other public relations activities may involve assisting with management of wide-ranging issues affecting tourism, such as conservation of natural resources and sociopolitical impacts of tourism; government relations, such as influencing pertinent legislation pending with local and foreign governments; and community relations, such as convincing residents of a local community that tourism revenues can benefit them. In addition to traditional marketing communications activities directed at targeted travel buyers on behalf of travel seller clients, public relations practitioners may be engaged in the internal communications projects to build relationships with a travel-seller's own employees.

Besides generating publicity in the media, public relations techniques include direct communication tactics such as brochures, newsletters, Web sites, e-mail, and other Internet-based communications, as well as sales promotional items and giveaways; interpersonal and group communication tactics, such as personalized pitches, press trips, fam tours, and trade shows; photography, film and video production; and special events. Often, travel and tourism special events are designed to commemorate a new travel product, such as a celebrity tennis tournament held in conjunction with the opening of a resort, or are meant to increase tourism during a traditionally "low" or "shoulder" season, such as the annual Ernest Hemingway Look-Alike contest designed to boost tourism to Key West, Florida, in the summer, or the annual Pirates Week to increase tourism to the Cayman Islands each October.

Crisis management is also a critical responsibility in conjunction with travel and tourism public relations and involves managing communications associated with crises ranging from viral infections infecting cruise ship passengers to airplane crashes and hijackings and terrorists bombing resorts or any other crises conceivably affecting the tourism and travel organization represented.

—*Lynne M. Sallot*

Bibliography

Cohen, E. (1972). Toward a sociology of international tourism. *Social Research, 39*(1), 164–182.

Society of American Travel Writers. Retrieved July 24, 2003, from http://www.societyofamericantravelwriters.com

Wilcox, D. L., Cameron, G. T., Ault, P. H., & Agee, W. K. (2003). Travel promotion. In *Public relations: Strategies and tactics* (7th ed., pp. 465–471). Boston: Allyn & Bacon.

World Tourism Organization. Retrieved July 24, 2003, from http://www.world-tourism.org/market_research/facts/menu.html

TRAVERSE-HEALY, TIM

The end of World War II signaled the beginning of modern-day public relations practice, not only in the United States but also around the world. In the

United Kingdom, Professor Tim Traverse-Healy, OBE, has earned his place as one of the modern-day architects of that global practice, beginning in the United Kingdom and extending to six continents and dozens of countries. Throughout his distinguished career as a practitioner and educator, Traverse-Healy shared his vision and insights into public relations as a profession, stressing philosophy over tactics.

Born in 1923, Traverse-Healy first studied medicine before earning his diploma in communications from London University. Traverse-Healy said his introduction to public relations arrived as an air-dropped package behind the German enemy lines in France during World War II, where he served as a Royal Marine Commando in Special Forces. Among other things in the package was a book by the Christopher Fathers listing public relations as a career. Traverse-Healy put the practice of public relations together with his Jesuit school training and parental influences to form his own personal mission of "honoring God by serving man" (personal interview, July 1998).

Back in London after the war ended, Traverse-Healy set up shop with his partner, Denis Lyons, in 1947, establishing the first recognized postwar public relations consultancy. His military training served him well as he developed his practice around the strategy (the "thinking") rather than the tactics (the "doing") of public relations. The new focus on intelligence, research, and strategy garnered Traverse-Healy myriad corporate, global clients including Conrad Hilton, National Westminster Bank, plc., AT&T, Airbus Industrie, Cadburys, Ford Motor Company, Unilever, and the U.S. Department of Commerce. Ever expanding his understanding of the developing public relations practice around the world, he traveled to and interacted with the leading practitioners from all types of organizations, studying their best practices while refining his philosophy of what practice should be. "The 1950s was a time to invest the craft of public relations with social values and social force and rebuild the world after the catastrophe of the war," Traverse-Healy said (personal interview, July 1998).

Traverse-Healy's influence has also been felt in the development of modern-day public relations education. He has been a professor at the University of Stirling in its fledgling days as the first public relations master's degree in the United Kingdom, and as a visiting professor and consultant to the University of Wales; the University of Westminster; the Faculty European Aviation Industry Management School in Toulouse, France; and Ball State and Baylor universities in the United States. In addition, Traverse-Healy has served on a wide range of educational commissions and boards, including secretary of the UK Public Relations Research Network, chairman of the UK Public Relations Education Trust, president of the International Public Relations Research and Education Foundation, and president of the International Foundation for Public Relations Studies. As in business, his emphasis in education was on the philosophy, strategy, and thinking involved in socially responsible practice. Traverse-Healy described this emphasis as "the difference between a profession and a craft" (personal interview, July 1998). Establishing his practice and sharing his expertise with education soon thrust Traverse-Healy onto the professional development stage. Underlying his business success was his growing reputation in questioning and nurturing the professional standards of public relations practice over the commercial practices and success of the field. He was a founding member of the Institute of Public Relations (IPR) in 1948, earned Fellow designation in 1956, and served as president in 1967–1968. He held offices in the European Public Relations Federation, the International Public Relations Association (IPRA) where he served as the founding secretary in 1950 to 1961, and twice was elected president of the World Public Relations Congress in 1970 and 1973. From 1952 to 1998, Traverse-Healy made more than 100 speeches on the social responsibilities of public relations practitioners to consider the public good as well as the organization's welfare to groups ranging from the Arthur Page Society in the United States to his 2003 keynote address to the World Public Relations Festival in Rome. His emphasis on codes of conduct and ethical behavior became the basis for the Code of Ethics & Professional Charter in the United Kingdom, adopted by the Public Relations Consultants Association in 1990 and the Institute of Public Relations in 1991. He also drafted the European Code of Conduct for the International Consultants Association and the European Consultants Association, adopted in 1991.

Numerous awards document and support Traverse-Healy's contributions, including the prestigious Order of the British Empire (OBE), the Tallents Gold Medal, the International Public Relations Association Presidential Gold Medal, and a place in the U.S. Arthur W. Page Society's Hall of Fame.

Since he put out his nameplate more than 50 years ago, Traverse-Healy's emphasis on ethical standards remains his key theme. In his 2003 address in Rome he summed up his concerns: "But on . . . our societal value and social values I am deeply concerned as to our record of behaviour as a group over the setting, monitoring, and policing of our profession's moral, cultural, and civic obligations" (personal correspondence, June 2003).

In 2000 Traverse-Healy donated his vast collection of books, manuscripts, articles, and speeches to the School of Journalism, Media and Cultural Studies at Cardiff University, where he holds an honorary professorship and advised the school on a new master's degree in International Public Relations. In honor of Traverse-Healy's 80th birthday, Professor Shirley Harrison of Leeds Metropolitan University in the United Kingdom edited more than 50 years of his papers and posted them to the Web site http://www.pr-50years.co.uk.

—*Barbara DeSanto*

See also Europe, practice of public relations in

TRUST

It was in *The Philosophy of Money* that Georg Simmel had written the sentence that could be said to be a necessary starting point for every contemporary investigation of the phenomenon of trust: "Without the general trust that people have in each other, society itself would disintegrate, for very few

Tim Traverse-Healy

SOURCE: Professional in Public Relations: 50 Years of Principles and Practice, http://www.pr-50years.co.uk. Reprinted with permission.

relationships are based entirely upon what is known with certainty about another person, and very few relationships would endure if trust were not as strong as, or stronger than, rational proof or personal observation" (1978, pp. 178–179). Harold Garfinkel, in his experiments with trust, elaborated that "'trust' as a condition of stable concerted actions" (1963, p. 187) can be transformed into "attitude of daily life" (1963, p. 210).

Originally, trust (*fiducia*) was a personal phenomenon that, at least since Peter Lombard (1100–1160), denoted the volitional aspect (*facultas voluntatis*) of medieval Christian faith (*fides*). In medieval Christianity,

every act of religious faith shows two sides or aspects—a cognitive and volitional. It is at once an affirmation of truth and a surrender to the truth affirmed. Apart from the first, it would be blind; apart from the second, without any practical significance. The fact that the emphasis is sometimes placed on the one and sometimes on the other leads to two relatively distinct notions of faith. When the volitional aspect is emphasised, we have the notion commonly denoted by the word "trust" . . .; when the cognitive, that denoted by the word "belief." (Morgan 1921, p. 689)

For Saint Thomas Aquinas (1225–1274), who accepted Lombard's phrase that man is endowed with both volitional and rational capacities, *facultas voluntatis et rationis,* it is the will that guides reason in the human search for the final meaning of life in acceptance and love of God.

In his work *Gemeinschaft und Gesellschaft,* originally published in 1877 with a subtitle "A Treatise on Communism and Socialism as Empirical Forms of Culture," which in the second edition, in 1902, was changed to "Basic Concepts of Pure Sociology," a German sociologist, Ferdinand Toennies, secularized the notion of will and placed it on a societal level: "The scope of social will is the whole of the environmental conditioning of social interaction" (1971, p. 94). This way trust also lost its personal character and became the foundation and property of social order. The French sociologist Emile Durkheim adopted this redefinition of trust from a personal to a social fact that "is to be recognised by the power of external coercion which it exercises or is capable of exercising over individuals" (1972, p. 58). This notion, that the underlying reality of trust is "irreducibly sociological" (Lewis & Weigert, 1985, p. 456), is still present in contemporary sociological approaches to trust.

In the second half of the 20th century, it was recognized in economics that trust as a form of social control has an economic value. Economic activities, as well as having "production costs," also have "transaction costs" (Williamson, 1985, pp. 18–19), which are the costs of running economic activities and correspond to the notion of friction in physics. Trust serves as a lubricant that smoothes transactions and is therefore a cost-saving device. As we can monetarize transaction costs, so we can monetarize savings we get from applying trust—instead of personally investing in monitoring and control. Trust thus becomes a commodity itself and we can draw its utility function: trust and transaction costs are inversely related. Instead of transaction costs, E. L. Khalil wrote of "organisational costs" as "the cost of distrust and the cost to minimize it" (1994, p. 392). Although the economic notion of trust as a cost-saving device stands on the sociological notion of trust as a social control that limits the permissible and available repertoire of human behavior, Francis

Fukuyama applied the economic notion of trust to sociological theory in 1995, paralleling economic (transaction or organisational) costs with social costs: trust in a society is inversely related to the costs associated with monitoring and controlling its members (police, courts, etc.).

In psychology, trust had often been used as a personality variable. Some people are said to be more trusting and trustworthy than others, who are said to be suspicious and untrustworthy. When Erik Erikson published his theory of "eight ages of man" (1950/1955, p. 223) that a person goes through from infancy to maturity, he wrote that children at the age of around one or two live through the first developmental stage in which they develop a basic sense of trust or mistrust toward the world around them and toward themselves. This assumption of introjection and projection regulating trust-mistrust polarity and through it managing human tensions and anxieties had led others to associate trust with prosocial and mistrust with antisocial personality traits: a trusting person evaluates others positively, "as essentially 'good' until proved otherwise" (Adorno, Frenkel-Brunswik, Levinson, & Sanford, 1950, p. 411), and a mistrusting person evaluates them negatively, as dangerous and hostile. The subconscious, primarily affective evaluative meaning of trust had been copied from psychology into sociology. Talcott Parsons wrote of trust as "affectively motivated" (1978, p. 59) and Anthony Giddens incorporated it into his theory of structuration as "basic trust" (1984, pp. 51–60), a defining property of human ontological security, on which three other forms of trust depend: elementary or interpersonal, abstract or impersonal, and active trust—with each having its own evaluative mechanism that differentiates between "good" and "bad" objects of trust (elementary trust through kinship—the in-group is good, abstract trust through expert systems—experts are good, and active trust through "a process of mutual narrative and emotional disclosure"—"opening out" is good).

In public relations, trust is an important concept in both the United States mainstream relational and in European views. In *Guidelines for Measuring Relationships in Public Relations.* James E. Grunig and Linda Childers Hon defined trust as "one party's level of confidence in and willingness to open one-self to the other party" and composed of "integrity, the belief that an organization is fair and just," "dependability, the belief that an organization will do what it says it will do," and "competence, the belief that an organization has the ability to do what it says it will do" (1999, p. 19). According to Günter Bentele (2003), in Europe, the notion of trust more often operates on a societal level as public trust.

—*Dejan Verčič*

Bibliography

Adorno, T. W., Frenkel-Brunswik, E., Levinson, D. J., & Sanford, R. N. (1950). *The authoritarian personality.* New York: Harper & Brothers.

Bentele, G. (2003). *Public trust: Theory and empirical results in Germany.* Paper presented to the 10th International Public Relations Research Symposium, BledCom 2003. 4–6 July, Bled, Slovenia.

Durkheim, E. (1972). *Selected writings.* New York: Cambridge University Press.

Erikson, E. H. (1950/1995). *Childhood and society.* London: Vintage.

Fukuyama, F. (1995). *Trust: The social virtues and the creation of prosperity.* London: Hamish Hamilton.

Garfinkel, H. (1963). A conception of, and experiments with, "trust" as a condition of stable concerted actions. In O. J. Harvey (Ed.), *Motivation and social interaction: Cognitive determinants* (pp. 187–238). New York: Ronald Press.

Giddens, A. (1984). *The constitution of society: Outline of the theory of structuration.* Cambridge, UK: Polity Press.

Grunig, J. E., & Hon, L. (1999). *Guidelines for measuring relationships in public relations.* Gainesville, FL: Institute for Public Relations, Commission on PR Measurement and Evaluation.

Khalil, E. L. (1994). Trust. In G. M. Hodgson, W. J. Samuels, & M. R. Tool (Eds.), *The Elgar companion to institutional and evolutionary economics* (Vol. L–Z, pp. 339–346). Aldershot, Hants, UK: Edward Elgar.

Lewis, J. D., & Weigert, A. J. (1985). Social atomism, holism, and trust. *Sociological Quarterly, 26*(4), 455–471.

Morgan, W. (1921). Faith (Christian). In J. Hastings (Ed.), *Encyclopaedia of religion and ethics* (Vol. 5, pp. 689–694). Edinburgh: T. & T. Clark.

Parsons, T. (1978). *Action theory and the human condition.* New York: Free Press.

Simmel, G. (1978). *The philosophy of money.* London: Routledge.

Toennies, F. (1971). *On sociology: Pure, applied, and empirical: Selected writings.* Chicago: University of Chicago Press.

Verčič, D., van Ruler, B., Bütschi, G., & Flodin, B. (2001). On the definition of public relations: A European view. *Public Relations Review, 27,* 373–387.

Williamson, O. E. (1985). *The economic institutions of capitalism: Firms, markets, relational contacting.* New York: Free Press.

TWO-STEP FLOW THEORY

To public relations practitioners, the two-step flow theory of communication highlights the importance of identifying and targeting opinion leaders when disseminating messages to audiences through mass media.

In 1944, sociologists Paul F. Lazarsfeld, Bernard R. Berelson, and Hazel Gaudet published a paper titled *The People's Choice,* which analyzed voter decision making during President Franklin Roosevelt's 1940 reelection campaign. Study findings suggested that messages did not flow directly from mass media to target audiences, as previously assumed. Rather, media information first reached opinion leaders, who evaluated the information and formed opinions that were then conveyed to others in their social circles through interpersonal channels. Only 5 percent of voters were swayed by direct exposure to media messages, the study found.

Based on the 1940 election campaign study, Lazarsfeld and fellow scholar Elihu Katz developed the two-step flow theory of communication, published in the book *Personal Influence* in 1955. Research by Katz and Lazarsfeld confirmed that face-to-face interactions with opinion leaders were more influential in shaping others' views than mass media. Herbert Menzel, a pioneer in scientific communication, suggested that target audiences were confused by the flood of information transmitted by media on a daily basis, leading people to turn to knowledgeable peers for assistance in sifting through and interpreting media content. The notion that media messages had minimal direct influence on opinion formation became known as the "limited effects paradigm."

Sociologists typically distinguish between two types of opinion leaders: those with formal authority, such as corporate executives and government officials, and those with informal influence over others in their sphere. A 1949 study by American sociologist Robert K. Merton showed that opinion leaders came from various social, economic, and educational backgrounds but shared the common characteristic of specialized interest and expertise on the topic under discussion. Lazarsfeld and colleagues also found that opinion leaders had greater access to sources of information outside their immediate circles, a disproportionate amount coming from mass media. Thus, opinion leaders did not replace media but rather functioned as discussion guides and interpreters of media content.

Early work by Lazarsfeld and associates suggested several reasons why personal conversations with opinion leaders exert greater influence over opinion formation than mass media. The informal nature of face-to-face communications, as well as the ability to judge the expertise and trustworthiness of the communicator, can contribute to greater openness on the part of the recipient of communications. At the same time, personal contact provides opinion leaders with the opportunity to adjust to the receiver's personality, counter any resistance, and employ friendly persuasion to achieve the desired response.

Two-step flow studies conducted in the 1940s have provided the basis for several recent theoretical developments. Communication scholars Hans-Bernd Brosius and Gabriel Weimann (1996) explained the setting of public agendas as a two-step flow, with influential individuals facilitating the flow of information between mass media and the public. Everett Rogers's (2003) theory of diffusion is also derived in part from the two-step flow concept, with the innovation behavior of near-peers influencing adoption of new ideas by other members of a social system.

Although the two-step flow theory was rapidly adopted and continues to be highly influential, critics have noted several shortcomings. According to Weimann (1991, 1994), observing the flow of communications in real-world settings is difficult, as is identifying the many factors that qualify a person as an opinion leader on a particular issue. Individuals can be opinion leaders on some topics but not on others, as Werner J. Severin and James W. Tankard pointed out.

Otis Baskin, Craig Aronoff, and Dan Lattimore (1997) also criticized the two-step flow theory for being overly simplistic, in that it assumes that the flow of information is unidirectional, linear, and limited to two levels: opinion leaders and followers. In fact, Lazarsfeld and his colleagues envisioned a multiple-step flow, with opinion leaders sharing media information with other influentials, who in turn disseminated the information to attentive followers. Some members of other, less attentive publics may become aware of and interested in the issue as well. Later research confirmed that the delivery of messages from mass media to the public involved a varying number of stages.

In applying the two-step flow theory to campaign planning, the challenge for public relations practitioners becomes to identify the individuals who are acting as opinion leaders on specific issues and to develop targeted messages to reach them, to stimulate the person-to-person communication that will influence target audiences.

—*Cindy T. Christen*

See also Agenda-setting theory; Diffusion of innovations theory; Media effects; Public opinion and opinion leaders

Bibliography

Baskin, O., Aronoff, C., & Lattimore, D. (1997). *Public relations: The profession and practice* (4th ed.). Madison, WI: Brown & Benchmark.

Brosius, H.-B., & Weimann, G. (1996). Who sets the agenda? Agenda setting as a two-step flow. *Communication Research, 23*(5), 561–580.

Katz, E., & Lazarsfeld, P. F. (1955). *Personal influence: The part played by people in the flow of mass communications* (1st ed.). Glencoe, IL: Free Press.

Lazarsfeld, P. F., Berelson, B. R., & Gaudet, H. (1944). *The people's choice.* New York: Columbia University Press.

Lazarsfeld, P. F., & Menzel, H. (1963). Mass media and personal influence. In W. L. Schramm (Ed.), *The science of human communication: New directions and new findings in communication research* (pp. 94–115). New York: Basic Books.

Merton, R. K. (1949). Patterns of influence: A study of interpersonal influence and of communications behavior in a local community. In P. F. Lazarsfeld & F. N. Stanton (Eds.), *Communication research* (pp. 180–215). New York: Harper & Brothers.

Rogers, E. (2003). *Diffusion of innovations* (5th ed.). New York: Free Press.

Severin, W. H., & Tankard, J. W., Jr. (2001). *Communication theories: Origins, methods and uses in the mass media* (5th ed.). New York: Addison-Wesley Longman.

Weimann, G. (1994). Is there a two-step flow of agenda setting? *International Journal of Public Opinion, 6*(4), 323–341.

Weimann, G. (1991). The influentials: Back to the concept of opinion leaders? *Public Opinion Quarterly, 55*(2), 267–279.

TWO-WAY AND ONE-WAY COMMUNICATION

Two-way and one-way communication represent two basic methods or "styles" of communication and also serve as two key concepts for categorizing James E. Grunig and Todd T. Hunt's (1984) "Four Models of Public Relations." Grunig and Hunt created the four models to show not only that different organizational settings require different means of evaluating their success, but also to show different stages in the history of public relations. For them, the major difference between two-way and one-way models is feedback. There is no explicit feedback component from communication receivers in the one-way models.

For Grunig and Hunt, one-way communication includes two models: press agentry or publicity, and public information. Using the press agentry or publicity model, practitioners believe that telling the whole truth is not essential. Sources release information with the idea of changing the receivers' behavior or beliefs. The information is often incomplete, distorted, or consists of half-truths. For the public information model, telling the complete truth is of the utmost importance. The public information model is used simply to inform, not persuade the receiver.

Grunig and Hunt worried about the paradigm of public relations often associated with the early practitioners: The role of practitioners was to inform and convince publics and markets of the rightness of the sponsoring organization's position on key matters. The use of one-way communication flatly rejects the possibility that the organization could be wrong in its stance, policies, and activities.

From Grunig and Hunt's perspective, two models feature two-way communication: two-way asymmetric and two-way symmetric. While both of the two-way models include feedback, asymmetric and symmetric models rest on the question of intent. In an asymmetric model, feedback is important to the shaping of the message. Feedback from the receiver will be used by the source to better tailor the message, maximizing results and providing an outcome that is beneficial to the message source. The symmetric model allows for the possibility that, through feedback, both the source and the receiver may change. There is one thing unique to the two-way symmetric model: It is the only one of the four models that is actually a dialogue—which also makes it the most ethical.

Along with the explicit four-model paradigm, there is an implied moral or ethical issue that practitioners are challenged to consider. What is acceptable (ethically honest and moral) behavior for public relations practitioners? Grunig and Hunt maintain that a genuine dialogue must happen for effective public relations to occur; to be specific, a two-way symmetric setting. They are not alone (Scott Cutlip and Allen Center are another example) in suggesting that good communication occurs when "good" people are the ones communicating.

Most people agree with the concept that it is best to be forthright and ethical (honest and moral) in the practice of public relations. Accomplishment of that goal, at least in part, requires two-way communication. Cutlip and Center offered the following definition of public relations: "Public relations is the planned effort to influence opinion through good character and responsible performance, based upon mutually satisfactory two-way communication" (1978, p. 16). This definition, emphasizing good character and two-way communication, preceded (and probably inspired) J. E. Grunig and Hunt's models.

When public relations is looked at in an ethical sense, symmetry and asymmetry cloud, rather than clarify, the issue. To work from Cutlip and Center's definition, if the communication is genuinely two-way, an ethical public relations attempt can be made. Symmetry and asymmetry simply become two variables of one-way communication. Two-way asymmetrical behavior simply becomes an unethical subterfuge, belonging in the same category with press agentry or publicity.

To further complicate matters, there is the question of public relations being defined as a process or a culture. Cutlip and Center noted that "public relations is often used interchangeably with propaganda, information, communications, public affairs, advertising, or persuasion" (1978, p. 4).

Discussion of what distinguishes two-way from one-way communication must precede a more current analysis of how public relations can foster, and engage in, dialogue. If openness is a major factor in improving organizational effectiveness, then the organization must engage in two-way communication. It must listen to and use research to gain insights, alerting the organization to problems and matters of contention. This prospect also requires strategic tactics beyond publicity, promotion, and the simple provisions of public information.

—*Michael Nagy*

See also Dialogue; Press agentry; Publicity; Symmetry

Bibliography

Cutlip, S. M., & Center, A. H. (1978). *Effective public relations* (5th ed.). Englewood Cliffs, NJ: Prentice Hall.
Grunig, J. E., & Hunt, T. (1984). *Managing public relations.* New York: Holt, Rinehart & Winston.

UNCERTAINTY REDUCTION THEORY

The concept of uncertainty reduction suggests that individuals are motivated to seek information to reduce uncertainty. The concept has implications for exploring communication as a means for resolving incompatibilities and inconsistencies in human relationships as well as experiences and behaviors in various settings. Through communication, individuals reduce uncertainty that emerges when experiences do not correspond to expectations or when relationships change. This concept can also be applied to public relations, which is primarily concerned with public relationships.

In 1986, Richard L. Daft and Robert H. Lengel posited that message ambiguity is a critical concept and that people will select a mode of communication that assists with clarification of ambiguity (i.e., how people seek information about one another in interpersonal communication). Further, James J. Bradac indicated, in 2001, that a major assumption of uncertainty reduction theory is the human motivation to reduce uncertainty about oneself and others in initial interactions. *Uncertainty* refers to a person's subjective framework of the number of alternative predictions available when thinking about another person's future behavior. A greater number of perceived alternatives produce a greater sense of uncertainty and a stronger drive for uncertainty reduction. Gaining individual knowledge, about human nature and the surrounding world, is aligned with this process but, ultimately, the person is moving in the direction of increasing simplicity so that assessed alternatives will be reduced.

From the uncertainty reduction perspective, a high level of uncertainty is a stimulus for seeking information as well as an inhibitor of attraction. The theory predicts that lack of knowledge about other people leads to attempts to reduce uncertainty through information seeking. Attraction for others (consistencies in organizational relationships, friendships, romantic interests) is suspended until knowledge about the individual is gained. In the course of human affairs, total uncertainty reduction is impossible because past experiences do not always accurately predict future behaviors. However, each person has a threshold in terms of how much uncertainty one is willing to accept in a relationship. This threshold will vary, depending on assessments of the behaviors of others, past experiences, and general tolerance for risk.

Generally, the most widely held uncertainty reduction principle is that increased information seeking corresponds with decreased levels of uncertainty. Intuitively, this seems to make sense, but according to Kathy Kellermann and Rodney A. Reynolds (1990), there is some inconsistency in the research results. The authors indicate, however, that both uncertainty reduction and question asking jointly decrease as the number of conversations increase.

In terms of organizations and public relationships, the concept of environmental uncertainty is often reviewed. Environmental uncertainty can be viewed in two ways, externally and internally. External uncertainty is primarily concerned with perceptions about the nature of changes in the external environment (i.e., market situations, competitor reviews, regulatory constraints) as well as informational quality. Internal uncertainty, according to J. D. Jorgensen and J. L. Petelle, refers to daily operations and interactions within an organization. This type of uncertainty involves items such as employee behavior, information load, and job security. The authors argue that the notion of relational uncertainty is critically important in these organizational relationships. For example, the reduction of uncertainty in dyads merits attention, because it may be linked to openness within these relationships. These relationships could be among team members, between a supervisor and his/her subordinate, or between a public relations account executive and a client representative.

Avoiding costs while maximizing benefits is a motive that competes with uncertainty reduction. For example, limited time and energy may prevent information seeking. A person may want to gather information about a particular subject, but he or she may be facing a barrage of committee work and e-mail messages. Impression management may also play a role. Maintaining a positive image with other employees and the supervisor may be compared with the costs of asking another "dumb" question. The request might suggest that the employee is incompetent. Other employees might have this perception but impression management may be rooted in that person's insecurities.

The landscape of public relations is not always stable, due to changing conditions in organizational relationships. Priscilla Murphy (2000) argued that organizational/public relationships are, essentially, complex adaptive systems. Many employees interact both locally and globally in their efforts to adapt to various situations. These adaptations form large-scale patterns that affect society. She posits that outcomes are unpredictable because the effects of actions leading to them are nonlinear. In other words, there is not necessarily a proportional relationship between a decision and its eventual outcome. Thus, uncertainty reduction is constantly challenged. Furthermore, coevolution complicates the process. According to Murphy, individual interactions coevolve; they are shaped by a number of variables such as personal history, norms, and resources. Each interaction is open-ended and persons need to adjust to continuous, reflexive states. Thus, total reduction of uncertainty is impossible.

Even though total reduction is impossible to achieve, uncertainty in organizational/public relationships can be managed. Robert L. Heath and Christine Diana Gay reviewed the area of risk communication in 1997, which corresponds to how much risk people are willing to assume in their interactions with others. Using the concept of environmental scanning, highly involved persons are more strategic in their choice of information sources. Employees may use mediated (e.g., Internet) and interpersonal sources as part of this scanning process to manage risk and uncertainty. According to Heath and Gay, persons who strongly espouse or oppose a source of risk demonstrate high levels of involvement. If individuals perceive that their self-interest is affected, they prefer authoritative sources (account executives, supervisors) and interpersonal contact to determine what they should know in order to hold appropriate opinions on a risk topic (i.e., crisis/issue situations). The risk and uncertainty concepts are necessarily intertwined. Heath and Gay note that key publics' information seeking is motivated by the desire to reduce uncertainty and limit risks.

According to a 1998 piece by Nicholas DiFonzo and Prashant Bordia, uncertainty can be managed by engaging in collective planning. Management can clarify the values and commitments behind change decisions (rather than preparing vague memos that leave much room for interpretation), the people who will make these decisions, and the timeline on which these decisions will be implemented. Managers can also involve staff members in the process of finding solutions for change issues (e.g., a committee to review revised accreditation procedures for the business). This policy can divert the anxiety that feeds the rumor mill and channel this agitated uncertainty into productive work, thus planning for change.

Open discussions in staff meetings can also provide an opportunity for the collective resources of the group to solve potential organizational dilemmas. Thus, internal public relations can be strengthened through such uncertainty management tactics. Even though these suggestions are designed for internal employees of an organization, how the organization handles change will be projected to the external environment. Stakeholders, such as the media, community groups, and clients, will learn through various sources (e.g., the media, spokespersons, employees) and will adapt their actions accordingly.

As a final note on uncertainty reduction in both external and internal situations, DiFonzo and Bordia (1998) provided the following communication strategies:

1. Announce changes as early as possible for all stakeholders who may be affected.

2. Establish an information timeline.

3. Comment on the inability to provide further information (this is especially important in crisis situations).

4. Try to clarify all decisions and the protocol for such decisions.

5. Engage in actions that facilitate trust (e.g., informing employees first).

—*Brian C. Sowa*

Bibliography

Bradac, J. J. (2001). Theory comparison: Uncertainty reduction, problematic integration, uncertainty management, and other curious constructs. *Journal of Communication, 51,* 456–476.

Daft, R. L., & Lengel, R. H. (1986). Organizational information requirements, media richness, and structural design. *Management Science, 32,* 554–571.

DiFonzo, N., & Bordia, P. (1998). A tale of two corporations: Managing uncertainty during organizational change. *Human Resource Management, 37,* 295–303.

Heath, R. L., & Gay, C. D. (1997). Risk communication: Involvement, uncertainty, and control's effect on information scanning and monitoring by expert stakeholders. *Management Communication Quarterly, 10,* 342–372.

Jorgensen, J. D., & Petelle, J. L. (1992). Measuring uncertainty within organizational relationships: An analysis of the CLUES instrument. *Management Communication Quarterly, 6,* 180–203.

Kellermann, K., & Reynolds, R. (1990). When ignorance is bliss: The role of motivation to reduce uncertainty in uncertainty reduction theory. *Human Communication Research, 17,* 5–75.

Kramer, M. W. (1993). Communication and uncertainty reduction during job transfers: Leaving and joining processes. *Communication Monographs, 60,* 178–197.

Murphy, P. (2000). Symmetry, contingency, complexity: Accommodating uncertainty in public relations theory. *Public Relations Review, 26,* 447–462.

UNITED KINGDOM, PRACTICE OF PUBLIC RELATIONS IN

The emergence of professional public relations in the United Kingdom is the outcome of a centuries-old process engaged in previously by the monarchy, the Church, and the state, encompassing propaganda, intelligence, and censorship. Pageantry, special events, pronouncements, and the publication of tracts and pamphlets were the weaponry of those past days.

Following the Reformation, the powers to persuade previously held by the Crown and the Church shifted to the Parliament. The Post Office, which in earlier times had been employed to spy, became the means of circulation, externally of official policies and internally of reporting on public sentiment and response.

Concerned over the years primarily with domestic matters, governmental action was also influenced by international affairs. An early instance of crisis management, for instance, occurred when the establishment took steps to counter the propaganda promulgated in England by the Revolutionaries during the American Revolution in an attempt to harness public opinion. Later, the establishment acted to counter the philosophical and theoretical basis of the French Revolution, fearing its effect on the British populace. During the American Civil War, when both of the warring parties undertook propaganda programs in Britain and in Europe in an attempt to gain popular support, the British government of the day moved to circulate its views.

In the years prior to the outbreak of World War I in 1914, there was in evidence a number of campaigns mounted by various movements of a social or political nature—for example, the suffragettes and the pro-temperance interests.

On an international level, the authorities were forced to take propagandist action to counter antagonistic programs. Witness the anti-British campaign mounted in Europe as a result of the inhumane treatment of the old, infirm, women, and children, and the burning of homesteads and invention of concentration camps.

During the late 1800s, the British Civil Service underwent an extensive process of reform that resulted in the strengthening of its nonpartisan nature. At the same time, it had also undergone considerable expansion to take account of developing social programs such as health, education, and benefits. A number of departments created embryonic information units that adhered to the principle of political impartiality. They were staffed invariably by public servants, and as early as 1906, a central committee was formed to oversee and coordinate the publication and distribution of official reports and the like.

But, as later occurred in the United States, the outbreak of World War I brought about significant changes in this area. A Home Office Press Bureau and a Foreign Office News Department were created, followed shortly by a Neutral Press Committee and a secret unit targeting foreign opinion. Meanwhile, various departments of government were strengthening their in-house information and publicity teams, increasingly employing outsiders from the fields of journalism and advertising to augment the efforts of the career officials.

In 1917, three years into the war, Prime Minister Lloyd George ordered the foundation of the Department of Information, which was promoted to a full ministry a year later. At the same time, a separate Department of Enemy Propaganda was also created. (It is worth noting that when the Americans

entered the war in 1917, they set up their propaganda organization, the Committee of Public Information, under the leadership of George Creel, a journalist. He described his activities as "a plain publicity proposition . . . the world's greatest adventure in advertising" [Creel, 1920, p. 4]).

In Britain, immediately following the Armistice in 1918, although the central ministry was disbanded, the various individual departments reshaped their information units (which nevertheless remained reactive rather than proactive in nature).

One of the phenomena of the interwar years (1918–1939) was the emergence of the Special Expert Committee. The Cabinet had decided that whereas advertising should be centralized, publicity should remain at the departmental level.

One such committee dealt with government advertising and included representatives of both media owners and agents. Such involvement, however, resulted in a number of the senior advertising figures becoming familiar with the full range of publicity activities, particularly press agencies. One outcome was that a few of the bigger advertising agencies—London Press Exchange, Crawfords, Highams, and Barkers, for instance—formed editorial publicity departments. During the same period, some of the commercial companies appointed individuals or created small departments to handle publicity and external relationships generally— steel, coal, shipping, chemicals, and railways, for example. Meanwhile, a small handful of independent consultants went into business, notably Freddie Lyons, who handled Unilever, and Sir Basil Clark, an ex-government official who set up Editorial Services Limited with a wide range of clients. Also expanding very visibly were the activities of the utilities—gas, electricity, and public services, such as the London Underground.

But of greater significance in the development of the information and publicity function during the interwar period were the programs activated by the Board of Education and the ministries of Housing, Health, and Agriculture, campaigns aimed at promoting the consumption of milk, care of teeth, infant health, and diphtheria inoculation. To these were added the very visible efforts and considerable success of the publicity activities of the Empire Marketing Board, dedicated to promoting British products overseas under the leadership of a career civil servant, Sir Stephen Tallents.

By the outbreak of World War II, in 1939, a number of experienced executives from industry and commerce were serving on the advisory committees of the various government ministries, departments, and agencies, and the titles *public relations officer* and *press officer* were in common usage.

With the onset of hostilities, the Ministry of Information was reinstituted to cover matters and, as might be expected of a nation committed to total war, branches concerned with enemy and neutral propaganda commenced operations. The public relations departments of the various government offices blossomed, as did the units of the various governments in exile.

The professional effect was that, after the war, there existed a network of trained individuals, many of whom knew each other. Although the Ministry of Information was disbanded, the government departments were retained and even expanded, and a Central Office of Information was created to service them.

Demobilized practitioners began to offer their services, some as independent consultants, and others who had previously been in advertising returned to their agencies, determined to open departments or create subsidiary companies.

Industry and commerce began to pay increased attention to press relations and public relations matters. A considerable spur to this process was the policy practices of the political party in power—the Socialists—who implemented considerable state controls over business and announced their intention of either nationalizing or referring to the Monopoly Authority a whole raft of industries and individual companies. Those industries slated were the Economic League and Aims of Industry, involving companies in the coal, steel, railway, sugar, insurance, and even the undertaking businesses. Companies under threat included the chemical and pharmaceutical companies, suppliers of industrial gases, the fishing industry, and the leading birth-control concern.

Cooperative action apart, leading corporations realized that they also had to consider their public stance and harness public sentiment, with the result that the hitherto predominantly reactive press departments were transformed gradually into proactive, full-fledged public relations units, often taking in the publicity and general advertising activities of the concern in the process. By 1947, it was estimated that, including national and local government officials, some 200 professionals were active in the field, broken down roughly equally between the public and private sectors. Public and parliamentary affairs specialists began to emerge, and several members of Parliament joined consultancies, becoming directors of corporations. By 1948, there was a call for a body to be formed to represent publicly the whole area of practice. Believing themselves to be threatened by postwar economies, the most active proponents were the local government public relations practitioners, who took on the heavy administrative load involved in forming an association. At the outset, there existed a degree of dissension between officials and private-sector executives, between so-called independent consultants and those working for advertising agencies, between those who saw themselves as senior and experienced, and those they viewed as junior (but who saw themselves as the "new wave").

Tallents, the man considered the pioneer of professional public relations in the United Kingdom, became the first president of the fledgling Institute for Public Relations in 1947, after being persuaded that there was indeed a genuine call for such an organization. In the years immediately following, presidents of accepted note were elected: Roger Wimbush in local government, Alan Hess with the motor industry, Lex Hornsby with the Ministry of Labour, and two independent consultants—Alan Campbell-Johnson, sometimes advisor to Lord Mountbatten, and Maurice Buckmaster, head of the French section of the Special Operations Executive in wartime. In 1958, added to this group was Sir Tom Fife Clark, former director general of the Central Office of Information. As might have been anticipated, the half-dozen agency-connected units dominated the early years of consultancy expansion, with about five independent consultancies of note also operating. In-house, the leadership came from the aviation, automotive, energy, and airline sectors, with their international approach and expertise setting industry standards of performance.

Editorial publicity and special events figured prominently in the various programs, and home economists, nutritionists, designers, and other specialists were soon brought into play. In the late 1950s and 1960s, it became popular for various sectors to mount cooperative campaigns. Notable among these industries were wool, cotton, steel, glass, cement, retail fashion, man-made fibers, fish, hats, and hairdressing.

In the 1970s and 1980s, with the economic changes that had taken place and the increased competition in the marketplace, cooperative campaigns became less in vogue, with major corporate players preferring to mount their own distinctive programs via either consultancies or strengthened in-house departments. Toward the end of this period and into the 1990s, two developments occurred. First, within the craft sector, specialists began to emerge, covering such areas as high technology and information technology, health care, and pharmaceuticals. Second, functional specialists began to be appointed to cover such areas as public relations and crisis and issue management.

Although the international consultancies—mostly American—such as Hill & Knowlton and Burson-Marsteller, had by the mid-1970s opened for business in London, the scene was still dominated by local concerns, only a few of which had gone international, such as Shandwick. The last two decades witnessed two trends. First, the ownership of the major consultancies has come into the hands of the major international advertising groups, dominated by the Americans. Second is the breaking down of the field into a large grouping of individuals and concerns who consider themselves communications practitioners, and a minority who consider themselves to be corporate affairs professionals concerned with social responsibility programs and community reportage.

Currently, the professional membership of the British Institute of Public Relations stands at 7,500, and 126 firms are members of its Public Relations Consultants Association.

PR Week, the profession's newspaper, estimates that there are upwards of 50,000 individual practitioners and 300 consultancy firms active in the field. *PR Week* also puts the annual fee income at 500 million pounds sterling, with the top 10 consultancies billing about half of that figure.

Additionally, the craft now supports a thriving infrastructure of specialist suppliers covering such areas as research, special events, printing, audio and video production, content analysis and evaluation, mailing and distribution, training, and recruitment. In-house and consultancy appointments seem to have peaked; the new areas of growth include health and education, local government, the social services and voluntary section, the arts, entertainment, and sports.

Presently, a fierce public debate is raging that threatens to embroil the whole industry. In essence, the Blair Labour Administration is being accused of putting spin before substance. Central to the affair is the political decision to insert a comparatively large number of so-called special advisors on short-term contracts into the administrative apparatus between the ministers and the permanent civil service. The tasks of these political appointees are twofold: first, to monitor that the various departments deliver according to the set political objectives, and second, to ensure that policies are understood and performance recognized by the electorate. The result has been to put at risk the delicate balance between official impartiality and partisanship.

—*Tim Traverse-Healy*

Bibliography

Creel, G. (1920). *How we advertised America.* New York: Harper & Brothers.

Grant, M. (1994). *Propaganda and the role of the state in inter-war Britain.* Oxford, UK: Oxford University Press.

L'Etang, J. (2003). *PR in Britain: History of professional practice in the 20th century.* Mahwah, NJ: Lawrence Erlbaum.

Taylor, P. (1995). *Munitions of the mind.* Manchester, UK: Manchester University Press.

UNITED PRESS INTERNATIONAL (UPI)

See News services

UNITED STATES GOVERNMENT AND PUBLIC RELATIONS

Although seldom straightforwardly identified as such, public relations activities are deeply ingrained in the fabric of government at all levels. In fact, the public relations industry has developed concomitantly with the practice of public relations by government. As government has grown, so has the use of public relations specialists to inform and persuade a diverse and sometimes fractured populace about the work of government.

Government public relations also includes the flow of information and persuasive messages from diverse stakeholders back to government agencies. Whether it is the corporate sector, the nonprofit sector, or foreign entities, the need to communicate to government decision makers has created a thriving public relations industry in Washington, DC, and across the nation. This two-way flow of information from the government to the governed and back again provides a useful, if somewhat oversimplified, heuristic for understanding this highly specialized field of public relations.

EVOLUTION OF FEDERAL GOVERNMENT PUBLIC RELATIONS

The use by government of public relations is hardly a recent invention; indeed, as William Rivers wrote in 1970, it has been an integral arm of government since the earliest days of the republic. The early efforts in the American colonies to stir up resentment against England, win popular support for the independence movement, and mobilize citizens to action were among the most sophisticated and successful public relations efforts in American history. Historians offer varied accounts of this first public relations campaign. The small band of Revolutionaries instigating unrest in the colonies was adept at building public support for its cause, causing the British authorities to respond that the revolution was simply an elite conspiracy. The Revolutionaries kept the populace informed by using tactics such as widely distributed printed materials authored by Samuel Adams, staging events such as the Boston Tea Party, or giving impassioned speeches in various colonial assemblies.

The history of the development of the public relations field itself is intertwined with the use of public relations by the government. President Andrew Jackson was the first chief executive to hire a former journalist to help explain his administration to the population.

The first federal government press bureau was established in 1905 by the U.S. Forest Service, a subsidiary of the United States Department of Agriculture (USDA). It was, perhaps, the creation of this office that led the U.S. Congress to pass an amendment regulating the use of public relations experts in the 1913 Appropriations Act for the U.S. Department of Agriculture. This amendment was the beginning of a tug-of-war between Congress and the executive branch about the appropriate use of public relations in federal policy formation.

The amendment was in response to a Civil Service Commission help-wanted advertisement for a "publicity man" for the Bureau of Public Roads, then part of the USDA. The amendment stated that appropriated funds could not be used to pay a publicity expert, unless specifically appropriated for that purpose. Known as the Gillett Amendment (38, U.S.C. 3107), this little-known codicil continues to govern the use of public relations in the federal government today. Although the provision does not prohibit government public relations, it has been used to limit some activities and has certainly slowed the use of the term *public relations* in federal government parlance. It may also explain why many government agencies today use such titles as information officers, press officers, public affairs experts, communications specialists, and press secretaries.

A second federal law restricting public relations was passed in 1919. It was designed to limit executive branch lobbying of members of Congress (18, U.S.C. 1913). In 1973, Congress reaffirmed the anti-lobbying rule in Public Law 92-351. This federal law prohibits the use of any appropriation for publicity designed to influence members of Congress in their attitude toward legislation or appropriations.

These restrictions notwithstanding, public relations in government has a long and storied tradition. The early 20th century was a watershed of sorts for the successful practice of public relations by the government. Although the history of public relations in government is best known for its role in building support for war, it has also been used as a tool for social welfare. In 1912, the U.S. Children's Bureau undertook a 10-year communications campaign to improve child and maternal health. This effort resulted in the successful passage of a key piece of social welfare legislation.

Shortly after the start of World War I, President Woodrow Wilson created the Committee on Public Information. George Creel, the primary architect of public will campaigns before and during World War I, was recruited to co-chair the committee and to mobilize public opinion in support of the war, particularly in persuading Americans to buy war bonds and enlist. Subsequent presidents made equally extensive use of public relations to sell the New Deal; tax cuts (as well as tax increases); international military incursions in Germany, Korea, Vietnam, Panama, Grenada, and Kuwait (to name only a few); domestic wars on poverty, drugs, and AIDS (also to name only a few); impassioned defenses against charges of impropriety (e.g., Watergate and "Clintongate"); and a host of other domestic and international communications initiatives.

Today, the U. S. government has one of the largest public relations operations in the world, with the U.S. Office of Personnel Management reporting nearly 15,000 public relations–related jobs. The National Association of Government Communicators estimates that across all levels of government, 40,000 professionals work as communicators. This total represents more than half of the total number of people that the Bureau of Labor Statistics reports as working in the field.

Much of the day-to-day work in government public relations involves the routine dissemination of information collected by the government. For example, the government Web site FedStats (www.fedstats.gov) provides easy access to statistics and information produced by more than 100 government agencies. In 1966, a public relations program was started to assist citizens in getting information about the government. Christened the Federal Information Center, this program has been funded for over 30 years and now includes a Web site (www.FirstGov.gov). In 2001, the Federal Information Center reported approximately 30 million contacts between its Web site and its national call center (GSA, 2002, p. 317, as reported in Lee, 1999).

At the federal level, government communicators are both political appointees and career civil service employees. Political appointees at the federal level generally stay in their positions for approximately 18 months and are often perceived as "political hacks" or dilettantes by the career staff. Career staff, on the other hand, are often perceived as intransient bureaucrats by the political staff. These relationships effectively form the first barrier to the creation and implementation of effective public relations strategies.

At the USDA, for example, some 150 employees report to the director of communications, a politically appointed position hired by, and reporting directly to, the Secretary of Agriculture. Each of the agencies of the USDA has its own communications staff, reporting to the agency administrator. In general, a typical communications office of a federal agency houses a press office, a community relations office, and an internal communications function.

Another example is the U.S. State Department, which, according to a recent Government Accounting Office (GAO) report, spends $1 billion a year on what is called *public diplomacy,* or public relations efforts designed to inform and educate people outside of the United States. The armed forces have the largest public relations staff in the federal government; their staff is also charged with recruiting functions, in addition to more typical public relations activities. Recent research has examined the use of public relations by the armed forces as an essential component of the 2003 war in Iraq. The Pentagon, according to Ray Hiebert, comprehensively planned for a war waged in the media, introducing the innovation of reporters embedded with troops during the actual fighting.

The legislative and judicial branches of government also have public relations professionals as part of their operational staffs. The office of a typical member of Congress includes a director of communications and a press secretary, as well as junior-level staff members. Members of Congress use a wide range of public relations tools to promote their own bills and to win reelection; these tools include the traditional ones of staged events and public speaking.

At the state level, the structure of public relations is generally the same, with a combination of political appointees in management jobs staffed by a group of civil servants at the executive level. State agencies also maintain public relations staffs, as do the offices of state legislators. In the state legislative setting, these offices often consist of a single person.

In large cities, the office of the mayor (as chief executive) will most likely be staffed by a press secretary or a director of communications, positions that are generally filled by the executive. City agencies, on the other hand, are most likely staffed by career public relations people, mirroring the state and federal systems.

A useful description of government public relations—at all levels—comes from one of the most prolific researchers on the topic, Mordecai Lee, who identified the following broad functions in 1973:

1. The implementation of public policy

2. Assisting the news media in the coverage of government

3. Reporting to the citizens on agency activities

4. Increasing the internal cohesion of the agency

5. Increasing the agency's sensitivity to its public

6. Mobilization of support for the agency itself

PUBLIC RELATIONS TO INFLUENCE GOVERNMENT

The second major strand of government public relations activities deals with efforts to influence the trajectory and outcome of various social, political, and economic issues in various decision-making arenas. One of the first public relations firms was started in the nation's capital in 1902 as a reaction to the progressive policies of the United States government. What started as a two-person firm over 100 years ago has burgeoned into several hundred public relations firms and a legion of lobbyists some 50,000 strong. In 1912, one of the founding practitioners of public relations, Ivy Lee, mounted a campaign on behalf of the private railroad companies to win a rate increase from the Interstate Commerce Commission. Today, the government itself contracts with a large number of public relations firms to conduct a wide range of communications activities.

Although lobbyists specialize by issue, some functions remain constant across the field. These include mining government data for important information; interpreting government actions or plans of action; explaining corporate actions to the government; advocating positions to benefit a company or issue group; using Washington, DC–based news media for organizational publicity; and the facilitation of selling products to the government. The rules governing lobbying were written in 1947 and incorporated into the federal Lobbying Act, which, among other things, requires the registration of lobbyists. Informing and educating members of Congress and the executive branch, however, is an activity undertaken by all manner of special interest groups.

Grassroots lobbying is a tactic used by many groups to influence the government. From Common Cause to the Sierra Club to the National Rifle Association, these nongovernmental organizations (NGOs) motivate their members to contact members of Congress and the executive branch on issues important to their constituencies. Grassroots lobbying, although as diverse as the interest groups themselves, uses tactics such as organizing fly-ins for their members to spend a day on Capitol Hill; catalyzing letters, phone calls, and e-mails to members of Congress; and placing stories in the news media. More aggressive influence efforts, often conducted by groups seeking more substantial degrees of political change, can involve rallies and demonstrations, marches, sit-ins and other dramatic special events designed to capture media attention.

It is clear that the public relations function—both to and from government—is increasing in both scope and size. In the future, some researchers believe that additional skills will be needed by public managers to do their work. Expected competencies include more traditional public relations activities and encompass the role of a policy entrepreneur. Additionally, public managers will need to prepare for the new media realities of life in the Internet age and a refocusing on public reporting.

—Aileen Webb and Charles T. Salmon

Bibliography

Caywood, C. (1997). *The handbook of strategic public relations and integrated communications*. New York: McGraw-Hill.

Cutlip, S. M., Center, A. H., & Broom, C. M. (2000). *Effective public relations* (8th ed.). Englewood Cliffs, NJ: Prentice Hall.

Cutlip, S. (1994). *The unseen power: Public relations. A history (Lea's communication)*. Hillsdale, NJ: Lawrence Erlbaum.

Hiebert, R. (2003). Public relations and propaganda in the framing the Iraq War: A preliminary review. *Public Relations Review, 29*, 243–255.

Jacobson, L. (2001, August 6). Public relations firm takes a second look at federal clients. *The National Journal*. Available online at http://www.govexec.com/dailyfed/0801/08060111.htm

Lee, M. (1999). Reporters and bureaucrats: Public relations counter strategies by public administrators in an era of media disinterest in government. *Public Relations Review, 25*(4), 451–463

Lee, M. (2003). A public relations program even Congress could love: Federal Information Centers. *Public Relations Review, 30*, 61–73.

Rivers, W. (1970). *The adversaries: Politics and the press*. Boston: Beacon.

U.S. NEWSWIRE

See News services

USES AND GRATIFICATIONS THEORY

As radio, film, and television became mainstream items in 20th-century American life, researchers found new topics to study, particularly the way these new media devices and genres fit into the structure or routines of daily life. This outgrowth of the functional paradigm stressed that nature incorporates new parts into existing systems in ways that adjust to and maintain the equilibrium of the systems through repetitive, patterned actions. In essence, the theory argues that viewers, listeners, and readers select and use various media options and programming to gratify their needs. This view of media theory reasons that audiences are active and attentive when media content serves some function they believe to be valuable.

Soon after radio became a standard fixture in American homes, Paul Lazarsfeld's Office of Radio Research sponsored a series of studies to see what radio meant in listeners' lives. The core studies, conducted by Herta Herzog, involved researching who listened to radio soap operas and for what reasons (satisfactions). The studies identified three main gratifications: (1) emotional release, (2) wishful thinking, and (3) advice regarding listeners' own lives. From these self-revealed satisfactions, the term *uses and gratifications* was coined.

This extensive, innovative study of a new media technology and its role as a part of society languished somewhat in research circles until 1959. Then sociologist Elihu Katz, Lazarsfeld's colleague in the 1940s Erie County election studies, again suggested that examination of how the new media were incorporated into the routine of life might begin at the end of the media chain. The new focus was on the users of media forms and technologies, rather than beginning with the technologies and forms being introduced into the system and seeking users. In other words, the suggestion was that end users make choices about (uses of) the media and content to satisfy their social and psychological needs (gratifications). He made his observations from 1959 to the 1970s. Katz further explored the uses and gratifications perspective with his colleagues Jay Blumler and Michael Gurevitch. The threesome's collaborative research resulted in one of the first books about the perspective, *The Use of Mass Communication: Current Perspectives on Gratifications Research,* published in 1974. The authors summarized the book's main premise: "Studies have shown that audience gratifications can be derived from at least three distinct sources: media content, exposure to the media per se, and social context that typifies the situation of exposure to different media" (Katz, Blumler, & Gurevitch, 1974, p. 24).

Katz, Blumler, and Gurevitch's book outlined their original five basic assumptions about the uses and gratifications perspective. First, the audience is an active component of the process rather than a passive recipient. This tenet is based on the idea that individuals have reasons to incorporate media as tools to achieve certain goals. Second, individuals must take the initiative to select and incorporate media into their lives—in other words, exert effort, which demonstrates that individuals are inviting that influence into their lives and therefore are determining what they will and will not allow. Third, media are in competition with other sources of gratification for individuals' attention; therefore, individuals place a high enough value on media to include them while excluding or limiting other sources of gratification, such as face-to-face communication. Fourth, the data showed that individuals "are very aware of their motives and choices and are able to explain them" (Katz et al., 1974, p. 17). This reinforces the idea that people are well aware of their part in creating and maintaining media as part of their system. Fifth, the three theorists believed that to fully understand the effects of media, the motives of the audiences (users) must be explored to discover the values the users place on the media and the content. Only through asking media users can the real value be discovered.

These five major tenets of the original research underlying the uses and gratifications perspective are based on the premise that people have free will to see numerous ways in which media may satisfy their needs and so make conscious choices to expose themselves to these influences. Whether they use the media for news, entertainment, background noise, or social status is secondary to the fact that the choice is theirs. The value in this approach is that through individual choice users can control the influence media have on their lives and the amount of influence the media might have in their lives. This approach is a direct contradiction of earlier theories such as the magic bullet, which emphasized that the media have a direct, uncontrollable, and often powerful effect on its audience members.

Subsequent studies involving the uses and gratifications theory focused on different genres of media technology, particularly television and the Internet, and identification of specific social and cultural variables that influence people's media use. Jennings Bryant and Dolf Zillmannn studied the effect of individuals' moods on media choice; Denis McQuail, Jay G. Blumler, and J. R. Brown explored the gratifications of TV quiz shows; McQuail developed a typology of common reasons for media use; James Lull constructed a typology of the social uses of television; and Richard Kilborn enumerated reasons for watching television soap operas.

The uses and gratifications perspective has spawned its own set of criticisms. Patrick Barwise and Andrew Ehrenberg concluded that media use is often not the totally conscious, selective choice that uses and gratifications theory originally suggested it was. Their conclusion was that media use is often habit bound and set in ritual, such as turning on the television upon walking in the room or listening to the radio while in the automobile. They further posited that selectivity was also ritualistic, in that individuals often did not consciously select what was on radio or television, but kept it on because it had become a habit.

McQuail suggested that in addition to the availability of media and individuals' access to media channels, personal circumstances and psychological makeup could also be factors that play a part in individuals' media choices and use. David Morley continued this line of thought by exploring the idea that subcultural socioeconomic influences play a role in how individuals use media, particularly in the way that people relate their experiences with those of television characters. This expands the narrow focus of uses and gratifications to include the perspective that people use media to identify with characters and scenarios in their surroundings and incorporate those values via cultural codes. This suggests that the media channels and content are not the only powerful elements in users' choices; the individuals' surroundings can also be a powerful influence affecting the media's power. The challenge here is isolating these variables to measure the true strength of the media effects versus environmental influences.

The general nature of the uses and gratifications perspective has led some researchers to dispute that uses and gratifications is a theory at all, and to contend it is more of an umbrella term for further study to develop specific theories with identifiable variables.

Working with colleague Karl Rosengren, Philip Palmgreen used his work in attitude orientation to develop the expectancy-value theory, which posits that individuals have a group of beliefs and evaluations (attitudes). The beliefs determine what an individual thinks he or she will get from a medium, and evaluations determine whether that medium provided the gratification sought. For example, if an individual watches a television program because he or she wants to be entertained, he or she will evaluate whether the time spent was worthwhile and make future decisions about more or less viewing, creating what Stephen Littlejohn calls a cycle of viewing/judging. Palmgreen developed this line of thought into the expectancy-value model of gratifications, demonstrating that uses and gratifications is not a simple linear process, as was first thought, but a complex cycle and network of effects.

Sandra Ball-Rokeach and Melvin DeFleur used the basic assumption of uses and gratifications to explore just how powerful the effects of this approach were. The result was the creation of dependency theory, which posits that users will become more dependent on media that seem to meet more of their needs and less dependent on media that meet fewer of their needs. A critical factor here is what importance the user places on different information in his or her life; for example,

die-hard sports fans will probably spend more time with ESPN than with the *CBS Evening News*. Another consideration is social circumstances, such as when outside events intrude in an individual's world and create an unstable situation—for example, the 9/11 destruction of the Twin Towers. The rabid sports fan will then most likely find his or her attention drawn away from ESPN to some type of news coverage. Depending on the severity of the social change, the resulting effect can be the creation of a new dependency, which may or may not create a permanent shift in media use and focus.

Leo Jeffers concluded that future study in uses and gratifications will focus on moving to higher research and theoretical levels, particularly in the area of "linking changes in patterns of uses and gratifications sought with changes in media content patterns and shifts in media organizations" (Jeffers, 1994, p. 260). This commentary sums up the focus of uses and gratifications research: The emphasis will be on the discovering patterns in relationship to the changing media scene while incorporating the social-psychological-environmental influences on individuals.

—*Barbara J. DeSanto*

Bibliography

Barwise, P., & Ehrenberg, A. (1988). *Television and its audience.* London: Sage.

Bryant, J., & Zillmann, D. (1994). *Media effects: Advances in theory and research.* Hillsdale, NJ: Lawrence Erlbaum.

DeFleur, M. L., & Ball-Rokeach, S. J. (1989). *Theories of mass communication* (5th ed.). New York: Longman.

Jeffers, L. W. (1994). *Mass media processes* (2nd ed.). Prospect Heights, IL: Waveland Press.

Katz, E., Blumler, J., & Gurevitch, M. (1974). *The use of mass communication: Current perspectives on gratifications research.* New York: Sage.

Kilborn, R. (1992). *Television soaps.* London: Batsford.

Littlejohn, S. W. (2002). *Theories of human communication* (7th ed.). Belmont, CA: Wadsworth Thomson Learning.

Lull, J. (1990). *Inside family viewing: Ethnographic research on television's audiences.* London: Routledge.

McQuail, D. (2000). *McQuail's mass communication theory* (4th ed.). London: Sage.

McQuail, D., Blumler, J. G., & Brown, J. R. (1972). The television audience: A revised perspective. In D. McQuail (Ed.), *Sociology of mass communication* (pp. 135–165). Middlesex, UK: Penguin Books.

Morley, D. (1992). *Television, audiences and cultural studies.* London: Routledge.

Palmgreen, P. (1984). Uses and gratifications: A theoretical perspective. In R. N. Bostrom & B. H. Westley (Eds.), *Communication yearbook 8* (pp. 20–55). Beverly Hills, CA: Sage.

UTILITARIANISM

Advocates of greater professionalism in public relations have long emphasized the practice's value to the public interest. The most recent code of ethics adopted by the Public Relations Society of America (PRSA) includes values associated with public service: advocacy, honesty, expertise, independence, loyalty, and fairness. Indeed, code provisions advocate the free flow of information, competition, and disclosure; safeguarding confidences; eschewing conflicts of interest; and enhancing the profession. Inherent in the concept of professionalism is a moral obligation to serve the public interest. Public relations serves the public when it provides information people need to make decisions, encourages commerce, and discloses financial and business dealings affecting stockholders and the public. Working on behalf of the common good is consistent with utilitarianism, a theory of morality based on improving the general welfare of humanity.

Among the best-known proponents of utilitarianism are John Stuart Mill (1806–1873) and Jeremy Bentham (1748–1832). In his 1863 book *Utilitarianism,* Mill identified happiness as the ultimate goal of human existence.

The creed, which accepts utility, or the greatest happiness principle, as the foundation of morality, holds that actions are right in proportion to their tendency to promote happiness, and wrong in proportion to their tendency to promote the reverse of happiness (Mill, 2002, p. 239).

Mill defined happiness as pleasure or the absence of pain. The rightness of an action is based on the amount of pleasure produced for society by the action. Unlike deontological theories, the focus of utilitarian ethics is on the outcome of one's action, not the act itself. An act is judged right if it produces more good than evil or more pleasure than pain. In this sense, the theory combines the two main concepts of ethics—right and good. The good is defined independently from the right, and the right is defined as that which maximizes the good.

Because happiness is the goal of human existence, producing the greatest amount of happiness for the greatest number of people serves as the moral obligation for humanity. Utilitarianism falls into a larger category of teleology in which maximizing the good is the goal of human action. On face value alone, wrote philosopher John Rawls (a critic of utilitarianism), teleological theories have merit.

Teleological theories have a deep intuitive appeal because they seem to embody the idea of rationality. It is natural to think that rationality is maximizing something and that in morality it must be maximizing the good. Indeed, it is tempting to suppose that it is self-evident that things should be arranged to lead to the most good (Rawls, 1971, pp. 24–25).

As the leader of England's philosophical radicals, a group of social reformers, Jeremy Bentham sought to reform England's legal system. He advocated a theory of justice in which right was measured by the effects of an action on the public welfare. He saw far too many judges basing punishment on the rule violated rather than on the crime's impact on society. For him, the level of punishment should be equivalent to the harm caused by the crime. Bentham even used a mathematical equation to determine which actions produced the most utility. His *hedonic calculus* determined right action by estimating the units of pleasure and pain produced by an action. If one action produced 10 units of pleasure (+10) as opposed to seven units of pain (−7) and another action produced five units of pleasure (+5) and three units of pain (−3), the first action with three overall units of pleasure would be considered more right than the latter action producing two units of pleasure (Munro, 1999, pp. 97–104).

Among the philosophical radicals adopting Bentham's utilitarianism was James Mill, whose son would reform Bentham's theories and give them relevance and vitality (Schneewind, 1999, p. 658). At age 3, John Stuart Mill began reading

Greek and in his late teens contributed articles to scholarly journals, including Bentham's *Westminster Review*. In his 1863 book, *Utilitarianism,* Mill dismisses Immanuel Kant's rule-based system of ethics, arguing that deducing moral duties from rules, without accounting for contradictions, is a logical impossibility. "All he shows is that the *consequences* of their universal adoption would be such as no one would choose to incur" (Mill, 2002, p. 236).

What Kant lacked, according to Mill, is proof that the rules were right in and of themselves. For Mill, that proof came only from the good produced by adhering to those rules. The medical art is good because it leads to health, and the art of music is good because it produces pleasure. The proof lies in the effect of the medical care and the music played.

Mills differed from Bentham in that he placed a greater value on higher mental pleasures than bodily pleasures. The quality of pleasures was just as important as the quantity of pleasures.

A being of higher faculties requires more to make him happy, is capable probably of more acute suffering, and is certainly accessible to it at more points, than one of an inferior type; but in spite of these liabilities, he can never really wish to sink into what he feels to be a lower grade of existence (Mill, 2002, p. 242).

In other words, cultivating the higher faculties opens the door to frustration and discontent— indeed, to recognition of one's imperfections. "It is better to be a human being dissatisfied than a pig satisfied; better to be Socrates dissatisfied than a fool satisfied" (Mill, 2002, p. 242). Mill does not mean that happiness requires someone to become a philosopher or scholar, but it does demand an interest in the world, nature, history, poetry, and the future. The utilitarian would resist isolation from the community and the world. To withdraw inside the gates of one's organization and work solely for personal gain would run counter to happiness. "When people who are tolerably fortunate in their outward lot do not find in life sufficient enjoyment to make it valuable to them, the cause generally is, caring for nobody but themselves" (Mill, 2002, p. 246).

One's obligation to the general welfare increases in proportion to the benefits one reaps from society.

The demands of utility would differ depending on the size and scope of the organization. Major corporations, enjoying the benefits of special laws, are obligated to do more for the greater good than smaller firms. Each, as a part of society, has an obligation to give back. Utilitarianism would place a heavy moral burden on multinational corporations, expecting them to benefit all living species. One's moral obligation would extend to animal life and the environment.

For Mill, the key to utility was benefiting society according to one's capabilities. He explained,

> The multiplication of happiness is, according to the utilitarian ethics, the object of virtue: the occasions on which any person (except one in a thousand) has it in his power to do this on an extended scale, in other words, to be a public benefactor, are but exceptional; and on these occasions alone is he called on to consider public utility; in every other case, private utility, the interest or happiness of some few persons, is all he has to attend to. (Mill, 2002, p. 252)

Contemporary utilitarianism provides two options when faced with a moral decision. One may adopt an act utilitarian approach or apply rule utilitarianism. The act utilitarian analyzes each situation and chooses the course of action that will likely bring about the best consequences. Act utilitarians "are to moralists as radar is to the storm-tossed airline pilot, furnishing general indicators but not a detailed and specific description of forces impinging on his aircraft" (Lambeth, 1986, pp. 15–16). Act utilitarianism appeals to industries that have no hard and fast rules of ethical conduct.

Rule utilitarians make decisions based on moral rules that have been shown over time to produce the greatest good. Unlike deontology, these rules are not based on the right action but on the consequences of right action. A good example of rule utilitarianism is ethics codes. They often represent what the profession or discipline has determined to have historically produced the best results. Honesty is the best policy because it increases trust and improves the quality of communication.

For most public relations practitioners, utilitarianism has an intuitive appeal. It advocates a responsibility to society without forfeiting one's responsibility to client organizations. Indeed, the organization is a part of society and, therefore, promoting its success would serve the greater good because society depends on healthy competition. If the organization acts contrary to the public welfare, then one's obligation would be to reconcile by coming clean and righting the wrongs caused by organizational behavior. Indeed, serving the greater good of one's organization would mean, for Mill, serving the greater good of society. If a conflict between the two occurs, one would have to rely on one's moral character and experience to choose which action would promote the greatest happiness.

If the PRSA Member Code of Ethics were a utilitarian standard, then the public relations practitioner would adhere to it because it has been shown to produce the greatest amount of happiness for the greatest number of people. In a free market society, businesses require advocates to help their voices be heard. By advocating the organization's cause, one serves the greater good. If the cause were unjust, however, its advocacy would also be unjust. Honesty would serve as a rule to guide action unless a situation arises in which withholding information might be in the best interests of society. Once the moral justification for withholding the information no longer applies, utilitarianism obligates full disclosure—not only of the information, but the reason for withholding the information in the first place. If the public agreed with the decision, one might feel justified in having withheld the information, but public disapproval and condemnation would expose one's mistake and lead to its correction when a similar situation arises in the future.

Expertise and independence would have utility as long as they were used to benefit the greater good. One could never justify their use for selfish reasons. Loyalty would serve the greater good because

loyalty is critical to a family, organization, and society; but if loyalty required immoral action, it would no longer serve the greater good. Fairness fits with the utilitarian goal of justice, and it would require practitioners not to use their power in such a way as to create inequity in society. While utilitarianism appears to emphasize the needs of the majority, it has never been in the majority's interest to oppress a minority.

The practicality of utilitarianism is that it allows public relations to promote the interests of the few and the many. It allows practitioners to serve as a moral conscience for the organization while advocating the organization's self-interests. One could feel comfortable serving the interests of those within one's company, knowing that doing good work for local interests benefits global interests. As one's position and influence increases, one's obligation to the public interest would proportionally increase. For utilitarians, where much is given, much is required.

—*Kevin Stoker*

Bibliography

Frankena, W. K. (1973). *Ethics* (2nd ed.). Englewood Cliffs, NJ: Prentice-Hall.

Lambeth, E. B. (1986). *Committed journalism: An ethic for the profession.* Bloomington: University of Indiana Press.

Mill, J. S. (2002). *The basic writings of John Stuart Mill: Utilitarianism.* New York: The Modern Library. (Original work published 1863)

Munro, D. H. (1999). Bentham, Jeremy. In D. M. Borchert (Ed.), *Philosophy and ethics* (pp. 97–104). New York: Macmillan Library Reference USA.

Rawls, J. (1971). *A theory of justice.* Cambridge, MA: The Belknap Press of Harvard University Press.

Schneewind, J. B. (1999). Mill, John Stuart. In D. M. Borchert (Ed.), *Philosophy and ethics* (pp. 658–672). New York: Macmillan Library Reference USA.

VAIL, THEODORE NEWTON

Theodore Newton Vail (July 16, 1845–April 16, 1920) was a senior executive with the company now known as AT&T at two of the most critical moments in its history:

- From 1878 to 1887, when the telephone began its voyage from fledgling invention to ubiquitous home and office appliance
- From 1907 to 1919, when the company, beset by competitors and despised by its customers, moved from the brink of financial ruin to a de facto monopoly affectionately known as "Ma Bell"

Vail was hired for his experience in managing complex operations, but his real success stemmed from his view of public relations as a critical component of business strategy.

Vail was born in Ohio and raised in Morristown, New Jersey, where his father supervised an uncle's ironworks. His cousin, Alfred Vail, was a close associate of Samuel F. B. Morse and helped develop the telegraph at the ironworks, devising the dot-and-dash alphabet of Morse code. So it's not surprising that Theodore Vail was interested in telegraphy as a young man and took a job as a telegraph operator for Western Union in New York City when he was 19. In 1866, his father purchased a farm in Iowa, and young Vail moved with the family. After two years of farming and teaching, he became a night telegraph operator for the Union Pacific Railroad at a supply station in Wyoming territory as the railroad pushed its way west. The following year, he married a cousin from Newark, New Jersey, and they moved to Omaha, Nebraska, where he landed a job as a clerk with the Railway Mail Service. Vail devised a system for presorting mail on railroad cars and attracted the attention of the Railway Mail Superintendent in Washington, DC, who made him his special assistant in 1873. Vail applied his new system to rail routes across the country, and in 1876 he was promoted to Railway Mail Superintendent himself, becoming the youngest officer in the Railway Mail Service.

That same year, Congress established a commission to devise a better system for paying railroads to transport mail. Vail worked closely with the commission's chairman, Gardiner Greene Hubbard, who happened to be Alexander Graham Bell's father-in-law and one of his original backers. Hubbard was impressed with the young postal executive's energy and creativity. For his part, Vail was fascinated by the telephone, which had just been invented. In February 1878, Hubbard hired Vail as the Bell Telephone Company General Manager. At that point, the Bell Telephone Company was less than one year old and controlled by a small group of Boston-based investors. It was assigning franchises in major cities, renting telephone sets to the local operators, and taking an ownership position in their companies. But it was low on cash; its principal assets were the four basic patents Bell had filed less than two years earlier, and it was suing the powerful Western Union Company for infringing them.

Bell and Western Union settled their suit in 1879, basically agreeing to stay out of each other's business. With a patent position that would not expire for 17 years, the company reorganized itself into the American Bell Telephone Company, with Vail as its chief operating officer. By then, the company managed 133,000 telephones, including 55,000 turned over to it by Western Union, and it had a capitalization of over $7 million.

Vail applied the same management skills to the telephone business that he had to the post office, including a strong sense of public service. His 1883 letter to the presidents of the Bell operating companies demonstrates a focus on customer relations uncharacteristic of the times. He asked them to assess "the tendency of the relationship between the public and the local companies for the past year. . . . Is telephone service as it is now being furnished satisfactory to the public? . . . Where there has been any conflict between the local Exchange and the public, what has been the cause?"

Vail also brought with him a conviction that a single company was the surest way to ensure reliable and ubiquitous service. He began building the Bell System with regional companies providing local service, a long-distance company interconnecting them, and a captive supplier manufacturing all the necessary equipment. In 1885, AT&T was incorporated as American Bell's long-distance subsidiary with Vail as president. Vail reasoned that Bell could maintain a virtual monopoly after the expiration of its patents by limiting access to AT&T's long-distance network to its licensed companies, isolating the independent telephone companies.

But American Bell's Boston investors were impatient to see a return on their capital and refused to fund further expansion. When they passed over Vail and named someone else president, as documented by J. Edward Hyde, Vail resigned. In an unusual parting shot, he wrote, "We have a duty to the public at large to make our service as good as possible and as universal as possible, and [our] earnings should be used not only to reward investors for their investment but also to accomplish these objectives" (Hyde, 1976, p. 23).

In the following years, American Bell milked the business Vail had built, raising rates and allowing service quality to slip. When the Bell patents expired in 1894, its disaffected customers couldn't wait to give their business to competitors. In 1899, the company's long-distance arm, AT&T, acquired the assets of its parent, American Bell, and became the parent company of the Bell System.

By 1907, AT&T was in sorry financial condition. Financier J. P. Morgan, who had acquired a major stake in the company, asked Vail to return as the company's president. Vail was 62 years old, his wife and only son had recently died, and he had made a fortune in South American transit development. No one would have blamed him if he had chosen to stay on his farm in Lyndonville, Vermont. But some of the original American Bell directors, now quite elderly themselves, took the train to Lyndonville and convinced Vail that the pieces were in place to realize his dream of a single, nationwide telephone system. But they needed him to pull it together and make it work.

Vail accepted the job and bought independent companies by the dozens, folding them into the Bell regional companies. And within two years, he even bought control of Bell's old rival, Western Union.

But Vail knew that the public, still reeling from the era of the "robber barons," mistrusted big business and was particularly skeptical about monopolies. He believed good public relations were based on understanding public opinion and helping to educate and shape it. So, according to AT&T's 1908 Annual Report, he undertook a systematic program of public education, working from the principle that "if we don't tell the public the truth about ourselves, somebody else will."

Thus began an unusual series of advertisements designed to sell not products or services but the company itself. The first of these ads, prepared by the N. W. Ayer advertising agency of Philadelphia, appeared in the summer of 1908 and set forth the campaign's objective in its subhead: "A perfect understanding by the public of the management and full scope of the Bell Telephone System can have but one effect, and that a most desirable one—a marked betterment of the services."

On a trip to Denver, Vail discovered that the town's business leaders were well acquainted with their local phone company, but knew little of AT&T and its Bell System. Vail ordered a logo prepared to spell it all out and signed every ad with it. Thus was the Bell seal born.

One of the first ads to appear with the new logo ran in the fall of 1908 under the headline "One Policy. One System. Universal Service." When one of the agency people worried that the ad's monopoly overtones might get the company embroiled in the national elections then under way, Vail asked if the ad was truthful. According to a 1936 unpublished memoir of James Drummond Ellsworth, AT&T's first publicist, Vail said, "Then print it and beat [the politicians] to it" (p. 68).

By promoting the customer benefits of "universal service," Vail had hit on a way to make a telephone monopoly acceptable to a wary public. He recast the company's vast reach—its very bigness—as a virtue, giving every Bell telephone user a connection to the wider world. Vail used every available technique, including publicity, pamphlets, speakers bureaus, and even the relatively new medium of moving pictures to tell the Bell System story. In 1912, when most companies preferred to operate in secrecy, Vail established what was probably the first corporate "Public Relations Bureau" to centralize information about the company and to track public opinion. "Take the public into your confidence," Vail was quoted as saying in Albert Bigelow Paine's In One Man's Life, "and you win the confidence of the public" (1921, p. 238.)

Business philosophy had come a long way since William Vanderbilt's oft-quoted answer when he was asked if he worked for the public or his shareholders—"The public be damned."

In January 1913 the U.S. Department of Justice notified AT&T that its string of acquisitions had put it in danger of violating the Sherman Antitrust Act.

Since the Interstate Commerce Commission had been investigating its acquisitions for three years, Vail could see the handwriting on the wall. Further, although the company operated in only a third of the country, it serviced 83 percent of American telephones. So in a daring move, Vail sued for peace. He promised to stop buying independent companies without government approval, offered to sell the company's 30 percent interest in Western Union, and agreed to allow the independent telephone companies to interconnect with AT&T's long-distance network at reasonable fees. In return, the government closed its investigations and accepted AT&T as a limited national monopoly.

Vail retired as president of AT&T in June 1919 at the age of 74. He died less than a year later. But the business system he built survived for another 65 years, becoming the richest company in the world by the time of its centennial in 1976. The Bell System was dismantled in an antitrust agreement in 1984, but the principles by which Vail conducted business—openness, candor, and customer service—survive in the DNA of numerous companies it spawned.

—Dick Martin

See also Block, Ed; Ellsworth, James Drummond; Laurie, Marilyn; Page, Arthur W.

Bibliography

Brooks, J. (1976). Telephone: The first hundred years. New York: HarperCollins.

Danielian, N. R. (1974). AT&T: The story of industrial conquest. New York: Arno Press.

Dresser, C. (1882, October 9). Interview with William H. Vanderbilt. Chicago Daily News.

Garnet, R. W.(1991). The telephone enterprise: The evolution of the Bell System's horizontal structure, 1876–1920. Baltimore: John Hopkins University Press.

Hyde, J. E. (1976). The phone book: What the telephone company would rather you not know. Chicago: Henry Regnery.

Paine, A. B. (1921). In One Man's Life. New York: Harper and Brothers.

Stone, A. (1991). Public service liberalism: Telecommunications and transitions in public policy. New Jersey: Princeton University Press.

von Auw, A. (1983). Heritage and destiny. New York: Praeger.

Theodore Newton Vail

SOURCE: Property of AT&T Archives. Reprinted with permission of AT&T.

VALIDITY

In general, validity refers to the accuracy of a quantitative research project. Validity is a concern in public relation research any time a survey instrument or sample is used. Use of a survey instrument raises questions about internal validity, as the accuracy of a research project is influenced by the planning, design, and execution of the project. A number of factors influence internal validity that are controlled through the experimental design. Few public relations research projects are true experiments, so this entry concentrates on the measurement aspect (i.e., surveys) of internal validity. The validity of a survey centers on whether or not you are actually measuring the concept you intended to measure.

An example will help to clarify the ideas related to validity. As part of a revision of an organization's employee communication system, suppose you decide to assess "communication satisfaction" with the various communication vehicles. A survey can be used to measure a variable such as communication satisfaction. But how do you know you are actually measuring the desired variable, in this case communication satisfaction? This is an issue related to internal validity. One check is called face validity. You, as an expert, carefully examine the survey to see if it captures the variable—that the survey reflects how you have defined the variable. A second check is content validity, where a group of experts on the topic review the survey. You could have experts on employee communication review the survey to determine if they think it captures communication satisfaction. A third check is criterion-related validity, in which your survey is proven to be related as anticipated to other established measures. You compare the results of your survey with the results of previously validated scales to see if they are related as predicted. The idea is to determine if the scores on your survey are consistent with the other scales. For instance, communication satisfaction should be positively related to job satisfaction, a variable that has validated measures. You would assess whether the communication satisfaction scores are positively correlated with job satisfaction scores. When two surveys correlate as predicted and correlate positively, this is known as convergence. You can also select a measure for a variable that you believe should correlate negatively with your survey, and this is called divergence. Although time consuming, testing validity is important when you create a new survey that is crucial to your public relations effort. It is better to invest the time and money in validating the scale than using inaccurate data—collected data that do not truly measure the intended variable.

External validity is the ability to generalize results from your sample to a larger population. Samples are used frequently in public relations research. For instance, you survey a small number of your customers, not all of them, to assess their knowledge of or attitudes toward an organization. External validity requires proper sampling techniques. The key is to use a sampling strategy that helps to ensure a representative sample—that is, the characteristics of your sample are the same as those of the population from which it was drawn. Your sample of customers should be representative of your customer population. If your primary customers are women from 20 to 35 years of age and your sample is mostly men 40 to 50 years of age, the sample is not representative. Refer to the "Sampling" entry for a discussion of proper sampling strategies for external validity.

—*W. Timothy Coombs*

See also Experiment/experimental methods; Quantitative research; Scales; Survey

Bibliography

Austin, E. W., & Pinkleton, B. E. (2001). *Strategic public relations management: Planning and managing effective communication campaigns.* Mahwah, NJ: Lawrence Erlbaum.

Stack, D. W. (2002). *Primer of public relations research.* New York: Guilford Press.

VOTER AND CONSTITUENT RELATIONS

Elected officers in the United States, from the city council to the presidency, communicate with their constituents. There are two phases to this relationship: the campaign and post-election. Yet for the candidate who is elected, these two phases may overlap: Voters become constituents, who are potentially voters again for the next election. This circular process has resulted in some observers categorizing constituent communication efforts as part of "the permanent campaign," "the continuous campaign," or "the invisible campaign." Once a candidate is put in office, the distinctions between a "voter" and a "constituent" blur. Since elected officers are provided some budget for communicating with constituents, the advantage for the incumbent grows exponentially: Not only are the communication efforts with constituents rewarded in the polling booth at the next election, but such efforts are subsidized by taxpayers themselves.

For a challenger facing an incumbent officeholder or for a candidate in an open race (where neither candidate is the current officeholder), the only phase of communication that matters is the election campaign itself. If the candidate does not establish and maintain satisfying relationships with voters at this stage, the opportunity to establish an effective constituent relations program will not exist.

VOTER RELATIONS

A political campaign is a communications event with important and enduring public policy consequences. How do candidates establish relationships with potential voters? In the 21st century the answer is equally divided between advanced technology and old-fashioned grass roots; it is concurrently accomplished through expensive advertising campaigns and heavy reliance on free news coverage and personal voter contact programs.

Since 1998 there has been a proliferation of the use of Web sites and e-mail contacts with potential voters in campaigns from the mayor's office to the Senate. Although these applications vary in sophistication and are used by voters who are typically highly involved in campaigns, they are becoming increasingly important.

At the same time that technology is facilitating voter relations, old-fashioned grassroots activities are resurfacing, also at all levels of office. Grassroots activities include all types of direct contact with voters: cookouts, door-to-door canvassing, and meetings. They typically rely on personal contact and communication between potential voters and the candidate or his or her surrogate. It is generally believed that the most persuasive grassroots activity provides personal contact with the actual candidate; surrogates who are directly linked to the candidate (spouse, family member) are the next tier; and anonymous volunteer surrogates follow. All personal contact via grassroots activities is highly regarded as an important element in electoral victory. One Republican political consultant, in an interview following the 2002 U.S. House of Representatives elections, indicated that a primary reason the Republicans did so well is that they've finally learned the grassroots techniques Democrats have practiced for years, and they're using them more effectively.

Political advertising appears across all broadcast and print media, as well as in outdoor, personal apparel and pre-recorded telephone messages. The amount and style of political advertisements are generally determined by the campaign budget combined with the availability and coverage of a particular medium. Although many Americans maintain that they dislike most political advertising, such ads on television are an important source of information for a majority of voters.

Obtaining free news coverage is an important element in most campaigns. Yet due to its unreliability in carrying a desired message to potential voters, it is considered a risky strategy to rely on extensively. Underfunded campaigns are more likely to seek free media than well-funded ones.

CONSTITUENT RELATIONS

Once elected, an officeholder has a continuing obligation to communicate with the people he or she is serving. Constituent relations are mutually beneficial to all involved parties. Constituents benefit from information they receive about various issues of governance and public policies, as well as occasional personal assistance from the officeholder. Officeholders benefit from the build-up of goodwill established through ongoing constituent communications efforts.

Staples among the tools of constituent relations may be categorized as (1) those conducted within the home district, state, or locale; and (2) those conducted within the office itself, often located geographically distant from the constituents. Within the home district or locale, many constituent relations functions are handled by a local office with a staff that operates independently (yet under the direction) of the elected officer. This local office provides much personal attention to local constituents and serves as the "home base" for the representative when he or she is in town. For U.S. congressmen and senators these local offices are often the point of first contact for a constituent

seeking assistance from the representative. One of the most important elements of constituent relations is the personal visit to the district, state, or locale by the elected representative; town meetings, drop-in visits, and events that attract constituents to meet with their represented official are often planned during such visits. One newly elected congressman in Georgia rides with a UPS delivery truck one day a month and visits every business stop on the route. Such creative tactics facilitate communication between the elected representative and constituents and are mutually beneficial to the corporation, the politician, and the citizenry. Many "within home area" activities carry the additional benefit of becoming subject matter for news media attention.

Much constituent relations activity occurs when the elected person is geographically distant from the home area. Central to effective communications handled by the primary office staff, these tools include newsletters, Web sites and e-mail, telephone contacts, and on-site visits from constituents.

Many public relations personnel are increasingly occupying central staff positions at all levels of public offices as managers of the voter and constituent relations functions.

—*Ruthann Weaver Lariscy*

Bibliography

Blumenthal, S. (1982). *The permanent campaign.* New York: Simon & Schuster.

Drew, D., & Weaver, D. (1998). Voter learning in the 1996 presidential election: Did the media matter? *Journalism & Mass Communication Quarterly, 75*(2): 292–301.

Fenno, R. F. Jr. (2003). *Home style: House members in their districts.* New York: Longman.

Hackney, A. J. (2003, April). Personal interview. Washington, DC.

Weaver Lariscy, R., & Tinkham, S. F. (1991). News coverage, endorsements, and personal campaigning: The influence on non-paid activities in congressional elections. *Journalism & Mass Communication Quarterly, 68*(3), 432–444.

Weaver Lariscy, R., Tinkham, S. F., Edwards, H. H., & Jones, K. O. (2001). *The "ground wars" of political campaigns: Grassroots activities in US state legislative campaigns.* Paper presented to the Political Communication Division of the International Communication Association, Washington, DC, May 2001.

WARFARE AND PUBLIC RELATIONS

When nations go to war, their citizens go with them. Modern warfare requires the commitment of a nation's resources and the sacrifice and support of its population. Democratic nations, in particular, must win the support of their citizens before committing armed forces to battle, and maintain that support for the duration of hostilities and beyond. Even in peacetime, the government and industries responsible for military preparedness must justify continued investment in weapons and forces. For these reasons, public relations strategies and tactics have long been associated with the waging of war. Historically, wartime has fostered pivotal developments in public relations strategies and tactics, as well as the careers of notable public relations figures. As warfare has changed, so too has the way in which these strategies and tactics have been used. However, the field's connection to warfare has raised ethical questions about the means and ends of public relations in pursuit of war.

Historically, the call to arms has helped develop the careers of notable public relations practitioners and, more important, the understanding of the use and effects of various strategies and tactics. Although some trace the connection between public relations and warfare to ancient Rome or the American Revolution, the rise of the modern public relations practice in the early 20th century is intimately connected to warfare.

President Woodrow Wilson formed the Committee on Public Information (CPI) during World War I. More commonly known as the Creel Committee—after its chair, newspaper editor George Creel—the CPI comprised leading newspaper editors, advertising writers, and several figures in the nascent public relations field, including Edward Bernays and Carl Byoir, who was the CPI's associate chair.

The Creel Committee is noteworthy for several reasons. First, it clearly established the three purposes to which governments put communication efforts in wartime: to build domestic public support for the war; to communicate U.S. intentions to foreign nations, with the aim of building support among allies and acquiescence among enemies; and to censor, or control the flow of, information reaching the media and, by extension, the public. Second, the CPI used a comprehensive range of communication tactics to achieve its aims, from personal appearances and staged events to the mass media of the day. This marked one of the first times that a public relations campaign used such a wide range of tactics, from newspaper articles, editorials, and advertisements warning against enemy spies to the "Four Minute Men," a corps of trained public speakers who blanketed the country with propaganda in support of the

President Woodrow Wilson (left) and George Creel, Committee on Public Information (more commonly known as the Creel Committee), leave the Royal Train at a station in the Alps on January 2, 1919, for exercise. Wilson formed the committee during World War I, made up of leading newspaper editors, advertising writers, and members of the public relations field as a means of spreading propaganda.

SOURCE: © Bettmann/CORBIS

war. Finally, the CPI nurtured the careers of Bernays and Byoir. Bernays, who played a relatively small role in the CPI's division, found some of his ideas about mass influence and the engineering of consent reinforced by the success of the CPI's campaign. Byoir staged a number of events designed to build support for the war among European immigrants. The events included a July 4, 1918, celebration in Philadelphia for the newly independent Czechoslovakia. What was truly impressive about the Creel Committee, in addition to its winning widespread financial and emotional support for the war, was the fact that its messages reached nearly every corner of the country despite the lack of a national mass media or universal literacy.

During World War II, the United States again called upon public relations and media professionals to galvanize support for the war effort. This time, the effort was directed by the Office of War Information (OWI), which served functions similar to the Creel Committee. The OWI had more media tools with which to work, including feature length motion pictures, newsreels, and radio broadcasts.

For example, director Frank Capra's "Why We Fight" films were designed to explain to the American public the aims of the war and events leading up to America's involvement. In addition to the OWI, public relations practitioners played significant roles in communicating U.S. policy. Former AT&T public relations chief Arthur W. Page drafted President Harry Truman's announcement of the first use of atomic weapons.

After World War II, the U.S. military's public relations activities were centralized in the newly renamed Department of Defense. With each branch of the service developing its own public information officers, the military no longer relied on ad hoc committees composed of civilians and military personnel. These ad hoc committees had essentially acted as public relations consultancies to the military effort; however, the history of both the CPI and the OWI was marked by infighting among the various military branches and the civilian experts. Centralizing the military's public relations operation was meant to reduce the rancor. This reflected a trend in corporate public relations during the same period in which an increasing number of large corporations sought to establish their own internal public relations departments. Public relations agencies still thrived, but this was an era of rapid growth in internal public relations operations. Although centralizing the public information function reaped some benefits for the military, such as a more unified message and streamlined operation, it also meant that news media professionals were no longer a formal part of the government's war efforts. The media were now outsiders and, spearheaded by the rise of a more critical generation of journalists, were more likely to investigate and criticize the military.

By the 1960s, the U.S. Defense Department employed more public information specialists than any other organization in the world. Over 1,000 members of the armed forces were assigned public information or public affairs duties. However, the Vietnam War was largely seen as both a military and a public relations failure. The United States' involvement in the war developed slowly, beginning in the late 1950s, and its aims were more difficult to explain. Further, the media, now working outside the official government public relations apparatuses, were covering the war from the front lines. In previous wars, the military was able to censor newsreel film footage showing American casualties and the horrors of war. In Vietnam, such footage was shown on evening newscasts. In addition to media coverage of the war, the antiwar movement also received extensive coverage and legitimacy. Every war from the American Revolution onward has had its opponents. The opponents often use public relations strategies and tactics to gain recognition and influence opinion. During the Vietnam War, the antiwar movement was able to leverage media coverage and direct influence tactics to turn opinion against the war.

It was widely believed among military professionals that if public opinion had not turned against the war, the United States might have prevailed. Although it is impossible to ascertain the veracity of this judgment, the perception that media coverage of battle adversely affected public opinion was to influence military public relations policy from that point forward. For example, in the United States' invasion of Grenada and the 1991 Persian Gulf War, the military strictly controlled media access to the battlefields. Much of the information about the war was gleaned from press briefings conducted by the Defense Department, which included military-edited videotape of successful U.S. attacks. Although reporters dutifully covered these press conferences, they also chafed at the restrictions and tacit censorship.

Both corporate and military public relations efforts are influenced by trends. Businesses are affected by sociological, cultural, economic, and technological changes. Similarly, the connection between public relations and warfare has been influenced by changes in the nature of warfare and media technology. These changes, in turn, have influenced both the strategies and tactics employed by the military to meet their goals.

Three trends in the nature of warfare have influenced the public relations strategies of combatants. The first trend is a shift in the kind of wars that nations—or, more frequently, populations—fight. Traditional wars fought between nations or groups of nations have given way to civil wars that pit one ethnic, religious, economic, or racial group against

another in the same country or region. After the end of the Cold War in the early 1990s, the geopolitical magnetism that aligned nations East and West against each other dissolved, giving way to a number of conflicts in the Balkans, Africa, and Asia. From the perspective of public relations strategy, the impact has been twofold. First, factions that can control the media in a region can influence local opinion about the war and rally one faction to take up arms against another. Thus Bosnian President Slobodan Milosevic used the state-controlled media to rally his armed forces and the local civilian population to engage in ethnic cleansing against Albanians. Second, the factions in these conflicts attempt to appeal to international media to bring international pressure to bear on their opponents or to bring an end to the conflict. Occasionally, nongovernmental organizations, especially relief or refugee groups, try to draw world attention to a war by drawing media attention to the plight of its victims. With the spread of global media outlets such as the BBC and CNN, the opportunities to gain media attention for civil wars have increased. This trend prompted one veteran journalist to warn others to "beware of thugs, warlords, and P. R. agents" (Gjelten, 2001).

A second trend in public relations and warfare has been the increasing need for nations to make their case in the world court of opinion. Combatants often require the support of other nations, and thus they seek to influence governments through international media. In some respects, this is a continuation of the ongoing propaganda many countries use to project a national image. Such examples include Radio Free Europe/Radio Liberty, the service that broadcasts pro-U.S. views into the former Soviet Union. In the prelude to wars, however, nations seek to justify the use of force and to elicit the support of other nations. In some cases, nations have hired public relations firms to influence government officials' opinions. For example, the government of Kuwait employed the services of Hill & Knowlton to help make the case that the United States should come to Kuwait's aide after Iraq invaded in 1990. Some have labeled the effort to explain a country's foreign policy *public diplomacy*.

Periods of relative peace between major nations have given rise to the need to justify the existence and continued investment in a large military. Thus, the third influence on public relations strategy is the need to position the military and those industries that support it as necessary in both peace and wartime. During the 1980s, for example, military contractor General Dynamics ran a series of image advertisements that celebrated the values of freedom and community involvement. The ads were meant not to sell weapons systems per se, but rather to position the organization as a valuable contributor to a peacetime economy. The switch to all-volunteer armed forces required the military to position itself as an attractive employment alternative to suitable recruits. Thus, in addition to the "Be All That You Can Be" advertising campaign, the military engaged in media relations programs that identified the armed forces as a source of jobs and support for further education.

Although wars have impelled nations to create more efficient and effective weapons technology, they have also been proving grounds for new tools of communication. For example, the telegraph became an essential tool for disseminating American Civil War news, and the case for the Spanish-American War was made largely in Hearst-owned newspapers. The technological innovations that have changed the way in which the media cover the news have also resulted in tactical opportunities and challenges for military public information specialists. On the one hand, global communication has given nations a global reach with their messages. From public diplomacy efforts to after-battle press briefings that are beamed around the world, the military has developed sophisticated techniques to broadcast its message. On the other hand, mobile technology and the spread of the Internet have made it nearly impossible for the military to censor news from the front lines. The United States' invasion of Iraq in 2003 illustrated the military's adaptation to these new technological realities. Rather than attempting to control media access to troops in action, the military actually "embedded" journalists with combat units. Dramatic images of the battle demonstrated the ferocity of war, U.S. firepower, and troops at work. However, foreign media outlets beamed news reports of the battle that represented views contrary to the U.S. media's view. Satellite broadcasting resulted in a wider range of viewpoints, including those of countries that opposed the war or were sympathetic to the Iraqi cause. The result was one of the most comprehensively covered wars in history, which required military public affairs officers to monitor and respond to a greater range of media queries.

The public relations field's connection to warfare raises critical ethical questions. The dual role of military public relations is to justify military action to the domestic and international publics as well as to control information that might undermine that cause. The Creel Committee, for example, was charged with influencing public opinion and censoring reports about the war. Both of these aims can be viewed as ethically muddled. War is serious business, and everyone from philosophers and theologians to public officials have debated the morality of warfare. To the extent that one views war as immoral, public relations' involvement in promoting war becomes ethically questionable. These concerns are exacerbated when it is believed that the justifications for war are based on misleading or false information. The line between public relations and propaganda is thin in these instances. For example, before voting to authorize U.S. military action in the 1991 Gulf War, senators heard testimony from a supposed Kuwaiti eyewitness who claimed she saw Iraqi troops commit atrocities during the invasion, including dumping babies from hospital incubators. After the war, it was discovered that the testimony was stage-managed by Hill & Knowlton, acting on behalf of Citizens for a Free Kuwait, an organization supported by the Kuwaiti royal family. The "eyewitness" was not in the country during the invasion, and no evidence of vandalized hospitals or dumped babies was found.

Related to this concern is the fact that the military seeks to influence the content of media reports or to shape the official statements issued during a conflict. Free and open access to government information by the media has always been a contentious issue. During times of war, the government generally enjoys greater freedom to restrict information to which the media—and, by extension, the public—has access. The military can restrict information on the basis of national security, operational secrecy, and the safety of the personnel involved. However, the media contend that sometimes information that is unfavorable or embarrassing to the military and its government is hidden.

—Michael F. Smith

See also Bernays, Edward; Byoir, Carl; Davis, Elmer, and the Office of War Information; Propaganda; United States government and public relations

Bibliography

Dennis, E. E., Stebenne, D., Pavilik, J., Thalhmer, M., La May, C., Smillie, D., FitzSimon, M., Gazsi, S., & Rachlin, S. (1991). *The media at war: The press and the Persian Gulf conflict.* New York: Gannett Foundation.

Gjelten, T. (2001, Summer). Beware of thugs, warlords, and P.R. agents. *Media Studies Journal,* 78–83.

Hiebert, R. E. (1993, Fall). Public relations, propaganda, and war: A book review and essay on the literature. *Public Relations Review, 3,* 293–302.

Hixson, W. L. (1997). *Parting the curtain: Propaganda, culture, and the Cold War, 1945–1961.* New York: St. Martin's Press.

Mock, J. R., & Larson, C. (1939). *Words that won the war: The story of the Committee on Public Information, 1917–1919.* New York: Russell and Russell.

Page, C. (1996). *U.S. official propaganda during the Vietnam War, 1965–1973: The limits of persuasion.* London: Leicester University Press.

WEB SITE

A Web site is a computer-generated document designed for graphic computer interfaces. The graphic interface used by the Internet is called the World Wide Web. Web sites can contain combinations of text, images, color, sound, and video. The basic logic of the Web is to enable individuals and organizations to easily create universally accessible visual and auditory documents using a discrete set of formatting commands.

In its purest form (i.e., using universally accepted formatting commands), Web sites can be read by any computer platform. As Elizabeth Castro (2000) explained, "Universality means that because HTML documents are saved as ASCII or Text Only files, virtually any computer can read a Web page. It doesn't matter if your visitors have Macintosh or Windows machines . . . a Unix box or even a hand-held device like a Palm Pilot" (Castro, 2000, p. 12). Occasionally, however, Web sites do not load properly. Typically, errors occur because the site creator (usually called the Web Master) has used nonstandard or nonuniversal coding commands.

The basic programming language for the Web is called *HyperText Markup Language* or, more commonly, HTML. HyperText refers to the ability to create documents that connect to other documents by means of *links*. Links can be placed on either text or images. Links direct users who click on them with their mouse to jump to other parts of the same Web page or frame, to open a document in a new window or frame, or to direct the visitor to a new Web page. A frame refers to a portion of a larger window.

Documents created using HTML may contain tables, numbered and bulleted lists, forms, and subroutines called *applets* and *scripts* that allow a Web Master to add special effects such as page counters, contingent logic (if . . . then), and special graphic effects (onMouseOver . . . , onclick . . .).

Other programming protocols, such as image maps, allow Web Masters to create an assortment of visual effects (pop-up windows, expanding menus, and enhanced document navigation). *Cascading style sheets* are another, more recent HTML feature and give Web Masters greater control over how Web pages are displayed. Cascading style sheets direct Web browsers to load pages using fonts that have been designated by the Web Master who created the page, rather than the generic fonts the browser might use by default.

Web pages are accessed via an electronic addressing system called a *Uniform Resource Locater,* or URL. A typical URL, such as the Public Relations Society of America's, might be *http://www.PRSA.org* (or *http://www.prsa.org*—most browsers are not case sensitive). The first part of the URL, called the *protocol,* tells the browser what sort of document to go looking for. In the case above, the protocol *http://* is HyperText (or HyperText transfer protocol). Other protocols include *https,* or *secure* HyperText transfer protocol, and *ftp,* or file transfer protocol.

The second part of the URL is the name of the server or the *domain name.* In the above example the domain name is *www.prsa.org*. The *www* in a domain name refers to the World Wide Web. Domain names may be registered for a fee and are essentially rented each subsequent year for an additional fee. There are several types of suffixes attached to domain names that identify the type of organization and country of origin. Common suffixes include *.com* (company), *.edu* (educational), *.org* (organization), and *.gov* (government).

Most countries, except for the United States, utilize country suffixes as part of their URLs and have their own designations for each type of Web site. For example, a Web site in the United Kingdom might be *http://www.[DomainName].co.uk*—other designations include *.fr* for France and *.nl* for the Netherlands.

The final parts of a URL, everything that follows the protocol and the server name, are file names and the path(s) to a specific file. For example, the membership page for PRSA's site might be *www.prsa.org/membership.html*. Alternatively, a particular file or page might be located within another directory (or folder). For example, PRSA's membership page might be found in a directory named *services* and look like this: *www.prsa.org/services/membership.html*. The *html* at the end of the file name refers to the type of page being displayed—html for HyperText Markup Language, doc for a text file, pdf for Portable Document Format file, and so on.

Recent Internet research suggests that there are now more than one billion discrete Web pages and millions of Web sites. Virtually all organizations now have Web presences. Because of the ubiquity of organizational Web sites, public relations and organizational professionals need to be aware of their importance and how to use them effectively.

—Michael L. Kent

See also Home page.

Bibliography

Castro, E. (2000). *HTML 4 for the World Wide Web: Visual quick start guide* (4th ed.). Berkeley, CA: Peachpit Press.

Dunn, A. (2000, January 20). It's a very wide Web: 1 billion pages worth. *Los Angeles Times*, p. C7.

Kent, M. L. (2001). Essential tips for searching the Web. *Public Relations Quarterly 46*(1), 26–30.

Kent, M. L., & Taylor, M. (1998). Building dialogic relationships through the World Wide Web. *Public Relations Review, 24*(3), 321–334.

Kent, M. L., & Taylor, M., (2003). Maximizing media relations: A Web site checklist. *Public Relations Quarterly 48*(1), 14–18.

Kent, M. L., Taylor, M., & White, W. (2003). The relationship between Web site design and organizational responsiveness to stakeholders. *Public Relations Review 29*(1), 63–77.

Lemay, L. (1996). *Teach yourself web publishing with HTML 3.0 in a week* (2nd ed.). Indianapolis, IN: Sams.net.

WHITAKER, CLEM

See Baxter, Leone, and Whitaker, Clem

WIRE SERVICE

Wire services are often called news-gathering agencies, a term that describes well the function of these agencies, which disseminate news that is generated and shared by subscriber or owner media. The Associated Press (AP) and United Press International (UPI) are two United States–based wire services; the former is member owned and far larger than the latter. Reuters, which is headquartered in Great Britain and which bills itself as the world's largest international multimedia news agency—with 2,400 editorial staff, journalists, photographers, and camera operators in 197 bureaus serving 130 countries—is one of several major wire services that evolved elsewhere in the world. Bureaus of these wire services send news stories and photographs to their subscribers, and wire services may offer specialized coverage (e.g., sports, financial, and feature services). Their broadcast wires offer news in a form appropriate for those media. Supplemental wire service syndicates are also formed by the major metropolitan newspapers, which may offer these services nationwide.

A public relations practitioner is indeed fortunate when a story she has placed in a local medium is "picked up" by a wire service, which disseminates it to other media regionally or nationally. Of course, public relations practitioners can also send releases directly to wire service bureaus.

In addition to these wire services, the public relations practitioner may elect to pay specialized public relations wire services to send news releases to news media. Such news wires available to public relations clients have the advantage of offering simultaneous transmission of news releases to regional and national news media. The public relations practitioner is charged for this service, but public relations news wires operate much as other wire service news bureaus do. They provide journalists with news releases as well as other information that public relations practitioners want sent to media (e.g., photos, graphics, spreadsheets, and audio and video, as well as advisories and invitations to news conferences). Many public relations wire services also supply basic news data banks for storing releases and published stories, which can give a news story a longer shelf life. The public relations news wire services also track media use, for example, as does a clipping service that provides clients with tear sheets of print media coverage.

Public relations wire services have increased credibility compared with news releases sent by public relations practitioners because news release copy is again checked by the public relations wire services, which value their reputation for reliability among the media they serve. Further, many large-circulation newspapers have public relations news wire computer feeds, and this electronic link to a newsroom can be an advantage over mailed news releases, which reporters and editors may never even open and which are vulnerable to weekend and holiday delays. Thus, many public relations practitioners consider the expense of public relations news wires to be worth the price when broad coverage and convenience are important.

—Marina Vujnovic and Dean Kruckeberg

See also News and newsworthy; News services; News story

Bibliography

Brooks, B. S., & Sissors, J. Z. (2001). *The art of editing* (7th ed.). Boston: Allyn & Bacon.

A United Press International (UPI) Unifax machine was an early type of fax machine that used early photocopier technology, enabling the sending of picture data over phone lines and turning UPI into a "wire service."

SOURCE: © Bettmann/CORBIS

Newsom, D., Turk, J. V., & Kruckeberg, D. (2004). *This is PR: The realities of public relations* (8th ed.). Belmont, CA: Thompson/Wadsworth.

WOMEN IN PUBLIC RELATIONS

Historically, men were the majority in public relations, but since the 1980s, women have been entering the profession in droves and currently make up over 70 percent of the field. Over 90 percent of undergraduate students majoring in public relations are female. This influx of women in the field is called the feminization of public relations.

The feminization of public relations has sparked serious debate about what the dramatic changes will be in public relations, both in the profession and in research. On one hand, feminization has lowered professional reputation. Its main effects have included a decline in salaries and status, an increased likelihood of encroachment from other professional fields, the exclusion of public relations from primary decision making in organizations, and the denial of feminine characteristics as valuable to the field. On the other hand, feminization has increased the possibilities for alternative perspectives on public relations, symmetrical management, and an ethical worldview. Women know both the dominant male reality and their own reality; this "dual consciousness" may encourage women to be more sensitive to the perspectives of different organizational publics and, therefore, be more ethical in their practice of public relations. The push for relationship building with publics can be seen as a direct result of feminization—it is argued that women are socialized to be naturally inclined towards sensitivity, collaboration, and, hence, relationship building.

Current understanding about women in public relations and the impact of feminization has derived from a body of research that began in 1986 with the release of the first comprehensive gender study in public relations, *The Velvet Ghetto,* authored by Carolyn Cline, Elizabeth L. Toth, Judy Vanslyke Turk, Lynne Masel Walters, Nancy Johnson, and Hank Smith. An edited follow-up volume titled *Beyond the Velvet Ghetto* was published in 1989. Along with a few other articles published in the late 1980s, these two landmark publications encouraged several researchers to begin examining how women in public relations experience their work and life. A few of the authors who have significantly contributed to the field's understanding of women in public relations include Pam Creedon, Larissa A. Grunig, Linda Hon, Marilyn Kern-Foxworth, and E. L. Toth. A compilation of research on women in public relations can be found in the 2001 book by Larissa A. Grunig, E. L. Toth, and Linda C. Hon, *Women in Public Relations: How Gender Influences Practice,* and in Linda Aldoory's 2003 article in *Communication Yearbook.*

Most of the research on women in public relations has described women's status, roles, and perceptions of public relations. In particular, the following issues have been addressed: leadership, roles, job satisfaction, salaries, promotion, hiring, sexual harassment, women of color in the profession, historical contributions of women, and

public relations education. For example, dozens of studies have shown that there are main differences between men and women concerning technical and managerial roles. For years, the term *glass ceiling* has been used to describe the invisible barriers women face when seeking promotions. Although women comprise most of the jobs in public relations, they do not comprise a comparable percentage of higher positions in public relations. To assess perceptions of gender and promotion, the Public Relations Society of America (PRSA) funded research in 1990, 1995, and most recently, 2000. In all three studies, women agreed, more strongly than did men, that men were promoted more quickly in their organizations. Women believed this to be the case throughout public relations. Men disagreed that they were promoted more quickly in their organizations, but they were uncertain about the field itself. In addition, women considered it more difficult for them to reach the top, in their organizations and throughout public relations. Men agreed, more than women did, that they had a fair shot at promotion in their organization. Studies examining salary have also found a significant difference in the mean and median salaries between men and women, with men earning more than women. Women were still paid less when years of experience, age, job interruptions, and level of education were taken into consideration. Men were more satisfied with their incomes as public relations practitioners than women were.

In the late 1990s, studies began searching for explanations for the discrepancies between men and women with regard to roles, salaries, promotions, and other professional characteristics. One pivotal study in this area was L. C. Hon's, published in 1995 in the *Journal of Public Relations Research,* on the factors explaining discrimination against women in public relations. Through qualitative research, Hon found that women in public relations experienced several obstacles to job satisfaction and promotion. These included the marginalization of the public relations function, a male-dominated work environment that led to women's exclusion from men's networks, women's lack of self-esteem, too few female role models, outmoded attitudes of senior men, conflicting messages for women, women's balancing career and family, gender stereotypes, sexual harassment, and ageism. Following Hon's study, other research indicated that women perceived themselves as insecure decision makers, which caused difficulty for them in moving up to management. Women were less inclined to stay late at work, due to family commitments. Women who were still the major caregivers of their family also had lower salaries. Some authors have argued that women tended to cluster in technician roles because of their interests in the creative arts, but others have claimed that women were as interested in status-related careers as men were and expressed a desire not to perform technician roles. Another factor was that men were offered more money for recruitment and retention purposes. Finally, historical disparity was difficult to remove and, therefore, might contribute to lower salaries for women. In other words, if women started out making lower salaries in the past—when there was overt sex discrimination—then they would continue to make lower salaries as they changed jobs or moved up to management. In general, women's inability to reach top management positions and gain equal salaries has been explained by socialization, women's lack of skills and knowledge about male-defined rules for advancement, and discrimination based on gender alone.

While empirical research throughout the 1990s was directed at understanding the role of women in public relations, authors were also writing feminist critiques that positioned the feminization of the field within larger organizational and societal perspectives. In writings by Pam Creedon, L. A. Grunig, Lana Rakow, and E. L. Toth, it has been argued that the discourse, theory, and research in public relations actually helped to sustain gender stereotypes and women's devaluation. For example, by dichotomizing the field into only two roles, those of manager and technician, and by emphasizing the managerial role as the one that the profession should strive for, women's main role—technician—was minimalized and devalued. The connection between the devaluing of the profession and the growth of the number of women in the field is in itself a discriminating practice governed by societal and organizational norms. Due to the fear of lower status and salaries

across the profession, critics had begun proposing as a solution the push for more male students in public relations and more male practitioners. However, feminist scholars have asserted that this push for more men only increased the devaluation of women's contributions to public relations. Scholars questioned whether the call for gender balance was an argument for the maintenance of the status quo and an attempt to maintain personal positions of power by men. Some writers encouraged organizations to structurally adapt to help nurture women's careers (e.g., implementing flextime policies, formal mentoring programs, and maternity leave). Organizations were also called on to have equitable numbers of female practitioners in management roles.

There has been minimal work in public relations examining the particular experiences of women of color in the field. In her research, published in 1989 in *Public Relations Review,* M. Kern-Foxworth found that African American males are paid more than African American females, but, overall, people of color have not attained the same status and salary level as their white counterparts. She found a gap between the roles that her research participants assigned themselves—middle-level management—and the one they actually fulfilled—technician. She argued that larger organizations did not allow minorities the opportunities to advance in their careers: the larger the organization, the lower the salaries and the less chance of becoming managers there is for people of color. In a follow-up study five years later, Kern-Foxworth, Oscar Gandy, Barbara Hines, and Debra A. Miller reported in *Journal of Black Studies* that about one-half of the African American female public relations practitioners they surveyed spent time giving advice and counsel. The authors of this study stressed that their findings supported the idea that black women may not share the same experiences as others who work in the profession, and, therefore, research samples should be segmented between white and black women. Although the topic of women of color in public relations has been subject to study more recently, there is a paucity of published research in mainstream public relations that examines the experiences of women of color.

Similarly, very little has been done to uncover the history of women in public relations and the contributions that female figures have historically made to the field. In textbooks, female historical figures are scarce. Few women or women's issues are depicted in public relations textbooks, and the available information can be less than accurate. What is known about women in public relations is based on the historical work conducted by Susan Henry, Karen Miller, and Karla Gower. Henry's series of articles about Doris Fleischman Bernays, published in the *Journal of Public Relations Research,* has been the most prolific historical work on women in public relations. Bernays was the wife and partner of Edward Bernays for 58 years and made great contributions to public relations as well as to Edward's business, and yet she went unnoticed. Jane Stewart, another profiled historical figure, served as vice president and then president of Group Attitudes Corporation, an independent consulting firm that became a subsidiary of Hill & Knowlton of New York. In Gower's piece, published in *Journalism History* in 2001, women in public relations were examined through their images in *Public Relations Journal* from 1945 through 1972. Women were established and active in PRSA, and were shown as such in the *Journal.* However, in the late 1950s, when societal expectations of women included staying home with children, the number of women represented in the magazine decreased. This gave the impression that the field of public relations was a male profession. The positive representations and the numbers of women increased again in the late 1960s.

An important issue for women in public relations has been the future of the profession and the future professionals, who are predominantly women. The number of undergraduate students majoring in public relations has increased, and the majority of these students are female. Published studies in this area span a decade, and have consistently shown little difference in how serious minded and management oriented female students were compared with male students. There was also no difference in salary expectations for first jobs, but there were significant differences in salary expectations after five years in the profession: male students expected to be making more than the female students. Male students were also more confident than female students. Female students expected slower promotions than did male students and believed they would have to postpone raising a family so that they could be promoted.

Research in the 21st century reflects the accomplishments of women in public relations. More women are in management and executive positions, more women teach and study public relations, and more professionals and scholars are aware of potential discrimination by gender and by race and ethnicity. Given the enduring feminization of the field, the experiences of women in public relations will continue to be a critical part of the discourse of the field.

—Linda Aldoory

See also Bernays, Edward; Fleischman, Doris Elsa; Public Relations Society of America

Bibliography

Cline, C. G., Toth, E. L., Turk, J. V., Walters, L. M., Johnson, N., & Smith, H. (1986). *The velvet ghetto: The impact of the increasing percentage of women in public relations and business communication.* San Francisco: IABC Research Foundation.

Creedon, P. J. (1991). Public relations and "women's work": Toward a feminist analysis of public relations roles. *Public Relations Research Annual, 3,* 67–84.

Grunig, L. A., Toth, E. L., & Hon, L. C. (2001). *Women in public relations.* New York: Guilford Press.

Henry, S. (1998). Dissonant notes of a retiring feminist: Doris E. Fleischman's later years. *Journal of Public Relations Research, 10,* 1–33.

Hon, L. C. (1995). Toward a feminist theory of public relations. *Journal of Public Relations Research, 7,* 27–88.

Kern-Foxworth, M. (1989). Status and roles of minority public relations practitioners. *Public Relations Review, 5,* 14–22.

Kern-Foxworth, M., Gandy, O., Hines, B., & Miller, D. A. (1994). Assessing the managerial roles of black female public relations practitioners using individual and organizational discriminants. *Journal of Black Studies, 24*(4), 416–434.

Toth, E. L., & Cline, C. G. (Eds.). (1989). *Beyond the velvet ghetto.* San Francisco, CA: IABC Research Foundation.

Toth, E. L., & Grunig, L. A. (1993). The missing story of women in public relations. *Journal of Public Relations Research, 5,* 153–175.

WRITING

Among the many tasks performed by public relations practitioners, writing most certainly tops the list. Practitioners develop various written pieces—media releases, brochures, promotional materials, business correspondence, and proposals—to communicate information to people inside and outside of the organization. Public relations writing should educate, persuade, or motivate. To accomplish these goals, writers must be functional and write with a purpose, while maintaining a creative flair.

Because of the wide variety of writing formats, versatility is an essential skill for public relations writers. They must know which format is the most appropriate for a project and the best way to construct a message so that the audience will understand it.

USING APPROPRIATE FORMATS

The most common writing formats in public relations are those used in publicity, marketing, advocacy, organizational communication, and business correspondence. Each has a certain style and purpose. To determine the best format to use, three things should be considered before beginning a writing project:

- What is the purpose of the piece?
- Who is the audience?
- What is the message?

The Purpose

Before they start writing, public relations practitioners must decide whether the purpose of the piece is to educate, persuade, or motivate. What is the desired result of the piece? To create awareness, gain support for an issue, or prompt behavior?

Writing that seeks to educate usually consists of straightforward information, whereas writing that aims to persuade or motivate takes on a more emotional tone. For example, the purpose of an article that lets employees know about a new benefit would be educational; however, a piece that tries to convince legislators why they should support a bill would require persuasive tactics.

The Audience

The purpose of the piece will determine who should receive it, which in turn will determine how it should be written. In most cases, a reporter doesn't want to receive a brochure and a customer doesn't want to receive a media release. Media formats (e.g., media releases, media advisories, pitch letters) should be used in writing for the media. Use creative brochures when marketing to customers, internal newsletters for informing employees, and business-like memos when communicating with management.

The Message

More than anything else, the message will determine the most appropriate writing format to use. Does the message need to be straightforward or is there creative license? Customers will want to read information that reinforces their decision to patronize an organization. This requires the use of persuasive tactics. Such tactics, however, would not be appropriate for a media release, which should contain factual, objective information.

Is the message brief or lengthy? How much space will be needed to adequately deliver the message? How will it reach the target public? Detailed information aimed at persuading a specific audience is better suited for a brochure or position paper than a one-page flyer. A flyer, on the other hand, might be more appropriate for announcing the date and time of a special event.

BEING UNDERSTOOD

Public relations practitioners who don't write in a way that their audience can understand are wasting their time. If readers find a piece too complicated, they will stop reading and will not receive the intended message. To increase the chances that the piece will be understood, write simply; use proper grammar, punctuation, and spelling; and adopt an appropriate style.

Simplicity

Readers can get confused by lengthy sentences and multisyllabic words. Using short words, sentences, and paragraphs will help focus the writer on writing concisely, which will enhance the simplicity of a piece. Jargon or clichés not familiar to an audience should be avoided.

There are several formulas that can be used to determine the simplicity of a written piece. These readability studies, such as the Flesch Formula, the Gunning Fog Index, and the Fry Formula, usually involve calculating word syllables and sentence length to determine the grade level at which the piece is written.

Grammar and Spelling

Using improper grammar and misspelling words reflects negatively on a writer. The credibility of the writer may be questioned, as well as the credibility of the information being presented. In addition, poor grammar and punctuation affect how a sentence is structured, and poor sentence structure leads to difficult reading and confusion. Writers should ensure that their writing is easy to read. Some common grammatical errors include the following:

- Using inconsistent nouns and pronouns
- Using inconsistent subjects and verbs
- Using faulty parallel structure
- Confusing *that*, *which*, and *who*
- Using run-on sentences or sentence fragments
- Overusing commas
- Misusing colons and semicolons

Carefully proofread your writing to avoid errors in grammar and punctuation, as well as spelling.

Although a spell checker is a wonderful computer tool, it should never be used as the final check. Nothing can take the place of a dictionary.

Style

The format of a written piece will determine its style. Media releases focus on facts written in pyramid style whereas marketing pieces feature more colorful language and creative structure. How the reader is addressed (in personal terms or as a neutral third party) is another style consideration.

The writing style used by the Associated Press (AP) has long been followed in the journalism and public relations fields. The *AP Stylebook* provides information on the standard use of such things as capitalization and abbreviations. Public relations practitioners who follow these guidelines, especially when writing for the media, enhance their credibility and make it easier for the media to edit public relations–generated copy.

—Ann R. Carden

See also AP style; Persuasion theory; Stylebook

Bibliography

Goldstein, N. (Ed.). (2002). *The Associated Press stylebook and briefing on media law* (Rev. ed.). Cambridge, MA: Perseus.

Smith, R. D. (2003). *Becoming a public relations writer* (2nd ed.). Mahwah, NJ: Lawrence Erlbaum.

Strunk, W., & White, E. B. (1999). *The elements of style* (4th ed.). Boston: Allyn & Bacon.

Zappala, J. M., & Carden, A. R. (2004). *Public relations worktext: A writing and planning resource* (2nd ed.). Mahwah, NJ: Lawrence Erlbaum.

ZONES OF MEANING

Zones of meaning are the fibers in the fabric of public opinion—the collective opinions of many markets and publics that make up a society. One of the problems perplexing activists, public relations practitioners, and scholars is understanding the nature of public opinion. Early in the 20th century the term *public opinion* was formalized as a research concept. It was coined to describe broadly what is on the mind of members of a society. What do they know, believe, prefer, dislike, like, aspire toward, value, and use as motives?

Further thinking and empirical investigations of public opinion revealed that a single "public" does not exist, and what we think of as "the public" certainly is not of one mind. For instance, poll data reveal that some people like any president of the United States, and others don't. Some people like baseball, and others don't. Some people support activist constraints on business practices, and some don't.

A zone of meaning is the shared knowledge, experience, preferences, motives, opinions held in the mind of some people in society, which may be quite unique to them. One of the ways to think about zones is as the result of experience. People who have lived their life in a dense, hot, and humid jungle share a zone of meaning quite different from people whose experience consists only of the vast regions near the Arctic Circle. Generations differ from one another because they have different zones of meaning, because their experiences are different. The same can be true for gender, race, and religion, to use a very short list. Labor shares a different zone of meaning from management.

Nevertheless, labor and management may share some zones. For instance, labor and management in the aircraft construction industry have a different zone of meaning than would exist for labor and management in the segment of the electricity-generating industry that uses nuclear fuel to generate power.

People in any society may like or dislike sports, in general or of various kinds. People who like basketball will share a zone of meaning quite different from that of those do who enjoy baseball. Players' names and team histories are part of each unique zone. The rules of the game differ from other games. The dynamics of league play and championship differ. Also, some sports are a part of certain people's lifestyle, and not part of other people's.

Surveys of communities reveal that some people within the community know or believe something quite different from the knowledge or beliefs of people who don't live in that community. People who live in a community with a heavy concentration of chemical manufacturing and refining facilities may understand the sirens that alert them to a safety danger. They may know when and how to shelter-in-place in the event such an emergency occurs. People who don't live in that community have less reason and opportunity to share this zone of meaning.

Likewise, in such communities, people who work in the industry are taught shelter-in-place procedures that are to be followed in a work site in the event an emergency occurs. Visitors to this site are required to learn those measures (come to share a zone of meaning) before they can enter. Plant managers have routine drills and training to ensure that workers and visitors know what the warning siren is and what actions must be taken in the event the siren sounds.

Citizens in the community also need such information, but they are likely to learn it through means other than company training. Industry may use an animal, such as a turtle, to attract attention to the shelter-in-place procedures. When in danger, turtles "shelter in place"; they go inside their shell. Such tools appeal to children. Thus, if a survey is done, it may well reveal that mothers and children know—share the zone—the meaning of the turtle and what to do, even if they don't know the term *shelter-in-place*. Plant personnel may know *shelter-in-place* but not know about the turtle and its recommendations. Both zones can lead to safety measures, but each is a different zone.

Differences of opinions, knowledge, experience, motives, and such are a fact of life. Not everyone knows all of the same "stuff." But society can not function without shared meanings. Thus, zones are like veins of ore (a zone of meaning) in a rock formation throughout which various threads of ore and other materials can be identified. Similar knowledge can help practitioners to understand where agreement or disagreement occurs and people whose ideas, knowledge, and experience differs from others'.

Faculty members sitting around a lunch table share zones of meaning about students' behavior. Despite being from different disciplines, they can share stories about academic excellence and about cheating. They share that zone. However, they may not share much of the zone of meaning that constitutes their respective academic disciplines. Historians undoubtedly know less biology than a distinguished biologist does. These faculty members share views on students, academic procedures, and administration. That allows them to work together in doing their jobs. When they go back to their offices, they enter quite a different zone of meaning.

The term *zone of meaning* can help academics and practitioners to understand the threads of opinions of key publics and markets. This insight can help practitioners to understand where agreement and disagreement exist, and perhaps why. Gaining such insights into the fabric of public opinion gives practitioners the perspectives they need to work with people based on their unique zones of meaning, zones that may create unity and friction, those that become part of the dialogue that can lead to agreement and the co-creation of meaning.

—*Robert L. Heath*

See also Marketing; Publics

The Public Relations Society of America Code of Ethics

The primary obligation of membership in the Public Relations Society of America is the ethical practice of Public Relations.

The PRSA Member Code of Ethics is the way each member of our Society can daily reaffirm a commitment to ethical professional activities and decisions.

- The Code sets forth the principles and standards that guide our decisions and actions.
- The Code solidly connects our values and our ideals to the work each of us does every day.
- The Code is about what we should do, and why we should do it.

The Code is also meant to be a living, growing body of knowledge, precedent, and experience. It should stimulate our thinking and encourage us to seek guidance and clarification when we have questions about principles, practices, and standards of conduct.

Every member's involvement in preserving and enhancing ethical standards is essential to building and maintaining the respect and credibility of our profession. Using our values, principles, standards of conduct, and commitment as a foundation, and continuing to work together on ethical issues, we ensure that the Public Relations Society of America fulfills its obligation to build and maintain the framework for public dialogue that deserves the public's trust and support.

The Members of the 2000 Board of Ethics and Professional Standards

Robert D. Frause, APR, Fellow PRSA
Chairman BEPS
Seattle, Washington

James R. Frankowiak, APR
Tampa, Florida

Jeffrey P. Julin, APR
Denver, Colorado

James E. Lukaszewski, APR, Fellow PRSA
White Plains, New York

Kathy R. Fitzpatrick, APR
Gainesville, Florida

PRSA Member Code of Ethics 2000

Linda Welter Cohen, APR
Tucson, Arizona

Patricia Grey, APR
Columbus, Ohio

Ralph Thomas Kam, APR
Kaneohe, Hawaii

Roger D. Buehrer, APR
Fellow PRSA
Las Vegas, Nevada

W. Thomas Duke, APR, Fellow PRSA
Greenville, South Carolina

PRSA MEMBER STATEMENT OF PROFESSIONAL VALUES

This statement presents the core values of PRSA members and, more broadly, of the public relations profession. These values provide the foundation for the Member Code of Ethics and set the industry standard for the professional practice of public relations. These values are the fundamental beliefs that guide our behaviors and decision-making process. We believe our professional values are vital to the integrity of the profession as a whole.

ADVOCACY

- We serve the public interest by acting as responsible advocates for those we represent.
- We provide a voice in the marketplace of ideas, facts, and viewpoints to aid informed public debate.

HONESTY

- We adhere to the highest standards of accuracy and truth in advancing the interests of those we represent and in communicating with the public.

EXPERTISE

- We acquire and responsibly use specialized knowledge and experience.
- We advance the profession through continued professional development, research, and education.
- We build mutual understanding, credibility, and relationships among a wide array of institutions and audiences.

INDEPENDENCE

- We provide objective counsel to those we represent.
- We are accountable for our actions.

LOYALTY

- We are faithful to those we represent, while honoring our obligation to serve the public interest.

FAIRNESS

- We deal fairly with clients, employers, competitors, peers, vendors, the media, and the general public.
- We respect all opinions and support the right of free expression.

PRSA CODE PROVISIONS

FREE FLOW OF INFORMATION

Core Principle

Protecting and advancing the free flow of accurate and truthful information is essential to serving the public interest and contributing to informed decision making in a democratic society.

Intent

- To maintain the integrity of relationships with the media, government officials, and the public.
- To aid informed decision making.

Guidelines

A member shall:

- Preserve the integrity of the process of communication.
- Be honest and accurate in all communications.
- Act promptly to correct erroneous communications for which the practitioner is responsible.
- Preserve the free flow of unprejudiced information when giving or receiving gifts by ensuring that gifts are nominal, legal, and infrequent.

Examples of Improper Conduct Under this Provision:

- A member representing a ski manufacturer gives a pair of expensive racing skis to a sports magazine columnist, to influence the columnist to write favorable articles about the product.

- A member entertains a government official beyond legal limits and/or in violation of government reporting requirements.

COMPETITION

Core Principle

Promoting healthy and fair competition among professionals preserves an ethical climate while fostering a robust business environment.

Intent

- To promote respect and fair competition among public relations professionals.
- To serve the public interest by providing the widest choice of practitioner options.

Guidelines

A member shall:

- Follow ethical hiring practices designed to respect free and open competition without deliberately undermining a competitor.
- Preserve intellectual property rights in the marketplace.

Examples of Improper Conduct Under This Provision

- A member employed by a client organization shares helpful information with a counseling firm that is competing with others for the organization's business.
- A member spreads malicious and unfounded rumors about a competitor in order to alienate the competitor's clients and employees in a ploy to recruit people and business.

DISCLOSURE OF INFORMATION

Core Principle

Open communication fosters informed decision making in a democratic society.

Intent

- To build trust with the public by revealing all information needed for responsible decision making.

Guidelines

A member shall:

- Be honest and accurate in all communications.
- Act promptly to correct erroneous communications for which the member is responsible.
- Investigate the truthfulness and accuracy of information released on behalf of those represented.
- Reveal the sponsors for causes and interests represented.
- Disclose financial interest (such as stock ownership) in a client's organization.
- Avoid deceptive practices.

Examples of Improper Conduct Under this Provision:

- Front groups: A member implements "grass roots" campaigns or letter-writing campaigns to legislators on behalf of undisclosed interest groups.
- Lying by omission: A practitioner for a corporation knowingly fails to release financial information, giving a misleading impression of the corporation's performance.
- A member discovers inaccurate information disseminated via a web site or media kit and does not correct the information.
- A member deceives the public by employing people to pose as volunteers to speak at public hearings and participate in "grass roots" campaigns.

SAFEGUARDING CONFIDENCES

Core Principle

Client trust requires appropriate protection of confidential and private information.

Intent

- To protect the privacy rights of clients, organizations, and individuals by safeguarding confidential information.

Guidelines

A member shall:

- Safeguard the confidences and privacy rights of present, former, and prospective clients and employees.

- Protect privileged, confidential, or insider information gained from a client or organization.
- Immediately advise an appropriate authority if a member discovers that confidential information is being divulged by an employee of a client company or organization.

Examples of Improper Conduct Under This Provision:

- A member changes jobs, takes confidential information, and uses that information in the new position to the detriment of the former employer.
- A member intentionally leaks proprietary information to the detriment of some other party.

CONFLICTS OF INTEREST

Core Principle

Avoiding real, potential, or perceived conflicts of interest builds the trust of clients, employers, and the publics.

Intent

- To earn trust and mutual respect with clients or employers.
- To build trust with the public by avoiding or ending situations that put one's personal or professional interests in conflict with society's interests.

Guidelines

A member shall:

- Act in the best interests of the client or employer, even subordinating the member's personal interests.
- Avoid actions and circumstances that may appear to compromise good business judgment or create a conflict between personal and professional interests.
- Disclose promptly any existing or potential conflict of interest to affected clients or organizations.
- Encourage clients and customers to determine if a conflict exists after notifying all affected parties.

Examples of Improper Conduct Under This Provision

- The member fails to disclose that he or she has a strong financial interest in a client's chief competitor.

- The member represents a "competitor company" or a "conflicting interest" without informing a prospective client.

ENHANCING THE PROFESSION

Core Principle

Public relations professionals work constantly to strengthen the public's trust in the profession.

Intent

- To build respect and credibility with the public for the profession of public relations.
- To improve, adapt, and expand professional practices.

Guidelines

A member shall:

- Acknowledge that there is an obligation to protect and enhance the profession.
- Keep informed and educated about practices in the profession to ensure ethical conduct.
- Actively pursue personal professional development.
- Decline representation of clients or organizations that urge or require actions contrary to this Code.
- Accurately define what public relations activities can accomplish.
- Counsel subordinates in proper ethical decision making.
- Require that subordinates adhere to the ethical requirements of the Code.
- Report ethical violations, whether committed by PRSA members or not, to the appropriate authority.

Examples of Improper Conduct Under This Provision:

- A PRSA member declares publicly that a product the client sells is safe, without disclosing evidence to the contrary.
- A member initially assigns some questionable client work to a non-member practitioner to avoid the ethical obligation of PRSA membership.

RESOURCES

Rules and Guidelines

The following PRSA documents, available online at www.prsa.org provide detailed rules and guidelines to help guide your professional behavior. If, after reviewing them, you still have a question or issue, contact PRSA headquarters as noted below.

- PRSA Bylaws
- PRSA Administrative Rules
- Member Code of Ethics

QUESTIONS

The PRSA is here to help. Whether you have a serious concern or simply need clarification, you can contact us confidentially at:

Chairman
Board of Ethics and Professional Standards
Public Relations Society of America
33 Irving Place, Floor 3
New York, NY 10003
212–460–1414
212–995–0757 Fax
or
AskBEPS@prsa.org

PRSA MEMBER CODE OF ETHICS PLEDGE

I pledge:

To conduct myself professionally, with truth, accuracy, fairness, and responsibility to the public;

To improve my individual competence and advance the knowledge and proficiency of the profession through continuing research and education;

And to adhere to the articles of the Member *Code of Ethics 2000* for the practice of public relations as adopted by the governing Assembly of the Public Relations Society of America.

I understand and accept that there is a consequence for misconduct, up to and including membership revocation.

And, I understand that those who have been or are sanctioned by a government agency or convicted in a court of law of an action that is in violation of this Code may be barred from membership or expelled from the Society.

SOURCE: © 2000 Public Relations Society of America. Reprinted with permission.

Appendix 2

International Association of Business Communicators Code of Ethics

PREFACE

Because hundreds of thousands of business communicators worldwide engage in activities that affect the lives of millions of people, and because this power carries with it significant social responsibilities, the International Association of Business Communicators developed the Code of Ethics for Professional Communicators.

The Code is based on three different yet interrelated principles of professional communication that apply throughout the world.

These principles assume that just societies are governed by a profound respect for human rights and the rule of law; that ethics, the criteria for determining what is right and wrong, can be agreed upon by members of an organization; and, that understanding matters of taste requires sensitivity to cultural norms.

These principles are essential:

- Professional communication is legal.
- Professional communication is ethical.
- Professional communication is in good taste.

Recognizing these principles, members of IABC will:

- engage in communication that is not only legal but also ethical and sensitive to cultural values and beliefs;

- engage in truthful, accurate and fair communication that facilitates respect and mutual understanding; and,
- adhere to the following articles of the IABC Code of Ethics for Professional Communicators.

Because conditions in the world are constantly changing, members of IABC will work to improve their individual competence and to increase the body of knowledge in the field with research and education.

Articles

1. Professional communicators uphold the credibility and dignity of their profession by practicing honest, candid and timely communication and by fostering the free flow of essential information in accord with the public interest.

2. Professional communicators disseminate accurate information and promptly correct any erroneous communication for which they may be responsible.

3. Professional communicators understand and support the principles of free speech, freedom of assembly, and access to an open marketplace of ideas; and, act accordingly.

4. Professional communicators are sensitive to cultural values and beliefs and engage in fair and balanced communication activities that foster and encourage mutual understanding.

5. Professional communicators refrain from taking part in any undertaking which the communicator considers to be unethical.

6. Professional communicators obey laws and public policies governing their professional activities and are sensitive to the spirit of all laws and regulations and, should any law or public policy be violated, for whatever reason, act promptly to correct the situation.

7. Professional communicators give credit for unique expressions borrowed from others and identify the sources and purposes of all information disseminated to the public.

8. Professional communicators protect confidential information and, at the same time, comply with all legal requirements for the disclosure of information affecting the welfare of others.

9. Professional communicators do not use confidential information gained as a result of professional activities for personal benefit and do not represent conflicting or competing interests without written consent of those involved.

10. Professional communicators do not accept undisclosed gifts or payments for professional services from anyone other than a client or employer.

11. Professional communicators do not guarantee results that are beyond the power of the practitioner to deliver.

12. Professional communicators are honest not only with others but also, and most importantly, with themselves as individuals; for a professional communicator seeks the truth and speaks that truth first to the self.

Enforcement and Communication of the IABC Code for Professional Communicators

IABC fosters compliance with its Code by engaging in global communication campaigns rather than through negative sanctions. However, in keeping with the sixth article of the IABC Code, members of IABC who are found guilty by an appropriate governmental agency or judicial body of violating laws and public policies governing their professional activities may have their membership terminated by the IABC executive board following procedures set forth in the association's bylaws.

IABC encourages the widest possible communication about its Code.

The IABC Code of Ethics for Professional Communicators is published in several languages and is freely available to all: Permission is hereby granted to any individual or organization wishing to copy and incorporate all or part of the IABC Code into personal and corporate codes, with the understanding that appropriate credit be given to IABC in any publication of such codes.

The IABC Code is published in the association's annual directory, *The World Book of IABC Communicators.* The association's monthly magazine, *Communication World*, publishes periodic articles dealing with ethical issues. At least one session at the association's annual conference is devoted to ethics. The international headquarters of IABC, through its professional development activities, encourages and supports efforts by IABC student chapters, professional chapters, and districts/regions to conduct meetings and workshops devoted to the topic of ethics and the IABC Code. New and renewing members of IABC sign the following statement as part of their application: "I have reviewed and understand the IABC Code of Ethics for Professional Communicators."

As a service to communicators worldwide, inquiries about ethics and questions or comments about the IABC Code may be addressed to members of the IABC Ethics Committee. The IABC Ethics Committee is composed of at least three accredited members of IABC who serve staggered three-year terms. Other IABC members may serve on the committee with the approval of the IABC executive committee. The functions of the Ethics Committee are to assist with professional development activities dealing with ethics and to offer advice and assistance to individual communicators regarding specific ethical situations.

While discretion will be used in handling all inquiries about ethics, absolute confidentiality cannot be guaranteed. Those wishing more information about the IABC Code or specific advice about ethics are encouraged to contact IABC World Headquarters (One Hallidie Plaza, Suite 600, San Francisco, CA 94102 USA; phone, 415-544-4700; fax, 415-544-4747).

Milestones in the History of Public Relations

MILESTONES IN THE HISTORY OF PUBLIC RELATIONS (TIMELINE)

Because public relations did not just begin at any point in history, scholars and practitioners have chronicled some of the most important and identifiable moments in the history that led up to the start of public relations by that name. As indicated in the entry entitled "Antecedents of modern public relations," the practice as we know it today is part of a living legacy. The key moments indicate those communicative events that preceded and fostered today's public relations. This history indicates the enduring efforts of some person or organization to communicate with others. At times, the efforts of public relations are geared to serve the larger interest of the community. At other times they are narrowly applied to serve the interest of some leader or organization. The following list is illustrative. No one should think that it is exhaustive. Nevertheless, it demonstrates how public relations, for better or worse, is a vital part of the enduring fabric of human society in its many facets.

Many of the moments mentioned in the timeline below are either featured entries in this encyclopedia or important parts of such entries. This timeline should encourage the reader to learn more about these moments and think of them as stepping-stones in the stream that is the history of public relations.

1800 B.C.—In Sumeria, a farm bulletin telling farmers how to grow crops is one of the earliest examples of mass distribution of educational materials.

100 B.C.—A signal of the rise in importance of pubic opinion, the Romans coin the phrase *Vox populi; vox Dei,* "the voice of the people is the voice of God."

52 B.C.—Julius Caesar sends reports, including "Caesar's Gallic Wars," to the Romans in preparation for his crossing the Rubicon River to invade Italy in 49 B.C.

A.D. 1215—Stephen Langton, Archbishop of Canterbury, mobilizes a disgruntled group of barons who confront King John with ultimatums that eventually mature into the Magna Carta.

A.D. 1315—John Wycliffe calls for reforms by the Catholic Church, including the publication of the Bible into the vernacular.

1500s—In the wake of the invention of printing with movable type by Johann Gutenberg in 1446, handbills and broadsides are used to promote various causes.

1517—Martin Luther starts the Reformation when he nails 95 theses proclaiming wrongdoings of the Roman Catholic Church to the door of the castle church in Wittenberg, Germany.

1622—Pope Gregory XV creates the Congregatio de Propaganda Fide (College for Propagating the Faith), an effort by the Roman Catholic Church to retain followers and solicit converts in the aftermath of the Reformation. This was the origin of the term *propaganda.*

1641—Harvard College launches first systematic fundraising effort in the United States, sending students door-to-door to raise money.

1748—The first news release to solicit press coverage is sent by King's College (now Columbia University) in New York.

1773—Sixty colonists dressed as Mohawk Indians demonstrate rising dissatisfaction with British tax policies by staging the Boston Tea Party, dumping 342 chests of tea valued at 10,000 pounds into Boston Harbor.

1787—The Federalist Papers, a series of 85 pamphlets that were also reprinted as articles in newspapers, were produced to generate support for the formal creation of the United States and passage of its Constitution.

1807—Thomas Jefferson, third president of the United States, combined *public* with *relations* in a statement about the obligation of government to the governed.

1829—Amos Kendall serves as the first presidential press secretary as a member of Andrew Jackson's "kitchen cabinet." In 1829 he was appointed fourth auditor of the Treasury, in addition to writing speeches, state papers, and news releases, conducting opinion polls, and developing the administration's own newspaper.

1840s—P. T. Barnum becomes the first press agent, promoting local appearances by his touring circus.

1850s—American railroads use publicity, advertising, and printed materials to attract tourists and settlers to the American West.

1882—Attorney Dorman Eaton first uses the term *public relations,* referring to an organization's role

in service to the public welfare, in an address to Yale Law School graduates on "The Public Relations and Duties of the Legal Profession."

1888—Mutual Life Insurance Company creates a "species of literary bureau" to coordinate advertising and publicity.

1889—The first corporate public relations department is established by Westinghouse. Westinghouse ultimately prevailed in the ensuing "battle of the currents" to promote the benefits of alternating current (AC) versus the direct current (DC) invented earlier by Thomas Edison and the General Electric Company.

1895—Ford Motor Company pioneers press product previews for product promotion.

1896—The use of modern publicity in political campaigns begins with the presidential election between William McKinley and William Jennings Bryan when both candidates establish campaign headquarters in Chicago.

1897—General Electric creates a publicity department.

1900—The first public relations firm, Publicity Bureau of Boston, is established by George Michaelis, Herbert Small, and Thomas O. Marvin.

1902—H. S. Adams's article, "What Is Publicity?" is published in the *American Review.* It is believed to be the first magazine article about public relations.

1903—Ford Motor Company uses auto races for product promotion; Chicago Edison, under the direction of President Samuel Insull, does the same via an external magazine.

1906—Ivy Ledbetter Lee is hired to represent the coal industry in the anthracite coal miners' strike. Lee issues his "Declaration of Principles," considered the birth of modern public relations counseling.

1909—Chicago Edison uses films for product promotion; Pendleton Dudley opens his public relations agency on Wall Street, a firm (Dudley-Anderson-Yutzy) that was sold to Ogilvy & Mather in 1983.

1912—Chicago Edison uses stuffers inserted in customer bills for promotional purposes.

1914—The "Ludlow (Colorado) Massacre." State militia kill 20 people—striking Colorado Fuel and

Iron Company miners, along with their wives and children—a tragedy that helped establish the value of corporate public relations. Ivy Lee represented Colorado Fuel and Iron owner J. D. Rockefeller's interests. No perpetrators are convicted, but many miners and union leaders are fired and blackballed.

1917—The Committee on Public Information, a government agency headed by George Creel (and also know as the Creel Committee), promotes public support of American involvement in World War I; Former Atlanta journalist Edward Clarke and ex-madam Bessie Tyler form the Southern Publicity Association to promote World War I fund drives. After the war, they built up membership in the Ku Klux Klan by offering a $10 induction fee to Klansmen for every new member they signed up.

1923—Edward L. Bernays publishes *Crystallizing Public Opinion,* the first book on professional public relations, and teaches the first public relations course at New York University.

1927—Arthur W. Page is named vice president of public relations at AT&T, accepting the job on the condition that he be allowed to be involved in policy making. Page would distinguish himself as the leading corporate practitioner of the century by emphasizing the importance of cooperation with the public and of disclosure about corporate activities; John W. Hill founds Hill & Knowlton.

1929—Edward Bernays stages two major public relations events as marches: the "Torches of Freedom" March in New York to promote smoking for women, and the "Golden Jubilee of Light" in Dearborn, Michigan, to celebrate the 50th anniversary of the invention of the electric light bulb.

1931—Paul Garrett becomes the first public relations director at General Motors, inspiring other large corporations to make similar appointments.

1933—Campaigns, Inc., the first political campaign firm, is founded by husband and wife Clem Whitaker and Leone Baxter in California; President Franklin Delano Roosevelt uses his famous "fireside chats" to instill confidence in the American people; Edward Bernays develops the "Green Ball" campaign for Lucky Strike cigarettes, urging women to (1) wear green clothing as a fashion statement and (2) smoke Lucky Strikes, as the green packaging would mesh with their outfit.

1936—The first widespread use of public opinion polling, with companies conducting selected consumer interviews. Small-sample Crossley, Gallup, and Elmo Roper polls predict Franklin D. Roosevelt's presidential victory over Alf Landon, while the 2 million–ballot *Literary Digest* poll predicts a Landon victory, proving that proper sampling is more important than sample size.

1939—Rex Harlow of Stanford University becomes the first full-time public relations educator.

1941—The first noncommercial opinion research agency, The National Opinion Research Center, is established.

1942—The Office of War Information, headed by Elmer Davis, promotes public support of and involvement in World War II.

1945—The Advertising Council (formerly the War Advertising Council) is reorganized to create information campaigns on behalf of various social causes; the United States government announces via press release that an American plane dropped an atomic bomb on Hiroshima.

1948—The Public Relations Society of America (PRSA) is founded.

1950—The PRSA Code of Professional Standards is adopted.

1953—The United States Information Agency (USIA) is created by President Dwight Eisenhower to disseminate news and cultural information abroad.

1955—The International Public Relations Association (IPRA) is founded.

1957—Anne Williams Wheaton is appointed associate press secretary to President Eisenhower, the first time a woman has held that position.

1960—In opposition to his earlier pro-smoking campaigns, Edward Bernays leads an effort to inform the public about the dangers of smoking.

1963—John Marston's four-step management process for public relations, RACE—research, action, communication, evaluation—is published in his book *The Nature of Public Relations.*

1965—PRSA accreditation is established.

1970—The International Association of Business Communicators (IABC) is founded.

1973—Carl Byoir and Associates becomes the first of several large public relations firms to become a subsidiary of an advertising company (Hill & Knowlton).

1980—Inez Kaiser becomes the first African American female to open a national public relations firm, Inez Kaiser & Associates.

1982—Six people in a Chicago suburb die of cyanide poisoning from Tylenol capsules they ingested, causing a public relations crisis for McNeil Laboratories and Johnson & Johnson

1989—The *Exxon Valdez* grounds at Bligh Reef, rupturing 8 of its 11 cargo tanks and spewing some 10.8 million gallons of crude oil into Prince William Sound. Although the spill is ranked 34th on a list of the world's largest oil spills over the previous two decades, the environmental damage makes the accident one of the largest public relations crises in United States history.

1993—A Seattle television station reports that a local couple found a syringe in a can of Diet Pepsi, inspiring a host of similar reports across the United States. Pepsi responds by working closely with the Food and Drug Administration to rule out product tampering as the cause. Throwing open their doors to the press, they demonstrate the impossibility of placing an object in a can, and the nationwide "scare" is determined to be a hoax.

1998—The Council of Public Relations Firms is founded.

1999—Anheuser-Busch unveils a public-service campaign against driving under the influence of alcohol.

2000—The PRSA Code of Ethics is revised as a list of "inspirational guidelines."

2002—The PRSA promulgates Universal Accreditation as the standard for practice.

SOURCE: Adapted from *A Short Timeline of Key People and Events in Public Relations History,* http://lamar.colostate.edu/~hallahan/hprhist. htm; PRHistory.com,http://www.camdencc.edu/breve/teachlc/archive/ humanities/ prhistory/timeline/second.htm; Institute of Public Relations, http://www .instituteforpr.com/pdf/HistoryofPublic%20Relation—Institute.pdf; Pioneers In Public Relations, http://facstaff.buffalostate.edu/smithrd/PR/ pioneers.htm

Appendix 4

Public Relations Education for the 21st Century: A Port of Entry

INTRODUCTION

Why a "Port of Entry" Report?

Public relations has come of age, and with that has come a critical need for broadly-based education that is relevant and connected to the practice.

The changes in public relations practice since the 1987 Commission on Public Relations Education Report are numerous and profound. At root, these changes reflect nothing less than the way the world has changed and continues to change, seemingly spinning ever faster and veering in new directions. But, happily, the changes also reflect a broad acceptance of the validity of modern public relations practice to a global society that is increasingly interdependent, increasingly interconnected.

By any measure, the growth of the public relations profession over the past decade has been astonishing. Public relations firms not only proliferate but also reach a size and scope undreamed of in the 1980s. Membership in established and new professional societies and trade associations spirals upward. And, most important, virtually every kind of institution, for-profit and not-for-profit alike, recognizes the need for dialogue with the groups of people who can and will influence its future.

This growth, evolution and maturation of public relations is sure to continue. Elements are in place for impressive incremental growth and change in the next century: the spread of democratic institutions around the world; the growing importance of communicating with internal as well as external publics; the veritable explosion of one-to-one communication and the technology to implement it; and the steady advance of the public relations body of knowledge, especially analysis of public awareness and change in attitudes and behavior.

PUBLIC RELATIONS' NEXT CRISIS?

The future is indeed bright for the field of public relations. But there is one major qualification—having enough trained people to meet the expanding demand for public relations services and counsel. In fact, one expert observer of the field has called this "public relations' next crisis."

EDITOR'S NOTE: *Public Relations Education for the 21st Century: A Port of Entry* is the work product of the 1999 Commission on Public Relations Education, 47 educators and practitioners for use by "academic programs and faculty to evaluate and develop their curricula; by practitioners who hire graduates of public relations programs; and by academic and professional associations which set standards for academic program certification and accreditation and for the chartering of student public relations organizations." The final report, below, was introduced at the October, 1999 International Conference of the Public Relations Society of America in Anaheim, CA.

Hyperbole aside, there is no doubt that providing qualified practitioners will be a serious problem. Law and medicine have methods, admittedly long-term, to deal with the supply and demand for their professionals. Public relations doesn't. In fact, public relations is a long way from what Dr. Clark Kerr, former chancellor of the University of California at Berkeley, has articulated as a model for such a flow: "Some new professions are being born; others are becoming more professional, for example, business administration and social work. The university becomes the chief port of entry for these professions. In fact, a profession gains its identity by making the university the port of entry." (Clark Kerr, *The Uses of the University,* 4th edition, Harvard University Press, Cambridge, MA/London, 1995.)

It is not the Commission's purpose here to rekindle the ever-smoldering embers of the debate as to whether public relations is a profession. The Commission cites Dr. Kerr only to identify the "use of the university" as one important potential solution to the problem of having enough trained public relations practitioners in the next century.

Other sources of public relations talent, mined successfully for some time, are, indeed, still productive. Former journalists, once a primary candidate cohort, offer valuable skills but, perhaps, limited conceptual understanding of the scope of public relations. Professionals from law, medicine, government, management consulting and other parallel fields often offer relevant attributes but are frequently most valuable in narrowly focused areas of public relations practice.

And therein lies the opportunity, at the entry level and higher, for well-prepared graduates of the public relations academy. Grounded in the liberal arts and sciences. Well-prepared in public relations theory and practice. Tested not only in the classroom but in the field. Understanding the inherent connection between public relations and management, sociology and the many other pillars of modern society. But also with the necessary skills—writing, analyzing, thinking—sharpened and ready for use.

This is the kind of public relations education the Commission has attempted to design. Its recommendations have their roots in earlier Commission reports and in the public relations curricula that in recent years have been producing an increasing number of successful practitioners. But the Commission has gone beyond the present to suggest what public relations education in the future can and must look like if it is to meet the needs of the profession as the new century begins.

The Commission hopes its report will be used by academic programs and faculty to evaluate and develop their curricula; by practitioners who hire graduates of public relations programs; and by academic and professional associations which set standards for academic program certification and accreditation and for the chartering of student public relations organizations.

A final word: this "Port of Entry" report embraces not only the education appropriate for that literal first entry into public relations but, by extension, re-entry or continued service in public relations through graduate study or continuing education.

In short, the public relations education of the next century envisioned by the Commission, like public relations itself, is a matter of continuous professional growth and development. The Commission invites students and potential students, faculty and other academic leaders, certification and accreditation bodies and public relations practitioners to buy into and profit from the greatly improved "Port of Entry" education this report describes.

1. SUMMARY OF THE REPORT—PURPOSE AND GOALS OF THE 1999 COMMISSION

The Commission saw its purpose as determining curricular guidelines and recommendations that, if followed, will prepare public relations students of all ages and levels of ability for the professional challenges of the 21st century as public relations practitioners carry out their fundamental responsibility of building understanding, credibility and trust between organizations and their publics.

The Commission's goals were to determine the knowledge and skills needed by practitioners in a technological, multicultural and global society, and then to recommend learning outcomes—what students should know and be able to do—for undergraduate, graduate and continuing education. The Commission also sought to address appropriate teaching methods, faculty credentials and resources to deliver these learning outcomes. Finally, the Commission sought to suggest methods appropriate for evaluating both student learning and the quality of the academic programs in which public relations is taught.

The Commission based its deliberations and recommendations in large part upon what it learned from an omnibus survey of public relations practitioners and educators co-sponsored by the National Communication Association in connection with its 1998 "Summer Conference on Public Relations Education."

Recommendations for Undergraduate Education

The Commission recommends that students graduating with undergraduate degrees possess both knowledge (what graduates should know and understand) and skills (areas of competence necessary to enter the profession).

Necessary knowledge includes:

- communication and persuasion concepts and strategies
- communication and public relations theories
- relationships and relationship building
- societal trends
- ethical issues
- legal requirements and issues
- marketing and finance
- public relations history
- uses of research and forecasting
- multicultural and global issues
- organizational change and development
- management concepts and theories

Necessary skills include:

- Research Methods and Analysis
- Management of Information
- Mastery of Language in Written and Oral Communication
- Problem Solving and Negotiation
- Management of Communication
- Strategic Planning
- Issues Management
- Audience Segmentation
- Informative and Persuasive Writing

- Community Relations, Consumer Relations, Employee Relations, other Practice Areas
- Technological and Visual Literacy
- Managing People, Programs and Resources
- Sensitive Interpersonal Communication
- Fluency in a Foreign Language
- Ethical Decision-Making
- Participation in the Professional Public Relations Community
- Message Production
- Working with a Current Issue
- Public Speaking and Presentation
- Applying Cross-Cultural and Cross-Gender Sensitivity

The Commission recommends that the undergraduate public relations curriculum be grounded in a strong traditional liberal arts and social science education. A minimum of five courses should be required in the major. Coursework in public relations should comprise 25 to 40 percent of all credit hours, with at least half of these courses clearly identified as public relations courses—the remaining 60 to 75 percent in liberal arts, social sciences, business and language courses.

The Commission strongly encourages a minor or double major in the liberal arts, social sciences or business.

The ideal undergraduate major in public relations would include these courses:

- Introduction to Public Relations
- Case Studies in Public Relations
- Public Relations Research, Measurement and Evaluation
- Public Relations Writing and Production
- Public Relations Planning and Management
- Public Relations Campaigns
- Supervised Work Experience in Public Relations (internship)
- Directed electives

Realizing that many if not most academic programs would find it difficult to offer seven courses devoted entirely to public relations, the Commission concludes that the topics of the courses listed above are the essence of a quality public relations education. The Commission acknowledges that two or more of these topics might be combined into one course or that they might be taught in courses that also address other topics.

If public relations is offered as an undergraduate emphasis or focus rather than as a full major, the Commission recommends these courses:

- Introduction to Public Relations
- Public Relations Research, Measurement and Evaluation
- Public Relations Writing and Production
- Supervised Work Experience in Public Relations (internship)

Recommendations for Graduate Education

The Commission recommends that students studying for master's degrees in public relations learn and appreciate the role of public relations as part of the management team, and learn relevant management and communications competencies and the skills needed to build effective relationships between organizations and their publics. Master's degree students should, says the Commission, gain advanced knowledge and understanding of the body of knowledge in public relations as well as theory, research, communication processes, planning, production and advanced communications management abilities.

The Commission recommends that the curriculum for a master's degree in public relations be a program of 30 to 36 credit hours. Students should master these content areas at a level beyond that expected of undergraduates:

- Public Relations Theory
- Public Relations Law
- Public Relations Research Methods
- Public Relations Management
- Public Relations Programming and Production
- Communication Processes
- Management Sciences
- Behavioral Sciences
- Public Relations Ethics
- A Public Relations Specialty
- An Internship or Practicum Experience and/or Comprehensive Examinations
- A Thesis with Comprehensive Examination and/or a Capstone Project

The Commission suggests these content areas in one sample 36-hour master's program:

- Public Relations Theory
- Public Relations Research
- Public Relations Management
- Public Relations Law
- Integrated Communications
- Accounting
- Finance
- Marketing
- Strategic Planning

The Commission suggests these content areas in a second sample 30-hour program:

- Research Methods in Communication
- Research Design in Public Relations
- Theories of Mass Communication
- Seminar on Public Relations Management
- Seminar on Public Relations Publics
- Seminar on Ethics and Philosophy in Public Relations
- Two electives
- A thesis

The Commission, noting that a doctoral degree is a theory and research degree, concludes that doctoral education should foster an awareness of not only the body of knowledge in public relations, but also the relationship of that body of knowledge to those of other communication-related bodies of knowledge. Doctoral students also should be expected to demonstrate awareness of the breadth and depth of disciplines that influence, and are influenced by, public relations and to be able to integrate that in their teaching and research. Finally, doctoral students should be prepared to develop and contribute to the public relations body of knowledge through formal quantitative and qualitative research, and to foster the development of competing paradigms of public relations based on differing theoretical and philosophical foundations.

The Commission recommends that the core curriculum of a doctoral program, either one focusing exclusively on public relations or the more common variant that includes public relations as part of a broader mass communication or communication doctorate, include courses in:

- Communication Theory
- Philosophy of Science
- Research Methods

- Statistical and Qualitative Research Tools
- Specialized Seminars in Public Relations
- Specialized Seminars in Related Social, Behavioral and Business Sciences
- Dissertation Research

The Commission also recommends that doctoral programs prepare their students to teach by involving them in the classroom and developing their teaching skills.

Recommendations for Continuing Education

Acknowledging that many professional organizations and private vendors offer workshops and seminars that are legitimate continuing education opportunities, the Commission focused its discussion of continuing education, however, on continuing education offered for academic credit or as part of a certificate program.

Continuing education courses pegged to students at a level of ability similar to that of an undergraduate (such as an individual with little or no public relations training or experience) might do well to follow its recommendations for undergraduate education, the Commission suggests. Similarly, graduate-level continuing education might adopt the Commission's recommendations for graduate education.

Continuing education lends itself especially well to distance education (any instruction that takes place with the instructor and student physically separated from each other). For that reason, the Commission notes that a greater variety of teaching methods and technologies may be appropriate in continuing education courses. The resources needed to offer distance education and the special training and preparation demanded of instructors also are special considerations for those offering continuing education courses.

Recommendations for Teaching Methods

The Commission enumerates more than a dozen different ways in which instructors can deliver instruction to students, ranging from traditional lectures to simulations, games and the use of small-group projects.

The Commission also identifies a number of instructional media, assignments and in-class

activities that can create a bridge between theory and practice.

Recommendations for Evaluation

The Commission identifies normative, formative and summative assessment tools and techniques that can be used to determine whether students have learned what their academic program intended. Techniques range from required entrance or exit examinations to internship performance to capstone courses to portfolio review.

The Commission notes that all academic programs should practice self-assessment of their effectiveness by means such as examining student evaluations, faculty-student ratios, placement and graduate school admission rates, alumni and employer satisfaction and input of advisory boards.

In addition, the Commission recommends that public relations programs seek external review from one of three available sources: the certification program of the Public Relations Society of America (available to all public relations programs), the National Communication Association (available to public relations programs in communications colleges, schools or departments) and the Accrediting Council on Education in Journalism and Mass Communications (available to public relations programs in journalism and mass communications colleges, schools or departments).

Recommendations for Faculty Qualifications

The Commission suggests that both academic and professional credentials and experience are important qualifications for public relations faculty. While the ideal full-time faculty member is an individual with both the academic credential of a terminal degree (usually a Ph.D.) and the professional credential of significant work experience in public relations, the Commission concludes that it is more realistic for programs to have among their full-time public relations faculty a balance of those with terminal degrees and those without terminal degrees whose professional experience is significant and substantial.

Adjunct faculty should have at least an undergraduate degree and professional public relations experience, the Commission notes, and suggests that accreditation or certification of adjuncts is highly desirable.

The Commission recommends that both full-time and part-time faculty be active participants in professional and/or academic associations and that both be contributing to the public relations body of knowledge through scholarship and professional or creative activity.

The Commission repeats a recommendation from the 1987 Commission report: "Public relations courses should not be taught by people who have little or no experience and interest in the field and have no academic preparation in public relations."

Recommendations for Resources to Support Public Relations Programs

The Commission urged that public relations students have the same access to both faculty and resources as students in other academic programs in the academic unit where public relations is taught.

Workloads of public relations faculty, the Commission recommends, should reflect the full range of responsibilities assigned to them: teaching, advising, research, service, administrative assignments and the supervision or advising of students organizations such as the Public Relations Student Society of America.

The Commission notes specifically that public relations education requires these administrative and financial resources:

- personnel: faculty, both full-time and part-time, paid commensurably
- staff support
- equipment and facilities in classrooms, labs and faculty offices
- travel and professional development funding
- operating support, such as telephone, FAX and photocopying capability
- library materials to inform both teaching and research

Identification of Global Implications

The Commission identifies seven factors that, regardless of nation or culture, can be considered to have an impact on public relations education. The impact will, of course, differ from culture to culture. The factors are:

- cultural values and beliefs
- laws and public policies
- external groups, organizations and associations
- organizational factors
- small group factors within an institution
- interpersonal factors within an institution
- intrapersonal factors within individuals

The Commission's Call to Action

The Commission concludes with a series of seven recommendations for interaction between public relations education and the professional practice of public relations:

1. Public relations practitioners should take a new look at the "products" of today's public relations education, for they are likely to be impressed with the breadth and depth of knowledge and skill students bring to internships and entry-level employment.

2. There is a great need for significantly increased support from practitioners for accreditation/certification of public relations programs, particularly through attaining additional representation of public relations organizations on the Accrediting Council on Education in Journalism and Mass Communications.

3. The practice should establish additional endowed chairs in public relations at academic institutions with outstanding public relations programs.

4. Successful individual public relations professionals should consider making significant contributions to public relations programs.

5. Public relations educators and professionals can advance the appreciation of the field among influentials and the general public by jointly developing and participating in projects of topical and long-term social significance.

6. Joint research projects, administered by educators and funded by the practice, can not only advance the educator-practitioner relationship but also expand the public relations body of knowledge.

7. "Traditional" support programs for public relations educators, their students and their programs—scholarships, paid internships, support of PRSSA and faculty enrichment programs—must be redoubled.

2. BACKGROUND

The Practice

While its roots can be traced to ancient civilizations, the emergence of public relations as a profession is essentially a twentieth century phenomenon. Immediately following World War II, pent-up demand for consumer goods and services exploded in the United States, triggering a parallel demand for public relations, primarily in the form of publicity support for sales and marketing efforts.

Few practitioners in the late '40s and '50s had studied this evolving practice. Since only a handful of colleges and universities offered formal courses in public relations, the industry reached out to men and women experienced in writing for newspapers and magazines, most having studied journalism. These professionals turned their skills toward a kind of "in-house journalism" for corporations or toward roles as publicists and promoters for clients. By 1950, an estimated 17,000 men and 2,000 women were employed in these endeavors.

Responding to the needs of their employers and clients, public relations practitioners began to expand their activity into such areas as financial relations (annual reports, shareholder meetings and presentations to the financial community) and internal communications (publications, special events and awards programs) to support efforts to enhance employee productivity and commitment.

During the 1960s, social issues and problems forced government, business, labor and other powerful organizations to act and react, creating new public relations emphases on community relations, consumer relations, social responsibility programs and research and analysis to identify issues which could affect the progress and survival of an organization. In this changing, confrontational and contentious era, public relations practitioners were expected to plan for, and manage, crises. Public relations communication itself evolved from one-way message delivery into a two-way exchange involving listening to publics; assessing their needs, expectations and demands; resolving conflicts between groups, and affecting public opinion and behavior.

In recent years, public relations professionals have moved toward an emphasis on building and maintaining relationships and on becoming skilled, active counselors at management's decision-making table. Driving this latest evolutionary movement are influential societal trends: global business operations; mergers, acquisitions and consolidations; the empowerment of public opinion within the global village; segmented, fragmented audiences; the information explosion that has led to uncontrolled, gateless dissemination of messages; increasing government regulation and oversight; issues of diversity and multiculturalism in the workplace, marketplace and town hall, and the introduction of technology, including automation and computerization.

The U.S. Bureau of Labor Statistics estimates that public relations is one of the fastest growing professional fields in the country, and that growth trend is mirrored in other countries as well.

Formal Study in Public Relations

Recognizing a lively and promising career market for their students, colleges and universities began to offer formal education for public relations. In the early 1950s, about a dozen schools offered public relations programs. In 1969 the Public Relations Society of America began to charter student chapters at colleges and universities; initially there were 14, all agreeing to offer at least two courses in public relations.

In 1975, the first Commission on Public Relations Education, comprised of eight educators and practitioners, was formed by PRSA to develop guidelines for public relations education. One of the Commission's primary recommendations was that programs offer at least 12 semester hours, the equivalent of four courses, in public relations at the undergraduate level. Thus, four courses became the new requirement for chartering chapters of the burgeoning Public Relations Student Society of America (PRSSA).

The 1987 Commission on Undergraduate Public Relations Education deliberated three years before issuing updated guidelines. Its 25 members represented such communications organizations as PRSA and its Educators Section (now the Educators Academy); the International Association of Business Communicators (IABC); the American Management Association; the American Marketing Association; the Foundation for Public Relations Research and Education (now the Institute for Public Relations); the International Communication Association (ICA); the Speech Communication Association (now the National Communication Association, NCA), and the Association for Education in Journalism and Mass Communication (AEJMC).

One of the primary recommendations of this 1987 Commission was a sequence of 15 semester hours, the equivalent of five courses, in formal public relations study for undergraduates. This also became the requirement for PRSSA chapters. Today there are 214 PRSSA chapters at colleges and universities.

Graduate curricula recommendations were addressed by PRSA commissions in 1990 and 1995 as more schools added advanced programs to their offerings. Today approximately 70 schools offer master's degrees or a graduate emphasis in public relations. Four universities offer doctoral programs specifically in public relations, with the majority of their graduates seeking careers in teaching and academic research.

The 1999 Commission and Its Process

The 1999 Commission on Public Relations Education was comprised of 47 educators and practitioners representing a consortium of eight allied communications organizations: PRSA and its Educators Academy; the Institute for Public Relations; NCA; AEJMC; the Association for Women in Communication (formerly Women in Communication, Inc.); IABC; the International Communications Association; and the International Public Relations Association (IPRA). PRSA served as the coordinating organization and a staff member served as an ex officio member of the Commission. (Members are listed in Appendix A.)

While many academic programs in public relations are housed in departments or schools of journalism and mass communication, an increasing number—almost half—are now in departments or schools of communication, a discipline which has its roots in rhetoric, interpersonal communication and persuasion. As a result, NCA, the leading U.S. academic society in communication, played a pivotal role in the Commission's work. In 1998, NCA sponsored a summer conference on public relations education, which drew, in part, on an extensive, jointly-sponsored survey of educators and practitioners seeking their views on public relations education. Deliberations and discussions at that NCA conference helped guide the final recommendations of the Commission.

The Commission conducted its work through called meetings, through conferences such as this NCA event; through open discussion sessions during annual meetings of its allied groups and through correspondence, conference calls and exchange of information over the Internet.

The Commission's final report was introduced at the October 1999 International Conference of PRSA in Anaheim, CA. The report also has been presented to all other organizations represented on the Commission and is being widely distributed to schools, educators and practitioners in the United States and around the world.

3. VISION AND PURPOSE

In the future, public relations professionals will not only be skilled communicators but leaders who will help their organizations build and maintain relationships with strategic publics. They will fulfill dual roles of managing communication and counseling top management. Excellent public relations education will be the foundation for preparing new professionals for this dual responsibility.

Therefore, it is important that public relations education grow in sophistication throughout the 21st Century. Public relations as an academic discipline should be equal in status to professionally-oriented academic programs in journalism, marketing, advertising, law and medicine. Academic programs at the graduate level may become comparable in length, complexity and intensity as MBA programs. Faculties for public relations programs may be increasingly interdisciplinary, representing not only a diversity of communications backgrounds but also diversity in academic degrees. Public relations programs may require greater structural and decision-making autonomy.

From the outset, the 1999 Commission on Public Relations Education saw its purpose as determining curricular guidelines and recommendations that will prepare students at all levels of education—undergraduate, graduate and continuing—for the professional challenges of the 21st century. Throughout its two years of study and planning, the Commission diligently sought to fulfill that purpose. Its work reflected the commitment of both educators and practitioners alike to the fundamental responsibility of public relations to build understanding, credibility and trust between organizations and their publics in democratic societies that now are linked globally.

4. MISSION AND GOALS

The mission of the 1999 Commission on Public Relations Education was to provide guidelines, recommendations and standards for public relations education—undergraduate, graduate and continuing—for the early 21st century. Specific concerns of the Commission were desired student outcomes (what students should know or be able to do as a result of their public relations education), curriculum, pedagogy (teaching methods) and assessment of both student learning and academic programs in public relations.

The Commission set six goals.

- Goal 1 Determine needs for public relations education in a technological, multicultural and global society.
- Goal 2 Recommend outcomes for public relations education at the undergraduate and graduate levels.
- Goal 3 Recommend curricula for undergraduate and graduate education.
- Goal 4 Recommend characteristics of appropriate academic "homes" for public relations education.
- Goal 5 Recommend required faculty credentials for public relations educators at the pre-professional level and in continuing education, and provide criteria for evaluating faculty.
- Goal 6 Identify minimal and desired resources for public relations education, and provide criteria for evaluating resources.

5. THE COMMISSION'S ASSUMPTIONS

The 1999 Commission on Public Relations Education was guided by 12 assumptions on which its members reached consensus.

1. The ethical practice of public relations is the context in which and for which education must occur.

2. Public relations helps organizations and publics adapt to each other.

3. Public relations education requires an interdisciplinary foundation that includes liberal arts, languages, social sciences and management.

4. Public relations communication is a two-way process influencing attitudes, behavior and relationships.

5. Graduates of public relations programs should be passionate about the profession, responsible self-managers, flexible in attitude, team participants and ethical leaders appreciative of cultural diversity and the global society.

6. Students must be prepared to operate in a multi-cultural environment.

7. Public relations education is a continuum that goes beyond undergraduate education to include graduate studies, professional development and continuing education.

8. Public relations educators have an obligation to seek professional refresher experience, and practitioners have a responsibility to support and provide opportunities for educators to retool.

9. Practitioners have a significant responsibility to support and participate in undergraduate and graduate public relations education.

10. In the coming years, the teaching of public relations will be significantly affected by new technologies and methods such as "distance learning."

11. Effective preparation of public relations practitioners will not be accomplished by curriculum content alone, but only when content is provided by competent instructors, when it is supplemented by hands-on experience and when it is subject to evaluation.

12. Public relations practitioners and educators should be leaders in building understanding that

public relations has a fundamental responsibility to society and adds value to society.

6. RESEARCH CONDUCTED BY THE COMMISSION

The 1999 Commission on Public Relations Education relied heavily on the findings of the largest and most comprehensive survey ever undertaken on public relations education. The study was co-sponsored by the Commission and the National Communication Association as part of NCA's 1998 "Summer Conference on Public Relations Education." Funding was contributed by PRSA and the University of Miami's School of Communication.

The three goals of the study were to: a) report what skills, knowledge and concepts practitioners and educators think are currently being taught in public relations curricula; b) compare these with what educators and practitioners think should be taught; and c) document the level of agreement between practitioners and academics as to what is taught and what should be taught. More than 100 academics and practitioners used the results of this study in the four-day NCA conference as the basis for making recommendations for public relations curricula in four types of academic programs: a) undergraduate programs based in journalism/mass communication units, b) undergraduate programs based in communication/rhetoric units, c) professional master's programs, and d) theory-based master's and doctoral programs. Those recommendations weighed heavily in the Commission's work.

Questionnaires were mailed to a stratified random sample of 564 educators and 748 practitioners, yielding a sample of 1312. Questions addressed both existing and desired student outcomes (skills and knowledge of graduates), curriculum (course content), pedagogy (teaching methods), and assessment (measuring what has been learned). The response rate ranged from 30 percent for academics to 12 percent for practitioners. While low, the overall response rate of 20 percent is within expected parameters for a questionnaire of this type and length when using a national random sample composed largely of practitioners.

The most significant conclusions of the study were:

Outcomes

Practitioners and educators strongly agree that current public relations education is on track. Students are learning what they should and what they need.

Consistent with those generally positive feelings about public relations education, only 19.8 percent of educators and 14.4 percent of practitioners disagree or strongly disagree that "PR education is keeping up with currents trends in the profession."

Practitioners also value public relations graduates, with only 18.1 percent disagreeing or strongly disagreeing that "Most PR practitioners have very positive attitudes toward PR college graduates." One in five educators (20.8 percent) disagreed with the statement.

Practitioners and academics generally agreed on 24 desirable skills/attitudes for entry level employees. The most highly desired skill was writing news releases (practitioner mean = 6.47, educator mean = 6.77, with 7 being "highly desired.") Second most desired skill was being a self starter (practitioner M = 6.33, educator M = 6.60), and the third most desired skill was critical thinking and problem solving (practitioner M = 6.49, educator M = 6.63).

It is significant that educators saw 18 of the desirable 24 skills/attitudes with a rating of 6 or greater as even more desirable than did practitioners.

On the whole, practitioners and academics also agree that they are not satisfied that desirable skills/knowledge are actually found in graduates, with only three—good attitude, word processing/E-mail, and typing skill—scoring above 5 on the 7-point scale. Although the data is by no means definitive, survey results indicate public relations educators may be focusing too much on mechanical skills (e.g., typing and word processing) and not enough on the half dozen entry level skills that are more important in the eyes of practitioners: being a self starter (M = 6.61), writing news releases (M = 6.53), critical thinking and problem solving skills (M = 6.49), and flexibility (M = 6.44).

The six most highly valued content areas that can be taught in a public relations curriculum, with their overall mean score on the 7 point scale, were: planning, writing, producing and delivering print communication to audiences (M = 6.51), setting goals/objectives/strategic planning (M = 6.49), ethical and legal credibility (M = 6.42), audience segmentation (M = 6.37), publicity and media relations (M = 6.35), and problem/opportunity analysis (M = 6.33).

Practitioners and educators were in noticeably close agreement on conceptual content of public relations education, with no differences exceeding one-half point on the 1–7 scale. Only one item of the 89 communication theory/concepts/models items had a difference of 0.50 or more between practitioners (M = 5.62) and educators (M = 6.12), with both valuing the area, but educators valuing it more. Another nine items had a difference of 0.40 between practitioners and educators, with the three most valued—audience segmentation, public opinion polls and surveys, and research design/process/techniques—being valued by both, with educators again valuing them more.

Practitioners and educators share far more working experience than most think. Practitioner respondents averaged 17.42 years of experience, while those teaching public relations averaged 10.35 years of professional experience and 7.79 years in their present teaching position.

PRSA's accreditation program is accepted and credible among educators more so than among practitioners; only 27.7 percent of practitioner respondents held the APR, while 36 percent of educator respondents are APR.

Assessment

Both educators and practitioners were in general agreement that assessment of student learning was important, that it should be done systematically and that it should include measures other than classroom forms of assessment. Educators placed more emphasis on systematic evaluation, informal assessment techniques and specific outcome assessment than did practitioners; practitioners placed more emphasis on portfolio assessment, inclusion of area

professionals in the process and annual student assessment.

Only internships as an assessment technique were rated 6.00 or higher among the 19 assessment techniques listed.

Educators were asked to report on their program assessment plans; fewer than half reported having assessment plans in place for their programs and even fewer (30 percent) reported having student assessment programs in place.

While more than three-quarters of the practitioners reported they participated in hiring decisions, fewer than a quarter had actually been asked to participate in the assessment of undergraduate or graduate public relations programs or students.

Curriculum

Educators and practitioners were in general agreement with how the public relations curriculum should look. Respondents organized the public relations curriculum around these areas: evaluation/measurement, specialty areas, photography/filmmaking, persuasion and propaganda, departments/firms/careers, research, political public relations, ethics, general social sciences, publicity, information technology, mass communication, special events, and principles of public relations.

Educators and practitioners differed on only 5 of 90 items, with practitioners seeing courses in journalism, radio/TV/film, and filmmaking as more essential than educators and educators seeing courses in communication theory/models and graphic design more essential than practitioners.

When asked what the purpose of an undergraduate major and minor in public relations should be, the majority of respondents said the major prepared the student for an entry-level job in public relations; the minor laid a foundation of public relations skills for students in other majors who might work in the field. The master's degree was seen in two ways, first as a way for practitioners to move into management and second as a way to better understand theory and research as applied to the profession. The doctorate in public relations was seen basically as providing entry to teaching public relations and as a means of advancing the theoretical base of the profession.

Teaching and Pedagogy

Respondents who taught either full or part time reported access to most teaching resources, with the exception of on-line research services (e.g., Lexis/Nexis), satellite links, access time to cable TV and specialized tutors (e.g., research, statistics, writing).

Two-thirds of the respondents reported using the Web or Internet for class use, primarily as supplemental resource links or for class assignments. Nevertheless, data suggested that public relations educators, while having access to both rudimentary and advanced media, still rely primarily on rudimentary media: videotapes, handouts and use of whiteboards or chalkboards.

Almost half of the respondents reported teaching "introduction to public relations," followed closely by writing/techniques classes (14.6 percent) and campaigns classes (12.8 percent). Most often classes were small (20–25 students).

When specific instructional techniques were compared between educators and practitioners who taught part time, only five differences emerged: practitioners reported greater use of lectures, guest lecturers, individual presentations/speeches, case studies and running complete campaigns than full-time educators.

Demographics

The sample was balanced by sex (Males = 51.4 percent; Female = 48.1 percent). Respondents' average age was 48.04 (median = 48; mode = 50). The vast majority were Caucasian (84.5 percent) and held graduate degrees (77.4 percent, a function of the educator subsample). Most had majored in a communication-related major; only 3.3 percent were business majors.

In terms of current position, half of the educators were assistant, associate or full professors, the other half lecturers or instructors. Practitioners reported being senior management (CEO, owner, partner, 19.4 percent), directors/managers (middle-level

management, 19.4 percent), and "other" (technicians, account executives, etc., 61.2 percent).

Most of the practitioners reported never having taught part time. Almost two-thirds, however, reported lecturing to a public relations class. Over half reported supervising an intern over the last five years.

The full study is available on the National Communication Association's home page (www.natcom.org) and a condensed version was printed in the Spring 1999 issue of *Public Relations Review*.

7. RECOMMENDATIONS FOR UNDERGRADUATE EDUCATION

Purpose of an Undergraduate Degree

The purpose of an undergraduate degree in public relations is to prepare students for an entry-level position in public relations and to assume a leadership role over the course of their careers in advancing the profession and professionally representing their employers. Students must be educated broadly in the liberal arts and sciences, and specifically in public relations, so that they are fully employable upon graduation.

Desired Outcomes

Specific educational outcomes are categorized as knowledge and skills. Knowledge outcomes identify what graduates should know and understand; skill outcomes address the areas of skill and competence necessary to enter the profession.

Like any other advanced professional field, public relations needs as its practitioners individuals with high ethical standards and a passion for their profession. Graduates should be responsible, flexible and professionally oriented self-managers. They should be curious, conceptual thinkers and appreciative of cultural and gender diversity and of global cultures. They must be trustworthy team participants and leaders, and good communicators.

Because of the interdisciplinary nature of public relations and the realities of its practice in society, it is important for graduates to be grounded in disciplines beyond journalism, communications and public relations. For that reason, the best preparation for the profession would include a minor or double major in a related area. It is expected that graduating students would be able to integrate the preceding professional attributes and demonstrate familiarity and comfort with the knowledge and skills that follow.

Knowledge

Undergraduate majors should master the following knowledge:

- Communication and persuasion concepts and strategies including mass media, organizational, small group and interpersonal channels of communication
- Communication and public relations theory, including public relations' role in society and in an organization
- Relationships and relationship building
- Societal trends
- Ethical issues
- Legal requirements and issues
- Marketing and finance
- Public relations history
- Uses of research and forecasting
- Multicultural and global issues
- Organizational change and development
- Management concepts and theories

Skills

Undergraduates should be competent in the following skills:

- Research, including methods, analysis, recommendations, reporting, environmental and social assessment and statistics
- Management of information including its role in the public relations process and assessment of message credibility
- Mastery of language in written and oral communication
- Problem solving and negotiation
- Management of communication
- Strategic planning
- Issues management, including environmental scanning, issue anticipation, risk analysis and change methodology

- Audience segmentation
- Informative and persuasive writing for various audiences
- Area emphases such as community relations, consumer relations, investor relations, employee relations, government relations, and media relations
- Technology and visual literacy (including the Internet and desktop publishing), and development of new media/message strategies and the design and layout of messages
- Managing people, programs and resources
- Sensitive interpersonal communication
- Fluency in a second language
- Ethical decision-making
- Participation in the professional public relations community
- Writing and production of specific communication messages
- Working within a current issue environment
- Public speaking and presentation
- Applying cross-cultural and cross-gender sensitivity

Curriculum

Because educational institutions are so diverse in their structures and organization, the Commission felt it more appropriate to address the content of curriculum rather than to prescribe specific courses. The content may be contained in various courses both internal and external to public relations programs and their curricula.

Sample curriculum configurations, to be used as guidelines only, follow these content recommendations.

In any case, a strong traditional liberal arts and social science education is a necessary foundation for public relations education. It also is requisite that a multicultural and global perspective pervades the curriculum, and that public relations be taught within the framework of ethical issues and behavior.

Coursework in a public relations major should comprise 25 to 40 percent of all undergraduate credit hours. Of those, at least half should be clearly identified as public relations courses.

Five clearly identifiable public relations courses should be the minimum, and programs should move to include more than five if at all possible.

A student's program of study should be comprised 60 to 75 percent of liberal arts, social science, business and language courses.

The student's program of study should include a minor or double major in another discipline. Especially suggested are business and the behavioral sciences.

Content

The following topics are all deemed essential to a strong undergraduate education in public relations, regardless of the course(s) in which they may be taught:

• Theory, Origin, Principles and Professional Practice of Public Relations: Content in this area specifically pertains to the nature and role of public relations, the history of public relations, the societal forces affecting the profession and its practice and theories of public relations. Also included are practitioner qualifications (including education and training), responsibilities and duties, functioning of public relations departments and counseling firms, and career-long professional development. Addressed here as well are specializations in public relations such as community relations, employee relations, consumer relations, financial and investor relations, governmental relations, public affairs and lobbying, fund raising and membership development, international public relations, and publicity and media relations.

• Public Relations Ethics and Law: Content here includes codes of ethics and practice in public relations and in other professions; specific legal issues such as privacy, defamation, copyright, product liability, and financial disclosure; legal and regulatory compliance, and credibility.

• Public Relations Research, Measurement and Performance Evaluation: Content should address both quantitative and qualitative research designs, processes and techniques including public opinion polling and survey research; experimental design and research; fact-finding and applied research; observation and performance measurement; social, communication and employee audits; issue tracking; focus groups and interviews; use of external research services and consultants; media and clipping analysis, and historical research. It should also focus on results-based decision making, measuring program effectiveness, measuring staff and counselor performance, developing criteria for performance, tools and methods for measurement and evaluation and reporting on results of public relations efforts.

• Public Relations Planning and Management: Content of the curriculum in planning and management should be theory, techniques and models related to setting long- and short-term goals and objectives, designing strategies and tactics, segmenting audiences, analyzing problems and opportunities, communicating with top management, developing budgets, contingency planning for crises and disasters, managing issues, developing timetables and calendars and assigning authority and responsibility. This content area also requires inclusion of the philosophy and culture of organizations, and knowledge of business or corporate culture including finance, theory, practice and terminology.

• Public Relations Writing and Production: Public relations writing is an essential, discrete skill not addressed in journalistic writing, composition or creative writing. Content here should address communication theory; concepts and models for both mass, interpersonal, employee and internal communication; organizational communication and dynamics; persuasion and propaganda; controlled versus uncontrolled communication, and feedback systems. It must include development of competency in such skills as layout and graphics, speechwriting and delivery, spokesperson training, speakers bureaus, corporate identity, photography, filmmaking and working with outside suppliers. It requires a solid understanding of media, media channels and the societal role of media. It includes message strategy and delivery (i.e., planning, writing, producing and delivering print communication to audiences; and planning, writing, producing and delivering audiovisual, electronic, videotape and multimedia communication to audiences). It also is essential that content address new public relations tools and techniques, especially current and emerging technology and its application in the practice of public relations.

• Public Relations Action and Implementation: This area of content includes actual implementation of campaigns; continuing programs (product publicity, safety, etc.); crises and isolated incidents; individual activities of practitioners and firms, clients or employers; meetings and workshops, and special events.

• Supervised Work Experience in Public Relations: It is imperative that public relations students have the opportunity to apply the skills and principles they learn to the professional arena. These practical experiences must be supervised by faculty and practitioners who cooperate to provide professional experience directed by learning objectives and assessed throughout to assure a quality practical educational experience.

- Disciplines Related to Public Relations: Supporting disciplines appropriate to public relations programs include political communication, organizational communication, interpersonal communication, rhetorical communication, small group communication, psychology, sociology, marketing, management and organizational behavior, finance, journalism, radio and television production, advertising, mass communication law, photography, filmmaking, art, design and graphics, information technology, hypertext and Web design.

- Directed Electives: Certain content in other disciplines should be considered essential for the development and preparation of public relations professionals. It is recommended that such content be recommended or directed as elective courses to supplement the core public relations and communication courses. Recommended directed electives include: business management and marketing, accounting, finance, economics, consumer behavior, political science and the political system, public administration, social psychology, sociology, cultural anthropology, English and English writing, political science, including government and political campaigns, and international business and communication.

Sample Content Configuration

As the practice of public relations becomes increasingly sophisticated, more institutions of higher learning will begin to define majors, rather than just sequences or emphases of study, in public relations. Given this projection, the Commission identified a sample curriculum following the above content recommendations for a bachelor's degree in public relations. Following is a recommendation for a minimum acceptable array of courses for a major in public relations with supplementary courses within the broader major and minor.

Ideally, an undergraduate degree in public relations would include these courses:

- Introduction to Public Relations (including theory, origin and principles)
- Case Studies in Public Relations that review the professional practice

- Public Relations Research, Measurement and Evaluation
- Public Relations Law and Ethics
- Public Relations Writing and Production
- Public Relations Planning and Management
- Public Relations Campaigns
- Supervised Work Experience in Public Relations
- Directed Electives

In a program where public relations is an emphasis or focus, integrated with related disciplines such as communication or journalism to form a major, some of this content may be included in courses with content that is broader than public relations alone. In these instances, the Commission recommends, as a minimum, that the public relations emphasis or focus include these courses:

- Introduction to Public Relations (including theory, origin and principles
- Public Relations Research, Measurement and Evaluation
- Public Relations Writing and Production
- Supervised Work Experience in Public Relations
- At least one additional public relations course in law and ethics, public relations planning and management case studies or campaigns

Programs that offer minors should make it clear that a minor in public relations is not sufficient to prepare a student for the professional practice of public relations. However, programs may offer minors in public relations to enhance the understanding of students majoring in professional disciplines that use or cooperate with public relations. A minor in public relations should specifically address the knowledge outcomes previously stated rather than just the skill outcomes.

8. RECOMMENDATIONS FOR GRADUATE EDUCATION

Purpose of a Master's Degree

The purpose of a master's degree is to enable students to acquire advanced skills and knowledge in research, management, problem solving and issues, and to obtain management level expertise.

For some students, the master's degree also is preparation for doctoral level education.

The master's degree program thus prepares individuals for public relations management leadership, career development and on-going contributions to the profession and to society in a global context. It guides the individual in knowing and appreciating the role of public relations as part of the management team, in gaining relevant management and communications competencies and in building effective relationships between organizations and their publics.

Desired Outcomes of a Master's Degree

Master's students should gain advanced knowledge and understanding of the body of knowledge in public relations, including theory, research, communication processes, planning, production and advanced communications management abilities.

Students should be taught within an environment in which they learn to provide leadership through use of communication, social and behavioral science theory and research techniques to help organizations analyze and solve problems and take advantage of opportunities that have public relations consequences.

To enter a master's degree program, individuals should hold an undergraduate degree in public relations or its equivalent: i.e., a combination of an undergraduate communications degree and public relations experience. Individuals with undergraduate degrees in other fields without public relations knowledge and competencies should be required to demonstrate proficiencies such as those listed in the undergraduate section of this report. Options could be provided to prepare new students for advanced study and/or to build upon their current competencies to the point they are ready for graduate-level study of public relations.

The Master's Degree Curriculum

The curriculum for the master's level graduate student must have a great deal of flexibility. It should be tailored to graduate student career objectives and personal interests. While many students will choose a master's degree as their final degree,

the master's curriculum should be able to prepare students who so desire to enter doctoral programs (e.g., by choosing a specific set of courses and/or completing a thesis).

The basic curriculum of the master's degree in public relations should be a program of study requiring between 30 to 36 credit hours of graduate coursework.

The Curriculum Composition

The following content areas should provide advanced, intensive focus upon the primary area of interest: public relations. All that has come before, through general education and public relations studies, will be here. The expectation is that students will develop further abilities to critically analyze and synthesize the body of knowledge in public relations management by producing critical essays and original research projects, and will enhance their professional performance through the application of theory and research.

The student should master the following content areas beyond the undergraduate competencies.

- Public Relations Theory: This area should familiarize students with the leading theories of public relations scholarship, including social science, rhetorical and communication theories (i.e., models of public relations, public relations roles theories, theories of publics, theories of public relationships), public relations history, and public relations issues (encroachment, feminization of the field, paradigm struggle, impact of social, political, and economic environments).
- Public Relations Law: This area should address regulatory, constitutional and statutory laws of public relations, risks of free expression and communications law related to public relations.
- Public Relations Research Methods: This area should include the application of social science research methods to the planning, implementation and evaluation issues of public relations practice. Quantitative and qualitative methods, an understanding of experimental design, sampling, use of standard statistical packages, report writing and research ethics should be taught.
- Public Relations Management: This area should include public relations strategic management

principles and issues (e.g., planning, organizing, evaluating, staffing, counseling, leadership, budgeting principles and such advanced subjects as reputation management), concepts of organizational effectiveness (strategy, size, technology, environment and the dominant coalition), public relations as a political process and how it is related to other functions such as integrated communications and to the mission of the organization, rhetorical-critical approaches; culture and globalization; building relationships with internal and external audiences; issues and crisis management; activism, mediation, negotiation, and conflict resolution.

- Public Relations Programming and Production: This area should include advanced programming and production principles, particularly related to new technology, the Internet and telecommunications as well as the practices and theories of message preparation, visual communications principles, and other communications techniques. Students should apply research and evaluation models to this practical side of public relations.
- Communication Processes: Here students should learn theories and practices of communication (organization, interpersonal, small group, mass, persuasion, rhetorical, conflict resolution).
- Management Sciences: This area should include accounting, finance, marketing and integrated marketing/advertising communication applicable to both for-profit and non-profit organizations.
- Behavioral Sciences: This area should acquaint students with social psychology, cultural anthropology, sociology and political science. It should also include courses that build an understanding of group behavior, global trends, evolving global codes of conduct, organizational culture, behavioral change and knowledge of local, state, national and international political systems.
- Public Relations Ethics: Some of the ethical issues that merit attention are philosophical principles, international ethical issues, concealment vs. disclosure, divided loyalties, social responsibility, accountability, professionalism, codes of ethics, whistle-blowing, confidentiality, ethical dealing with the media, solicitation of new business, ethics of research, logical arguments and multicultural and gender diversity.
- Public Relations Specialty Options
- Internship or Practicum Experience and/or Comprehensive Examination

- Thesis and/or Comprehensive Exam and/or Capstone Project

The graduate student should be required to conduct some original research in her/his particular area of interest, resulting in a thesis or graduate capstone project of acceptable quality. If a thesis is optional, the student should be required to take a comprehensive examination. It is recommended that no credit hours be awarded for comprehensive examinations.

One Sample Master's Program Content Outline (36 credit hours)

Public Relations Content:

- Public Relations Theory
- Public Relations Research
- Public Relations Management
- Public Relations Law
- Integrated Communications

Management Science Area Content:

- Accounting
- Finance
- Marketing
- Strategic Planning

When the Master's Degree is Terminal:

- Leadership Studies (New Technologies, Conflict Resolution, International Relations)
- Capstone Project

When the Master's Degree is Preparation for the Doctorate:

- Thesis

An Alternative Sample Master's Program Content Outline (30 credit hours)

- Research Methods in Communication
- Research Design in Public Relations
- Theories of Mass Communication
- Seminar on Public Relations Management
- Seminar on Public Relations Publics
- Seminar on Ethics and Philosophy in Public Relations

- Seminar on Global Public Relations
- Two Electives
- Master's Thesis (6 credits)

The Purpose of a Doctoral Degree

A doctoral degree in public relations is a theory and research degree. The purpose of the Ph.D. program is to help students develop the theoretical and research skills they will need to add to the body of public relations knowledge.

A doctoral degree should prepare graduates for academic positions in universities and for advanced management and applied research positions in major public relations departments, opinion research companies and other organizations.

Historically, the doctoral curriculum in public relations has been a specialized option within a broader Ph.D. program, usually titled "mass communication" or "communication."

But communications Ph.D. programs have not produced a sufficient supply of graduates with a public relations specialty, primarily because few educators with an interest in researching public relations problems have been involved in those Ph.D. programs. The result has been a shortage of public relations researchers. The addition of public relations researchers to university faculties would render the existing framework of most Ph.D. programs adequate for a public relations specialty.

Desired Outcomes of a Doctoral Degree

Students completing a doctoral program should be:

- prepared for roles as senior managers and as future college faculty who can deliver course content and evaluate student work effectively.
- aware of not only the body of knowledge in public relations, but the relationship of that body of knowledge to those of other communication-related (e.g., interpersonal, rhetorical, organizational and small group) bodies of knowledge as well. In addition, students should demonstrate awareness of the breadth and depth of disciplines that influence, or are influenced by, public relations and ability to integrate that knowledge in their teaching and research.

- prepared to develop and contribute to the body of knowledge through formal quantitative and qualitative research and to develop the ability to disseminate that information to the academic and practitioner communities in a clear, usable fashion through conferences and professional publications.
- prepared to develop competing paradigms of public relations based on differing metatheoretical and philosophical foundations in response to the maturation of the field.

Because doctoral programs are generally an array of courses tailored to the academic and professional backgrounds of individual students, it is expeted that appropriate attention will be given in these individualized programs to ensuring a foundation in public relations concepts, theories and professional practices.

Curriculum

The core curriculum of most Ph.D. programs in communication or mass communication stresses research and theory building through courses in communication theory, philosophy of science, research methods and statistical and qualitative research tools.

A public relations Ph.D. candidate should also take the bulk of his or her coursework in these core areas of research skills. It is essential that the instructors of these core courses understand public relations, encourage new research on public relations problems and encourage the building of public relations theories. This has seldom been the case in current Ph.D. programs.

In addition, the Ph.D. program should offer several specialized seminars in public relations on topics such as public relations management and its appropriate place in the organizational structure; behavior of publics; public relations roles, law, history and operations; and global perspectives on public relations.

Public relations Ph.D. students should be encouraged to take research seminars in related social, behavioral and business sciences that are particularly relevant to public relations in order to learn the theories and methods of those related disciplines. These courses, for example, could include the sociology of organization, organizational communication, operations research and management science, political behavior, sociology of collective behavior, public opinion, language usage and communication and social psychology.

Finally, the public relations Ph.D. candidate should conduct dissertation research in which he or she studies theory applicable to the solution of important public relations problems and in specific topic areas in public relations such as investor relations, crisis management, issues management, social responsibility, marketing public relations and integrated communications.

However, a doctoral program also has the obligation to prepare students to teach by involving students in the classroom and developing their teaching skills because many, if not most, graduates will accept positions as public relations faculty.

9. RECOMMENDATIONS FOR CONTINUING EDUCATION

Purpose of Continuing Education

Continuing education has been an important aspect of professional education throughout the evolution of public relations in the 20th century. In the historical sense, continuing education has meant education for the adult learner outside the traditional degree programs of a college or universities. Continuing education in public relations might well be identified as "lifelong learning" because it seeks to add to or refresh the knowledge or skills of those familiar with and/or already working in the practice of public relations. The purpose of this instruction should be to provide for the ongoing professional development and advancement of public relations professionals, from entry-level beginners through senior executives. It is important that continuing education courses, faculty and resources be of comparable quality with those of degree-granting public relations programs, as described elsewhere in this report.

Desired Outcomes of Continuing Education

Sometimes continuing education is provided on a college or university campus, although often it is not. Sometimes it is provided by traditional modes of instruction, although increasingly it is being provided by "distance education" or "distance learning" that the Commission defines as any instruction that takes place with the instructor and student physically separated from each other. Sometimes it is a one-hour workshop or a half-day seminar, sometimes carrying CEUs (continuing education units).

Increasingly important in continuing education is the growing number of certificate programs; while not degree programs per se, they group a number of courses together into a logical program of study. The Commission suggests that academic criteria in certificate programs should be no different from those in degree programs, especially when the courses used in certificate programs are the same courses that traditional students might use to meet undergraduate or graduate degree requirements.

The 1999 Commission on Public Relations Education focused solely on continuing education offered as for-credit instruction, acknowledging that many professional associations and private vendors also offer workshops and seminars not linked to academic credit that are legitimate continuing education opportunities.

As a result of their participation in for-credit continuing education courses or programs, public relations practitioners should add to their knowledge of the concepts, theories and practices of the profession.

Curriculum

In continuing education, just as in traditional degree programs, curriculum models differ from institution to institution. No one model can serve all.

For undergraduate-level continuing education offerings, the guidelines presented by the Commission certainly are appropriate. Likewise, when the continuing education offerings are at an advanced level and offered to practitioners who already have undergraduate degrees, the master's degree guidelines suggested by the Commission are relevant.

Continuing education is offered using perhaps a greater variety of teaching methods than traditional undergraduate or graduate courses. Typically, continuing education has led the way in pioneering new teaching methodologies, particularly distance education methods. Active learning often is enhanced through student involvement with new technologies such as the Web.

In addition to traditional teaching techniques, continuing education often utilizes Internet transmission of course material by either asynchronous or synchronous course delivery; video-assisted instruction; a combination of Web and television instruction; satellite or broadcast instruction; delivery by compressed video, or other technology-based modes of delivery. Often traditional and distance education modes are combined in one course: a week-long face-to-face introduction to the course might be followed with additional meetings on-line or through E-mail interaction.

Continuing education courses in public relations often have been provided by public relations faculty who teach them on an overload basis, as "extra" assignments for which they receive extra compensation. An exception has been at some land-grant institutions whose mission is heavily outreach-oriented; some of these schools have made continuing education instruction part or all of a full-time faculty member's regular responsibilities.

When continuing education is offered by distance education technologies, the model of faculty overload doesn't always work well. It takes considerable effort to teach Web-based or television-delivered courses, and incentives beyond a bit more salary need to be developed to encourage faculty to develop and teach these courses.

Because continuing education is likely to be offered increasingly through new technologies, state-of-the-art hardware and software are essential for those institutions offering continuing education courses and for those students enrolling in them.

Professional societies and associations, such as PRSA and IABC, would do well to partner with colleges and universities to ensure that appropriate continuing education modules are developed and offered. These associations and public relations foundations, notably the Institute for Public Relations and the PRSA Foundation, are encouraged to provide seed money for the development of continuing education courses and certificate programs to ensure that public relations learning is, indeed, lifelong.

10. TEACHING METHODS

The teaching of public relations at all levels should emphasize active learning. Given the fact that much public relations work is done by teams of practitioners, team-based and service learning also should be encouraged.

Teaching involves the delivery of instruction; the creation of student assignments and learning activities; and the application of instructional media to the classroom, laboratory and distance learning environment.

The 1999 Commission on Public Relations Education presents these recommendations on teaching methods because it believes it is not only important to address curriculum content but also to address how that content can best be transmitted.

Delivery of Instruction

Lectures are a delivery technique familiar to students, especially helpful in introducing and examining a broad range of material, particularly abstract concepts. The best lecturers will incorporate a lively and informative style, and encourage interactivity with students through discussion, dialogue and questioning.

Guest lecturers and speakers add fresh voices to the classroom, which increases student interest. Practitioners can bring the practice of public relations into the classroom and provide a bridge between student and professional associations. The pool of available guest lecturers for most programs is typically large, and professionals usually are enthusiastic about assisting in this way.

Simulations and role-playing also are very effective teaching methods for selected topics. Both encourage student involvement (affective learning) and aid in student retention of material. The teacher can control the simulation in ways he or she could not if students were working with an actual client or situation.

Games are useful ways to simplify abstract concepts and are particularly useful for teaching remedial skills and history or for review sessions, such as those that might be held to help students prepare for an examination.

Small group discussion and in-class exercises provide essential learning opportunities in the area of team building and group dynamics. This teaching method also helps develop brainstorming and analytical skills as students learn to give and receive critiques.

Having students make oral presentations in class provides them with practice in a skill that will be vital to them as practitioners, making client presentations and defending their ideas in meetings. Oral presentations offer a good opportunity for peer or practitioner evaluation of student work, and also for interaction and networking with both peers and practitioners. They also can be useful in helping students learn to create and use computer-aided presentations and visual aids.

Teaching writing and design or production skills in a computer classroom or lab gives students an opportunity to build their skills and their computer literacy.

The use of field trips is another teaching method that provides an opportunity for interactive learning as students see the practice of public relations in process and interact with practitioners.

Instruction is increasingly being delivered through distance education, as described in Part 9 of this report, using a variety of techniques: on-line Internet delivery of lectures and readings, chat rooms and E-mail interaction between student and professor, combinations of video-Web-television instruction and delivery of entire courses by broadcast media or satellite.

Assignments and Activities

Case studies, an excellent bridge between theory and application, can be used at all class levels to promote learning. Regardless of the model, case studies teach analytical and critical thinking skills.

Incorporating the planning (and sometimes even the implementation) of campaigns into public relations courses adds depth and detail, and provides opportunities for students to translate theory into practice. Carrying a plan through to implementation adds the dimension of learning about client relationships and, when the client is "real," provides another opportunity for professional networking.

Instructional Media

Audio and video recordings are useful not only because they present important material in an interesting way, but because by listening or viewing, students also learn to recognize production quality.

The Internet (and when available an intranet) has many applications in public relations teaching: as the source of case studies and research data, as a means of contact with practitioners and as an interactive communication channel between faculty and students. Its potential for interactivity makes it especially appealing in distance education settings.

11. EVALUATION

Both academic programs and the students enrolled in them should be evaluated. In the case of students, the objective is to ascertain whether students learned what the curriculum and their faculty intended. In the case of programs, the objective of the evaluation is to ascertain and ensure quality of the curriculum, how it is taught, the quality of that instruction and the resources provided to support the educational effort.

Evaluation of Students

Student evaluation may be normative, formative and/or summative.

Normative assessment is usually undertaken to determine which students are eligible to enter or to advance within the public relations program. Normative assessment tools might include:

- required entrance exams
- assessment of the extent to which the student possesses the attitudes and behaviors of professionals
- screening through standardized test scores and placement tests in subjects such as English, spelling and math
- high school and projected college GPA
- performance in pre-requisite classes
- writing and speaking apprehension
- internship performance as a screen for subsequent internships
- Formative assessment is evaluation that provides continuing feedback throughout a student's

degree program. Formative assessment tools might include: faculty evaluation and grading of assignments

- tests that screen for skill proficiency
- capstone courses to measure ability to conceptualize and apply knowledge
- case study analysis to measure critical thinking
- oral and computer-aided presentations to measure presentation skills
- evaluation of internships by both faculty and site supervisors
- review of a portfolio of student work
- examination of career objectives, expectations, knowledge, preparation and future plans
- measurement of sensitivity to multicultural environments and diversity, perhaps using a standardized test such as that used by the U.S. Navy to test for multicultural sensitivity
- Summative assessment is conducted at the time a student completes a degree program. Appropriate tools might include review of a portfolio of student work to assess writing and presentation skills, research skills, analytical ability and ability to complete projects or campaigns
- faculty assessment of strengths and weaknesses, either in writing or as an exit interview
- administration of an organizational simulation of a public relations work environment
- review of professional experience gained through course assignments, internships or other work experience

Evaluation of Programs

Program evaluation can be accomplished through self-assessment and external review.

1. Self-Assessment

Public relations programs should continually measure their effectiveness in delivering instruction in both degree-oriented and continuing education courses by utilizing the following self-assessment tools:

- Teacher-course evaluations by students, peers and administrators
- Faculty-student ratios
- Job placement rates

- Percent of public relations graduates working in the field
- Graduate school admissions
- Exit interviews and surveys
- Alumni satisfaction surveys
- Employer satisfaction surveys
- Professional accreditation of alumni
- Input of advisory boards

Programs also are advised to monitor such quality indicators as instructional innovations, particularly integration of new technologies; student access to courses in related disciplines (e.g., business); vitality of student organizations; involvement of professionals; and equitable distribution of resources. Finally, programs should periodically compare the content of the courses they offer to the Commission's recommendations.

2. External Review

Three organizations currently provide external review of academic programs in public relations education: PRSA, NCA and the Accrediting Council for Education in Journalism and Mass Communications (ACEJMC). PRSA's Certification of Education in Public Relations (CEPR) provides professional association certification for programs housed in any academic discipline, including communication, journalism and business. NCA's Program Review, on the other hand, provides educator assessment for programs housed in communication colleges, schools or departments. Similarly, ACEJMC examines programs housed in journalism and mass communication units. ACEJMC is the only one of the three authorized by the U.S. Department of Education to grant professional accreditation. Review by any of the three organizations is at the invitation of the program unit.

PRSA's certification process is coordinated by its Educational Affairs Committee, which consists of both educators and practitioners. After receipt of a required self-study, the committee assigns a visiting team of two or three members who examine the public relations program on site over three to four days. Criteria for evaluation are based on the most recent guidelines of the Commission on Public

Relations Education. Among program elements reviewed are curriculum, faculty/student ratio, resources, internships, student counseling, job placement and involvement and support of professionals. Team members visit classes, check records and interview faculty, administrators, students, alumni and practitioners. At the conclusion of the on-site review, the team makes a preliminary report of its findings, including strengths and weaknesses of the program, to the program's coordinator. A written report with the team's recommendation is submitted to the Educational Affairs Committee, which decides whether or not to grant certification. The committee's decision is then forwarded to PRSA's Board of Directors for approval.

In ACEJMC accreditation, the entire academic unit—college, school or department—is evaluated through a review of all programs in the unit, which might include advertising, broadcasting, newspaper journalism, magazine journalism and public relations. The process begins with a self-study based on 12 standards. A three-day site visit is conducted by a team of three to six educators and practitioners who represent the unit's various disciplines. When the unit has a public relations component, an effort is made to include a public relations educator or practitioner on the team.

During its campus visit, the ACEJMC team examines the unit's compliance with the 12 standards, which deal with governance/administration, budget, curriculum, student records/advising, instruction/evaluation, faculty credentials and qualifications, internships and work experience, faculty scholarship/research/professional activities, public service, graduates/alumni, and minority and female representation, respectively. As in the PRSA process, team members monitor classes, check records and interview faculty, students and representatives of other relevant groups. The team prepares a written draft report of its findings before leaving campus and presents copies of the report to the unit administrator and the institution's president. Responses from the unit and institution are considered before the report is finalized and submitted to ACEJMC's Accrediting Committee, which recommends full accreditation, provisional accreditation (meaning the unit must

correct specified deficiencies in one year) or denial of accreditation. The committee then forwards its recommendation to ACEJMC's Accrediting Council for a final decision. Institutional representatives are invited to the meetings of both groups. Units must be reaccredited every six years.

Of the 24 professional, practitioner organizations which are dues-paying members of ACEJMC, only one—PRSA—represents the profession of public relations. Thus the profession has only one voice and one vote on decisions made by ACEJMC's Accrediting Council. In contrast, other disciplines are represented by multiple professional organizations, each with one or more votes. For example, advertising is represented by two organizations (American Academy of Advertising and American Advertising Federation), broadcasting by four (Broadcast Education Association, National Association of Broadcasters, National Association of TV Program Executives and Radio-Television News Directors Association) and newspaper journalism by eight (American Society of Newspaper Editors, Associated Press Managing Editors, National Conference of Editorial Writers, National Newspaper Foundation, Newspaper Association of America, Society of Professional Journalists, Southern Newspaper Publishers Association and the Inland Press Association).

Only a minority of academic programs in public relations are certified by PRSA or accredited by ACEJMC. As noted earlier in this report, approximately one half of all public relations programs are housed in communication units, which are not eligible for ACEJMC accreditation. Such programs are eligible for PRSA certification; however, relatively few programs have sought CEPR status to date. Furthermore, of the hundreds of journalism and mass communication units that teach public relations, only 109 currently are accredited by ACEJMC.

The NCA process bridges the gap between self-assessment and external review. The association provides the Communication Programs Rationale and Review Kit (1997), which presents questions to guide self-assessment (for example, "Has our department kept pace with the discipline?"), lists

NCA resources and services to aid evaluation (for example, contact information for nationally recognized communication specialists in teaching, research and service), and offers the association's Program Review Service. More collegial than the processes of PRSA and ACEJMC, NCA's on-site Program Review brings "consultants" to campus rather than "evaluators." The service allows the host unit to determine the number of consultants, choose their specialization and geographic location, and even select named individuals (NCA also will recommend team members if a host unit desires). The consultants' report goes to the unit requesting the review, not to NCA.

All of these program evaluation processes would be more valuable if:

- More public relations programs sought accreditation and/or certification.
- Additional public relations organizations, such as the Arthur W. Page Society, IABC, Council of Public Relations Firms, Institute for Public Relations, PRSA Foundation, and International Public Relations Association (IPRA), obtained membership in ACEJMC. Representation should also be solicited from educator associations with large public relations memberships, such as NCA and ICA.
- ACEJMC teams better reflected the composition of the student body of the unit reviewed, particularly those in which public relations is a major component.

12. FACULTY QUALIFICATIONS

Both academic and professional credentials and experience are important qualifications for public relations faculty. It also is critical that public relations faculty share the understanding that public relations is practiced in an interdisciplinary, multicultural and global context.

Programs may use both full-time and part-time faculty to teach public relations courses. It is important, however, that the majority of public relations instruction be provided by full-time faculty.

Perhaps the ideal full-time faculty member is an individual with both the academic credential of a terminal degree, usually the Ph.D., and the professional credential of significant work experience in the field of public relations. And to the extent that they exist—they do, but in relatively small number—academic programs would do well to hire individuals with both sets of credentials.

What is perhaps more realistic is for academic programs to have among their full-time public relations faculty a balance of those with terminal degrees and those who may not have terminal degrees but whose professional experience is significant and substantial. Particularly in programs that offer graduate degrees, it is critical that there be full-time faculty with Ph.Ds capable of teaching public relations theory and research and qualified to direct graduate thesis and dissertations in public relations. When no graduate faculty who specialize in public relations research are available to guide and mentor graduate students, they may be diverted into a thesis or dissertation that does not encourage an interest in public relations.

Adjunct (part-time) and temporary full-time faculty should, in every case, have at least an undergraduate degree and relevant professional public relations experience. It is highly desirable that they be personally accredited or certified by a professional public relations organization, especially when their college degree is in a field other than public relations.

Most adjunct faculty will be drawn from the ranks of those currently working in public relations, so their professional expertise is being updated and refined on a daily basis. Because they are often not experienced teachers, it is essential that adjuncts be provided with appropriate training for the classroom.

Full-time faculty must create their own opportunities—one would hope with the enthusiastic leadership of practitioners and professional organizations—to keep up with current public relations practices through "professor in residence" programs, faculty-professional exchanges, participation in professional development programs and sabbaticals.

All faculty, both full-time and adjunct, should be members of and participate in professional and/or academic associations and conferences.

And all faculty, both full-time and adjunct, should be contributing to the public relations body of knowledge through scholarship and professional or creative activity. The form that contribution may take will, of course, vary depending on whether the faculty member has primarily academic or professional credentials.

The Commission repeats a recommendation from the 1987 Commission report: "Public relations courses should not be taught by people who have little or no experience and interest in the field and have no academic preparation in public relations."

13. RESOURCES NEEDED FOR PUBLIC RELATIONS PROGRAMS

Public relations faculty and students should have resources comparable to those available to faculty and students in other academic programs in the academic unit where public relations is taught.

It also is important that faculty in public relations programs have responsibility for those matters and decisions that directly affect public relations faculty, students and the units of which they are a part.

Workloads of public relations faculty should reflect the full range of responsibilities assigned to them: teaching, advising, research, service, administrative assignments and the supervision or advising of student organizations such as PRSSA or student public relations agencies.

Administrative and financial resources necessary to support public relations education include:

- personnel: faculty, both full-time and part-time, who are paid commensurate with faculty in other programs in the academic unit
- staff support: secretarial and technical support personnel
- equipment and facilities in classrooms, labs and faculty offices: computer hardware, software and peripherals; classrooms specially equipped for presentations; research facilities, particularly a telephone bank for surveys and space suitable for simulating or conducting focus groups, and space for student organizations
- travel and professional development support; funding for travel to academic and professional conferences, for payment of professional association dues, for participation in workshops or other professional development programs
- operating support: telephone, books and other materials used in teaching, postage, photocopying, faxes
- library: materials to inform both teaching and research

Faculty-student ratios should conform to those recommended by national accrediting bodies (such as the Accrediting Council on Education in Journalism and Mass Communications) and those that certify programs (such as Public Relations Society of America). There should be qualified full-time faculty members teaching public relations when it is offered as a major, emphasis or focus, the number of those faculty dependent on student enrollment. Full-time public relations faculty should teach the majority of required courses.

Scholarships and financial aid should be available to students. This is particularly critical in graduate programs where funding is perhaps the deciding factor as programs compete for the best students for assistantship and fellowship awards.

While most administrative and operating expenses are the responsibility of academic units, there are other resources that must be provided by the profession. Among these are providing internship and professional residency programs for students and faculty, supporting and serving on advisory boards, endowing chairs and faculty positions in public relations and providing examples and samples of public relations work, especially audio-visual materials, for classroom use.

14. GLOBAL IMPLICATIONS OF THE COMMISSION'S RECOMMENDATIONS

A major assumption of the Commission was that its report would focus primarily on higher education in the United States. The Commission's members were principally associated with USA-based institutions, and, given the range of factors that can affect higher education in public relations, the Commission did not want to presume to make recommendations for other nations and cultures.

However, the Commission did want to enable educators and practitioners in other countries to adapt or adopt its recommendations if they so choose. To that end, the Commission identified the following factors that affect public relations higher education, to a greater or lesser extent, in all societies and cultures.

The following list is not exhaustive. The factors are presented in the hopes that others may find them helpful in explaining and guiding public relations higher education not only in the USA but also elsewhere in the world.

Cultural Values and Beliefs

- Importance within society of truth-telling, fairness, justice and the concept of doing no harm to the innocent.
- Degree of comfort with uncertainty within society as seen in the collective attitudes toward centralized or decentralized control.
- Attitudes toward men and women.
- Degree of acceptance (or not) of class differences and assumptions about an individual's duties and responsibilities to others in society.

Laws and Public Policies

- Structure of and support for higher education, including the degree of politicization of higher education within society.
- Public support for technological infrastructure within the economy.
- Freedom of press and individual rights to free speech and related issues.
- Policies regarding free markets and "transparent" economic exchanges, especially in the areas of corporate disclosure.

External Groups, Organizations and Associations

- Employer demand for university graduates who have majored or specialized in public relations.
- Number of professional associations in the field and their support for higher education.
- Number of organizations in region, including activist publics, that emphasize and appreciate public information, public relations, and public affairs.
- Number of competing institutions of higher education.

Organizational Factors

- Size, complexity and sources of resources for the institution, be it a university or college.
- The historic, legal mandate or stated function of the institution.
- Technological infrastructure of the institution.

Small Group Factors Within Institutions

- Qualifications of the faculty and how they relate to students—for example, the degree of power differentiation or egalitarianism experienced in the classroom.
- Qualifications of faculty and staff and how they relate to each other—for example, the "natural tension" often experienced between journalism and public relations faculty.
- Worldview of the institution's dominant coalition: do senior administrators at the university encourage change and innovation, or not.

Interpersonal Factors Within Institutions

- Role expectations between individual administrators and faculty members.
- Role expectations between an individual faculty member and a student.
- Role expectations outside the university between clients and practitioners—for example, is the practitioner expected by the client to be a technician or a problem solver?

Intrapersonal Factors and Traits Within Individuals

- Intelligence of the students, faculty members, practitioners.
- Sex/gender—physical traits and internalized sex roles.
- Maturity (not the same as age).
- Eagerness and willingness to learn.

In sum, public relations both as a professional practice and as an academic discipline may be considered protean—readily assuming various roles and structures depending on its internal and external environments. The wide variety of social environments and public relations practices around the world means that inevitably there are, and will continue to be, a variety of models of public relations higher education.

15. A CALL TO ACTION: PUBLIC RELATIONS EDUCATION AND THE PRACTICE

Symbiosis is not too strong a descriptor of the relationship between public relations education and the professional practice of public relations. Yet there is much to do to realize the full potential of this mutually-beneficial relationship.

The key to progress here, the Commission suggests, is to base future cooperative efforts on a simple, practical statement of respective needs: Public relations educators need additional resources and recognition; the practice needs a steady flow of graduates who are prepared to enter, or re-enter, the profession and, as the saying goes, "hit the ground running."

So what is to be done?

The 1999 Commission on Public Relations Education recommends a seven-point interactive program:

1. Public relations practitioners should take a new look at the "products" of today's public relations education. Those who have, are impressed with the breadth and depth of knowledge and skill students bring to internships and entry-level employment. Those who haven't, are missing what is quite often a good hiring "bet."

2. There is a great need for significantly increased support from practitioners for accreditation/certification of public relations programs. In the year 2000, three to five additional public relations seats on The Accrediting Council on Education in Journalism and Mass Communications (ACEJMC) should be sponsored by the practice. This will generate added practitioner participation on campus accreditation site visit teams as well as in the final decisions on which programs are to be accredited.

3. The practice should establish additional endowed chairs in public relations at academic institutions with outstanding public relations programs. A chair is costly and may require the pooling of financial assistance from several organizations and their clients, but chairs represent prestige externally and clout internally.

4. Successful individual public relations professionals, especially those who have benefited handsomely from public relations practice, should consider making significant contributions to the public relations programs

of their choice. Such philanthropy, common in other professional fields, would mark public relations as a field in which one generation of practitioners is tied to succeeding generations by commitment to the development of the profession.

5. Public relations educators and professionals can advance the appreciation of the field among influentials and the general public by jointly developing and participating in projects of topical and long-term social significance. Educators bring intellectual legitimacy and credibility to such projects; practitioners—individually and through organizations such as PRSA, The Arthur Page Society, the newly formed Council of Public Relations Firms and the various public relations institutes and foundations—can add strategic input and needed resources. The "outside world" must be engaged on hot macro issues: for example, ethical communications conduct in the age of global interdependence. Structures for such activities already exist. They include the PRSA/CPRF Socratic Dialogues (in April, 1999 such a dialogue was held at The Annenberg School). Partnering organizations have included the Ethics Officers Association and several national trade associations.

6. Joint research projects, administered by educators and funded by the practice, can not only advance the educator-practitioner relationship but also expand the public relations body of knowledge. Moreover, when the research subjects are of topical interests—say, on employee behavioral response to key messages—they provide an opportunity for positive exposure of the true gravitas of the profession. And if adequately funded ($50,000–$500,000 or more), the research can impress academic influentials.

7. Finally, "traditional" support programs for public relations educators, their students and their programs must be re-doubled. This means more practitioner-funded scholarships, more paid internships, more support of PRSSA to benefit students, and more faculty enrichment programs including inter-term employment and other imaginative cooperative efforts.

Other kinds of such professional support also must be considered, such as the valuable expenditure of professionals' time on campus to strengthen public relations programs. Both individual practitioners and professional associations can be invaluable in providing advice and feedback to programs and their faculties. Advisory boards also can provide financial and other resources that enhance program quality.

These programs, and others like them, will further enhance the likelihood that public relations education, through its own growth and development, will produce more successful public relations practitioners and leaders and advance the profession's contribution to society.

APPENDIX A: THE 1999 COMMISSION ON PUBLIC RELATIONS EDUCATION

Dean Kruckeberg, Ph.D., APR, Fellow PRSA
University of Northern Iowa
Co-Chair of the Commission
Represented PRSA

John L. Paluszek, APR, Fellow PRSA
Ketchum Public Affairs
Co-Chair of the Commission
Represented PRSA

Bill C. Adams, APR, Fellow PRSA
Florida International University
Represented PRSA

David K. Allred, APR
Utah Jazz Basketball Club
Represented PRSA

Gail Baker, Ph.D., APR
University of Florida
Represented PRSA

John R. Beardsley, APR
Padilla Speer Beardsley Inc.
Represented PRSA

Sue Bohle, APR, Fellow PRSA
The Bohle Company
Represented PRSA

Carl Botan, Ph.D.
Purdue University
Represented ICA

Joan L. Capelin, APR, Fellow PRSA
Capelin Communications, Inc.
Represented PRSA

Clarke L. Caywood, Ph.D.
Chair, Integrated Marketing Dept.
Represented PRSA

Timothy W. Coombs, Ph.D.
Illinois State University
Represented NCA

William J. Corbett, APR, Fellow PRSA
Corbett Associates, Inc.
Represented PRSA

H. J. (Jerry) Dalton, Jr., APR, Fellow PRSA
Optima Strategies Division
Represented PRSA

Kathleen Fearn-Banks, Ph.D.
University of Washington
Represented PRSA

John W. Felton, APR, Fellow PRSA
Institute for PR Research & Education
Represented Institute for Public Relations

James E. Grunig, Ph.D.
University of Maryland
Represented PRSA

Larissa A. Grunig, Ph.D.
University of Maryland
Represented AEJMC

Barbara A. Hines, Ph.D.
Howard University
Represented PRSA

Stanton H. Hudson, Jr., APR
Hudson & Associates
Represented PRSA

Kathleen S. Kelly, Ph.D., CFRE, APR, Fellow PRSA
University of Southwestern Louisiana
Represented PRSA

Dan L. Lattimore, Ph.D., APR
University of Memphis
Represented PRSA

Wilma Mathews, ABC
Arizona State University
Represented IABC

Mark P. McElreath, Ph.D., APR
Towson University
Represented IABC

Arthur P. Merrick, APR, Fellow PRSA
The Rockey Company
Represented PRSA

Dan Pyle Millar, Ph.D., APR
Indiana State University
Represented NCA

Debra A. Miller, Ed.D., APR
University of Portland
Represented PRSA

Bonita Dostal Neff, Ph.D.
Valparaiso University
Represented WICI

Douglas Ann Newsom, Ph.D., APR,
    Fellow PRSA
Texas Christian University
Represented PRSA

Coral M. Ohl, Ph.D., APR
California State University, Fullerton
Represented PRSA

Isobel Parke, APR, Fellow PRSA
Jackson, Jackson & Wagner
Represented PRSA

Judith Turner Phair, APR, Fellow PRSA
University of Maryland/Biotechnology Institute
Represented PRSA

Betsy Plank, APR, Fellow PRSA
Betsy Plank Public Relations
Represented PRSA

Cheryl I. Procter, APR
Home Box Office
Represented PRSA

Shirley A. Ramsey, Ph.D., APR
University of Oklahoma
Represented PRSA

Maria P. Russell, APR, Fellow PRSA
Syracuse University
Represented PRSA

Kenneth Seeney
EIERA
Represented PRSA

Melvin L. Sharpe, Ph.D., APR, Fellow PRSA
Ball State University
Represented IPRA

Don W. Stacks, Ph.D.
University of Miami
Represented PRSA

Elizabeth Lance Toth, Ph.D., APR
Syracuse University
Represented ICA

Joseph V. Trahan III, Ph.D., APR
Defense Information School
Represented PRSA

Judy Van Slyke Turk, Ph.D., APR, Fellow PRSA
University of South Carolina
Represented AEJMC

James K. Van Leuven, Ph.D., APR
Colorado State University
Represented PRSA

Dennis L. Wilcox, Ph.D., APR, Fellow PRSA
San Jose State University
Represented PRSA

Laurie J. Wilson, Ph.D., APR, Fellow PRSA
Brigham Young University
Represented PRSA

Nancy B. Wolfe, APR, Fellow PRSA
Elon College.
Represented PRSA

Donald K. Wright, Ph.D., APR, Fellow PRSA
University of South Alabama
Represented PRSA

Frank W. Wylie, APR, Fellow PRSA
California State University, Long Beach
Represented IPRA

Elaine Averick
Commission Staff Liaison
PRSA

APPENDIX B: RESEARCH AND REPORTS USED BY THE 1999 COMMISSION

Research and Reports

International Public Relations Association (Sept., 1990). *Public relations education— Recommendations and standards.* Gold Paper No. 7.

Foundation for Public Relations Research and Education (April, 1985). *Advancing public relations: Recommended curriculum for graduate public relations education.* New York: Author.

Public Relations Society of America (1987). *Design for undergraduate public relations education: 1987 report of the Commission on Undergraduate Public Relations Education.* New York: Author.

Special Issue of Public Relations Review, (1999), *24*(1).

Schwartz, D., Yarbrough, J. P. & Shakra, M. T. (1992). Does public relations education make the grade? *Public Relations Journal 48*(9), 18–20, 24–26.

Stacks, D. W. (1998, July). *Perceptions of public relations education: A survey of public relations curriculum, outcomes, assessment, and pedagogy.* Paper presented to the 1998 PR Summer Conference, Arlington, VA.

Other Suggested Resources for Public Relations Educators and Administrators

Berth, K. & Sjoberg, G. (1997). *Quality in public relations.* Quality Public Relations Series No. 1. Copenhagen, Denmark: The International Institute for Quality in Public Relations.

Bianco-Mathis, V. & Chalofsky, N. (ed.) (1996). *The adjunct faculty handbook.* Thousand Oaks, CA: Sage.

Public Relations Society of America (1987). *Demonstrating public relations professionalism: A report of the PRSA Task Force on demonstrating professionalism* New York: Author.

Haworth, J. G., & Conrad, C. F. (1997). *Emblems of quality in higher education: Developing and sustaining high-quality programs.* Boston: Allyn & Bacon.

Conrad, C. F. & Wilson, R. W. (1985). *Academic program reviews: Institutional approaches, expectations and controversies.* ASHE-ERIC Higher Education Rep. No. 5. Washington, DC: Clearinghouse on Higher Education, The George Washington University.

Cox, B. (1994). *Practical pointers for university teachers.* London: Kogan Page.

Glazer, Judith. (1986). *The master's degree: Tradition, diversity, innovation.* ASHE-ERIC Higher Education Rep. No. 6. Washington, DC: Clearinghouse on Higher Education, The George Washington University.

McArthur, D. J., & Lewis, M. D. *Untangling the Web: Applications of the Internet and other information technologies to higher learning.* Available on the World Wide Web at: http://www.rand.org/publications/MR/MR975/

Meagher, L. D., & Devine, T. J. (1993). *Handbook on college teaching.* Durango, Colorado: Hollowbrook Publishing.

Menges, R. J., & Weimer, M. (1996). *Teaching11. Evaluation.*

International Public Relations Association. (1982). *A model for public relations education for professional practice.* Gold Paper No. 2.

Oeckl, A. (1976). *Public relations education worldwide.* Gold Paper No. 2. International Public Relations Association.

Porter, Lynette R. (1997). *Creating the virtual classroom: Distance learning with the Internet.* New York: Wiley Computer Publishing.

Sallot, L. M. (ed.). (1998). *Learning to teach: What you need to know to develop a successful career as a public relations educator* (2nd ed.). New York: Public Relations Society of America.

Sharp, M. L. (1985, Feb.). Public relations education: its needs and advancement. *IPRA Review, 9*(1), 4–7.

GLOSSARY OF ORGANIZATIONS CITED IN THE REPORT

Accrediting Council on Education in Journalism and Mass Communications (ACEJMC)

American Management Association

American Marketing Association

Arthur Page Society

Council of Public Relations Firms (CPRF)

Institute for Public Relations (formerly the Institute for Public Relations Research and Education)

International Association of Business Communicators (IABC)

International Communication Association (ICA)

International Public Relations Association (IPRA)

National Communication Association (NCA)

Public Relations Society of America (PRSA)

Public Relations Student Society of America (PRSSA)

BENEFACTORS

The Commission on Public Relations Education gratefully acknowledges the following organizations, which provided valuable support for the Commission's work:

Hilton Hotels Corporation

Northwest Airlines

Southwest Airlines

National Communication Association

Public Relations Society of America

University of Miami

Institute for Public Relations (formerly the Institute for Public Relations Research and Education)

SOURCE: Public Relations Society of America. Reprinted with permission.

Appendix 5

The Corporate Annual Report

An Evolution

THE CORPORATE ANNUAL REPORT: AN EVOLUTION

At its essence, the corporate annual report is the financial statement issued yearly by a publicly owned corporation, showing assets, liabilities, revenues, expenses and earnings.

Over time, the annual report has emerged as an art form, a visual, colorful expression of a public company's fiscal year, its products and its workers. On the pages that follow, the evolution of the corporate annual report is shown through the juxtaposition of the entire 11-page 1881 American Bell Telephone Company Annual Report and excerpts from the 92-page 2002 AT&T Annual Report.

SOURCE: Property of AT&T Archives. Reprinted with permission of AT&T.

REPORT

OF THE DIRECTORS

OF THE

American Bell Telephone Co.

TO THE STOCKHOLDERS,

MARCH 29, 1881.

BOSTON:
ALFRED MUDGE & SON, PRINTERS,
34 SCHOOL STREET.
1881.

OFFICE OF THE AMERICAN BELL TELEPHONE CO.,
BOSTON, March 29, 1881.

To the Stockholders:

The business of the company since its organization in May, 1880, has been in every respect satisfactory.

Up to the present time the chief development of the telephone has been for exchange systems, but there is reason to expect a large use of the instrument for private lines, branch lines and speaking-tube purposes; and to this, during the coming year, especial attention should be directed.

For purposes of comparison, statistics have been prepared for twelve months, ending Feb. 28, 1881, including the last two and a half months of the work of the *National* Bell Telephone Company.

The general manager's report shows that on the 1st of March, 1880, 138 exchanges were in operation or about to open, and on Feb. 28, 1881, the number was 408; an increase of 270.

The number of instruments in the hands of our licensees in the United States,

Feb. 20, 1880, was   60,873
Feb. 20, 1881   132,692

Showing an output for the year of 71,819 instruments. This number includes 20,885 taken over from the Gold and Stock Telegraph Company, and in use by our licensees.
The number of instruments sold for export purposes

up to Feb. 20, 1880, was   2,800
During the past year   16,041

In the United States there are only nine cities of more than 10,000 inhabitants, and one of more than 15,000, without a telephone exchange.

2

The total number of cities and towns for which licenses to build exchanges have been issued, is 1,523 ; and there is no reason to doubt that, in most of these points of any imp r-tance, the system will within a few months be put in operation.

With the exception of Camden, New Jersey, which is still in process of settlement, there is no exchange in the United States now being operated or built under any license except that of this company.

The business of connecting cities and towns by telephone wires has been taken up in the past year with some vigor, and the prospect is good for a large increase in these lines. Boston, for example, is now in communication with seventy-five cities and towns, including Providence, Worcester, Springfield, Lawrence, Lowell, and other important places.

It will take some time yet to get first-rate service in a large network of towns, as the practical difficulties at least equal those which were met in giving prompt connection within the limits of one city, but nothing but experience and tests of various methods are needed to enable such groups of exchanges to reach satisfactory results. Thirty-two contracts have been given to other companies for this class of work, and the reports to date show 1,398 miles of wire and 731 miles of pole line in use.

The connection of exchanges with the telegraph lines has been begun in a small way all over the country, and although it will take time to accustom people to the use of the telephone for the sending of telegraph messages, the commission from this source will undoubtedly grow and become of substantial value.

The company has now a stock interest in the companies in New York, Chicago, Philadelphia, St. Louis, San Francisco, Elmira, New Haven and Canada, amounting, in the aggregate, at par, to $1,300,300, and owns the whole of the Boston Exchange, which has cost, with the Edison Exchange bought from the opposition, $130,358.97.

The business of all these companies is now upon a paying

3

basis, although the requirements for new construction and for the cost of putting together two systems in New York, Chicago and Boston, have thus far absorbed all net earnings in these places, while in consequence of these changes the service in these cities is not yet fully satisfactory.

In New York and Chicago the local companies will probably at once make provision for their new construction outside of their net earnings, and put themselves in a position to pay dividends upon their capital.

In Boston some $15,000 will be required from the treasury for construction, after which it is expected that the business will be sufficient to provide for its own further growth.

The business of the New York company already promised handsome results, when, on the 21st of January, a sleet storm, more severe than any known since the telegraph came into general use, prostrated the wires and many poles in all parts of the city, and inflicted severe direct and indirect loss upon the company.

The executive committee of that company, however, feel every confidence that its business will prove of very great value, and that beyond certain important questions of construction, which are somewhat difficult of solution in that city, we have no serious obstacles to a great success.

In settling with the Western Union Company it was necessary, in order that the competing interests should be harmonized, that all their exchange systems should be bought, and it was estimated at the time of the settlement that we might have to sustain a loss of some $50,000 in completing these arrangements.

With one unimportant exception, that of Camden, N. J., before mentioned, we have settled all of these cases and have either bought and resold to or procured to be bought by our licensees, fifty-five exchanges, costing   . $325,160 06

of which we have kept Boston, costing   . $26,000 00
and have recovered upon the remaining fifty-
four 267,187 98

leaving a loss of $31,972 08

4

This may be considered a satisfactory settlement, as there was much waste and bad building on the part of the opposition exchanges for which our licensees were unwilling to pay, and yet it was of the greatest importance to get the whole country settled, and under one system.

It is hoped that before the next annual meeting a valuable business will be developed in Canada. It seemed to the directors of importance to control the license of instruments in the Dominion, in order to prevent the smuggling of telephones across the border. Two companies have been formed in that country; one to hold the patents and issue licenses, and the other to develop the business. Our company holds and should continue to hold a majority of the capital stock of the former; and as considerable delay occurred in settling the competition between the Bell and the Gold and Stock licensees in the Dominion, it was found necessary to advance enough money to the second company to get the contest ended, the plant of both parties under one control, and the business under some headway. All this has been done, and the development of exchanges is proceeding with much enterprise; and it is probable that the Bell Telephone Company of Canada will, erelong, be in such a position that we can readily sell such part of the stock which we have received for our investment there as it may not be thought best to keep. It is, however, as yet too early to give any exact report upon the business in Canada, but we are advised that 4,496 telephones are in use, and 2,082 subscribers are connected with the various exchanges, and the managers of the company feel entirely confident of success.

In regard to claims for telephone patents advanced by other parties, the directors are advised by Messrs. Chauncey Smith and James J. Storrow, the counsel of the company, as follows : —

" MARCH 23, 1881.

" W. H. FORBES, Esq., *President American Bell Telephone Co.:*

" *Dear Sir,* — The condition of the patent controversies which the company is concerned in in relation to the Bell patents is as follows : —

5

" These patents cover every apparatus capable of transmitting articulate speech by electricity which has yet been devised, and the more carefully the subject is examined the more certain it appears that no instrument can do it except by copying the method invented by Mr. Bell and patented to him by his patent of March 7, 1876. For eighteen months after the grant of that patent no one publicly, at least, disputed his claims to originality.   After his telephones had gone into general use, the Western Union Telegraph Company set up three claimants, and pushed these claims in the Patent Office and in the courts.   But after the facts of the case had been fully brought out in evidence, the acute and sagacious counsel of the Western Union Telegraph Company were satisfied that Mr. Bell would prevail.

" This particular question, though the most important part of the controversy with the Western Union, was only a part of it, and the contract of Nov. 10, 1879, settled the whole controversy. The settlement was based upon the assumption and concession that the Bell patent was valid, and that it covered all the apparatus known, and upon the recognition of the advantage to the Telephone Company of the exclusive right to use certain subordinate inventions owned by your opponents, and upon the commercial advantages likely to arise from other provisions of the contract in the then condition of your company.

" It was necessary that the controversies thus originated in the Patent Office should be proceeded with, but there is no doubt whatever about the result.   Moreover, the American Bell Telephone Company own the exclusive right to use those inventions of your opponents.

" W. L. Voelker, of Philadelpha, has since been added to those who claimed the great invention, but his evidence has been taken and his dates are too late to leave him any ground for contest.

" Recently a new claimant has appeared.   The People's Telephone Company, formed in the summer of 1880, acquired the right to prosecute a claim for Daniel Drawbaugh, who alleges that he preceded Mr. Bell by six or seven years.   But we consider them to be absolutely without chance of success.   This claim was not heard of until the summer of 1880.   Every one remembers the attention which Mr. Bell's discovery at once attracted, and it is absurd to suppose that practical telephones existed in the suburbs of Harrisburg for ten years before anybody published the fact.

6

" It is the common fortune of important patents, after they have developed great commercial value, to be the subject of similar claims, but such tardy attacks on such valuable patents have invariably failed. It always turns out that such claimants have done something, but have stopped short of the successful result which the patentee had reached.

" We are satisfied, as we have already advised you verbally, that the People's Company have nothing to sell which is worth buying.

" The Drawbaugh applications now stand rejected in the Patent Office.

" In October last we obtained a preliminary injunction against the People's Company after a contest. The suit has been pushed, our evidence taken, and case only waits such proof as the defendants may have to offer.

" We have also obtained three other injunctions on the Bell patents in New York, one in Boston, and one in Chicago.

" There are other interference controversies on some minor features of the Bell patents, but they give us no anxiety, because the evidence taken shows the strength of Mr. Bell's case, and because, if we fail in any of them, you will obtain the patents of the other parties at a moderate cost.

" The company is concerned in other patent controversies, but in view of the evidence which has been taken in all the important ones, we perceive no cause for alarm in any of them.

" Yours truly,

" (Signed)   CHAUNCEY SMITH.
" (Signed)   JAMES J. STORROW."

A large amount of work has been done in the electrical and experimental department, both in examining new inventions and testing telephones and apparatus, and in studying the question of overhead and underground cables, and the improvement of telephones and lines, for both short and long distance service. This work is expensive, but it is of the first importance to our company, and must be continued.

The report of the General Inspector upon this department shows that we own or control, either by purchase or by inventions made by our own electricians, 124 patents, and have applications in the Patent Office for 77 more. Among these a considerable number are of great value as a

7

protection to our business, and from them a substantial revenue has already been received by royalties from our licensees. This source of income will be materially increased, and should eventually more than cover our experimental and electrical expenses.

Immediately after the settlement with the Western Union Company the policy of making only five-year contracts was adopted, in order that our company could have time to learn the best permanent basis for the relations between the company and its licensees, and to see which of them would prove satisfactory as associates. Many applications are now being made for permanent licenses, and we have begun to give such permanent contracts in places where the business is being prosecuted with energy and success, in exchange for a substantial interest in the stock of the local companies. By pursuing this plan, the company will gradually acquire a large permanent interest in the telephone business throughout the country, so that you will not be dependent upon royalties for a revenue when the patents shall have expired.

The treasurer's report shows that the total receipts, including sales of stock and loans, for the year ending Feb. 28, 1881, have been $2,058,184 08

And the total expenditures, including construction account 1,957,430 97

Balance on hand $100,753 11

The capital or construction accounts include settlements with the Western Union and Gold and Stock Telegraph Companies for instruments and exchange plant, purchase of new telephones, purchase of exchange interests, patents, plant in Canada, and sundry smaller items, and amount to $1,537,456 93

The earnings of all kinds for the same period have been 605,184 01

Expenses of operating, including royalty to Western Union and associates .   .   .   339,425 44

Dividend, Jan. 1, 1881   .   .   .   .   178,500 00

8

The increase in earnings has been steady from $28,151.54 per month, in March, 1880, to $61,244.93 in February, 1881. And the net earnings for these twelve months show an increase of $193,037.44 over those of the previous year.

Much of the electrical and legal work of these first years of the company, and indeed some of our expenses incurred in studying and classifying the business, are substantially for the establishment of the property, and might be charged to construction and capitalized, but the directors have preferred the more conservative policy of charging everything to operating which could reasonably be put there, although the result upon the books appears less favorable, in consequence, than the business prospects might warrant us in exhibiting.

If this course is continued, when the suits in progress become settled, and the rush to secure patents for all the early inventions is over, our operating expenses in the legal and electrical departments can be much lessened, and a business of far greater volume than that of the past year can be done with no increase in our expense account.

No reason is now apparent for any increase of consequence in the construction account, beyond the limit provided for by the $500,000 loan negotiated last October, and the directors do not foresee any occasion for raising any further amounts of money.

The treasurer's accounts show that the company is earning something more than a three per cent dividend for the current six months, and if the net increase of telephones producing rental continues at over 4,000 per month, the latter half of the year will give a still better result.

After two years passed in a struggle for existence, and a third largely devoted to the settlement of disputes inherited from that contest, the owners of the telephone patents, at the beginning of their fourth year, for the first time find themselves free from all serious complications, with nothing to prevent the company from directing its whole working force

9

to the development of the business, and with a defined policy for its future operations, which seems to be working well in all parts of the country.

In conclusion, the directors wish to express their appreciation of the ability, fidelity, and zeal with which the general manager and his assistants have grappled with the unusually perplexing difficulties encountered in systematizing our affairs.

The statement of the treasurer for the year ending Feb. 28, 1881, and the report of the auditing committee, are appended.

For the directors,

W. H. FORBES,

President.

Statement of the American Bell Telephone Company for Year ending Feb. 28, 1881.

EARNINGS AND OPERATING EXPENSES.

EARNINGS.

Rental	$535,754 84	
Sales of instruments and supplies .	29,379 51	
Royalties from manufacturers . .	20,353 45	
Exchange dividends . . .	11,200 00	
Miscellaneous	8,496 21	
		$605,184 01

EXPENDITURES.

Expenses of management . .	$130,672 66	
Legal expenses	44,283 58	
Interest and taxes	34,486 73	
Royalty on switches, etc. . .	12,097 58	
Commission (chiefly royalty to W. U. Telegraph Co. *et als.*, contract of Nov. 10, 1879)	94,406 11	
Depreciation	23,478 78	
Dividend	178,500 00	
		$517,925 44

NOTE. — The word *exchange* means *telephonic exchange system.*

The words *exchange interests* mean *interests in local companies operating such systems.*

10

CASH STATEMENT.

RECEIPTS.

Cash balance March 1, 1880	$130,500	46
Sales of stock	850,000	00
Loan of 1880	296,100	00
Temporary loans	137.660	42
Rental	402,794	18
Sales of instruments and supplies	45,040	35
Royalties	21,603	90
Exchange dividends	11,200	00
Extra territorial lines and telegraph commissions	3,472	60
Transfer of Western Union exchanges	112,658	37
Exchange interests	24,425	24
Loans paid	11,330	25
Miscellaneous	11,398	31

EXPENDITURES.

Operating expenses—				
General (including salaries, office, travelling, electrical and experimental)	$126,660	73		
Legal expenses	46,284	89		
Interest and taxes	20,805	51		
Commission and royalty (includes royalty to the Western Union Telegraph Company, *et als.*, contracts of November 10, 1879)	35,114	30		
			$228,865	43
Instruments purchased and manufactured		....	305,651	19
Transfer of exchanges		....	188,715	57
Patents		....	123,371	32
Exchange interests		....	441,363	30
Office furniture and library		....	4,859	31
Loans paid		....	477,110	87
Loaned		....	10,000	00
Dividend		....	173,595	00
Miscellaneous		....	3,898	98
Cash on hand		....	100,753	11
	$2,058,184	08	$2,058,184	08

11

SUMMARY.

RECEIPTS.

Cash balance March 1, 1880 .	.	$130,500 46
Capital accounts . . .	.	1,432,424 28
Current accounts . . .	.	495,259 31

EXPENDITURES.

Capital accounts	....	$1,537,456 93
Current accounts	....	419,974 04
Cash balance Feb. 28, 1881 .	. ...	100,753 11
	$2,058.184 08	$2,058,184 08

Boston, March 28, 1881.

To the Directors of the American Bell Telephone Co.:

Gentlemen, — Your committee, appointed to audit the accounts of the treasurer, with authority to employ an expert, has attended to that duty, and herewith presents the report of Mr. C. T. Plimpton, the expert employed for that purpose.

Very respectfully submitted,

CHARLES P BOWDITCH, *Committee.*

Boston, March 21, 1881.

I hereby certify that I have audited the books and accounts of the Treasurer of the National Bell Telephone Company, from March 1, 1880, and of the books and accounts of the American Bell Telephone Company from their commencement in May, 1880, to March 1, 1881, as follows : —

The cash books, their debits and credits, journalizings, postings, stock ledger, bank accounts, trial balances and cash on hand.

In my investigations have found everything in connection with the above correct, and that all disbursements as entered in cash books are sustained by approved vouchers, and that the books are kept with accuracy.

CHARLES T. PLIMPTON, *Auditor.*

Networking
Makes
Our Customers
Strong

Customers
Make
Us Strong

AT&T:
The World's
Networking
Company

Networking Makes Our Customers Strong

Our customers continue to benefit from our leadership role in networking.

o Continuing to outperform the industry in customer satisfaction and innovation

o Ongoing investment to meet the needs of enterprises and individuals who place a high value on communications

o Offering unmatched capabilities in managing end-to-end mission critical business applications

o Growing in our role as the industry-leading Internet protocol (IP) provider

o Continuing to be recognized as a critical partner and a preeminent provider of high-quality services

o Applying AT&T Labs expertise to networking solutions of tomorrow while meeting customer needs today

o Delivering to customers a real return on their communications investment through more than 36,000 networking experts

o Delivering international direct-dial service to more than 250 countries and territories, and in-bound calling services for travelers in 200 countries through AT&T Direct Service

o Offering real competitive choice in local, long distance and Internet services

Customers Make Us Strong

AT&T continues to benefit by satisfying the needs of its customers.

o Managing nearly 50 million consumer relationships and 4 million business customers

o Creating one of the strongest financial structures and best balance sheets in the industry

o Realizing annual revenue of more than $37 billion

o Leading the industry in customer satisfaction

o Forming a unified communications services company with approximately 71,000 employees in 56 countries

o Ranking as one of the largest online billers with more than 1 million residential customers billed online

o Serving as the official provider of personal telecommunications services to military personnel serving at 529 military bases and camps worldwide and on more than 200 U.S. Navy ships

o Serving more than 2.4 million households, with residential AT&T Local Service in California, Georgia, Illinois, Michigan, New Jersey, New York, Ohio and Texas as of December 2002, with more states to follow

AT&T: The World's Networking Company

AT&T continues to operate the most sophisticated and reliable global network.

o Having one of the most experienced leadership teams in the industry

o Carrying more than 310 million long distance calls on an average business day, with more than 99.99 percent completed on the first try

o Handling approximately 2,700 trillion bytes (terabytes) of data on an average business day

o Leading in long distance backbone optical fiber, with more than 50,000 route miles, plus more than 19,600 route miles of local metro fiber

o Leading the industry in IP traffic growth

o Operating 18 Internet data centers on three continents

o Having approximately 2,900 points of presence in 850 cities across 60 nations

o Operating with 95 intelligent optical switches online

o Providing, first ever, 10-gigabit-per-second service (OC-192) coast-to-coast

o Leading in Dense Wave Division Multiplexing with 1,600 systems deployed, including Ultravailable Networks for enterprise customers

With significant financial strength and leverage, a world-class network and one of the most qualified management teams focused on transforming the business, AT&T is committed and poised to meet the needs of its customers better than anyone in the industry.

To my fellow shareowners: AT&T launched a new era in 2002 – an era marked by more than just a change in the chairman's office. We spun off our broadband operations. We completed our restructuring plan. And we introduced a new management team focused on serving customers and building shareowner value.

At the same time, we accelerated our efforts to transform AT&T from a primarily voice-services business to the largest provider of data services globally. We reached out to expand our relationships with clients around the world. And we realigned to focus less on individual products and more on integrated customer solutions.

In short, we rededicated ourselves to AT&T's 118-year legacy of service, quality, reliability and innovation. And we committed to fulfilling our mission as "the world's networking company."

While we focused on meeting our goals and seeking new market opportunities, waves of uncertainty crashed around us. The world braced for terror and war. The global economy stumbled. And the telecom industry suffered bankruptcies and accounting scandals that dragged down some of our major competitors.

Those telecom schemes conjured up phony market economics and phantom prices that no competitor could fairly match. The companies involved saw their reputations rightly ravaged.

AT&T, on the other hand, rose above the fray. We remained focused on our customers. And we met our financial commitments during every quarter of 2002, performing with both vigor and integrity. Today, we stand tall – proud to be one of the world's strongest telecommunications providers.

Our strength stems from our values, a set of principles we call "Our Common Bond." Formally adopted in 1992, the values of "Our Common Bond" have been hallmarks of the AT&T culture for more than 100 years: respect for individuals, dedication to helping customers, highest standards of integrity, innovation and teamwork. Our commitment to these principles cannot be compromised.

Nor can our commitment to our shareowners. That's why we diligently overhauled our balance sheet. Our restructuring effort reduced AT&T's net debt* from $56.2 billion entering 2001 to $12.9 billion at year-end 2002. We now enjoy the lowest overall net debt level among the major players in our industry. *In 2001, net debt of $56.2 billion was net of $0.1 billion of cash and $8.7 billion of monetizations. In 2002, net debt of $12.9 billion was net of $8.5 billion of cash, $0.5 billion of monetizations and $0.7 billion of fluctuations in foreign debt value.

To maintain and magnify our financial strength, we're taking a disciplined approach to our ongoing cost and capital structure. Our network investments are largely behind us. We spent $3.9 billion in capital expenditures in 2002, roughly half the 1999 level, and we'll continue to moderate our spending going forward.

With a focus on innovation and quality, AT&T Consumer is expanding its portfolio of services, including offering local service (with long distance) in more and more states. AT&T Consumer extended local service from two states in 2001 to eight states in 2002.

We expect the majority of our 2003 capital expenditures to be demand-driven and success-based. The primary focus for the remaining capital expenditures will be enhancing our products and processes to improve service and customer satisfaction. So while our distressed competitors struggle to keep the lights on, we'll continue to pump up productivity and make it easier for customers to do business with AT&T.

Our business customers are already seeing results from the $500 million we invested in process improvements in 2002. We slashed cycle times an average of 30 percent last year. That means we cut days – and in some cases weeks – off the interval between a customer's order and activation of their services. The result: We're setting new standards for sales, provisioning, billing, and service that our competitors simply can't match.

Our world-class standards and services are attracting new business customers, and winning back others concerned about our competitors' well-publicized troubles. We continue to gain market share as companies increasingly value the reliability, sustainability, integrity and quality behind the AT&T brand. And we will continue to promote these advantages as we target new customers and take additional market share in 2003.

Maintaining our scale and broad customer base will be critical as we face ongoing declines in both consumer and business long distance voice revenue. Several trends are driving these declines:

• Customers are relying increasingly on wireless and Internet communications.

• As the regional Bell operating companies (RBOCs) enter long distance, competition and price pressures mount.

• Our success in attracting quality wholesale customers has shifted the proportions of retail and reduced-priced wholesale minutes that run on our network.

• Consumers are taking advantage of lower-priced products, such as prepaid cards and optional calling plans.

We are managing through these declines by scaling our growth investments. In 2002, we outperformed the industry and gained share in all the key growth areas of our business – business local, data, Internet protocol (IP) and managed services. These services represent our future; their growth helps offset erosion in long distance voice.

These services are also at the heart of the AT&T Business portfolio, which will be the primary driver of our future revenue. A leading global provider of enterprise communications solutions, AT&T Business delivered nearly $27 billion to our top line in 2002.

○ | Meeting the communications needs of businesses worldwide, AT&T Business delivers the most reliable and secure enterprise networking solutions with local-to-global reach, end-to-end network management and world-class professional expertise.

For more than 4 million customers throughout the world, AT&T Business serves as a strategic partner. For large enterprise customers, we design, deploy, manage and enhance networks, ensuring industry-leading levels of continuity and security. Our services help these customers unlock the full value of their applications while managing complexity, improving productivity, and generating a return on their communications investments.

We are the undisputed industry leader in IP traffic, after being in sixth place only two years ago. Our IP traffic is growing at a rate three times faster than the rest of the industry. The AT&T network now carries one petabyte of IP traffic per day. To print that amount of data on paper, you'd need about 50 million trees – or a forest about the size of New Orleans. And you'd need to re-grow that forest every day.

The growth of AT&T Business will be fueled, in part, by AT&T Consumer, which contributed nearly $12 billion in 2002 revenue. AT&T Consumer manages nearly 50 million customer relationships with consumers, who count on us for long distance, local, Internet and transactional services such as prepaid cards and collect calling. If it were a standalone business, AT&T Consumer would rank among the Fortune 200.

We continue to expand our consumer-service portfolio. A key growth area is our local and long distance bundle for consumers and small businesses. We offer these combined services via the unbundled network elements platform, or UNE-P. That platform allows AT&T and other carriers to lease from the RBOCs the network elements needed to deliver services along the "last mile," which connects directly to the customer.

By the end of 2002, more than 2.4 million AT&T residential customers were enjoying the features and price benefits that result from UNE-P-based competition. As of this writing, our residential local customer base has grown to more than 2.7 million. We also have more than 500,000 access lines serving small businesses through UNE-P.

More consumers and small businesses will enjoy the benefits of competition thanks to a Federal Communications Commission decision announced in February 2003. The RBOCs lobbied furiously to eliminate UNE-P and reduce competitive choice. But the Commission voted to allow the states to decide what works and what doesn't, rather than impose a national "one-size-fits all" mandate. Now we will take our case to the states, and we will enter markets where the economic conditions allow us to make a reasonable return using UNE-P.

Our initial results prove that customers want choice and will support a competitive offer. We have earned mid single-digit market share or higher in our first eight markets. We doubled our number of all-distance customers in 2002. In the fourth quarter alone, the number grew more than 25 percent from the previous quarter.

3

With a shared commitment to Our Common Bond, values that bind the people of AT&T, we are dedicated to satisfying customer needs and building value for shareowners.

This pattern suggests strong opportunities for growth in new markets as well. We are confident that we will be offering all-distance service in a total of 14-17 markets by the end of 2003, with more markets to follow in 2004.

But getting there won't be easy. In the months ahead, the challenges facing our industry will continue. Current market signals point to ongoing economic weakness and lower information technology (IT) spending.

We recognize, however, that this downturn won't last forever. The economy will eventually rebound, IT spending will resume, and telecom's trials will end. We're preparing today for that turnaround by channeling our resources to keep our company strong and to position AT&T as one of the primary beneficiaries of an economic upswing.

We are the only long distance carrier upgrading its network and service portfolio. We are the only carrier enhancing its customer-facing processes and increasing its sales presence. And we are among the few carriers operating from a position of unquestioned financial flexibility and strength. So when the market recovers, our scale, scope and stability will make AT&T the company to beat.

That's why, despite the challenges, I feel so proud and privileged to be leading this company. While our competitors are still getting organized, we've already assembled all the ingredients for success – solid financials, a world-class global network, an intense customer focus and unshakable values.

Our people are passionate about satisfying customers and building shareowner value. We are working as one company, one network and one team to deliver a level of excellence that others must strive mightily to attain.

Outstanding innovation, enduring integrity, and a flawless customer experience... our customers, employees and you – our shareowners – should expect nothing less from the world's networking company.

David Dorman

David Dorman
Chairman and Chief Executive Officer

○ Financial Report Contents

AT&T CORP. AND SUBSIDIARIES

SEVEN-YEAR SUMMARY OF SELECTED FINANCIAL DATA[1]

	2002	2001	2000	1999	1998	1997	1996
				(Unaudited)			
			(Dollars in millions, except per share amounts)				
RESULTS OF OPERATIONS AND EARNINGS PER SHARE							
Revenue	$ 37,827	$ 42,197	$ 46,850	$ 49,609	$ 47,287	$ 46,226	$ 45,716
Operating income	4,361	7,832	12,793	12,544	7,632	6,835	8,341
Income (loss) from continuing operations.................	963	(2,640)	9,532	6,019	4,915	4,088	5,064
INCOME FROM CONTINUING OPERATIONS							
AT&T Common Stock Group:[2]							
Income	963	71	8,044	8,041	4,915	4,088	5,064
Earnings (loss) per basic share	1.29	(0.91)	11.54	13.04	9.18	7.65	9.60
Earnings (loss) per diluted share	1.26	(0.91)	11.01	12.61	9.10	7.65	9.60
Cash dividends declared per share	0.75	0.75	3.4875	4.40	4.40	4.40	4.40
Liberty Media Group:[2]							
(Loss) income	—	(2,711)	1,488	(2,022)	—	—	—
(Loss) earnings per basic and diluted share	—	(1.05)	0.58	(0.80)	—	—	—
ASSETS AND CAPITAL							
Property, plant and equipment, net.......................	$ 25,604	$ 26,803	$ 26,083	$ 25,587	$ 21,780	$ 19,177	$ 16,871
Total assets — continuing operations.................	55,272	62,329	90,293	89,554	40,134	41,029	38,229
Total assets	55,272	165,481	242,802	169,499	59,550	67,690	63,669
Long-term debt	18,812	24,025	13,572	13,543	5,555	7,840	8,861
Total debt....................	22,574	34,159	42,338	25,091	6,638	11,895	11,334
Shareowners' equity	12,312	51,680	103,198	78,927	25,522	23,678	21,092
Debt ratio[3]	64.7%	86.3%	122.1%	83.7%	36.7%	57.2%	61.6%
OTHER INFORMATION							
Employees — continuing operations[4]	71,000	77,700	84,800	96,500	94,500	116,800	117,100
AT&T year-end stock price per share	$ 26.11	$ 37.19	$ 27.57	$ 80.81	$ 79.88	$ 65.02	$ 43.91

[1] Prior period amounts have been restated to reflect the spin-off of AT&T Broadband and the 1-for-5 reverse stock split, as applicable, both of which occurred on November 18, 2002.

[2] In connection with the March 9, 1999 merger with Tele-Communications, Inc., AT&T issued separate tracking stock for Liberty Media Group (LMG). LMG was accounted for as an equity investment prior to its split-off from AT&T on August 10, 2001. There were no dividends declared for LMG tracking stock. AT&T Common Stock Group results exclude LMG.

[3] Debt ratio reflects debt from continuing operations as a percent of total capital, excluding discontinued operations and LMG, (debt plus equity, excluding LMG and discontinued operations).

[4] Data provided excludes LMG.

AT&T CORP. AND SUBSIDIARIES
CONSOLIDATED BALANCE SHEETS

	At December 31,	
	2002	2001
	Dollars in millions	
ASSETS		
Cash and cash equivalents..	$ 8,014	$ 10,680
Accounts receivable, less allowances of $669 and $754................................	5,286	7,153
Other receivables	173	1,431
Deferred income taxes..	910	1,192
Other current assets..	1,520	622
Current assets of discontinued operations	—	1,649
TOTAL CURRENT ASSETS	15,903	22,727
Property, plant and equipment, net	25,604	26,803
Goodwill, net of accumulated amortization in 2001 of $564............................	4,626	5,314
Other purchased intangible assets, net of accumulated amortization of $244 and $190	556	661
Prepaid pension costs...	3,596	3,329
Other assets	4,987	5,144
Non-current assets of discontinued operations	—	101,503
TOTAL ASSETS	$ 55,272	$165,481
LIABILITIES		
Accounts payable	$ 3,819	$ 4,156
Payroll and benefit-related liabilities	1,519	1,606
Debt maturing within one year...	3,762	10,134
Other current liabilities	2,924	3,929
Current liabilities of discontinued operations	—	5,801
TOTAL CURRENT LIABILITIES	12,024	25,626
Long-term debt..	18,812	24,025
Long-term benefit-related liabilities	4,001	3,459
Deferred income taxes..	4,739	2,438
Other long-term liabilities and deferred credits	3,384	7,159
Non-current liabilities of discontinued operations	—	43,071
TOTAL LIABILITIES	42,960	105,778
Minority Interest of Discontinued Operations...	—	3,303
Company-Obligated Convertible Quarterly Income Preferred Securities of Subsidiary Trust Holding Solely Subordinated Debt Securities of AT&T of Discontinued Operations	—	4,720
SHAREOWNERS' EQUITY		
AT&T Common Stock, $1 par value, authorized 6,000,000,000 shares; issued and outstanding 783,037,580 shares (net of 171,801,716 treasury shares) at December 31, 2002 and 708,481,149 shares (net of 170,349,286 treasury shares) at December 31, 2001	783	708
Additional paid-in capital	28,163	54,798
Accumulated deficit..	(16,566)	(3,484)
Accumulated other comprehensive loss...	(68)	(342)
TOTAL SHAREOWNERS' EQUITY	12,312	51,680
TOTAL LIABILITIES AND SHAREOWNERS' EQUITY	$ 55,272	$165,481

The notes are an integral part of the consolidated financial statements.

38

AT&T CORP. AND SUBSIDIARIES

CONSOLIDATED STATEMENTS OF CHANGES IN SHAREOWNERS' EQUITY

	For the Years Ended December 31,		
	2002	**2001**	**2000**
	Dollars in millions		
AT&T Common Stock			
Balance at beginning of year	$ 708	$ 752	$ 639
Shares issued (acquired), net:			
Under employee plans	6	3	1
For acquisitions	—	9	121
Settlement of put option	—	31	—
For exchange of AT&T Wireless tracking stock	—	(74)	—
For funding AT&T Canada obligation	46	—	—
Redemption of TCI Pacific preferred stock	10	—	—
Other	13	(13)	(9)
Balance at end of year	783	708	752
AT&T Wireless Group Common Stock			
Balance at beginning of year	—	362	—
Shares issued:			
For stock offering	—	—	360
Under employee plans	—	2	2
For exchange of AT&T Wireless tracking stock	—	438	—
Conversion of preferred stock	—	406	—
AT&T Wireless Group split-off	—	(1,208)	—
Balance at end of year	—	—	362
Liberty Media Group Class A Common Stock			
Balance at beginning of year	—	2,364	2,314
Shares issued (acquired), net:			
For acquisitions	—	—	62
Other	—	14	(12)
Liberty Media Group split-off	—	(2,378)	—
Balance at end of year	—	—	2,364
Liberty Media Group Class B Common Stock			
Balance at beginning of year	—	206	217
Shares issued (acquired), net	—	6	(11)
Liberty Media Group split-off	—	(212)	—
Other	—	—	—
Balance at end of year	—	—	206
Additional Paid-In Capital			
Balance at beginning of year	54,798	93,504	62,083
Shares issued (acquired), net:			
Under employee plans	328	291	100
For acquisitions	—	862	23,583
Settlement of put option	—	3,361	—
For funding AT&T Canada obligation	2,485	—	—
Redemption of TCI Pacific preferred stock	2,087	—	—
Other*	31	(1,054)	(2,804)
Proceeds in excess of par value from issuance of AT&T Wireless common stock	—	—	9,915
Gain on issuance of common stock by affiliates	—	20	530
Conversion of preferred stock	—	9,631	—
AT&T Wireless Group split-off	—	(20,955)	—
Liberty Media Group split-off	—	(30,768)	—

(continued on next page)

39

AT&T CORP. AND SUBSIDIARIES

CONSOLIDATED STATEMENTS OF CHANGES IN SHAREOWNERS' EQUITY (Continued)

	For the Years Ended December 31,		
	2002	2001	2000
	Dollars in millions		
AT&T Broadband spin-off	(31,032)	—	—
Exchange of AT&T Wireless tracking stock	—	(284)	—
Beneficial conversion value of preferred stock	—	295	—
Dividends declared — AT&T Common Stock Group	(569)	(265)	—
Other	35	160	97
Balance at end of year	28,163	54,798	93,504
Guaranteed ESOP Obligation			
Balance at beginning of year	—	—	(17)
Amortization	—	—	17
Balance at end of year	—	—	—
(Accumulated Deficit)/Retained Earnings			
Balance at beginning of year	(3,484)	7,408	6,712
Net (loss) income	(13,082)	7,715	4,669
Dividends declared — AT&T Common Stock Group	—	(275)	(2,485)
Dividends accrued — preferred stock	—	(652)	—
Premium on exchange of AT&T Wireless tracking stock	—	(80)	—
Treasury shares issued at less than cost	—	(7)	(1,488)
AT&T Wireless Group split-off	—	(17,593)	—
Balance at end of year	(16,566)	(3,484)	7,408
Accumulated Other Comprehensive (Loss)			
Balance at beginning of year	(342)	(1,398)	6,979
Other comprehensive income (loss)	266	1,742	(8,377)
AT&T Wireless Group split-off	—	72	—
Liberty Media Group split-off	—	(758)	—
AT&T Broadband spin-off	8	—	—
Balance at end of year	(68)	(342)	(1,398)
Total Shareowners' Equity	$ 12,312	$ 51,680	$103,198
Summary of Total Comprehensive (Loss) Income:			
(Loss) income before cumulative effect of accounting changes	$(12,226)	$ 6,811	$ 4,669
Cumulative effect of accounting changes	(856)	904	—
Net (loss) income	(13,082)	7,715	4,669
Other comprehensive income (loss) [net of income taxes of $(169), $(1,119), and $5,348]	266	1,742	(8,377)
Comprehensive (Loss) Income	$(12,816)	$ 9,457	$ (3,708)

AT&T accounts for treasury stock as retired stock.

We have 100 million authorized shares of preferred stock at $1 par value.

* Other activity in 2001 and 2000 represents AT&T common stock received in exchange for entities owning certain cable systems.

The notes are an integral part of the consolidated financial statements.

AT&T CORP. AND SUBSIDIARIES

CONSOLIDATED STATEMENTS OF CASH FLOWS

	For the Years Ended December 31,		
	2002	2001	2000
	Dollars in millions		
OPERATING ACTIVITIES			
Net (loss) income	$(13,082)	$ 7,715	$ 4,669
Deduct:			
Loss from discontinued operations	(14,513)	(4,052)	(4,863)
Gain on disposition of discontinued operations	1,324	13,503	—
Cumulative effect of accounting changes — net of income taxes	(856)	904	—
Income (loss) from continuing operations	963	(2,640)	9,532
Adjustments to reconcile income (loss) from continuing operations to net cash provided by operating activities of continuing operations:			
Net gains on sales of businesses and investments	(30)	(1,231)	(734)
Cost investment impairment charges	146	531	7
Net restructuring and other charges	1,418	973	577
Depreciation and amortization	4,888	4,559	4,538
Provision for uncollectible receivables	1,058	884	925
Deferred income taxes	2,631	(1,338)	1,005
Net revaluation of certain financial instruments	8	(150)	—
Minority interest income	(114)	(131)	(41)
Equity losses (earnings) from Liberty Media Group	—	2,711	(1,488)
Net losses related to other equity investments	512	7,783	51
Decrease (increase) in receivables	707	888	(2,382)
Decrease in accounts payable	(175)	(508)	(585)
Net change in other operating assets and liabilities	(1,400)	(2,126)	(148)
Other adjustments, net	(129)	(200)	(616)
NET CASH PROVIDED BY OPERATING ACTIVITIES OF CONTINUING OPERATIONS	10,483	10,005	10,641
INVESTING ACTIVITIES			
Capital expenditures and other additions	(3,878)	(5,767)	(7,025)
Proceeds from sale or disposal of property, plant and equipment	468	73	555
Increase in other receivables	—	—	(981)
Investment distributions and sales	10	1,585	414
Investment contributions and purchases	(2)	(101)	(1,787)
Net dispositions (acquisitions) of businesses, net of cash disposed/acquired	(18)	15	(23,742)
Decrease in AT&T Canada obligation	(3,449)	—	—
Proceeds from AT&T Broadband	5,849	—	—
Increase in restricted cash	(442)	—	—
Other investing activities, net	33	(100)	(112)
NET CASH USED IN INVESTING ACTIVITIES OF CONTINUING OPERATIONS	(1,429)	(4,295)	(32,678)
FINANCING ACTIVITIES			
Proceeds from long-term debt issuances, net of issuance costs	79	11,392	739
Retirement of long-term debt	(1,091)	(725)	(688)
(Decrease) increase in short-term borrowings, net	(7,157)	(17,168)	16,973
Repayment of borrowings from AT&T Wireless	—	(5,803)	—
Issuance of convertible preferred securities and warrants	—	9,811	—
Issuance of AT&T common shares	2,684	224	99
Issuance of AT&T Wireless Group common shares	—	54	10,314
Net issuance (acquisition) of treasury shares	—	24	(581)
Dividends paid on common stock	(555)	(549)	(3,047)
Other financing activities, net	(1)	(38)	(64)
NET CASH (USED IN) PROVIDED BY FINANCING ACTIVITIES OF CONTINUING OPERATIONS	(6,041)	(2,778)	23,745
Net cash (used in) provided by discontinued operations	(5,679)	7,683	(2,746)
Net (decrease) increase in cash and cash equivalents	(2,666)	10,615	(1,038)
Cash and cash equivalents at beginning of year	10,680	65	1,103
Cash and cash equivalents at end of year	$ 8,014	$ 10,680	$ 65

The notes are an integral part of the consolidated financial statements.

41

○ | AT&T Board of Directors

David W. Dorman, 49
Chairman of the Board and Chief
Executive Officer since
November 2002. Elected to the
Board in 2002.

Kenneth T. Derr, 66
Retired Chairman of the Board
and Chief Executive Officer of
Chevron Corporation, an
international oil company.
Director since 1995. 2, 3

M. Kathryn Eickhoff, 64
President of Eickhoff Economics,
Inc., an economic consulting firm.
Director since 1987. 1, 3

Frank C. Herringer, 60
Chairman of the Board and
former Chief Executive Officer of
Transamerica Corporation, a
financial services company,
which was acquired in 1999 by
Aegon N.V., an international
insurance organization. Elected
to the Board in 2002. 1, 2

Amos B. Hostetter, Jr., 66
Chairman of Pilot House Associates, LLC, a family investment
company. Director since 1999.
1, 2

Shirley Ann Jackson, Ph.D., 56
President of Rensselaer
Polytechnic Institute. Elected to
the Board in 2001. 2, 3

Jon C. Madonna, 59
Retired Chairman and Chief
Executive Officer of KPMG, an
international accounting and
consulting firm. Director since
2002. 1

Donald F. McHenry, 66
Distinguished Professor in the
Practice of Diplomacy at the
School of Foreign Service at
Georgetown University, and
President of IRC Group LLC,
international relations
consultants. Director since 1986.
1, 3

Tony L. White, 56
Chairman of the Board, President,
and Chief Executive Officer of
Applera Corporation, a life sci-
ences company. Elected to the
Board in 2002. 2, 3

1. Audit Committee
2. Compensation and Employee
   Benefits Committee
3. Governance and Nominating
   Committee

Ages are as of April17, 2003.

O | ## Senior Leadership Team

David W. Dorman
Chairman of the Board and
Chief Executive Officer

Betsy J. Bernard
President

James W. Cicconi
General Counsel and Executive
Vice President
Law and Government Affairs

Hossein Eslambolchi
President of AT&T Labs,
Chief Technology Officer and
AT&T Business Chief
Information Officer

Mirian Graddick-Weir
Executive Vice President
Human Resources

Thomas W. Horton
Senior Executive Vice President,
Chief Financial Officer

Frank Ianna
President
AT&T Network Services

John C. Petrillo
Executive Vice President
Corporate Strategy and
Business Development

John Polumbo
President and Chief Executive
Officer
AT&T Consumer

Kenneth E. Sichau
President
AT&T Business Sales

Constance K. Weaver
Executive Vice President
Public Relations, Brand &
Business Marketing

Other Corporate Officers

Nicholas S. Cyprus
Vice President and Controller

Edward M. Dwyer
Vice President and Treasurer

Robert S. Feit
Vice President, Law
and Corporate Secretary

Richard E. Sullivan, Jr.
Investor Relations Vice President

*David Dorman, Betsy Bernard,
Tom Horton*

*John Petrillo, Mirian Graddick-
Weir, John Polumbo*

*Jim Cicconi, Connie Weaver,
Frank Ianna*

*Hossein Eslambolchi,
Ken Sichau*

○ | Corporate Information

Corporate Headquarters
One AT&T Way
Bedminster, NJ 07921-0752

Business
AT&T Business has relationships
with about 4 million business customers worldwide who depend on
AT&T for voice, data, Internet and
managed solutions. For more
information about AT&T Business
and our products and services,
visit our Web site at www.att.com/
business. Small/medium business
customers can find the right
communications solution with
the convenience of on-line sales
and service by visiting
www.att.com/businesscenter/smb
ushome.html. Large/ global business customers can access our
expansive set of local to global
business solutions by visiting
www.att.com/businesscenter/lgbu
shome.html. Government customers can locate our suite of integrated technology solutions with
professional service expertise by
visiting www.att.com/gov.

Consumer
AT&T Consumer has nearly 50 million customer relationships and
offers services as diverse as long
distance and local services,
domestic and international calling
plans, prepaid and subscriber
calling cards, and dial-up and
broadband Internet access.
AT&T Consumer also offers customers the convenience of online
billing, ordering and customer service. To order a consumer service,
visit our Web site at
www.consumer.att.com.

AT&T on the World Wide Web
The AT&T Internet home page –
www.att.com – is your entry point
to a vast array of services and
information. One of the most visited sites on the Internet, att.com
gives you access to the latest
AT&T products for your home,
along with the convenience and
security of online ordering and
billing. The site connects business
customers to the services and
innovation that give their companies a competitive advantage. In
addition, you can navigate to current company news, connections
to investor and corporate information and the latest advances from
AT&T Labs.

AT&T Giving
For more than 100 years, AT&T
has built a tradition of investing in
local communities through our
ongoing support for education,
civic and community service, the
environment and the arts. In 2002,
the AT&T Foundation contributed
nearly $40 million to nonprofit
organizations in local communities
throughout the United States and
many other countries. Also in
2002, AT&T employees volunteered nearly 750,000 hours of
community service through the
AT&T CARES program. For more
information on the AT&T Foundation and AT&T CARES, visit our
Web site at
www.att.com/foundation.

Environment, Health & Safety
AT&T is dedicated to creating a
safe and healthy workplace for
AT&T employees and strives to
maintain our reputation as one of
the top corporate environmental
champions. More information
about AT&T's environment,
health and safety initiatives may
be found at our Web site:
www.att.com/ehs/.

TelecomPioneers
Since 1911, AT&T has been a
sponsor of TelecomPioneers (formerly Telephone Pioneers of
America), the world's largest,
industry-based volunteer organization. AT&T employees and
retirees comprise more than
57,000 of its members. In 2002,
TelecomPioneers awarded the
AT&T Pioneers its first President's
Innovation Award. For more information on the AT&T Pioneers, visit
our Web site at
www.attpioneers.org.

Supplier Diversity Initiative
As part of AT&T's Supplier Diversity initiative, approximately $870
million of AT&T's total purchases in
2002 were made from minority-,
women- and service-disabled vet-
eran-owned business enterprises.
More information is available at our
Web site:
www.att.com/supplier_diversity/.

AT&T Communications Action
Network (CAN)
On February 20, the FCC
announced its Triennial Review
decision, approving new rules to
give states more authority over the
$125 billion U.S. local-telephone
market. Jim Cicconi, AT&T Corp.
General Counsel and Executive
Vice President, Law and Government Affairs, said, "the result is
that consumers will see lower
prices and more choices in the
marketplace, and the economy will
experience more investment and
greater innovation." To learn more
about this and other important
AT&T public policy issues, visit the
CAN Web site at www.attcan.org.
While you're there, sign up and
join our Communications Action
Network!

O | ## Shareowner Information

Shareowner Services

You can get up-to-the-minute information about your AT&T investment 24 hours a day by visiting www.att.com/ir – the AT&T Investor Relations Web site – where you will find current stock quotes, historical stock prices, financial results, tax basis information, investor news and online access to your AT&T shareowner account. Get fast information about how to arrange for the direct deposit of dividends, change your address, reinvest your dividends or transfer ownership of your shares. If you need more information, send an e-mail to att@equiserve.com, or contact us by phone at 1-800-348-8288. Our interactive voice-response system can answer most of your questions 24 hours a day, seven days a week. Representatives are available Monday through Friday, 8 a.m. to 5 p.m. (Eastern), to assist you. Shareowners outside the United States may call 1-816-843-4282. Shareowners using a telecommunications device for the deaf (TDD) may call 1-800-822-2794. Our fax number is 1-781-575-3261, and our mailing address is: AT&T Shareowner Services, c/o EquiServe, P.O. Box 43007, Providence, RI 02940-3007.

Electronic Access to Proxy Materials

In an effort to reduce the printing and mailing costs associated with the distribution of the AT&T Annual Report and Proxy Statement, AT&T registered shareowners can electronically access, view and download the AT&T Annual Report and Proxy Statement and other materials at the AT&T Investor Relations Web site at www.att.com/ir. AT&T shareowners can choose this option by marking the "Electronic Access" box on the proxy card or by following the instructions provided when voting by telephone or the Internet. If you choose this option prior to each shareowner meeting, you will receive your proxy card, which provides a notice of meeting and a business-reply envelope. Beneficial owners can request the electronic-access option by contacting their broker or financial institution.

Dividend Reinvestment Plan

Participating in the AT&T Shareowner Dividend Reinvestment and Stock Purchase Plan (DRP) is a convenient, systematic way to build your investment. Under Dividend Reinvestment, all or a portion of your dividends are automatically reinvested to purchase additional shares of AT&T common stock. Participants receive periodic account statements tracking reinvestment transactions and account balances. Additional shares of AT&T common stock can be purchased with cash or automatic monthly investments from your bank account. Fees may apply to certain transactions. To obtain a Plan prospectus, contact EquiServe at 1-800-348-8288.

Direct Registration of AT&T Shares

AT&T shareowners are finding it convenient to have shares held in the Direct Registration System, which gives you full ownership of your shares. With Direct Registration, AT&T's transfer agent (EquiServe) holds the shares in your name. You retain full ownership and continue to receive all AT&T dividends, shareowner communications, annual reports and proxy-voting material. You can easily get your account balance or sell your shares by phone or via the Internet. It's safe and convenient. For more information on this service, contact EquiServe at 1-800-348-8288.

Stock Information

AT&T (ticker symbol "T") is listed on the New York Stock Exchange, as well as the Boston, Chicago, Cincinnati, Pacific and Philadelphia exchanges in the United States; and the Euronext-Paris, and the London and Geneva stock exchanges. As of December, 31, 2002, AT&T had approximately 783 million shares outstanding, held by more than 3.3 million shareowners.

Additional Financial Information

A copy of AT&T's Annual Report on Form 10-K, filed with the Securities and Exchange Commision, may be obtained free of charge by sending a request to:
One AT&T Way
Bedminster, NJ 07921
Attention: Investor Relations
or may be accessed electronically at www.att.com/ir/.

O | Our Common Bond

We commit to these values to guide our decisions and behavior:

Respect for Individuals
We treat each other with respect and dignity, valuing individual and cultural differences. We communicate frequently and with candor, listening to each other regardless of level or position. Recognizing that exceptional quality begins with people, we give individuals the authority to use their capabilities to the fullest to satisfy their customers. Our environment supports personal growth and continuous learning for all AT&T people.

Dedication to Helping Customers
We truly care for each customer. We build enduring relationships by understanding and anticipating our customers' needs and by serv-

ing them better each time than the time before. AT&T customers can count on us to consistently deliver superior products and services that help them achieve their personal or business goals.

Highest Standards of Integrity
We are honest and ethical in all our business dealings, starting with how we treat each other. We keep our promises and admit our mistakes. Our personal conduct ensures that AT&T's name is always worthy of trust.

Innovation
We believe innovation is the engine that will keep us vital and growing. Our culture embraces creativity, seeks different perspectives and risks pursuing new opportunities. We create and rapidly convert technology into products and services, constantly searching for new ways to make technology more useful to customers.

Teamwork
We encourage and reward both individual and team achievements. We freely join with colleagues across organizational boundaries to advance the interests of customers and shareowners. Our team spirit extends to being responsible and caring partners in the communities where we live and work.

By living these values, AT&T aspires to set a standard of excellence worldwide that will reward our shareowners, our customers, and all AT&T people.

Appendix 6

Public Relations Society of America Local Chapters

LOCAL CHAPTERS: PUBLIC RELATIONS SOCIETY OF AMERICA

For updated contact information, consult the Public Relations Society of America's Web site, www.prsa.org

ALABAMA

Base: Birmingham
HOME PAGE: www.alabamaprsa.org

ALASKA

Base: Anchorage
HOME PAGE: www.prsaalaska.org

ARIZONA

Southern Arizona

Base: Tucson
HOME PAGE: www.prsatucson.com

Phoenix

HOME PAGE: www.phxprsa.org
HOTLINE: 602–258–7772

ARKANSAS

Base: Little Rock
HOME PAGE: www.arkprsa.org

Northwest Arkansas

Base: Fayetteville
HOME PAGE: www.nwaprsa.org

CALIFORNIA

California Capital

Base: Sacramento
HOME PAGE: www.prsa-sacramento.org
FAX-ON-DEMAND: 800–776–3290

California Inland Empire

Base: Riverside
HOME PAGE: www.prsainlandempire.org

Central California

Base: Fresno Valley
HOME PAGE: www.prsacentralcal.org

Los Angeles

HOME PAGE: www.prsa-la.org

Oakland-East Bay

Base: Oakland
HOME PAGE: www.prsaeastbay.org

Orange County

Base: Santa Ana
HOME PAGE: www.ocprsa.org

San Diego County

Base: San Diego
HOME PAGE: www.prsasandiego.org
HOTLINE: 619–680–3990
FAX-ON-DEMAND: 800–776–3290

San Francisco

Base: San Francisco
HOME PAGE: www.prsasf.org
FAX-ON-DEMAND: 800–776–3290

Silicon Valley

HOME PAGE: www.siliconprsa.org

COLORADO

Denver

HOME PAGE: www.prsacolorado.org

Pikes Peak

Base: Colorado Springs
HOME PAGE: www.prsacoloradosprings.org

CONNECTICUT

Base: New Haven
HOME PAGE: None

Connecticut Valley

Base: Hartford
HOME PAGE: www.prsa-cvc.org

Westchester/Fairfield

Base: Westchester/Fairfield
HOME PAGE: www.prsa-wf.org

DELAWARE

Base: Wilmington
HOME PAGE: www.prsadelaware.org

FLORIDA

Gulfcoast

Base: Naples
HOME PAGE: None

Gulfstream

PO Box 677
Fort Lauderdale, FL 33302
HOME PAGE: www.prsagulfstream.org

North Florida

Base: Jacksonville
HOME PAGE: www.jax-prsa.org

Miami

HOME PAGE: www.prsamiami.org

Orlando Regional

PO Box 1212
Orlando, FL 32802–1212
HOME PAGE: www.prsaorlando.org

Palm Beach

PO Box 1212
Orlando, FL 32802–1212
HOME PAGE: www.prsapalmbeach.org

Tampa Bay

HOME PAGE: www.tampa.prsa.org

GEORGIA

Atlanta

HOME PAGE: www.prsageorgia.org

South Georgia

Base: Savannah
HOME PAGE: None

HAWAII

Base: Honolulu
HOME PAGE: www.prsahawaii.org

ILLINOIS

Central Illinois

Base: Bloomington
HOME PAGE: www.geocities.com/prsa_ci

Chicago

HOME PAGE: www.prsachicago.com

Suburban Chicago
HOME PAGE: www.prsasuburbanchicagoland.org

INDIANA

Base: Indianapolis
HOME PAGE: www.hoosierprsa.org
HOTLINE: 317–265–4887

IOWA

Cedar Valley

Base: Cedar Rapids/Waterloo
HOME PAGE: www.cvprsa.org

Central Iowa

Base: Des Moines
HOME PAGE: www.prsaciowa.org

Greater Dubuque

HOME PAGE: None

Quad Cities

Base: Eastern IA/Western IL
HOME PAGE: None

KANSAS

Base: Wichita
HOME PAGE: www.prsakansas.org

KENTUCKY

Bluegrass

Base: Louisville
HOME PAGE: www.bluegrassprsa.org

Thoroughbred

Base: Lexington
HOME PAGE: www.kyprsa.com

LOUISIANA

Baton Rouge

HOME PAGE: None

New Orleans

HOME PAGE: www.prsaneworleans.org
INFOLINE: 504–558–0034

North Louisiana

Base: Shreveport
HOME PAGE: None

MAINE

Yankee

Base: Concord, NH
HOME PAGE: www.yankeeprsa.org

MARYLAND

Annapolis/Anne Arundel

Base: Annapolis/St. Mary's
HOME PAGE: www.annapolisprsa.org

Chesapeake Bay

HOME PAGE: None

Maryland

Base: Baltimore
HOME PAGE: www.prsamd.org
MD residents only: 800–929–7680

National Capital

Base: Washington, D.C.
HOME PAGE: www.PRSA-ncc.org/

MASSACHUSETTS

Boston

HOME PAGE: www.prsaboston.org

MICHIGAN

Central Michigan

Base: Lansing
HOME PAGE: www.cmprsa.org

Detroit

HOME PAGE: www.prsadetroit.org

West Michigan

Base: Grand Rapids
HOME PAGE: www.wmprsa.org

White Pine

Base: Bay City/Saginaw
HOME PAGE: www.ecd.prsa.org

MINNESOTA

Base: Minneapolis
HOME PAGE: www.mnprsa.com

MISSOURI

Greater Kansas City

Base: Kansas City
HOME PAGE: www.kansascity-prsa.org

Mid-Missouri

Base: Columbia/Jefferson City
HOME PAGE: www.midmoprsa.org

St. Louis

HOME PAGE: www.prsastlouis.org

MONTANA

Base: Statewide
HOME PAGE: www.montanaprsa.org

NEBRASKA

Base: Omaha
HOME PAGE: www.nebraskaprsa.org

Siouxland

HOME PAGE: None

NEVADA

Las Vegas Valley

Base: Las Vegas
HOME PAGE: www.prsalasvegas.com

Sierra Nevada

Base: Reno
HOME PAGE: www.prsareno.org

NEW HAMPSHIRE

Yankee

Base: Concord, NH
HOME PAGE: www.yankeeprsa.org

NEW JERSEY

Base: Statewide
HOME PAGE: www.prsanj.org

NEW MEXICO

Base: Albuquerque
HOME PAGE: www.nmprsa.com

NEW YORK

Buffalo/Niagara

Base: Buffalo
HOME PAGE: www.prsabuffaloniagara.org

Capital Region

Base: Albany
HOME PAGE: www.timesunion.com/
communities/prsa

Central New York

Base: Syracuse
HOME PAGE: www.prsa-cny.org

Finger Lakes

Base: Corning/Elmira
HOME PAGE: None

New York

Base: New York City
HOME PAGE: www.prsany.org

Rochester

HOME PAGE: www.prsarochester.org

Westchester/Fairfield

HOME PAGE: www.prsa-wf.org

NORTH CAROLINA

Charlotte

HOME PAGE: www.prsacharlotte.org
HOTLINE: 704–3351–8874

North Carolina

Base: Raleigh-Durham
HOME PAGE: www.northcarolina.prsa.org

Tar Heel

Base: Greensboro
HOME PAGE: www.prsatarheel.org

OHIO

Akron Area

Base: Akron
HOME PAGE: www.prsaaa.org

Cincinnati

HOME PAGE: www.cincinnatiprsa.org

Central Ohio

Base: Columbus
HOME PAGE: www.centralohioprsa.org
HOTLINE: 614–470–2875

Dayton/Miami Valley

HOME PAGE: www.prsadayton.org

Greater Cleveland

Base: Cleveland
HOME PAGE: www.prsacleveland.org

Northwest Ohio

Base: Bowling Green/Toledo
HOME PAGE: www.ecd.prsa.org

OKLAHOMA

Oklahoma City

HOME PAGE: www.prsaokc.com

Tulsa

HOME PAGE: None

OREGON

Greater Oregon

Base: Eugene
HOME PAGE: None

Oregon Capital

Base: Salem
HOME PAGE: www.oregoncapitalprsa.org

Portland Metro

Base: Portland
HOME PAGE: www.prsa-portland.org
HOTLINE: 503–221–6202

PENNSYLVANIA

Central Pennsylvania

Base: Hershey/Harrisburg
HOME PAGE: http://cpaprsa.tripod.com

Philadelphia

HOME PAGE: www.prsa.philly.org

Pittsburgh

HOME PAGE: www.prsa-pgh.org

RHODE ISLAND

Southeastern New England

Base: Providence, RI
HOME PAGE: www.prsasene.org
HOTLINE: (401) 737–7772

SOUTH CAROLINA

Base: Columbia
HOME PAGE: www.scprsa.org

SOUTH DAKOTA

Siouxland

HOME PAGE: None

TENNESSEE

Memphis

Base: Memphis
HOME PAGE: www.prsamemphis.org

Lookout

Base: Chattanooga
HOME PAGE: www.lookoutprsa.org

Nashville

HOME PAGE: www.prsanashville.com
RESERVATION LINE: 615–963–1335

Tri-Cities

Base: Tri-Cities TN/VA
HOME PAGE: None

Volunteer

Base: Knoxville
HOME PAGE: www.volunteerprsa.org

TEXAS

Austin

Chapter Address
P.O. Box 684036
Austin, TX 78768
HOME PAGE: http://prsa.austin.org

Greater Fort Worth

HOME PAGE: www.prsa.austin.org

Central Texas

Base: Waco
HOME PAGE: None

Houston

HOME PAGE: www.prsahouston.org

Laredo-Gateway

Base: Laredo
HOME PAGE: None

Dallas

HOME PAGE: www.prsadallas.org

Rio Grande

Base: El Paso
HOME PAGE: None

San Antonio

HOME PAGE: www.prsanantonio.com
HOTLINE: 210–302–1000

UTAH

Greater Salt Lake

Base: Salt Lake City
HOME PAGE: www.slcprsa.org

Utah Valley

Base: Provo
HOME PAGE: None

VERMONT

Yankee

Base: Concord, NH
HOME PAGE: www.yankeeprsa.org

VIRGINIA

Blue Ridge

Base: Roanoke
HOME PAGE: www.prsa-blueridge.org/

Hampton Roads

Base: Hampton/Norfolk
HOME PAGE: www.prsahr.org

Richmond

HOME PAGE: www.prsarichmond.org

WASHINGTON

Greater Spokane

Base: Spokane
HOME PAGE: www.spokanepr.org

Puget Sound

Base: Seattle
HOME PAGE: www.prsapugetsound.org
FAX-ON-DEMAND: 800–776–3290

WEST VIRGINIA

Base: Statewide
HOME PAGE: www.prsawv.org

WISCONSIN

Madison

HOME PAGE: www.prsamadison.org

Northeast Wisconsin

Base: Neenah/Oshkosh
HOME PAGE: www.prsanewis.org

Southeastern Wisconsin

Base: Milwaukee
HOME PAGE: www.prsawis.org

SOURCE: Public Relations Society of America. Reprinted with permission.

Appendix 7

Public Relations Online Resources

American Society of Association Executives

World's leading membership organization for the association management profession.
www.asaenet.org

Canadian Public Relations Society

Professional organization with 1,700 members across Canada.
www.cprs.ca

Communications Roundtable

Association of public relations, marketing, graphics, advertising, training, information technology, and other communications organizations.
www.roundtable.org

Council of Public Relations Firms

Information source for members regarding the public relations industry.
www.prfirms.org

Holmes Report

Source of news, knowledge, and career information for public relations professionals.
www.holmesreport.com/

The Institute for PR

Promotes and encourages academic and professional excellence.
www.instituteforpr.com

The Institute of Public Relations

The largest public relations professional membership association in Europe.
www.ipr.org.uk

International Association of Business Communicators

Products, services, activities, and networking opportunities to help people and organizations achieve excellence in public relations, employee communication, marketing communication, public affairs, and other forms of communication.
www.iabc.com

International Public Relations Association

Provides professional development and personal networking opportunities for worldwide membership.
www.ipra.org

I-PR Discussion List

An online community of public relations professionals.
www.marketingwonk.com/lists/ipr/

National Investor Relations Institute

Advances the practice of investor relations and the professional competency and stature of its members.
www.niri.org

The PR Academy

An online course for prospective public relations practitioners.
www.learnpr.com

PR Bytes

A moderated forum for public relations professionals to discuss public relations/communications issues as they relate to the Internet.
http://groups.yahoo.com/group/prbytes

PR Week

The first weekly magazine to offer worldwide coverage of the public relations business.
www.prweek.com

Public Relations Consultants Association

Information about public relations consultants in the United Kingdom.
www.prca.org.uk/sites/prca.nsf/homepages/homepage

*Public Relations Division,
Association for Education in
Journalism and Mass Communication*

Web site for association of public relations educators in the United States and abroad.
http://lamar.colostate.edu/~aejmcpr/

Public Relations Institute of New Zealand

The national organization created to promote public relations in New Zealand and serve the best interests of the people who practice it.
www.prinz.org.nz

Public Relations Links

Links compiled by Kirk Hallahan, Fellow PRSA, at Colorado State University.
http://lamar.colostate.edu/~hallahan/j13pr.htm

Public Relations Society of America

The world's largest professional organization for public relations practitioners.
www.prsa.org

Public Relations Student Society of America

Cultivates mutually advantageous relationships between students and professional public relations practitioners.
www.prssa.org

Technology Events Information

List of important and influential technology-related gatherings worldwide.
www.catchpole.com/internetpr/events.cfm

Young PR Pros

An online forum for those new to the public relations field.
http://groups.yahoo.com/group/youngprpros

Westcoastprjobs.com

Job site for jobs in Arizona, California, and the Pacific Northwest.
www.westcoastprjobs.com

Workinpr.com

Recruiting and career site specifically for the public relations industry, offering credible industry research, career resources, and public relations tools.
www.workinpr.com

Writing That Works

Monthly how-to newsletter exclusively on practical business writing, editing, and communications.
www.apexawards.com/wtw.htm

Yearbook.com

Experts and sources on thousands of topics.
www.yearbook.com

Appendix 8

Where to Study Public Relations

The following **245** colleges and universities offer substantial programs of public relations at the undergraduate level. Each has met the criteria established by the Public Relations Society of America (PRSA) for chartering a chapter of the Public Relations Student Society of America (PRSSA). The purpose of PRSSA is to cultivate a mutually advantageous relationship between students and the professional practice. Named here are the PRSSA Faculty Advisors who can provide further information about public relations study at their respective schools. Please contact Liesel Enke at liesel.enke@prsa.org or by phone at 212/460-1474 if you have any questions or updates regarding this list. The schools listed here are chartered by PRSA for PRSSA chapters as of **February 2004**.

ALABAMA (3)
University of Alabama
Dept. of Communication Studies
Birmingham, AL 35294
Dr. John Wittig, APR
Phone: (205) 934-8917
wittig1939@hotmail.com

University of Alabama
Dept. of Advertising/PR
Tuscaloosa, AL 35487
Prof. Karla K. Gower
Phone: (205) 348-0132
gower@apr.ua.edu

Samford University
Dept. of Journalism & Mass Comm.
Birmingham, Alabama 35229
Dr. David Shipley, APR
Phone: (205) 726-2586
dsshiple@samford.edu

ALASKA (1)
University of Alaska
Dept. of Journalism/Public Comm.
Anchorage, AK 99508
Prof. Vivian Hamilton
Phone: (907) 694-0400
hamiltonpr@gci.net

ARKANSAS (4)
University of Arkansas
Dept. of Journalism
Fayetteville, AR 72701
Dr. Phyllis Miller
Phone: (479) 575-5213
pmiller@comp.uark.edu

University of Arkansas
Dept. of Journalism
Little Rock, AR 72204
Prof. Jamie Byrne
Phone: (501) 569-3392

Arkansas State University
College of Communications
State University, AR 72467
Prof. Lisa Moskal
Phone: (870) 972-3075
lmoskal@astate.edu

Harding University
Communication Department
Searcy, AR 72149
Prof. Jack Shock
Phone: (501) 279-4196
communication@harding.edu

ARIZONA (2)
Arizona State University
School of Journalism
Tempe, AZ 85282-1305
Prof. Renea D. Nichols
Phone: (480) 965-8799
reneanichols@asu.edu

Northern Arizona University
Dept. of Journalism,
Box 5619
Flagstaff, AZ 86011
Dr. Manny Romero
Phone: (520) 523-2507
manny.romero@nau.edu

CALIFORNIA (17)
Biola University
Department of Communications
13800 Biola Ave.
La Mirada, CA 90639
Todd V. Lewis
Phone: (562) 944-0351
todd_lewis@peter.biola.edu

California Polytechnic University
Dept. of Communication Arts
Pomona, CA 91768
Prof. John Kaufman
Phone: (909) 869-3534
jakaufman@csupomona.edu

California Polytechnic University
Journalism Department
Cal Poly
San Luis Obispo, CA 93407
Mark Hucklebridge
Phone: (805) 756-1196
mhuckleb@calpoly.edu

California State University, Bakersfield
Dept. of Communications
Bakersfield, CA 93311-1099
Dr. Andy O. Alali
Phone: (805) 664-2152
aalai@csub.edu

California State University, Dominguez Hills
Dept. of Communications
Carson, CA 90747
Prof. Donn E. Silvis
Phone: (310) 243-3682
dsilvis@csudh.edu

California State University, Fresno
Dept. of Mass Communications
Fresno, CA 93740-8029
Betsy Martinusen
Phone: (559) 278-6154
betsy_martinusen@csufresno.edu

California State University, Fullerton
Dept. of Communications
Fullerton, CA 92634
Joseph Massey
Phone: (714) 278-4609
jmassey@fullerton.edu

California State University, Hayward
25800 Carlos Bee Boulevard
Hayward, CA 94542
Dr. Valer Sue
Phone: (510) 885-3292

California State University, Long Beach
Dept. of Journalism
Long Beach, CA 90840

Prof. Mathew Cabot
Phone: (562) 985-7939
mcabot@csulb.edu

California State University, Northridge
Journalism Department
Northridge, CA 91330-8311
Prof. Scott Berman
Phone: (818) 677-3135
scott.j.berman@csun.edu

California State University, San Bernardino
5500 University Parkway
San Bernardino, CA 92407-2397
Donna Eileen Simmons
Phone: (909) 880-7379
dsimmons@csub.edu

Chapman University
Dept. of Communications
Orange, CA 92866
Prof. Janell Shearer, APR
Phone: (714) 997-6647
shearer@chapman.edu

University of the Pacific
Dept. of Communication
Stockton, CA 95211
Dr. Carol Ann Hackley, APR
Phone: (209) 946-2505
tchackley@aol.com

Pepperdine University
Communication Division
Malibu, CA 90265
Dr. Louella Benson-Garcia
Phone: (310) 506-4593
louella.benson@pepperdine.edu

San Diego State University
College of Prof. Studies
San Diego, CA 92182-0116
Kenn Ulrich, APR, Fellow PRSA
Phone: (619) 397-5471
tcuex@hotmail.com

San Jose State University
School of Applied Arts & Sciences
San Jose, CA 95192-0055
Prof. Kathleen Martinelli
Phone: (408) 924-3285
martinelli@jmc.sjsu.edu

University of Southern California
School of Journalism
Los Angeles, CA 90089-1695
Jennifer Floto
Phone: (310) 578-2642
floto@usc.edu

COLORADO (1)
Colorado State University
Dept. of Technical Journalism
Fort Collins, CO 80523
Dr. Kirk Hallahan, APR, Fellow PRSA
Phone: (970) 491-3963
Kirk.hallahan@colostate.edu

CONNECTICUT (2)
University of Hartford
School of Communication
West Hartford, CT 06117
Susan Grantham
Phone: (860) 768-4016
grantham@hartford.edu

Quinnipiac University
School of Communication
Hamden, CT 06518
Russell Barclay, Ph.D.
Phone: (203) 582-3210
russel.barclay@quinnipiac.edu

DELAWARE (2)
Delaware State University
Mass Communications Dept.
Dover, DE 19901
Prof. Marcia Taylor
Phone: (302) 857-6570
dsumtaylor@yahoo.com

University of Delaware
Dept. of Communication
Newark, DE 19711
Prof. Phil Wescott
Attn: PRSSA
Phone: (610) 338-2560

DISTRICT of COLUMBIA (2)
American University
School of Communication
Washington, DC 20016
Prof. b j Altschul, APR
Phone: (202) 885-2103
bja@american.edu

Howard University
School of Communication
Washington, DC 20059
Dr. Rochelle Ford
Phone: (202) 806-5124
r_tillery_larkin@hotmail.com

FLORIDA (7)
University of Florida
College of Journalism and Communications
Weimer Hall, P.O. Box 11840
Gainesville, FL 32611
Margarete R. Hall
Phone: (352) 392-1686
mhall@jou.ufl.edu

Florida A&M University
School of Journalism
Tallahassee, FL 32307
Dr. LaRae M. Donnellan, APR
Phone: (850) 561-2765
larae9411@hotmail.com

Florida International University
Dept. of Communication
North Miami, FL 33181
Prof. Catherine Ahles, APR, Fellow PRSA
Phone: (305) 919-5629
ahlesc@fiu-edu

Florida Southern College
Communication Department

111 Lake Hollingsworth Dr.
Lakeland, FL 33801
Kimberly Grady-Brock
Phone: (863) 680-4133
kimgradybrock@aol.com

University of Miami
School of Communications
Coral Gables, FL 33124
Dr. Donn Tilson, APR, Fellow PRSA
Phone: (305) 284-3153
dtilson@miami.edu

University of North Florida
College of Arts & Sciences
Jacksonville, FL 32224-2660
Prof. Roberta Reid-Doggett, APR
Phone: (904) 620-2624
rdoggett@unf.edu

University of South Florida
Dept. of Mass Communication
4202 East Fowler Ave. CIS1040
Tampa, FL 33620
Prof. Kelly G. Page
Phone: (813) 974-6790
kgpage@chumal.cas.usf.edu

GEORGIA (5)
Clark Atlanta University
Communications Department
Atlanta, GA 98926
Prof. Brenda Wright
Phone: (404) 880-8304
bwright@cau.edu

University of Georgia
School of Journalism
Athens, GA 30602
Betty Jones
Phone: (706) 542-1704
betjones@arches.uga.edu

Georgia Southern University
Communication Arts Dept.
PO Box 8091
Statesboro, GA 30458
Demare Gross

Phone: (912) 681-0126
ddemare@gasou.edu

Georgia State University
Communications Dept.
Atlanta, GA 30303-3098
Prof. Jennifer Jiles
Phone: (404) 651-5678
joujdj@langate.gsu.edu

Valdosta State University
Dept. of Communication Arts
Valdosta, GA 31601
Prof. David Blakeman, APR
Phone: (229) 333-5820
dblkaema@valdosta.edu

HAWAII (2)
Hawaii Pacific University
College of Communication
FHT 504-4
James Daniel Whitfield
Phone: (808) 256-5230
jwhitfie@campus.hpu.edu

University of Hawaii
Dept. of Journalism
Honolulu, HI 96822
Prof. Tom Kelleher, Ph.D.
Phone: (808) 956-8881
tkell@hawaii.edu

IDAHO (1)
Brigham Young University
258 Rigby Hall
Rexburg, ID 83460
Michael Cannon
Phone: (208) 496-1897
cannonm@byui.edu

ILLINOIS (9)
Bradley University
Dept. of Communication & Fine Arts
Peoria, IL 61625
Prof. Michael Thurwanger
Phone: (309) 677-2366
twanger@bradley.edu

Columbia College
Marketing/Communications
Chicago, IL 60605
Prof. Morton H. Kaplan
Phone: (312) 663-1600
mkaplan@pupmail.colum.edu

DePaul University
Dept. of Communications
Chicago, IL 60614
Kurt Wise, Ph.D., APR
Phone: (773) 325-2969
kwise1@depaul.edu

Eastern Illinois University
Journalism Department
Charleston, IL 61920
Brian Sowa
Phone: (217) 581-6943
Fax: (217) 581-5718
bcsowa@eiu.edu

Illinois State University
Dept. of Communications
Normal, IL 61761
Dr. Dean Kazoleas, APR
Phone: (309) 438-8953
drdeank@hotamil.com

Northern Illinois University
Dept. of Communication
DeKalb, IL 60115
Dr. Walter Atkinson
Phone: (815) 753-7009
tm0wla1@wpo.cso.niu.edu

Southern Illinois University
Dept. of Speech Communication
Mail code 6605
Carbondale, IL 62901-6605
Dr. Nilanjana Bardhan
Phone: (618) 453-1891
bardhan@siu.edu

Southern Illinois University
Dept. of Speech Communication
Edwardsville, IL 62025

Prof. Judith Meyer
Phone: (618) 650-5016
jkmeyer@plantnet.com

Western Illinois University
Dept. of English & Journalism
Macomb, IL 61455
Dr. Mohammed Siddiqi
Phone: (309) 298-1326
m-siddiqi@wiu.edu

INDIANA (6)
Ball State University
Dept. of Journalism
Muncie, IN 47306
Bob Pritchard
Phone: (765) 285-9104
rpritchardl@bsu.edu

Butler University
Dept. of Journalism
Indianapolis, IN 46208
Prof. Rose Campbell
Phone: (317) 940-8000
rcampbel@thomas.butler.edu

Indiana State University
Dept. of Communication
Terre Haute, IN 47809
Dr. Debra Worley, APR
Phone: (812) 237-8882
cmdebra@isugw.indstate.edu

Purdue University
Dept. of Communication
West Lafayette, IN 47907
Prof. Josh Boyd
Phone: (317) 494-3333
boyd@purdue.edu

University of Southern Indiana
Dept. of Communications
8600 University Blvd.
Evansville, IN 47711
Tamara L. Wandel, Ph.D.
Phone: (812) 464-8600
twandel@usi.edu

Valparaiso University
Communication Department
Valparaiso, IN 46383
Dr. Bonita Dostal Neff
Phone: (219) 464-6827
bonita.neff@valpo.edu

IOWA (6)
Drake University
School of Journalism & Mass Communications
Des Moines, IA 50311
Prof. Ronda Menke, APR
Phone: (515) 271-3167
ronda.menke@drake.edu

University of Iowa
School of Journalism
Iowa City, IA 52242
Ann Haugland
Phone: (319) 335-9195
Ann-haugland@uiowa.edu

Iowa State University
123B Hamilton Hall
Ames, IA 50011-1180
Erin Wilgenbusch, APR
Phone: (515) 294-0483
eew@iastate.edu

Mount Mercy College
PR Department
Cedar Rapids, IA 52402
Dave Klope
Phone: (319) 363-1323
dklope@mmc.mtmercy.edu

University of Northern Iowa
Dept. of Communications & Theatre Arts
Cedar Falls, IA 50614
Dr. Gayle Pohl, APR
Phone: (319) 273-6308
gayle.pohl@uni.edu

Simpson College
Dept. of Communication Studies
Indianola, IA 50125
Susanne Gubanc

Phone: (515) 961-1740
gubanc@simpson.edu

KANSAS (2)
University of Kansas
School of Journalism & Mass Communication
Lawrence, KS 66045
Prof. David Guth, APR
Phone: (785) 864-4755
dguth@ku.edu

Kansas State University
Dept. of Journalism
Manhattan, KS 66506
Joye Gordon
Phone: (785) 532-6890
gordon@ksu.edu

KENTUCKY (5)
Eastern Kentucky University
Dept. of Mass Communications
Alumni Coliseum, Rm. 108
Richmond, KY 40475
Mary Jo Nead
Phone: (859) 622-1143
Maryjo.nead@eku.edu

University of Kentucky
College of Communication
Lexington, KY 40592
Dr. Scott Witlow
Phone: (859) 257-9000
scott@uky.edu

Morehead State University
Dept. of Communications & Theater
Breckinridge Hall
Morehead, KY 40351
Shirley Serini, APR, Fellow PRSA
Phone: (606) 783-2694
s.serini@morehead-st.edu

Murray State University
Dept. of Journalism
Murray, KY 42071
Robin B. Orvino-Proulx
Phone: (270) 762-5308
robin.proulx@murraystate.edu

Western Kentucky University
Dept. of Journalism
Bowling Green, KY 42101
Ken Payne
Phone: (502) 745-5836
ken.payne@wku.edu

LOUISIANA (9)
Grambling State University
Dept. of Mass Communications
Grambling, LA 71245
Dr. Martin O. Edu
Phone: (318) 274-2189
edum@alpha0.gram.edu

University of Louisiana
Dept. of Communication
Lafayette, LA 70503
Phone: (337) 482-6103

University of Louisiana
Dept. of Communication Arts
Monroe, LA 71209
Dr. Bette Kauffman
Phone: (318) 342-1090
kauffman@ulm.edu

Louisiana State University
Manship School of Mass Communications
Baton Rouge, LA 70803-7202
Lori Boyer
Phone: (225) 578-3488
lboyer@lsu.edu

Louisiana State University
Communications Department
Shreveport, LA 71115
Prof. Ron Sereg
Phone: (318) 797-5375
resereg@hotmail.com

Loyola University
Communications Dept.
New Orleans, LA 70118
Dr. Cathy Rogers
Phone: (504) 865-3297
crogers@loyno.edu

McNeese State University
Dept. of Mass Communication
PO Box 90335
Lake Charles, LA 70609-0335
Dr. Leonard Barchak
Phone: (337) 475-5430
barchak@mail.mcneese.edu

Nicholls State University
Dept. of Mass Communication
Thibodaux, LA 70310
Felicia LeDuff Harry
Phone: (986) 448-4959
Maco-flh@nicholls.edu

Northwestern State University
Dept. of Language & Communication
Natchitoches, LA 71457
Paula Furr
Phone: (318) 357-5213
furrp@nsula.edu

MARYLAND (5)
Bowie State College
Dept. of Journalism
Bowie, MD 20715
Dr. Rev. Unnia Pettus-Hargrove
Phone: (301) 464-7869
revunnia@aol.com

Hood College
Dept. of Communication Arts
Frederick, MD 21701
Dave Medaris
Phone: (301) 360-2690
Medaris@aol.com

Loyola College
Writing & Media Dept.
Baltimore, MD 21210
Dr. Elliott King
Phone: (410) 617-2819
eking@loyola.edu

University of Maryland
College of Journalism
College Park, MD 20740

Dr. Bey-Ling Sha, APR
Phone: (301) 405-7447
profsha@hotmail.com

Towson University
Dept. of Speech & Mass Communication
Towson, MD 21252
Dr. Meg Algren, APR
Phone: (410) 830-2000
malgran@towson.edu

MASSACHUSETTS (5)
Boston University
School of Public Communication
Boston, MA 02215
Prof. Stephen P. Quigley, APR
Phone: (617) 358-0066
squigley@bu.edu

Emerson College
Communication & Performing Arts
Boston, MA 02116
Prof. Abbott Ikeler
Phone: (617) 824-3427
Abbott_Ikeler@emerson.edu

Northeastern University
School of Journalism
Boston, MA 02115-5000
Prof. Gladys McKie
Phone: (617) 373-4054
g.mckie@neu.edu

Salem State College
School of Arts & Sciences
Salem, MA 01970-5353
Dr. Robert Brown
Phone: (978) 542-6463
d28man@mindspring.com

Simmons College
300 The Fenway
Boston, MA 02115
Lynda A. Beltz
Phone: (617) 521-2831
Lynda.beltz@simmons.edu

MICHIGAN (9)
Adrian College
Communications Dept.
Adrian, MI 49221
Prof. Joanna Schultz
Phone: (517) 265-5161
jschultz@adrian.edu

Central Michigan University
Dept. of Journalism
Mt. Pleasant, MI 48859
Prof. Diane Krider
Phone: (989) 774-3153
kride1ds@cmich.edu

Eastern Michigan University
PR Area, Dept. of English
Ypsilanti, MI 48197
Dr. Melissa Motschall, APR
Phone: (734) 487-0147
melissa.motschall@emich.edu

Ferris State University
School of Business
Big Rapids, MI 49307
Prof. Ronald H. Greenfield, APR
Phone: (231) 591-2448
ronald_greenfield@ferris.edu

Grand Valley State College
School of Communication
Allendale, MI 49401
Tim Penning, APR
Phone: (616) 331-3478
penningt@gvsu.edu

Michigan State University
Advertising Department
East Lansing, MI 48824
Dr. Brenda Wrigley
Phone: (517) 355-7556
wrigley1@msu.edu

Northern Michigan Univ.
1401 Presque Isle
Marquette, MI 49855
Prof. Wally Niebauer
Phone: (906) 227-1057
niebauer@nmu.edu

University of Michigan, Dearborn
Dept. of Communications
Dearborn, MI 48128-1491
Susan L. Sheth
Phone: (313) 436-9177
susheth@umd.umich.edu

Wayne State University
Speech/Communication & Theatre
Detroit, MI 48202
Dr. Shelly Najor
Phone: (313) 577-1556
m.a.najor@wayne.edu

MINNESOTA (4)
University of Minnesota
School of Journalism & Mass Communication
Minneapolis, MN 55455
Dr. Albert Tims
Phone: (612) 625-0020
Timsx001@unm.edu

Minnesota State University, Moorhead
Mass Communication Dept.
Moorhead, MN 56560
Susanne Williams
Phone: (218) 291-4373
willmsu@mnstate.edu

St. Cloud State University
Dept. of Mass Communications
St. Cloud, MN 56301
Prof. Gretchen Tiberghien, APR
Phone: (320) 255-3293
gtib@stcloudstate.edu

University of St. Thomas
Dept. of Journalism
St Paul, MN 55105
Jeanne Steele
Phone: (612) 962-5265
jrsteele@stthomas.edu

MISSISSIPPI (2)
Univ. of Southern Mississippi
Dept. of Journalism
Hattiesburg, MS 39406-5121
Dr. Charles Mayo
Phone: (601) 266-6471
Charles.mayo@usm.edu

Mississippi State University
Dept. of Communication
P.O. Box PF
Mississippi State, MS 39762
Dr. John E. Forde, APR
Phone: (662) 325-8033
jeforde@ra.msstate.edu

MISSOURI (5)
Central Missouri State University
Dept. of Communication
Warrensburg, MO 64093
Dr. Tricia L. Hansen-Horn
Phone: (660) 543-8635
hansen-horn@cmsu1.cmsu.edu

Northwest Missouri State University
136 Wells Hall
Maryville, MO 64468
Dr. Melody Hubbard
Phone: (660) 562-1827
hubbar@mail.nwmissouri.edu

Southeast Missouri State University
Dept. of Mass Communication
Cape Girardeau, MO 63701
Dr. Susan Gonders
Phone: (573) 651-2486
sgonders@hotmail.com

Stephens College
Communications Department
Columbia, MO 65215
Prof. John S. Blakemore, APR
Phone: (573) 876-7104
johnb@stephens.edu

Missouri Southern State University-Joplin
Department of Comm. & Foreign Languages
Joplin, MO 64801

Prof. Brenda J. Kilby
Phone: (417) 625-9786
kilby-b@ mssc.edu

NEBRASKA (3)
Creighton University
Dept. of Journalism
Omaha, NE 68178
Prof. Eileen Wirth
Phone: (402) 280-3014
emw@creighton.edu

University of Nebraska
206 Avery Hall
Lincoln, NE 68588-0130
Prof. Phyllis Larsen
Phone: (402) 472-3041
plarsen1@unl.edu

University of Nebraska
Dept. of Journalism & Mass Communication
Omaha, NE 68182-0112
Prof. Karen Weber
Phone: (402) 554-2246
kweber@mail.unomaha.edu

NEVADA (2)
University of Nevada
School of Communications
4505 Maryland Parkway
Box 451024
Las Vegas, NV 89154-1024
John Naccarato
Phone: (702) 895-1333
John.naccarato@ccmail.nevada.edu

University of Nevada
School of Journalism
Reno, NV 89557-0040
Dr. Amiso George
Phone: (775) 784-4198
ageorge@unr.edu

NEW JERSEY (4)
Monmouth University
Dept. of Communication
West Long Branch, NJ 07764
Nancy Wiencek

Phone: (732) 571-7553
nwiencek@monmouth.edu

Rowan University
Communications Dept.
201 Mullica Hill Rd.
Glassboro, NJ 08028
Larry Litwin
Phone: (856) 256-4224
larry@larrylitwin.com

Rutgers University
Dept. of Journalism & Mass Media
New Brunswick, NJ 08903
Dr. W. David Gibson
Phone: (732) 932-7500 x 8114
gibson@scils.rutgers.edu

Seton Hall University
Dept. of Communication
South Orange, NJ 07079
Prof. Kathleen D. Rennie, APR
Phone: (908) 851-0804
kathdrenn@aol.com

NEW MEXICO (1)
University of New Mexico
Dept. of Communication & Journalism
Albuquerque, NM 87131
Dr. Dirk Gibson
Phone: (505) 277-2727
dirkgib@unm.edu

NEW YORK (14)
Buffalo State College
Communication Dept.
Buffalo, NY 14222
Marian Deutschman
Phone: (716) 878-6008
mardeu@localnet.com

Canisius College
Dept. of Communication Studies
2001 Main Street
Buffalo, NY 14208-1098
Prof. Stanton Hudson, Jr., APR
Phone: (716) 888-2589
hudsons@canisius.edu

City College of New York
Dept. of Communications
New York, NY 10031
Prof. Lynn Appelbaum
Phone: (212) 650-6561
lappelbaum@ccny.cuny.edu

Cornell University
Dept. of Communication Arts
Ithaca, NY 14853
Dr. James Shanahan
Phone: (607) 255-8058
jes30@cornell.edu

Fashion Institute of Technology (SUNY)
Advertising & Communication
New York, NY 10001
Prof. Roberta Elins
Phone: (212) 217-7705
Roberta_elins@fitnyc.edu

Iona College
Communication Arts Dept.
715 North Ave.
New Rochelle, NY 10801
Prof. Robert J. Petrausch
Phone: (914) 633-2000
rpetrausch@iona.edu

Ithaca College
School of Communications
Ithaca, NY 14850-5801
Jerry Engel, APR
Phone: (607) 274-1030
jengel@ithaca.edu

Long Island Univ. at C.W. Post
Communication Arts
Brookville, NY 11548
Prof. Abby Dress, APR
Phone: (516) 299-2984
Dress2@worldnet.att.com

New York University
Dept. of Journalism
New York, NY 10003
Dr. Joyce Hauser
Phone: (212) 998-5196
jh7@nyu.edu

SUNY at Geneseo
Dept. of Speech Communication
Geneseo, NY 14454
Mary Mohan
Phone: (585) 245-5223
mohan@geneseo.edu

SUNY at Oswego
Communication Studies Dept.
Oswego, NY 13126
Dr. Zoltan Bedy
Phone: (315) 425-9143
bedy@oswego.edu

Syracuse University
Newhouse School
Syracuse, NY 13244
Robert Kucharvy
Phone: (315) 443-2747
rmkuckar@syr.edu

Utica College
Dept. of Journalism & PR
Utica, NY 13502
Patricia Swann
Phone: (315) 792-3243
pswann@utica.edu

University of Buffalo
Dept. of Communication
359 Baldy Hall
Buffalo, NY 14260
Deborah Silverman, Ph.D., APR
Phone: (716) 645-2141, ext. 1181
debsilv@aol.com

NORTH CAROLINA (8)
Appalachian State Univ.
Dept. of Communication
Boone, NC 28608
Dr. Janice Pope
Phone: (828) 262-2391
popejt@appstate.edu

Campbell University
Dept. of Mass Communication
Buies Creek, NC 27506

Prof. Olivia Ross, APR
Phone: (910) 893-1526
ross@mailcenter.campbell.edu

East Carolina University
School of Communication
221 Joyner East
Greenville, NC 27858
Christine R. Russell
Phone: (252) 328-2670
russellc@mail.ecu.edu

Elon University
Campus 2850
Elon College, NC 27244
Jessica J. Gisclair
Phone: (336) 278-5724
jgisclair@elon.edu

University of North Carolina
School of Journalism
Chapel Hill, NC 27514
Larry Lamb
Phone: (919) 843-5851
llamb@email.unc.edu

University of North Carolina
Dept. of Communication
Charlotte, NC 28223
Dr. Alan Freitag
Phone: (704) 687-4005
arfreita@email.uncc.edu

North Carolina State University
Dept. of Communication
Raleigh, NC 27695-8104
Dr. Juliette Storr
Phone: (919) 515-9749
jmstorr@social.chass.ncsa

Western Carolina University
Dept. of Communication
Cullowhee, NC 28723
Debie Connelly
Phone: (704) 227-7491
dlconnelly@email.wcu.edu

NORTH DAKOTA (2)
University of North Dakota
School of Communication
Grand Forks, ND 58203
Michael Nitz
Phone: (701) 777-3053
dakotanitz@hotmail.com

North Dakota State University
Dept. of Mass Communication
Fargo, ND 58105
Paul Nelson
Phone: (701) 231-7705
Paul.nelson.1@ndsu.nodak.edu

OHIO (16)
University of Akron
Dept. of Communication
Akron, OH 44325
Dr. Nancy Somerick
Phone: (330) 972-6686
nmsomer@uakron.edu

Bowling Green State University
Dept. of Journalism
Bowling Green, OH 43403
Prof. Terry Rentner
Phone: (419) 372-2079
trentne@bgnet.bgsu.edu

Capital University
Dept. of Communications
Columbus, OH 43209
Dr. Steven Bruning
Phone: (614) 236-6323
sbruning@capital.edu

University of Dayton
Dept. of Communication
Dayton, OH 45469
Dr. Doris Dartey
Phone: (937) 229-3945
doris.dartey@notes.udayton.edu

University of Findlay
Dept. of Communication
Findlay, OH 45840-3695

Prof. Jeanette Drake, APR
Phone: (419) 434-6982
drake@findlay.edu

John Carroll University
Dept. of Communication
University Heights, OH 44118
Fred Buchstein
Phone: (216) 397-4378
fbuchstein@jcu.edu

Kent State University
School of Journalism
138A Taylor Hall
P.O. Box 5190
Kent, OH 44242-001
Michelle Ewing, APR
Phone: (330) 672-4288
meewing@kent.edu

Miami University
Dept. of Communication
Oxford, OH 45056
Dr. Marjorie K. Nadler
Phone: (513) 529-7175
nadlemk@muohio.edu

Ohio University
School of Journalism
Athens, OH 45701
Diana Knott
Phone: (740) 597-1294
knott@ohio.edu

Ohio Northern University
Dept. of Communication Arts
Ada, OH 45810
Dr. Stephen Iseman
Phone: (419) 772-2053
s-iseman@onu.edu

Ohio State University
School of Journalism
3016 Derby Hall
154 N. Oval Mall
Columbus, OH 43210
Daniel J. Steinberg, APR

Phone: (740) 344-8177
steinberg.28@osu.edu

Otterbein College
Dept. of Speech Communication
Westerville, OH 43081
Prof. Denise Shively, APR
Phone: (614) 823-1838
dshively@otterbein.edu

University of Toledo
Dept. of Communication
Toledo, OH 43606
Prof. Joseph L. Clark, APR
Phone: (419) 530-4794
jclark@utnet.utoledo.edu

Ursuline College
Communication Arts Dept.
Pepper Pike, OH 44124
Prof. Rosemary Rood-Tutt
Phone: (440) 449-4200
rtutt@ursuline.edu

Wright State University
Department of Communication
Dayton, OH 45435
Dr. Henry J. Ruminski, APR
Phone: (937) 775-2950
henry.ruminski@wright.edu

Xavier University
Communication Arts Dept.
3800 Victory Parkway
Cincinnati, OH 45207
Dr. Jennifer Wood
Phone: (513) 745-3704
jfwphd@aol.com

OKLAHOMA (5)
University of Central Oklahoma
Journalism Department
Edmond, OK 73034
Prof. Jill Kelsey, APR
Phone: (405) 974-5914
jkelsey@ucok.edu

University of Oklahoma
School of Journalism & Mass Communication
Norman, OK 73019
Prof. Kenneth McMillen, APR
Phone: (405) 325-3737
kmcmillen@ou.edu

Oklahoma State University
School of Broadcasting & Journalism
Stillwater, OK 74078
Prof. R. Brooks Garner, APR
Phone: (405) 744-8271
garnerr@okstate.edu

Oral Roberts University
Communication Arts Dept.
Tulsa, OK 74171
Dr. Johnny Mac Allen
Phone: (918) 495-6867
jallen@oru.edu

University of Tulsa
Dept. of Communication
Tulsa, OK 74104
Prof. Shari Weiss
Phone: (918) 631-3811
weisss@centum.utulsa

OREGON (1)
University of Oregon
School of Journalism
Eugene, OR 97403
Dr. Jim Van Leuven, APR
Phone: (541) 346-3752
jvanleuv@oregon.uoregon.edu

PENNSYLVANIA (19)
Bloomsburg University
Mass Communications Dept.
Bloomsburg, PA 17815
Dr. Richard Ganahl III
Phone: (560) 389-4783
rganahl@husky.bloomu.edu

California University
Communication Studies

California, PA 15419-1394
Dr. Sylvia Sholar
Phone: (724) 938-4227
sholar@cup.edu

Drexel University
Humanities/Communication
Philadelphia, PA 19104
Alexander G. Nikolaev
Phone: (215) 895-1823
Alexander.g.nikolaev@drexel.edu

Duquesne University
Dept. of Journalism
Pittsburgh, PA 15282
Dr. Kathleen Roberts
Phone: (412) 396-5698
robertskg@duq.edu

Edinboro University
Dept. of Speech & Communication - Studies
Edinboro, PA 16444
Dr. Anthony C. Peyronel
Phone: (814) 732-2116
apeyronel@edinboro.edu

Lehigh University
Division of Journalism
Bethlehem, PA 18015
Prof. Carole Gorney, APR,
Fellow PRSA
Phone: (610) 758-4178
cmg1@lehigh.edu

Mansfield University
Communication & Theater Dept.
Mansfield, PA 16933
Prof. Holly Pieper
Phone: (570) 662-4789
hpieper@mnsfld.edu

Marywood College
Communication Arts Dept.
2300 Adams Ave.
Scranton, PA 18509
Prof. Jay Hammeran

Phone: (570) 348-6209
hammeran@es.marywood.edu

Millersville University
Dept. of Communication and Theater
PO Box 1002
Millersville, PA 17551-0302
Prof. Thomas P. Boyle, APR
Phone: (717) 871-5448
thomas.boyle@millersville.edu

Pennsylvania State University
College of Communications
University Park, PA 16802
Prof. Anne Marie Major, APR
Phone: (814) 863-3069
amm17@psu.edu

Point Park College
Dept. of Journalism & Communication
Pittsburgh, PA 15222
Prof. Bob O'Gara, APR
Phone: (412) 392-3413
rogara@ppc.edu

University of Scranton
Dept. of Communication
Scranton, PA 18505
Dr. Jan Kelly, APR
Phone: (570) 941-7745
kellyj1@scranton.edu

Shippensburg University
Communication/Journalism
Shippensburg, PA 17257
Prof. Kathleen Williams
Phone: (717) 477-1594
kpwill@ship.edu

Slippery Rock University
Dept. of Communication
Slippery Rock, PA 16057
Dr. Mark Banks
Phone: (724) 738-2569
mark.banks@sru.edu

Susquehanna University
Communication Department
Selinsgrove, PA 17870
Dr. Randall Hines, APR
Phone: (570) 372-4079
hines@susqu.edu

Temple University
Dept. of Journalism
Philadelphia, PA 19122
Dr. Jean L. Brodey, APR
Phone: (215) 204-8757
brodey44@aol.com

Villanova University
Communications Dept.
800 Lancaster Ave.
Villanova, PA 19085-1699
William L. Cowen
Phone: (610) 519-7921
William.cowen@villanova.edu

Westminster College
Dept. of English
New Wilmington, PA 16172
Prof. Delores Natale
Phone: (724) 946-7348
nataleda@westminster.edu

York College
Dept. of Communication
York, PA 17405
Robert Carroll, Ph.D., APR
Phone: (717) 815-6451
rcarroll@ycp.edu

RHODE ISLAND (1)
Roger Williams University
Dept of Communication
Bristol, RI 02809
Robert J. Ristino, Ph.D., APR, Fellow PRSA
rristino@rwu.edu

SOUTH CAROLINA (2)
College of Charleston
Communication Department
Charleston, SC 29424

Vincent L. Benigni
Phone: (843) 953-7019
benigniv@cofc.edu

University of South Carolina
College of Journalism
Columbia, SC 29208
Prof. Beth Dickey
Phone: (803) 777-3320
beth_dickey@usc.jour.sc.edu

SOUTH DAKOTA (1)
University of South Dakota
Dept. of Mass Communication
Vermillion, SD 57069
Karen Thompson
Phone: (605) 677-6471
kthompso@usd.edu

TENNESSEE (9)
Austin Peay University
Dept. of Communication and Theatre
Clarksville, TN 37044
Dr. Frank E. Parcells
(931) 221-6308
parcellsf@apsu.edu

East Tennessee State Univ.
Dept. of Communications
Johnson City, TN 37601
Dr. John King
Phone: (423) 439-4169
johnking@etsu.edu

Lee University
Dept. of Communication Arts
1120 N. Ocoee Street
Cleveland, TN 37320
Prof. Patricia Silverman, APR
Phone: (423) 614-8228
psilverman@leeu.edu

Lipscomb University
Communication Dept.
Nashville, TN 37204
Dr. Kenneth R. Schott
Phone: (615) 279-5816
ken.schott@lipscomb.edu

University of Memphis
Journalism Dept.
Memphis, TN 38152
Dr. Rick Fischer, APR
Phone: (901) 678-2853
rfischer@memphis.edu

Middle Tennessee State University
Department of Journalism
Murfreesboro, TN 37132
Dr. Teresa Mastin
Phone: (615) 904-8239
mastinte@msu.edu

University of Tennessee
Dept. of Communications
Chattanooga, TN 37403
Prof. Rebekah Bromley
Phone: (423) 874-0896
Rebekah_bromley@utc.edu

University of Tennessee
School of Journalism
1345 Circle Park Drive, Room 476
Knoxville, TN 37966-0330
Dr. Bonnie Riechert
Phone: (865) 974-5108
breicher@utk.edu

University of Tennessee
Dept. of Communications
Gooch Hall, GH 305
Martin, TN 38238
Dr. Jeff Hoyer
Phone: (731) 514-3197
jhoyer@utm.edu

TEXAS (15)
Abilene Christian University
Journalism & Mass Communications Div.
Abilene, TX 79699
David A. Hogan
Phone: (325) 674-2045
Dave.hogan@acu.edu

Baylor University
Dept. of Journalism
P.O. Box 97353

Waco, TX 76798-7353
Dr. Michael Bishop, APR, Fellow PRSA
Phone: (254) 710-1469
Michael_Bishop@baylor.edu

Hardin-Simmons University
Dept. of Communication
Box 16022 HSU Station
Abilene, TX 79698
Dr. Randy Armstrong
Phone: (915) 670-1436

University of Houston
School of Communication
Houston, TX 77204-3786
Dr. Robert Heath
Phone: (713) 743-2873
rheath@uh.edu

Howard Payne University
Brownwood, TX 76801
Prof. Peter Seward
Phone: (915) 646-2502 ext. 5531
pseward@hputx.edu

University of North Texas
Dept. of Journalism
P.O. Box 311460
Denton, TX 76201
Dr. Richard Wells, APR
Phone: (940) 565-22167
wells@unt.edu

Sam Houston State University
Journalism Program
Huntsville, TX 77341
Prof. Franklin Krystyniak, APR
Phone: (936) 294-1833
frankk@shsu.edu

Southern Methodist University
Center for Communication Arts
Dallas, TX 75275
Prof. Chris Anderson, APR
Phone: (214) 768-3378

Southwest Texas State University
Dept. of Journalism
San Marcos, TX 78666
Dr. Bruce Renfro
Phone: (512) 245-2656
Rr08@stsw.edu

University of Texas
Dept of Communications/PRSSA-UTA Station
Box 19107
Arlington, TX 760190107
Alisa White
Phone (817) 272-5185
arwhite@uta.edu

University of Texas
Dept. of Advertising
CMA 7.142
Austin, TX 78712
Prof. Ron Anderson
Phone: (512) 471-1989
rba@mail.utexas.edu

University of Texas
Communication Dept.
San Antonio, TX 78249
Prof. Aimee Shelton
Phone: (210) 458-5348
ashelton@utsa.edu

Texas A&M University
Dept. of Journalism
College Station, TX 77843
Dr. Douglas Starr, APR, Fellow PRSA
Phone: (979) 845-5374
d-starr@tamu.edu

Texas Christian University
Dept. of Journalism
Fort Worth, TX 76129
Dr. Douglas Ann Newsom, APR, Fellow PRSA
Phone: (817) 257-6552
d.Newsom@tcu.edu

Texas Tech University
Dept. of Mass Communication
Lubbock, TX 79409

Dr. Michael Parkinson, APR
Phone: (806) 742-6500
michael.parkinson@ttu.edu

UTAH (4)
Brigham Young University
Dept. of Communications
Provo, UT 84602
Prof. Rich Long
Phone: (801) 422-2924
commsec@byugate.byu.edu

University of Utah
Dept. of Communication
Salt Lake City, UT 84112
Julia Corbett
Phone: (801) 581-4577
fleener@aol.com

Utah State University
Department of Journalism
Logan, UT 84322
Les Roka
Phone: (435) 797-0369
lroka@cc.usu.edu

Weber State University
Dept of Communication
1605 University Circle
Ogden, UT 84408-1605
James Andrew Lingwall
(801) 626-8128
alingwall@weber.edu

VIRGINIA (7)
George Mason University
Dept of Communications
4400 University 3D6
Fairfax, VA 22030
Katherine Rowan
Phone: (703) 993-4063
krowan@erols.com

Hampton University
Dept. of Mass Media
Hampton, VA 23668
Pro. Rosalynne Whitaker-Heck

Phone: (757) 727-5405
rosalynne.whitaker-heck
@hamptonu.edu

Liberty University
School of Communications
1971 University Blvd. Lynchburg, VA 24502
Deborah Wade Huff
Phone: (804) 582-2428
dwhuff@liberty.edu

Norfolk State University
Dept. of Journalism
Norfolk, VA 23504
Prof. Francis McDonald, APR
Phone: (757) 683-9559
francis.mcdonald@hamptonu.edu

Radford University
PO Box 6932
Radford, VA 24142
Dr. Kristin K. Froemling
Phone: (540) 831-5282
kfroemling@hotmail.com

Virginia Commonwealth University
School of Mass Communication
Richmond, VA 23284-2034
Dr. Ernest F. Martin, Jr.
Phone: (804) 828-6000
Martinef99@yahoo.com

Virginia Polytechnic Institute
Communications Studies
Blacksburg, VA 24061
Dr. Rachel Hollaway
Phone: (540) 231-9828
rhollowa@vt.edu

<u>WASHINGTON (5)</u>
Central Washington Univ.
Communication Dept.
Ellensburg, WA 98926
Prof. Beatrice Coleman
Phone: (509) 963-1070
profcoleman@hotmail.com

Eastern Washington University
Dept. of Communication
Cheney, WA 990042431
Dr. Patricia Chantrill
Phone: (509) 359-2313
patricia.chantrill@mail.ewu.edu

Gonzaga University
Communication Arts Dept.
AD Box 70
Spokane, WA 99258-0001
Dale Goodwin
Phone: (509) 328-4220
dgoodwin@gonzaga.edu

Washington State University
Dept. of Communications
Pullman, WA 99164-2520
Moon J. Lee
Phone: (509) 335-4225
Moonlee@wsu.edu

University of Washington
School of Communication
Seattle, WA 98195
Prof. Kathleen Fearn-Banks
Phone: (206) 543-7646
kfb@u.washington.edu

<u>WEST VIRGINIA (4)</u>
Bethany College
Communication Dept.
Bethany, WV 27032
Prof. Ted Pauls, MBA
Phone: (304) 829-7000
    tpauls@mail. bethanywv.edu

Marshall University
School of Journalism
400 Hal Greer Blvd.
Huntington, WV 25755-2622
Kim Carico-Simpson
Phone: (304) 696-4636
carico3@marshall.edu

West Virginia University
School of Journalism
Morgantown, WV 26506-6010

Dr. Ivan Pinnell
Phone: (304) 293-3505
Ivan.pinnell@mail.wvu.edu

West Virginia State College
Communication Department
Institute, WV 25112
Dr. Trevellya Ford-Ahmed
Phone: (304) 766-3327
tfordahmed@mail.wvsc.edu

WISCONSIN (6)
Marquette University
Dept. of Advertising & PR
P.O. Box 1881
Milwaukee, WI 53201-1881
Dr. Daradirek "Gee" Ekachai
Phone: (414) 288-3649
ekachaid@mu.edu

University of Wisconsin
School of Journalism & Mass Communication
Madison, WI 53706
Michelle Nelson
Phone: (608) 263-3397
mrnelson@facstaff.wisc.edu

University of Wisconsin
Dept. of Journalism
Oshkosh, WI 54901

Dr. Julie Henderson, APR
Phone: (920) 424-1105
henderso@uwosh.edu

University of Wisconsin
Journalism/Mass Communication Dept.
UWM Chapter PRSSA
Milwaukee, WI 53201-0413
Prof. Becky Crowder, APR
Phone: (414) 229-5794
bcrowder@csd.uwm.edu

University of Wisconsin-SP
Division of Communication
219 CAC, UWSP
1101 Reserve Street
Stevens Point, WI 54481
Dr. Richard M. Dubiel
Phone: (715) 346-2007
rdubiel@uwsp.edu

University of Wisconsin
Dept. of Communication
Whitewater, WI 53190
Dr. Peter Smudde
Phone: (414) 472-1234
smuddep@uww.edu

SOURCE: Public Relations Student Society of America. Reprinted with permission. For the most recent listings, visit the Society's Web site, www.prssa.org

Appendix 9

Dictionary of Public Relations Measurement

A

Alpha Level (α) The amount of error or chance allowed in sampling or inferential testing

Analysis of Variance (ANOVA) An inferential statistical test of significance for continuous-measurement dependent variables against a number of groups as independent variables

Attitude A predisposition to act or behave toward some object; a motivating factor in public relations composed of three dimensions: affective (emotional evaluation), cognitive (knowledge evaluation), and connotative (behavioral evaluation)

Attitude Research The measuring and interpreting of a full range of views, sentiments, feelings, opinions, and beliefs that segments of the public may hold toward a client or product

Attitude Scale A measure that targets respondent attitudes or beliefs toward some object; typically interval-level data, and requires that an arbitrary or absolute midpoint ("neutral" or "neither agree nor disagree") be provided to the respondent; also known as Likert or semantic differential measures

Audience A specified group from within a defined public targeted for influence

B

Baseline An initial measurement against which all subsequent measures are compared

Behavioral Objective (1) An objective that specifies the expected public relations campaign or program outcome in terms of specific behaviors; (2) a measure that is actionable in that it is the behavior requested of a target audience

Belief A long-held evaluation of some object, usually determined on the basis of its occurrence; clusters of beliefs yield attitudes

Benchmarking (Benchmark Study) A measurement technique that involves having an organization learn something about its own practices and the practices of selected others, and then compare these practices

Bivariate Analysis A statistical examination of the relationship between two variables

BRAD British Rate and Data measure, providing circulation and advertising cost data

C

Campaign (Program) The planning, execution, and evaluation of a public relations plan of action aimed at solving a problem

Case Study Methodology An informal research methodology that gathers data on a specific individual, company, or product with the analysis focused on understanding its unique qualities; not generalizable to other cases or populations

Categorical Data Measurement data that are defined by their association with groups and are expressed in terms of frequencies, percentages, and proportions (*see* Nominal data, Ordinal data)

Category In content analysis, the part of the system where the units of analysis are placed; also referred to as *subjects* or *buckets*

Causal Relationship A relationship between variables in which a change in one variable forces, produces, or brings about a change in another variable

Census Collection of data from *every* person or object in a population

Central Tendency A statistic that describes the typical or average case in the distribution of a variable (*see* Mean, Median, Mode, Range, Standard deviation, Standardized score, Variance, Z-score)

Characters A manifest unit of analysis used in content analysis consisting of individuals or roles (e.g., occupations, roles, race)

Chi-Square (X^2) An inferential statistical test of significance for categorical data (nominal or ordinal)

Circulation Number of copies of a publication as distributed (as opposed to read)

Closed-Ended Question A question that requires participants to supply selected and predetermined responses (e.g., "strongly agree," "agree," "neither agree nor disagree," "disagree," "strongly disagree")

Clustered Sample A type of probability sample that involves first breaking the population into heterogeneous subsets (or clusters) and then selecting the potential sample at random from the individual clusters

Coefficient Alpha (α) A statistical test for a measurement's reliability for interval and ratio data; also known as Cronbach's coefficient alpha

Cohort Survey A type of longitudinal survey in which some specific group is studied over time according to some criterion that stays the same (e.g., age $= 21$) while the samples may differ

Column Inches Total length of an article if it were all in one column, measured in inches (or centimeters); determines the total "share of ink" that a company or brand has achieved

Communication(s) Audit A systematic review and analysis of how effectively an organization communicates with all of its major internal and external audiences by identifying these audiences, by identifying the communication programs and their communication products utilized for each audience, by determining the effectiveness of these programs and their products, and by identifying gaps in the overall existing communication program; uses accepted research techniques and methodologies (*see* the following methodologies: Case study, Content analysis, Experimental, Focus group, Formal, Historical, In-depth interview, Informal, Secondary, Survey, Participant-observation)

Community Case Study An informal methodology whereby the researcher takes an in-depth look at one or several communities—subsections of communities—in which an organization has an interest by impartial, trained researchers using a mix of informal research methodologies (i.e., participant-observation, role-playing, secondary analysis, content analysis, interviewing, focus groups)

Confidence Interval In survey methodology based on a random sampling technique, the range of values or measurement within which a population parameter is estimated to fall (e.g., for a large population we might expect answers to a question to be within ±3 percent of the true population answer; if 55 percent responded positively, the confidence interval would be from 52 to 58 percent); sometimes called *measurement error*

Confidence Level In survey methodology based on a random sampling technique, the amount of confidence we can place on our confidence interval (typically set at 95 percent, or 95 out of 100 cases truly representing the population under study, with *no more than* 5 cases out of 100 misrepresenting that population); sometimes called *sampling error*

Construct Validity A statistically tested form of measurement validity that seeks to establish the dimensionality of a measure

Content Analysis (1) An informal research methodology (and measurement tool) that systematically tracks messages (written, spoken, broadcast) and translates them into quantifiable form using a systematic approach to defining message categories via specified units of analysis; (2) the action of breaking down message content into predetermined components (categories) to form a judgment capable of being measured

Content Validity A form of measurement validity that is based on other researchers' or experts' evaluations of the measurement items contained in a measure

Contingency Question A survey question that is to be asked only to some respondents, determined by their responses to some other questions; sometimes called a *funnel question*

Contingency Table A statistical table for displaying the relationship between variables in terms of frequencies and percentages; sometimes called a *cross-tabulation table* or *cross tab*

Continuous Data Data measured on a continuum, usually as interval data

Convenience Sample A non-probability sample where the respondents or objects are chosen because of availability (e.g., "man on the street"); a type of non-probability sample in which whoever happens to be available at a given point in time is included in the sample; sometimes called a "haphazard" or "accidental" sample

Correlation (*r*) A statistical test that examines the relationships between variables (either categorical or continuous)

Correlation Coefficient A measure of association that describes the direction and strength of a linear relationship between two variables; usually measured at the interval or ratio data level (e.g., Pearson Product Moment Coefficient, *r*) but can be measured at the nominal or ordinal level (e.g., Spearman-Rho)

Cost per Thousand (CPM) Cost of advertising for each 1,000 homes reached by the media

Covariation A criterion for causation whereby the dependent variable takes on different values depending on the independent variable

Criterion Variable The variable the research wants to predict

Criterion-Related Validity A form of validity that compares one measure against others known to have specified relationships with what is being measured; the highest form of measurement validity

Crossbreak Analysis A categorical analysis that compares the frequency of responses in individual cells

Cross-Sectional Survey A survey based on observations representing a single point in time (*see* Snapshot survey)

Cumulative Scale (Guttman Scale/Scalogram) A measurement scale that assumes that when you agree with a scale item you will also agree with items that are less extreme

Cyber Image Analysis (1) The measurement of Internet content via chat rooms or discussion groups in cyberspace regarding a client or product or topic; (2) the measurement of a client's image everywhere on the Internet

D

Data The observations or measurements taken in evaluating a public relations campaign or program (*see* Interval data, Nominal data, Ordinal data, Ratio data)

Deduction A philosophical logic in which specific expectations or hypotheses are developed or derived on the basis of general principles

Delphi Technique A research methodology (usually survey or interview) where the researcher tries to forecast the future based on successive waves of interviews or surveys with a panel of experts in a given field as a means of building a "consensus" of expert opinion and thought relating to particular topics or issues

Demographic Analysis Analysis of a population in terms of special social, political, economic, and geographic subgroups (e.g., age, sex, income level, race, educational level, place of residence, occupation)

Demographic Data Data that differentiate between groups of people or things (e.g., by sex, race, or income)

Dependent Variable The variable that is measured or collected as the outcome of changes in the independent variable

Depth Interview An extensive, probing, open-ended, largely unstructured interview, usually conducted in person or by telephone, in which respondents are encouraged to talk freely and in great detail about given subjects; also known as an *in-depth interview*

Descriptive Research A form of research that gathers information in such a way as to paint a picture of what people think or do

Descriptive Statistics The reduction and simplification of the numbers representing research, to ease interpretion of the results

Descriptive Survey A type of survey that collects in quantitative form basic opinions or facts about a specified population or sample; also known as a *public opinion poll*

Double-Barreled Question A question that attempts to measure two things at the same time; a source of measurement error

E

Environmental Scanning A research technique for tracking new developments in any area or field by carrying out a systematic review of what appears in professional, trade, or government publications

Equal Appearing Interval Scale A measurement scale with predefined values associated with each statement; also known as a *Thurstone Scale*

Equivalent Advertising Value (AVE) Equivalent cost of buying space devoted to editorial content

Ethnographic Research An informal research methodology that relies on the tools and techniques of cultural anthropologists and sociologists to obtain a better understanding of how individuals and groups function in their natural settings (*see also* Participant-observation)

Evaluation Research A form of research that determines the relative effectiveness of a public relations campaign or program by measuring program outcomes (changes in the levels of awareness, understanding, attitudes, opinions, and/or behaviors of a targeted audience or public) against a predetermined set of objectives that initially established the level or degree of change desired

Events A community affairs or sponsorship output

Experimental Methodology A formal research methodology that imposes *strict* artificial limits or boundaries on the research in order to establish some causal relationship between variables of interest; is not generalizable to a larger population

Explanatory Research A form of research that seeks to explain why people say, think, feel, and act the way they do; concerned primarily with the development of public relations theory about relationships and processes; is typically deductive

Exploratory Research A form of research that seeks to establish basic attitudes, opinions, and behavior patterns or facts about a specific population or sample; is typically inductive and involves extensive probing of the population, sample, or data

F

Face Validity A form of measurement validity that is based on the researcher's knowledge of the concept being measured; the lowest form of measurement validity

Facilitator An individual who leads a focus group; also known as a moderator

Factor Analysis A statistical tool that allows researchers to test the dimensionality of their measures; used to assess a measure's construct validity

Field Study Methodology A formal research methodology that imposes fewer restrictions, limits, or boundaries on the research in order to test some causal relationships found in experimental research and generalize them to a larger population

Filter Question A question used to move a respondent from one question to another; a question that is used to remove a respondent from a survey or interview; also known as a *funnel question*

Focus Group Methodology An informal research methodology that uses a group approach to gain an in-depth understanding of a client, object, or product; is not generalizable to other focus groups or populations

Formal Methodology (1) A set of research methodologies that allow the researcher to generalize to a larger audience but often fail to gain in-depth understanding of the client, object, or product; (2) a set of methodologies that follow the scientific or social scientific method; (3) a set of methodologies that are deductive in nature

Frequency A descriptive statistic that represents the number of objects being counted (e.g., number of advertisements, number of people who attend an event, number of media release pickups)

F-Test An inferential test of significance associated with Analysis of Variance (ANOVA)

Funnel Question A question used in a questionnaire or schedule that moves an interviewer or respondent from one part of a survey to another (e.g., "Are you a registered voter?" If the respondent says yes, certain questions are asked; if not, then other questions are asked)

G

Goal (Objective) The explicit statement of intentions that supports a communication strategy and includes an intended audience/receiver, a proposed measurable outcome (or desired level of change in that audience), and a specific time frame for that change to occur

Gross Rating Points (GRP) Measures of weight, readership, or audience equivalent to audience exposure among 1 percent of the population (*see also* Targeted Gross Rating Points [TGRP])

Guttman Scale (Cumulative Scale/Scalogram) A measurement scale that assumes (1) unidimensionality and (2) that people, when faced with a choice, will also choose items less intense than the one chosen

H

Historical Methodology An informal research methodology that examines the causes and effects of past events

Hypothesis An expectation about the nature of things derived from theory; a prediction of how an independent variable changes a dependent variable; formally stated as a predication (e.g., "males will purchase more of X than females") but tested via the null hypothesis ("males and females will not differ in their purchases of X")

Hypothesis Testing Determining whether the expectations that a hypothesis represents are indeed found in the real world

I

Image Research A research program or campaign that systematically studies people's perceptions toward an organization, individual, product, or service; sometimes referred to as a *reputation study*

Impressions The number of people who might have had the opportunity to be exposed to a story that has appeared in the media; also known as *opportunity to see*, usually refers to the total audited circulation of a publication or the audience reach of a broadcast vehicle

Incidence The frequency with which a condition or event occurs in a given time and population or sample

Independent t-Test An inferential statistical test of significance that compares two levels of an independent variable against a continuous measured dependent variable

Independent Variable The variable against which the dependent variable is tested

In-Depth Interview Methodology An informal research methodology in which an individual interviews another in a one-on-one situation (*see* Depth interview)

Induction A philosophical logic in which general principles are developed from specific observations

Inferential Research Statistical analyses that test if the results observed for a sample are indicative of the population; the presentation of information that allows us to make judgments about whether the research results observed in a sample generalize to the population from which the sample was drawn

Inferential Statistics Statistical tests that allow a researcher to say within a certain degree of confidence whether variables or groups truly differ in their response to a public relations message (*see* Analysis of Variance [ANOVA], Bivariate Analysis, Chi-Square [X²], Correlation [r], Regression [REGR], t-Test)

Informal Methodology A research methodology that does not allow the researcher to generalize to a larger audience but leads to in-depth understanding of the client, object, or product

Informational Objective An objective that establishes what information a target audience should know or the degree of change in knowledge levels after the conclusion of a public relations campaign or program

Inputs The research information and data from both internal and external sources applied in the conception, approval, and design phases of the input stage of the communication production process

Inquiry Research A formal or informal research methodology that systematically employs content analysis, survey methodology, and/or interviewing techniques to study the range and types of unsolicited inquiries that an organization may receive from customers, prospective customers, or other target audience groups

Instrumental Error In measurement, error that occurs because the measuring instrument was poorly written

Interval Data Measurement data that are defined on a continuum and assumed to have equal spacing between data points (*see* Ratio data); examples include temperature scales and standardized intelligence test scores

Interview Schedule A guideline for asking questions in person or over the telephone

Issues Research A formal or informal research methodology that systematically studies public policy questions of the day, with the chief focus on those public policy matters whose definition and contending positions are still evolving

Item A manifest unit of analysis used in content analysis consisting of an entire message (e.g., an advertisement, story, or press release)

J

Judgmental Sample A type of non-probability sample in which individuals are deliberately selected for inclusion in the sample by the researcher because they have special knowledge, positions, or characteristics or represent other relevant dimensions of the population that are deemed important to study; also known as a *purposive sample*

K

Key Performance (Performance Result) The desired end effect or impact of a program of campaign performance

Known Group t-Test An inferential statistical test of significance that compares the results for a sampled group on some continuous-measurement dependent variable against a known value

KR-20 A reliability statistic for nominal- or ordinal-level measurement; also known as *Kuder-Richardson Formula 20*

L

Latent Content From content analysis, an analysis of the underlying idea, thesis, or theme of content; the deeper meanings that are intended or perceived in a message

Likert Scale An interval-level measurement scale that requires people to respond to statements on a set of predetermined reactions, usually "strongly agree," "agree," "neither agree nor disagree," "disagree," "strongly disagree"; must possess an odd number of reaction words or phrases; also called *summated ratings method* because the scale requires at least two, if not three, statements per measurement dimension

Longitudinal Survey A type of survey involving *different* individuals or objects that are observed or measured over time (e.g., multiple snapshot samples)

M

Mail Survey A survey technique whereby a questionnaire is sent to a respondent via the mail (or Internet) and the respondent self-administers the questionnaire and then sends it back

Mall Intercept Research A special type of person-to-person surveying in which in-person interviewing is conducted by approaching prospective participants as they stroll through shopping centers or malls; a non-probability form of sampling

Manifest Content From content analysis, an analysis of the actual content of a message exactly as it appears as opposed to latent content that must be inferred from messages

Market Research Any systematic study of buying or selling behavior

Mean (1) A descriptive statistic of central tendency that describes the "average" of a set of numbers on a continuum, also called *average*; (2) the process of applying a precise number or metric, which is both valid and reliable, to the evaluation of some performance

Measurement A way of giving an activity a precise dimension, generally by comparison to some standard; usually done in a quantifiable or numerical manner

Measurement Error For surveys, *see* Confidence interval

Measurement Reliability The extent to which a measurement scale measures the same thing over time (*see* Coefficient alpha [α], Split-half reliability, Test-retest reliability)

Measurement Validity The extent to which a measurement scale actually measures what it is believed to measure (*see* Construct validity, Content validity, Criterion-related validity, Face validity)

Media Includes newspapers, business and consumer magazines and other publications, radio and television, the Internet; company reports, news wires, government reports and brochures; Internet Web sites and discussion groups

Media Evaluations The systematic appraisal of a company's reputation, products, or services, or those of its competitors, as measured by their presence in the media

Median A descriptive statistic of central tendency indicating the midpoint in a series of data, the point above and below which 50 percent of the data values fall

Mention Prominence An indication of how prominently a company, product, or issue is mentioned in the media, typically measured in terms of percentage of article and position within the output (e.g., headline, above the fold, first three minutes)

Mentions Counts of incidence of company, product, or person appearances in the media; one mention constitutes a media placement

Message Content (1) The verbal, visual, and audio elements of a message; (2) the material from which content analyses are conducted; (3) a trend analysis factor that measures what, if any, planned messages are actually contained in the media (*see also* Message content analysis)

Message Content Analysis Analysis of media coverage of messages regarding a client, product, or topic on key issues

Message Strength A trend analysis factor that measures how strongly a message about a client or product or topic was communicated

Mode A descriptive statistic of central tendency indicating the most frequently occurring, or the most typical, value in a data series

Moderator An individual who leads a focus group; also known as a *facilitator*

Motivational Objective An objective that establishes the desired level of change in a target audience's specific attitudes or beliefs after a public relations campaign

Multivariate Analysis An inferential or descriptive statistic that examines the relationship among three or more variables

N

Network Analysis A formal or informal research method that examines how individuals or units or actors relate to each other in some systematic way

Neutral Point In attitude measurement scales, a point midway between extremes; in Likert-type scales usually defined as "neutral" or "neither agree nor disagree"

Nominal Data Measurement data that are simple categories in which items differ in name only and do not possess any ordering; data that are mutually exhaustive and exclusive; the simplest or lowest of all data; categorical data; example: male or female, where neither is seen as better or larger than the other

Nonparametric Statistics Inferential and descriptive statistics based on categorical data

Non-Probability Sample A sample drawn from a population wherein respondents or objects do not have an equal chance of being selected for observation or measurement

Nonverbal Communication That aspect of communication that deals with messages that are *not* a part of a natural language system (e.g., visual, spoken [as opposed to verbal], environmental)

Normal Curve Measurement data reflecting the hypothetical distribution of data points or cases based on interval- or ratio-level data that are "normally distributed" and error free; every continuous or parametric data set has its own normally distributed data that fall under its specific normal curve

Null Hypothesis The hypothesis of no difference that is formally tested in a research campaign or program; its rejection is the test of the theory

O

Objective (1) A measurable outcome in one of three forms: informational (cognitive), motivational (attitudinal/belief), or behavioral (actionable); (2) an explicit statement of intentions that supports a communication strategy and, to be measurable, includes an intended audience/public, a proposed change in a communication effect, a precise indication of the amount or level of change, and a specific time frame for the change to occur

Omnibus Survey An "all-purpose" national consumer poll usually conducted on a regular schedule (once a week or every other week) by major market research firms; also called *piggyback* or *shared-cost* survey

Opinion A verbalized or written evaluation of some object

Opportunities to See (OTS) The number of times a particular audience has the potential to view a message, subject, or issue; also known as *impressions*

Ordinal Data Measurement data that are categories in which items are different in name and possess an ordering of some sort; data that are mutually exhaustive and exclusive and ordered; categorical data; example: income as the categories of under $25K, $26K–$50K, $51K–$75K, $76K–$100K, over $100K

Outcomes (1) Quantifiable changes in awareness, knowledge, attitude, opinion, and behavior levels that occur as a result of a public relations program or campaign; (2) an effect, consequence, or impact of a set or program of communication activities or products, that may be either short term (immediate) or long term

Outgrowth The cumulative effect of all communication programs and products on the positioning of an organization in the minds of its stakeholders or publics

Outtake (1) Measurement of what audiences have understood and/or heeded or responded to with regard to a communication product's call to seek further information from public relations messages prior to measuring an outcome; (2) audience reaction to the receipt of a communication product, including favorability of the product, recall and retention of the message embedded in the product, and whether the audience heeded or responded to a call for information or action within the message

P

Paired t-Test An inferential statistical test of significance that compares data that are collected twice on the same sample

Panel Survey (1) A type of survey that consists of the *same* individuals or objects that are observed or measured over time; (2) a type of survey in which a group of individuals are deliberately recruited by a research firm because of their special demographic characteristics for the express purpose of being interviewed more than once over a period of time for various clients on a broad array of different topics or subjects

Parameter In sampling, a characteristic of a population that is of interest

Parametric Statistics Inferential and descriptive statistics based on continuous data

Participant-Observation An informal research methodology where the researcher takes an active role in the life of an organization or community, observes and records interactions, and then analyzes those interactions

Percent of Change A measure of increase or decrease of media coverage

Percentage A descriptive statistic based on categorical data; defined as the frequency count for a particular category divided by the total frequency count; example: 10 males out of 100 people = 10%

Percentage Point The number by which a percentage is increased or decreased

Performance The act of carrying out, doing, executing, or putting into effect; a deed, task, action, or activity is a unit of a program of performance

Performance Indicator A sign or parameter that, if tracked over time, provides information about the ongoing results of a particular program of performance or campaign

Performance Measure A number that shows the exact extent to which a result was achieved

Performance Result (Key Performance) The desired end effect or impact of a program of campaign performance

Performance Target A time-bounded and measurable commitment toward achieving a desired result

Periodicity A bias found in sampling due to the way in which the items or respondents are chosen; example: newspapers may differ by being daily, weekly, weekday only, and so forth

Poll (1) A form of survey research that focuses more on immediate behavior than on attitudes; (2) a very short survey-like method whose questionnaire asks only very brief and closed-ended questions

Position Papers Print output

Positioning Trend analysis factor that measures how a client, product, or topic was positioned in the media (e.g., leader, follower)

Probability Sample A sample drawn at random from a population such that all possible respondents or objects have an equal chance of being selected for observation or measurement

Probe Question A question used in a questionnaire or schedule that requires the participant to explain an earlier response, often in the form of "why do you think this?"

Product (Communication Product) The end result of the communication product process resulting in the production and dissemination of a brochure, media release, video news release, Web site, speech, and so forth

Program (Campaign) The planning, execution, and evaluation of a public relations plan of action aimed at solving a problem

Prominence of Mention Trend analysis factor that measures how prominently a client or product or topic was mentioned and where that mention occurred (e.g., headline, top of the fold, certain part of a broadcast)

Proportion A descriptive statistic based on categorical data, defined as the fraction out of 1; example: 10 males out of 100 people represent 10 hundredths (.01) of the sample

Psychographic Research Research focusing on a population or sample's nondemographic traits and characteristics, such as personality type, lifestyle, social roles, values, attitudes, and beliefs

Public Opinion Poll A type of survey that collects basic opinions or facts about a specified population or sample; also known as a *descriptive survey*

Purposive Sample A non-probability sample in which individuals are deliberately selected for

inclusion based on their special knowledge, position, characteristics, or relevant dimensions of the population

Push Poll A survey technique in which an interviewer begins by acting as if the telephone call represents a general survey but then asks the respondent a question implying questionable behaviors or outcomes of a person or product

Q

Q-Sort A measurement instrument that focuses on respondent beliefs by asking the respondent to sort through opinion statements and sort them into piles on an 11-point continuum usually bounded by "most like me" and "most unlike me"

Qualitative Research Usually refers to studies that are somewhat to totally subjective, but nevertheless in-depth, using a probing, open-ended response format or reflecting an ethnomethodological orientation

Quantitative Research Usually refers to studies that are highly objective and projectable, using closed-ended, forced-choice questionnaires; research that relies heavily on statistics and numerical measures

Question A statement or phrase used in a questionnaire or schedule that elicits either an open- or closed-ended response from a research participant (*see also* Funnel question, Probe question)

Questionnaire A measurement instrument that contains exact questions and measures that an interviewer or survey researcher uses to survey through the mail, Internet, in person, or via the telephone; may be closed ended or open ended, but typically employs more closed-ended questions

Quota Sample A type of non-probability sample that draws its sample based on a percentage or quota from the population and stops sampling when that quota is met; a non-probability sample that *attempts* to have the same general distribution of population characteristics as the sample

R

Range A descriptive central tendency statistic that expresses the difference between the highest and lowest scores in the data set; example: responses to a question on a 1-to-5 Likert-type scale where all reaction categories were used would yield a range of 4 (5 minus 1)

Ratio Data Measurement data that are defined on a continuum and possess an absolute zero point; examples: number of children, a bank account, absolute lack of heat (0° Kelvin = –459.67°F or –273.15°C)

Reach Refers to the scope or range of distribution and thus coverage that a given communication product has in a targeted audience group; in broadcasting, the net unduplicated (also called "duplicated") radio or TV audience for programs or commercials as measured for a specific time period

Readership The number of people who actually read each issue of a publication, on average

Regression (REGR) An inferential statistical test of significance that predicts dependent variable (measured) outcomes for independent variables that may be either categorical (e.g., bivariate) or continuous (interval) in nature

Reliability In general, the extent to which results would be consistent, or replicable, if the research were conducted a number of times (*see also* Measurement reliability)

Research The systematic effort before (formative research) or during and/or after (summative or evaluative research) a communication activity aimed at discovering and collecting the facts or opinions pertaining to an identified issue, need, or question; may be formal or informal

Response Rate In survey methodology, the number of respondents who actually completed an interview

S

Sample A group of people or objects chosen from a larger population (*see* Convenience sample, Longitudinal survey, Non-probability sample, Panel survey, Probability sample, Snapshot survey)

Sampling Error For surveys, *see* Confidence level

Scale A measurement instrument consisting of attitude or belief items that reflect an underlying structure toward some attitude or belief object

Scalogram (Guttman Scale/Cumulative Scale) A measurement scale that assumes (a) unidimensionality and (b) that people, when faced with a choice, will also choose items less intense than the one chosen

Scattergram A descriptive statistic based on continuous data that graphically demonstrates how data are distributed between two variables; also known as a *scatter diagram* or *scatterplot*

Schedule (1) The timeline on which a public relations program or campaign is conducted; (2) a list of questions, usually open ended, used in focus group and in-depth interviews to gather data

Screener Question One of several questions usually asked at the beginning of an interview or survey to determine if the potential respondent is eligible to participate in the study (*see also* Funnel question)

Secondary Methodology An informal research methodology that examines extant data in order to draw conclusions; a systematic re-analysis of a vast array of existing data; often used in benchmarking and benchmark studies

Semantic Differential An attitude measure that asks respondents to evaluate an attitude object based on bipolar adjectives or phrases separated by a continuum represented as consisting of an odd number of intervals; developed by Osgood, Suci, and Tannenbaum

Semantic Space The idea that people can evaluate an attitude object along some spatial continuum

Share of Ink (SOI) Measurement of the total press/magazine coverage found in articles or mentions devoted to a particular industry or topic as analyzed to determine what percent of outputs or opportunities to see (OTS) is devoted to a client or product

Share of Voice (SOV) Measurement of total coverage devoted to radio/television coverage to a particular industry or topic as analyzed to determine what percent of outputs or opportunities to see (OTS) is devoted to a client or product; also known as *share of coverage*

Simple Random Sample A type of probability sample in which numbers are assigned to each member of a population, a random set of numbers is generated, and then only those members having the random numbers are included in the sample

Situation Analysis An impartial, often third-party assessment of the public relations and/or public affairs problems, or opportunities, that an organization may be facing at a given time

Skip Interval The distance between people selected from a population based on systematic sampling; usually defined as the total population divided by the number of people to be sampled (e.g., for a sample of 100 people to be drawn from a population of 10,000 people, the skip interval would be 100/10,000 = 100 individuals skipped between selected participants)

Snapshot Survey A type of survey that consists of individuals or objects that are observed or measured once (*see also* Cross-sectional survey)

Snowball Sample A type of non-probability sample in which individuals who are interviewed are asked to suggest other individuals for further interviewing

Sources Mentioned Trend analysis factor that measures who was quoted in media coverage; also known as *quoteds*

Speaking Engagements Print or broadcast or Internet communication product output

Split-Half Reliability A test for a measure's reliability where a sample is randomly split and one

segment receives a part of the measure and the second segment receives the rest

Standard Deviation (σ) A descriptive statistic of central tendency that indexes the variability of a distribution; the range from the mean within which approximately 34 percent of the cases fall, provided the values are distributed along a normal curve

Standardized Score (Z-Score) A descriptive statistic based on continuous data that expresses individual scores based on their standard deviations from the group mean; the range of scores is usually −3.00 to +3.00

Statistical Significance Refers to the degree to which relationships observed in a sample can be attributed to sampling error or measurement error alone; expressed in terms of confidence that the relationships are due to error X percent of the time (e.g., 5 percent) or expressed in terms of the confidence that we have that the results are due to what was measured X percent of the time (e.g., 95 percent confident)

Stratified Sample A type of probability sample that involves first breaking the total population into homogeneous subsets (or strata) and then selecting the potential sample at random from the individual strata; example: stratifying on race would require breaking the population into racial strata and then randomly sampling within each strata

Survey Methodology A formal research methodology that seeks to gather data and analyze a population's or sample's attitudes, beliefs, and opinions (*see* Cohort survey, Longitudinal survey, Panel survey, Snapshot survey); data are gathered in-person or by telephone (face-to-face), or the survey is self-administered via the mail, e-mail, or fax

Symbols/Words A manifest unit of analysis used in content analysis consisting of specific words (e.g., pronouns, client name, logotypes) that are counted

Systematic Sample A type of probability sample in which units in a population are selected from an available list at a fixed interval after a random start

T

Target Audience A very specific audience differentiated from "audience" by some measurable characteristic or attribute (e.g., sports fishermen)

Targeted Gross Rating Points (TGRP) Gross Rating Points (GRP) targeted to a particular group or target audience

Test-Retest Reliability A test of a measure's reliability carried out by testing the same sample with the same measure over time

Themes A latent unit of analysis used in content analysis that measures an underlying theme or thesis (e.g., sexuality, violence, credibility)

Throughputs The development, creative, and production activities (writing, editing, creative design, printing, fabrication, etc.) as part of the throughput stage of a communication product production process

Time/Space Measures A manifest unit of analysis used in content analysis consisting of physically measurable units (e.g., column inches, size of photographs, broadcast time for a story)

Tone Trend and content analysis factor that measures how a target audience feels about the client or product or topic; typically defined as positive, neutral/balanced, or negative

Trend Analysis Tracking of performance over the course of a public relations campaign or program; a survey method whereby a topic or subject is examined over a period of time through repeated surveys of independently selected samples (snapshot or cross-sectional survey)

t-Test An inferential statistical test of significance for continuous-measurement dependent variables against a bivariate independent variable; used when the total number of observations is less than 100 (*see* Independent t-test, Known group t-test, Paired t-test)

Type of Article (1) Categories of a publication such as "product review," "bylined article," "editorial," "advertorial," "feature story"; (2) trend analysis factor that measures the nature of client, product, or topic coverage (e.g., column inches, broadcast time)

U

Unit of Analysis The specification of what is to be counted in content analysis methodology; consists of symbols/words, time/space measures, characters, themes, and items; may be *manifest* (observable) or *latent* (attitudinal)

Univariate Analysis The examination of only one variable at a time

V

Validity In general, the extent to which a research project actually measures what it is intended or purports to measure (*see also* Measurement validity)

Value An underlying cultural expectation; usually directs an individual's beliefs

Variance (σ^2) A descriptive statistic of central tendency that measures the extent to which individual scores in a data set differ from each other; the sum of the squared standard deviations from the mean (σ)

W

Word/Symbol In content analysis, a unit of analysis

Z

Z-Score (Standardized Score) A descriptive statistic of central tendency that takes data from different types of scales and standardizes them as areas under the normal curve for comparison purposes

SOURCE: ©2002, The Institute for Public Relations, University of Florida, P.O. Box 118400, Gainesville, FL 32611-8400. Reprinted with permission. This dictionary, prepared and edited by Don R. Stacks, is updated regularly by the Institute at its Web site, http://www.instituteforpr.com.

Index

Grunig, James E., 1–2, 5–6, 78, 82, 146, 169–170, 182, 197, 200, 210, 306, 326, 333, 430, 453–455, 506, 534, 539, 580, 593–594, 646–647, 690–691, 704, 706, 718–720, 744, 778–780, 801, 803, 819, 837–840, 842, 852, 866–867, 869

Grunig, Larissa A., 2, 6, 82, 182, 207, 290, 297, 306, 324–325, 333, 534, 539, 580, 593–595, 690–691, 788, 803, 839–841, 900–901

Guanxi, 44

Gudykunst, William, 430

Guillery, J. M., 160

Gunter, B., 656

Gunton, George, 448

Gurevitch, Michael, 881

Gusella, Mary, 114

Gutenberg, Johannes, 177–178, 915

Guth, D. W., 56

Guyer, Paul, 245

Gyan, Margaret, 17

Habermas, Jürgen, 207, 226–227, 284, 299, 486, 539, 704, 707–708, 710–712, 841

Hachigian, D., 588, 592

Hackney, A. J., 892

Hagar, Nicky, 51

Haggerty, James F., 638, 677

Hairline rule, 94

Haldeman, Bob, 266

Hales, Colin P., 500

Haley, Russell, 656

Hall, Edward, 429

Hall, Richard B., 440

Hall, Stuart, 257–258

Hall, Wendy, 233

Hallahan, Kirk, 11–14, 81, 91–94, 150–152, 166, 168, 171–174, 236, 253–254, 281–283, 341–343, 426–428, 455–457, 520–521, 588, 591–592, 611, 664, 691, 854–855

Ham, George, 112

Hamal, G. F., 390

Hambrick, Donald C., 824

Hamlin, C. H., 155

Hammon, D., 278

Hammond, George, 107, 379–382, 467. *See also* Counseling; Publicity; Spin; Strategy

Hammond, Ruth, 112

Hammond, Sharon, 672

Hamrefors, Sven, 833

Hanily, M. A., 690

Hansen-Horn, Tricia L., 477–478, 492–493, 632–634

Harding, Sandra, 325

Harlow, Rachel Martin, 410–412

Harlow, Rex, xxv, 82, 397, 467, 683, 689, 696, 917

Harlow, William Forrest, 319, 522–523, 804–806

Harper and Row Publishers, Inc. v. Nation Enterprises, 202

Harris, Barbara, 59, 534

Harris, Lou, 89

Harris, Thomas, 505

Harris, Tom, 366

Harrison, Benjamin, 607–608

Harrison, Shirley, 865

Hart, Joy L., 47–49, 232–235, 327–328, 441–442, 446, 557–559

Hartman, C., 768

Hartman, Johnny, 59

Harvey, M. G., 510

Hasling, J., 616

Hauss, Deborah, 431

Hawthorne effect, 545

Hawthorne Works, 545

Hawver, Carl F., 467

Hayakawa, S. I., 696

Hayes, Glenn C., 686

Hays, Scott, 22

Haywood, Roger, 294

Hayworth, Rita, 639

Hazelwood, Joseph, 315

Hazleton, Vincent, 444

HBM. *See* Health Belief Model (HBM)

Health, safety, and environment (HSE) reports, annual, 31–32. *See also* Activism; Goodwill; Public interest

Health Belief Model (HBM), 382–385

Health Care Public Relations Association of Canada, 115

Health communications, 173

Health planning approach, 669

Health Plus, 333

Health sites, 588

Hearing, 385–387

Hearit, Keith Michael, 38–40, 68–70, 122–124, 147–150, 224, 301–302, 595–596

Heath, Henry, 747

Heath, Perry, 304

Heath, Rebecca Piirto, 656

Heath, Robert L., xxiii–xxvii, 8, 122, 417–419, 453, 455, 488, 537, 564–567, 691, 705–707, 786–787, 849–851, 854, 872

about, xxxi

Agenda Online, 21

age of deference (end of), 17–21

annual health, safety, and environment (HSE) reports, 31–32

antecedents of modern public relations, 32–37

Beat, 72–73

best practices, 80

bill stuffer, 83

co-creation of meaning theory, 135–136

commodifying information, 157–158

control, 193–196

corporate conscience, 208

corporate public relations department, 501–504

counseling, 214–216

deadline, 239–240

differentiation, 251–253

dramatism and dramatism theory, 261–263

Dudley, Pendleton, 267–269

encroachment theory, 278

evolution of publicity agencies, 303–306

executive management, 308–310

Exxon and the Valdez crisis, 315

function of public relations, 350–353

government relations, 370